清华映像

2017

主编 覃川 张佐
执行主编 卢小兵 程曦
副主编 张歌明 张莉

清华大学出版社
北 京

内容简介

本书是清华大学主页“清华映像”栏目2017年年度合集，用精美的图片和中英文原创文章全面报道清华发展建设及改革创新的重点任务、重大事件和重要成果，介绍清华在教学、科研、社会服务等方面的成就，捕捉师生生活亮点，纵览清华历史风物。本书的读者对象包括高等学校和科研机构的师生、研究人员，以及关注清华和中国高等教育发展的社会大众。

图书在版编目(CIP)数据

清华映像. 2017 / 覃川，张佐主编. — 北京：清华大学出版社，2019
ISBN 978-7-302-53299-6

Ⅰ. ①清… Ⅱ. ①覃… ②张… Ⅲ. ①清华大学—概况 Ⅳ. ①G649.281

中国版本图书馆CIP数据核字（2019）第137802号

责任编辑：梁　斐　高翔飞
封面设计：李　娜
责任校对：刘玉霞
责任印制：宋　林

出版发行：清华大学出版社
网　　址：http://www.tup.com.cn, http://www.wqbook.com
地　　址：北京清华大学学研大厦A座　　**邮　　编**：100084
社 总 机：010-62770175　　**邮　　购**：010-62786544
投稿与读者服务：010-62776969, c-service@tup.tsinghua.edu.cn
质量反馈：010-62772015, zhiliang@tup.tsinghua.edu.cn
印 装 者：三河市龙大印装有限公司
经　　销：全国新华书店
开　　本：210mm × 260mm　　**印　　张**：24.25　　**插　　页**：1　　**字　　数**：1259千字
版　　次：2019年10月第1版　　**印　　次**：2019年10月第1次印刷
定　　价：188.00元

产品编号：083433-01

前 言

打开本书封面上镂空的窗口，您一定已经看到一幅幅或灵动或沉静、或清新或深邃的图片——它们，都来自 2017 年清华大学主页头条“清华映像”栏目。

“清华映像”诞生于 2011 年清华大学百年校庆之际，以精美的设计图和精练的中英文原创文章，全面报道清华发展建设及改革创新的重点任务、重大事件和重要成果，介绍清华在教学、科研、社会服务等方面的成就，捕捉师生生活亮点，纵览清华历史风物。

自 2011 年 3 月至 2018 年 4 月清华主页改版，长达 7 年多的时间里，“清华映像”栏目一直是清华大学中英文主页（www.tsinghua.edu.cn）一道亮丽的风景线——点击日历条上每一个工作日的日期，就会看到当天“清华映像”的图片和标题；每隔一到两周，还会推出一期以动画形式呈现的选题——如同一幅流动的画卷，随着清华新百年的发展进程，不断延展更新。

2017 年，是清华大学党委宣传部（新闻中心）负责统筹制作“清华映像”栏目的第一年。

这一年，我们着重提升了“清华映像”的时效性，从清华发起成立亚洲大学联盟到清华领衔团队斩获世界高性能计算最高奖“戈登 · 贝尔”奖，都有“清华映像”第一时间的生动呈现。

这一年，我们着力加强系列策划，将“清华映像”纳入围绕学校中心工作展开的一系列重大选题报道整体策划中，相继推出校庆年度回顾特别策划、清华新百年教学成就奖系列报道、砥砺奋进看清华系列报道、本科教学工作审核评估系列报道等系列专题，为及时展现清华综合改革和“双一流”建设成果、特别是教育教学和科学研究成绩留下了丰富而生动的记录。

这一年，我们还将精品教材、科研成果、探访实验室、特等奖学金获得者、学生社团、社会实践、后勤优质项目、清华名人名言及名人故居、清华二十四节气等系列选题穿插推进，推出了一组组图文并茂的高质量原创报道。

2017 年，“清华映像”栏目篇均访问量提升了 30%，单篇访问量稳定在 15000 次以上，单篇最高访问量突破 90000 次，体现了广大读者对栏目的持续关注和充分认同。

2017 年，邱勇校长在清华大学 106 周年校庆致辞中强调，清华正朝着“更创新、更国际、更人文的目标奋力迈进”。纵观这一年的 185 期“清华映像”，直接涉及“更创新”的有 42 期，直接涉及“更国际”的有 15 期，直接涉及“更人文”的有 46 期。“挑战杯”特等奖“天格计划”跨学科学生团队挑战基础科学前沿领域的勇气与实践，苏世民书院首批毕业生以中英双语亲手写下清华一年的满满收获，用八年心血灌溉清华园诗风词韵、在报道发布当天不幸辞世的王步高教授……都是 2017 年“清华映像”中令人难忘的剪影。

可以说，“清华映像”这一独特的栏目形式，本身就是“更创新、更国际、更人文”的清华新形象的写照。它浓缩了清华园的今与昔、师与生、知与行，传承着清华的风骨，传递着清华的温度。

通过这本合集，我们期待着与您一道，重新走进 2017 年清华园的春夏秋冬，触摸清华人夜以继日、奔跑向前的坚定身影。

覃川
2019 年 8 月

目 录

2 1月3日 世纪清华 再续地缘
4 1月4日 研究生精品课程“现代智能信息处理”
6 1月6日 影响清华的演讲之蒋南翔校长就职演说
8 1月9日 精仪系本科生米璐在生物微机电领域著名期刊发表封面文章

10 1月10日 校园歌手大赛：用一年的时间只为做好这一件事
12 1月11日 《合同法》：做读者进一步深造的引路石
14 1月12日 材料学院陈娜副研究员等在室温磁性半导体及器件研究中取得重要进展

16 1月13日 清华名人名言之梁思成：有所专而又多能，精于一而又博学
18 1月20日 清华名人名言之周诒春：维能耐劳忍苦，斯能建功立业
20 1月27日 家乡的春节美食

22 2月3日 清华名人名言之章名涛：治学严谨，为人清正
24 2月10日 清华名人名言之季羡林：只有知不足的人才能为人类文化做出贡献

26 2月17日 清华名人名言之潘光旦：我的钱全都买书了
28 2月20日 又是一年开学时
30 2月21日 热动42班：我们的书生时代
32 2月22日 优秀教材《工程材料（第5版）》：历史视野，与时俱进
34 2月23日 航院李群仰课题组发文揭示二维材料摩擦演化之谜

36 2月24日 三院遗址
38 2月27日 郑德焰：实践之路，造“桥”之行
40 2月28日 周立柱：花甲之年筚路蓝缕，投身西部志在教育

42 3月1日 普通高等教育精品教材《电子商务概论》：将最新的成果带给学生
44 3月2日 薛平教授研究组研制成功一种新型高速光学相干层析成像系统

46 3月3日 清华名人故居之吴晗故居：通向光明的小屋——西院12号
48 3月6日 姚维坤：一个清华博士的乡村情怀
50 3月7日 女生节：记忆集体情感的符号
52 3月8日 “中国青年女科学家奖”获得者周树云：做科学秘境中的女探险家

3 Centennial Tsinghua Rekindling Relationship with Geoscience
5 Quality Course for Postgraduate Students: Modern Intelligent Information Processing
7 Influencing Tsinghua: President Jiang Nanxiang's Inauguration Speech
9 Undergraduate Student from DPI Published Cover Article for Well-known Journal in the Field of Biological Micro-electromechanical System
11 Campus Singing Contest: Using One Year's Time to Do Just One Thing
13 Course Book *Contract Law*: Further Leading the Way for Readers
15 Dr. Chen Na from the School of Materials Science and Engineering Made an Important Progress in Research on Room-temperature Magnetic Semiconductors and Devices
17 Famous Quotations in Tsinghua History: Multi-Talented Yet a Specialist, Versatile Yet Master of One
19 Famous Quotations in Tsinghua History: Only by Being Able to Withstand Hard Work Can One Gain Great Results
21 Spring Festival: Delicacy from Hometown

23 Famous Quotations in Tsinghua History: Rigorous Scholarship and Upright Personality
25 Famous Quotations in Tsinghua History: Only Those Who Are Never Tired of Learning Can Make Contributions Towards the Human Culture
27 Famous Quotations in Tsinghua History: I've Spent All My Money on Buying Books
29 New Semester: to Continue with Pursuing My Dream
31 Our Reading Time
33 The Recommended Course Book: Engineering Materials (Fifth Edition)
35 Dr. Li Qunyang Research Group of the School of Aerospace Engineering Issued an Article to Reveal the Mystery of Friction Evolution of Two-Dimensional Materials
37 No. 3 Courtyard
39 Ph.D. Candidate Zheng Deyan: Road of Practicability — Forming "Bridges"
41 Professor Zhou Lizhu: to Dive Straight into the Western Regions of China

43 Tertiary Textbook Topics of E-commerce: Bringing the Latest Findings to the Students
45 Research Group of Professor Xue Ping Successfully Developed a New Type of High-Speed Optical Coherence Tomography System
47 Tsinghua Celebrity Wu Han's Former Residence: No. 12 of the West Yard
49 Yao Weikun: a Feeling for the Villages and Countryside from a Tsinghua Ph.D. Student
51 Girls' Day: a Symbol of Our Collective Memory
53 Recipient of L'Oréal-UNESCO Women in Science China Award—Shuyun Zhou: to Be That Female Explorer in the World of Science

54 3月9日 清华、米兰理工携手共建中意设计创新基地
56 3月10日 植树节：清华的绿色大学梦
58 3月13日 清华大学2016年特等奖学金获得者陈立杰：立志为人类智慧添砖加瓦
60 3月14日 清华冬泳队：冰水彻骨寒，健儿绽笑颜
62 3月15日 多功能教学楼的“七十二变”
64 3月16日 韩美林教授设计《丁酉年》邮票：清华与生肖邮票的不解之缘
66 3月17日 清华名人名言之蒋南翔：不仅是给干粮，更应给猎枪
68 3月20日 水清木华又春分
70 3月21日 计34班：小小中厅凝聚集体力量
72 3月22日 精仪系智能微系统团队：培养“顶天立地”的复合型人才
76 3月23日 谢道昕、饶子和及娄智勇等合作阐明植物分枝激素独脚金内酯的感知机制奥秘
78 3月24日 王国维故居：国学大师在西院度过的时光
80 3月27日 博士生郑云：书本之外，是更广阔的产业世界
82 3月28日 清华紫荆花车队折桂中国节能竞技大赛
84 3月29日 岳光溪院士：站在中国这块土地上做科研
86 3月30日 高温气冷堆技术，中国领跑
88 3月31日 顾毓琇：心系国家，眷念清华

90 4月5日 清明祭礼，不失不忘；先烈遗志，薪火相传
92 4月6日 106周年校庆：更好的清华等你来
94 4月7日 浸润东非，拥抱热土
96 4月10日 校园绿色出行：行到哪里，就把环保意识带到哪里
98 4月11日 2016年清华大学特等奖学金获得者马冬昕：水滴穿石，双肩筑梦
100 4月12日 乃哥麦提·伊加提：在梦想的道路上踏实前行
102 4月13日 新版工程硕士学位课程拥抱“学堂在线”
104 4月14日 电子系杨知行团队：中国产业腾飞，中国标准先行
106 4月17日 朗读亭走了，读书仍在继续
108 4月18日 清华大学106周年校庆致辞
112 4月21日 校园马拉松：奔跑吧，青春！
114 4月24日 《算表》：历史留在清华简上的数学之美
116 4月25日 特别策划：不忘初心，砥砺前行——2016年清华大学党的建设工作回顾
118 4月26日 你的清华，为你订制，由你创造
120 4月27日 清华大学数学学科90周年庆：歌行砥砺，华章再续
122 4月28日 世界，清华与你同行
124 4月29日 清华发起成立亚洲大学联盟
126 4月30日 清华大学106周岁生日快乐！

128 5月8日 清华科研关键词：改革·创新·引领
130 5月9日 行健新百年，共筑中国梦
132 5月10日 百年清华，人文日新

55 Tsinghua University and Politecnico di Milano Jointly Established a Hub for Sino-Italian Design Innovation
57 Arbor Day: Tsinghua's Green Dream
59 Chen Lijie, 2016 Top Grade Scholarship Winner: Determined to Contribute to the Wisdom of Mankind
61 Winter Swimming in Tsinghua: No pain, No Gain
63 Transformation of Multi-functional Teaching Buildings
65 The "Year of the Rooster" ("DingYou Nian") Stamps Designed by Professor Han Meilin
67 Jiang Nanxiang's Educational Philosophy Continues to Influence Tsinghua Students
69 Spring Comes to Tsinghua Campus
71 Computer Class 34: Small Space, Big Ideas
74 The Team of Intelligent Micro System: Allowing Students to Be Truly Useful
77 Unveiling the Mystery of the Perception Mechanism of Strigolactone Hormone
79 Wang Guowei's Former Residence: The Master of Chinese Culture's Time in the West Yard
81 Learn to Apply Beyond the Textbooks Teachings
83 Tsinghua Bauhinia Energy Efficient Fleet Wins Honda China Eco-Car Competition
85 Yue Guangxi: at the Forefront of CFB Technology
87 China Takes the Lead in High-temperature Gas-cooled Reactor Technology
89 Gu Yuxiu: Tsinghua, Where the Heart and Soul Belongs

91 Qingming Festival: Remembering the Martyrs, Passing Down Traditions
93 Tsinghua's Anniversary: a Better Tsinghua Awaits You
95 Venturing into East Africa, Embracing Her Hot Land
97 Eco-Friendly Transport: Go Green on Campus
99 Taking the Road Less Traveled: Ma Dongxin Awarded Tsinghua's 2016 Top Grade Scholarship
101 Nighmat Ijat: En-route to My Dreams
103 XuetangX Released a New Version of Online Master of Engineering Courses
105 Yang Zhixing's Team Raises the Bar for International Digital TV Standards
107 Tsinghua's Reading Booth: Reading to Become a Better You
110 President's Message for Tsinghua's 106th Anniversary
113 Tsinghua Campus Marathon: Youthful and Historical
115 Mathematical Trails Left Behind on Historical "Tsinghua Bamboo Slips"
117 Tsinghua University CPC Review 2016: Creating a World-class University with Chinese Characteristics
119 Tsinghua's "Personal Tailor" Programs Offer Infinite Possibilities
121 Tsinghua's Mathematical Sciences Discipline Celebrated Its 90th Anniversary
123 Tsinghua and the World: Looking Back at 2016
125 AUA Officially Launched at Tsinghua
127 Tsinghua University: Happy 106th Birthday!

129 Overview: Tsinghua Innovative Research 2016
131 Tsinghua Students' Work 2016 Review: Working Together towards the Chinese Dream
133 Tsinghua Enters New Phase for Humanities After a Century of Establishment

134 5月11日 “北京榜样”程京院士：健康梦，中国芯
136 5月12日 施滉：真理所在，即趋附之
138 5月15日 邺架轩开业：清华是个读书的好地方
140 5月16日 庆106岁诞辰，清华开放百个实验室
142 5月17日 开放交流时间：营造更有温度的校园文化
144 5月18日 艺术与科技的交融，让“非遗”传承回归生活
146 5月19日 马约翰故居：体育，从庭院出发
148 5月22日 特等奖学金获得者张祎蕊：大学生活是一场旅行
150 5月23日 无偿献血：清华人十五载血脉相承
152 5月24日 清华x-lab：做创新时代的探路者、引路者、带路者
154 5月25日 “万园之园”的数字化重生
156 5月26日 清华历史上的人和事：钱锺书是这样做读书笔记的
158 5月31日 志合者，不以山海为远——清华大学新雅书院侧记

160 6月1日 “长城友谊奖”获得者罗忠敬：探寻燃烧之美，搭建科学桥梁
162 6月2日 清华北院，幽香如故
164 6月5日 赵小凡：拿下特等奖学金的博士妈妈
166 6月6日 探寻航院校庆开放实验室：玄秘星空、精妙大脑与蓝色风洞

168 6月7日 跨越时空：平均年龄93岁的一次朗读
170 6月8日 地学系张强教授：探究空气污染复杂来源
172 6月9日 张奚若：学问要往大处着眼
174 6月12日 特等奖学金获得者张晓声：专注科研，多元发展
176 6月13日 绿色清华“三联画”：绿色教育，绿色科技，绿色校园
178 6月14日 老师当“绿叶”，同学变“红花”——一堂别开生面的思政课翻转课

180 6月15日 化学系石高全教授领衔石墨烯研究项目获国家自然科学奖二等奖

182 6月16日 邱勇校长：有你的清华会更好——致2017年高考考生的邀请信

184 6月19日 15年，清华大学博士生学术论坛在路上
186 6月20日 同声传译实验室：培养更国际、更顶尖的外语人才

188 6月21日 夏至：昼晷已云极，宵漏自此长
190 6月22日 曾哲妮：清华，我的“刷新”之旅
192 6月23日 世界和平论坛：为世界安全这个古老命题寻找新的钥匙
194 6月26日 清华国学研究院院长陈来：优秀传统文化的传承者
196 6月27日 追记清华大学水利系教授谷兆祺：化作滴水汇江河
198 6月28日 毕业纪念品：可触摸的清华记忆
200 6月29日 苏世民书院这一年，重新定义了我对中国的了解

135 "2016 Beijing Role Model" Cheng Jing: Biological Chip Is for a Healthy Future
137 Shi Huang: The Truth Endures
139 Ye Jia Xuan Reading Center Opening: Enjoy the Pleasure of Reading
141 A Hundred of Tsinghua Laboratories Open to the Public on Homecoming Day
143 Open Office Hours Build Stronger Student-Faculty Relationships
145 Key Laboratory of Traditional Craft Techniques and Materials Research: Blending Art and Technology
147 Ma Yuehan's Residence: Continuing Tsinghua's Sporting Spirit
149 2016 Top Grade Scholarship Winner: Zhang Yirui and Her Journey
151 Red Cross Blood Donation: 15 Years of Tsinghua's Support
153 Tsinghua x-lab: Leading the Way in the Innovative Era
155 The Digital Rebirth of the Old Summer Palace
157 Stories of Tsinghua People: Qian Zhongshu's Note-taking Methods
159 Xinya College: Aspirations and Commitments

161 Chung K. Law: Explore the Beauty of Combustion and Build a Scientific Bridge
163 Charm and History at the North Yard of Tsinghua University
165 Doctorate Mum Zhao Xiaofan Wins Top Grade Scholarship Award
167 Explore Open Laboratories of the School of Aerospace Engineering: Mystery Stars, Secret Brain, Blue Wind Tunnel
169 Marching Out of Time: Reading at an Average Age of 93
171 Professor Zhang Qiang: Exploring the Complex Sources of Air Pollution
173 Zhang Xiruo: Knowledge Is About Being Far-sighted
175 Top Grade Scholarship Winner Zhang Xiaosheng: Focus on Scientific Research and Develop with Diversity
177 Green Tsinghua: Education, Technology and Campus
179 Special Ideological and Political Course: The Teacher Will be the Green Leaves and the Students Will Become Red Flowers
181 Professor Shi Gaoquan from the Department of Chemistry Was Granted State Natural Science Award for Graphene Research
183 The President of Tsinghua University Qiu Yong's Letter to 2017 Prospective Students—a Tsinghua with You Is a Much Better Tsinghua
185 15 Years, Tsinghua University's Doctoral Student Academic Forum Still Well on the Road
187 Simultaneous Interpretation Laboratory—the Cultivation and Training of Talents Who Are More Sharp and International
189 Celebrating the Summer Solstice at Tsinghua
191 Zeng Zheni: Hitting the "Refresh" Button in the Tsinghua Experience
193 World Peace Forum: Finding a New Key for the Age-old Propositions of Global Security
195 Dean of the Tsinghua Academy of Chinese Learning Chen Lai: Inheriting the Excellence of Our Traditional Culture
197 Remembering Gu Zhaoqi: a Selfless Professor in the Department of Hydraulic Engineering
199 Graduation Souvenirs: Your Tangible Tsinghua Memory
201 A Reflection on My Year at Schwarzman College, Tsinghua University

202 6月30日 毕业季：没有人是佩妥剑再入“江湖”

204 7月3日 热烈庆祝中国共产党清华大学第十四次党员代表大会胜利召开！
206 7月10日 清华艺术博物馆“奇妙日”：从莫奈到苏拉热
208 7月17日 春去夏犹清，美味伴暑假
210 7月24日 赵元任故居：想国想家，教我如何不想他
212 7月31日 于婉莹：给你不一样的手绘清华

214 8月7日 立秋：朱明送夏，少昊迎秋
216 8月14日 无体育，不清华：清华体育小史
218 8月21日 致七字班新生：欢迎你，在更好的清华园
220 8月28日 蔚然百年的清华学风

222 9月4日 “清华创客”王世栋：让每个人的3D创想变成现实
224 9月11日 “清华大学新百年教学成就奖”颁奖
226 9月12日 行为与沟通实验室：打造自我实验、自我提高的平台
228 9月13日 彭凯平：幸福是一种有意义的快乐
230 9月14日 周济团队：用钻研挑战材料王国的不可能
232 9月15日 温馨雅室别样红——梁思成林徽因故居
234 9月18日 钱易：最大的幸福是后生可“慰”
236 9月19日 曾攀：把“有限元”讲得“出神入化”
238 9月20日 程文浩：教学是生命，是信仰
240 9月21日 彭林：清华学生太优秀，老师多努力都不过分
242 9月22日 华罗庚：天才出于积累，聪明在于勤奋
244 9月25日 阎学通：“为人”是一辈子的学问
246 9月26日 赵青：清华体育传统是从教的力量源泉
248 9月27日 邓俊辉：精致的趣味，师者的情怀
250 9月28日 于歆杰：执匠人之心，铺设育人“电路”
252 9月29日 一封家书

254 10月9日 全球胜任力课程——走在“一带一路”上的课堂
256 10月10日 清华国际本科新生拓展营：感受中华文化，传递清华精神
258 10月11日 全球创新学院教研大楼在西雅图落成启用
260 10月12日 清华大学艺术博物馆开馆一周年，迎来设计者马里奥·博塔
262 10月13日 回忆园中好风景——梅贻琦故居
264 10月16日 张强课题组：化学领域版“小蝌蚪找妈妈”
266 10月17日 全运赛场上的清华“学生兵”
268 10月18日 清华师生喜迎中国共产党第十九次全国代表大会胜利召开！

203 Graduation: Entering into "Jianghu" from Tsinghua

205 Celebrating the Success of the 14th Party Congress of Tsinghua University of the CPC
207 A Wonderful Day at Tsinghua Art Museum: from Monet to Soulages
209 This Summer, Tsinghua Launched New Dishes
211 Former Residence of Zhao Yuanren : His Nation, His Home, His Deep Affection
213 Yu Wanying: Here's an Amazing Hand-painted Tsinghua Campus

215 Autumn Begins: Goodbye to Summer, Hello to Autumn
217 No Sports, No Tsinghua: Tsinghua's Sporting History
219 To the Class of 2017: Welcome to a Better Tsinghua
221 One Hundred Years of Study at Tsinghua University

223 Tsinghua Maker Wang Shidong: Materializing Everyone's 3D Creative Imagination
225 Tsinghua University New Century Teaching Achievement Award
227 Behavior and Communication Laboratory—a Platform for Self-experiment and Self-improvement
229 Peng Kaiping: Happiness Is a Form of Meaningful Joy
231 Zhou Ji: Challenging the Impossible in the Material Kingdom
233 No. 8 of Xinlin Yard： Witness of New China's Architectural History
235 Qian Yi: Surpassed by Excellent Students Is Great Happiness
237 Zeng Pan: Bringing Mechanical Engineering Classes to Life
239 Cheng Wenhao: Teaching Is Life, Teaching Is Faith
241 Peng Lin: Tsinghua Students Are So Good, and It Is Perfectly Fine That Teachers Work Hard
243 Hua Luogeng: Genius Comes from Accumulation, Intelligence Comes from Diligence
245 Yan Xuetong: Learning Integrity Is a Lifelong Pursuit
247 Zhao Qing: Tsinghua's Sports Tradition Is the Source of Motivation as a Teacher
249 Deng Junhui: Bringing Delicacy into Teaching
251 Yu Xinjie: Sharing His Greatest Joy in Teaching
253 A Letter to Home

255 Global Competence Course on the Belt and Road
257 International Undergraduate Enhancement Camp : Feel the Chinese Culture and the Spirit of Tsinghua
259 The GIX（Global Innovation Exchange）Building in Seattle Opens
261 Tsinghua University Art Museum Welcomes Her Designer Mario Botta for 1st Anniversary Celebration
263 Former Residence of Mei Yiqi: in the Garden of Memory
265 Zhang Qiang's Team: Chemical Version of "Baby Tadpoles Looking for Their Mothers"
267 Tsinghua's Students in the National Sports Game
269 Tsinghua Teachers and Students Warmly Welcomed the 19th CPC National Congress

270 10月19日 砥砺奋进看清华·教育教学篇：努力培育肩负使命、追求卓越的人
272 10月20日 砥砺奋进看清华·学术科研篇：推进科研体制机制改革，催生一流创新成果

274 10月23日 砥砺奋进看清华·学生思政篇：点亮理想之灯，照亮前行之路
276 10月24日 砥砺奋进看清华·人事制度改革篇：激发人才引擎动力，助推世界一流大学建设

278 10月25日 砥砺奋进看清华·全球战略篇：风从清华来，吹向全世界
280 10月26日 清华美院向帆：“艺术与科技的春天”就是当下
282 10月27日 杨学诚：我这支蜡烛，不求点得长，只求点得亮
284 10月30日 “会飞的盒子”实践支队：带着山区的孩子飞到更远的地方

286 11月1日 王步高：清华园的诗风词韵，离不开他的心血灌溉
288 11月2日 数学系扈志明：当一名教师一直都是我的心愿
290 11月3日 “双一流”背景下的一流本科教育：清华倾全力培养肩负使命、追求卓越的人
292 11月6日 聂建国院士：传递土木工程的广博与厚重
294 11月7日 假如清华只有100个本科生
296 11月8日 本科教学大家谈
298 11月9日 清华本科生的一天
300 11月10日 张仃：先生之风，山高水长
302 11月13日 “八度阳光”创业团队：以光汇电，助力扶贫
304 11月14日 “赤子初心”致敬党的光辉历史
306 11月15日 筑梦成网，织就光明未来
308 11月16日 清华大学张学工团队入选首批“人类细胞图谱计划”项目
310 11月17日 清华大学第一级学生：为人垂一范，为学报国恩
312 11月20日 清华领衔团队斩获世界高性能计算最高奖“戈登·贝尔”奖，创新战略+学科交叉打造一流超算平台

316 11月21日 清华美院实验室：艺术“美”梦实现的地方
318 11月22日 小雪：盼望
320 11月23日 当数字技术遇上甲骨文——清华美术学院陈楠设计汉仪陈体甲骨文
322 11月24日 清华最早的图书馆：梦开始的地方
324 11月27日 “挑战杯”特等奖“天格计划”：基础科学也可以很“酷”
326 11月28日 清华学生手语社：用手画出彩虹，让爱成为行动
328 11月29日 初探电子系微纳光电子学实验室：光子的世界，精致的诺言
330 11月30日 航天航空学院教授郑钢铁：钢铁是怎样炼成的

332 12月1日 西区体育馆：清华精神的“见证者”
334 12月4日 李稻葵做客“人文清华”讲坛：在新时代用新思维看待中国经济
336 12月5日 十年星星之火，初成燎原之势
338 12月6日 探访核研院核化学化工实验室：从岁月的溶液里萃取记忆

271 The Teachings of Tsinghua: Cultivating Talents and Always Be in the Pursuit for Excellence
273 Tsinghua's Research Achievements: Scientific Research System Reform to Promote First Class Results in Innovation
275 The Ideological and Political Work Towards Tsinghua Students: Lighting up a Path of Illumination
277 Tsinghua's System Reform of Human Resources Management: Stimulating the Engine for Talents and Boosting the Construction of a World-class University
279 An International Look at Tsinghua: the Tsinghua Wind Blows to the World
281 Xiang Fan: Now Is the Spring Time of Both Art and Technology
283 Yang Xuecheng: Like a Candle, I Only Desire It Burns Brightly
285 "The Flying Box" Team: Take Children in the Mountainous Area Fly Farther

287 Wang Bugao: The Poems of Tsinghua, a Part of His Soul
289 Department of Mathematics, Hu Zhiming: Being a Teacher Has Always Been My Wish
291 Tsinghua: Top Undergraduate Education Aligned with "Double World-class" Development
293 Academician Nie Jianguo: The Improvement of Teaching Is a Never-ending Journey
295 If Tsinghua Had Only 100 Undergraduates
297 Experts Share Essentials of Undergraduate Teaching at Tsinghua
299 One Day as a Tsinghua Undergraduate Student
301 Revolutionary Artist and Art Educator Zhang Ding: His Spirits Last Forever
303 Eight Sunshine Startup Team: Lighting the Way for Poverty Alleviation
305 Art Exhibition Pays Respects to Party History
307 Dream Grid, Building a Bright Future
309 Zhang Xuegong Team of Tsinghua University Is Selected in the "Human Cell Atlas" Program
311 First Class of Tsinghua: for Oneself, for Others and for the Nation
314 A Tsinghua-led Team Won "Gordon Bell Prize" (the World's Most Prestigious Award in High Performance Computing)
317 The Laboratories of Tsinghua Academy of Arts and Design: Where Art Dreams Come True
319 Yearning for Light Snow
321 Chen Nan's "Digital Oracle Bone Inscriptions" Design: When Digital Technology Meets Oracle Bone Inscriptions
323 Tsinghua's Earliest Library: The Place Where Dreams Begin
325 The "Challenge Cup" Top Grade Award — "Grid Project": Basic Science Can Be Really Cool
327 Sign Language Association: Use Hands to Paint Rainbows, Transfer Love into Action
329 The World of Photons: What Is the Micro-nano Optoelectronics Lab Like?
331 Prof. Zheng Gangtie from the School of Aerospace Engineering: How Is Steel Tempered?

333 The West District Gymnasium: a "Witness" to the Tsinghua Spirit
335 Li Daokui Attended the Humanitas Tsinghua Forum: New Thinking for China's Economy in the New Era
337 Ten Years of "iSpark", It is Just the Beginning
339 The Laboratory of Nuclear Chemistry and Nuclear Chemical Engineering: Extracting Tsinghua's Distant Past in Nuclear Chemistry Research

340 12月7日 二十四节气之大雪
342 12月8日 忆“一二·九”运动骨干、清华大学校友陆璀
344 12月11日 2017年清华大学特等奖学金获得者胡耀文：“大满贯”是怎样炼成的
346 12月12日 清华大学学生粉刷匠工作室协会：改造校园，粉刷梦想
348 12月13日 “为祖国健康工作五十年”提出60周年：清华体育精神60年的接力
350 12月15日 王文显：清华园里的“话剧教父”
352 12月18日 “闯世界”本科生海外学术研修支持计划：学术人才的“清华设计，全球培养”
354 12月19日 清华大学学生清源协会：运用专业知识，促进可持续发展

356 12月20日 探访模拟法庭实验室：法学实践的第二课堂
358 12月21日 鲍捷：老一辈科学家的影子，新一代赤子的心
360 12月22日 饺子们，温暖整个冬天吧！
362 12月25日 2017年清华大学特等奖学金获得者余天呈：做有人文精神的科学家
364 12月26日 本科生课程咨询委员会：学生是教改的主角
366 12月27日 戏曲进清华：给我一天，还你千年
368 12月28日 交叉信息院金奇奂研究组刷新单量子比特储存相干时间世界纪录

370 12月29日 2017，我们与清华一起走过

372 后记

341 Heavy Snow, the 21st Solar Term of the Year
343 Lu Cui: Backbone of the December 9th Movement
345 Hu Yaowen, The Recipient of 2017 Tsinghua Top Grade Scholarship: The Grand Slam
347 KidStudio: Transform the Campus and Paint the Dream
349 "To Work Healthily for 50 years for Our Motherland": 60 Years of Tsinghua's Sportsmanship
351 John Wong-Quincey: Father of Stage Play in Tsinghua
353 "Top Open" Program: Cultivating Academic Talents in Global Culture
355 Rural International Student Exchange of Tsinghua University: Using Professional Knowledge to Promote Sustainable Development in China
357 Moot Court Laboratory: the Second Classroom of Law Practice
359 Young Scholar Bao Jie Inheriting the Older Generation Scientists' Spirit
361 Dumplings, Warm up This Winter!
363 Winner of Tsinghua Top Grade Scholarship Yu Tiancheng: to Be a Scientist with Humanistic Care
365 Advisory Committee of Undergraduate Courses: Students Are the Protagonists of Education Reform
367 Traditional Chinese Opera in Tsinghua: a Day in Exchange for a Thousand Years
369 Kihwan Kim's Group from the Institute of Interdisciplinary Information Sciences Breaks the World-record in the Coherence Time of a Single Quantum Bit Storage
371 The 10 Most-read Tsinghua Spotlights Stories of 2017

清华映像 2017

1月3日

世纪清华　再续地缘

供稿 | 地学系

文字 | 地学系

图片 | 支剑元

时隔 64 年，清华大学迎来了地学系的回归。2016 年 11 月 30 日，清华大学地球系统科学系成立。这是百年清华高起点、高水平复建地学学科，建设世界一流大学的又一重要举措。

清华大学拥有悠久辉煌的地学历史，是我国最早开展地学学科教育和科学研究的高校之一。1928 年，清华大学地学系成立，著名地质学家翁文灏担任首任系主任。其后，清华大学地学系经历数次重组调整，抗战时期也曾一度中断，在 20 余年的发展中，共培养毕业生 200 多人。据不完全统计，共有 41 位毕业生当选为中国科学院地学学部院士，其中包括荣获 2003 年世界气象组织最高奖及 2006 年国家科学技术最高奖的气象学家叶笃正先生。1952 年，清华大学地学系和气象系被调整到北京大学；地质学系被调出，参与组建北京地质学院。此后，清华大学地学学科的发展处于空白状态。

2009 年 3 月，清华大学决定复建地学学科，成立了清华大学地球系统科学研究中心。清华大学充分发挥自身的综合优势，在较短时间内凝聚了一批人才。截至目前，清华大学地学系拥有教研系列教师 28 人，其中包括“千人计划”入选者、“何梁何利奖”获得者、国家杰出青年科学基金获得者等多名人才。

2016 年 11 月，基于“神威·太湖之光”系统的“千万核可扩展全球大气动力学全隐式模拟”论文一举拿下了超级计算应用领域世界最高奖——“戈登·贝尔奖”！地学系教师付昊桓是论文通讯作者之一。此外，地学系在世界上率先建成最高分辨率（30 米）的全球地表覆盖和农地数据库，被世界科研机构广泛应用和引用。地学系与环境学院联合建立的大气污染防治动态评估与管理平台为决策提供实时动态支持，提升地方“精准治霾、科学治污”的能力。地学系师生还在共同努力下，获得了一批地学领域的新认识。

未来，清华大学地球系统科学系的发展将突破以往地学的单圈层、孤立研究、多以定性研究为特点的传统，以系统的、多圈层相互作用、定量化的观点去认识地球这一复杂的、开放的巨系统；围绕地球系统过程、地球系统模式、地球系统观测和全球变化经济学等领域探索新知，培养学生，教育大众，为维护地球生态环境安全与人类可持续发展做出新的贡献！

Centennial Tsinghua Rekindling Relationship with Geoscience

On November 30, 2016, the Department of Earth System Science (DESS) at Tsinghua University was officially established. The establishment of DESS is another crucial step as this centurial university works to promote the discipline of geoscience nationally, and contributes to the continued construction of a world-class university.

Tsinghua University has a long and splendid history of geoscience studies. As one of the earliest centers of geoscience education and research in China, Tsinghua University has cultivated many experts of global renown. The Department of Geography at Tsinghua University was officially founded in September 1928 and the first group of students enrolled the following year. The first dean, Dr. Weng Wenhao, was one of the founders of modern Chinese geology. The Department of Geography was renamed as the Department of Geoscience in 1933, which was consisted of three groups: geography, geology, and meteorology. Meteorology separated to form an independent department in 1947, followed by geology in 1950. More than 200 students graduated from the Departments of Geoscience, Geology, and Meteorology. Among these, at least 41 graduates of geoscience disciplines at Tsinghua University were elected as academicians of the Division of Earth Sciences at the Chinese Academy of Sciences. One of the most outstanding representatives is the meteorologist Dr. Ye Duzheng, who won the top prize of the World Meteorological Organization in 2003 and the National Top Science and Technology Award in China in 2006. In 1952, the Department of Geoscience and Department of Meteorology were reassigned to Peking University, while the Department of Geology became the foundation of the Beijing Institute of Geology. Geoscience research at Tsinghua University ceased after these reconfigurations.

In March 2009, the Center for Earth System Science (the predecessor of DESS) at Tsinghua University was founded. Drawing on the comprehensive advantages of Tsinghua University and a clear understanding of the frontiers of earth system science, DESS has gathered an outstanding group of talents in climate dynamics and change, biogeochemistry, earth system observation and simulation technology, high performance computing, global change economics, and related disciplines. DESS has grown into a distinctive and internationally influential department within a relatively short period. DESS now has 28 faculty members, including 10 professors, 15 associate professors, and 3 assistant professors. Among DESS faculty, there are three foreign teachers, two recipients of "thousand talents plan" fellowships, one winner of the "HO LEUNG HO LEE" Award, five recipients of National Outstanding Youth Natural Science Funding, two winners of the "young thousand talents plan" , two winners of "top young talent" awards, and one winner of National Excellent Youth Natural Science Funding.

DESS faculty and students have achieved a series of results with international impacts, publishing over 500 *SCI* papers since 2000. Among these, more than 21 papers have appeared in internationally renowned journals such as *Nature*, *Science*, *Lancet*, and *Proceedings of the National Academy of Science*. DESS has also taken part in the management and operation of the National Supercomputer Center in Wuxi. Therefore, members of DESS won this year's ACM Gordon Bell Prize, the highest award in supercomputing, for the development of a "10M-Core Scalable Fully-Implicit Solver for Nonhydrostatic Atmospheric Dynamics" on the Sunway TaihuLight system. This is the first time that a Chinese team has won this award, with a DESS Professor Fu Haohuan among the corresponding authors of the prizewinning study. DESS has also produced the highest resolution (30 meters) global land cover map and agricultural land database to date. This database is widely used and has been cited by scientific institutions worldwide. In cooperation with the School of Environment, DESS has set up a dynamic evaluation and management platform for policymakers to prevent and control atmospheric pollution. This initiative has greatly improved local capabilities to "precisely control haze and scientifically control pollution" .

The multi-disciplinary faculty brought together in DESS will facilitate innovative research at the frontiers of earth system science, replacing traditional single-sphere qualitative studies with systematic quantitative analyses that track interactions among a wide range of variables and processes. This approach places DESS along the forefront of efforts to understand the immense and complicated environmental systems that make up our planet and the surrounding universe. Future explorations toward understanding, modeling, and observing earth systems and related economies will foster student development, educate the public, and contribute to environmental protection and the sustainable development of the human race.

Contributor | Department of Earth System Science

Translation and revision | Department of Earth System Science

Image | Zhi Jianyuan

1月4日

研究生精品课程“现代智能信息处理”

供稿丨精仪系

采访、文字丨胡颖

图片丨陈稳杰

“现代智能信息处理是十分活跃和具有挑战性的领域，世界范围内，伯克利加州大学是最早开设相关课程的学校之一。”研究生精品课程“现代智能信息处理”授课教师王雪教授笑着说。

王雪老师介绍，伯克利开设的这门课程名为“软计算”。在当时的背景下，“软计算”是一个很新的名词——传统计算（硬计算）的主要特征是严格、确定和精确，但是传统计算并不适合处理现实生活中的许多问题。而软计算及后续发展形成的现代智能信息处理方法，通过对不确定、不精确及不完全真值的容错建模，取得低代价的解决方案和鲁棒性，并模拟自然界中智能系统的信息处理过程来有效处理日常工作，可以说是实现人工智能的基础和关键。而人工智能的概念发展也已历经了 60 余年，其历程并非一帆风顺，曾经历低谷时期，直至近年来随着深度学习理论等的出现，再次成为人们关注的热点之一。2016 年上半年，谷歌智能机器人 Alpha Go 和李世石进行人机大战之后，人工智能的概念再度在全球范围内走红。在前不久刚结束的第三届世界互联网大会上，国内互联网界巨头都提出了要将人工智能作为非常重要的未来热点和发展方向。

王雪老师说，当年自己的博士课题就是面向人工智能专家系统及其应用方面的研究，在清华任教的 20 余年也一直在该领域埋头苦干、努力积累。王雪教授目前担任精密测试技术及仪器国家重点实验室副主任、精密仪器系副主任，承担着多项国家重大重点科研项目，多次获得国际顶级期刊与会议的最佳论文奖、最高引用奖，2015 年和 2016 年连续两年入选爱思唯尔中国高被引学者。

“现代智能信息处理”课程由王雪老师自 2002 年起开设，已经有近 15 年的发展历程。作为清华研究生精品课，该课程深度结合了人工智能的基础理论和智能信息的处理技术，与传感测试、智能制造领域紧密融合，是学科间相互结合与渗透的产物，具有广阔的应用前景。课程介绍了测试计算智能、人工智能的基础理论和方法。具体内容包括：测试系统的组成和信息获取过程、人工智能的起源及发展、数据融合的基本原理；神经计算基础和基本方法、实现技术和支持向量机方法；模糊计算中的模糊逻辑与模糊推理、模糊计算应用和粗糙集；进化计算中的遗传算法、粒群智能、蚁群智能等方法和实例等。

王雪老师说：“人工智能虽然看似很‘高大上’，但最重要的是如何应用到实际应用领域。”因此，现代智能信息处理课程开设的实验在这门课程中扮演着必不可少的角色。课程开设了“神经计算信号模式识别”“遗传算法非线性全局优化”“模糊逻辑非稳态系统运动控制”等创新型挑战实验，与讲授的人工智能基础理论和方法相配合，让学生理论联系实际，提高学生动手能力，将深刻而枯燥的理论以最浅显、最直观、最生动的方式呈现出来，做到真正地学以致用，从而激发学生的学习兴趣。在王雪老师、助教和学生的共同努力下，课程连续被评为清华大学研究生精品课，出版获奖教材，课程实验系统获得专利与软件著作权，指导学生入围 NI 学生设计大赛全球 Top10。此外，为了使知识传授的形式更为丰富多彩，王雪老师在课堂教学中融入了大量师生互动、短时演讲、学术研讨与翻转课堂等特色环节，实现课堂教学成果的实时反馈评估。

新的时代不断赋予课程新的内容，为了始终保持与时俱进的步伐，王雪老师也持续对课程做出相应的变革与发展。在课堂上，王雪老师总是及时向学生传达该领域的最新资讯和对学科未来的预测，并将自己的学术理念展示给学生，启发学生思考这样几个问题：为什么要学这门课？学这门课的用处何在？未来如何利用所学知识服务于实践？

通过理论、实践与思考结合的多元化授课形式，“现代智能信息处理”课程真正达到了“价值塑造、能力培养、知识传授”三位一体的授课目标，对提高清华研究生课程的整体水平起到了示范作用。最后，王雪老师还不忘表扬一下参与课程的同学：“多年的教学过程中，清华学生的好学、机敏、勤奋和刻苦让人印象深刻，期待他们将课程中的所学所思所悟，切实地转化为科研的助力，为学校、为所在学科领域的进步做出贡献。”

Quality Course for Postgraduate Students: Modern Intelligent Information Processing

"Modern intelligent information processing is a hot issue worldwide. UC Berkeley is one of the first universities to launch the relative courses." Professor Wang Xue from the Department of Precision Instrument (DPI), said with a smile.

Professor Wang Xue said, when UC Berkeley launched this course, "soft computing" was a new term. Different from the hard computing realizing accurate and strict computation, soft computing and the proposed modern intelligent information processing methods aim to solve the actual problems by ambiguous and fuzzy algorithms inspired by natural intelligent systems such as human brain. Modern intelligent information processing is the base stone of artificial intelligence The concept of artificial intelligence was developed 60 years ago. It also has experienced a tough period, and until recently, with the breakthrough in deep learning, it appears in the public again. After the man-machine match between Alpha Go and Lee SeDol in 2016, artificial intelligence became popular in the world once again, and will reach a peak of development in the future. In the 3rd World Conference on Internet held recently, many Internet giants have put forward that China will take artificial intelligence as the future focus and development trend.

Professor Wang mentioned that his doctoral thesis was the applications of artificial intelligence and expert systems. After graduation he became a faculty member in Tsinghua University and has been dedicated to this field for more than 20 years. Currently, he holds the position of the vice director of the State Key Laboratory of Precision Measurement Technology and Instruments, and the vice dean of the Department of Precision Instrument, undertaking a number of national key scientific research projects. In the two consecutive years of 2015 and 2016, he was awarded Top 100 highly cited scholars of Elsevier China.

The course "Modern Intelligent Information Processing" was launched by Professor Wang in 2002. As one of the quality courses for postgraduate students in Tsinghua University, "Modern Intelligent Information Processing" combines artificial intelligence and intelligent information processing, as well as advanced sensing technology and intelligent manufacturing. The course has broad application prospects. The main content of this course includes the theories and methods in artificial intelligence, such as neural network, evolution computing and fuzzy computing.

"In fact, the most important thing is how to apply these theories to the actual field." said Professor Wang. Therefore, experiments play an essential role in this course. There are three novel experiments for students which are neural network based signal pattern recognition, genetic algorithm based nonlinear global optimization and fuzzy computing based unstable system control. These experiments intend to let students get started quickly, and present the profound and boring theories in the simple, intuitive and vivid way, releasing study for applications, to stimulate students' interest in learning. Under the joint efforts of Professor Wang, teaching assistants and students, this course has been included in the excellent course list twice and has obtained the teaching prize, the software copyright and the national invention patent. In addition, in order to make the knowledge imparted in the form of a richer and more colorful way, Professor Wang has integrated teacher-student interaction, short speeches, academic discussions, flipped classroom characteristics and other characteristic links into classroom teaching, to achieve real-time feedback evaluation of classroom teaching results.

The new content of the course has been given by the new era, and in order to keep pace with the times, Professor Wang has also made corresponding changes and development of the course continuously. In the class, Professor Wang always conveys the latest consultation in the field and the prediction of the future of the discipline in a timely manner to the students, and show his academic ideas to students, to inspire students to think about these issues: Why should we learn this course? What is the use of this course? How to use the knowledge we have gained to solve the actual problems in the future?

Through diversified teaching modes of the combination of theory, practice and thinking, modern intelligent information processing course achieves the three-in-one teaching goal "value shaping, ability training, knowledge imparting" , which is the exemplary role for improving the overall level of graduate courses at Tsinghua. Finally, Professor Wang emphasized that he was impressed by the smart and hard-working students in Tsinghua university and sincerely hope that they could utilize the relative theories and methods in their own fields and make contributions to the development of industries.

Contributor | Department of Precision Instrument

Translation and revision | Brice Icigumije

Image | Chen Wenjie

1月6日

文字 | 张铮

图片 | 李娜

影响清华的演讲之蒋南翔校长就职演说

在今天的清华园中，有很多师生们耳熟能详的教育理念和人才培养制度，都创立于蒋南翔担任清华校长的时期。例如：倡导学生积极参加体育锻炼的“为祖国健康工作五十年”的口号和“强制锻炼”的要求，由高年级本科生和研究生担任本科生班级辅导员的“双肩挑”制度，要求本科生将毕业设计与生产生活实践相结合的“真刀真枪做毕业设计”的“教育、科研、生产三结合”的方法，等等。由蒋南翔一生的教育实践总结提炼的“蒋南翔教育思想”，至今仍然在清华大学发挥着重要的作用。

1952 年 12 月，蒋南翔出任清华大学校长。当年 12 月 31 日，在全校教职工和学生代表为他举办的欢迎会上，他发表了一篇简短的致辞，精练地阐述了自己的教育理念和对清华未来发展的期盼。他在致辞中提到的很多想法，后来也在他的工作中得到充分的印证。

在演讲一开始，蒋南翔谈道：“清华大学是我的母校。在 1932 年到 1937 年期间，我在这里度过了自己的大学生活。也正是在这个强敌压境、我们祖国处在风雨飘摇的困难时期，我在这里开始参加了革命活动，参加了共产主义青年团和中国共产党。”1932 年，19 岁的蒋南翔从江苏宜兴考入清华大学中国文学系，1933 年加入中国共产党，参与主编《清华周刊》和《北方青年》等进步刊物，并在 1935 年的“一二·九”运动中成为重要的领导者之一。正是他，在起草的《清华大学救国会告全国同胞书》中发出了“华北之大，已经安放不得一张平静的书桌了！”这样振聋发聩的呐喊。

随后，蒋南翔在致辞中说：“清华大学当前迫切的任务就是要深入教育改革，破除英美资产阶级的旧教育传统，逐步地把自己改造成为社会主义的新型工业大学。”在这样的理念下，蒋南翔后来在师生中进行系统的马克思主义理论教育，并亲自讲授相关课程，而且他提出清华大学应该成为“红色工程师的摇篮”，培养“又红又专、全面发展”的社会主义建设者和接班人。在强化“思想与专业都要过硬，工程教育与生产实践相结合”的同时，他也注重学生人文素养的提升。他曾坚决制止把清华大学的文科图书迁出，在学生的联欢会上演奏二胡，认为清华要加强理科的基础，文化素养也不能降低。

在致辞的最后，蒋南翔强调在清华的高等教育改革要“坚持党的领导，忠实地正确地执行各项教育政策”，并号召“全校师生员工团结一致，把我们的学校不断推向前进。”确实，在他担任清华校长期间，近 3 万名毕业生从清华园奔赴祖国最需要的地方，靠着过硬的政治素质、身体基础和业务能力，成长为各行各业的骨干和主力。

Influencing Tsinghua: President Jiang Nanxiang's Inauguration Speech

At present, many concepts of education and talent training systems that are well-known among Tsinghua's teachers and students were established in the period when Jiang Nanxiang served as the president of Tsinghua University. For example, the slogan of "work healthily for 50 years for our motherland" and requirement of "compulsory exercise" are to encourage students to actively participate in physical exercise, the "double responsibility" program means selecting the senior undergraduates and postgraduate students to act as student counselors, the method of "combination of education, research, and production" is to require undergraduates to combine graduation design, production and life practice, namely "to do graduation design with real things" , and so on. Today, the "Jiang Nanxiang's education thought" still plays an important role in Tsinghua University.

Jiang Nanxiang had served as the president of Tsinghua University for nearly 14 years, starting from the end of 1952. On December 31, 1952, Jiang Nanxiang delivered a brief speech in a welcoming meeting held by the faculty members and student representatives for him, elaborating on his educational concepts and expectation on the future development of Tsinghua University. Many of the ideas he mentioned in his speech were fully confirmed in his work afterwards.

At the beginning of the speech, Jiang Nanxiang said, "Tsinghua University is my alma mater, and I spent my university life here from 1932 to 1937. It was also in this difficult time when powerful enemies were invading us and our country was in an unstable situation. I participated in the revolution from here, joined the Youth League and the Communist Party of China." In 1932, 19-year-old Jiang Nanxiang was admitted to Tsinghua University; in 1933, he joined the CPC and took part in editing journals such as *Tsinghua Weekly* and *Northern Youth*; and in 1935, he became one of the important leaders in the "December 9th Movement" . It was him who cried "North China is such a vast area, but already no place to put a desk for quiet reading!"

Jiang Nanxiang said in his speech, "the current urgent task of Tsinghua University is to deepen its educational reform, to break the old educational tradition, and to gradually transform our university into a socialistic industrial university." Under this concept, Jiang Nanxiang later started giving systematic education of Marxist theory to teachers and students, and personally taught the relevant courses. He also proposed that Tsinghua University should become "the cradle of red engineers" , and cultivate "both socialist-minded and professional, and comprehensively developed" graduates. At the same time of strengthening that "both ideology and professional skills must be perfect, engineering education and production practice should be combined" , he also paid attention to the improvement of students' humanistic qualities. He once resolutely put a stop to the moving-out of the liberal arts books of Tsinghua University, and played urheen at student get-togethers. He considered Tsinghua University should strengthen both liberal arts education and science education.

Indeed, during Jiang's tenure as the president of Tsinghua University, nearly 30,000 graduates went to the most talent-needed places of the motherland, and relying on good political quality, physical condition and professional ability, they grew into the backbone and primary forces in all walks of life.

Contributor | Department of Earth System Science

Translation and revision | Anish Vincent Pandey

Image | Li Na

1月9日

供稿 | 精仪系

文字 | 刘书田

图片 | 陈稳杰

精仪系本科生米璐在生物微机电领域著名期刊发表封面文章

在生物微机电领域，单细胞捕获技术在生物细胞操作和分析中具有重要的应用，这一技术近年来也获得了极大的关注和显著的发展。

但在以往的研究中，当细胞悬浮液注入生物芯片后，细胞往往以随机的方式进入流道，少量细胞通过窄口或流道中的凹槽被限制在流道内，而其他多数细胞随悬浮液流出出口。细胞在流道中能否进入捕获单元的概率呈现为高斯分布，因此此类方式的捕捉效率非常有限。

而精密仪器系 2013 级本科生米璐则在单细胞捕获方面的研究上有了进一步的突破。她以第一作者身份撰写的论文《基于流阻网络的高效率大规模单细胞捕获技术》在生物微机电领域著名期刊 *Lab on a Chip* 上发表，并入选当期封底展示论文。精仪系博士生黄亮为本文的共同第一作者，精仪系“青年千人”王文会为本文通讯作者，生命学院研究员吴琼等为本文合作作者。

“我们在研究中主要提出了一种新颖的单细胞捕获器件。”米璐介绍道。这种器件巧妙地利用等效电阻网络原理设计了数以万记的大规模捕获单元矩阵，遵循最小流阻原理捕获单细胞，每个单元均可以保证很高的捕获效率，并且单元之间相对独立，最终实现高效和灵活的大规模和图案化单细胞阵列操作。

米璐的研究成果得到了审稿人的一致高度肯定，这篇论文被评价为有望解决单细胞捕捉中同时满足大规模阵列和高效率要求 (it can be scaled up and still keep a high trapping efficiency) 这一挑战性问题，而她也为之付出了难以想象的努力。

尽管在最初的研究中，米璐花费了大量的时间不断优化实验方案，却未能取得任何突破，科研最艰难的时候她甚至被建议更换课题。但凭着一股不愿服输的精神，米璐一有时间就会到实验室开展工作，经常熬夜做实验、改文章。2016 年暑假，米璐得到清华“闯世界”计划的支持，到哈佛大学 David A. Weitz 教授实验室从事相关的研究工作。

探索未知的热情和想要攻克难题的坚定信念让她最终收获到了科研的硕果，论文所刊登的期刊 *Lab on a Chip* 是英国皇家化学学会 (RSC) 旗下的旗舰期刊之一，在生物微机电研究领域拥有很高的声誉和地位。值得一提的是，该论文的前期工作在 2016 年 7 月召开的 Optofluidics2016 国际会议上也获得了最佳会议论文奖，并申请了一项国家专利。

对于此次论文的发表，米璐感到倍受鼓舞。但兴奋之后，她又回到了实验室，希望基于已有的单细胞捕获芯片，对在单细胞层面上的细胞迁移等问题进行更深入的研究。米璐也期待着能将已有的技术真正转换成生物研究中有意义的发现。

Undergraduate Student from DPI Published Cover Article for Well-known Journal in the Field of Biological Micro-electromechanical System

In the field of bio-microelectronics, single-cell traps have important applications in biological cell manipulation and analysis. Such technology has also, in recent years, gained much attention and significant development.

However, from previous studies, when the suspension cell was injected into the bio-chip, the cells often enter in a random manner. While a majority of cells do enter successfully, a small number of them do not. Whether the cells can fully enter and given the probability of the Gaussian distribution, this type of capture efficiency is very limited.

The 2013's undergraduate student Mi Lu from the Department of Precision Instruments (DPI) at Tsinghua University has made further breakthroughs in this field. She is the first author of the article *A fluidic circuit based, high-efficiency and large-scale single cell trap*. This research paper was published in the journal *Lab on a Chip* and it was selected to be part of the outside back cover. Huang Liang and Dr. Wang Wenhui from DPI are the co-first author and corresponding author correspondingly. Professor Wu Qiong from the School of Life Sciences at Tsinghua University is the co-author of the research paper as well.

"We proposed a novel device for single cell trapping in our study." said Mi Lu. Through large-scale captures, this device is able to ensure high capture efficiency and relative independence between each single cells which allows more effective use and flexibility.

Mi's research achievements gained much praise from the editors and the paper is considered to be a great proposal in solving single cell trapping with high efficiency and flexibility for large scale cell patterning. It can be scaled up and still keep a high trapping efficiency. Mi has made unimaginable efforts in order to tackle such challenges.

In the initial phase, despite spending a lot of time in optimizing the experiment scheme, Mi was unable to make any breakthroughs. Scientific research is difficult and people have suggested that she change the research topic. Yet, Mi refused to give up and spent all her time working in the lab. She often stay up late for experiments and writing articles. In the summer holidays of 2016, Mi gained support from Tsinghua's "Into the world" plan where she will be continuing with her research in Professor David A. Weitz's Laboratory at Harvard University.

Wishing to explore the unknown and being passionate in overcoming difficulties led Mi to eventually harvesting the fruit of scientific research. The journal *Lab on a Chip* is one of the flagship journals under the Royal Society of Chemistry (RSC). In the field of bio-MEMs research, it holds high reputation and status. It is worth mentioning that the preliminary work of the paper also gained the best conference paper award at July 2016's Optofluidics International Conference. Application has been made for it to be a national patent.

With regards to the publication of this paper, Mi Lu felt greatly encouraged. Yet after all the excitement, she returned back to the laboratory and desired to carry out more in-depth studies in the field of single-cell capturing as well as cell migration at a single-cell level. Mi also hopes to make more meaningful discovery and convert existing technology into more biological research.

Contributor | Department of Precision Instrument

Translation and revision | Min Weiyuan

Image | Chen Wenjie

1月10日

供稿 | 团委

文字 | 冯婉婷

图片 | 梁露文

校园歌手大赛：用一年的时间只为做好这一件事

“清华大学校园歌手大赛已经走过二十六个年头，从‘大梦响家’到‘廿四声’，从‘音本位’到今天的‘留声纪’，校歌赛每年都吸引着数以千计的老师和学生的关注，堪称清华一年一度的音乐盛会……”2016年12月10日，在学校综合体育馆举办的第二十六届校园歌手大赛“留声纪”的开场视频里，主持人带着观众们一起回顾了校园歌手大赛走过的二十多载春秋。

清华大学校园歌手大赛是清华校内的传统大型文艺活动，自1990年创办以来，目前已经成功举办了二十六届。经过二十多年的成长，校园歌手大赛作为一项文艺活动在校内深受同学们的欢迎和喜爱，在国内高校学生文艺活动中也有相当高的知名度。在校园歌手大赛的舞台上，每一年都会涌现出许多优秀的校园歌手，他们用心唱出自己对音乐的爱与执着，并持续活跃在校园内外，其中还有不少选手发展成为职业歌手，推出个人专辑。

在过去十多年里，校园歌手大赛的影响力不断扩大，邀请到不少知名歌手担任嘉宾，高质量和高水准的现场比赛也吸引了不少来自校外的观众，这与长达一年的筹备过程以及台前幕后众多工作人员的付出密不可分。每一届校园歌手大赛从上半年的外围赛、预选赛，到下半年的新生赛、复赛，最后到十二月的决赛，每一场比赛都凝结着校学生会文艺部工作人员的精心策划与用心付出。他们来自不同年级，为了校园歌手大赛这个共同的爱好与目标而聚在一起。“我们用了一年只为做好这一件事。”第二十六届校园歌手大赛主要负责人之一、校学生会文艺部前任部长邓经纬同学在回顾这一年的工作时如是说。作为学校知名度颇高的学生活动，校园歌手大赛从初赛到决赛都由同学们自己筹办，即便是决赛现场具体的舞台、灯光、音响等工作，也主要是同学们自己担任工作人员。学生文艺活动的“学生”二字，不仅体现在参赛选手是校内优秀的音乐爱好者，也体现在活动的举办得益于同学们的策划与实践。

清华学生的文艺热情与基因向来都是有的，从大家耳熟能详的水木年华、李健到近年来走上职业歌手道路的廖国铱、丁芙妮，清华一直不乏热爱音乐、热爱文艺的人。从1990年到现在，每一届校园歌手大赛都涌现出许多让人惊喜的声音，每一年的比赛也在继承的基础上不断有发展与创新。校园歌手大赛为清华校内热爱音乐的人们提供了表现的舞台，也传承着清华的文艺传统，这体现在参与校园歌手大赛的每一位选手和工作人员身上。“校园歌手大赛的舞台给了我可以专注于自己音乐的感觉。”第二十六届校园歌手大赛冠军宿涵这样说道。一群有音乐执着和文艺热情的人用一年时间呈现一场精妙的音乐盛会，这或许可以作为对清华校园歌手大赛传统的概括。

Campus Singing Contest: Using One Year's Time to Do Just One Thing

"The Campus Singing Contest of Tsinghua University has gone through twenty-six years. From the 'big dreams' to the 'choir' to the 'sounds', the contest attracts thousands of teachers and students every year. It is called the Tsinghua Annual Music Event... ." On the December 10th, 2016, Tsinghua's gymnasium saw the opening of the 26th Singing Contest. The host reminded the audience and participants about the importance of this event and the significance of it being the 26th Singing Contest.

The Campus Singing Contest is a traditional large-scale cultural activity for Tsinghua. Since its establishment in 1990, it had since held 26 successful contests. After more than 20 years of development, the contest is welcomed and loved by the whole university and as a cultural activity, it enjoys high reputation even outside of Tsinghua campus. As a major art and cultural event, there are many outstanding campus singers who showcase their love for music on the stage. Many continue with their passion and remain both active in and out of the campus. Many have developed into professional singers and some have launched their own music album.

In the past ten years, the influence of this contest has been expanding. Many well-known singers have been invited as special guests. Such high quality and high standard of live shows also attracted a lot of audiences outside of Tsinghua. Preparation process is closely guarded by staff who work tirelessly behind the scene. Each year, the contest holds a qualification round then various competitions, semi-finals and eventually the final in December. Each was selected painstakingly by arts department at Student Union of Tsinghua University. "We have spent one year's time for this contest." said the former director of arts department Deng Jingwei, who was also the principal person in charge of the 26th Singing Contest. From the preliminary rounds to the final show, students were in charge and organized everything from stage design, lighting, sound and other necessary works. Such event not only reflect the students' passion for music and art but also the ability of them to plan, organize and execute major large-scale events.

Tsinghua students have always been passionate. From various singers such as music group Shuimunianhua, Li Jian, Liao Guoyue, Ding Funi and many more, Tsinghua has never had a lack of passion for the arts, literature and music. Since 1990, surprising talents have emerged from every competition and every new event has been based on the succession of continuous development and innovation. The contest provides a stage for performance as well as a way for Tsinghua to inherit literary and artistic traditions. "The stage allows me to focus on my music." said Su Han who won the champion of the 26th Singing Contest. A group of musicians and passionate individuals used the time of a whole year to present a fantastic music event which summarized the glory of the Tsinghua spirit and tradition.

Contributor | Youth league

Translation and revision | Min Weiyuan

Image | Liang Luwen

1月11日

供稿 | 法学院

文字 | 梁乐萌

图片 | 宋晨

《合同法》：做读者进一步深造的引路石

大学教育在“传道授业解惑”的基础上更加注重学生自主学习、研究，因此一本好的教材也就扮演着更为重要的角色。清华大学法学院崔建远教授希望他主编的教材《合同法》能“启迪思维，做读者进一步深造的引路石”。

《合同法》对应着法学院开设的“合同法”和“债法”两门课程，既适用于法学专业的本科生，也适用于研究生。这本教材以解释论为主，辅之以立法论，系统且全面地介绍了我国合同法的内容，阐释了我国合同制度及规则的意义，也挖掘了合同法及各项具体制度和规则的深层依据和价值。同时，它还反映了最新的民商立法与司法解释的精神及规定，吸收了最新的科研成果。

“拓展”“探讨”“反思”“论争”等板块是本书最大的特色。这些极具丰富性与创新性的板块起到了“引路石”的作用，通过真实多样的案例素材引导学生扩展视野，独立思考。《合同法》不仅在形式与思路上加以创新，填补了国内教材的空白，还在合同履行的抗辩权、合同变更、合同解除、违约责任等方面矫正了不适当的看法。书中许多观点被《法学家》《政治与法律》《人民司法案例》等学术刊物所刊载的论文多次引用。

崔建远教授曾经荣获第二届“全国杰出中青年法学家”称号，曾获教育部高等学校优秀青年教师奖、清华大学教书育人奖、清华大学良师益友奖等荣誉，并于2011年被聘为“长江学者奖励计划”特聘教授。谈到自己的学术研究，崔建远认为，中国正处在民事立法这个阶段，所以他的很多研究就是为立法服务的。而《合同法》书中的若干观点已被最高人民法院的司法解释所采纳。

《合同法》教材自2013年7月出版后经三次重印，得到了多个院校师生及众多法律实务工作者的广泛好评。在“亚马逊”“京东”“当当”等各大图书网站，该教材都获得了90%以上的好评率。“精益求精”“逻辑缜密”“难易适中”“文字流畅”等，是在商品评论中高频出现的词语。“编者有独立而严谨的思考，这在如今良莠不齐的教材市场中是难得的精品。”在“当当网”，一位不知名的网友这样评论道。

Course Book *Contract Law*: Further Leading the Way for Readers

On the basis of "reassuring knowledge" , higher education is set to pay more attention to students' autonomous learning and research. Therefore, good teaching materials play a more important role. Professor Cui Jianyuan from the School of Law at Tsinghua University hopes his edited course book *Contract Law* can "enlighten thinking and further lead the way for readers."

The course book *Contract Law* is for both courses "Contract Law" and "Law of Obligation" . This is applicable for both undergraduate and postgraduate students. The textbook gives priority to explaining the theory and is supplemented by legislative theory. It systematically and comprehensively introduces contract law in our country. It illustrates the significance of contract system as well as exploring the rules of contract law and the deep foundation, system and value that it holds. At the same time, it also reflects the latest legislation and judicial interpretation of regulation so that the latest scientific research and achievements could be better understood by all.

The four sections, namely "expansion" , "investigation" , "reflection" and "argument" , are the core characteristics of the book. These sections guide the readers through a variety of case materials and guide students to expand their field of vision. It trains students to adopt independent thinking and promote students' understanding of contract law. The course book *Contract Law* is not only being innovative in the form and way of thinking but it also fills the gaps found in domestic teaching materials. It corrects and adopts new approaches in areas such as contract performance, contract changes, termination and breaches of contracts. Many views in the book are cited by articles in reputable academic journals.

Professor Cui Jianyuan has been awarded the honor of "National Outstanding Young Jurist" , and won the "Outstanding Young Teachers from the Ministry of Education" and many more honors. In 2011, he has been selected as the distinguished professor of Chang Jiang Scholar Program. When it comes to his own academic research, Professor Cui argues that China is currently at the stage of civil legislation which is why many of his research is focused on services for such legislation. Many of the viewpoints in *Contract Law* have been adopted by judicial interpreters from the Supreme People's Courts.

Since published by Peking University Press in July 2013, the course book *Contract Law* has been reprinted thrice. It has received much favorable comments from law practitioners, teachers and students. In Amazon, JD.com, Dangdang.com and other web-based booksellers, the textbook has gained consistently more than 90% of positive rating. Comments such as "nearly perfection" , "logical" and "smooth read" are some of the most used words to describe the textbook. One anonymous netizen commented on Dangdang.com: "It is a rare thing to find on the market these days when an author is independent and rigorous in his thinking. When there is an abundance of mediocre teaching materials, this one is unique and no doubt, stands out."

Contributor | School of Law

Translation and revision | Min Weiyuan

Image | Song Chen

1月12日

供稿 | 材料学院

改编 | 杨茂艺

图片 | 李筱甜

材料学院陈娜副研究员等在室温磁性半导体及器件研究中取得重要进展

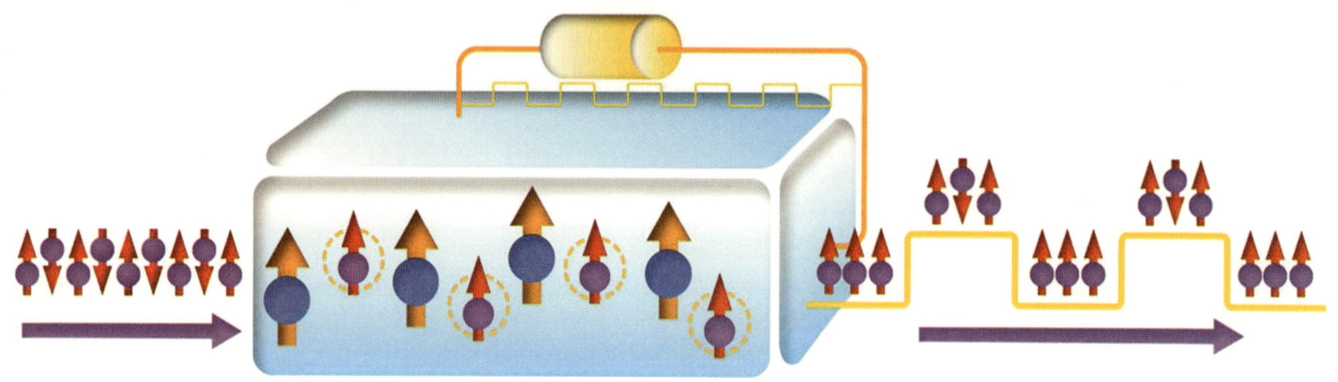

多年前，《科学》杂志曾提出 125 个重要科学问题，其中之一是“有没有可能创造出在室温下能够工作的磁性半导体材料”。近日，清华大学材料学院材料加工研究所非晶合金研究组陈娜副研究员及其合作者，通过诱导磁性金属玻璃发生金属 - 半导体转变的方式，开发出居里温度高于 600K 的 p 型磁性半导体，并基于此磁性半导体实现了室温 p-n 结和电控磁器件的制备。

研发室温实用型磁性半导体的重要性在哪里呢？

首先，磁性半导体兼具磁性和半导体特性，可以满足人们对电荷和自旋同时调控的期望，为信息的处理、存储和运输提供了一种全新的导电方式。磁性半导体的运用对于开发新一代电子器件（自旋场效应管、自旋发光二极管等）具有重要意义，将会大幅降低能耗、增加集成密度、提高数据运算速度，在未来的电子行业具有非常诱人的应用前景。

其次，探索室温实用型磁性半导体，并基于此材料开发室温实用型自旋电子器件一直是自旋电子学领域的关键科学问题。然而，到目前为止最为引人关注的稀磁半导体，尤其是基于Ⅲ - Ⅴ族半导体的稀磁半导体材料居里温度仅仅为 200K，无法满足电子器件在室温下工作的需求。

针对这一瓶颈，陈娜及其合作者采用“逆向思维”，通过氧化已有高居里温度磁性金属的方法制备新型磁性半导体，在保留磁性金属原有高温内禀磁性的同时使之获得半导体特性，由此开发出了居里温度高于 600K 的新型 $Co_{28.6}$ $Fe_{12.4}$ $Ta_{4.3}$ $B_{8.7}$ O_{46} 磁性半导体。

该磁性半导体为 p 型，带隙约为 2.4 eV，具有室温光致发光现象。进一步地，通过该 p 型磁性半导体与 n 型单晶硅的集成，制备了 p-n 异质结和 p-n-p 结构，表明该新型磁性半导体可以和现有硅基半导体工业兼容。除此之外，基于此新型磁性半导体制备的电控磁器件通过外加门电压调控其载流子浓度，实现了室温磁性的显著调控。

陈娜说：“我们的发现为制备具有独特功能特性的高居里温度磁性半导体材料开辟了一条新的路径。”该成果于 2016 年 12 月 8 日在《自然 - 通讯》在线发表，论文标题为《源于铁磁金属玻璃的室温磁性半导体》。

Dr. Chen Na from the School of Materials Science and Engineering Made an Important Progress in Research on Room-temperature Magnetic Semiconductors and Devices

Many years ago, the journal *Science* raised 125 important scientific issues. One of the questions was "is it possible to create magnetic semiconductor materials that can work at room temperature." Recently, Dr. Chen Na, an associate professor from the School of Materials Science and Engineering at Tsinghua University, and her co-workers, developed a p-type magnetic semiconductor with a Curie temperature higher than 600K by inducing the metal-semiconductor transition in ferromagnetic metallic glasses. Based on this magnetic semiconductor, the preparation of the room-temperature p-n junction and the electronically controlled magnetic device was realized.

What's the significance of Research & Development on practical room-temperature magnetic semiconductors?

Firstly, a magnetic semiconductor has both magnetic and semiconductor properties, and can meet people's expectations of control of the charge and spin at the same time. It provides a brand new way of realizing information processing, storage and transportation in one single material. The use of magnetic semiconductors is important for the development of a new generation of spintronic devices (spin field effect transistor, and spin light-emitting diodes, etc.), and will significantly reduce energy consumption, increase the integration density, and improve data computing speed, which can then allow it to have a very attractive applicative prospect in the future of electronics industry.

Secondly, it has always been a key scientific issue in the field of spintronic to explore useful room-temperature magnetic semiconductors, and to develop practical room-temperature spintronic devices based on this material. However, the most eye-catching diluted magnetic semiconductors to date, especially those based on III-V semiconductors, have a Curie temperature of only 200K, which cannot meet the requirement of electronic devices to work at room temperature.

In response to this bottleneck, Dr. Chen and her co-workers used "reverse thinking" by oxidizing magnetic metals with high Curie temperature to produce new types of magnetic semiconductors, making it obtain the semiconductor property while retaining the high-temperature intrinsic magnetic property of magnetic metals. Thus, a new type of $Co_{28.6}Fe_{12.4}Ta_{4.3}B_{8.7}O_{46}$ magnetic semiconductor with a Curie temperature higher than 600K was developed.

This magnetic semiconductor is p-type, and has a bandgap of about 2.4 eV and a room-temperature photoluminescence phenomenon. Furthermore, p-n heterojunction and p-n-p structure were prepared through the integration of this p-type magnetic semiconductor with the n-type single-crystal silicon, indicating that this new type of magnetic semiconductor can be compatible with the existing silicon-based semiconductor industry. In addition, the electronically controlled magnetic device, prepared based on this new type of magnetic semiconductor, regulates its carrier concentration through externally applied gate voltage, and achieves a significant regulation of its room-temperature magnetism.

"Our findings have opened a new path for the preparation of high-Curie-temperature magnetic semiconductor materials with unique functional properties." said Dr. Chen. This result was published online in *Nature Communications* on December 8th, 2016, titled "A room-temperature magnetic semiconductor from a ferromagnetic metallic glass" .

Contributor | School of Materials Science and Engineering

Translation and revision | Anish Vincent Pandey

Image | Li Xiaotian

1月13日

改编｜刘书田

图片｜梁露文、郭祥

清华名人名言之梁思成：有所专而又多能，精于一而又博学

梁思成先生（1901—1972）是我国建筑学界一代宗师。1901 年 4 月他出生时，正值其父梁启超流亡日本。他的出生给这个动荡不安的家庭带来了欣慰；梁启超给他取名“思成”，希望他多思而事业有成。

1915 年，梁思成考入清华学校，开始了 8 年的清华求学生涯。在清华学习期间，梁思成才华出众，爱好广泛，对音乐、美术、体育都有浓厚兴趣，曾在全校运动会上获得过撑竿跳高第一名，也曾担任学校管弦乐队的第一小号手兼队长。他的美术尤其出色，曾被美术老师指定和闻一多等人组织一个“研究艺术及其与人生关系”的艺术团体，活跃了学校文化艺术氛围。

梁思成不但多才多艺，还是学生运动领袖之一。1919 年五四运动中，他是清华“爱国十人团”和“义勇军”等社团的中坚分子，凭借其冷静而敏锐的政治头脑，被同学誉为“一个有政治头脑的艺术家”。

1923 年，梁思成从清华毕业，并于次年到美国宾夕法尼亚大学建筑系学习深造，开始了作为建筑家的光辉生涯。

在 20 世纪 30 年代的动荡岁月里，梁思成和林徽因以及他们的同仁，以简陋的交通工具，奔波于穷乡僻壤与山峦沟壑中，从事艰辛的古建筑踏勘与测绘调查，从总结匠人抄本经验起步，用现代的建筑表现方法，记录整理古代建筑遗产，成为我国古建筑研究的先驱者之一。

梁思成也是我国近代建筑教育事业的奠基者之一。他先后创办了东北大学建筑系和清华大学建筑系，培养、发掘和团结了一大批人才。1961 年，他撰文教导清华学生“求学问需要精，但是为了能精益求精，专的更好就需要博”。

梁思成认为，建筑是人类文化的综合体，最本质的是建筑师应当是有文化修养的综合艺术家。他主张建筑师必须有广泛深厚的文化修养，建筑师的认识领域要广，要有哲学家的头脑、社会学家的眼光、工程师的精确与实践、心理学家的敏感、文学家的洞察力。在建筑系课程设置上，梁思成有意识地加强专业课程与人文、社会科学的结合，认为学术修养要博精结合，“‘专’不等于把自己局限在一个‘牛角尖’里，既有所专而又多能，能精于一而又博学，这是我们每个人在求学上应有的修养”。

梁思成先生将自己一生的心血投入教育事业，在以后的几十年中结出了丰硕成果，而清华建筑系的人才辈出就是对先生最好的汇报。

注：本文改编自《梁思成：有所专而又多能，精于一而又博学》（原作者：金富军，载于 2008 年 12 月 9 日清华新闻网）。

Famous Quotations in Tsinghua History: Multi-Talented Yet a Specialist, Versatile Yet Master of One

Mr. Liang Sicheng (1901—1972) is a great master in China's architecture studies. When he was born, his father Mr. Liang Qichao (1873—1929), a well-known scholar in China, was in exile in Japan. His birth brought solace to a time of turmoil for the Liang family. His father gave him the name "Si" (think, ponder), "Cheng" (success, accomplished), hoping that he would be a thinker and successful in life.

In 1915, Mr. Liang Sicheng was admitted into Tsinghua School (the predecessor of Tsinghua University), and began his 8-year-long academic journey. While studying at Tsinghua, he was a talented and outstanding student, with varied interests in music, arts and sports. He once won the pole vault champion in the school sports game and also served as the captain and chief trumpet of the school orchestra. His abilities in fine arts was especially outstanding. He was once appointed by his arts professor to form a research team with illustrious artists and literary figures to study the relationship between arts and life, invigorating the arts atmosphere of whole school.

Mr. Liang was not only multi-talented; he was also a leader in student movements. In the May 4th Movement of 1919 (an anti-imperialist, anti-feudal, political and cultural movement in China), he became a backbone member of Tsinghua's "Patriotic Ten-People" and "Army of Volunteers" groups.

In 1923, Mr. Liang graduated from Tsinghua. In the next year, he was admitted into the School of Architecture at University of Pennsylvania, where he began his studies as an architecture student.

In the turbulent years in the 1930s, Mr. Liang Sicheng, Ms. Lin Huiyin and their colleagues, through the primitive transportation methods, traveled across poor remote villages and mountain ranges and ravines, engaging in arduous architecture field work and cartography survey. Starting from summarizing copied scripts of ancient craftsman, and through modern architecture methods, they recorded ancient Chinese architecture, and became pioneers of China's ancient architecture researcher.

Mr. Liang Sicheng is also one of the pioneers in China's modern architecture education. He established architecture majors in Northeast University and Tsinghua University, nurturing and discovering a great number of talents. In 1961, he wrote in an article, "in the pursuit of knowledge, one must learn the essence in a field, but to be constantly improving and be a master in the field, one must also have a wide-range of knowledge."

In Mr. Liang's mind, architecture is a reflection of the civilization of mankind. The most basic requirement of an architect is the study of culture, knowledge, and art. He added that an architect must have wide and deep cultural knowledge and self-cultivation. An architect's sphere of knowledge must be extensive. He needs to have the mind of a philosopher, the eyes of a sociologist, the precision and experience of an engineer, the sensitivity of a psychologist, and the observation skills of a literary man. In designing architecture curriculum, Mr. Liang saw the need to complement architecture courses with humanities and social sciences. He believed in both a liberal education and specialization. "Specialized learning does not equal limited learning; being both specialized and multi-skilled should be an accomplishment in everyone's academic pursuit."

Mr. Liang Sicheng invested his whole life in the teaching of architecture, reaping great fruits of success in the following decades. Architecture talents that emerged from Tsinghua University is the best reward for him.

Translation and revision | Alexis See Tho

Image | Liang Luwen, Guo Xiang

1月20日

改编 | 冯婉婷

图片 | 霍巍、郭祥

清华名人名言之周诒春：维能耐劳忍苦，斯能建功立业

“维能耐劳忍苦，斯能建功立业，贪安好逸者无济于社会也。”20世纪初建校的清华曾在社会上有“贵族学校”之称，为了树立勤俭朴实的风气，周诒春担任清华第二任校长后常常用这句话来教导清华的学生，告诉学生们应以课业为重，不要追求物质享受。

周诒春，字寄梅，1883年12月29日生于湖北汉口；1907年毕业于上海圣约翰大学，后赴美入威斯康星和耶鲁等校学习教育、心理等专业；曾参与颜惠庆主编的我国第一部《英汉大字典》的编纂工作。1913年10月至1918年1月，周诒春担任清华校长。在任期间，他积极推行完全人格之教育，实行严格管理，改革留美学生选拔机制，提出向完全大学过渡，许多优良传统在此时期奠基，使清华学校稳步发展。

为了让学生养成勤俭朴实的优良风气，在当时的清华，学生身上不许带钱，钱要存在学校银行里，只有平常的零用钱可以留少许在身上；但花费每分钱都要记明细账，月底结算完要呈送斋务室，备核盖印后发还。在周诒春的身体力行与严格管理下，清华学生逐步养成勤奋勤俭、朴实无华的风气。当时社会人士均认为，蓝布衫及粗布鞋乃清华学生的制服。有校友回忆，当时清华校内全体布衣布鞋，无一例外，即便达官富贾之子弟，在校园内亦绝不敢公然衣着华服。

清华在成立之后，经过二十余年的发展，快速成为国内著名的高等学府，这与早期几任校长的辛勤耕耘密不可分。其中，周诒春在学生德育工作方面的贡献尤多。他为人威严方正，不因循苟安，在德育工作方面以身作则。周诒春极力提倡德、智、体三育并举，在清华推行“造就完全人格之教育”，鼓励学生全面发展，提高综合素质，成为适应现代社会的国家公民。他一直强调，清华学生既受特别权利，当奋发有为，力戒虚骄自大、贪安好逸；当群策群力，同气同声，以回报国家。他在鼓励学生养成勤俭勤奋的好习惯的同时，极力提倡团体活动，注重培养学生着眼于大体，不谋小团体利益的集体精神与合作意识；注重培养学生的爱国主义精神、良好的社会公德与团结协作精神。

在周诒春的极力倡导和以身作则下，清华学生逐渐树立了勤勉勤俭的良好风气。正是因为校风朴实，学生用功勤奋、全面发展，社会各界子弟均视能在清华读书为荣。清华逐渐发展成为中国高等学校中的新军，并在经历了百年发展之后成为当今世界著名高校之一。这些都离不开当年奠定的稳固基础和代代相传的优良传统。维能耐劳忍苦，斯能建功立业，这是多年来清华培育出的同学们引以为豪的清华精神，也将成为更多清华人未来发展的准则之一。

注：本文改编自《周诒春：维能耐劳忍苦，斯能建功立业》（原作者：金富军，载于2008年4月21日清华新闻网）。

Famous Quotations in Tsinghua History: Only by Being Able to Withstand Hard Work Can One Gain Great Results

"Only by being able to withstand hard work can one gain great results. Those who slack off and escape from responsibilities will not be needed in society." During its early years, Tsinghua was known as an "elite school." In order to set up such high standards, Mr. Zhou Yichun, the second president of Tsinghua, often used this quote to educate students. He wanted Tsinghua students to place emphasis on coursework and knowledge instead of material comforts.

Mr. Zhou Yichun was born on December, 29th, 1883 in Hankou, Hubei Province. In 1907, he graduated from Saint John's University in Shanghai and later went to study in the University of Wisconsin and Yale University in courses such as education and psychology and much more. He once worked alongside the renowned writer and diplomat in China Mr. Yan Huiqing (1877—1950) and edited China's first *English-Chinese Dictionary*. From October 1913 to January 1918, Mr. Zhou served as the president of Tsinghua. During that time, he actively promoted and adopted strict management, made reforms in the selection of young talents and helped with the transition between school and society as well as laid foundations to many Tsinghua traditions. Under his leadership, Tsinghua saw steady and holistic developments.

In order to create a good atmosphere, Tsinghua students were banned from carrying on cash, instead, they needed to place their money into the school's bank. They could only carry a tiny amount of pocket money and they must clearly write down every expenditure. At the end of month, an official stamp must be given to indicate such monitoring and record. Under the guidance and strict management style of Tsinghua, students adopted ethos that is both hard-working and humbly simple. Blue plain clothing, shoes and shirts became the uniform of the students. This is the same for all the students regardless of their economic background. No one dared to openly wear any stylish or "expensive-looking" clothing. This simplicity and modesty became a campus culture. It was strictly abided by everyone.

After its establishment in 1911, Tsinghua rapidly became a well-known university in China. This result is closely connected to the work and philosophy of the early presidents of Tsinghua. Mr. Zhou made great efforts in cultivating the students' moral education. He set a good example for moral work and advocated intellectual and physical education and launched a kind of Tsinghua education that encourages "complete personality and all-round development." This helped students to be able citizens of the great nation. He stressed to students that one must avoid arrogance and greed and learn to be an able individual to save one's country. He encouraged students to adopt good habits in being thrifty, diligent and encouraged group activities so that students can focus and learn to have team spirit and a conscious for cooperation. He also paid attention to the students' patriotic spirit and ensured that they have good social ethics and a spirit of solidarity.

Under the leadership of Mr. Zhou, Tsinghua students gradually formed a positive atmosphere. With this spirit and holistic development, students from Tsinghua are able to become capable citizens for China. Tsinghua has set a new standard for institutions of higher education in China and after more than 100 years, it has become a world-class university. The solid foundation and fine traditions have been handed down from generation to generation. This spirit and pride will only be maintained and carried down by more Tsinghua people.

Translation and revision I Min Weiyuan

Image I Huo Wei, Guo Xiang

1月27日

文字 | 杨茂艺
图片 | 唐蓓蓓

家乡的春节美食

丙申终曲已奏响，荷塘夜色冰犹凉，清华学子纷纷收拾行囊踏上回家的旅程。春节，一个如中国社会活力泵一样的节日，年复一年，抚平过去的悲欣，为新的一年注入鲜活的血液。然而，和所有人一样，清华学子们对春节最深、最甜蜜的印象，也少不了一道道家乡年夜饭特色菜。

河北临西清炖羊肉——新雅书院 · 常文治

老家多回族，若是回老家过年就随了回族的俗。我们那里的回族人不讲究过年三十儿，过正月初一。大年初一一家老少一定要团坐一起，吃上一桌“八大碗”：烧肉、圈巧阁、清炖羊肉、松花羊肉、黄焖鸡、黄焖肉、清汆丸子和肉杂拌。当然，八大碗不局限于此，有时稍有出入，例如，把酥肉、松花、焖子、粉条饼切好炖在一起也是“一碗”。其中清炖羊肉窃以为最佳，八大碗偏油腻，但清炖羊肉却鲜而不膻，加之以汤水的清淡，鲜香至极，也可谓是荤菜里的清流了。在特别的日子，守着特别的习俗，也是很不一样但有意义的过年体验。

广西桂林糍粑——人文学院 · 何青翰

我们老家最富特色的地方小吃莫过于糯米做的糍粑了。外婆做糍粑之前，会把糯米浸泡一天以上，滤干水，放在木甑里蒸。熟的时候，只见浓厚的水蒸气腾出来，小孩子们激动地纷纷拍手，外婆会拈出一小块米糕，给孩子们尝尝。蒸熟的糯米要倒入石臼舂烂，在干净的器皿上洒些糯米粉，将舂烂的糯米加馅置其上揉搓，捏成小团或饼状，这糍粑就做好了。无论是用井水煮着吃、用柴火烤着吃，还是同甜酒一起煮沸加糖再吃，都会成为除夕夜守岁时的一大美味。一路向南的我此刻正靠着车窗，惦念着那盘年味醇厚的糍粑。

四川乐山烧白——航院 · 屈颖钢

白斩鸡、老鸭汤、红烧鱼、粉蒸肉，这几道经典川菜是每年年夜饭开场的主角；而乐山人嗜辣，这开头几道菜里也总要有一点辣味，才算得上鲜香。我最爱烧白，大块五花肉扣在糯米饭上蒸入味，做出两份，一份咸的加上梅菜和淡盐，一份甜的放上白糖芝麻和干桂圆。就连习惯了在除夕夜里四处乱跑、不爱吃饭的小孩也会眼巴巴地望着这道菜，非得等老人夹上一筷子放进嘴里，才心满意足地离去。

西藏林芝——新闻学院 · 次仁曲吉

藏历新年大年初一的一早，家庭主妇已经煮好了放有红糖、碎奶渣、糌粑的“观颠”（青稞酒的一种）。首先，供灯祭祀神灵后，全家人先共饮新年第一杯酥油茶。接着，晚辈向长辈敬“切玛”并献上哈达。之后，大家一起喝“观颠”，吃传统藏式点心“卡塞”——一种酥油制的裹了砂糖的饼干，分耳朵形、蝴蝶形、条形、方形、圆形等形状。就这样，藏族人在酥油茶的甘醇、青稞酒的清冽和“卡塞”的甜蜜之中迎来了新的一年。

其实，我们每个人心中都有一间温暖的厨房、一张明亮的餐桌、一盘盘佳肴……春节将至，愿一年的疲惫能随油盐米醋一起溶解，愿深藏的记忆能被激动的味蕾再次唤醒。那些家乡特有的春节美食，早已成为我们挥之不去的思念。

Spring Festival: Delicacy from Hometown

The year of the Monkey is at the end. The lotus pond of Tsinghua campus has frozen as students get ready to return home for the Spring Festival. Like everyone else, Tsinghua students often have the sweetest and deepest impression during this time since there is nothing more soothing than to think about the unique and rich dishes and delicacies found in the many and different hometowns of the Tsinghua students.

Hebei Linxi's Stewed lamb—Chang Wenzhi from Xinya College

My home is where you will find many Hui people so we follow the Hui customs when it comes to celebrating the Spring Festival. The Hui people in my hometown do not pay attention to the New Year's Eve, the first day of the first lunar month is the most important day for them. On that day, young and old sit together to eat the "eight big bowls" : roast meat, lamb stew, yellow braised chicken, meat balls and mixed meat plates. Of course, food is not limited to just these big eight. There are also the crispy meat, vermicelli, cake and others. The stewed lamb is the best. Fresh mutton combined with soup makes anyone's mouth water. On such a special day and with such unique customs, this is simply a very different and meaningful New Year experience.

Guangxi Guilin's "Ci Ba"—He Qinghan from School of Humanities

Our home is where you can find the best "Ci Ba" or glutinous rice cake. As the local snack for Guilin, this is something that everyone must try. Before making it, grandmother would soak the rice for more than a day then drain the water and cook it. The kids would clap excitedly when they see the steam then grandmother would take out a piece of the cake for the kids to try. The steamed glutinous rice would be poured then stuffed and kneaded into smaller cake like portions. It is after such steps that the "Ci Ba" is ready. Whether you eat it boiled or cooked or with sugar, it has become an inseparable part of New Year celebration. As I make my way South, all that I could think of are these cakes.

Sichuan Leshan's Shao Bai—Qu Yinggang from School of Aerospace Engineering

Baizhan chicken, old duck soup, braised fish and steamed pork with rice, these classical Sichuan dishes make their mark in every New Year celebration. The people from Leshan love spicy food and these dishes have always been spicy and regarded to be delicious. Shao Bai is my favorite, braised streaky pork with chunks of steamy glutinous rice along with a bit of salt and some preserved vegetable. And, let's not forget some white sugar sesame and dried longan. Such food is irresistible for even those kids who are not fond of eating. They would be staring at these dishes and wait for the elders to give them a bite before running off into the night to celebrate the New Year.

Tibet Nyingchi – Tsring Chokyi from School of Journalism and Communication

Early morning of Tibetan New Year's Day, housewives have already finished cooking. What is it? Brown sugar, milk residue and roasted barley known as "Guan Dian" (a type of barley wine). After paying respects and making offers to the deities through the lamp ceremony, the family will drink the first butter tea to mark the New Year. Then, the youngsters will pay their respects "Che Ma" to the elders and present to them the hada. After drinking the "Guan Dian" ,they would eat the "Ka Sai" . "Ka Sai" is a type of butter cake wrapped in sugar. There are many shapes from the butterfly to the strip to the square, the circle and many more. So in this way, the Tibetan people usher in the New Year with butter tea, barley wine and "Ka Sai" sweets.

In fact, there is a kitchen, a table and dishes after dishes of great food in all of our minds. As the Spring Festival approaches, we hope that a whole year's fatigue can be dissolved with salt, rice, vinegar and other ingredients. Such flavors will surely provoke memories that we have with food and awaken our taste buds. These New Year delicacies have become our ever lasting memories.

Translation and revision | Min Weiyuan

Image | Tang Beibei

2月3日

改编 | 刘兰

图片 | 李筱甜、郭祥

清华名人名言之章名涛：治学严谨，为人清正

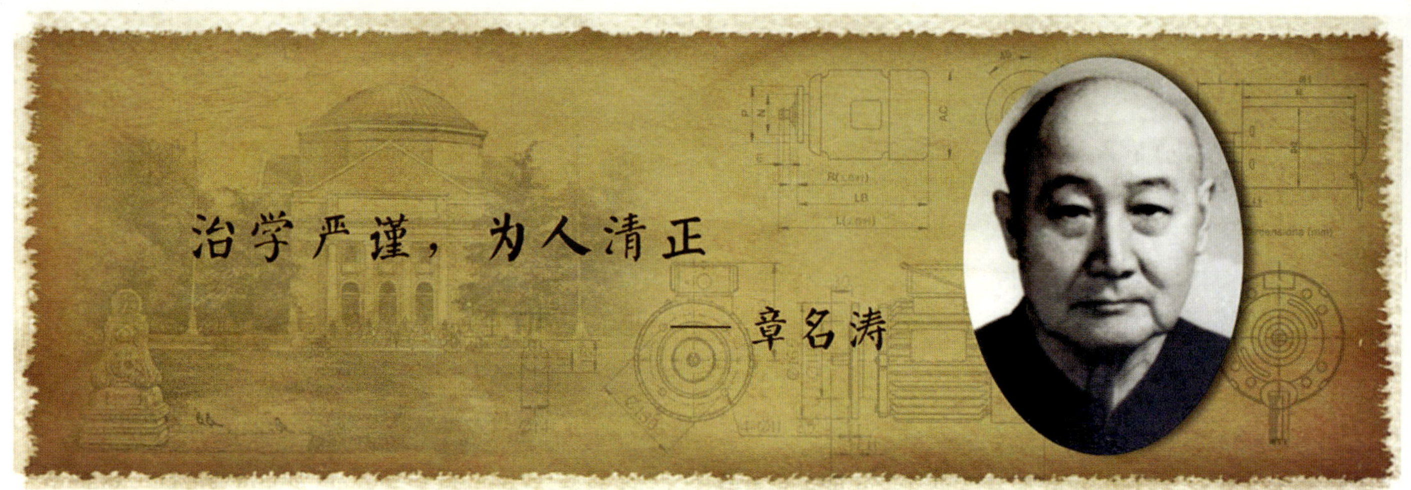

1992年，时任国务院副总理的朱镕基在参加清华大学电机系60周年系庆时题写了“为学与为人”的赠言，并进一步解释说：“为学在严，严格认真，严谨求实，严师可出高徒。为人要正，正大光明，正直清廉，正己然后正人。”这充分表达了朱镕基学长和广大清华师生对章名涛教授的怀念，更生动诠释了章名涛教书育人的一生——“治学严谨，为人清正”。

章名涛（1907—1985）从小怀抱“科学救国”的志向。1924年到1929年，他留学英国，先后获得工程科学学士和硕士学位。为报效祖国，1930年他毅然回国，1932年开始在清华执教，被聘为教授，筹建电机系。在西南联大时期，他与师生共甘苦，并于1942年开始担任系主任。其后他几经辗转，于1948年9月返回清华园，并继续担任电机系主任。他先后担任清华大学电机系主任20余年，为电机系的发展做出了卓越贡献。章名涛先生的一生都坚定地投入中国教育和科技事业之中，他不仅身体力行，更身教先于言传地为师生们树立为人的师表、做事的榜样。

面对教学，章名涛先生一丝不苟，追求尽善尽美。他把课堂教学当作艺术，比如“交流电机”课程是众多学生害怕的“老虎课”，但是他将艰深的理论阐释得深入浅出，概念清晰，深受同学推崇。他还特别重视教材建设，亲自编写了很多教材，如我国第一部《电机学》《电机设计》等。直到晚年，他仍坚持坐在轮椅上孜孜不倦地工作，花费大量精力与年轻教师俞鑫昌一起将《异步电机中谐波磁场的作用》（英文版）一书译成中文，并纠正了书中313处错误，全部在“译者注”中标明。

面对科研，章名涛先生高瞻远瞩，致力于清华大学电机系和中国电机工程技术的发展。解放之初，电机系只有电力和电讯两个组，在他的领导下，电机系逐步发展了一些新的学科，并建立了新的教研组，专业学科配置逐步完善，及时地适应了我国电力工业发展的现实需求。1954年，他指出工业发展要求学校提高师资水平，根本要提高教师的科学水平。他先后安排多位年轻教师主攻新的学科方向，主张教师要充分利用图书馆，并到实验室去。1956年，他参加了周恩来总理主持的制定全国十二年科学技术发展规划的工作，回校和教师们研究讨论，确定了电机工程方面的两个主攻方向，对电机系今后的战略发展起到了关键性作用。改革开放之后，尽管他早已重病缠身，但还是坚持发挥余热。

“哲人已逝，言犹在耳”，朱镕基学长曾深情回忆道，“母校电机系主任章名涛教授在一次会上对我们讲过这样一段话：你们来到清华既要学会怎样为学，更要学会怎样为人。青年人首先要学‘为人’，然后才是学‘为学’。为人不好，为学再好，也可能成为害群之马。学为人，首先是当一个有骨气的中国人。”

章名涛用自己的一生诠释了什么叫“治学严谨，为人清正”，怎样“当一个有骨气的中国人”，也为清华师生永久地留下一句为学为人的至理名言。

注：本文改编自《章名涛：治学严谨，为人清正》（原作者：周襄楠，载于2008年3月25日清华新闻网）。

Famous Quotations in Tsinghua History: Rigorous Scholarship and Upright Personality

In 1992, Mr. Zhu Rongji, the Vice Premier of the State Council at the time, wrote the sentence, "Scholarship and Personhood" for the Department of Electrical Engineering at Tsinghua University, when he participated in the 60th anniversary of the Department of Electrical Engineering. He explained that, scholarships need to be rigorous; which signifies being rigorous and serious, rigorous and realistic, and also be rigorous in cultivating excellent students; while personhood needs to be upright; which signifies being upright and conscientious, being upright and honest, and being upright to self, then upright to others. With this sentence, Mr. Zhu Rongji and Tsinghua alumni from the Department of Electrical Engineering fully expressed the memory of deceased Professor Zhang Mingtao, and vividly interpreted the entire educating life of Professor Zhang — "rigorous scholarship and upright personality" .

Zhang Mingtao (1907—1985), studied abroad in the United Kingdom and got his Bachelor and Master degree in Engineering from 1924 to 1929. In 1930, he returned home to serve the motherland and took on a professor position from Tsinghua University in 1932, where he participated in the establishment of the Department of Electrical Engineering. In 1942, he began to serve as the dean of the Department of Electrical Engineering. He was involved in the establishment of the Department of Electrical Engineering at Tsinghua University, and had served as the dean of the Department of Electrical Engineering for more than 20 years. He had made outstanding contributions towards the development of the Department of Electrical Engineering. Professor Zhang Mingtao firmly committed his entire life to the cause of China's education, science and technology. He not only earnestly practiced what he preached, but also influenced by doing deeds before teaching by words to set an example for the teachers and students on how to be a man and how to implement actions.

As for teaching, Professor Zhang Mingtao was meticulous and always in pursuit of perfection. He treated teaching as an art. For instance, many students feared the course "Alternating Current Motor" as a particularly difficult lesson, but he explained the difficult theory in a simple way, and the concept then became clear to the students, therefore he was also very popular with the students. He also attached great importance to teaching materials construction. He compiled a lot of teaching materials by himself, such as China's first *Electromechanics, Design of Electric Machine,* and so on. In his later years, he insisted on working from his wheelchair, and spent a lot of energy in translating a book named *The Role of Harmonic Magnetic Field in Induction Motor* (English version) into Chinese, together with the young teacher Yu Xinchang, during which he corrected 313 errors in the book, which were all marked in the "Translator's Notes" .

In the face of scientific research, Professor Zhang Mingtao had foresight and was committed to the development of the Department of Electrical Engineering and China's electrical engineering technology. At the beginning of the liberation, the Department of Electrical Engineering only had two institutes, electrical power and telecommunications. Under his leadership, the Department of Electrical Engineering gradually developed a number of new disciplines and established a new teaching and research group. The professional discipline settings were gradually improved, and timely adapted to the real demand of China's power industry development. In 1954, he pointed out that the industrial development required educational institutions to improve the level of teachers, fundamentally, to improve the scientific level of teachers. He had successively arranged a number of young teachers to focus on the new discipline, and advocated teachers to make full use of the library and laboratory. In 1956, he took part in the establishment of the 12-year National Science and Technology Development Plan, which was chaired by Premier Zhou Enlai. After he returned to Tsinghua, he discussed with professors and determined the two primary directions that should be focused for the electrical engineering, which had played a key role in the future strategic development of the Department of Electrical Engineering. After the reform and opening up, although he had been seriously ill, he still insisted on devoting his remaining energy.

"A wise man has gone, but his words remain," Mr. Zhu Rongji recalled, "Professor Zhang Mingtao once told us that, when you come to Tsinghua, you have to learn how to study, and moreover, learn how to be a man. Young people must learn the essence of personhood first, and then the one of scholarship. A bad man with a good scholarship can also be a black sheep. For being a good man, first of all, you have to be a backboned Chinese."

Professor Zhang Mingtao interpreted "rigorous scholarship and upright personality" and how to be "a backboned Chinese" with his entire life, and left words of wisdom on scholarship and personality for Tsinghua people.

Translation and revision | Anish Vincent Pandey

Image | Li Xiaotian, Guo Xiang

2月10日

改编丨杨晨晞

图片丨霍巍、郭祥

清华名人名言之季羡林：只有知不足的人才能为人类文化做出贡献

1911 年 8 月 2 日，季羡林出生在山东省清平县（现临清市）一个贫困农民家庭。1930 年，他以优异的成绩考入清华西洋文学系。在清华的四年时光中，季羡林结识了陈寅恪、朱光潜、吴宓等名师，还知不足地旁听了很多外系的课程。名师的言传身教和清华良好的学术氛围对他产生了深远的影响。从他的《清华园日记》不难看出，作为一名二十出头的大学生，那时的季羡林已经在文学方面颇有见地，但是他从没停下前进的脚步。

从清华毕业一年后，季羡林赴德国哥廷根大学学习。那里自由的学习氛围和浓郁的文化气息促使他将自己的学习目标最终定在了难度不小的梵文领域。与此同时，知不足的他先后学习吐火罗语、英语、俄语、塞尔维亚 - 克罗地亚语等多门语言，不断用学习来充实自己。1941 年，季羡林获得博士学位，其论文《〈大事〉中伽陀部分限定动词的变化》在学术界引起了轰动。由于当时“二战”正酣，季羡林无法回国，在“上有飞机轰炸、下有饥肠辘辘”的境况下，他仍然不忘钻研佛教混合梵语，还用德文完成了几篇有创见的论文，由此奠定了他在世界梵文学界的地位。

1945 年秋，季羡林辗转回到了阔别十年的祖国，被聘为北京大学教授，并兼任新组建的东方语言文学系主任。然而当时资料缺乏，人员不足，加之政局混乱、经济拮据，他深感痛楚和无奈。即使在这种情况下，他仍然坚持进行学术研究，在两年多时间里发表了 40 余篇涉及各种题材的文章。

即便在“文革”时期受到批斗和不公正待遇，他仍坚持用五年时间“偷偷”地翻译了长达八万行的印度著名史诗《罗摩衍那》，这部译著成为中国翻译史和中印文化交流史上的一座丰碑。在那样的历史条件下，正是知不足的精神鼓舞着他为世界文化做出新的贡献。

改革开放后，身兼数职的季羡林仍将学术作为自己人生的重点。他每天坚持凌晨 4 点起床，读书、写作或是翻译，8 点去上班，晚上加班加点读书、写作，甚至把开会、吃饭、接待等“边角”时间也利用起来从事研究。年逾古稀、满头银发的他每天骑自行车来往于图书馆和家之间，看上去仍旧精神矍铄。他在 80 多岁高龄还完成了《糖史》等三部著作。至 2003 年，季羡林的全部著作约有 1200 万字，并有多部作品在国内外产生了重大影响，但是他从不只满足于学术方面的建树，知不足的精神让他在诸多领域都有所成就，成为一位“杂家”。

季羡林说：“只有知不足的人才能为人类文化做出贡献。”他自己便是一直秉持着这种知不足的精神，一路坎坷奋进，成就颇丰依然壮心不已、孜孜以求。这种“知不足”精神也将永远流传在清华校园中，成为一代又一代清华人宝贵的精神财富。

注：本文改编自文章《季羡林：只有知不足的人才能为人类文化做出贡献》（原作者：周襄楠，原载于 2008 年 6 月 16 日清华新闻网）。

Famous Quotations in Tsinghua History: Only Those Who Are Never Tired of Learning Can Make Contributions Towards the Human Culture

Ji Xianlin was born in a poor peasant family in Qingping County, Shandong Province, on August 2, 1911. In 1930, he was admitted to the Department of Western Literature at Tsinghua University with excellent grades. During his tenure of four years in Tsinghua, Ji Xianlin met Mr. Chen Yinque (1890-1969), Dr. Zhu Guangqian (1897-1986), Mr. Wu Mi (1894-1978) and other renowned scholars, and tirelessly attended a lot of courses from other departments. Academic masters' words and deeds and stable academic atmosphere in Tsinghua had a profound impact on him, and also contributed towards his writing *Diary of My Time at Tsinghua*, which still to this date has a unique value. From those words in his diary, it is not difficult to see that as an undergraduate in his early twenties, he has been very insightful in the literature. However, he never stopped his paces forward.

After graduation for one year, Ji Xianlin went to Georg-August-University of Goettingen for further studies in 1935. The free learning atmosphere and cultural richness there prompted him to finally set his goal of learning in a difficult field, a unique language field of Sanskrit. At the same time, he had tirelessly learned Tocharian, English, Russian, Serbian, Croatian, and other languages, enriching himself with constant learning. In 1941, he received his Ph.D. At that time, the World War II was still in full swing, Dr. Ji could not return home. Under the circumstances of suffering aircraft bombing and starvation, he still did not forget to study Buddhist hybrid Sanskrit, and had completed several original papers in German, which had laid his position in the academia of Sanskrit across the world.

In 1945, Dr. Ji Xianlin finally returned home. He took on a professor position from Peking University and served as the dean of the Department of Oriental Language and Literature. However, due to the lack of materials and personnel, plus political chaos and financial constraints, he felt helpless. But in his heart, he could not be more aware that there were still a lot of academic blanks required him to fill in. Therefore, he resolutely decided to devote himself to academic research, and published more than 40 articles related to various topics within around a two-year period.

Even during the period of the Cultural Revolution, Dr. Ji spent 5 years in "secrecy" translating 80,000 lines of India's well-known epic *Ramayana*, which is known to be a massive monument in the Chinese translation history and cultural exchanges history between China and India. Under such historical conditions, it was just the spirit of tireless learning that inspired him to make new contributions towards world culture.

After the reform and opening up, in spite of holding several posts, Dr. Ji Xianlin still took the academics as the primary priority of his life. He insisted on getting up, reading, writing or translating at 4:00 every morning, going to work at 8:00, working overtime for reading and writing at night, and even took full advantage of the time for meetings, meals, reception and created other spare time to do research. Over seventy years of age, silver-haired, cycling between the library and home every day, he still looked hale and hearty. He even completed three famous books, including the *Sugar History* in his 80 years old. Till 2003, all of Dr. Ji's writings have about 12 million words, and a number of his works have had a significant impact at both home and abroad. But he was never satisfied with his achievements in the academic aspects. His spirit of tireless learning helped him gain achievements in many areas, and also made him become known as a "miscellaneous expert" .

Dr. Ji Xianlin said, "Only those who are never tired of learning can make contributions towards human culture." He is one of those people who uphold this brilliant spirit and continues to push ahead. With abundant achievements, he was still ambitious and assiduous. This spirit of "tireless learning" will always be popular in Tsinghua and become valuable spiritual wealth for the future generations of Tsinghua.

Translation and revision | Raj Lamar

Image | Huo Wei, Guo Xiang

2月17日

改编 | 张智伟

图片 | 郭祥

清华名人名言之潘光旦：我的钱全都买书了

在闻一多看来，他是科学家；在梁实秋看来，他的作品体现了“自然科学与社会科学之凝合”；在费孝通看来，他是一个人文思想家、人类学家，是一位并世罕见的通才。他就是我国著名的社会学家、优生学家、民族学家潘光旦。

潘光旦，1899 年出生于江苏省宝山县（今上海宝山区），14 岁考入清华。彼时，他已是远近闻名的“书痴”，其阅读面广，文理兼具，尤其对性心理学方面的知识具有特别的兴趣。

1920 年，在“各门功课都名列前茅，英文更是全级之冠”的基础上，潘光旦在性心理学学术领域开始崭露头角。当时，在费了很大一番周折之后，潘光旦将图书馆中还不公开的英国心理学家蔼理士的《性心理学研究录》六大册逐一借出啃完，成为全校首位通读此书的学子，俨成此中权威。蔼理士不仅是学术巨子，亦是欧西文豪，其书向来以难读知名，而潘光旦年当弱冠就通读原著，其不易自可想见。

翌年，他又读了精神分析派的论著，颇有斩获。读到支如增的《小青传》时，他便试用其手法写了一篇《小青的分析》，当成作业交给梁启超。梁大为激赏，批曰：“以子之才，无论研究文学、科学乃至从事政治，均（可）大有成就。”转年，他又将此文整理成书，交梁审阅，梁又批语大加赞赏和鼓励。

1922 年，潘光旦赴美留学，1926 年学成归国，此后一直在大学任教，1934 年又被母校清华延聘。由于博览群书，他被同行亲切地称为“活字典”。在西南联大这大师云集之地，遇有难题，大家都不约而同地说：“走，问潘光旦去！”

在长期的治学过程中，潘光旦将读书演化成了一种生活习惯。平日里，潘光旦几乎足不出户，除了吃饭，就是看书。潘光旦近视达一千二百度，看书时书几乎要贴着鼻尖。家人都笑话他，说这已不是“看”书，而是“闻”书了。

对潘光旦而言，读书、买书已经成为他的一种癖好，他的生活费大部分都用来买书了，以至于口袋里有时只剩下一点点生活费用，但藏书却堆满了几间屋子。

1936 年，潘光旦住在清华园新南院 11 号时，门前藤萝架上曾结出过一对并蒂的葫芦，他欣喜之余便将个人书房命名为“葫芦连理之斋”，坐拥书城，藏书上万余册。潘光旦经常说的一句话是——“读书要有废寝忘食的精神，才有成功的希望”。他是这么说，也是这么做的。

“文革”中，潘光旦时常被拉去批斗。有一次，红卫兵来抄家，搜来搜去，只搜出一百几十元存款。他们简直不相信。潘光旦回答说：“我就这么点钱，我的钱全都买书了。”

注：本文在史飞翔的文章《潘光旦：我的钱全都买书了》（原载于《科技日报》2014 年 6 月 28 日）基础上略有删改。

Famous Quotations in Tsinghua History: I've Spent All My Money on Buying Books

Mr. Wen Yiduo (1899-1946) regards him as a scientist while Mr. Liang Shiqiu (1903-1987) feels that his work is "an embodiment of both natural science and social science" . Dr. Fei Xiaotong (1910-2005) believes that he is a humanistic thinker, an anthropologist and a rare talent. He is Mr. Pan Guangdan (1899-1967), the renowned sociologist and ethnologist in China.

Mr. Pan was born in Baoshan County of Jiangsu Province in 1899. He was admitted to Tsinghua School (the predecessor of Tsinghua University) at the age of 14. At that time, he was already known as a "book fan" . As a lover of both literature and arts, he had read many books already and was particularly passionate about psychology.

In 1920, on the basis of "having the most excellent homework results and achieving the highest level of English" , Pan began to emerge academically in the field of psychology. At that time, after a lot of twists and turns, Mr. Pan Guangdan finished reading the six-book series of the *Studies in the Psychology of Sex* by British psychologist Havelock Ellis (1859-1939). He became the first student out of the whole university to complete reading this series. Mr. Ellis was not only an academic giant, but also a well-known writer. It is well known that Mr. Ellis's work is hard to read. It was surprised to many that Pan was able to read Mr. Ellis' work at such a young age.

In the following year, Mr. Pan Guangdan read psychoanalytic works. He read the book *The Biography of Xiaoqing* written by Zhi Ruzeng and wrote an analysis on the character. He handed it in as homework to Mr. Liang Qichao (1873-1929). Mr. Liang wrote: "This young man is a talent. No matter if he chooses to do research or study science or commit himself to the world of politics, he will be of great use." Later on, Pan turned this analysis into a book and earned more praises and encouragement from Liang after he finished reading the book.

After returning to China in 1926, Mr. Pan Guangdan once taught at some universities and took on a professor position from Tsinghua University in 1934. Due to his appetite for reading, he was affectionately known as the "walking dictionary" by his peers. In many gatherings, Pan was the go-to person whenever people encounter a problem. They would always say: "Let's go to ask Pan Guangdan!"

Professor Pan Guangdan's biggest hobby was reading. He rarely left home and apart from eating, he would always be reading. He had myopia up to 1,200 degrees and whenever he was reading, the book would always be right up to his nose. Family members would always joke around and say that he wasn't reading but "smelling" books. For Pan, reading and buying books has become a hobby and most of his living expenses have gone towards his books. He only kept a few for his living expenses since his biggest hobby was collecting and reading books.

In 1936, Professor Pan lived in No. 11 Xinnanyuan of Tsinghua campus and a pair of gourd hanged in front of his home. He dubbed his study as the "quiet gourd corner" and with a collection of more than 10,000 books. Pan would often say "Only with passion can you find the hope of success from reading!" He does what he says.

During the "Cultural Revolution" , Professor Pan Guangdan was often placed under public humiliation. One time, the Red Guards barged into his home and after conducting searches, they only ended up finding no more than 100 RMB. Professor Pan said, "This is all I have. I've spent all my money on buying books!"

Translation and revision | Min Weiyuan

Image | Guo Xiang

2月20日

文字 | 杨晨晞

图片 | 赵存存

又是一年开学时

春天的脚步近了，开学的日子也来临了。还习惯于家里的温暖被窝、家人的悉心照料和旧友的谈笑往来的我们，也要开始规划新学期的日程了。年味还未散去，元宵节的灯火仿佛还在眼前，但是我已经踏上北上的列车，期待新学期的未知旅程。

虽然我来到园子才一个学期，是名副其实的新人，但是回首这过去的半年，我们在园子里的一幕幕景象还历历在目。拎着沉甸甸的箱子报道、参加盛大的开学典礼、做团队训练营破冰活动、师生见面会聆听专业介绍，以及长达三周的苦中作乐的军训，这些都是我们 6 字班共同拥有的关于清华的一段初始记忆，也是大家在大学校园中难得的一段集体生活。

随着军训的结束，大家逐渐打破了集体生活条条框框的束缚，开始在园子中探索属于自己的新生活。也许我们在学校还迷迷糊糊地犯着路痴，也许我们还为生活的不适应而困扰，也许还有些许对大学新的学习方式的不习惯，但是，校园中早已随处可见我们的印记：演讲比赛上的振臂高呼、赤足运动会上的忘我奔跑、歌手大赛上的嘹亮歌声，都有着 6 字班的闪亮身影。

刚刚入学的我们，在老师和学长们的鼓励下，开始找寻属于自己的通向梦想之路。潜心学术的同学们将空闲时间毫无保留地奉献给了图书馆，专心社工的同学来回奔走为集体和组织献策献力，热心公益的同学们在志愿服务的各大窗口挂满了他们的微笑，留心实践的同学也在不同的实践平台上开始迈出自己社会实践的第一步。清华为我们提供了无限种可能，让我们去探索，找到自己前行的路，我们也就无所畏惧，奋力前进。

在这平凡又有意义的半年里，我在园子里最大的收获要数结识了一群志同道合又活泼有趣的朋友。他们来自天南海北，因为共同向往着这个园子，我们聚集在了一起，也因为有着共同渴望的未来而凝聚在了一起。我们可能不会天天见面，但是每一次小组作业、每一次阳光长跑、每一场集体班会我们都彼此陪伴着。开心时我们会一起吃火锅，烦恼时我们曾彻夜长谈，迷茫时我们会互相鼓励……虽然我们同在异乡，但未来的路有大家一起前行，就不会感到孤单。

园子里的第一个学期已经过去，我们努力朝着自己想要的模样成长。新学期开始啦，我们要尝试更多未曾体验的校园生活，奔向心中的梦想！

New Semester: to Continue with Pursuing My Dream

Spring is right around the corner and the beginning of a new semester is about to begin. For us who are used to our warm bed, the care from our family and the laughter from our friends, it is time to start a new semester. The Chinese New Year still lingers and it was as if the festive atmosphere started yesterday. However, I'm already on the train to start a new semester.

Although I have only been at Tsinghua for one semester and I am considered a new student, looking back at the past 6 months made me realize that everything about the campus is somewhat fresh yet also familiar. Carrying heavy boxes for my enrolment, the grand opening ceremony, the presentations by teachers and students, the 3-week military training and the various ice-breaking activities became my fond memories of Tsinghua so far. It is also a collective memory for all Tsinghua students.

With the end of military training, we gradually began to explore our lives within campus. Maybe we still get lost finding our classrooms and struggle in some aspects to adapt to life on campus, but we have already left our marks in Tsinghua. Whether it is during competition or games, you can see our presence.

We have just entered Tsinghua, and under the encouragement of our teachers and seniors, we began our path to our dreams. We devoted ourselves to quiet self-study in the library, to organizing various activities, to volunteering and to participating in other events. Tsinghua has provided much warmth and guidance so that we are still able to search within ourselves and determine which path and dreams to follows. We explore, we find our way, we have fears, we struggle and we move forward.

In the past ordinary and meaningful 6 months, I've gained so much. I've came to know a group of like-minded and lively friends. We came from all over the country and since we are in the same university, we are able to share our dreams together. It is true that we might not see each other every day but every lesson, every jog, every group activity, every hot pot, every chat and every words of encouragements...allow us to find out common goals and confidence in achieving our dreams. We share a common footprint and we are not alone.

After one semester, we are working hard towards our own goals. As new semester starts, we are ready to experience the next phase and ready to chase our own dreams!

Translation and revision | Min Weiyuan

Image | Zhao Cuncun

2月21日

文字 | 冯婉婷
图片 | 任帅

热动42班：我们的书生时代

"原来以为上了大学之后会有很多时间读书，但是感觉过去一年好像读书的时间并不多。"当热动42班的班委们聚在一起开大二学年第一次班委会时，大家纷纷提出了"没有时间读书"的问题。也正是这次班委会，让他们决定把"读书"这件事作为陪伴他们一年的班级活动。

"氛围的营造和习惯的养成不是一日之功，所以我们决定让读书成为这一年我们每一天的坚持。"时任热动42班团支书的邹逸宁介绍说，他们想用集体的力量去鼓励和监督大家做这件"想做却没有时间做"的事情，还给这次活动取名为"我们的书生时代"。这个名字在包含活动主题的同时，更像是号召大家一起沉下心来读书的口号。

"要让大家都积极参与进来，就要保证活动有理解，有趣和有收获。"邹逸宁说。这三点是他们在筹备活动时一直奉行的。

"有理解"意味着班级活动是建立在对同学们理解的基础上的。一方面，活动要对大家有意义；另一方面，活动不应给大家徒增压力。"我们的书生时代"在第一个学期的主要活动是由班委负责提醒大家每日读书，学期末举行读书分享会和鼓励同学们提交读书报告。为了让大家更好地体会到读书活动的意义，班委们并没有规定具体的书目。但为了方便交流，他们推荐了《看见》这本书。"这是因为我们发现社会上的各种言论和立场常常会让我们感到困惑，所以选择了这本书。"邹逸宁说。班委们不仅是这次活动的组织者，更是发挥带头作用的参与者。而为了让大家可以更好地进行时间分配，班委们提前六七周就公布了活动计划，这样既保证大家有充裕的准备时间，也使得同学们可以更加深入地阅读。"我想最后分享会时大家精彩的展示和提前准备有很大关系。"邹逸宁说。班级活动本身就是一个组织者与参与的同学之间相互理解、共同努力的过程。

"有趣"体现为活动形式的丰富性。到了第二学期，热动42的同学们将读书的主题确立为"人生"，建议每名同学至少读一本名人传记。为了更好地把"读万卷书，行万里路"结合起来，班委们还组织同学们去天津探访了曹禺故居等名人故居。在探访之前，同学们根据自己的阅读，专门制作了有关名人故事的宣传册，并带到了名人故居当地免费发放给前来参观的游客。"我们走的时候，故居的管理员还专门把我们剩下的宣传册保留下来作纪念呢。"邹逸宁说起这件事时充满了自豪。此外，即便在寒假，同学们也没闲着，大家建立了寒假读书的微信群，每天读书打卡，相互监督和交流，并且班委们还每周定期组织线上读书微沙龙，让大家在假期中也时刻惦记着读书这件事。

"有收获"不仅蕴含在热动42班获得的诸如校级素拓银奖、院系甲级团支部等一个个奖项中，也蕴含在班级同学逾万字的读书报告和亲手制作的文集中，更蕴含在每一名同学这一年中最真实的感受中。"我很喜欢和大家一起交流读后感的氛围……""很感谢这次活动，一年来我真的读了不少书……"邹逸宁说，当她看到同学们写的这些感受时十分感动。"这次读书活动虽然结束了，但是大家读书的习惯会一直延续下去，我们的书生时代没有结束。"

Our Reading Time

"I thought I would have lots of time to read in university, but in fact, it seemed like I barely had any time to read in the past year." Members of the class committee, the Class 42 of Department of Thermal Engineering (DTE Class 42), presented the issue of "no reading time" during the first committee meeting in their sophomore year. Inspired by this meeting, the class committee decided to put "reading" as the theme for the next year's class activities.

"Reading atmosphere and habits are not built in a single day, that's why we call on daily persistence on reading for the entire year." Zou Yining, the League branch secretary of DTE Class 42, said that they wished the collective strength could encourage and supervise everybody to read, which was "desired but with no time to do". The event was entitled "Our Reading Time" , which contains the theme and serves as a slogan to call on deep reading.

"To assure everyone's active participation, it should be understandable, interesting and fruitful." Zou said that they had always born these three principles in mind when the event was under preparation.

"Understandable" means the class event is based on students' understanding; it should be meaningful without any burden of pressure. The "Our Reading Time" event in the first half of the year was taken in the form that the organizers reminded the students of daily reading and held reading sessions near the end of term and encouraged the class members to hand in their reading reports. To achieve the better understanding, the organizers did not require a fixed bibliography. In the meantime, for the convenience of communication, the organizers recommended the book *To See* written by Ms. Chai Jing, a known journalist in China. "We chose this book because we found that we sometimes got confused by various opinions and views in the society." Members of the class committee were not only the organizers but also the leading participants, said Zou. They announced the plan six or seven weeks earlier to guarantee plenty of time for preparation and deep reading. "The marvelous presentations showed on the reading session have a lot to do with earlier preparations." Zou said that the event itself was a process of mutual understanding and joint effort made by the organizers and participants.

"Interesting" manifests the richness in event forms. In the second half of the year, DTE Class 42 set up a new reading theme called "life" . Here each student was required to read a biography of a celebrity. To read and travel as much as possible, students also went to Tianjin to visit the former residence of the renowned playwright Cao Yu (1910-1996) and other celebrities. Before the visit, based on their reading, students produced brochures of celebrity stories and freely distributed them to visitors. "The administrator there had kept our brochure as a souvenir." Zou was very proudly. In addition, even during the winter vacation, students formed a WeChat group of vacation reading; they signed every day, supervised and communicated with each other. The class committee also held weekly online salons to remind class members of reading during the vacation.

"Fruitful" is highlighted not only in many awards, but also in students' splendid reports, essays as well as in the most authentic personal experience of every class member. "I like the atmosphere to share reading reports with others..." "I really appreciate the event, as I have read a lot during the year..." Zou felt extremely touched witnessing such expressions. "The reading event itself has come to an end but our reading habits will last for a long time, we are still in our reading time."

Contributor | Department of Thermal Engineering

Translation and revision | Sarthak Pyakurel

Image | Ren Shuai

2 月 22 日

文字 | 杨茂艺

图片 | 薛雅芳

优秀教材《工程材料（第 5 版）》：历史视野，与时俱进

人类社会的每一次进步，都以新材料的运用为标志，从 100 万年前的旧石器时代，到 5000 年前的青铜时代，再经过铁器时代、钢铁时代，直至 20 世纪中叶以来高分子材料、半导体的崛起……材料，一直是关系经济建设、科学研究和人们日常生活的重大话题。

改革开放初期，中国独立的材料学科处于起步阶段，国内针对高分子、复合材料领域的研究几乎是一片空白。1983 年，清华大学出版第一本《工程材料》教材，填补了这一空白。其后，此书 4 次再版。2011 年，由朱张校、姚可夫主编的《工程材料（第 5 版）》出版，成为国家级“十一五”“十二五”规划教材、北京市精品教材，被国内外诸多高校的本科生、研究生作为教材和参考书，受到师生的普遍欢迎。

《工程材料（第 5 版）》由理论、知识、应用三部分内容组成：基本理论部分阐述了工程材料的结构、组织、性能以及它们之间的关系，其中，重点阐述了金属材料组织与性能的影响因素和规律；知识部分介绍了常用金属、高分子、陶瓷、复合材料的成分、组织、性能及其应用知识；应用部分介绍了机械零件失效与选材知识以及工程材料在汽车、机床、仪器仪表、热能、化工和航空航天等领域的应用情况。

与同类教材相比，《工程材料（第 5 版）》特点鲜明，不仅人文情怀显著，而且逻辑性强，图文并茂。教材开篇就回溯了中国古代历史，配以东汉青瓷、西汉淬钢、唐代丝绸等插图和《天工开物》等古籍文字介绍，帮助读者自然而然地进入相应章节的学习。此外，教材中除了基础知识和理论的详密叙述外，还插入了诸如晶体结构表、钢的若干种热处理示意图等图表来减轻学生的阅读负担，调动学习的热情。

从第 1 版到第 5 版，《工程材料》历经 28 年的岁月，每一次编撰出版都离不开作者的勤劳心血和求真精神。从计算机技术在材料制热中的运用到激光表面改性，再到纳米陶瓷的剪裁研究，全书贯穿着“问题－思考”模式，以介绍国际材料学的前沿成果为开端，提出相应问题，对学生进行创新思维教育。

迄今，《工程材料（第 5 版）》已连续 11 个学期被运用到清华大学机械、精仪、热能、汽车、航天航空、材料等 6 个院系的本科生教学中。依托此教材所制作的网络精品课程也已在各大学习网站上线，让更多人享受到了高品质课程所带来的学习的喜悦。

The Recommended Course Book: Engineering Materials (Fifth Edition)

From the Paleolithic age (one million years ago) to the Bronze Age (5,000 years ago) to the Iron Age to the mid-20th century, every advancement in human society is marked by the use of new materials. The rise of semiconductors and new materials significantly influence the relationship in economic construction, scientific research and everyday lives.

At the beginning of China's reform and opening up, China's independent study in materials science is still at a stage of infancy. Domestic research in polymer and composite materials is almost on a blank page. In 1983, Tsinghua published the first set of teaching materials *Engineering Materials*. After that, the book has been reissued for four times. In 2011, the fifth edition edited by Zhu Zhangxiao and Yao Kefu has been published.

The *Engineering Materials (Fifth Edition)* consists of three parts: theory, knowledge and application. The basic theory part is about structure, organization, performance and their relationships. The knowledge part is about the understanding of various materials from metal to ceramics to other components. And the application part is about using such knowledge and applying it in industries and sectors such as aerospace, chemistry, automobile and much more.

Compared with other course books, the *Engineering Materials (Fifth Edition)* is comprehensive, logical and well-illustrated. The book starts off in Ancient China with explanations on celadon which dates back to Eastern Han Dynasty, steel from Western Han, silk from Tang Dynasty and other materials written in ancient texts such as *Tiangong Kaiwu* (a Chinese encyclopedia compiled in 17th century). Instead of the usual boring structure, the book is filled with tables, diagrams and other visual stimuli which allows the students to understand this seemingly dry topic through different perspectives. Reading no longer becomes a burden.

Materials, information and energy are known as the pillars of human civilization in 21st Century. Teaching materials should also advance with the changing times. From the first to the fifth edition, 28 years of constant refinement, compilation and final publication cannot be separated from the hard work and dedication of the authors. From modified materials under heat to laser computer technology to research in ceramics, the thinking mode behind this textbook is about introducing advanced international achievements and innovation and putting forward corresponding problems.

The course book *Engineering Materials (Fifth Edition)* has been applied to the teaching of undergraduate students in Department of Mechanical Engineering, Department of Precision Instrument, Department of Automotive Engineering, Department of Thermal Engineering, School of Aerospace Engineering and School of Materials Science and Engineering for the past 11 semesters. At present, such materials have been used online so that more people are able to experience the joy of learning.

Contributor | Academic Office

Translation and revision | Min Weiyuan

Image | Xue Yafang

2 月 23 日

航院李群仰课题组发文揭示二维材料摩擦演化之谜

供稿 | 航天航空学院
文字 | 梁乐萌
图片 | 任帅

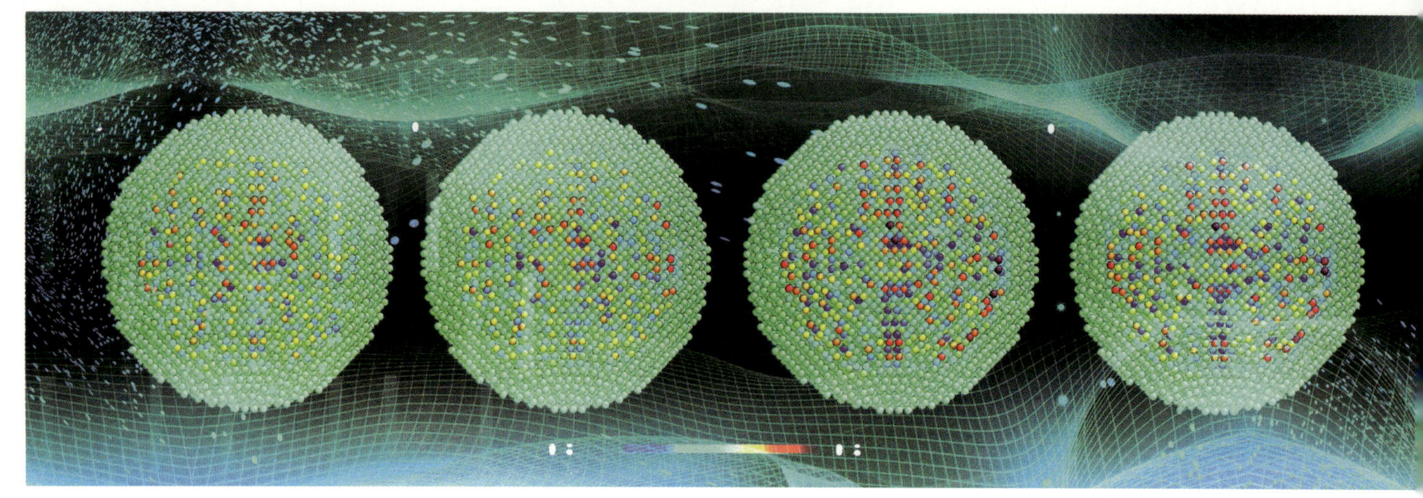

“摩擦”这一物理现象在日常生活中处处可见，人们习以为常的走路、穿衣都离不开摩擦，没有它，我们的生活可以说是“寸步难行”。可是，不知你是否想过，我们对于摩擦的认识大都是建立在宏观经验情况下的。如果走进纳米尺度的微观世界，走近独特神秘的二维材料，看似简单的“摩擦”也会变得奇妙无比。

二维材料是指厚度仅有单层原子 / 分子的晶体材料。自 2004 年石墨烯首次被成功分离以来，以它为代表的二维材料因其独特的电、磁、热、力、光学等性质成为学术研究的新热点，科学家甚至预言石墨烯将“彻底改变 21 世纪”，并且“极有可能掀起一场席卷全球的颠覆性新技术产业革命”。

因此，无数学者致力于揭开二维材料摩擦的秘密，不懈探索、研精钩深，清华航天航空学院李群仰课题组就是其中之一。2016 年 11 月 24 日，他们于《自然》杂志在线发表题为《石墨烯摩擦接触界面的状态演化》的文章，首次重现了石墨烯摩擦行为的所有核心现象，并提出了二维材料可能存在的一种全新的摩擦演化及调控机制。

李群仰课题组的研究表明，界面的咬合“质量”，即上下表面原子间的局部钉扎强度和整个界面咬合作用的协同性，是影响摩擦行为的关键因素。在滑动过程中，石墨烯由于具有超强的面外变形能力，能够动态地调整其构型，从而改变与压头原子之间紧密接触和协同钉扎程度。这一机制超越了摩擦学中二维材料粘着褶皱效应的经典解释，即在摩擦过程中二维材料由于样品层数不同导致表面变形能力的差异，进而影响其真实接触面积大小以及最终的摩擦阻力。

该研究工作首次阐述了石墨烯摩擦演化行为的机理，其“接触质量”理论对于其他拥有超柔力学特性的二维材料也具有普适性——二维材料由于其超薄的几何特性和超大的柔性，能够从界面的“质”而不仅是“量”上来调控其摩擦性能，对进一步理解固体界面摩擦行为的物理机制具有重要的指导意义。此外，作为新一代的固体润滑剂，石墨烯在诸多方面都表现出优于传统材料的特性，本工作对于石墨烯在摩擦和磨损领域更为有效的应用也提供了相应的理论支持。

这项研究由李群仰副教授与麻省理工学院李巨教授和宾夕法尼亚大学罗伯特·卡皮克教授合作，并指导西安交通大学李苏植博士完成，西安交通大学、德国卡尔斯鲁厄理工大学的部分教授也参与了工作。该论文的通讯作者为李群仰副教授、罗伯特·卡皮克教授和李巨教授。

Dr. Li Qunyang Research Group of the School of Aerospace Engineering Issued an Article to Reveal the Mystery of Friction Evolution of Two-Dimensional Materials

"Friction" is a common occurrence in our daily lives. Movements such as walking and getting dressed are all related to friction, without which, our lives would in fact be unimaginable. However, our understandings about friction are mostly based on our daily experiences on the macro-scale. If you step into a microscopic world, playing with the unique and mysterious two-dimensional materials, the seemingly simple and mundane friction becomes rather complicated and intriguing.

Two-dimensional materials are crystalline materials consisting of a single layer of atoms/molecules. Since its first successful demonstration in 2004, two-dimensional materials represented by graphene have become a hot topic of scientific research, due to their unique properties of electricity, magnetism, heat, force, and optics. Scientists have even predicted that graphene will change the 21st century in the sense that it would be very likely to set off a globe-sweeping revolution in industry with disruptive technologies.

To explore full potentials of two-dimensional materials, researchers are carrying out extensive studies on these wonderful materials. Dr. Li Qunyang's research group from the School of Aerospace Engineering at Tsinghua University is one of the groups on that mission. On November 24th, 2016, they published an article online titled "The evolving quality of frictional contact with graphene" on the journal *Nature*. Their atomistic simulations, for the first time reproduced all the key phenomena of frictional behavior of graphene; based on a careful statistical analysis the research team proposed a unique mechanism that governs the friction process of floppy two-dimensional materials.

The study by Dr. Li and co-workers shows that interfacial contact qualities, namely the local pinning capability between the atoms on the upper and lower surfaces and the cooperation of the pinning forces along the entire interface, are the key factors affecting frictional behavior. During the sliding process, graphene could dynamically adjust its configuration owing to its superior out-of-plane deformability, so as to change the state of the intimate contact and commensurability of the interface. This finding offers a brand new mechanism beyond the well-known puckering effect in the friction of two-dimensional materials. For the puckering argument, a thinner sample will have a smaller bending rigidity; therefore it will have a larger contact area when interacting with a slider, which leads to higher friction force and more dissipation.

The new mechanism revealed by this work fully explains the evolution effect in graphene friction for the first time. The contact quality argument is also applicable to other ultra-flexible two-dimensional materials. Two-dimensional materials, with outstanding deformability originating from their ultra-thin atomic structures, can regulate their friction property, not just from the "quantity" of the contact interface, but also from the "quality" . This is conceptual breakthrough in understanding of the physical mechanisms of frictional behavior on solid surfaces. As graphene and other two-dimensional materials have been proposed to be the next-generation solid lubricants, this study also provides a theoretical guidance for more effective application of these atomically thin materials in the field of friction and wear.

This work was led by Associate Professor Qunyang Li from Tsinghua University, Professor Ju Li from Massachusetts Institute of Technology, and Professor Robert Carpick from the University of Pennsylvania; and the computational work was completed by Dr. Li Suzhi from Xi'an Jiaotong University. Professors from Xi'an Jiaotong University and Karlsruher Institut für Technologie also participated in the research. The corresponding authors of this article are Dr. Li Qunyang, Professor Robert Carpick and Professor Li Ju.

Contributor | School of Aerospace Engineering

Translation and revision | Raj Lamar

Image | Ren Shuai

2 月 24 日

改编 | 杨鹏成

图片 | 郭祥

三院遗址

2016 年 12 月 30 日，在清华大学图书馆逸夫馆东南门和西南门之间的草坪上矗立起一座造型为中国的经幢形式且融合西方的方尖碑形式的塔形纪念物。纪念物正面，镌刻着百岁老学长宋平题写的“三院遗址”以及魏碑体的“清华第一个中共支部诞生地”。纪念物顶部，三院主体建筑浮雕渐显，象征党的革命立场，逐步发出耀眼光芒；从另一个角度看，则是渐隐，象征随着时代前行，老三院在岁月中慢慢隐去，为新的建筑代替。

虽然现在已经无缘一睹清华三院的风光，但每当人们回忆起三院中的往事、想起清华人与国家共命运同呼吸的岁月，都情深意切，无限感慨。

三院是清华园内最早的建筑物之一，与清华学堂、同方部等为同期建筑，位于大礼堂以北，图书馆以西。初建时，三院的总面积为 5117 平方米，共有前后四排。第一排为教室，第二三排为学生宿舍，第四排为食堂和厨房。三院为中等科（相当于四年制中学的头三年）学生(男生)的主要活动场所，所以历史上也叫“中等科”。改办大学以后，清华园内文、法学院的许多著名学者，如冯友兰、朱自清、陈寅恪、闻一多、陈岱孙等，都曾在这里授课。后来，这里也曾被学生用来开展文艺活动。

三院值得铭记，不仅因为它是老一辈大师和学生们思想交流和碰撞的场所，三院的教室也是清华人爱国精神的见证者。1926 年，清华第一个中共支部就是在三院教室秘密诞生的。自建立以来，清华党组织紧密团结师生员工，奋力拼搏，开拓进取，谱写了辉煌篇章。从“一二・九”运动的中坚力量到西南联大时期抗战大后方的“民主堡垒”，清华党组织始终走在最前面。

抗战期间，三院遭日寇破坏。抗战胜利后，三院的后几排建筑因已属危险房屋而被拆除，但人们将第一排修缮后留作纪念。20 世纪 80 年代为建设图书馆逸夫馆，将这仅有的一排三院建筑也予以拆除了。三院由此走入历史长河，仅留下遗址任后人遐思缅怀。

注：本文根据清华大学校史馆提供的文章《“三院遗址・清华第一个中共支部诞生地”纪念物介绍》和《清华校友对三院的生动回忆》（载于 2017 年 1 月 3 日清华新闻网）改编。

No. 3 Courtyard

Dec 30th, 2016 marked a significant day in Tsinghua's history. On the grass field to the south of Yifu Library, a stone monument was unveiled in remembrance of the No.3 Courtyard. On it is inscribed "The Birth Place of Tsinghua's First Communist Party Branch" .

Although fate didn't bring us to witness the glory to the No.3 Courtyard, a former academic compound on campus, every time Tsinghua's former generation of faculties and students reminisce the old tales of the now gone buildings, thoughts of breathing the same revolutionary air and walking in step with the nation's fate stir up deep emotions and longings for the past.

The No.3 Courtyard was one of the earliest structures in the original Tsinghua campus. Built during the same period as Tsinghua Xuetang and Tongfangbu Building (the first auditorium of Tsinghua), it was located to the north of the Auditorium and to the west of the Library.

When it was first built, its area encompassed 5,117 square meters, with four rows of buildings. The first row were classrooms, second and third rows housed student dormitories, and the last row was the canteen and kitchen. The No.3 Courtyard was initially a middle school (equal to the first three years of the current middle school system in China) and was the main activity center for students.

After Tsinghua became a university, many scholars such as Feng Youlan, Zhu Ziqing, Chen Yinque, Wen Yiduo and Chen Daisun, once lectured at the No.3 Courtyard. Later, the No.3 Courtyard was also where students held literary and art events.

It's important to inscribe the No.3 Courtyard in our minds, not only because it was where teachers and students of the past exchanged ideas, but also because the No.3 Courtyard's classrooms were once witnesses of the patriotism of Tsinghua people. In 1926, the No.3 Courtyard classrooms became the birth place of Tsinghua's first CPC branch. After the Party branch was established, its members delved into revolution work, fervently pushing for the party's progress.

The Party branch of Tsinghua united faculty members and students in a struggle and strive to pioneer revolutionary work, composing glorious chapters of history. For example, during the "Dec 9th Movement" and later to the War of Resistance against Japan under the banner of the National Southwest Associated University, the Party members of Tsinghua were always in the forefront.

However, during the War of Resistance Against Japan, the No.3 Courtyard was destroyed by the invading army. After the war when Tsinghua was reopened, a few rows of buildings within the No.3 Courtyard were on the brink of collapse and were demolished as a result. However, the first row of buildings was retained as a memorial. It was in the 1980s when the last of No.3 Courtyard was torn down to make way for the construction of the Yifu Library.

Today, the stone monument on the lawn of Yifu Library is for the generations to come to remember No.3 Courtyard's past.

Translation and revision | Alexis See Tho

Image | Guo Xiang

2月27日

供稿 | 精仪系
文字 | 蒋佩妍
图片 | 任帅

郑德焰：实践之路，造“桥”之行

社会实践是清华大学博士研究生的必修课程，以培养博士生全面素质为核心，结合博士生的培养特点采用项目化的方式。实践项目由清华大学在全国各地建立的近70家校级实践基地统一提供，博士生从中自主选择与专业相关或者自己擅长的科研课题，到实践单位工作六周完成课题。在精仪系直博三年级学生郑德焰看来，实践之路就是一个需要不断造桥的行程。

2016年暑期，郑德焰作为队长带领清华大学江苏金坛博士生实践支队赶赴“小桥流水人家”的江南，走进常州亿通分析仪器制造有限公司。自2010年开始，每年都有清华博士生来到亿通实习、实践；亿通的大部分产品——监测空气质量的环保仪器——都是清华博士生利用短短六周时间研发的。

郑德焰和队员们的目标是开发一个数据采集仪，在位于区域内不同位置的不同仪器之间“架起桥梁”，让数据可以通过这架“桥梁”传递到电脑上，方便使用者实时监控整个区域的空气质量。既要帮助公司进行产品的更新换代，又要把师兄师姐们为清华博士生实践树立的优秀形象传承下去，郑德焰无比兴奋又倍感压力。

六周以内做成产品，郑德焰在解决实际问题的过程之中体会到，逢山开路，遇水架桥，实践不仅是服务企业的过程，更是迅速学习知识并立即用于实践的过程。在亿通，他和另外两名队员吃住都在厂里，并和在学校一样，保持着晚上继续攻关完成任务的习惯。2016年8月6日，在亿通实践的最后一天，他凌晨四点起床工作，终于在早餐前把整个系统调试通过。

最初的设计目标已经实现，然而实践并未就此结束。亿通公司的技术人员在接下来的调试过程之中，发现新产品在功能上存在瑕疵。“好马登程跑到头，好汉做事干到底。”已经回家的郑德焰继续思考改进的方法，并且在返校之前再次来到亿通，修复之前的漏洞，并增加新的功能。在一千多平方米的厂房里，深夜一个人加班，这样的经历，他调侃说：“一个人住这么大的房子，还好大脑一直在运转，没有时间去想恐怖故事。”第二天晚上，郑德焰终于将产品调试成功。

实践结束之后，郑德焰依然与亿通公司保持着联系，解决技术问题。而他带领实践支队研发的亿通数据采集仪也已进入市场销售。亿通公司的陈总对清华的博士生们很是赞扬：“你们用六周的时间，帮助一个公司经营发展下去，帮助一个厂里的工人解决就业问题，我们非常感激。”他希望将这台仪器连同其他环境监测仪器，推广到中小学校中，实时监测空气数据，保障孩子们的健康。

Ph.D. Candidate Zheng Deyan: Road of Practicability —Forming "Bridges"

In 2016, Zheng Deyan, the leader of Tsinghua University's Jiangsu Jintan doctoral in-field team underwent 6 weeks of in-field practicum at Jiangsu's Changzhou Yitong Equipment Manufacturing Co., Ltd. The goal is that in the end, a bridge could be built to link schools, enterprises and future prac-teams and such experience could be passed down to the next generation of students.

Social practice is a compulsory course for Tsinghua's Ph.D. students. This is to cultivate and improve the overall quality of doctoral students. Such training and project-oriented characteristics is something that Tsinghua place great emphasis on. For doctoral students, Tsinghua University provides nearly 70 practicum bases all over the country so that students can choose their own research project or specialties and finish relative tasks in 6 weeks. In doctoral student Zheng Deyan's view, the road of practicability is where the "bridge" must be in a continuous process of construction.

In the summer of 2016, Zheng Deyan from the Department of Precision Instruments led a practice team to Jiangsu's Changzhou Yitong Equipment Manufacturing Co., Ltd (Yitong Co.). Since 2010, Yitong Co. receives Tsinghua students annually for such in-field practicum. Yitong Co.'s main products - equipment that monitors air quality, are the product of such in-field study by Tsinghua students.

The goal of the team is to develop an acquisition instrument that "bridge" the various data located at different places in the region. The data is transmitted to the computer through the "bridge" and allow the user to monitor air quality in real time. Helping companies to upgrade their products and also establishing a positive image and working attitude for future Tsinghua students was something that excited Zheng. Yet, simultaneously, he felt great pressure.

In the process of solving practical problems, the team realized that it is not only about the process of serving the enterprise but also the process of quickly learning the knowledge and applying it into practice. In Yitong Co., he and the other two team members lived in the company and completed tasks well into the night. On the 6th of August, 2016, which is the last day of the practicum, Zheng got up at 4 a.m. and completed debugging the entire system before breakfast.

The original design goal has been achieved but the practicum did not end there. After the debugging process, Yitong Co.'s technical staff discovered new functional flaws. The saying goes "a good horse finish its entire journey and a responsible man complete all related tasks" . Zheng returned home already but he kept on thinking about ways to make improvements and then went back to Yitong Co. to analyze the loopholes and add on new features. Sitting in the 1,000 square meter factory, he worked into the night. He recalled his experience and jokingly said: "I was by myself in such a huge factory and thank goodness I was working all night long. Otherwise, given the setting I'd be thinking about some horror story."

After leaving, Zheng still maintains contact with the company so that technical problems could be resolved. Meanwhile his data acquisition instrument has entered the market. "We are very grateful for your help and your efforts during the 6 weeks at our company." said Mr. Chen (CEO of Yitong Co.). It is with great hope that such equipment could be used by primary and secondary schools so that real-time monitoring of air quality data can be further used to protect the health of the children and the nation.

Contributor | Department of Precision Instrument

Translation and revision | Min Weiyuan

Image | Ren Shuai

2月28日

供稿 | 计算机系
文字 | 张智伟
图片 | 陈稳杰

周立柱：花甲之年筚路蓝缕，投身西部志在教育

2007年，青海大学计算机技术与应用系正式成立，实现了教育部“清华大学－青海大学”对口支援计划的一个重要的学科部署。经过慎重考虑，年过花甲的清华大学计算机系周立柱教授接受了学校和青海大学交付的重任，牵头创建青海大学计算机技术与应用系，开启了自己与西部的一段教育情缘。

拥有丰富管理经验的周立柱老师在创系之初就明确指出：“最大问题不是生源质量，而是教师队伍建设。”组织清华教师前往青海授课只能解决某些课程的燃眉之急，积极为青海教师开设各类辅导课程，切切实实地打造和培养青海大学的骨干教师，才是授人以渔。此外，周老师还积极安排青年教师进修访问、攻读在职博士，以此提升科研能力和教学水平。经过近五年的时间，青海大学计算机系的教师队伍已经初具规模，周老师带领着同事们探索出了“三年基础，一年实践”的培养模式，源源不断地为当地输送高素质的毕业生。

在狠抓教师队伍建设的同时，周立柱教授还四处奔走、积极协调，在多方大力支持下，很快建成了计算机硬件、软件、网络等教学实验室。利用清华捐赠的超级计算机，建成了大规模计算集群研究环境。特别是以此为基础，随后陆续建立了“青海省信息技术应用与工程研究中心”“青海大学三江源数据分析中心”等科研机构，开启了利用信息技术，服务青海经济的研发之路。周立柱教授将自己的一份赤诚、毕生经验都毫无保留地奉献给了青海大学计算机技术与应用系，使得这个系自创立之时就站在了高起点上。

即使卸任青海大学计算机系主任后，周立柱教授仍旧奔走在推动西部地区计算机教育发展的路上。2011年清华百年华诞之际，他抓住时机，在学校的支持下，策划并组织实施了“清华携手谷歌助力西部教育”项目，促进了青海大学、新疆大学、宁夏大学、云南大学、贵州大学等五所西部高校计算机学科在师资队伍、精品课程、本科生培养等方面的发展。他经常告诫自己并鼓励学生：要勇于为国家奉献自我、做出贡献，要有改变落后地区面貌的社会使命感和担当。尽管可能会有牺牲，但人生也同样可以收获很多，赢得充分的成就感。

注：本文改编自姜伟峰、刘丹《周立柱：花甲之年筚路蓝缕　执着奉献不忘初心》（原载于2016年9月21日，清华新闻网）。

Professor Zhou Lizhu: to Dive Straight into the Western Regions of China

In 2007, the Department of Computer Technology and Application at Qinghai University was established. In spite of being over his sixtieth, Professor Zhou Lizhu took the position as the dean of this new department at Qinghai University, who once served as the dean of the Department of Computer Science and Technology at Tsinghua University.

"At the beginning of the establishment, the biggest problem that we've faced is about the quality of the teaching team." said Professor Zhou. In order to solve this problem, he organized Tsinghua teachers to take charge of training at Qinghai so that the overall teaching ability at Qinghai could be drastically improved; meanwhile, he asked Tsinghua teachers to personally teach important courses and not only guide but also help with the preparation of the courses alongside Qinghai teachers. Through watching and learning, Qinghai teachers became the backbone of such courses and fully take charge in the future alongside Tsinghua teachers who will continue to provide remote support.

Just as this problem was solved, lagging teaching conditions posed another challenge. After several requests, Professor Zhou successfully secured donations from Tsinghua to Qinghai in facilities such as computer equipment. This will allow a large-scale computer lab and positive learning environment be installed at Qinghai. Such favorable learning conditions for students help to boost quality as well as provide technical support for subjects such as meteorology and other research work. Subsequently, Qinghai University also established the "Information Technology and Engineering Research Center" for Qinghai Province, "Qinghai University Source Data Analysis Center" and many other research institutions which are used to support the economic development of information technology services in Qinghai Province.

Even after left his office, Professor Zhou was still busy running around for the computer education in the western region. In the Centennial Anniversary of Tsinghua back in 2011, Google began a partnership in the field of education with Tsinghua's Computer Science and Technology Department. Professor Zhou seized the opportunity and formed a "Tsinghua and Google supported education project" . Led by Tsinghua, the project helps to provide resources and funding for Qinghai University, Xinjiang University, Ningxia University, Yunnan University and Guizhou University. It helps to promote the teaching exchanges, course work and development of undergraduate trainings amongst these five universities. He often tells students that "it is worth working in the area that has great potential. There will be sacrifices but there will also be fruitful results and a sense of tremendous achievement".

Contributor | Department of Computer Science and Technology

Translation and revision | Min Weiyuan

Image | Chen Wenjie

3月1日

普通高等教育精品教材《电子商务概论》：将最新的成果带给学生

供稿 | 教务处

文字 | 张智伟

图片 | 梁晨

“你准备好迎接电子商务了吗？”1998年，IBM公司以一则响亮的广告在全球掀起了电子商务的热潮；1999年，阿里巴巴、携程、当当网等日后在中国电子商务领域做得风生水起的电子商务企业相继成立，中国电子商务正式步入实质性的商业阶段，这一年甚至被部分人称为“中国电子商务元年”。电子商务在商业领域蓬勃发展的同时，电子商务研究与教育也随之进步，国内最早的一批电子商务教材出现在高校课堂。清华大学覃征教授主编的《电子商务导论》（人民邮电出版社出版）便是其中之一。

2000年，为了填补国内电子商务学科基础理论教材领域的空白，覃征教授主编出版了《电子商务导论》，该书成为国内最早的电子商务教材之一。此后十余年，随着电子商务领域日新月异的变革，相关教材也在不断地与时俱进。由于研究的深入和知识的扩展，书名从《电子商务导论》改为《电子商务概论》（高等教育出版社出版），版次也从第一版发行到了第五版。为了能让最新科研成果进入教材，教材再版时，内容甚至经历了“伤筋动骨”的改变。

2015年出版发行的《电子商务概论（第4版）》就采用了新的知识体系，从电子商务基础、技术、管理、实践、案例、战略6个层面重新组织内容体系。教材编写组还基于教学实践和科学研究，不断对新取得的科学研究成果进行分类总结、创建案例并将之纳入教材，建立了“学中练、练中学、练中闯、练中创”的教材理念。

目前，国内以《电子商务概论》命名的教材有不下十余种，覃征教授组织的编写组在对教材十余年的精耕细作中，不断地构建独特的知识体系。例如，教材中“移动电子商务”“面向服务体系的软件架构”“电子商务文化”等新知识内容，在国内电子商务教学及国内领导干部的培训中起到了引领和示范作用，获得了国家精品课程教材和清华大学优秀教材特等奖荣誉称号。

经过十余年坚持不懈的努力，目前该教材连续更新，再版次数在同类教材中处于国内领先位置。与此同时，教材编写课题组与国际著名的施普林格出版社合作，相继出版英文专著*Introduction to E-commerce*（2009年）和*E-commerce Strategy*（2013年）、韩文专著《전자 상거래》（2013年），成为首部作者为国内人士的全球发行外文版电子商务专著。

Tertiary Textbook Topics of E-commerce: Bringing the Latest Findings to the Students

"Are you ready for E-commerce?" In 1998, this IBM's advertisement launched an E-commerce boom in the world. In 1999, Alibaba, Ctrip, dangdang.com along with other E-commerce companies entered into a stage of fast development and expansion. 1999 became known as the first year when China stepped into the era of E-commerce. As E-commerce developed alongside commercial development, research and education in this field saw the first batch of related teaching materials being made available for tertiary institutions. Tsinghua University's Professor Qin Zheng's *Introduction to E-commerce* is one of them.

In order to fill the blank of E-commerce theory teaching and learning, Professor Qin Zheng edited and published *Introduction to E-commerce* in 2000. It became one of the first textbooks on E-commerce. After more than ten years, changes in E-commerce has been ongoing and fast-paced. Teaching materials has been "updated and changed non-stop" . From *Introduction to E-commerce* to *Topics of E-commerce*, the First edition evolved into a Fifth edition.

In 2015, the *Topics of E-commerce* (Fourth Edition) is based on a new teaching framework where the contents are divided into 6 sections. These are E-commerce foundation, technology, management, practice, case studies and strategy. Teaching practice and scientific research is also based on the latest results. Contents are summarized and case studies are included to ensure that students are able to apply theory into practice. "Learn through practice, practice and learn, refine through learning and innovate through practice" is the core idea behind the new textbook.

At present, there are more than a dozen different kinds of teaching materials on the titles of *Topics of E-commerce*. For more than a decade of intensive research and meticulously organizing the latest contents, Professor Qin Zheng continues with constructing a high quality curriculum which is not only rich in content but also up to date. For example, the book mentions mobile E-commerce, service-oriented software, E-commerce culture and other new related knowledge. The material has played an exemplary role in E-commerce training.

With more than ten years of perseverance, the teaching material and the updated version is currently the first of its kind in the country. At the same time, the textbook team along with Springer Press jointly published *Introduction to E-commerce* (English, 2009) , *E-commerce Strategy* (English, 2013) and 전자 상거래 (Korean, 2013).

Contributor | Academic Office

Translation and revision | Min Weiyuan

Image | Liang Chen

3 月 2 日

文字丨杨鹏成

图片丨李娜

薛平教授研究组研制成功一种新型高速光学相干层析成像系统

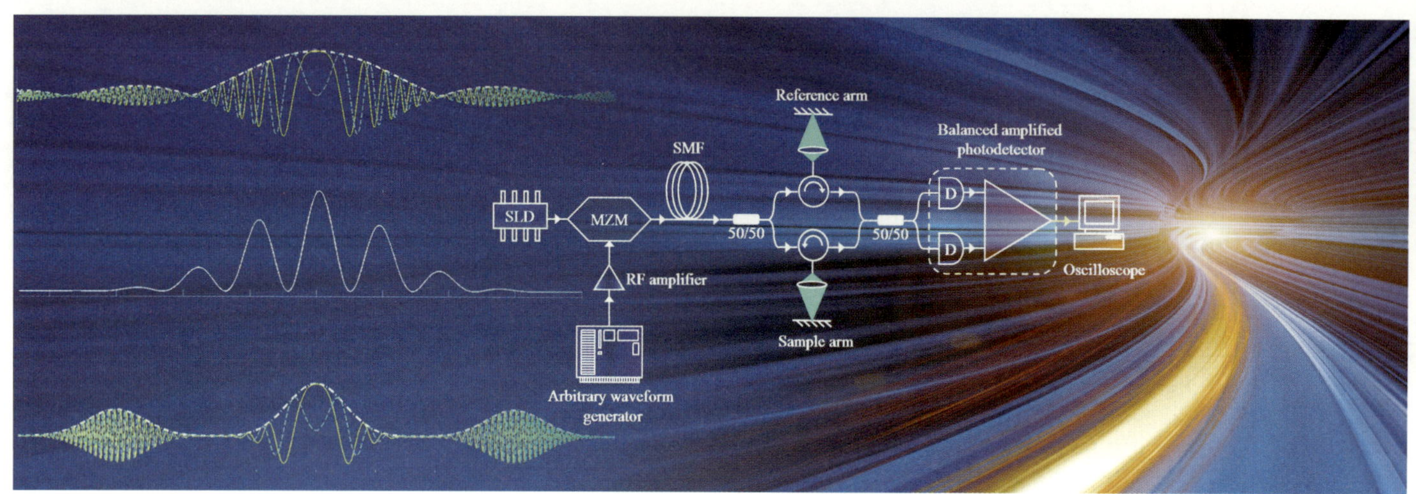

传统的临床影像方法包括超声、X 光、CT 和核磁共振成像 MRI 等。而国际上新出现的“光学活检”是一种比传统医学成像高近百倍分辨率的光学相干层析成像技术（OCT）。它不需要切取待测组织样品，只需对活体进行光扫描即可得到细胞分辨水平的组织断层图像，分辨出细胞层次结构和形态。

光学相干层析成像技术（OCT）作为一种新型的无损、高分辨率光学断层三维成像方法，在生物、医学、材料等许多领域具有非常重要的应用，是光学影像领域的研究热点。

但在薛平教授研究组研制成果出现之前，OCT 技术一直存在一个成像速度的瓶颈问题。对于一些医学、生物学上的快变过程，如果成像速度不够快，会导致图像的模糊与失真，从而难以进行相关的分析。因此，对快速动态过程的检测，成像速度起着至关重要的作用。但要实现实时高清三维光学相干层析成像，当前每秒数百帧的成像速度仍然不够。其中的瓶颈在于图像数据处理速度受限于现有图像传感器（CCD）获取数据的速度及中央处理器（CPU）、图形处理器（GPU）的运算速度。如何进一步提高光学相干层析成像的处理速度，成为目前相关领域的关注焦点。

为了解决这个问题，物理系博士后张晓等人在导师薛平教授指导下，独辟蹊径地提出一种新型的高速光计算方法，首次应用于光学相干层析成像并得到了实验验证。新技术使用具有计算功能的光路，高速处理包含样品三维结构信息的海量数据，彻底摆脱了传统方法中图像传感器（CCD）和高性能中央处理器（CPU）、图形处理器（GPU）的运算速度对成像速度的制约，实现了 1000 万次线扫描 / 秒（相当于 1 万帧 / 秒高清图像）的高速光学相干层析成像，为实现实时三维高清光学相干层析成像提供了一条全新的道路。

目前，这是世界上最快的光学相干层析成像速度。

清华大学物理系教授薛平研究组于 2016 年 11 月 21 日在《科学报告》（*Scientific Reports*）期刊在线发表题为《用于光学相干层析成像的光计算技术》的研究论文，报道了这种新型基于光计算的高速光学相干层析系统。该领域著名媒体《光学相干层析成像新闻》（*Optical Coherence Tomography News*）将该成果列为“每周特色”（feature of the week）进行了重点介绍，认为这是本领域的重要进展。

Research Group of Professor Xue Ping Successfully Developed a New Type of High-Speed Optical Coherence Tomography System

Internationally, the "optical biopsy" is an optical coherence tomography (OCT) technique, which has a resolution ratio nearly 100 times higher than conventional clinical imaging methods, such as ultrasound, X-ray and CT. It does not need to cut the tissue samples to be tested. Only by light scanning in the body, cellular resolution tomographic images of tissue can be obtained with clear cellular structure and tissue morphology.

Optical coherence tomography (OCT), as a new non-invasive and high-resolution three-dimensional imaging method, has very important applications in many fields, such as biology, medicine, materials and so on. It is a hotspot in the field of research on optical imaging.

However, before the research result of Professor Xue's research group, OCT technology always had a bottleneck problem of imaging speed. If the imaging speed is not fast enough, the image may get blurred and distorted and thus make the related analysis very difficult for some fast processes in medical and biological study. Therefore, imaging speed plays an important role in the study of rapid dynamic process. But current imaging speed of hundreds of frames per second is still not enough to achieve real-time, high-definition, and three-dimensional optical coherence tomography. The bottleneck is that the speed of image data processing is limited by the speed at which the current charge coupled device (CCD) acquires data and the arithmetic speed of the central processing unit (CPU) and graphics-processing unit (GPU). How to further improve the processing speed of optical coherence tomography has become the focus of current research.

In order to solve this problem, Zhang Xiao, who is a postdoctoral researcher of physics, under the guidance of Professor Xue, proposed a new type of high-speed optical computing technique, which was for the first time applied to optical coherence tomography and proved experimentally. The new technique completely gets rid of the imaging speed constraints due to the limited speed of CCD, high-performance CPU and GPU in traditional methods. The new technique uses an optical path with a computational function, achieving high-speed optical coherence tomography of ten million line scans per second (equivalent to high-definition imaging of ten thousand frames per second). High-speed optical processing of massive data of three-dimensional structure information of samples provides a new path to achieve real-time, three-dimensional, and high-definition optical coherence tomography.

To date, this is the fastest optical coherence tomography in the world.

Research group of Professor Xue Ping under Faculty of Physics at Tsinghua University, published a research paper entitled "Optical Computing Technology for Optical Coherence Tomography" online on November 21, 2016 in the journal of *Scientific Reports*, reported this new type of high-speed optical coherence tomography system based on optical computing technique. Optical Coherence Tomography News, the well-known medium in this field, lists the result as an important progress in the field and gives it a focused introduction as "feature of the week" .

Translation and revision | Raj Lamar

Image | Li Na

3月3日

改编 | 梁乐萌

图片 | 李娜

清华名人故居之吴晗故居：通向光明的小屋——西院 12 号

进入清华西门，自西向东走在清华路上的人们恐怕没有几人会想到要去北侧的西院看一看。那是一片宁静的地方，原始的平房掩映在不高的柏树下，似乎与清华整体的现代化气质风格迥异。然而，这些平凡的小屋中，有一所却因为吴晗的居住被赋予了不平凡的意义。

吴晗是中国著名历史学家、社会活动家，于 1931 年考入清华历史系，1934 年毕业留校任教。抗战爆发后，他先后任云南大学、西南联大教授，并开始积极投身爱国民主运动。1946 年西南联大解散，吴晗返回北平继续在清华历史系讲授中国通史，不久，他被分配到清华园西院 12 号居住。

“分到的这所住房并不算好，但比较宽敞，又是独门独院，院子也不小，面对一片树林。三间正房铺着地板，旁边有盥洗室、厨房，还有两间西房。这与昆明相比，已是天渊之别了。”吴晗很喜欢这所房子。西院 12 号不仅是吴晗一家的栖身之所，还是那个风雨如晦的年代无数进步青年的精神寄托之处。中共地下党、民主青年同盟等组织常在西院 12 号聚会。除了清华的同学，燕京、北大的同学也常来，屋子里坐不下，就坐在院子里，实在没处坐，青年们就直接坐在地板上，照样畅谈当前的斗争形势，激浊扬清、挥斥方遒。

“就在这所房子里，我度过两年多黑暗的岁月。尽管外面是黑的，这所房子里却经常有明朗的笑声，热烈的争论……有许多次运动的宣言、声明、通电等等，是在这所房子里起草的……”在《清华杂忆》中，吴晗这样回忆。

进步青年们在西院 12 号组织了读书会，吴晗曾多次为其演讲。此时他担任了共产党领导下的“通识学社”的导师，常常在读书会上分享研究马列主义、毛泽东思想的体会，引导大家提高学习革命理论的兴趣。在白色恐怖的威胁下，西院 12 号还是许多革命同志的避难所。以这所房子为起点，吴晗等人帮助一批批青年通过封锁线、到达解放区，为解放区输送了大量人才。他还以革命思想影响、团结了一批教授，使越来越多的教授与中国共产党接近。他们经常在西院 12 号讨论至深夜，共同迎接新中国的曙光。

1948 年，吴晗被列入国民党“剿总”黑名单，不得已离开清华奔赴解放区。次年 3 月，他再次回到清华，为新时期清华的建设做出了重要贡献。

70 年过去了，西院 12 号早已不复当年的热烈与激情，争论声已不再，只有声声鸟鸣与隐隐约约的汽车鸣笛声。但是，它与近春园红色花岗岩雕刻的吴晗塑像，与邓小平题写的“晗亭”二字一起，见证了吴晗由学者、民主战士成长为优秀共产党员的人生历程。

注：本文根据“清华史苑”专栏文章《含笑遥望着远方——吴晗故居》（原载于 2007 年 10 月 9 日清华新闻网）改编。

Tsinghua Celebrity Wu Han's Former Residence: No. 12 of the West Yard

Upon entering the west gate of Tsinghua, on the pathway from the west to the east, there aren't many people who would particularly go to the west yard at the north side to take a glance. It is a rather quiet place, and the original bungalows there, nestled in the shadow of not-too-high cypress tree. The area also seems rather out of tune compared to the overall modernization of Tsinghua campus. However, such an ordinary cabin received extraordinary significance because of it being Wu Han's residence.

Wu Han was a famous Chinese historian and a social activist. He was admitted to Tsinghua University in 1931, and later stayed in Tsinghua to teach after graduating in 1934. After the outbreak of the anti-Japanese war, he had successively served as a professor in Yunnan University and the National Southwest Associated University, and began to actively join the patriotic democratic movement. In 1946, when the National Southwest Associated University ended, Wu Han returned to Peking and continued to teach Chinese history in Tsinghua. No. 12 of the West Yard in Tsinghua was where he lived.

"The house cannot be considered great, but it is spacious. It has its own yard, which is not too small and which faces the forest. Three rooms are covered with floorboards, and next to them, there is a bathroom, kitchen, and two west rooms. It is miles ahead, when compared to the one in Kunming." Wu Han liked the house. No. 12 of the West Yard was not only the residence of Wu Han, but also a spiritual sustenance of countless progressive youth in an era of unrest. The Chinese Communist Party, the Democratic Youth Alliance and other organizations often gathered at No. 12 of the West Yard. In addition to Tsinghua students, students from Yanjing and Peking University also often came to the yard, sitting either in the house or in the yard when the house was already full. If the yard was also filled, young students sat directly on the floor, talking about the happenings and being passionate about their dreams.

"In this house, I spent more than two very dark years. Despite the darkness outside the house, inside was filled with mostly laughter, and heated debates. Manifestos, declarations, and telecommunications, etc. of many movements were also drafted in this house..." Wu Han recalled in the *Tsinghua Memory*.

Progressive youth organized different reading parties at No. 12 of the West Yard, and Wu Han had the opportunity to give them many speeches. At that time, he served as a tutor of the "General Education Society" under the leadership of the Chinese Communist Party, and often shared his study of Marxism-Leninism and Mao Zedong's thoughts at the reading parties, guiding others into gaining interest of learning some more revolutionary theory. Under the threat of the white terror, No. 12 of the West Yard was also a refuge for many revolutionary comrades. Taking this house as a starting point, Wu Han helped a group of young people pass the blockade line and arrive in the liberated areas, having transported a lot of talents along the way.

In 1948, Wu Han was included in the suppression blacklist by the Nationalist Party, and forced to leave Tsinghua and go to a liberated area. In the following March, he returned to Tsinghua once again, and made important strides towards the construction of Tsinghua University in the new era.

Seventy years have passed, No. 12 of the West Yard had already lost all its warmth and passion. There were no more debates. Merely the sounds of birds and vague car whistles could be heard. However, with the sculpture of Wu Han on the red granite in Jinchunyuan and the inscription of "Han Ting" written by Deng Xiaoping, the place blossomed with Wu Han's development from a scholar and a democratic soldier to an outstanding communist, and also showcased the light he had brought to this yard and the entire Chinese society.

Translation and revision | Sarthak Pyakurel

Image | Li Na

3月6日

文字 | 蒋佩妍

图片 | 梁晨

姚维坤：一个清华博士的乡村情怀

“我想用我的足迹，丈量家乡农村的每一寸土地，参与到污水治理的每个环节，为美丽乡村建设鼓与呼，贡献一份力。”2016 年暑期，清华大学环境学院 2015 级博士生姚维坤顶着 40℃的高温，赴安徽省蚌埠市实地调查“美丽乡村建设”中农村污水处理现状。

半个月的实践结束之后，他用一周时间编辑整理出一份 30000 多字的《蚌埠市乡镇污水处理设施运营情况调查报告》递交给实践单位蚌埠市规划设计院，其中对农村水污染治理问题的建议就有 10000 多字。

国家当前对美丽乡村建设的倾力投入，使农村环境得到明显改善，但是依旧存在比较严重的水污染问题，而农村生活污水是重要的污染源。未经处理的生活污水直接排放到河道里，其中的病菌虫卵引起疾病传播，使村民的身体健康受到威胁，这让来自农村的姚维坤痛心不已。利用自身所学的水处理专业知识，为农村水污染治理鼓与呼，姚维坤认为这是作为一名清华人的责任和担当。

“真没我想象中的那么容易。”姚维坤说。在调研开始前的资料收集环节，他投入了大量的准备工作。为了让调研的村庄具有代表性，他必须全面了解蚌埠地区农村污水处理站的建设现状，而这些建设资料分散在市级和县级的环保局、建设局和美好办等部门。整整两周，姚维坤不得不奔波各地，协调关系，一点点地搜集到全部资料，精心筛选出 54 个典型村的污水处理站，调研范围覆盖了固镇、怀远、五河 3 个县所有乡镇。

地点筛选完毕后，新的难题又出现了。姚维坤说，有几个村庄因为实在偏远，都没法依靠导航找到，只能一路走一路问人。有个最远的村庄，问了 10 多个村民才找到它的污水处理站。除了路远，路还不好走，有些村庄只有土路或者石子路。极差的路况加上蚌埠夏季 40℃的高温酷暑，直接导致了车辆爆胎。

即使“身心疲惫，特别想就这么放弃了”，姚维坤依旧坚持了下来。15 天时间，行程 5000 多公里，姚维坤走遍了这些污水处理站，从污水特征、处理工艺、建设时间、处理规模、总投资、流动方式、设计出厂水质标准等维度采集了大量真实数据，拍摄照片 500 多张，手写的调查笔记超过 10000 字。

姚维坤在调查中发现，农村现行的污水处理方式大都套用城市污水的治理模式，并且每个村的污水处理建设规模基本一致，未能结合农村的实际情况，因此治理效果不理想。姚维坤在报告中以专业视角提出低碳式农村污水处理模式，他认为在现阶段，美丽乡村示范村特别需要研究开发建设成本低、处理效果好、运行无费用或低费用、适合分散型处置的处理技术。

“希望我的这份报告能发挥作用，为蚌埠市农村污水治理提供翔实的参考依据。”姚维坤说。

Yao Weikun:
a Feeling for the Villages and Countryside from a Tsinghua Ph.D. Student

"I want to use my footprint to measure every inch of land in China's rural areas. I want to participate in the sewage treatment of this area and contribute to creating a beautiful countryside for my country." In the summer of 2016, Yao Weikun, a 2015 Ph.D. student from Tsinghua's School of Environment braved the scorching heat of 40 degrees and went to Anhui Province's Bengbu to conduct a field survey of the beautiful countryside. He was there for the installation and construction of a sewage treatment.

After half a month, he compiled a 30,000 word plus report on *Bengbu Township*'s *sewage treatment*. He submitted this to the Design and Planning Institute of Bengbu Township. His notes on the challenges and control of rural water pollution took up more than 10,000 words.

The current construction of a "beautiful countryside" in the country is about making investments and ensuring that rural areas are significantly improved. However, water pollution is still a serious problem and sewage is that source of pollution. Untreated sewage is directly discharged into the river which spread diseases and germs. This threatens the villagers' health and saddens Yao. Due to his own study in water treatment and pollution control, Yao believes that as a Tsinghua student, this is his responsibility.

"It was not as easy as I thought it would be." said Yao. He placed a lot of preparatory work before his survey. In order to conduct his investigation, he must fully understand the current situation of the construction of sewage treatment in Bengbu. Such information are scattered throughout various departments such as the Municipal and County Environmental Protection Bureau. For a total of two weeks, Yao had to collect information and select 54 typical village sewage treatment stations to gain a more comprehensive overview of the situation. In the end, his scope of research covered Guzhen, Huaiyuan and Wuhe County.

After the site screening, new problems emerged. Yao said that some villages are extremely remote and it was not easy to find. He had to ask people one by one. In one case, he asked 10 villagers to finally locate the local sewage treatment station. Moreover, road conditions are not good. Poor road conditions and extreme heat led to tires bursting and a slow journey.

Even "if it was so physically and mentally tiring to the point that one would just give up" , Yao didn't. 15 days and 5000 km, Yao visited all the sewage treatment stations and from the treatment process to construction time and scale, to total investment, water quality standards, factory design and the finalization stage, Yao was there. He collected real data and took more than 5000 photos and hand-wrote more than 10,000 words of observation notes.

Yao found that the current rural sewage treatment mode is like the ones in the city. When it came to the station's scale, all the villages are the same. Treatment is not ideal. From a professional perspective, Yao suggested a low-carbon sewage treatment mode for the rural setting. He believes that at the present stage, a beautiful countryside requires the initial investment to be low in cost.

"I hope that this report can play an important role in providing a detailed reference for the sewage treatment in rural Bengbu." said Yao.

Translation and revision I Min Weiyuan

Image I Liang Chen

3月7日

文字 | 张智伟
图片 | 赵存存

女生节：记忆集体情感的符号

“男孩子们为我挂起了一条长长的横幅，这条横幅是那年‘女生节’唯一一个有名字而且只送给一个女生的横幅；上午第一节课后回到寝室，发现宿舍门口已经用气球拼出了一个星星的形状，上面写着祝福的话；中午聚餐的时候还收到了一把心仪很久的油纸伞……”回忆起大学本科四年里的“女生节”，徐梦茵——法学院2012级国防生班唯一的一位女生，总是毫不吝啬地称赞男生：“对我超级好，每年‘女生节’都觉得没人比我更幸福了。”

起源于20世纪90年代的3月7日“女生节”在清华有20多年历史了。从某种意义上来说，这个定于“三八”国际劳动妇女节前一天的节日，对所有女生意味着一种独立、自信的生活态度，也体现了男性对女性的尊重与两性平等的观念。这种尊重女性和两性平等的观念也是清华的传统。1928年，清华正式招收的第一批女生入学后，学生们专门写了《四级级歌》（清华男女同校的第一级是当时的“第四级”），其中写道：“春来大地兮遍紫黄，共坐春风兮男女一堂，男女一堂兮吾级始创，始创，始创，吾级之光。”

“女生节”里，男生们想尽办法“讨好”女生，女生则可以大方接受男生们的百般“殷勤”，男女生们从平日的繁忙中抽出身来，共同享受这个特殊日子的轻松。徐梦茵现在还清晰地记得，第一次女生节，班里所有男生集合在一起，请她“随意点歌”，“五音不全”的男生也欣然接受了她点歌的要求。从大学一年级到四年级，她在“女生节”时的心情从好奇、喜悦变成了依恋、不舍。对于校园里的男女生而言，“女生节”也成为彼此敞开心扉、增进友谊的节日，即使是已经毕业，很多男生还会在“女生节”这一天向曾经的女同学表达祝福。

每年“女生节”横幅的海洋里，毕业班的横幅总是格外引人注目：“清华四载成何事，韶光尽付眼前人”“明年，给你们写横幅的就不是我们了”……俏皮中难掩依依惜别之情，“女生节”也悄然成为记忆集体情感的符号。

2016年3月7日，男生们为徐梦茵过了本科阶段最后一个“女生节”，当天晚上，徐梦茵在朋友圈里写道：“希望以后，我们还可以一起唱一首《依然爱你》。”

Girls' Day: a Symbol of Our Collective Memory

"The boys hung up the long banner. The banner is the only one among all banners on this special day, which is delivered to only one girl. After returning to my dorm, I found balloons arranged in the shape of a star right outside the dorm door. There were words of blessings written all over the balloons. At lunchtime, I even received a traditional Chinese umbrella which was something that I've wanted for a long time..." When it came to "Girls' Day" during all of her four years of study, Xu Menghan has nothing bad to say about the boys in her class. As the only girl and member of the 2012 Law-National Defense Class, Xu praised the boys since "they pamper me" . "On every Girls' Day, no one is happier than me!"

Started on the March 7th in the 1990's, Tsinghua already has more than 20 years of history of Girls' Day. In a way, having the day before The International Working Women's Day is seen as a symbol of the girls having an independent and confident attitude towards life. It also reflects Tsinghua's tradition of gender equality and respect for women. In 1928, Tsinghua officially enrolled girls for the first time. After the first enrolment, the students wrote a song called "*Grade Four Song*" (Tsinghua's first co-ed class was known as Grade Four). "Spring time saw colors of purple and yellow spread out across the plain...girls and boys share on classroom...together, they share common goals...and together, they try to find that light..."

On "Girls' Day" , the boys try their best to please the girls. Girls are able to make requests. Both genders enjoy and celebrate the special day. Xu Menghan still remembered that on the first Girls' Day, the boys in her class gathered together and asked her to "randomly select songs" for them to sing. Those who can't sing accepted the challenge and did so anyway. From her first year at Tsinghua to the fourth year, she went from being curious about the day to being happy to missing it and being all sentimental. For the students, this special day is about friendship and remembrance. Even after years of graduation, many of the boys still remember to send their wishes to their former classmates.

The annual "Girls' Day" is always about eye-catching banners. "Four years at Tsinghua and all I care is the person in front of me." "Next year, we will no longer be the ones who will write the banner for you." Girls' Day has quietly become a collective memory.

On March 7, 2016, the boys held the last Girls' Day for Xu. Xu wrote in her social media update the following: "I hope that in the future, we could still find that chance to sing *I Still Love You*."

Translation and revision | Min Weiyuan

Image | Zhao Cuncun

3月8日

文字 | 胡颖　徐静
图片 | 郭祥

“中国青年女科学家奖”获得者周树云：做科学秘境中的女探险家

“我感谢同行们对我过去工作的认可，这个奖也是对我继续努力做出更好工作的一个鼓励。”对于自己获得的第十三届“中国青年女科学家奖”，清华大学物理系教授周树云笑着说。

2017 年 2 月 28 日，“中国青年女科学家奖”颁奖典礼在北京举行，周树云因在新型二维材料及异质结的新奇电子结构研究方面的贡献而获此殊荣。

“中国青年女科学家奖”由全国妇联、中国科协、中国联合国教科文组织全国委员会和欧莱雅中国于 2004 年设立，每年评选 10 位在基础科学领域和生命科学领域取得重大科技成果的、45 岁以下的优秀青年女科学家。对于自己获得的这个奖项，周树云更看重它对女性科研人员的激励作用：“从某种意义上来说，‘中国青年女科学家奖’让一些女性研究人员进入公众视野，对于提升学生的信心和推动女性在科学领域的发展具有积极作用。”

在科研的道路上，周树云走得踏实且坚定。从高中时代起，她就对物理很感兴趣，并对力学、电学有着强烈的好奇心。读大学时，她毅然选择了物理系，师从朱邦芬院士。在做本科毕业设计的时候，她对凝聚态物理研究产生了浓厚兴趣，由此踏上科研求索之路。从清华大学本科毕业后，周树云在美国加州大学伯克利分校继续深造。获得博士学位之后，她成为美国劳伦兹伯克利国家实验室的同步辐射光源“先进光源”的博士后研究员和材料科学部的项目科学家。2012 年，前途一片光明的周树云决心报效祖国，毅然回到清华大学物理系。

回国后，周树云带领自己的课题组，着力研究具有重大潜力的新型二维材料及由不同层状材料通过人工构筑形成的范德华异质结。近年来，研究组在第二类外尔半金属的实验证明及范德华异质结的能带结构调控研究方面取得了重要进展。

“女性适不适合从事科研从来都不是我考虑的问题。我只需要问自己喜不喜欢科研，能否从科研中得到一些乐趣和成就感。物理系的女生很少，女教师更少。我希望女同学们在学习、生活上遇到困难时，我能给她们提供一个倾诉和解决问题的机会，能给她们正面的影响，告诉她们女生一样可以兼顾科研与家庭。”周树云说。

对于未来的发展，周树云目标明晰：“二维材料和异质结构是我感兴趣的新兴前沿研究领域，还有很多我想要继续探索的奥秘，我希望能从中得到更多的乐趣和成就感。”面对未来可能的挑战，周树云异常坚定与自信：“无论遇到什么困难，我都从未想过放弃，物理学是我挚爱一生的事业和选择！”

Recipient of L'Oréal-UNESCO Women in Science China Award—Shuyun Zhou: to Be That Female Explorer in the World of Science

"I would like to thank the committee for their recognition of my work. This award is a great encouragement to me, and I will keep striving for excellence in science." Professor Zhou Shuyun made this comment after being awarded the 13th L'Oréal-UNESCO Women In Science China Award.

The award ceremony was held on February, 28th, 2017, in Beijing. Zhou Shuyun was recognized for her contribution to the electronic structure of novel two-dimensional crystals and heterostructures using angle-resolved photoemission spectroscopy.

"L'Oréal-UNESCO Women in Science China Award" was jointly established in 2004 by the National Women's Federation, China Association of Science and Technology, China UNESCO National Committee and L'OREAL China. Each year, 10 young female scientists under age of 45 who have made major contributions to life science, fundamental science and technology are selected. Zhou Shuyun viewed the award as a positive action to motivate young women researchers in science. "In some sense, this award brings more female researchers into public view. This not only boosts the confidence of female students but also plays a positive role in promoting women's development in the field of science."

Zhou's interests in science started ever since her high school days. During her undergraduate study at Tsinghua University, she developed a keen interest in condensed matter physics after an undergraduate thesis project with Prof. Zhu Bangfen. After graduating from Tsinghua University, Zhou Shuyun continued her Ph.D. studies at the University of California, Berkeley. After earning her doctorate degree, she became a postdoctoral fellow of the Advanced Light Source and later a project scientist of the Materials Sciences Division at Lawrence Berkeley National Laboratory. In 2012, Zhou Shuyun decided to return to Tsinghua and start her own research group in the Physics Department.

Zhou's group at Tsinghua University focuses on the electronic structure and ultrafast dynamics of novel two-dimensional materials and heterostructures, which hold great promise for future electronics and spintronics applications. In recent years, her research group has made important progress in the study of superlattice bands in graphene/h-BN van der Waals heterostructure, and the experimental realization of Lorentz violating type-II Weyl semimetal.

"Whether or not women are suitable for scientific research has never been an issue for me. All I ask myself is whether I like it or not, and whether I can get fun and satisfaction out of it. There are not many girl students in the Physics Department, and women faculties are even less. I hope that female students can turn to me for support and help, should they encounter difficulties in their study or in life. I want to tell them that girls can have both a career in research and a family." said Zhou.

Looking forward, Zhou Shuyun has a clear goal about where to go next in science: "I am really excited about two-dimensional materials and heterostructures. This is an emerging research field with many opportunities. With the state-of-art sample growth techniques and advanced spectroscopies, there is really a lot to be discovered." In the face of possible challenges, Zhou said with firm confidence that "No matter what difficulties I've encountered, I never thought about giving up. Physics is the love of my life. It is my career and my choice" .

Translation and revision | Min Weiyuan

Image | Guo Xiang

3 月 9 日

文字 | 蒋佩妍

图片 | 陈稳杰

清华、米兰理工携手共建中意设计创新基地

继西雅图全球创新学院、苏世民书院、深圳国际校区之后，清华新百年“更创新、更国际、更人文”的蓝图上又增添了浓墨重彩的一笔——清华大学与米兰理工大学将在意大利米兰合作建设中意设计创新基地。清华校长邱勇与米兰理工校长费卢奇奥·内斯塔于 2017 年 2 月 22 日在人民大会堂签署了合作协议。

作为文艺复兴的发源地，意大利以艺术与设计创意著称，米兰更是被誉为世界设计之都。米兰理工大学创建于 1863 年，其工科排名意大利第一，艺术与设计学科位列世界第十。中意设计创新基地选址于米兰理工大学著名的设计校区（Bovisa Campus）内，与米兰理工大学设计学院在地理位置上无缝对接，并将与米兰理工大学的各类顶尖实验室实现资源共享。

利用这一基地，我校将与米兰理工大学和意大利设计产业界开展全方位深度合作，把中意设计创新基地打造成国际化高端人才培养平台、艺术设计创新研究平台和艺术设计原创成果展示发布平台。该基地将成为清华教师在欧洲的工作室和创作基地、清华学生的海外实习实践基地。

中意设计创新基地的实现，得益于清华大学与米兰理工大学多年来的交流合作以及两校在设计领域的共同优势。清华大学与米兰理工大学联合培养的双学位硕士生项目已经持续七年；清华美院师生也频频在米兰设计周、米兰国际设计三年展等设计前沿阵地亮相；2015 年米兰世博会，由清华美院教师担纲设计的中国国家馆，其外形如同希望田野上的金色麦浪，诠释了中国人对农业、饮食、自然的看法，让中国文化随着中国设计真正“走出去”。

“中意设计创新基地的建立，是清华的全球战略在欧洲的延伸，表明清华的全球战略正在逐步全面推开，向着‘更创新、更国际、更人文’的目标又迈出了坚实的一步。”清华校长邱勇说。

Tsinghua University and Politecnico di Milano Jointly Established a Hub for Sino-Italian Design Innovation

After the Global Innovation Exchange institute in Seattle, Schwarzman College and the Global Campus in Shenzhen, Tsinghua's blueprint of "more innovative, more internationalized and more humanity-oriented" witnessed another colourful addition — the Sino-Italian Design Innovation Hub jointly established by Tsinghua University and Politecnico di Milano.

As the birthplace of the Renaissance, Italy is famous for her art and design. Milan is known as the Design Capital of the world. Politecnico di Milano was founded in 1863. Her Engineering course is ranked first in Italy with Art and Design disciplines ranking tenth in the world. The Sino-Italian Design Innovation is located in Bovisa Campus and is within close proximity to the School of Design at Politecnico di Milano. The Hub will share resources along with various leading laboratories at Politecnico di Milano.

With this research and education base, Tsinghua will carry out comprehensive in-depth cooperation with not only Politecnico di Milano but also the design industry in Italy. The goal of the base is to provide a high-end training platform for future talents as well as a research base and innovative drive for art design and exhibitions. It will also serve as the studio and creative base for Tsinghua teachers in Europe as well as an option for Tsinghua students to carry out their internship.

Sino-Italian Design Innovation Hub was made possible due to the many years of exchanges and cooperation in design between Tsinghua University and Politecnico di Milano. A double Master Degree held by both universities has lasted for 7 years and many Tsinghua teachers and students have had their debut at Milan Design Week, Milan International Design Exhibitions and much more. The China Pavilion at 2015 Milan World Expo was designed by Tsinghua teachers. Like a gold wheat field, it symbolizes prosperity and hope as well as an interpretation of Chinese views on agriculture, food and nature. That was a great way to allow culture to "venture out" and make its mark in Chinese designs.

"The establishment of the Sino-Italian Design Innovation Hub is an extension of Tsinghua University's global strategy in Europe. It indicates that Tsinghua University is gradually and comprehensively implementing its global strategy and making solid steps towards the goal of being 'more innovative, more internationalized and more humanity-oriented'." concluded Qiu Yong, President of Tsinghua University.

Translation and revision | Min Weiyuan

Image | Chen Wenjie

3月10日

文字 | 刘书田

图片 | 霍巍

植树节：清华的绿色大学梦

清华园有个绿色的梦。

1998年5月，清华成为中国“绿色大学”的首创者。对于“绿色大学”的概念，清华大学环境学院钱易院士认为：“绿色大学”有时会被简单地理解为绿化，但“绿色大学”的真正含义远远超越这一理解，所谓“绿色”，是指一种保护环境、保护资源、可持续发展的理念。

经过近二十年的建设和完善，清华学生如今能够通过参与多样化和独特的实践教育、聆听高端论坛、参与SRT（“大学生研究训练计划”）和各类竞赛活动、参加协会组织等形式，在丰富多彩的活动中享受绿色教育。

从理念到行动，绿色教育的成果也在清华人的生活、学习和工作中体现出来：一次性筷子在清华园中“黯然离场”，取而代之的是可重复利用的筷子；坚持了近十年的废纸换再生纸活动，已成为许多同学的习惯；废旧自行车通过重新清洗组装，再度出现在学堂路上；为了减少燃油污染，校内交通环线客车以电为动力，它驶到哪里，就将环保的意识带到哪里。

清华还有一群坚持“绿色行动”的组织，其中知名度最高的是学生绿色协会。绿色协会以“绿色实践，行胜于言”为口号，组织绿色环境教育、栽培“屋顶农场”，致力于宣传环境知识，倡导校园绿色生活，把环保与可持续发展的理念融入同学的生活中。寒暑假期间，清华学子们奔赴祖国各地，进行环境专业类、生态考察类、环保宣教类的社会实践，为美丽中国的发展贡献力量。

在我国第37个植树节之时，学生绿色协会曾组织清华学子“种植”过“我为祖国添新绿”的“誓语树”，同学们在誓语树上写下了保护环境的愿望，发表了自己的治霾宣言。

在人才培养的漫漫征途中，清华大学的绿色教育体系只是一个开始，正如钱易院士所说：“如果首先把清华建成一个符合环保和可持续发展要求的社区，那么，她就会成为一个模板，逐渐地，‘绿色中国’将不再是梦想。”

又到一年植树节，让我们从点滴做起，呵护身边的一草一木，圆美丽的清华园一个绿色大学梦。

Arbor Day: Tsinghua's Green Dream

Tsinghua has a green dream.

In May 1998, Tsinghua University became the pioneer of adopting the concept of "Green University" in China. The concept of "Green University" is often understood to be simply about greenery. However, Academician Qian Yi from the School of Environment at Tsinghua University believes that the meaning of a "Green University" is far beyond that. This "greenery" refers to environmental protection, resource protection and a concept of sustainable development.

After nearly twenty years of refinement and improvement, students can now integrate in an educational practice that is diverse and unique such as listening to high-end forums to participating in SRT (Students' Research Training Program), associations and other forms of activities which offers rich and colorful activities that helps to improve "Green Education" .

Going from concept to practice, the results of "Green Education" are reflected in the life, study and work of Tsinghua people. Disposable chopsticks were replaced with reusable chopsticks across Tsinghua and papers have been recycled. Old and unused bicycles have been fixed and reused. New environmentally friendly vehicles have been employed on campus to minimize fuel pollution.

Apart from small details which reflect environmental protection, there is also a special group in Tsinghua who focuses on "green action" . This Green Association bears the slogan of "Green practice - action speaks louder than words" . They are committed to the promotion of environmental knowledge, the concept of green campus life and ensuring that students are aware of sustainable development. During the holiday, Tsinghua students also travelled throughout the country to promote and raise awareness about the environment, ecology and the crucial need in ensuring that China remains beautiful.

On the 37th Chinese Arbor Day, the Association played an active role in cultivating and ensuring that our motherland stays green. They wrote their desires to protect the environment and pledged their oath in reducing smoggy days which is a constant threat and challenge for the country.

When it comes to talent development, Tsinghua's Green Education is just the beginning. Like what Qian Yi stated: "If a community need to have sustainable development and awareness in environmental protection, then Tsinghua needs to be that template. Gradually, a 'Green China' will no longer be a dream."

This is another Arbor Day:

Let us start with ourselves first.

Let us protect every grass, every flower, every tree and every plant.

Let us work towards a greener future and a greener Tsinghua!

Translation and revision | Min Weiyuan

Image | Huo Wei

3月13日

文字 | 刘书田

图片 | 霍巍

清华大学2016年特等奖学金获得者陈立杰：立志为人类智慧添砖加瓦

“大一的时候，我经常在紫荆操场漫步，思考我是谁？我要做什么？”2016年特奖答辩会的现场，一位激情澎湃的少年刚说完这句话，台下便自发响起了掌声。

这位语惊四座的少年名叫陈立杰，来自交叉信息研究院计科30班。

陈立杰的大三学年学分绩排名年级第一，专业核心课学分绩达98.3分，曾以第一作者身份在计算机领域顶级会议AAMAS和COLT上发表论文，曾率领清华代表队参加第38届ACM/ICPC国际大学生程序设计竞赛世界总决赛并获得铜牌，是大家眼里的“学神”，是老师眼中的“学术新秀”。

竞赛、学业、科研，串联起了陈立杰的大学生活。

从初中开始参加信息学竞赛，陈立杰一直都是信息学奥林匹克竞赛界的传奇人物之一。他一路靠自学击败各路强手，揽获各种奖牌。高一时，他曾拿到全国青少年奥林匹克竞赛的金牌，顺利保送清华大学；高三时，参加第25届国际信息学奥林匹克竞赛，他以全场第一名的成绩获得金牌。

进入清华后，陈立杰认真对待所有课程的学习，夯实自己的基础。大二下学期，他选修了研究生课程“高等理论计算科学”。初次参与算法研究，点燃了陈立杰的研究兴趣。尽管难度很大，他仍然坚持为这门非常有挑战性的课程每周花费近20小时。

功夫不负有心人，陈立杰对这门课的学习内容进行深入探究，写成《关于拟阵限制下多臂老虎机的最优探索问题》这一学术论文，发表于理论机器学习领域的国际一流会议COLT2016，他还前往纽约会场作了专门的口头报告。

陈立杰真正令众人佩服的，不是在信息竞赛中屡获佳绩，也不是独占鳌头的专业课成绩，而是他身上“能够独立寻找问题”的科学家气质。

大三在麻省理工学院访问期间，陈立杰和导师合作，利用传统计算理论，找到了证明量子计算优越性的理论框架，解决了著名量子信息学者约翰·沃特罗斯（John Watrous）在2002年提出的开放问题（open problem），在学术界引起了相当大的反响。

科研不总是一帆风顺的，陈立杰坦言，苦苦思索却没有结果的日子占了绝大多数，他有时也会陷入沮丧和迷茫之中。但抱着“成为一名理论计算机科学家”的远大理想，陈立杰一步一脚印走了过来。

“我们的院长姚期智先生曾经说过，现在是计算机科学的黄金时代，也是人类的黄金时代。”陈立杰说。如今，他即将赴美国攻读博士学位，期待成为这个黄金时代大潮中闪现的一朵浪花，在计算机科学领域绽放出最独特的智慧之光，为人类的智慧添砖加瓦。

注：本文改编自《我立志为人类智慧添砖加瓦——访清华大学2016年本科生特等奖学金获得者、交叉信息研究院2013级本科生陈立杰》，2016年11月22日发表于“小五爷园”微信公众号。

Chen Lijie, 2016 Top Grade Scholarship Winner: Determined to Contribute to the Wisdom of Mankind

"In the freshman year, I often walked in the Zijing playground, thinking who I was and what I really wanted to do." On the scene of Top Grade Scholarship Defense Meeting of 2016, applause filled the room after a passionate young man said this sentence.

The teenager is named Chen Lijie and is from class 30 of Computer Science and Technology under the Institute for Interdisciplinary Information Sciences.

Chen Lijie's grades in the junior year ranked the first and his average grade of professional courses reached 98.3. He once published papers in AAMAS and COLT, top meetings in the field of computer science, as the first author, and led the Tsinghua team to participate in the 38th ACM / ICPC International College Students Programming Competition World Finals and won the bronze medal. In the students' eyes, he is the "smartest student" and in his teachers' eyes, he is an "academic rising star" .

Chen Lijie began to participate in informatics contests from middle school, and has always been one of the legends in Informatics Olympiad Competitions. By self-study, he beat talents from other places and won a variety of medals. At the first year in high school, he once won the gold medal in National Youth Olympic Competition, and was admitted to Tsinghua University without the entrance exam. At the third year in high school, he ranked first place and won the gold medal in the 25th International Informatics Olympiad Competition.

After entering into Tsinghua University, Chen Lijie studied all courses seriously to consolidate his academic foundation. In the sophomore year, he selected the postgraduate course of "Higher Theoretical Computational Science" . The initial participation in the algorithm research ignited his research interest. Despite the difficulty, he insisted on putting in nearly twenty hours a week on this very challenging course.

Hard work does pay off. With in-depth study based on learning of the course, Chen Lijie wrote an academic paper entitled "Optimal research issue on multi-armed slot machine under the matroid limit" , published it in COLT2016, an international first-class meeting in the theoretical machine learning field, and also went to the New York meeting place and gave a special oral report.

What really Chen Lijie makes everyone admire is not about the awards he has won in the information competitions, nor his top grades in the professional courses, but the scientists' temperament of "ability to find the problem independently" in him.

During the MIT visit in his junior year, Chen Lijie cooperated with his tutor and found a theoretical framework to prove the superiority of quantum computing by using the traditional computing theory, which solved the "open problem" proposed in 2002 by John Watrous, who is a famous quantum information scholar, and aroused a considerable response in the academic community.

Scientific research is not always smooth. Chen Lijie frankly said that, in most days, hard thinking doesn't come with a result, and he also felt frustrated and confused sometimes. But with the dream of "becoming a theoretical computer scientist" , Chen Lijie moves forward one step at a time.

"Our dean Andrew Chi-Chih Yao once said that nowadays is the golden age of computer science, and also the golden age of mankind." said Chen Lijie. Now, he is about to go to the United States for a doctorate, looking forward to becoming a flash in the tide of this golden age, blooming the most unique light of wisdom in the field of computer science, and contributing to the wisdom of mankind.

Translation and revision I Raj Lamar

Image I Huo Wei

3月14日

文字 | 杨茂艺

图片 | 郭祥

清华冬泳队：冰水彻骨寒，健儿绽笑颜

春花已绽，回首寒冬，那份畏惧烈风冷霜而不得不躲在暖气屋子里的记忆仍然清晰，自己的四肢似乎也还停留在疏于锻炼而瑟瑟发抖的状态。

似乎一到寒冷季节，我们就默许了自己的懒怠与静止，忘了给生命以继续蓬勃的动力。然而，清华西湖游泳池畔的那群人却时刻提醒着我们——天行健，君子以自强不息……

清华冬泳协会自1987年成立以来，已走过了三十个年头，现有的200多名会员中，既有风华正茂的清华学子，也有步履不再那么矫健的耄耋老人。每到仲冬时节，他们相约西湖畅游，在路人诧异又艳羡的注视下，一头扎进冰冷刺骨的池水，在笔直的泳道里开始自己英雄般的征程。

当裹着厚棉衣的人们呼着热气在北风中摇晃难定，他们却头顶冰碴儿、双臂袒露，像一条条快活自如的鱼一样，一往无前。

日复一日、年复一年的冬泳不仅考验着会员们的身体素质，也从多方面磨炼着他们的意志品质。从岸上做准备运动到破冰开游，从水中互相鼓励到泳后齐喝羊汤，他们之间渐渐形成了一种特殊的默契和友谊，让冬泳团体愈发坚强和包容。而那经历低温浸泡之后回到岸上的疯狂喜悦，也只有勇者才能体会得到——花花绿绿的泳衣在冬日午后的暖阳下闪耀着光彩，盖上浴巾浴袍开始互相打趣，打开收音机哼着小曲儿……

清华冬泳队的一位学生道出了他们的感受：“很冷，可就是很快乐，‘痛’并快乐着！”

如果你目睹过那群80多岁的老人如何坚持冒着零下十几度的严寒天气，在冰水里舒展身躯，恐怕会心生敬佩或羞赧。关节炎、腰椎病、术后伤甚至失聪……这一系列病痛都挡不住他们对生命活力的追求，阴冷的雨雪也浇不灭他们内心深藏的火焰。

老校长梅贻琦的秘书沈刚如先生开创了清华冬泳的历史，他本人到了96岁仍然风雨无阻地在西湖里坚持冬泳，精神矍铄。他曾为清华冬泳协会赋诗《冬泳赞》一首，诗中写道：“余少体质弱，遍求健身术，球类太极拳，游泳冷水浴，最好是冬泳，人与水拼搏。空气既新鲜，日光亦灼灼，神经要冷静，热昏疾病出，血管要柔软，硬化难求药。奋斗冷水中，循环自加速，多种慢性病，无医自痊愈，坚持数十年，身心都活跃。学习有精神，智力更开拓，献身现代化，健康不能缺。我今七十九，顽躯仍矍铄，现身来说法，冬泳炼体魄。”

冬泳，一项挑战自我的运动，一次意志精神的淬炼。每一滴彻骨寒凉的水珠都以绝美的方式滋润着健儿们的脸颊，笑颜灿烂，竟不觉生之艰难。

Winter Swimming in Tsinghua: No pain, No Gain

Spring has come, but thoughts of the strong and dreaded wind that kept us holed up indoors is not far from our memory. Then, we walked around with trembling hands and feet - a proof of the much-needed exercise.

Almost every winter, we somehow give way to laziness and live in physically inactivity. But a group of people by Tsinghua's West Lake is a constant reminder of a phrase in the Chinese classic, "As heaven maintains vigor through movement, a gentleman should constantly strive for self-perfection."

The Tsinghua Winter Swimming Club was established in 1987 and currently boasts more than 200 members—the elderly who is wobbly in his step, and the young and energetic students.

Once mid-winter arrives, they would gather at Tsinghua's West Lake for a casual swim. The group of winter swimmers dive in unison into the biting cold water while astonished passers-by gawk and simultaneously admire their courage. Forming perfectly straight swimming lanes, they begin their fearless journeys.

While people are wrapped in thick cotton-padded coats, puffing out vapors, trudging through strong winds, shards of ice sprinkle the heads of these winter swimmers, and with bare shoulders, they swim on with an iron will, gliding freely like fishes in the water. Day after day and year after year, the winter swimming club not only puts its members' physique to the test, it also trains their mental will.

From warm-up exercises on the lakeshore to encouragements while swimming and to drinking warm lamb soup after a swim, these activities have gradually created a unique friendship between the members, strengthening relationships and creating inclusiveness in the club.

It's the brave ones who have experienced the piercing cold waters and the unexplainable kind of delight after a swim who will truly appreciate and enjoy the lakeside scene of people in colorful swimwear wrapped in towels under the warm rays of the sun. They tease each other and hum to music blaring from a radio.

A winter swimmer perfectly captures the scene: "Ah, it's so cold, but it's so fun. It's a pleasurable kind of pain. "

Whenever I think of a group of 80 year-olds persistently swimming in waters well, below zero degrees, I would secretly feel ashamed. It's as if arthritis, spinal problems, surgical wounds and hearing loss is a non-factor that could prevent them from their enjoyments in life. The fire hidden deep within their hearts cannot be extinguished by gloomy rain and the chill of snow.

The club was founded by Mr. Shen Gangru, secretary to the former Tsinghua president Mei Yiqi. Even when he was 96, rain or shine, he would swim in the Tsinghua West Lake. He once penned a poem about Tsinghua's Winter Swimming Club titled "Ode to Winter Swimming" . He wrote:

A weak-bodied youth I was,

searched far and wide for ways to build strength;

Ball games and Tai Chi, swimming in cold waters,

The best is winter swimming - man's struggle with water;

The air fresh, the sun radiant.

...

Winter swimming is a sport that challenges the self and a refiner of mental will. Every drop of freezing water pierces to the bone yet moistens the cheek. The swimmer's face wears a brilliant smile and life's misery strangely dims.

Translation and revision | Alexis See Tho

Image | Guo Xiang

3月15日

文字 | 左烜晅
图片 | 赵存存、李娜

多功能教学楼的“七十二变”

“六教又升级自习空间了！”

“对啊，我也看到了，分隔走廊和自习空间的木板很有设计感呢。”

刚开学，就有很多同学发现教学楼的变化，好评不断。其实，除了六教（即第六教学楼）的自习讨论空间之外，教学楼内还有很多我们鲜少注意到的改变。

从绿植、沙发、榨汁机、六教指示牌到讨论区、教室内的多媒体设备等，教学楼的“变身”远不只这些——

14 间讨论教室内配置了可变形的活动桌椅，根据不同的课程需求打造不同功能的教室。师生讲座、分组讨论和大组讨论，想要的模式应有尽有。

打造教学楼多功能公共空间，改造讨论空间六处，休闲空间四处，教师答疑休息室六间，助力学生学业，激发学习兴趣。

更有四教的学生作业展，展示建筑学院大师班作业 18 组，教学楼公共空间创业大赛作品 170 件以及美术学院作品近 200 幅，充分挖掘教学楼内文化载体的功能，让同学们在教学楼内就能欣赏艺术，陶冶情操……

而这一切都源于物业管理中心对于师生需求的深刻体察。随着课堂教学工作不断由“以教为主”向“以学为主”转变，师生对教室格局的需求也发生了变化。

“我参加过物业中心的问卷调查，并提出了建议，我希望可以在六教增添一些讨论区。这样可以方便下课后小组讨论，也不用担心影响教室内自习的同学。”来自新闻与传播学院的何雪冰说。

追求优质的教学、生活环境是物业管理中心的核心目标，其下属教学办公区事务科负责全校 276 间公共教室的卫生、秩序和安全。物业管理中心曾主动开展调研，了解师生需求，吸收国内外知名高校教学楼的建设和管理理念，结合我校特点，努力为师生提供舒适的教学环境、丰富的人文环境、朴实的育人环境。

校学生会生活权益部的微信公众号“艾生权”有学生留言说：“在‘小艾’的印象中，‘大清’的教学楼似乎从来没有停止过变身的步伐。各种配套设施贴心地解决同学们的需求，越来越人性化的设计方便着每一位师生，真正达到了高端大气上档次，低调奢华有内涵。”《自然》杂志的主编在六教零层新改造的教室讲学后表示：“这里的教室从设计、家具到设备，都是世界一流的。”

Transformation of Multi-functional Teaching Buildings

"The self-study spaces have been upgraded in Building 6!"

"Yes, I saw it too. The design of the corridors and self-study space are great."

School just started and many students spotted the changes. Praises were constant. In fact, apart from the self-study space at Building 6, there are many more subtle changes to the multi-functional teaching building.

From green plants to sofas to juicers to signs to discussion areas and multimedia equipment set up for the classrooms, changes in the building are from just these examples.

14 discussion rooms are equipped with foldable tables so that classroom layout could be altered and changed to suit various functions, courses and corresponding activities. The classroom design would suit all types of interactions between teachers and students whether in smaller group discussions or in a bigger lecture type design.

Teaching and public spaces were increased in the building. 6 discussion rooms were renovated along with 4 rooms for leisure and 6 Q&A lounges where teachers can assist with study and stimulate the students' interest in further learning.

There is also an exhibition space for students' work from Building 4. 18 groups of work are on display from the School of Architecture. Moreover, there are 170 works entered into competitions along with nearly 200 artworks from the Academy of Arts and Design on display in the building's public space. These fully utilize the building's other function which is to be a platform for cultural and artistic exchange. This allow students to appreciate art as well as cultivate their own artistic sentiments through such displays.

All of this is derived from the experiences gathered by staff at the property management center. The teaching function is changing from "teaching is the focus" to "learning is the focus" . This means that needs for classroom layout is also changing.

"I've participated in the questionnaire and made some suggestions, saying that I hope the university can add more discussion rooms in the teaching buildings which will help with after-class discussions. This also means that students who are self-studying will not be disturbed." said He Xuebing from Tsinghua's School of Journalism and Communication.

The pursuit of quality teaching and living environment is the main goal of the property management center. Its affairs department is responsible for the hygiene, order and safety of the 276 classrooms. It has taken the initiative to carry out research to understand the needs of the teachers and students. It also carried out research into the management concepts and designs of well-known colleges and universities both at home and abroad so that teachers and students are provided with a more comfortable, educationally rich and simple environment.

Students have mentioned that "Tsinghua's teaching buildings has never stopped transforming. A variety of supporting facilities and user-friendly designs bring only greater comfort and convenience to the teachers and students. The environment and design is low-key yet at the high-end of scholarly luxury." The editor of the magazine *Nature* said after his lecturing in one of the rooms at Building 6 that, "the designs from the classrooms to the furniture to the equipment are all world-class" .

Translation and revision | Min Weiyuan

Image | Zhao Cuncun, Li Na

3月16日

文字 | 冯婉婷

图片 | 霍巍

韩美林教授设计《丁酉年》邮票：清华与生肖邮票的不解之缘

对于集邮爱好者而言，生肖邮票一直是备受追捧的题材，每年生肖邮票的设计者与图稿也一直受到邮迷们的关注。2017 年 1 月，《丁酉年》生肖邮票首发，精美的鸡年邮票迅速得到广大邮迷的喜爱。该套邮票的设计者，是我国著名艺术家、国家一级美术师、清华大学美术学院教授韩美林先生。

《丁酉年》特种鸡票一套两枚，一枚为白色底色，一枚为彩色底色，延续了第四轮生肖邮票的设计风格。《丁酉年》鸡票第一枚图案展现了一只威武强壮、高傲奔放的雄鸡，第二枚则为呵护幼崽的母鸡与抽象可爱的小鸡组成的“合家欢”形象。《丁酉年》生肖邮票表现的是生肖鸡幸福美满的一家子，既突出了雄鸡起舞、大吉大利的生肖贺岁主题，又展现了和谐团圆的家庭生活。在此次创作中，韩美林先生使用了他最擅长的装饰画风格，同时为了体现“合家欢”的整体氛围，他还突破以往创作的雄鸡风格，创作了母鸡与小鸡的形象。

“我从 1956 年开始集邮，1983 年设计了猪年生肖邮票，时隔 33 年后，再次参与生肖邮票的设计工作，我感觉这是一种缘分，是我和民族传统文化与艺术的缘分。”韩美林先生为此次设计《丁酉年》生肖鸡年邮票前前后后绘制了上千幅手稿。最终，精美的彩墨画稿结合韩美林先生亲自选出的流畅精致的雕刻布线稿，呈现出精妙活泼的《丁酉年》生肖邮票。

正如白岩松在主持《丁酉年》特种邮票首发仪式时所说：“生肖邮票的诞生，是艺术设计、印制工艺与传统文化内涵的深刻融合。一套具有艺术价值的邮票精品，是在不断的理念创新、设计创新和工艺创新中诞生的。”

实际上，清华美院与生肖邮票的设计渊源已久：美院吴冠英教授曾参与《辛卯年》《癸巳年》和《乙未年》等多套生肖邮票的设计；2014 年发行的马年生肖邮票则由清华美院视觉传达系的王红卫副教授和他的研究生郝望舒共同设计。

从 1980 年发行首枚生肖邮票——庚申猴邮票起，每轮生肖邮票都从猴年开始、羊年结束，吴冠英教授完成了第三轮生肖邮票的“收官”之作，韩美林教授设计的第三轮生肖邮票《丁酉年》在 2017 年的央视元宵晚会上为更多人所知。这一套套生肖邮票传承着中华文明的独特基因，也不断延续着清华与中华民族传统文化的深厚缘分。

The “Year of the Rooster” (“DingYou Nian”) Stamps Designed by Professor Han Meilin

For collectors, zodiac stamp has always been popular. Stamp designs and artworks have always been of interest. January 2017, “DingYou Nian” which featured rooster stamp was made publically available for the first time. The exquisite design and artwork is loved by many. The artist and designer behind the stamps is renowned in China. He is Mr. Han Meilin, a professor from Tsinghua's Academy of Arts and Design.

There are two sets of “DingYou Nian” stamps. One has a white background and the other, a more colourful one. This continues the design style of the fourth round of lunar year stamps. The first design shows a powerful and proud rooster. The second stamp is a hen surrounded by chicks. It is drawn in an abstract fashion and symbolizes a “happy family” . The “DingYou Nian” stamps represents happiness as well as prosperity shown in the pose of the rooster. During this design, Professor Han employed his distinctive style to reflect the overall feel of “homely happiness” . He added a different style to the drawings of the rooster, the hen and the chicks.

“I started collecting stamps in 1956 and designed Year of the Pig stamps in 1983. After 33 years, I participated in the design of stamps again, so this is fate. This is my fate with traditional culture and art.” For the “DingYou Nian” stamps, Han Meilin painted thousands of manuscripts. The final design was handpicked by Han himself.

Renowned TV presenter Bai Yansong who presided over the opening ceremony of these “DingYou Nian” stamps said: “The birth of such lunar year stamps is a profound integration of artistic design, printing technology and deep cultural traditions. This is the result of innovation in concept, design and technology.”

There is a long history between these designs and Tsinghua's Academy of Arts and Design. Professor Wu Guanying from the Academy was involved in the design of “XinMao Nian” , “GuiSi Nian” and “YiWei Nian” . The 2014 Year of the Horse stamp was designed by Associate Professor Wang Hongwei and his postgraduate student Hao Wangshu.

Since the issuance of the first zodiac stamp (Year of the Monkey) in 1980, zodiac stamps have continued year after year, cycle after cycle. It has always started with the Monkey and ended with the Goat. Professor Wu Guanying completed his top work as part of the third cycle and Professor Han Meilin's design took over. His work was made well known during the CCTV Lantern Festival Gala. This set of stamps continues the tradition of Chinese zodiac stamps and keeps the Chinese heritage in a special way. The design is also a way for Tsinghua University to preserve herself with our traditional culture.

Translation and revision | Min Weiyuan

Image | Huo Wei

3月17日

文字 | 刘书田

图片 | 任帅

清华名人名言之蒋南翔：不仅是给干粮，更应给猎枪

1952年11月，受中央人民政府任命，马克思主义教育家、中国青年运动的著名领导者蒋南翔（1913—1988）担任清华大学校长，重回清华园。

对于清华，蒋南翔一直怀有深厚的感情，这里不仅是他的母校，也是他革命生涯开启的地方。1932年，他考入清华中文系；1933年秋加入中国共产党，并逐渐成长为清华及北平学生运动的重要领导人；1935年参与领导了“一二·九”运动；抗战爆发后，蒋南翔奔赴民族解放的战场，长期领导青年工作。

清华的求学生涯和革命经历，为他日后从事教育事业奠定了重要基础。蒋南翔在清华工作的13年是其教育思想形成与实践的重要时期，在他的带领下，清华认真贯彻执行党的教育方针，在建设社会主义多科性工业大学的过程中，探索出了一条独具特色的办学之路。

新中国成立后，教育领域开始学习苏联的教育经验，重视实践环节是一大特点，蒋南翔对此非常认同。他始终认为，学校不但要给学生提供“干粮”，更重要的是要教会学生使用不断获取干粮的“猎枪”。

因此，蒋南翔一直重视学生基础理论和知识的学习，强调学生基本技能的训练、解决实际问题能力的培养。在学生进校伊始，蒋南翔就谆谆告诫同学们，作为一所工科大学，清华培养的学生要“能活学活用书本知识，既能动脑又能动手，善于在实践中创造新的经验，做掌握理论武器的主人，不做书本的奴隶”。

蒋南翔曾明确提出在教学计划的制订中一定“要加强理论和实践的联系”。1958年，经过多年的探索，清华在贯彻党的教育与生产劳动相结合的方针过程中，开始提出结合实际生产任务进行毕业设计，“真刀真枪的实际作战”，不但为国家完成了相当数量的实际生产和科研任务，而且使清华学生的政治、业务水平和工作能力得到了全面提高。

正是遵循这样的教育理念，清华致力于培养学生又红又专全面成长，为他们日后献身祖国建设事业奠定了坚实基础。

十年树木，百年树人。蒋南翔校长的教育理念深深地影响着一代代清华学子。同学们时常想起老校长当年的叮嘱：“你们进入大学要学知识，要提高能力。就像一个人要穿过原始森林，重要的不仅是给他一袋干粮，更应给他一支猎枪。因为干粮吃光了，不会再有；而用猎枪，可以不断地获得新的食物。”

注：本文改编自刘惠莉所著文章《蒋南翔：不仅是给干粮，更应给猎枪》，原载于《新清华》2008年4月4日第1718期第4版。

Jiang Nanxiang's Educational Philosophy Continues to Influence Tsinghua Students

In November 1952, Jiang Nanxiang (1913-1988) was appointed by the Central Government to be the Dean of Tsinghua University. As a Marxist educator and a well-known leader of the Chinese Youth Movement, he headed back to Tsinghua.

Jiang Nanxiang has always harboured deep feelings for Tsinghua. It is not only his alma mater but also where he first started his revolutionary career. In 1932, he was admitted by Tsinghua's Chinese Department and later joined the Communist Party in the autumn of 1933. He gradually became an important student leader and participated in the December 9th Movement in 1935. After the outbreak of the war, Jiang stayed at the front of the battlefield and was committed to youth work.

Tsinghua experience and his own revolutionary work laid solid and important foundation for his future career in education. He formed and practiced educational thoughts during his 13 years of work at Tsinghua. Under his leadership, Tsinghua conscientiously implemented the party's education policy and through exploration of integration, he added in unique approaches of multi-disciplinary education curriculum with socialist characteristics.

After the founding of the People's Republic of China, education began to take on the Soviet model and practice became a major feature. Jiang agrees since he believes that a school is not only about giving one food but above all, it should be about giving one a shotgun so that they have continuous access to food.

Therefore, Jiang Nanxiang has always attached importance to basic theory work and learning. Jiang placed great emphasis on the basic skills of students training and the ability to solve practical problems. When the students first enter into Tsinghua, Jiang would tell them that as a Tsinghua student, one need to learn and use knowledge, one need to have both brain and hands and not only be good at theory work but also excel at creating new experience through hands-on practice. "You need to be the master of a weapon and not the slave of a book!"

Jiang has explicitly highlighted the point that "we must merge both theory and practical work" . In 1958, after years of exploration, Tsinghua University along with the party's education direction began to propose the combination of both theory and actual practice. They asked graduate works to be a reflection of a "real battle" . It is not only about accomplishing research and practice tasks for the nation but also about comprehensively improving Tsinghua's overall political, business and high work-level abilities.

It is with such an educational philosophy that Tsinghua students have fully grown as individuals and dedicated themselves to the construction of the motherland. Such solid foundation has been laid.

A decade for one tree and a century for one individual - Jiang's educational concept has had great influences on generations of Tsinghua students. Students often recall the famous words of this former Dean: "You go to university to learn knowledge and to improve competency. Like someone who is trekking through a forest, you need to give him food but most importantly, you need to give him a shotgun so that even if he has finished all the food, he can still find more and be self-sustainable."

Translation and revision | Min Weiyuan

Image | Ren Shuai

3 月 20 日

文字 | 刘书田

图片 | 梁露文

水清木华又春分

三月的清华园春光正好，桃李芬芳，春意盎然。

清华园的春天是一树树的花开。照澜院的梨花、情人坡的桃花、新斋前的玉兰花、学堂路的李花，白的、粉的、紫的、红的，一簇簇摇曳在春风中，仿佛争先恐后地想要汇报春日到来的讯息。

清华园的春天是一幅幅色彩斑斓的有声水墨画。二校门汉白玉的光彩、大礼堂厚重的砖红、礼堂前泛起青绿的草坪、澄澈湛蓝的天空，明媚却不耀眼。主干道上此起彼伏的自行车铃声，枝叶间、草地上叽叽喳喳的鸟鸣声，学子们谈笑风生的爽朗笑声……闭上眼睛也能体会到春意的降临。

春天园子里最美的地方便是"水木清华"一带。清华园取义于"水木清华"，而"水木清华"又出自东晋谢混的《游西池》诗句"水木湛清华"。青翠的林山环拢着一池秀水，几缕绿柳低垂，山林之间掩映着两座玲珑典雅的古亭，幽雅静谧。这里往往是令游人们驻足停留最久的地方，也是清华学子们挚爱的景色。

"一年之计在于春"，园子里到处洋溢着蓬勃的朝气。有的呼朋唤友，在偌大的园子里寻一方净地，读诗填词，共享大好春光；有的捧起相机，找寻园子里最美的瞬间，用镜头捕捉春天的踪影。情人坡前听涛声，老馆门前听鸟鸣，万泉河畔看垂柳，西操傍晚赏日落，每时每刻都不禁让人慨叹一声"春光无限好"。青春不歇地在每一年的春天，如约绽放。

有人说，春日的清华园也象征着永葆青春的清华精神。园子里萦回的，是长风拂起的年轻志士们的衣襟，是昨夜西风中先贤们的蓦然回首，也是青春年华破土时不变的西山晴好。园子的面貌日新月异，但那种青春盎然的气息却从未离开过清华园。

走过百年，今天的清华依旧青春洋溢，生机勃勃。春光可惜莫轻抛，趁春日正好，何不携三五好友一同去赏大好春光呢？

Spring Comes to Tsinghua Campus

A March in spring is the most beautiful season in Tsinghua. Aromas from peach blossoms and the colors from flowers all point to one thing: Spring is in the air!

Spring in Tsinghua is the time when flowers bloom. The pear flowers at Zhaolan Yuan, the peach blossoms at Lover's Slope, the magnolias in front of Xinzhai Building, and the plum tree along Xuetang Road...all the white, pink, purple and red flowers sways gently in the wind in a manner as if to say that this sight is too splendid to behold.

Tsinghua's spring is a colourful tapestry. The white marbles of the Old Gate, the red bricks from the Auditorium, the green lawn that sits in front of it and the clear blue sky provides everyone with a dazzling sight. Close your eyes and listen to the bells from the bikes, the chattering of the birds and the laughter of the students. Do you not feel the arrival of spring?

The most beautiful Tsinghua Campus in spring is Shui Mu Tsinghua (SMTH). Shui Mu Tsinghua not only reflects the Lotus Pond and the Tsinghua Campus but is also a line from the poem *The tour around the Western Pond* by Xie Hun, a poet from the Eastern Jin Dynasty. The jade forest surrounded by mountains and springs...the green willows...the exquisite pavilion: all a scene of elegance and tranquility. Such sights make everyone want to linger longer.

"The work for the year is best begun in spring." Tsinghua is full of vigorous vitality. There are friends finding places within campus for a quiet afternoon. There are those reading and writing poems whilst taking in the sight of spring. Some venture out into the campus with their cameras to seek for the best shots. Whether it is at the Lover's Slope or the Old library, spring is everywhere. The willow trees along the little stream and the daily sunset draws everyone's attention. We couldn't help but exclaim "Oh! How delightful spring is!"

Some say that spring in Tsinghua is the symbol of that eternal youthful Tsinghua spirit. The campus is filled with the breeze that grace the coat of the young scholars. It is a breeze that once touched the ancient sages and now returns for a visit. It is also a reminder of that unchangeable youthful time and delightful scenery. With the passage of time, Tsinghua might have changed yet that young lively atmosphere will never leave our campus.

After a century, there is still much youthful vitality in Tsinghua. The light that shines during spring marks the best moment for some agreeable trip. Thus, what could be more pleasing than to enjoy the season with a friend or two?

Translation and revision | Min Weiyuan

Image | Liang Luwen

3月21日

文字丨梁乐萌、杨鹏成

图片丨李娜

计34班：小小中厅凝聚集体力量

清华的本科生大多集体居住在位于校园北端的紫荆学生公寓，住宿格局为四人一间，相邻两间共享一个中厅。同学们对中厅有各自不同的利用方式，计34班的同学们则充分利用这一空间，举办别具一格的“中厅讲座”，将小小的中厅建设成同学们交流学习、共同进步的平台。

计34班的“中厅讲座”开始于大二上学期，累计共开展43场。班里各路“大神”——某门课程基础较强、成绩突出的同学——以讲座的形式为大家讲解知识，解答疑难。除了课业辅导，他们还曾邀请学校摄影队队员和图片编辑方面的“大牛”为同学们讲解相关技巧，丰富同学们的业余生活。

“这个想法最初是在干部培训时受学长启发产生的，当传统的集体自习开展遇到困难时，我们就转而尝试这种方式。”该班前任团支书马也介绍说，他本人也担任了第一次中厅讲座的主讲人之一。“同学们参与度都很高，每次到场的同学都超过班级人数的三分之二。班里唯一的女生每次都去，我们专门给她留了凳子。”

第一次“中厅讲座”主讲大学物理与数据结构两部分知识，由于恰巧举办于期中考试前，对同学们来说恰似一场“及时雨”。此后讲座逐渐定期化，内容也由最初的知识梳理、考前复习扩展到往年精题分享甚至大作业交流。计算机专业常有难度高、工作量大的大作业，同学中流传的“奋斗三星期，造台计算机”就是形容大作业之难的经典“段子”之一。针对这一情况，计34班班委会安排提前完成大作业的同学在“中厅讲座”中分享经验教训，协助每个同学按时、高效地完成大作业。

活动放在中厅举办，是这个活动的“精髓”之一。班委从同学角度考虑，将讲座时间定在周末晚上九点到十点，地点在男生宿舍中厅，为喜欢在宿舍学习的同学们提供了便利。中厅空间不大、设备不足，同学们就自愿贡献出自己的电脑和显示器，不仅为讲座提供了便利，还可以在讲座后把电子版笔记直接分享给同学们，方便大家随时温习。

从中厅出发，计34班团结一心，坚定而自信地稳步前行。连续三年，计34班在期中、期末考试中名列年级第一，过硬的学习成绩无声而有力地证明了“凝聚集体力量”这一理念的效果。

计34班不仅有学习成绩的“硬实力”，还有班级活动的“软实力”——在班团干部和同学们的共同努力下，计34班连续三年获得校甲级团支部、优良学风班称号，并曾获得北京市“先锋杯”优秀团支部、北京高校“优秀基层学生组织”等荣誉。

步入大四，计34班的部分同学担任了五字班、六字班的辅导员，“中厅讲座”这一特色活动随之得到了宣传与推广。今后，或许有更多小小的中厅将在夜晚亮起灯光，而它所凝聚的温情与集体意识，也将一并在清华园得到传承。

Computer Class 34: Small Space, Big Ideas

Most of Tsinghua's undergraduate students stay at Zijing Apartment located in the northern end of the campus. Four students stay in one room and there is a common room between every two rooms. Students make use of this space through different ways. Computer Class 34 use the space to establish a "lecture salon" so that it becomes a platform for students to communicate, learn and make progress together.

Class 34's "lecture salon" starts in the second year and has accumulated so far, 43 sessions in total. The various "experts" in the class (those students with greater understanding of the course) hold lectures so that queries could be answered. "This idea was originally raised by more senior students. During the more traditional collective self-study mode, when difficulties arise, this lecture salon becomes the answer." said Ma Ye. Ma is the former group secretary and also one of the lecturers. "There is very high participation rate from the students. In fact, more than two-thirds of the students from normal weekday classes attend these sessions. The only girl in the class never misses out on a single session. We would always save a seat for her."

Ma also recalled that the first lecture was like a "much needed rain" for those who find physics and data structure to be dry and hard to grasp. Since then, the lectures became gradually regular, the contents more in-depth and previous reviews and coursework were shared to increase clarity in the learning content and to reduce unnecessary workload. Students jokingly said that one example is spending "three weeks to build a computer" . The lecture committee arranges for the students who have completed the homework in advance to share their learning and assist others so that work could be completed with efficiency.

Having the lecture salons being held in that dorm room is in many students' views, an essential and convenient location. Held at the boy's dormitory and during weekends from 9p.m. to 10p.m., it saves time and allow the mostly male students to access the location with ease. Taking into account the lack of resources and space, many students voluntarily contribute their own computers to better equip the room with resources. Notes taken at the end of every session are shared with the participants to ensure that self-study could be continued.

Class 34 advances in unity and confidence. "While individual efforts helped us to achieve great results, the main reason is collective power." Ma further added: "Such academic performances effectively proved that group efforts outweighs anything." For three consecutive years, Class 34 came first in mid-term and final exams.

Such great results from the students in combination with "soft power" and efforts from the lecture salons resulted in Class 34 being recognized and awarded the "Excellence Award" . It was also awarded Beijing Municipality's "Pioneer Cup" "Outstanding grassroots student organization" and many more.

As students head into their final years, students from Class 34 became counsellors for Class 5 and 6. The "lecture salon" has been promoted throughout Tsinghua due to its effectiveness in boosting coursework understanding as well as being a unique learning component. There will be many more lecture salons where students will continue the Tsinghua spirit.

Translation and revision | Min Weiyuan

Image | Li Na

3月22日

文字丨刘兰、冯婉婷

图片丨梁露文

精仪系智能微系统团队：培养“顶天立地”的复合型人才

题记：清华大学精仪系智能微系统团队围绕国家人才战略和“顶天立地树人”的研究生培养理念，重点解决工科研究生教育中培养模式与指导方法单一、学术培养与工程实践结合不紧、科学精神与人文素养联系不够等问题，成功培养了一批高层次的复合型工科创新人才，并在2016年获得了研究生教育成果一等奖。

清华大学精仪系智能微系统团队在1994年大致成型，以智能微系统技术作为总的研究方向，二十多年来，团队在尤政院士的带领下，逐步摸索出了一条“培养顶天立地的复合型工科创新人才”的道路。“顶天”是指把握国家发展战略、瞄准国际学术前沿，从事世界一流的学术探索；“立地”则指在学术研究的基础上，集中精力、脚踏实地地进行高水平的应用开发，解决实践中的实际问题。在已经毕业的70名研究生中，获得国家级科技奖的有8人次，共承担国家重大/重要科研项目15项；35名已经毕业的博士生中，有11名在清华大学、航天科技集团的关键岗位工作。

团队教师的共识是，面向不同工程与应用需求去进行发现、思考，进而提炼其中的科学问题，是工科院系学术型硕士和博士研究生培养的重要特点与核心。单纯为了发表论文去做研究的状况容易泛滥，必须加以注意和引导，“纸上谈兵”最不可取。

团队教师深刻体会到，“广育祖国和人民需要的各类人才”非常重要，是实现中华民族伟大复兴的必要条件。这其中，科学探索人才能够为原创性学术思想及科研成果的产生贡献力量，为我国科技未来的发展提供“制高点”；工程技术人才能够有效解决我国经济社会发展面临的诸多实际问题，是促进生产力发展的主力军；社会治理人才具有优秀的综合素养和科学的治理理念，是我国现代社会治理体系不可或缺的中坚力量。

在方法论上，团队教师牢固把握工科研究生培养的四个关键要素——从教师这方面来讲，要做到传授科技知识，培养科研技能，形成全面能力，提升综合素养；从学生这方面来说，则要经历从看着“师傅”干、跟着“师傅”干，到自己当“师傅”、做“中国好师傅”这四个阶段。

在这个理念的指引下，团队在研究生的培养过程中一直坚持突出多学科交叉融合与多层次系统复合的学科特点。多学科融合不仅体现在智能微系统技术本身需要多个领域的专业知识，更体现在团队的导师组成上。团队由十名不同学科背景的教师组成，涵盖机械、电子、材料、化学等多个学科。丰富的导师资源在研究生的培养过程中发挥了巨大的优势。具体来说，团队的博士生在通过资格考试后、硕士生在完成课业学习后，可以与导师共同确定一位辅导教师，并由导师、辅导教师、研究生所承担项目的负责人共同组成导师组，即形成了“导师联合指导制度”。每个研究生既是团队专业技术组的一员，又是具体项目组的一员，在学术科研与工程实践两个层面汲取知识与经验，有利于工科研究生的全面成长。

团队在培养过程中特别强调，导师不仅提供专业上的指导，在学生的学习生活和未来选择方面也要发挥重要作用。为了更好地落实“树人”的理念，团队根据每名学生的知识背景和个人潜能制订了不同的学术成长路线，实现因材施教。研究生入学确立导师之后，导师不会立即指定具体的研究课题，而是让学生们自愿参与到团队里的某一科研项目中，熟悉科研流程，激发科研兴趣，找到适合自己的科研方向。在过去的十余年中，有20余名学生参与了NS-1卫星、NS-2卫星系列、微型高性能星敏感器、MEMS太阳敏感器等多个重要科研项目。这个过程中，对于有能力、有想法的学生，导师主要负责把握方向、创造条件；对于有能力、“没想法”的学生，导师会安排具体工作帮助他们凝练思想；对于有想法、没能力的同学，导师则通过激发他们的问题意识来帮助他们进行深入思考——这是因材施教的具体体现。

此外，团队在培养人才过程中对于“复合型”十分重视。他们认为，工科是应用学科，学生不仅要有很强的业务能力，也需要具备团队合作、人际交往等其他方面的能力。在科研与论文工作之外，团队一方面支持研究生适当参加社会工作、加入学生社团——2000 年至 2015 年期间，团队培养的研究生一半以上参加过研究生团委、研究生会、学生会、辅导员等公共服务工作；另一方面强调军民融合和国际化培养方面的并重。团队在国防预研、重大专项等研究发面发挥了十分重要的作用，学生们也有机会参与到具体项目中。同时，团队将眼光放远到国际，为学生创造国际交流的机会和国际化的资源，其目的在于希望学生们“成为有用的人，做出有用的东西”。让研究成果能够在国家和产业的发展中实实在在发挥作用，并在国际上产生影响，这不仅是团队近年来一直努力的方向，也是团队培养人才和进行科研的最终目标。

The Team of Intelligent Micro System: Allowing Students to Be Truly Useful

Note: The team of Intelligent Micro System at Tsinghua's Department of Precision Instrument holds onto the goal of "Cultivating talents with an insurmountable spirit". As part of the national strategy, Tsinghua established a training mode and provided a guide on cementing academic training with engineering practice along with ensuring that individuals truly embody the scientific spirit. The Department has cultivated groups of high-level talents and as a result, was awarded the 2016 Postgraduate Education Achievement Award.

The team of Intelligent Micro System at Tsinghua's Department of Precision Instrument was established in 1994. For more than 20 years, the team under the leadership of Academician You Zheng undertook intelligent micro system as the research direction and worked out a path to achieve the goal of "Cultivating talents with an indomitable spirit". "Indomitable" in this case refers to students being able to grasp national development strategy aimed at the international academic front and then engage and apply it into cutting-edge research. "Spirit" is based on academic research, applying development with a focus on solving challenges through real practice. Out of the 70 postgraduate students, 8 were awarded the National Science and Technology Awards and took on 15 major national-level scientific research projects. Out of the 35 doctoral students, 11 gained key positions at Tsinghua University and China Aerospace Science and Technology Corporation (CASC).

Under such guidance, the team has always insisted on multi-disciplinary integration. Multi-disciplinary integration is not only reflected in micro system technology, since it requires a combination of expertise, but also in the composition of the team's mentors. The team is comprised of 10 mentors all with varying disciplines. These covers machinery, electronics, material science, chemistry and others. Rich teacher resource is a huge advantage in the cultivation process of postgraduate students. Doctoral students who have successfully passed their qualification exams and postgraduates who have completed their academic learning can get a tutor with approval from the mentor. The student's supervisor, the tutor, and the principle investigator of the project that the student is working on forming a "supervisory team". The team would help students to find their research direction and ensure that academic progress is going smoothly.

In addition, with particular emphasis on "mentoring", teachers not only provide professional guidance on learning but also on life and the choices that students make.

In order to better implement a cultivation concept, the team look at each students' background and potentials to develop a different academic growth path. After establishing tutors, they will not immediately specify which research topics the students should undertake but allow them to participate in research, to be familiar with the process of scientific research so that they can find their interests and own research directions. In the past 10 years, there are more than 20 students who participated in the NS-1 satellite, NS-2 satellite star sensor, sun sensor series and other important research projects. During this process, tutors are mostly responsible for finding that direction for students with competencies and ideas. They create a learning environment for those with clearer goals. For those who require additional help, tutors would try to highlight the problems and further encourage deeper thinking. The team believes that this type of mentoring based on individualization is important.

In addition, the team attaches great importance to the development of talents in terms of multi-disciplinary learning. They believe that engineering is an applied discipline and students should not only have strong professional research abilities but also other skills such as cooperation, teamwork and interpersonal skills. Apart from research and thesis work, the team also encourage students to participate in social work. From 2000 to 2015, students participated in various public services with emphasis in the military field and other international events. For national defense research projects, student participation played a very important role. Students also have the chance to participate in specific projects. At the same time, the team look for international exchanges, resources and opportunities. The purpose is to train students to "become a useful person and do useful things" . Research is about influencing and supporting actual developments in the nation and across industries. This is not only the recent goal of the team but also the ultimate goal of training and further research.

Translation and revision | Min Weiyuan

Image | Liang Luwen

3 月 23 日

文字 | 梁乐萌

图片 | 梁晨

谢道昕、饶子和及娄智勇等合作阐明植物分枝激素独脚金内酯的感知机制奥秘

“疏影横斜水清浅，暗香浮动月黄昏。”“春色满园关不住，一枝红杏出墙来。”日常生活中，交错有致的枝条为植物平添了婀娜与灵动，总是给人们以美的感受。而植物分枝是受到激素调节控制的。阐明激素感知机制，是生物学领域的重大科学问题，对于揭示生命现象的本质、提高生物的生存和发展能力具有重要意义。

激素是如何调节植物生命活动的？这一直是各国生物学家孜孜以求的奥秘。2016 年 8 月 1 日，清华大学生命科学学院谢道昕教授与医学院饶子和院士、娄智勇教授等合作在《自然》杂志在线发表了题为《DWARF14 蛋白是植物激素独脚金内酯的受体》的研究论文，率先阐明了植物分枝激素独脚金内酯的识别机制，发现 D14 是具有生成和感知独脚金内酯活性分子双重功能的新型受体。该文揭示了 D14 感知植物分枝激素独脚金内酯的分子机制：D14 蛋白既参与生成独脚金内酯活性分子，又不可逆地共价结合该活性分子，发生变构、招募下游蛋白、触发信号传导链、调控植物分枝。

独脚金内酯不仅调控植物分枝、决定植物株型、影响作物产量，还调控共生真菌生长及寄生杂草萌发。寄生杂草每年造成世界粮食生产数百亿美元的损失，对独脚金内酯感知机制的研究，能够为研发新型除草剂、防治寄生杂草提供指导作用，有助于解决世界范围内寄生杂草严重危害农作物的问题；同时也对作物株型的遗传改良具有重要的指导意义。

该文首次揭示了新型的“受体 - 配体”不可逆识别规律。此前发现的所有动植物激素活性分子，都是可逆地结合其受体，调控各种生命活动。该文所发现的“受体 - 配体”不可逆识别新规律，丰富了生物学领域过去百年内建立的配体可逆地结合受体并循环触发传导链的“配体 - 受体”识别理论，为创立生物受体与配体不可逆识别的新理论奠定了重要基础，是生命科学领域的重大突破。

该工作得到《自然》《科学 · 信号》《植物生物学年鉴》和《中国科学：生命科学》杂志的高度评价，同时入选 2016 年度全球生物信号转导领域重大突破、中国生命科学领域十大进展、中国高校十大科技进展。

清华大学生命学院博士生姚瑞枫、医学院博士毕业生明振华、医学院闫利明博士和生命学院博士生李素华为本文共同第一作者，谢道昕教授、娄智勇教授及饶子和院士为共同通讯作者。研究工作由国家自然科学基金会和国家科技部的项目资助。

Unveiling the Mystery of the Perception Mechanism of Strigolactone Hormone

As famous poem goes, "Few shadows inverted in clear water, subtle aroma fragrance floating in the dim moonlight" , "Spring sneaks out of the garden, a branch of red plum climbs outside the wall" , in daily life, staggered branches make the plant graceful and vivid, and always make people sense its beauty. While branching of plants are controlled and regulated by hormones, clarifying the perception and recognition mechanism of hormones is a major issue in the field of biology, and is also of great significance to reveal the essence of biological phenomena and improve the survival and development ability of creatures.

How do hormones regulate life activities of plants? This has always been a mystery that biologists from different countries try to reveal. On August 1, 2016, Profs. Xie Daoxin, Rao Zihe and Lou Zhiyong cooperatively elucidated the recognition mechanism of the plant branching hormone strigolactone and published a research paper entitled "DWARF14 is a non-canonical hormone receptor for strigolactone" online in the *Nature* magazine. This work identifies a novel active strigolactone molecule CLIM, defines D14 as the non-canonical receptor of strigolactone, reveals an irreversible interaction mechanism of "receptor-ligand" , and elucidates that D14 possesses dual function to generate and perceive the active molecule of strigolactone.

Strigolactone, as a new plant hormone, not only regulates the important growth and development process of plant branch, but also serves as the rhizosphere signal to regulate the interaction between plants and symbiotic fungi and parasitic weeds. The research on the perception mechanism of strigolactone would generate valuable information for genetic modification of crop varieties with perfect architecture, and provide a structural basis for the development of new herbicides that might help to solve the problem of serious damages caused by parasitic plants to crop across the world.

All the previously identified animal and plant hormones follow the classic reversible recognition law of "ligand-receptor" discovered since 1880s. However, this work for the first time reveals a most unusual irreversible recognition mechanism of "receptor-ligand" , which was highlighted by several magazines such as *Nature*, *Science Signaling*, *Annual Review of Plant Biology* and *Science China- Life Sciences*, and selected as the "2016: Signaling Breakthroughs of the Year" , "2016 Top 10 Breakthroughs of Life Sciences in China" , and "2016 Top 10 Breakthroughs of Science and Technology in Universities of China" .

The co-first authors are Yao Ruifeng, Ming Zhenhua, Yan Liming and Li Suhua. The co-corresponding authors are Profs. Xie Daoxin, Lou Zhiyong and Rao Zihe. This work was financially supported by the grants from NSFC and MOST.

Translation and revision | Raj Lamar

Image | Liang Chen

3月24日

文字 | 杨晨晞

图片 | 李娜

王国维故居：国学大师在西院度过的时光

在清华园西侧，东临校河，坐落着一片整齐的平房，散布着十几户院落，这里便是清华的早期教师宿舍——西院。院落周围有着无数缠绕的常青藤和竹子，日光穿过，树影斑驳。国学大师王国维曾在环境如此清幽的西院中度过了他最后两年的学者人生。

王国维（1877—1927），字静安，号观堂，浙江海宁人。20世纪20年代，他在学术界声望极高，新学旧派无不赞誉。受聘清华后，1925年4月18日，他携夫人搬入西院16号与18号，两所住宅皆为平房，自成小院，两院紧邻，坐北向南，有朱漆门窗、廊柱和灰色瓦顶，是典型的北方四合院。

据王国维之子回忆，家人饮食起居都在18号，16号正房西屋则作为书房，三面墙壁都是高及屋顶的书架，放满线装书，内间小室也放满了书。书房南面窗下放置有一张书桌、一只藤椅、几把木椅，供学生来访时落座。另有一只藤质躺椅放在书架间空地，供王国维先生疲乏时或思考时使用。东间为塾师给家中子女授课的地方，放有几张小木书桌和老师的床铺。为了不打扰王国维先生研究，前院平常很少有人进去，大门常年关闭。后院则非常整洁，夫人侍弄花木，满院生香。

在如此宁静典雅的西院，王国维度过了人生的最后两年，这两年也正是他精力充沛、学术研究成就卓著的时期。早年研究成果在此汇聚，旧学新知再获心得。那时，他致力于边地少数民族金石文献考证，完成了近40篇著述，还整理和改订旧作，结集出版了《古史新证》，这成为他史学研究方面的代表作。书中运用“二重证据法”和“阙疑法”，作为开创中国现代史学的科学方法，从内容和方法上拓展了中国史的研究范畴。

除学术研究外，王国维在西院居住期间还致力于教育事业。他在清华国学研究院教授与指导研究生，主要负责经学、小学、上古史、中国史学方向，主讲“说文”“尚书”“古史新证”等课程。学生眼中的静安先生，拙于言辞，却学问笃实，他卓越的学术成就和深刻的传授之道，在学界有着至高的威望。他的学生、史学家姜亮夫回忆，他授课之专深，“要到毕业出来教书研究后，才越来越感到帮助很大”。

1927年6月2日，王国维在颐和园投湖自尽，国内外学术界同悲。他辞世后，家人退去西院16号的房屋，继续留住西院18号。在王国维逝世两周年之际，清华师生募款修建了“海宁王静安先生纪念碑”。碑集各界名家之大成，梁思成从东北大学回到清华勘定碑址、设计碑式，陈寅恪撰写碑文，林志钧书丹，马衡篆额，李桂藻刻石。清华园西院的王国维晚年故居，与浙江省海宁市盐官镇的王国维早年故居一起，共同见证了国学大师王国维人生不同时期的行迹。王国维的治学精神和教育理念也永远留存在清华园中，供一代代师生从中汲取力量。

注：本文改编自《清刚之气永在天壤——王国维》（2007年11月2日发表于《新清华》第1701期第4版）。

Wang Guowei's Former Residence: The Master of Chinese Culture's Time in the West Yard

On the west side of Tsinghua University, along the school river lays a line of orderly bungalows, scattering more than a dozen courtyards. This is the west yard, the Tsinghua teachers' dormitory in the early days. The courtyard is surrounded by numerous winding ivy and bamboo, with the mottled shades shaking as the sunshine filters through. Master of Chinese culture Wang Guowei once spent his last two years of scholarly life in this quiet west yard.

Wang Guowei (1877—1927), with styled name of Jing'an and assumed name of Guantang, is from Haining, Zhejiang Province. In the 1920s, he was highly regarded in academia, and praised by all the new and old schools. After being appointed by Tsinghua University, in April 18, 1925, he and his wife moved into No.16 and No.18 of the west yard, which were all bungalows with small courtyards. Those two were close to each other, sitting north to south and decorated with red-paint doors and windows, aisle columns, and grey tile roofs. They are in fact typical courtyards found in northern China.

As recalled by Wang Guowei's son, the entire family's diet and daily life were in No.18, and the west room of No.16 in the principal house was used as study room. Against three walls stood high-to-roof bookshelves, full of wire binding books, and the inner room was also full of books. Under the south window in study room, there was a desk, a rattan chair, and a few wooden chairs for students to sit on during their visit. There was also a rattan chair putting in the space among shelves for Mr. Wang Guowei when he got tired or was thinking. The east room is the place where the private teacher gave lessons to his children, equipped with a few small wooden desks and teacher's bed. In order not to disturb Mr. Wang Guowei's study, very few people went to the front yard, and the door was closed all year round. The backyard was very neat. His wife planted many flowers and trees, filling the yard with fragrance.

In such a quiet and elegant west yard, Wang Guowei spent his last two years of life, which was also a period when he was energetic and had outstanding academic research achievements. Early research results converged here, and new knowledge was acquired through classical learning. At that time, he was committed to the research on epigraphy literature of borderland minority, and had completed nearly 40 articles and books. He also sorted and revised old works, and collected them and published the *New Testimony of the Ancient I listory*, which became his masterpiece on historical research. In the book, the "*dual attestation*" and "Method of Leaving Question Open" are used to expand the study scope of Chinese history from the contents to methods, creating a scientific method to study modern Chinese history.

In addition to academic research, during the period of residing in west yard, Wang Guowei was also committed towards the cause of education. He was a professor and supervisor in the Tsinghua Academy of Chinese Learning, and mainly responsible for the study of Confucian classics, philology, ancient history, Chinese historiography, and giving lectures such as "Shuowen" , "Shangshu" and "New Testimony of the Ancient History" . In the eyes of students, Mr. Jing'an had clumsy words but sound scholarship, and his outstanding academic achievements and profound way of teaching had a high prestige in the academia. Jiang Liangfu, his student and a historian, recalled that, the profession and deep meaning in his teaching became more and more helpful when you started teaching and doing research after graduation.

In 1927, Wang Guowei's death aroused sadness across the domestic and foreign academia. After his death, his family returned the No.16 of west yard to Tsinghua University and continued to stay in the No.18 of west yard. Now in Tsinghua, Wang Guowei monument is still visible, and the monument is a work done by many masters. For instance, Liang Sicheng went from the Northeastern University to Tsinghua to set the site for the monument and designed the style, Chen Yinque wrote the inscriptions, Lin Zhijun wrote for stone inscriptions, Ma Heng sealed the script, and Li Guizao carved the stone. The old residence of Wang Guowei in Tsinghua west yard during his late years and the one in Yanguan Town, Haining, Zhejiang Province during his early years, witnessed the master's life in different periods. Wang Guowei's scholarship spirit and education concepts will always remain in the west yard, for generations of Tsinghua teachers and students to draw strength therefrom.

Translation and revision | Raj Lamar

Image | Li Na

3 月 27 日

文字 | 冯婉婷

图片 | 李娜

博士生郑云：书本之外，是更广阔的产业世界

“这 40 多天的企业实践，我们对你的工作十分满意。”清华大学核能与新能源技术研究院（简称“核研院”）博士生郑云结束 2016 年的暑期实践后，得到了实践单位的高度认可。这样的评价不仅源于他实践期间的踏实工作，更是对他较好地结合了理论知识与实际技术操作的肯定。

郑云的实践单位是武汉喜马拉雅光电科技股份有限公司。实践期间，他的课题主要内容是对核研院在氢能燃料电池方面的技术进行产业化研究，最终实现车用燃料电池的产业化和商业化。

到达实践单位后，郑云与企业技术负责人进行了充分沟通，进而结合自身专业特点和企业的具体需求，制订了两个方面的研究内容——燃料电池膜电极催化剂浆料的配比和工艺优化，以及点胶过程中的厚度、宽度和精度优化控制。

实践过程中，郑云深刻体会到学习所得与实际的产业研究是相辅相成的：“清华的学习让我掌握了相关领域的理论基础和解决问题的良好思维方式，对燃料电池的基本原理和应用非常熟悉，为具体的实践工作奠定了良好的基础；实践过程则让我了解了相关技术在实际应用中的具体情形和存在的一些问题，帮助我在返校学习后，更全面、更实际、更有针对性地考虑问题。”

在技术的实际应用过程中，郑云也曾遇到过难题，无法通过查阅文献直接找到答案，但他通过合理设计实验、咨询相关技术人员等方式，最终获得了更优化的解决方案。40 多天时间里，他不仅帮助企业解决了许多实际的工艺和技术问题，还完成了一项燃料电池相关技术的发明专利，撰写了一份 8000 多字的技术报告。

这次暑期实践不仅让郑云转换了思想，从根本上改变了他对科学技术产业化的认识；也让他增长了见识，增强了实际操作能力，拓宽了眼界和思考问题的维度。

“这次博士生社会实践工作给了我进入企业生产车间、接触社会基层的机会，能够将所学到的基本理论知识和科研方法应用到实际生产中，真正实现了‘研以致用’。”郑云十分感谢学校提供了这样的实践机会，也希望更多的博士生能像自己一样，在真正研以致用的实践中有所收获。

Learn to Apply Beyond the Textbooks Teachings

Zheng Yun, a doctoral student at Tsinghua University's Institute of Nuclear and New Energy Technology (INNET) received high recognition at the end of summer 2016 for his hard work. "We are deeply satisfied with your 40 days of in-field practice and work." This evaluation not only stems from his practical work but also the ability combining theory and practice.

For his in-field placement, Zheng Yun went to Wuhan Himalaya Polytron Technologies Inc. His main work there was to conduct further research in hydrogen fuel cell technology, something that was thoroughly discussed at INNET. The final goal is to achieve commercialization and industrialization of using such cells in vehicles.

After arriving at the company, Zheng Yun and the other technicians talked about the specific needs and goals of the company along with other professional characteristics to finally settle on two research directions. This includes the formulation and process optimization of fuel cell membrane electrode catalyst along with optimization control with process in rubber thickness, width and precision.

Zheng combined what he had studied at Tsinghua with industrial research during his time at the company in Wuhan. "Tsinghua allowed me to master the theory work of all related fields and helped me to solve problems through holistic ways of thinking. This meant that I'm familiar with the basic principle and application of fuel cells and thus have a solid foundation in such practice." Zheng said that Tsinghua's practice and theory fusion "allowed me to understand that technical issues encountered during practice may differ from theory. During this learning process, my ways of thinking have been more comprehensive, targeted and practical."

In the actual application of such technology, he did realize that sometimes, books and theory cannot give one the solution to a problem. Instead, it is through experiments and consultations with other technical staff that can eventually help the team to find a more optimal solution. During the 40 or so days, not only did Zheng help the enterprise with technical and practical issues, he also gained one patent relating to fuel cell technology as well as the completion of an 8000 words technical research paper.

This summer practice not only allowed him to think differently, it also fundamentally changed his understanding of science and technology. He gained much knowledge, broadened his horizons and became more capable in both theoretical and practical work.

"This in-field opportunity allowed me to work in the workshop and production floor. This allowed me to come in contact with those at the grass-root. I was able to refine my understanding and skills in both theory and practical work during actual production. I was able to put research into use." Zheng Yun is grateful to Tsinghua for providing him such opportunities and hope that more doctoral students like himself can find learning through practice.

Translation and revision | Min Weiyuan

Image | Li Na

3月28日

文字 | 杨晨晞

图片 | 李娜

清华紫荆花车队折桂中国节能竞技大赛

你是否曾为方程式跑道上风驰电掣的赛车场景血脉贲张？你是否也曾为节能汽车和新能源汽车所引领的绿色交通趋势心动不已？在2016年Honda中国节能竞技大赛中摘得桂冠的清华大学紫荆花节能车队，为我们诠释了这两者的完美结合。

2016年10月29日至10月30日，第10届Honda中国节能竞技大赛在广东省肇庆市广东国际赛车场举行，清华大学紫荆花节能车队共派出三辆车参加比赛，其中燃油车一辆（紫荆花一队）、电动汽车两辆（紫荆花二队、三队），经过两天的激烈角逐，紫荆花二队以优异成绩夺得了大学电动汽车组冠军。除此之外，紫荆花一队位列大学燃油组第7，紫荆花三队位列大学电动汽车组第22，整体水平位于大学组第一梯队。

清华大学紫荆花车队于2007年成立，每年面向全校范围招新，并参加壳牌亚洲汽车马拉松环保赛与Honda中国节能竞技大赛。车队由来自汽车、机械、环境等院系的30余名同学组成。在多年的理论学习和实践过程中，车队已经积累了相当丰富的研发和比赛经验。

2016年，依托汽车工程系和绿控传动有限公司的大力支持，队员们在汽车系高级工程师边明远的指导下，用一年时间完成了赛车的设计、加工与调试工作。不同专业背景的同学们充分利用各自的专业知识，在车身设计、轻量化、提高发动机和电机效率、提高传动效率等方面取得了巨大突破。他们把自己在汽车理论、发动机原理、汽车构造等课堂上学到的知识充分运用在赛车上，使用了发动机减摩、改善轴荷分配等理论方法，真正做到了专业学习与实践结合，锻炼了动手实践能力，实现了学以致用的目标。

在亲自动手实践的过程中，队员们也进一步升华了自己所学的知识。比如在减轻底盘重量和减小摩擦损失的尝试中，队员们总结了前人经验，设计使用了穿透式离合控制机构，取得了十分出色的效果，还申请了专利。而为了让电车更高效地利用有限的能量，队员们需要对电机的控制器进行设计，除了写代码、调代码之外，队员们还会亲自焊接电路，让自己编写的程序在实车上“跑起来”。

成立十余年来，紫荆花节能车队的队员们秉承“自强不息、厚德载物”的校训和“行胜于言”的校风，将节能理念与技术一代代传承，用实际行动在赛场上展示了清华汽车人的风采。在参加比赛之余，车队还以“紫荆花开，节能挑战未来”为口号，致力于节能环保理念的宣传，吸引更多的人关注汽车节能领域。

研发汽车新能源和实现汽车的节能技术是解决能源环境问题的重要途径之一，也是《中国制造2025》计划和国家长期发展的战略决策。可以说，紫荆花节能车队既是清华学子们接触节能技术的校园平台，也是未来汽车节能技术研究人才的“孵化器”。

Tsinghua Bauhinia Energy Efficient Fleet Wins Honda China Eco-Car Competition

Have you seen cars racing like the wind in formula runways? Have you sensed the significance of eco-cars in energy saving and emission reduction? Now, the perfect combination of both of these is taking place around us!

From October 29 to October 30, 2016, the tenth Honda China Eco-Car Competition was held in Guangdong International Circuit, Zhaoqing, Guangdong province. Tsinghua Bauhinia Energy Efficient Fleet sent three eco-cars to the competition, which contained one fuel vehicle (1st team) and two electric cars (2nd and 3rd team). After two days of fierce competitions, the 2nd team of Bauhinia Energy Efficient Fleet became the champion of the college electric car group while giving an outstanding performance. At the same time, the 1st team placed No.7 in fuel vehicle group and the 3rd team placed No.22 in college electric car group. The performance of the entire motorcade placed a frontier level in the college group.

Formed in 2007, Tsinghua Bauhinia Energy Efficient Fleet annually recruit new members from the entire university, participates in Shell Asia Eco-marathon and Honda China Eco-car Competition. More than 30 students from automotive, mechanical, environmental and other schools formed the team. The team has accumulated considerable R&D and competition experience after years of theoretical study and practice.

In 2016, supported by the Automotive Engineering Department and LVKON Co., Ltd., the team members, under the guidance of Senior Engineer Bian Mingyuan, completed the car design, processing and commissioning work within just one year. Students from varied backgrounds have made complete use of their professional knowledge, making great breakthroughs in body design, lightweights, and the improvement of engine and motor efficiency as well as transmission efficiency. Students applied what they learned from automobile theory, engine principle, automobile structure courses significantly well into the racing cars, they used the theory of engine friction reduction and axle load distribution, successfully combined professional learning with practice and also exercised practicing ability, while achieving the primary goal of learning.

During the practicing process, members also further sublimated their knowledge. For example, in the attempt to reduce chassis weight and friction loss, team members summed up the previous experience and designed penetrating clutch control mechanisms, which achieved perfect results and was also applied for a patent.

Over the ten years, members in Bauhinia Energy Efficient Fleet adhered to the university motto of "Self-Discipline and Social Commitment" and the university spirit of "actions speak louder than words" , inheriting the concept and technology of energy saving from generation to generation, presenting the talent of Tsinghua automobile researchers with practical actions.

R&D of new energy vehicle and adoption of energy-saving technology on automobile is one of the most important measures for solving our energy environment; while it is also a strategic decision of *Made in China 2025* and long-term national development, and an inevitable trend of development in the future. The eco-car competition offers students an opportunity to discover automobile energy-saving technology, while Bauhinia Energy Efficient Fleet serves as not only a platform on which students could reach energy-saving technology, but also an incubator for future researchers on automobile energy-saving technology.

Translation and revision | Raj Lamar

Image | Li Na

3 月 29 日

文字 | 曲田、张译丹

图片 | 李娜

岳光溪院士：站在中国这块土地上做科研

“站在中国的这块土地上，你就必须要说这块土地的话。”清华大学热能系岳光溪院士一直在工程第一线，践行着这样一份“红色工程师”的信念与执着。

1964 年，岳光溪考入清华大学动力农机系。“文化大革命”期间，他被调配到山西岚县电机厂做技术员。直到 1979 年，岳光溪才又考回清华，毕业后留在热能系热工教研组，1984 年转到热能工程教研组。经过长期的研习，岳光溪日益深刻地认识到，在一个传统的研究领域，要站在“巨人的肩膀上”谈创新。“创新的前提，是一个漫长的掌握别人的东西的过程。”岳光溪始终强调，面向应用的科研要抓住市场的需求，找到能够长期做下去的研究领域，这样才能获得持久的支持，使研究者形成系统的认识过程，继而才可能创新。

早在 20 世纪 90 年代初期，循环流化床——一种煤种适应性极强的清洁煤技术，已经初步发展并很快应用到产品中。我国由于投入不足、资金欠缺等多方面的原因，发展相对缓慢。掌握较先进的循环流化床技术的原芬兰奥斯龙公司曾向我国出售了几台循环流化床锅炉，我们一直想引进他们的技术，却被声称“只卖苹果不卖树”的奥斯龙公司一口回绝。“这句话我记了一辈子，也让我跟外国人‘赌’了 20 年，我就不信我们不能培养出自己的‘苹果树’！”回忆起这段经历，岳光溪目光灼灼，言语坚定。

不断提出问题、解决问题、再碰壁、再攻坚……经过漫长而艰辛的探索，2005 年，岳光溪和他的团队终于完成了全新的循环流化床燃烧理论体系骨架的搭建。不仅如此，他们还彻底弄清了循环流化床锅炉设计背后的原理，揭开了国外技术的缺陷和不适应中国企业情况的根本原因，使循环流化床锅炉设计从纯经验方式转向了“中国特色”的理论指导方式。我国锅炉制造行业接受了岳光溪的设计理念，生产的国产循环流化床锅炉占领了中国市场。岳光溪指导的国家团队完成了世界最大容量 600MW 超临界循环流化床发电示范工程，成为世界循环流化床燃烧技术的标志性工程；而且实现了中国循环流化床设计技术的第一次出口，在国际上赢得众多相关技术大国的瞩目。越来越多的国际公司找到岳光溪，希望与他的团队进行合作。岳光溪信心十足地说：“我们中国人的研究也能走到世界前列。”

尽管已经在循环流化床研究领域培育出累累硕果，但岳光溪并没有止步。近几年，他又带领团队进入了煤气化技术领域，研发出的分级给氧气化炉、水煤浆膜式壁煤气化炉和气化蒸汽联产炉，形成清华三代气化技术，在国内外“打出名气”。他们借鉴开发循环流化床技术的经验，走产学研结合的路，使得煤气化的研发在短期内实现了从产生最初的想法到推出工业装置和产业化推广。

“在高校做科研，尤其是工科应用科研，必须走一条产学研结合的道路。研究者不到第一线去，不亲自操作，永远得不到真知。”岳光溪认真地说。他用几十载栉风沐雨的坚守，亲身践行了自己的这一信条。

Yue Guangxi:
at the Forefront of CFB Technology

"If you are standing on this land called China then you need to speak the language of this land." Yue Guangxi has always adhered to this theory and maintained such faith and dedication as a "red engineer" .

In 1964, Yue Guangxi was admitted to Tsinghua University's Department of Agricultural Machinery. During the Cultural Revolution, he was deployed to Shanxi Lanxian Motor Factory to work as an on-site technician. In 1979, Yue Guangxi took the exam and was re-admitted back to Tsinghua. After graduation he worked at the thermal engineering research group and gradually realized that if one is to find innovation then they must do so by standing on the shoulder of giants.

"Innovation is a long process of mastering something else." said Yue Guangxi. He always stressed the application of research and meeting market demand so that lasting support could be gained and the process of system formation can be better understood. Only through that can researchers learn to innovate.

As early as the beginning of the 1990's, the circulating fluidized bed (CFB) technology was developed then applied to products. Due to lack of investment, funding and other reasons, its development in China was relatively slow when compared with the rest of the world. Finland's Ahlstrom Company, who mastered the advanced technology of circulating fluidized bed, once sold China a couple of boilers. We want to learn their technology but Ahlstrom told us that they "only sell apples and not the tree" . "I will always remember this. That marked the beginning of my 20 long years of bet with foreigners. I couldn't believe that we cannot cultivate our own 'apple tree'! " recalled Yue. Although it was a while ago, Yue can still remember that event with clarity.

During the process of exploration, finding solutions and continuing with research, Yue and his team finally completed the framework behind the system and combustion theory of the CFB. At the same time, Yue became clearer with the principle of the design of the boiler. This allowed better understanding of the defects in foreign design and technology and the reasons behind why it couldn't be adapted to suit China. This gave research some "Chinese characteristics" . Yue completed the design of the boiler and exported it to foreign country. This became the first time that China exported CFB design and technology into another foreign country and since then it has gained much international spotlight, more and more companies are finding ways to connect and work with Yue and his team. Yue said with full confidence that "We the Chinese and our research can also be at the forefront" .

"When you are conducting research in colleges and universities and especially if you are in engineering then you must take a path that is a combination of production, teaching and research. If the researchers do not venture to the forefront and personally operate and come in contact with their own research then they will never gain true knowledge." said Yue. This is indeed true for Yue since he has been guided by this philosophy for decades.

Translation and revision | Min Weiyuan

Image | Li Na

3月30日

文字 | 杨鹏成

图片 | 李娜、郭祥

高温气冷堆技术，中国领跑

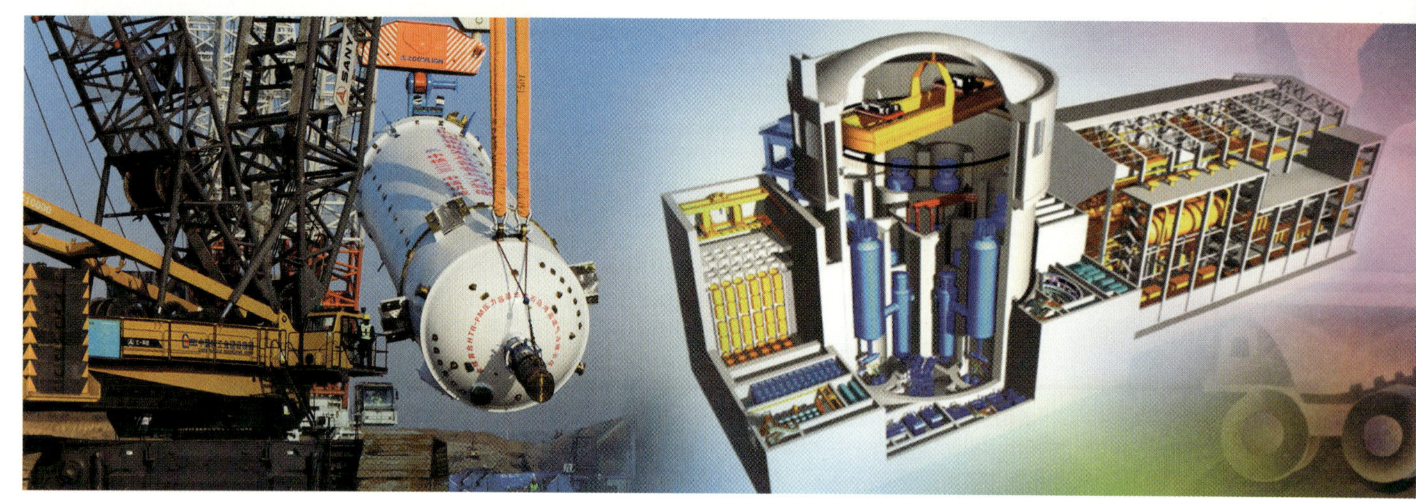

2016年12月21日，清华大学核研院发布的一条关于核电站技术方案的信息引起了热议——我国将在20万千瓦级模块式高温气冷堆核电站示范工程（HTR-PM）基础上，开发60万千瓦级模块式高温气冷堆核电站（HTR-PM600）。有媒体评论道："项目标志着我国高温气冷堆技术从'863'时期的'跟跑'位置，到示范工程阶段的'领跑'位置，再到正式跨入商用阶段。一旦建成，它将成为国际首个商用高温气冷堆核电站。"

目前国际一次能源消费总量中，用于发电的份额只有40%左右，其余是非电利用，包括工业热、民用热和交通能源等。而高温气冷堆除了可用于安全高效发电外，还可以单独或组合地运用在几乎所有工业领域。其中最有特点和潜力的领域包括核能制氢、石油化工、煤气化和液化、海水淡化、区域供热等。发展高温气冷堆具有独特的战略意义，也因此得到国际核能界的广泛重视。

我国高温气冷堆技术历经跟踪、跨越和自主创新，达到了在商业规模模块式高温气冷堆核电站技术上的世界领先地位。首先，我国经过国家"863"计划重点项目——清华大学核研院10兆瓦高温气冷实验堆（HTR-10）的建设和运行，掌握了自主发展高温气冷堆的技术基础。2006年，由清华大学核研院牵头研发和设计的HTR-PM又被列入国家科技重大专项，这一项目也是国际上高温气冷堆技术商业示范的首次尝试。2012年12月，项目在山东正式施工，预计于2018年建成发电。HTR-PM采用了具有固有安全特性（即堆芯不会熔毁）的模块式球床高温气冷堆设计方案，产生的高压过热蒸汽用于发电。该技术将拥有广阔的商业化应用前景。

在此基础上，清华大学核研院发展了高温气冷堆的后续机型——HTR-PM600。HTR-PM600充分借鉴HTR-PM在设计、制造、建造和执照申请方面的经验，利用模块式高温气冷堆的特点，实现标准化。HTR-PM600不仅标志着我国在推动高温气冷堆的市场应用和技术进步、着力建设国际一流具有自主知识产权的高温气冷堆产业体系方面又迈出了重要一步，也是高温气冷堆在国内外市场的产业化应用中的又一项突破。

China Takes the Lead in High-temperature Gas-cooled Reactor Technology

On December 21, 2016, a hot public discussion was observed with the release of the technical scheme of a nuclear power plant (NPP) by the Institute of Nuclear and New Energy Technology ("INET"), Tsinghua University - China will develop a 600 MW modular High-Temperature Gas-cooled Reactor (HTGR) nuclear power plant (HTR-PM600), on the basis of 200 MW modular HTGR demonstration power plant project (HTR-PM). A media outlet commented, "The project marks China's transition from a following position on HTGR technology in the 863 period to a leading position on the demonstration stage, and further on the commercial stage. Once completed, it will become the first commercial HTGR NPP in the world."

At present, the share for power generation in the international primary energy consumption only accounts for 40 percent or so, and the rest is for non-electric use, including process heating, civil heating and transportation energy. In addition to safe and efficient power generation, HTGR can also be used alone or in a combination in almost all industrial areas, among which, the most special and potential areas cover nuclear hydrogen, petrochemical, coal gasification and liquefaction, seawater desalination, regional heating, etc. Therefore, it has attracted wide attention in the international nuclear industry, and the development of HTGR has a unique strategic significance.

Through construction and operation of the 10 MW experimental High-Temperature Gas-cooled Reactor (HTR-10) in the National 863 Plan by INET, China has mastered the technology for independent development of HTGR. Since then, China's HTGR technology has gone through stages of following, transcending and independent innovation, and has reached the international leading position in the commercial field of HTGR NPPs.

In 2006, HTR-PM, with the R&D and design led by INET, was listed in the national major science and technology projects. This project is also the first attempt of commercial demonstration of HTGR technology in the world. In December 2012, the construction of the demonstration plant was commenced in Shandong and is expected to be completed by 2018 for power generation. HTR-PM adopts a modular pebble-bed HTGR design with inherent safety feature. The high-pressure superheated steam generated by the plant will be used for power generation. This technology will have a broad prospect for commercial application.

Based on this, INET developed a follow-up model of HTGR, namely the 600 MW modular HTGR NPP (HTR-PM600). HTR-PM600 has been developed based on the experience of HTR-PM in respect of design, manufacturing, construction and licensing. Standardization is expected to be realized given the features of modular high-temperature gas-cooled reactor.

HTR-PM600 is a milestone in promotion of HTGR market application and technology progress, and in building a world-class HTGR industry system with independent intellectual property rights in China. It is also another outstanding breakthrough in the industrial application both domestically and internationally.

Translation and revision | Raj Lamar

Image | Li Na, Guo Xiang

3月31日

文字 | 方之澜

图片 | 李娜

顾毓琇：心系国家，眷念清华

清华西门附近有一片平房，散布着十几户稍显老旧的院落。在靠河的一侧，一栋砖瓦房的门柱上，用绿色的漆刷上了大大的“16 号”字样。西院 16 号，这个对如今的清华学生来说已经有些陌生的地方，在 80 年前，曾一度是学校不少教育、科研乃至抗日救亡活动的重要见证。曾经居住在这里的人，是清华工学院院长，是现代话剧的先驱者之一，是一位古典音乐家，是“国际桂冠诗人”，是导演、史学家，还是一位杰出的教育家。而这些，都还不足以概括他的全部。

他是顾毓琇。1915 年考入清华学校，1923 年毕业后赴美攻读电机工程，1928 年获得麻省理工学院博士学位。他 26 岁时发明的“顾氏变数”以及随后发表的 100 多篇论文和专著，为他在国际电机领域中奠定了崇高的地位，他是第一个获得国际电工与电子界崇高荣誉“兰姆”奖章的中国人。

1932 年，顾毓琇回到母校任电机工程学系主任，翌年升任工学院院长，成为当时清华大学领导层核心成员之一。“利用工程的智识和方法来帮助国家解决国防和民生问题，便是我们工程师的天职。”时值“九一八”事变刚过，为日益严峻的中国局势深感忧虑的顾毓琇，发出了这样的高声疾呼。

他不仅积极推动学术研究为社会、国家服务，自觉地将学校发展与国家、民族命运结合起来，还亲力亲为，为抗日战争做出自己的贡献。1936 年 11 月，绥远战役爆发。傅作义发现原装备的意大利产防毒面具因天气冷而失效，请求清华制作防毒面具应急。军情紧急，清华立即动员起来，任命顾毓琇为总负责人，组织协调机械、化学等系师生研制出新的防毒面具。他代表清华亲赴前线，送给傅作义部 200 副试用。由于使用效果不错，傅作义部随即向清华定制 10000 副。清华组织近百名工人紧急制作，1937 年 2 月，这批防毒面具制成后送到一线将士手中。百灵庙大捷后，顾毓琇又亲往祝贺。

1937 年卢沟桥事变后，清华、北大、南开南迁长沙组建临时大学，顾毓琇随同；后于次年 1 月离开，担任教育部政务次长。顾毓琇虽然离开了清华，但对清华始终充满浓浓的感情。

2001 年，移居美国的顾毓琇已是一位年近百岁、住进医院的老人。他在毛笔上套了一个棉制圆环帮助握笔，写下了苍劲有力的“清华电机系七十周年”。这是他最后的题词，他把眷念永远留在了清华园。

Gu Yuxiu: Tsinghua, Where the Heart and Soul Belongs

Not too far from Tsinghua University's west gate is an area with old courtyards. The expanse of about ten residential blocks bring to mind historical ruin sites. On one side where it faces a river, bricks and tiles still hold up a house. On the top of its door frame is "No.16" in large print, painted in green. For today's Tsinghua students, this is not a familiar site, but 80 years ago, this was home to the university's various academic programs and research efforts.

This was once the home of the dean of Tsinghua's School of Engineering. A pioneer of modern Chinese plays, a classical musician, an acclaimed poet, a director, a historian, an outstanding educator and yet, all these fail to embody the whole of his being.

He was Gu Yuxiu. He entered Tsinghua University in 1915, left to study in the U.S. in 1923 and graduated in 1928 with a doctorate degree in electrical engineering from Massachusetts Institute of Technology. At 26, he created a mathematical variable named after himself, and had by then written more than a hundred journal articles and essays, establishing his international prominence in the field of electrical engineering. He was the first Chinese national to receive the prestigious Lamme Medal in International Electrical and Electronics Engineering (IEEE).

In 1932, Gu Yuxiu returned to his alma mater as the department head of the electrical engineering program. The following year, he was promoted as the dean of the school of engineering, making him one of the core leaders of the university.

"Employing engineering knowledge and methods to help the country solve national security issues and improve people's livelihoods is our duty as engineers." Gu had once said shortly after the September 18th incident in 1931 where Japanese troops seized the northeast city of Shenyang.

He not only advanced the university through fervent promotion of academic research, but also brought the nation and the fate of the people together. In November of 1936, the Battle of Suiyuan broke out. Then, General Fu Zuoyi realized that his Italian-made gas masks had become dysfunctional due to the cold weather. So he requested Tsinghua to produce new gas masks for his army. The military situation was pressing and Gu Yuxiu was appointed the chief person responsible for the research and production of the gas masks.

Bearing the name of Tsinghua, he delivered 200 gas masks to the front lines of the battlefield for trial tests. The general subsequently ordered 10,000 masks and through the labor of almost a hundred workers, they produced the masks a few months later and had them delivered to the hands of soldiers on the frontline.

In 1937, after the battle at Lugou Bridge, Tsinghua University, Peking University and Nankai University moved to the South and formed a provisional university in Changsha. The year after, Gu Yuxiu left Tsinghua to be the deputy ministry of government affairs in the Ministry of Education. Even though he left Tsinghua, he still held a deep affection for the university.

By 2001, the hundred-year-old former dean's fingers can only faintly grip his calligraphy brush, but he wrote firmly and heartily the characters "70th Anniversary of Tsinghua University Department of Electrical Engineering" . That was the last time he ever lifted his brush again, but he had forever left behind his nostalgia for Tsinghua.

Translation and revision | Alexis See Tho

Image | Li Na

4月5日

文字 | 张译丹

图片 | 陈稳杰

清明祭礼，不失不忘；先烈遗志，薪火相传

这是一个缅怀的日子，也是一个展望的日子；这是一个祭奠的日子，也是一个传承的日子。

每年清明节，清华师生都要自发祭扫英烈纪念碑，这早已成为清华人的精神传统。学校领导和各院系师生汇集在“祖国儿女，清华英烈”纪念碑前鞠躬献花，表达内心深深的敬意。

纪念碑下的平台上，镌刻着 43 位在民族独立和人民解放战争中献身的烈士姓名和简要档案。当年，他们满怀爱国主义豪情，以救国报国为己任，为国家独立、民族解放，为中华民族的伟大复兴前赴后继、死而后已；今天，一支支白菊、一个个花篮寄托着清华师生的缅怀与追思，传承着清华人爱国奉献、追求卓越的精神传统。

2013 年 4 月 5 日，清华原创话剧《马兰花开》剧组的 26 名师生曾经来到这里，深情缅怀和追忆“两弹一星”元勋邓稼先，以及所有为国家、民族、人民做出重要贡献，奉献了青春、热血与生命的清华英烈。

在 2015 年祭奠清华英烈的活动中，校党委副书记史宗恺对同学们说，清华先烈们的勇于担当首先是一种人生境界、一种家国天下的情怀；此外，勇于担当还要有为理想奋斗的勇气，更要有真才实学。“新中国成立以来，还有许多为国家建设奉献青春甚至生命的清华人，比如因公殉职的廖枝飞同志，我们应该永远铭记他们，向他们致敬。相信清华的担当精神能在一代代清华人身上传承下去并且发扬光大。”史宗恺说。

2016 年 4 月，大型原创史诗话剧《雨花台》在清华巡演，这部话剧集中展示了中国共产党早期青年运动领导人之一恽代英、清华留美生中第一批共产党员之一施滉等雨花台烈士为民牺牲的大无畏精神。话剧副导演、剧中人物施滉饰演者李竹也在清明这天来到清华英烈纪念碑前，与同学们共同朗诵了学生原创诗歌《我们不能忘记》，以昂扬的激情讴歌“烈士青春”，许下了继承先烈光荣传统、向着实现中华民族伟大复兴的目标不断拼搏前行的誓言。

悠悠艾草香，绵绵细雨情，清明又至……

Qingming Festival: Remembering the Martyrs, Passing Down Traditions

This is a day of remembrance. This is a day where we look towards the future. This is a day about legacy and above all, a very traditional day.

Every Qingming Festival, Tsinghua students and teachers take part in tomb-sweeping. This has always been the spiritual tradition of Tsinghua. School leaders and faculty members gather together to pay their respects to "Tsinghua martyrs" . They not only remember but also review the glorious history of Tsinghua's past heroic deeds. During periods of great revolutions, Anti-Japanese War, national struggles and liberations, Tsinghua has always played an important and active role. 43 heroes' names are engraved on the Tsinghua Martyrs Monument. These group of Tsinghua people are filled with true patriotism and pride. They devoted themselves to saving their country and played a crucial role in the great rejuvenation of the Chinese Nation.

This tradition continues...

In April 2013, Tsinghua's original drama *Ma Lan Flowers Bloom* made its debut. With some 26 teachers and students, they affectionately paid their respect to Comrade Deng Jiaxian in front of the "The sons and daughters of our Chinese Nation-The Tsinghua Heroes" monument. Every single one of these heroes has made important contributions to the country, to the people and gave much of their youth, passion and life to their land.

In 2015's Qingming Festival, Tsinghua's Deputy Party Secretary Shi Zongkai stressed the importance of Tsinghua people and the courage that they possess. This is the courage to be oneself and to pay respect to one's motherland. Also, it is about the courage to gain true skills and genuine knowledge. Mr Shi encouraged students to uphold such values, "There are many more names that did not make it on the monument. There are countless number of Tsinghua people who equally made heavy contributions to their motherland. Take the example of Comrade Liao Zhifei. I believe that Tsinghua's spirit can be passed down from generation to generation. It is up to us to carry it forward."

In 2016 Qingming Festival, the original drama show *Yuhuatai* came to Tsinghua. It tells the sacrifice and the stories of Yun Daiying *(known as one of the earliest leaders of the Communist Party)*, Shi Huang *(known as one of the earliest Party members among the Tsinghua graduates who had studied in the States)* and the Yuhuatai martyrs.

Li Yanwu, on behalf of all students, the President of Tsinghua's Graduate School expressed his respect on the behalf of all students to these heroes. He said: "Their heroic deeds and spirit will always be remembered and handed down from generation to generation. Let us be inspired by their deeds and let us inherit the glorious tradition and also achieve the goal of the great rejuvenation of the Chinese nation. Let us march forward!"

The grassy fragrance...the drizzles...Qingming is coming again...

Translation and revision | Min Weiyuan

Image | Chen Wenjie

4月6日

文字 | 杨晨晞
图片 | 薛雅芳

106 周年校庆：更好的清华等你来

跨过百年的风华，从“怀增进国力之愿”到踏上中国高等教育的探索之路，清华走过了 106 年的时光。水木明澈，花草葳蕤，丁香馥郁，紫荆竞妍，2017 年的四月天，更好的清华等你来！

更好的清华等你来，主题语简洁有力却意蕴丰富：一个“更”字，既展现了近年来学校改革发展的成效，又包含对于未来的期许；一个“等”字，不仅是对于校友回家的温情呼唤，还包含着共同建设好清华的愿景——明天会更好，清华会更好，未来会更好。

更创新的清华等你来。锐意改革、矢志创新是清华永葆活力的源泉，我们欣喜地目睹教育教学、科研、资源管理等各领域的改革正在全面深入推进，也亲身体验到公布开放交流时间、校园国际热岛建设、新生必修游泳等一系列新举措为清华带来更富活力的崭新面貌。

更国际的清华等你来。一如校歌所唱“立德立言，无问西东”，清华格外重视东西方学术交流，东西文化，荟萃一堂。典雅的苏世民书院培育着来自五洲的优秀学子，由清华发起成立的亚洲大学联盟即将在校庆期间正式诞生……清华在国际高等教育舞台上扮演着日益重要的角色。

更人文的清华等你来。百年清华，人文日新。“人文清华”系列讲坛携人文社科领域的大师巨擘，为全校师生定期带来精神的洗礼；主干道上数不清的文化素质教育讲座海报令人目不暇接；艺术博物馆开馆以来的系列展览诠释着彰显人文、荟萃艺术、涵养新风、化育菁华的理念。更加人文的校园文化氛围与理工气息交辉，创造多元而包容的文化环境，在宁静中创造美好未来。

更美丽的清华等你来。春夏两季参天白杨守护的南北主干道，秋冬东西主干道上活化石般的银杏，学堂朝晖，书馆春晓，荷塘月色，闻亭钟影，日晷悬针，水木华年，清华风物之美无须过多的表达。进一步完善校园规划、提升校园景观等一系列举措为更美的校园环境“保驾护航”——从富有弹性的健步小道踏上主干道，欣赏着一块块兼具科技与人文气息的太阳能照明双语导视牌，再回到增开晨间热水的学生宿舍淋浴间冲个热水澡，清新而充满能量的一天就此开始……

还有无数的“更”等待着我们去改变、去创造，而这些“更”的最终合力指向了“更好”。清韵华舞，歌饮百年，水木静好，清芬百年。清华 106 周年校庆，更好的清华等你来！

Tsinghua' s Anniversary: a Better Tsinghua Awaits You

With a century of elegance and the “aspiration of harboring national power” , the road of China's higher education development has always seen the presence of Tsinghua University. The Campus dotted with greenery and filled with blossoming flowers and its aroma welcomes the University's 106th Anniversary in this month of April. A better Tsinghua awaits all and we all look forward to that!

A better Tsinghua awaits you. This concise and powerful message is rich in meaning. The word “better” not only reflect the effectiveness of reform and development in recent years, but also future expectations. It is not only a warm welcome for future students and alumni but also contains a common vision for a future Tsinghua. Tomorrow will be better, Tsinghua will be better and so is the future.

A more innovative Tsinghua awaits you. We are delighted to see that the reform for teaching, research, resource management and other fields are in full swing. More exchanges and projects as well as the latest additional compulsory course of swimming is only a fraction of a series of new initiatives for a more dynamic Tsinghua.

A more internationalized Tsinghua awaits you. Tsinghua has always placed importance on academic exchanges between East and West. Things have always been holistic and an integration. The elegant Schwarzman Scholars welcome students from all continents. An Asian University Alliance will be formed soon which meant that Tsinghua is and will always be playing an increasingly crucial role in international higher education exchange.

A more humanity-orientied Tsinghua awaits you. A century of Tsinghua and her art-oriented teachings meant that humanities, history and literature courses have always improved the overall quality and knowledge of the Tsinghua teachers and students. With countless posters as well as series of exhibitions held at Tsinghua's own museum, the concept of education has always been refined and maintained. More scholarly atmosphere will create a more diverse and inclusive cultural environment. Thus, a better and innovative future is created amidst tranquility.

A more beautiful Tsinghua waits for your presence. The north and south main road is protected by poplar trees in the spring and summer while autumn and winter bear witness to the fallen ginkgo leaves, the moonlight reflection in the lotus pond that sits in front of the old buildings and the shuimu Tsinghua that becomes an inseparable part of Tsinghua. To further improve the planning of the campus, landscape has been enhanced and a series of initiatives have been put into place to ensure the maintenance and protection of the marvelous campus. In addition, to making improvement to the campus, initiatives have been put in place to “protect” and “navigate” the overall environment of Tsinghua. When students go for a run down the jogging paths in the morning, while taking in the gorgeous view of the campus with solar-powered bilingual signboards, they can now return to their dormitories to enjoy a hot shower and start the day fresh.

More “better” times awaits us in the future for change and new creations. These “better” will ultimately lead to great “positivity and improvement” . The Tsinghua song echoes throughout the centuries. Tsinghua's 106th Anniversary: a better Tsinghua awaits you!

Translation and revision | Min Weiyuan

Image | Xue Yafang

4月7日

文字 | 杨茂艺

图片 | 宋晨

浸润东非，拥抱热土

熔岩高原与裂谷错落，热带草原和淡水湖辉映，驰骋的角马踏起沙的骄傲，静默的金合欢树装点了天的蔚蓝……东非，神奇而瑰丽。600年前，郑和船队航至肯尼亚，揭开了中非交流的序幕；600年后，清华师生则以“丝路新探”海外实践项目的名义再次拜访，展望21世纪中非合作的未来。

自2017年2月6日起，14名本研学子与3名教师组成的清华赴东非实践支队在肯尼亚和埃塞俄比亚先后参观了蒙内铁路、亚吉铁路，拜访了中国土木工程集团有限公司、华为技术有限公司等企业，与新华社驻内罗毕分社等机构进行座谈，走访了内罗毕贫民窟与联合国环境署、人居署总部等机构。

非洲洋溢着对中国的热情——从公路铁路到城市供电供水，从消费用品到生产器械，无不渗透着中国元素。而亚吉铁路作为非洲第一条电气化铁路，则全部采用了中国标准和中国装备。当支队走进内罗毕贫民窟的长青造梦小学时，学生们一下子涌上来，跟队员们一起拍手、合影，不停地说着“China，你好”。那感觉，温暖而真实。

中国企业的活力也不容忽视——既有在员工聘用、采购、投资方面高度本地化的华为公司，也有在亚的斯亚贝巴工业园组织当地员工合唱“团结就是力量”的中国制鞋民企。通过与中土埃塞公司等企业管理层的座谈，同学们深刻认识到硬实力推广与文化内涵宣传在企业跨国发展中的重要性。

作为第一支到访中国驻埃塞俄比亚大使馆的国内大学生队伍，支队受到了大使腊翊凡的高度赞扬：“带领优秀青年学子走进非洲是极有远见的举措。”中国驻非盟使团团长旷伟霖则表示，希望进一步加强驻非盟使团与清华大学的合作，为国家战略提供更多的学术与人才支持。

世界之大，每一寸土地都值得用脚步丈量。以具备全球领导力、胜任力为重要成长目标的清华学子更应将自我命运融入时代浪潮，从拥抱东非这片热土开始，走向更广阔的未来。

Venturing into East Africa, Embracing Her Hot Land

Flowing lava and vast plateau, tropical grassland and freshwater lakes, the galloping of the wild beasts, the quietness of the Acacia trees...all under a limitless sky of blue. East Africa is both magical and magnificent. 600 years ago, Zheng He's fleet arrived in Kenya and launched the exchange between China and Africa. Now, 600 years later, under the "New Silk Road Discoveries" overseas in-field practicum project, Tsinghua teachers and students began their tour into Africa during this new century.

Since February 6, 2017, 14 students and 3 teachers from Tsinghua embarked on their project in Kenya and Ethiopia. For further studies and discussion, they visited Mengnei Railway, Yaji Railway, China Civil Engineering Group, Huawei, Xinhua News Agency in Nairobi and many more enterprises and institutions. The group also visited slums in Nairobi, the UN Environment Program and other attached headquarters.

Africa is filled with enthusiasm for China. From roads, railway, power supply, consumer goods to equipment, that Chinese touch is everywhere. Yaji Railway as Africa's first electrified railway uses equipment made in China and adheres to Chinese standards. It is worth mentioning that when the group paid visits to slums in Nairobi, students from local primary schools came up clapping, with smiling faces, asking for photos and they kept on saying "China! China!" That feeling was warm and very real.

Of course, the vitality of Chinese enterprises cannot be ignored. In addition to the employment of the locals, procurement, investment and high degree of localization made by Huawei, there are also other companies in the capital of Ethiopia's Industrial Park. One example is a shoe-making enterprise whose "unity is strength" slogan resonated with many. Through discussions about management with these enterprises, the students realized the importance of cultural promotion and hard power in transnational developments。

As the first group of university student to visit the Chinese Embassy in Ethiopia, the group was highly praised by the Ambassador, who found their ventures into Africa to be a very far-sighted initiative. "We hope to further strengthen the cooperation between the African Union Mission and Tsinghua University. Moreover, we wish to provide more academic and talent support for the national strategy," said Kuang Weilin, Head of the Chinese delegation to the African Union.

The world is huge and we need to leave behind our footprints on every inch of the land. With "cultivating global leadership and competencies" as the primary goal of these Tsinghua students, they should embrace current times and not only embrace the hot exotic land of East Africa but also think about the broader future.

Translation and revision | Min Weiyuan

Image | Song Chen

4月10日

文字 | 张智伟

图片 | 赵存存

校园绿色出行：行到哪里，就把环保意识带到哪里

2016年初，正当寒气逐渐散去、校园绿意盎然之时，清华园里的校园巴士由多年不变的乳黄色变成了紫色，在为校园平添几分勃勃生机的同时，也悄然间为绿色大学建设增添了新的元素。

早在1998年，清华就在全国高校中首创“绿色大学”理念，构想提出之时，电动校园巴士、自行车等绿色出行方式便成为其中一环。2000年，清华又率先尝试引进了第一批电动车，但由于当时的电动车无论能源消耗还是电池寿命都不能与现在同日而语，实用性不强，很快就被淘汰。校车在2005年被更换为燃油车。

2016年，学校启动绿色校园微循环电动车示范系统，22辆纯电动校园巴士投入使用，成为国内首个在大学校园内规模化实施的纯电动车应用系统。新能源电动车电池性能大幅提升，车辆运行成本是燃油车的1/4，一氧化碳年排放量可减少1711 kg。而且，由于采用信息化平台实施运行监测，车辆运行更加准点高效，负责新能源车运营的接待服务中心还在常规路线基础上，增加了“敬老专线”“温暖回家专线”等定制化线路，为绿色出行赋予了便捷、高效的新内涵。

谈起绿色出行，除校园通勤车外，清华园里的自行车也不得不提。曾有校友将自行车称为清华“三大件”之一：“成千上万的自行车是清华一道独特的景观……人手一辆，每天如此，日复一日，年复一年。毋庸置疑，以自行车作为代步工具，这是绿色出行、低碳生活，值得称道赞赏……清华的自行车，是令人肃然起敬的自行车，是作用非凡的自行车。”2010年，丹麦王子约阿希姆访问清华大学时，对清华园自行车数量之多表示“印象深刻”，他还与清华同学一起，骑自行车游校园，倡导绿色出行。

如今，清华的自行车不仅是代步工具，也逐渐成为师生员工绿色出行理念的载体——废弃自行车被重新清洗组装，循环使用；校园里的自行车协会、绿色协会等社团组织通过各种富有特色的活动，倡导绿色出行。

寒来暑往，在绿意掩映的校园里，绿色出行意识也正蔚然成风。园子里的人们行到哪里，就把绿色环保意识带到了哪里。

Eco-Friendly Transport: Go Green on Campus

At the beginning of 2016, when the cold weather quietly dispersed and spring brought vitality back, school buses on Tsinghua campus turned purple from their original creamy yellow, while increasing energy to the campus and silently adding new elements to the Green University.

In 1998, Tsinghua University introduced the concept of "Green University" for the first time, since then the electric buses, bicycles and other green travel modes had become a part of the movement. As early as 2000, ahead of most Chinese universities, Tsinghua University introduced their first electric vehicles. However, giving their negative performance on energy consumption and battery life compared to that of today, they were soon phased out and replaced by fuel vehicles in 2005.

In 2016, Tsinghua University launched micro-recycling electric vehicle system and 22 electric school buses went into service, which became the first application system of electric vehicles directed in Chinese universities.

However, the new-energy vehicles launched in 2016 consumed only one-forth energy of that of fuel vehicles in their operating costs, which means 1711kg less in annual emission of carbon monoxide. Besides, the monitoring system is based on information platform, therefore the punctuality and efficiency are guaranteed. Also, apart from regular routes, the service center in charge of new-energy vehicle operation designed several special routes such as "Respect The Old" and "Come Back Home" , adding new connotation as convenience and efficiency towards Green Travel.

When it comes to Green Travel, beside the commuter buses, bicycles are another aspect to mention. Bicycles were once regarded by alumnus as one of "Three Goods" on Tsinghua campus: "A bicycle for each one, day by day, year by year, thousands of bicycles have formed the unique landscape of Tsinghua University... Undoubtedly, as a tool of transport, bicycles are advocated for green travel and low-carbon life... Bicycles on Tsinghua campus are awesome and play a unique role." Joachim, Prince of Denmark, visited Tsinghua University in 2010 and said he was "impressed" by the number of bicycles in Tsinghua. He also toured the campus riding a bicycle together with the Tsinghua students to call on green travel.

From a simple tool of transport, bicycles have gradually become a carrier of green travel vision for all staff and students. Wasted bicycles were being cleaned, assembled and recycled in use. Bicycle association, Green Association and other campus communities also advocate green travel through a range of activities.

From season to season, when the campus is covered with green, the awareness of green travel is also enjoying its prosperity. The green environmental awareness is taken to wherever people go.

Translation and revision | Raj Lamar

Image | Zhao Cuncun

4月11日

文字 | 杨茂艺

图片 | 陈稳杰

2016年清华大学特等奖学金获得者马冬昕：水滴穿石，双肩筑梦

2008年“双胞胎姐妹花圆梦清华”，2011年当选校学生会副主席，2011年本科生特等奖学金获得者，化学系2012级直博生，北京高校优秀辅导员，“五四杯”首都青年学生乒乓球总决赛冠军，2016年清华大学特等奖学金获得者，“清华学神”……进入清华9年来，马冬昕的名字似乎总是与各种荣誉称号和媒体报道联系在一起。一路走来，旁人看到的多是繁花似锦，只有她自己知道脚下的土地经过了怎样的辛勤耕耘。

从本科阶段起，马冬昕就对自己的学习生活进行了严格的时间管理——与姐姐马冬晗相约6点半起床，自习到晚上10点教室关门；用小本子写下周一至周日各个时间段的学习生活安排；坚持每周6小时以上的乒乓球校队训练；利用各种社工会议之间的间隙来复习知识……只争朝夕的她把每天的零碎片段都竭力填充为斑斓的图画，从演讲比赛到马拉松，从学生节表演到原创诗歌朗诵，从暑假支教到校庆嘉年华……大学本科四年的生活于她而言，仿佛是六年、八年。

直博升入化学系的最初两年里，想要“练就一招制敌的绝技”的马冬昕屡屡受挫，实验记录本上写满了“失败”，沮丧的她曾一度有更换课题的念头。然而，在导师邱勇院士的鼓励下，她又做回了那滴固执顽强的水珠，以生命之柔韧挑战科研之艰美。读博的四年时光里，她总共合成了84种新材料，制备了近千块有机发光器件，撰写了14本、共计3000多页的实验记录。功夫不负有心人，马冬昕所在的团队在国际上首次提出了可蒸镀离子型过渡金属配合物的通用设计方法，马冬昕也以第一作者身份在国际著名期刊上发表SCI收录论文10篇，影响因子累计超过70。

学术成果累累的同时，作为清华“双肩挑”队伍的一员，马冬昕还先后担任了化学系2012级辅导员、学生工作组组长、学生学习与发展指导中心工作坊讲师，在与学弟学妹们的接触中，她细致认真的工作更是获得了如潮好评。

这位被身边同学评价为“眉清目秀，干净利落，学而不倦，精益求精”的女孩表示，直博阶段结束后自己想要出国从事博士后研究，学成回国后继续投身科研事业。

愿她终能以清华赤子之心，筑人生绮丽之梦。

Taking the Road Less Traveled: Ma Dongxin Awarded Tsinghua's 2016 Top Grade Scholarship

2008 "Twin sisters fulfill their Tsinghua dream" , 2011 Undergraduate Top Grade Award, Beijing University Excellent Counselor, "May 4 Cup" Table Tennis Championship, 2016 Postgraduate Top Grade Award... for 9 years, such dazzling titles and attentions have been attached to Ma Dongxin.

Ma Dongxin along with her sister Ma Donghan adheres to strict time management. They both wake up at 6:30a.m. and self-study until 10:00pm when the classroom shuts for the day. Ma Dongxin writes down other arrangements for the week in their small notebook and maintain more than 6 hours of table tennis practice every week. She uses every chance she gets to review and refine her learnt knowledge and ensure that day and night, her life is packed with self-fulfilling activities. From marathons to public talks to poetry recitation to summer practicums to other events, her 4 years of study at Tsinghua were very fulfilling.

The first two years of her Ph.D. was tough since it wasn't all easy. Words about "failure" were written all over her notebook. Frustrated, she thought about replacing the subject, however under the encouragement of her supervisor Professor Qiu Yong, she returned back to her former self and continued with her studies. During her 4 years of Ph.D., she synthesized a total of 84 new materials, prepared nearly a thousand pieces of organic light-emitting devices, wrote 14 experimental records totaling more than 3000 pages and became that tough water droplet with the ability to wear through rocks. In the end, Ma put forward design method of using evaporation in the ion transition metal complexes and became the first author in more than 10 international SCI listed papers.

Apart from great academic achievements, Ma is also the 2012 class counselor for Tsinghua's Department of Chemical Engineering. As the group leader and lecturer for workshops, Ma became grateful for the praise and influence that she was able to receive from her students.

Ma Dongxin wishes to continue with her research and go abroad after graduation. Then, she wishes to return to her motherland and continue with work in scientific research. For Ma, she wishes to continue with building her dream.

Translation and revision | Min Weiyuan

Image | Chen Wenjie

4月12日

供稿 | 公管学院

改编 | 刘书田

图片 | 李娜

乃哥麦提·伊加提：在梦想的道路上踏实前行

2011年夏天，乃哥麦提·伊加提收到了清华大学生物科学专业的录取通知书。他坐了50多个小时的火车，独自从新疆来到北京，开启了逐梦新征程。

来到清华后，乃哥麦提依然勤奋刻苦，图书馆、自习室和教室成为他日常生活的主要根据地，优异的成绩单也帮他褪去了初入学时的胆怯与自卑。学习之余，乃哥麦提重拾起了对足球的热爱，绿茵场上经常活跃着他矫健的身影。

然而，“夏花”般的生活突然迎来了“严冬”。大二下学期，乃哥麦提被一种慢性病缠身。先是头发开始毫无缘由地成把脱落，而后是眉毛快速脱落，迫不得已，乃哥麦提只能申请休学治疗。四个月的时间，他在医院的病床上度过，陪伴他的除了母亲，就是冰冷的光疗仪器、苦涩的中医药剂、收费单上一排长长的数字，以及埋在心底的悲伤和彷徨。

休学期已满，乃哥麦提迎来了又一个艰难的9月。他渴望尽快回到校园，但繁重的医疗支出，使得学费成为这个家庭的巨大压力。

庆幸的是在此时，国家助学金雪中送炭，帮助乃哥麦提重返校园。“那时国家助学金对我来说真的太重要了，以至于时至今日，我仍希望通过记述自己的故事来记住彼时受过的帮助。”乃哥麦提感慨地说。最令他感动的还有在毕业典礼前夕，学生处的老师打电话给他，邀请他的父母参加毕业典礼，并报销车票和三天住宿，父母甚是欢喜，他亦将学校和老师的真诚帮助铭记在心。

清华大学早在1997年就提出“绝不让一个勤奋而有才华的学生因为家庭经济困难而辍学”的目标。从2006年到2016年，清华大学建立“助、勤、奖、贷、补”的新资助体系，十年间资助总额增长了62.2%，8000余名在校家庭经济困难学生获得了资助，而乃哥麦提则是获益学生之一。

休学治疗期间，乃哥麦提突然意识到：“如果真的想要为这个世界做出些什么，我只能从改变自己开始。”于是他决定弃理从文，想要探寻更多的社会议题。

在时隔一年重新开始的大三生涯中，乃哥麦提着手准备，他选修了“组织理论”等社会科学方面的课程，阅读了《族群社会学》等大量社会科学方面的书籍，并与相关领域的老师交流自己的想法。最终，乃哥麦提免试推研至清华大学公共管理学院。

如今，乃哥麦提的身体已无大碍。他和生命学院足球队一起捧回了“马约翰杯”男子足球赛的冠军奖杯，继续在球场上挥洒汗水，亦能够在逐梦的道路上继续前行。这场疾病不仅让乃哥麦提邂逅了国家助学金，也以一种特别的方式改变了他前进的方向，使他踏上新的征途。

注：本文改编自《乃哥麦提·伊加提：清华园逐梦》（原作者何雪冰，2016年12月20日刊登于清华大学新闻网）

Nighmat Ijat:
En-route to My Dreams

In the summer of 2011, Nighmat Ijat received a Letter of Acceptance from Tsinghua University's School of Life Sciences. He sat alone on the train for more than 50 hours from Xinjiang to Beijing and began a new journey. He was on the road to his dreams.

After coming to Tsinghua, he studied hard. The library, study room and classroom became three top homes for him. His excellent result and report helped him to shake off a sense of low self-esteem and shyness. Apart from learning, Nighmat also had a passion for football.

However, winter quickly descended upon him since he was down with a chronic disease during his second year of study. At first, his hair began to fall off for no reason then his eyebrows. He had to suspend his studies and what followed was 4 months spent at hospital. Lying on the cold hospital bed with his mother beside him, the bitterness of the medicine and the cold therapy equipment along with the long expenses made him sad and lost. He ushered in another difficult September and was more than eager to return to Tsinghua and his studies as soon as possible. Yet with such heavy medical expenses along with the tuition fee, it placed great pressure on his family.

Fortunately, the State Scholarship offered much needed assistance during such times of difficulty. "At that time, the scholarship was extremely important for me. I hope that through my story, I'm able to remember forever the help that I've received." said Nighmat. He was also extremely moved by the fact that on the eve of the graduation ceremony, the teachers called him and invited his parents to attend the ceremony. The train tickets and 3 days of accommodation were fully reimbursed.

As early as 1997, Tsinghua made reforms to the tuition fees which meant that "not one diligent and talented student will be forced to drop out of school due to economic difficulties" . From 2006 to 2016, Tsinghua University set up a new subsidy system called "Assistance, Diligence, Award, Loan and Subsidy" . The total amount of subsidy increased by 62.2% during the ten years and more than 8,000 students received support. Nighmat was one of them.

When he was recovering, he realized that "If I really want to do something for this world, I can only start by changing myself." He decided to explore more about social issues. During his third year, he chose many social science courses such as "Organizational Theory" and read a lot of books on sociology and other related fields. In the end, he was accepted into Tsinghua's School of Public Policy and Management.

Now, Nighmat has recovered and continues to play football. He is still on the road towards his dreams. His illness changed his life and with support from the scholarship, he is now embarking on a new journey.

Contributor | School of Public Policy & Management

Translation and revision | Min Weiyuan

Image | Li Na

4 月 13 日

文字 | 方之澜

图片 | 郭祥

新版工程硕士学位课程拥抱“学堂在线”

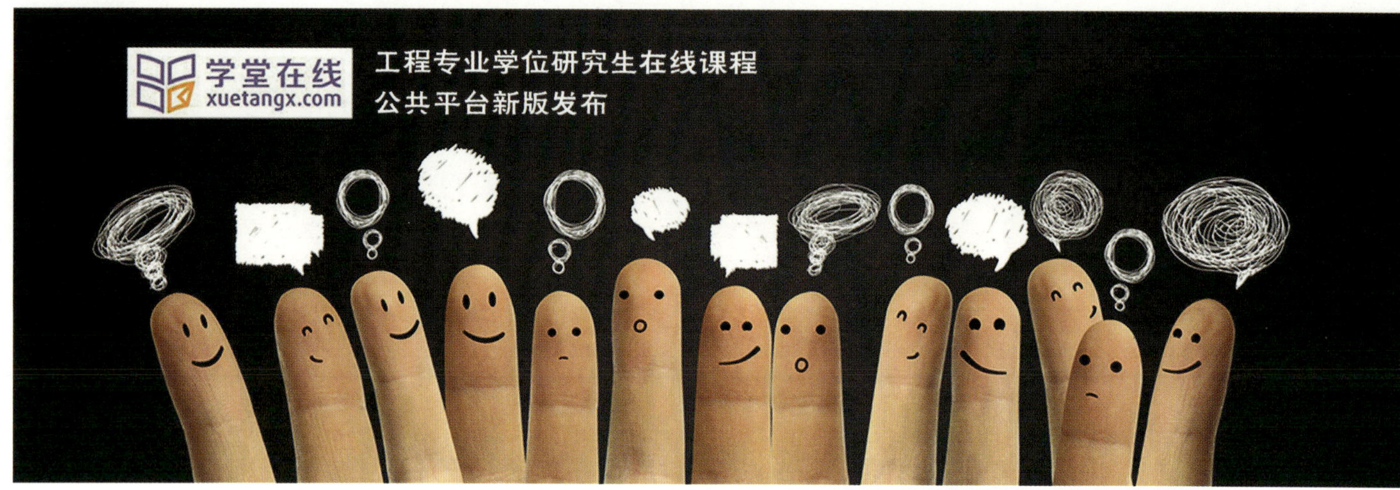

“互联网 +”“大规模”“开放式”“教育”……当这些词汇在脑海中一个一个闪过，你大概不难想到它们所共同描绘的一个对象——慕课（MOOC）。如今，这种跨专业、跨学校乃至跨国际的免费优质课堂，正在全球教育界掀起一场革新浪潮。

作为最大的中文慕课（MOOC）平台，清华大学“学堂在线”在推进课程发展完善的过程中，一直做着不懈的努力。2017 年 1 月 15 日下午，“学堂在线”2017 年在线教育行业发展分享会暨全国工程专业学位研究生在线课程公共平台新版发布会在清华举行。全国工程专业学位研究生教育指导委员会副秘书长、清华大学研究生院副院长张伟在会上宣布，全国工程专业学位研究生在线课程公共平台新版正式发布。

为贯彻落实教育部《关于加强高等学校在线开放课程建设应用与管理的意见》精神，进一步促进工程硕士专业学位研究生教育教学改革和培养模式创新，不断提高工程硕士专业学位研究生培养质量，2015 年 7 月，全国工程专业学位研究生教育指导委员会宣布启动工程硕士学位在线课程建设项目，依托“学堂在线”平台建设工程硕士学位在线课程，实施混合教育模式。

全国工程专业学位研究生在线课程面向全国工程硕士专业学位研究生乃至全球学习者，采取公开发布、免费学习、有偿资质认证和学分认证。截至 2016 年底，平台上已经有超过 30 多家合作院校的课程，覆盖 26 个工程领域。全国工程专业学位研究生在线课程公共平台新版的发布，将会为学习者带来更好的学习体验。

高等教育普惠大众，“全球校区”终身学习。近年来，“学堂在线”秉承着“创新教育、改变世界”的使命，不断探索，不断前进。暑期班课程、自主模式课程、全球首门 VR 课程、微慕课、直播课程、X- 学堂产品等相继上线，此外，“学堂在线”还设立了学堂萌芽奖学金，激励学员完成课程。

2017 年，“学堂在线”将继续探索创新，始终把用户需求放在第一位，提供多样性、个性化的教学和学习服务。

XuetangX Released a New Version of Online Master of Engineering Courses

Internet+, Massive, Open, Education...When these words flash in your minds, the object they are referring to, is quite evident - MOOC. The cross-professional, cross-school, and even transnational free quality courses are shaping a new era for global education.

As the largest Chinese MOOC platform, XuetangX always endeavors to promote the development of online courses. On the afternoon of January 15, 2017, XuetangX Sharing Session of Online Education Development and New Version Conference of National Master of Engineering Online Courses was held in Tsinghua University. In the session, Zhang Wei, the deputy secretary of steering committee on national master of engineering education and assistant dean of graduate school of Tsinghua University, announced the release of the new version of national masters of engineering online courses.

To implement the spirit of "Advice of Ministry of Education on Strengthening the Construction and Management of College Open Online Courses" , further promote the reform in engineering postgraduate education and innovation of training model, raise the training quality of master of engineering students, the steering committee on national master of engineering education announced the project of online masters of engineering courses on July, 2015, which aimed to construct online postgraduate courses based on the platform of XuetangX and adopt mixed educational patterns.

The national masters of engineering online courses are available to domestic masters of engineering students as well as global learners, the platform adopts public release, free learning, paid qualification certification and credit authentication. By the end of 2016, it had covered courses from 30 cooperative partners and 26 engineering fields. The release of the new version of masters of engineering online courses will bring better learning experience to all learners.

Higher education benefits the general public and global universities guarantee people's lifelong learning. In recent years, XuetangX has adhered to the mission of "innovate education and changing the world" , while continuing to explore and move forward. Products such as summer programs, independent programs, the first VR program in the world, micro-MOOC and XuetangX have been applied, XuetangX even set up a "XuetangX Sprout" scholarship to motivate the students to complete the course.

In 2017, XuetangX will continue to explore and bring quality-learning resources, flexible learning methods to all the learners. XuetangX will always prioritize its users first, providing diverse, personalized teaching and learning services to more MOOC teachers and learners.

Translation and revision | Raj Lamar

Image | Guo Xiang

4月14日

供稿 | 电子系
文字 | 梁乐萌
图片 | 陈稳杰

电子系杨知行团队：中国产业腾飞，中国标准先行

“这个项目从 1999 年开始已推进了 17 年，其中的曲折和艰辛犹如我脸上的皱纹，显而易见，密集而且深邃。”在 2016 年的总结会上，谈及本团队完成的“DTMB 系统国际化和产业化的关键技术及应用”课题，71 岁的清华大学教授杨知行说。2017 年 1 月 9 日，该项目在 2016 年度国家科技奖励大会上荣获科技进步一等奖，17 年漫漫征途终于迎来了光明。

DTMB 一词听起来陌生，却与我们的日常生活紧密相连。DTMB 是中国数字电视强制性国家标准，是数字电视丰富多样的声音、图像背后沉默却不可或缺的技术基础，其第一起草人正是杨知行。

电视的发展经历了黑白、彩色、数字三个阶段，前两个阶段中国都采用欧洲标准，没有核心技术知识产权使得国内相关产业只能赚取微薄的加工费。1996 年，美国和欧洲相继建立了数字电视技术标准。面对转型的挑战与机遇，以杨知行为代表的一批清华人决心迎头赶上，“在国民经济主战场打一个翻身仗”。

美国、欧洲数字电视标准分别采用全时域和全频域的处理方式，前者以时间轴为坐标表示动态信号的关系，后者以频率轴为坐标表示信号，两者各有短长。杨知行团队发挥后发优势，采用时域和频域信号协同处理的方式，创新研发出“时域同步帧头 + 频域数据帧体”的 TDS-OFDM 信号帧结构，各方面性能明显优于其他标准。2006 年，DTMB 正式成为国家标准。

然而，杨知行团队并没有满足于此，让 DTMB 走向国际是他们更大的心愿。“对于应用科学来说，标准就是一种前沿技术。这种技术的竞争不凭借论文，而是凭借市场。”杨知行说。怀着这样的信念，团队成员频繁前往中南美洲，在海边、高原、热带雨林进行测试。DTMB 不负众望，9 个测试点与美、欧、日标准的较量中全部取得胜利。2011 年，经过三次努力，DTMB 标准成为国际电联正式标准，与美、欧、日共同构成地面数字电视四大国际标准，这也被国际电联誉为“1972—2012 年全球数字电视发展 40 年的一个重大里程碑事件”。

“现在国际上已开始了第二代数字电视标准竞争，我们希望并将努力争取攀登新的高峰。”展望将来，杨知行说。

Yang Zhixing' s Team Raises the Bar for International Digital TV Standards

"This project has been conducted for 17 years, since 1999. The twists and turns and hardships in those years, just like wrinkles on my face, are obvious, intensive and deep" , said the 71-year-old professor Yang Zhixing at the wrap-up session of 2016, when talking about the topic of "The key technology and application for DTMB system's internationalization and industrialization" . On January 9, 2017, this project won the first prize for scientific and technological progress in the National Science and Technology Award Conference of 2016, and the long journey of 17 years finally came to light.

The word DTMB may sound unfamiliar, but it is closely linked to our daily lives. DTMB is China's mandatory national standard for terrestrial digital television and foundation technical for rich and varied voices and images in television. Its first drafter was Yang Zhixing.

The development of television has gone through three stages, including black and white, color and then digital. For the first two stages, China adopted European standards, and no core intellectual property makes related domestic industries merely earn meager processing fees. In 1996, the United States and Europe successively established digital television standards. In the face of the challenges and opportunities of transformation, a group of Tsinghua people, represented by Yang Zhixing, was determined to catch up and play a turnaround in the main battlefield of national economy.

The digital television standard of the United States and Europe respectively adopted full-timing domain and full-frequency domain processing methods. The former one uses the time axis as coordinates to show the relationship with dynamic signal and the latter uses the frequency axis as coordinates to show the signal. Both of them have their advantages and disadvantages. Yang Zhixing's team took advantage by adopting co-processing method of time domain and frequency domain signals, they innovated the TDS-OFDM signal frame structure of "time domain synchronous frame header and frequency domain data frame body" , of which the performances in all aspects are better than those of other standards. In 2006, DTMB was officially approved as the national standard.

However, Yang Zhixing's team did not stop on their step, making DTMB international was their primary wish. "For the applied science, the standard is a cutting-edge technology. The competition of this technology is not by virtue of papers, but the market itself." said Yang Zhixing. With this conviction, the team members frequently traveled to Central and South America to do the field tests by sea, at plateau, and in the jungle. DTMB lived up to expectations. In all the nine test points, it won in the competition with the standards of the United States, Europe and Japan. In 2011, after several times of efforts, DTMB standard became the International Telecommunication Union's formal standard, and constituted the four major international standards for terrestrial digital TV together with the standard from the United States, Europe and Japan, which is also known as "a major milestone event in 40 years of global digital TV development from 1972 to 2012" .

"Now the second generation of digital TV standard competition in the international community has started, we hope and will strive to ascend greater heights." Professor Yang Zhixing said when looking forward to the future.

Contributor | Department of Electronic Engineering

Translation and revision | Raj Lamar

Image | Chen Wenjie

4月17日

文字 | 冯婉婷

图片 | 梁晨

朗读亭走了，读书仍在继续

“我念了席慕蓉的诗《爱的絮语》，送给我未出生的孩子。希望孩子将来喜爱读书，做更好的自己。”葛老师走出朗读亭，轻轻抚摸着自己的腹部，脸上洋溢着幸福的笑容。

一个多月以前，央视《朗读者》栏目组在新清华学堂前设置了“朗读亭”。短短一周里，这个精致复古的小亭子迎来了许多老师和同学：校党委研究生工作部部长白本锋老师走进朗读亭，朗诵了朱自清的著名篇章《荷塘月色》，希望同学们能够记住清华这个可爱而美丽的园子；清华大学原创话剧《马兰花开》中许鹿希女士的扮演者蔡丹阳，通过朗读《两弹元勋邓稼先》，表达了对“两弹元勋”邓稼先的敬意；苏世民书院学生李施军朗读了《祖国不会忘记》，送给那些和他一样“到祖国最需要的地方去”的当代青年。

正如《朗读者》节目开播时所说，“朗读是传播文字，而人则是关注生命，将值得关注的生命和值得关注的文字完美结合，就是我们的朗读者”，一批又一批清华朗读者在这个小小的空间里以朗读的形式表达了自己对文字和生活的热爱。虽然朗读亭只在清华园里停留了七天，但是园子里朗诵和阅读的热情却从未停止。

杨绛先生曾说“读书是为遇见更好的自己”，并在清华设立了“好读书”奖学金，表达了她对同学们“好读书、读好书”的美好希冀；邱勇校长向新生赠送图书作为入学礼物，勉励同学们养成读书的好习惯，并承诺未来每一年都会以不同形式对清华学子进行赠书；读书类社团的成立、读书沙龙的举办、“水木书榜”的评选，都反映出近年来清华校内日趋浓厚的读书氛围。

读书之于人文校园的打造，如同春风化雨，润物无声。伴随“朗读亭进清华”活动，校园内举办了一系列丰富的读书活动，从用明信片的形式鼓励同学们列出自己的读书计划到开展“图书漂流”活动，读书已经成为清华人的一种生活方式，“人文日新”的清华正以日益浓厚的文化氛围滋养着这里的每一个人。

朗读亭走了，读书仍在继续……

Tsinghua's Reading Booth: Reading to Become a Better You

"I read Xi Murong's poem *The Endless Talk on Love*, dedicated to my future child. I hope that the little one will love reading poems and always strive to become better." said Ms. Ge as she walks out of a reading booth. She gently strokes her belly. She wears a wide and radiant smile.

A month ago, *The Readers*, a popular television program by the China Central Television (CCTV) featuring renowned Chinese personalities who recite their chosen piece of literature before an audience made its stop at Tsinghua University, setting up a booth in front of the Tsinghua Auditorium. Within a week, the small booth attracted droves of students and faculty members.

Head of the graduate students' party work committee Bai Benfeng read Zhu Ziqing's famous essay *Moonlight over the Lotus Pond* to remind students of Tsinghua's beauty. Cai Danyang, actress for Xu Luxi in Tsinghua's original play *Malan Flower Blooming* read *The Hero of two bombs Deng Jiaxian* to express her utmost respect for Deng. A Schwarzman Scholar, Li Shijun, read *The Motherland Will Never Forget* dedicating it to youths who have gone to places where China has the most need.

When the television program *The Readers* aired, its host had said: "reading is the broadcast of the written word, while the principle of mankind is to cherish life. This program is to bring together words and things in life that are worth our attention." One after another Tsinghua readers visited the booth to bring to life their love for literature and life. Although the booth was only on campus for a week, their appreciation for reading and literature will not see an end.

Ms. Yang Jiang once said "reading can help to be a better you" . During her time at Tsinghua, she even created an award for best readers, representing her hope for students to embrace reading, especially the good ones. Tsinghua University's president, Qiu Yong gives freshmen books as gifts, encouraging them to nurture a habit of reading and he promised to give books to Tsinghua students every year. The various reading clubs, reading salon activities and the choosing of most popular books by students reveal the love for reading on Tsinghua campus.

A Chinese idiom says, just as wind and rain give life in spring, reading can build up a campus where its people are cultured and well-read. While the reading booth leaves Tsinghua, the campus is organizing a series of reading activities where students share their reading plans and a book-sharing program amongst students. The booth set in motion a reading culture with the hopes that it will become a lifestyle amongst students, making it the very character of a Tsinghua graduate.

Translation and revision | Alexis See Tho

Image | Liang Chen

Photographer | Zhang Bo

4月18日

供稿 | 校长办公室

图片 | 唐蓓蓓、薛雅芳

清华大学106周年校庆致辞

在这温暖宜人、充满生机的四月，我们迎来了清华大学的106岁生日。我谨代表学校向海内外广大校友和全体师生员工致以亲切的问候和良好的祝愿，向多年来关心支持我校发展的各界人士和朋友表示衷心的感谢！

一年之前，在清华大学105周年校庆之际，习近平总书记给母校写来贺信。总书记充分肯定了清华大学一百余年来的办学成就和优秀传统，要求清华大学坚持正确方向、坚持立德树人、坚持服务国家、坚持改革创新，面向世界、勇于进取，树立自信、保持特色，广育祖国和人民需要的各类人才，深度参与创新驱动发展战略实施，努力在创建世界一流大学方面走在前列。这既是对所有清华人的极大鼓舞，更是对我们的巨大鞭策。

过去一年，在全校师生员工的共同努力下，清华大学全面推进综合改革，加快建设中国特色世界一流大学，朝着更创新、更国际、更人文的目标奋力迈进。

更创新的清华，全心培养拔尖创新人才，努力创造高水平的研究成果。推进大类培养，将49个本科招生专业整合为16个大类专业，强化通识教育，为创新人才培养搭建更加广阔的平台。实施博士生招生改革，采用“申请—审核”制，优先选拔具备浓厚学术志趣与良好学术潜质的学生。设立“开放交流时间”（open office hour），教师每周固定时间接待学生自由咨询，缩短师生距离，让师生在面对面交流中迸发思想火花。设立长聘教授讲坛，让最优秀的学者展示他们的学术水平和丰富的学养，推动跨学科、跨领域的交流。科研体制机制改革正式启动，聚焦学科交叉、军民融合、前沿部署和科技成果转化，创造有利于创新的学术生态。

首座高温气冷堆商业示范核电站建设工程进展顺利，核能技术继续领跑全球。量子计算、类脑计算、界面高温超导、下一代互联网等一批前沿研究布局到位，呈现出蓬勃的创新活力。杨知行教授领衔的团队获国家科技进步奖一等奖，3项科研成果入选2016年度中国高等学校十大科技进展。出土文献研究与保护中心发现的清华简算表被认定为世界上最早的十进制乘法表。薛其坤院士获得首届未来科学大奖。施一公院士获得何梁何利基金科学与技术成就奖。经管学院钱颖一教授获2016年中国经济学奖。

更国际的清华，全面深化全球交流合作，拓展学生的国际视野，更好地联结中国与世界。全球战略颁布实施，国际化办学能力和全球影响力持续提升。2016年9月10日，旨在培养未来世界领导者的苏世民书院正式开学，国家主席习近平和美国总统奥巴马分别发来贺信。与美国华盛顿大学、微软公司共建的全球创新学院招收了首批学生；与瑞士日内瓦大学开展全面合作，共建可持续发展研究中心，在日内瓦建立培养和输送中国大学生赴国际组织实习与就业的基地；推动与意大利米兰理工大学建立战略合作伙伴关系，在米兰共同打造中意设计创新基地；启动建设清华大学深圳国际校区，全面提升学校在前沿创新、国际合作和高端人才培养方面的水平。

支持学生广泛参与国际学术交流和文化交流，2016年学生出国学习交流人数再创新高。首次启动清华全球南方文化浸润系列项目，大力推进发展中国家研究博士生项目建设，积极推动学生到非洲、欧洲、中东等地开展社会实践活动。倡议成立亚洲大学联盟，共同谋划亚洲高等教育的未来，为打造亚洲命运共同体乃至人类命运共同体贡献力量。清华的倡议已得到日本东京大学、新加坡国立大学等15所亚洲名校的积极响应，联盟将于2017年4月29日在清华正式宣告成立。

更人文的清华，进一步深厚人文底蕴，提升学生的人文素养，推动文理渗透，培养更多能够真正肩负未来使命的优秀人才。“人文清华”讲坛开启一年多来共举办8场演讲，文学家格非、国学家陈来、社会学家李强、伦理学家万俊人、历史学家彭林、思想史家汪晖、国际关系权威专家阎学通等一批清华知名学者在讲坛上分享灼见，让清华新的人文之光照耀校园、辐射社会。

2016 年 9 月 10 日，艺术博物馆正式对外开放，推动艺术与科学的融合，展示艺术之美和科学之美，开启清华人文艺术新篇章。大力营造校园读书氛围，连续两年向本科新生赠书，实施学生深度阅读计划，发布首届“水木书榜”，推动学生热爱读书、勤于思考，建设更加人文、更加宁静的书香校园。顺利召开第五届世界和平论坛，国际影响力不断提升。格非教授的长篇小说《望春风》荣获《当代》年度最佳长篇小说。2017 年 3 月 30 日，时隔 15 年再次召开文科工作会议，着力提高基础文科水平，强化应用文科优势，推动文科建设迈入新的阶段。

回顾过去的一年，我们辛勤耕耘、成果丰硕。2017 年 3 月 16 日，清华大学召开新百年首次全校教职工大会，进一步凝聚了共识、鼓舞了士气，全校师生员工正满怀期待、充满信心，共同用扎实的工作，开创新百年发展的新格局。我相信，在所有清华人的共同努力下，清华大学的明天一定会更加美好！

清华大学校长

President's Message for Tsinghua's 106th Anniversary

This April, in the warm season brimming with vigor and vitality, we celebrate the 106th anniversary of Tsinghua University. On behalf of Tsinghua, I would like to extend my cordial greetings and best wishes to our students, faculty and staff, as well as all Tsinghua alumni at home and abroad. I also offer my heartfelt gratitude to all friends for their unfailing support to Tsinghua over the years.

One year ago, as we celebrated the 105th anniversary, CPC General Secretary Xi Jinping sent a congratulatory letter to Tsinghua, his alma mater. He praised Tsinghua for its fine traditions and outstanding accomplishments in its proud history of over 100 years, and encouraged Tsinghua to stay true to its mission and foster great virtues in our students. Tsinghua, as he said, should move forward with an unwavering commitment to the nation and embrace reform and innovation. Proud and confident, Tsinghua should keep its distinctive features as it reaches out to the world and cultivate talents with a diverse variety of skills that meet the needs of our country and people. General Secretary Xi also called on Tsinghua to be part of China's innovation-driven development and become a pacesetter as it grows to be a world-class institution of higher education. His message represents a tremendous source of inspiration and encouragement to the Tsinghua community as we continue to go forward.

Over the past year, with the concerted efforts of our faculty, staff and students, Tsinghua has carried out comprehensive reform across the board. We have accelerated the progress towards a world-class university with distinctive Chinese features, striving to become more innovative, more international and more humanity-oriented.

To become more innovative, we have given high priority to cultivating innovative talents and strived to produce cutting-edge research achievements. In so doing, we, as always, have remained ahead of the curve in innovative education. We have reformed the discipline categorization for the undergraduate admission purpose in order to facilitate general discipline education. The 49 original disciplines are consolidated into 16 for admitted students to study in the first two years, so the boundary of each discipline is broadened. By strengthening liberal education, we aim to open up more possibilities of fostering innovative talents. We have reformed the way in which doctoral candidates are admitted by adopting an "application-assessment" scheme to select candidates that have keen academic pursuits and impressive potential for academic excellence. We launched the "Open Office Hour" , which brings teachers and students closely together. Such advising sessions help generate new ideas and sparks of wisdom. We set up a "Lecture Room" for tenure-track professors. The idea is to allow the top professors to demonstrate their exceptional academic credentials. That is part of our efforts to promote exchanges across disciplines and fields of study. We started the reform of the management system for scientific research, with a focus on cross-discipline research, integration of defense and civilian technologies, cutting-edge research and the commercialization of technological advances. In so doing, we strive to create an innovation-friendly academic ecosystem.

Smooth progress has been made in building the first demonstration nuclear power station for commercial use, which features a high-temperature gas-cooled reactor. With that, we continue to be a world leader in nuclear power technology. We have mobilized sufficient resources for a variety of frontier research areas including quantum computing, brain-like computing, interface-induced high-temperature superconductivity and the next-generation internet. Professor Yang Zhixing's team was awarded the nation's first prize for scientific and technological advances. Three research results of our professors were listed among 2016 Top Ten Scientific and Technological Progress of China's Colleges and Universities. The decimal multiplication table discovered by Tsinghua Unearthed Documents Research and Protection Center has been identified as the world's earliest. Professor Xue Qikun, a member of the Chinese Academy of Sciences (CAS), received the Future Science Prize, which was presented for the very first time. Professor Shi Yigong, a CAS member, was awarded the 2016 Prize for Scientific and Technological Achievements of Ho Leung Ho Lee Foundation. Professor Qian Yingyi from the School of Economics and Management was awarded the 2016 China Economics Prize.

To become more international, we have pursued deeper international cooperation in all areas to help our students gain international perspectives and better connect China to the world. As we launch and implement the global strategy, we have improved our capability to run international programs and our global profile. On September 10th, 2016, Schwarzman Scholars officially opened its inaugural class. On that occasion, President Xi Jinping and U.S. President Barack Obama sent their messages of congratulations.

The Global Innovation Exchange (GIX) Institute, a partnership between Tsinghua, the University of Washington in Seattle and Microsoft Corporation, welcomed the first group of students. Tsinghua entered into a comprehensive partnership with the University of Geneva (UNIGE) in Switzerland. Together, we will establish a research center on Sustainable Development Goals (SDG), and have set up a base where we train and prepare Chinese students for internships and employment opportunities at international organizations in Geneva. We have also entered into a strategic partnership with Politecnico di Milano, with whom the China-Italy Design Innovation Hub will be created. We have launched Tsinghua University Shenzhen Global Campus (TUSGC), a move to elevate Tsinghua's capabilities in cutting-edge innovation, international cooperation and cultivation of high-caliber talents.

Tsinghua has assisted students in participating in international academic and cultural exchange programs. 2016 witnessed another record high in the number of our students who traveled abroad on study tours. For the first time, we implemented the Tsinghua Global South Culture Immersion Series. We have made robust efforts to develop Ph.D. programs on developing-world research and encourage our students to take part in field studies in Africa, Europe and the Middle East. We proposed to create the Asian Universities Alliance (AUA) to shape the future landscape of Asia's higher education and address regional and global challenges. Tsinghua's initiative has caught on among 15 prestigious universities across Asia, including the University of Tokyo and the National University of Singapore. The AUA will be officially inaugurated at Tsinghua University on April 29th this year.

To become more humanity-oriented, we have strived to further enrich our credentials in humanities. To improve our students' literacy in humanities, we have worked to create synergies between liberal arts and science programs. We aim to nurture more well-rounded graduates who can truly live up to their mission in the future. Since its inception more than 1 year ago, the Humanities at Tsinghua Lecture Series has offered 8 lectures. Among the renowned scholars at Tsinghua who have shared their insights under the lecture series were Ge Fei, a literary giant, Chen Lai, a veteran researcher on China studies, Li Qiang, a sociologist, Wan Junren, an ethicist, Peng Lin, a historian, Wang Hui, a historian of thought, and Yan Xuetong, an authority on international relations. These endeavors have stimulated widespread interest in humanities on the campus and beyond.

On September 10th, 2016, the Art Museum was officially inaugurated, in a move to foster fusion between art and science. The facility serves to display the beauty of art and science alike. A new chapter has been opened in Tsinghua's efforts to embrace humanities and art subjects. We have worked hard to encourage reading on campus. For two years in a row, a book has been presented to every freshman as part of a common reading program. A recommended Tsinghua reading list has also been released. Our goal is to create a tranquil campus environment that is ideal for reading and learning.

By successfully hosting the 5th World Peace Forum, we have steadily enhanced our international profile. *Spring Breeze*, Professor Ge Fei's novel, was rated the novel of the year by *Dangdai Bimonthly*, a literature magazine. On March 30 this year, we convened another work conference dedicated to liberal arts 15 years after the last such event took place. We have prioritized the need to improve the quality of our basic liberal arts programs and sharpen our edge in applied liberal arts subjects.

All in all, the past year was another fruitful year for Tsinghua. On March 16th this year, Tsinghua University convened its first faculty and staff congress since 2011. The congress built up consensus and instilled greater confidence in our faculty and staff members. Together, we are taking solid steps to open up new prospects in Tsinghua's second century. I am convinced that with the joint efforts of our university community, Tsinghua will embrace an even brighter future.

Qiu Yong

President of Tsinghua University

4 月 21 日

采访、文字 | 拜喆喆

图片 | 宋晨

校园马拉松：奔跑吧，青春！

2017 年 4 月 15 日下午，U-RUN 2017 清华大学校园马拉松鸣枪开赛。对清华人而言，这是一场迎接活力春夏的仪式，更是一年一度为母校庆生的独特方式。

3000 余名清华师生、校友身着各色代表服饰，跑过人文日新的图书馆、历史悠久的西体育馆，经过标志性建筑二校门和新清华学堂，一路上感受和煦春风，掠过校园风光，身后是厚重历史底蕴与青春气息的交错共生。

学生们最常去的锻炼地点之一——紫荆操场是校园马拉松的起终点。在这里，身着橙色 T 恤的志愿者们是赛场上的一道风景，他们要负责赛场布置、秩序维护、成绩牌发放等一系列工作。生命科学学院 2014 级本科生陈文燕就是其中一员，当天下午北京气温达到 30℃，灿烂阳光下，她一直笑眯眯地解答参赛运动员们的疑问。“其实我本来报名参赛了，可惜人太多没报上，于是决定来当志愿者。”和陈文燕一样，还有不少同学通过这种特殊的“参赛”方式，投入到校园马拉松的活动中。

比赛前一天，像是为了弥补一个遗憾，陈文燕和另外几个没有成功报名的朋友一起绕着校园跑了七八公里。对她而言，在清华跑步是一种独特的体验：“在清华就算一个人跑，也会和其他跑者遇到，经过彼此的时候很开心，不会孤独。”跑步也成为她学习生活中的一种仪式：“实验的一个阶段结束，就会选择出来痛快地跑跑步，即使实验失败，心里也没那么难受了。”

在这场“嘉年华”里，学生并不是唯一的参与者。起终点线上站着一群裁判员，其中一位胸前挂着十几个名次牌，经过的学生们会开心地跟她打招呼，她是清华大学体育部教师郭惠珍。校园马拉松举办的这三年，她每年都担当裁判工作，“感觉一次比一次红火”。说起这样的变化，她的脸上不无自豪：“从校领导到团委、学生会，再到每一位老师同学，大家都在为传承清华体育精神尽自己的一份力量。”

清华的体育传统已然延续了百余年。早在 1912 年，清华就提出了“德智体并重”的育人方针；20 世纪 50 年代，蒋南翔校长提出“为祖国健康地工作五十年”，激励了一代又一代的清华师生；进入新世纪，“育人至上，体魄与人格并重”“无体育，不清华”成为清华体育发展的重要理念。

2015 年起，顺应同学们日益高涨的马拉松热情，清华决定举办校园马拉松活动，校园马拉松由此成为每年校庆的一项特色活动。对一些毕业生而言，参加一场马拉松是和母校告别必不可少的仪式——在毕业倒计时的日子里，重新用脚步丈量他们曾骑着脚踏车经过的一草一木、建筑风物，大学时光里的人、事、景如同快退一般闪过。站上终点线的那一刻，仿佛又重新回到起点，青春依旧恰如其分。

Tsinghua Campus Marathon: Youthful and Historical

U-RUN 2017 Tsinghua University Campus Marathon began under the firing shot on the afternoon of the 15th of April, 2017.

For Tsinghua, this is one way for them to celebrate their alma mater's birthday. This is a way to celebrate spring with much vitality.

More than 3,000 Tsinghua teachers and students and alumni dressed themselves in various colors for the marathon. They ran past the Library, the Western Stadium, Tsinghua's landmark- the Old Gate and the New Auditorium. Apart from the warm spring and the beautiful campus scenery, they also saw themselves becoming a part of Tsinghua: one that is youthful and historical.

Zijing playground is the most common place for students to exercise thus, it was the starting point and the end of the marathon. Here, volunteers in their orange T-shirts became a nice scenery during the race. They are responsible for the layout, for handing out various result cards and for maintaining order... Chen Wenyan from the School of Life Sciences is one of the volunteers. During that 30°C afternoon in Beijing, Chen answered questions from the participants with a big smile on her face. "In fact, I was supposed to be a part of the participants but since too many people registered for the marathon, I didn't make it onto the list, so in the end, I decided to be a volunteer." Chen was not alone in this since many others were the same.

The day before the marathon, Chen and a few others who didn't make it into the final marathon ran 7 to 8 kilometers around campus to make up for the miss. For Chen, running around Tsinghua is a unique experience. "Even if you are running by yourself in Tsinghua, you can still bump into other runners. You would never feel alone." Running became a part of her life. "After an experiment, I would go for a run so even if I'm upset, I would always feel slightly better than before."

Students were not the only participants in this marathon. A group of referees stood at the finish line and students would cheerfully greet one particular individual whenever they ran past her. Who is she? She is Guo Huizhen, a teacher from Tsinghua's Sports Department. For three consecutive years, she was the referee for the Campus Marathon. "Every year is bigger and better than before!" When talking about changes, she would always say with pride: "From leaders to those in the Communist Youth League to individual teachers and students, everyone is doing their best for Tsinghua's sports culture."

Tsinghua's sports tradition has continued for more than 100 years. As early as 1912, Tsinghua put forward a "moral, intellectual and physical" education policy. In the 1950s, President of Tsinghua, Mr Jiang Nanxiang, put forward his goals in "To work healthily for 50 years for our motherland" and inspired generations after generations of Tsinghua teachers and students for work in this sector. In the new century, "physical education and moral education" and "no sports, no Tsinghua" became important concepts for the development of sports at Tsinghua.

From 2015 onwards and in line with the growing popularity of the marathon, Tsinghua decided to include the marathon as a special event during Tsinghua's celebration month. For some graduates, attending the marathon is a crucial ritual and link with their alma mater. It is not only a countdown to one's final graduation but also a way for them to re-visit the campus, the scenery and the people. Time flies and this is particularly true for university life. The finish line is like a signal which marks the starting point of our youthful days... .

Translation and revision | Min Weiyuan

Image | Song Chen

4月24日

文字 | 张译丹

图片 | 梁晨

《算表》：历史留在清华简上的数学之美

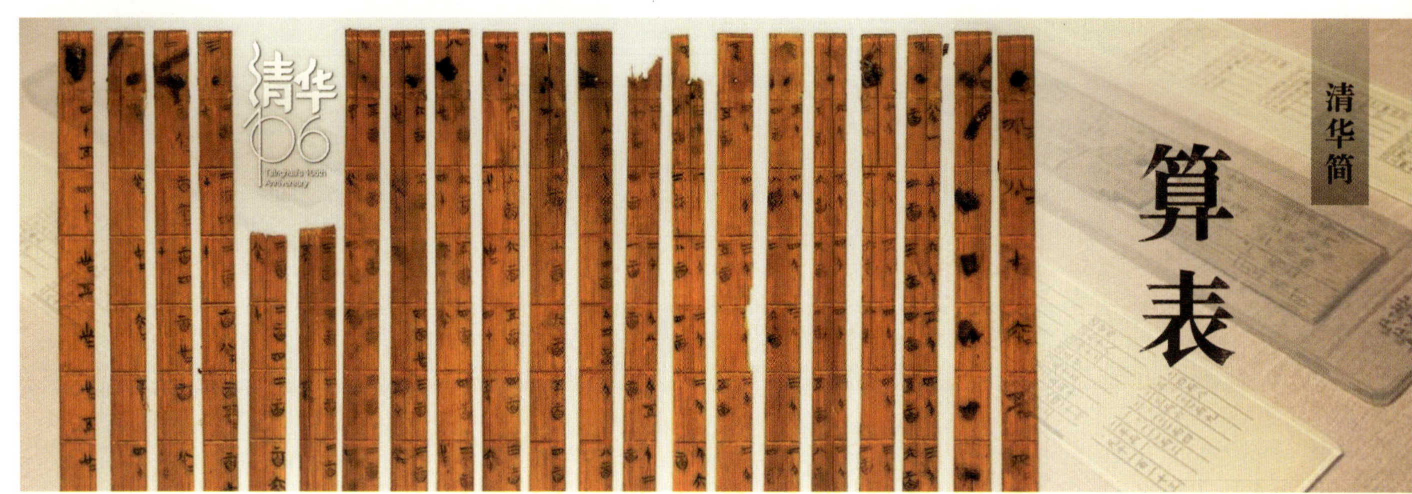

2017 年 4 月 23 日，清华大学举行第七辑清华简整理报告的成果发布会，清华简《算表》被吉尼斯世界纪录确认为“世界上最早的十进制乘法表”的认证仪式同时举行，作为古代文史研究热点的清华简再一次吸引了大众的目光。《算表》——这套被数学史专家认定为目前国内发现最早的实用算具，是中国乃至世界数学史上的重大发现。利用《算表》，不仅能够快速计算 100 以内的两个任意整数乘除，还能计算包含分数 1/2 的两位数乘法。

清华简是一批抄写于战国时期的竹简，总数约有 2500 枚，自从 2008 年入藏清华大学起，清华简就一直是古代文史学者的研究焦点。这批竹简由于很早就被随葬于地下，没有经历秦始皇焚书的劫难，因此保存了先秦典籍的原貌。

《算表》在清华得以“重见天日”，可以说是一种必然：拿到这批竹简后，由李学勤先生带领的出土文献研究与保护中心团队就紧锣密鼓地展开了辛勤的修复和调研工作。经过细心比对，团队在这批竹简中发现了一种形制很特殊的竹简，这类简共有 21 支，是迄今能见到的最早的计算器——《算表》。据李学勤先生介绍，《算表》中的 17 支保存完整，另外 4 支入藏时已有些残缺，但通过分析研究，还是能知道残缺部分的内容。

全国数学史学会理事长、中国科学院自然科学史研究所研究员郭书春说，《算表》能直接用于两位数的乘法及除法运算，还能对含有分数 1/2 的两位数进行乘法运算，“可能还可以用于开方运算，但还需进一步研究探索”。

清华出土文献研究与保护中心团队深知，《算表》的发现如一颗新星，照亮了中国乃至世界数学史上的一隅黑夜。而一旦锁定这颗星，看到的将会是更为浩瀚的璀璨星河。同时，团队也了然，《算表》科研工作任重道远：原简册已经散乱，整理者鉴于《算表》每简自上而下的数都按照自大到小的顺序排列，又仔细参照秦汉九九表，《算表》横向竹简的顺序也按照其相应数字由大到小排列，而全册背后有划痕可以作为原简册编联顺序的证据，经过多次反复检验，编联无误。清华大学多次主办《算表》学术研讨会，邀请权威大家共同参与其中，共同揭开藏在中国竹简中的奥秘。杨振宁先生参观研讨《算表》的性质、功能，丘成桐教授亲自考察《算表》，美国纽约市立大学数学史家道本周（Joseph Dauben）教授在访华时也指出：“这一发现意义非凡，它是世界上最早的十进制乘法表实物。”

李学勤先生和他带领的团队，用勤奋而富有创造性的研究拂去了笼罩在清华简上的一层层神秘面纱。清华简《算表》再一次让世界看到了古老中国的智慧，看到了穿越历史的数学之美。

Mathematical Trails Left Behind on Historical “Tsinghua Bamboo Slips”

On April 23rd, 2017, Tsinghua University presented a news conference on the 7th series of reports on Warring States bamboo slips (Tsinghua Slips for short). At the same time, the Times Table was confirmed by the Guinness world records as the “world's first decimal multiplication table” , meanwhile the certification ceremony was also held. As a grand attraction of research on ancient literature, Tsinghua Slips once again attracted public attention. Times Table, identified by mathematical historians as the earliest practical computing tool found in China, fills a gap which has hitherto existed in the mathematical literature of the Pre-Qin Period. It is a major discovery in the history of mathematics, not only in China but also in the entire world. The Times Table provides a method on the multiplication and division between two arbitrary integers within a 100 and even double-digit multiplication containing a fraction of 1/2.

The story of Times Table and Tsinghua University was an unexpected discovery. In July 2008, Tsinghua collected 2500 bamboo slips of Warring States, which were firstly found by tomb raiders and then were brought by a donor in the Hong Kong market.

The rediscovery of the Times Table in Tsinghua was inevitable. After the collection, researchers on unearthed literature spent a painstaking amount of effort on repairing and research work. They found 21 slips were in a unique form, which was the earliest calculator that had ever been seen - Times Table. From Prof. Li Xueqin, director of Tsinghua's Research and Conservation Center for Excavated Translation and revisions, 17 slips of Times Table were kept intact, the other four had been damaged, but they were able to know the contents of missing parts through analysis and study.

Guo Shuchun, chairman of the National Association for History of Mathematics, researcher of Institute of History of Natural Science, Chinese Academy of Sciences, thought that Times Table could be directly used towards the double-digit multiplication and division and even multiplication containing a fraction of 1/2, “It may also be used for root operation, but for that we still need to conduct further research” .

Relevant teams in Tsinghua University knew fully well that the discovery of Times Table was like a star, lighting up the night of the history of mathematics in China and also the entire world, once we locked the star, what we see would be a vast and bright galaxy. At the same time, the team was also adamant that there's a long way to go for the research work. The original volume has been scattered, researchers arranged the top-down numbers on each slip in a descending order, and they also sorted the lateral order of slips in the same way while referring to Qin-Han multiplication tables. The scratches on the reverse side of volume can be an evidence of original order; the order of the bamboo slips was corrected after the repeated tests. Tsinghua University has hosted several academic seminars on the topic of Times Table, inviting authorities to uncover the mystery hidden in the Chinese slips. Mr. Chen Ning Yang participated in the discussion of the property and function of the table; Prof. Shing-Tung Yau has personally visited the table; Prof. Joseph Dauben, mathematical historian from the City University of New York, pointed out during the visit to China, “This discovery is of great significance. It is the world's earliest decimal multiplication table.”

Times Table once again presented the world with the wisdom of ancient China, the mysterious beauty of mathematics and the historical power through time and space.

Translation and revision | Raj Lamar

Image | Liang Chen

4 月 25 日

原作者 | 赵晓杰、覃川

改编 | 刘书田

图片 | 宋晨

特别策划：不忘初心，砥砺前行——2016 年清华大学党的建设工作回顾

2016 年，是一个特殊而值得记忆的年份。中国共产党迎来了 95 岁的生日，清华大学党组织也已建立了整整 90 年。

从 2016 年 3 月起，学校按照中央部署，以党支部为基本单位，在全体党员中开展“学党章党规、学系列讲话、做合格党员”学习教育，推动党内教育从“关键少数”向广大党员拓展、从集中性教育向经常性教育延伸。

200 余场理论宣讲、11 期《学习参考资料》、3 辑《清华大学共产党员风采录》、全媒体学习内容推送、读原著学经典、听辅导报告、抄写党章、重温入党誓词、集体过“政治生日”、缅怀革命先烈、主题实践等丰富多彩的“两学一做”形式，让全体党员得到了系统性的学习，思想得到净化、精神得以提振，干事业、求发展的巨大热情进一步被激发出来。

这一年中，清华认真落实意识形态工作责任制，不断强化阵地管理。进一步加强干部队伍建设，落实从严要求，研究制定职务职级职数管理、领导干部选拔任用工作纪实、干部薪酬管理等制度，做到有据可查、责任明确。

这一年中，清华思想理论建设再绘新篇。各类干部学习班、支部书记研讨班、新任支委培训班和发展对象学习班内容丰富、形式多样。大力加强马克思主义学科建设和思想政治理论课建设，创办“清华思客”“微党建”“党建慕课”等新平台，精心打造新媒体矩阵，完善“合唱”“轮唱”机制。

这一年中，清华加强党风廉政建设，开展以“讲规矩、有纪律”为主题的宣传教育月活动。成立统一战线工作领导小组，召开全校统战工作会议和统一战线工作 80 周年纪念座谈会，制订《关于进一步加强和改进统一战线工作的若干意见》。

这一年中，清华大学坚持把立德树人作为中心环节，推动全员全过程全方位育人。扎实开展社会主义核心价值观教育，实施学生党建支持计划，持续开展“行健新百年，共筑中国梦”的主题教育，首次发布学生工作蓝皮书，积极推进学生荣誉体系与评价体系改革，构建全频谱学习发展支持体系，引领清华学子的逐梦之路。

这一年中，清华隆重举行庆祝中国共产党成立 95 周年暨纪念清华党组织建立 90 周年大会，扎实推进党的各项建设，并启动第十四次党员代表大会的筹备工作，为学校改革发展稳定提供了可靠的思想保障和强大的精神动力。

90 年风雨兼程，一代代清华共产党人不忘初心、砥砺前行，把理想信念镌刻得更加深邃而夺目……

Tsinghua University CPC Review 2016: Creating a World-class University with Chinese Characteristics

2016 was a special and memorable year. The Chinese Communist Party ushered in her 95th birthday. It also marked 90 years of the establishment of Tsinghua's CPC Party Committee.

More than 200 field theory talks, 11 editions of *References*, 3 series of *Records of Tsinghua University's Communist Party Members*, multimedia contents, original classics, counselling reports, papers, reviews, party oaths as well as collective celebrations to remember martyrs and various other activities not only boost the CPC spirit but also brings out the great enthusiasm needed from all to realize their individual dreams as well as those of their motherland.

This year, Tsinghua earnestly strengthened management, team building, the implementation of strict requirements as well as research and development duties, cadre selection and other management systems.

This year, Tsinghua's ideological and theoretical construction saw a new chapter. Various classes and workshops for cadres and secretaries are rich in content and diverse. The first "Campus Online Culture Festival" was also set up. This year, Tsinghua highlighted and made "rules and discipline" as the theme of many educational activities. Strict discipline is set to explore the overall management structure.

"To instill morality and cultivate talents" remain the crucial goal of Tsinghua. The theme "The new century is here for us to build a Chinese dream" saw tens of thousands of students ready to participate in social practice. The release of the first edition of the bluebook for student work laid a better path for Tsinghua students to follow so that they can find their dream.

This year, Tsinghua celebrated the 95th anniversary of the founding of the CPC. At the same time, Tsinghua commemorated the 90th anniversary of the establishment of Tsinghua's CPC committee.

In 2017, Tsinghua's teachers and students will stand in unity to uphold the spirit and goal of remembering the initial aspirations and to keep on moving forward. Let us work together to transform Tsinghua into a world-class university with Chinese characteristics!

Translation and revision | Min Weiyuan

Image | Song Chen

4月26日

原作者 | 周襄楠、徐静
改编 | 蒋佩妍
图片 | 宋晨

你的清华，为你订制，由你创造

置身园中观清华，时为岭，时为峰，可博大如鸿鹄高翔之青冥，可精深若蛟龙潜游之碧渊。所谓“孔子施教，各因其材”，清华为每一位学子私人订制的培养模式，为他们的成长之旅带去独一无二的风景。

如果你专注于学习，清华能够提供浩瀚的知识海洋。清华每年共有 9000 多门课程可选，济济名师倾囊相授。53 门课程入选教育部 2016 年 7 月公布的首批“国家级精品资源共享课”名单，网络资源免费向公众开放。截至 2016 年秋季，清华共上线 196 门慕课课程，连续两年位居全球高校之首。此外，清华已经开设 121 门混合式教学课程，实现了线上慕课与线下讲授讨论的结合，给予学子更大的学习自由度。2016 年，新雅书院正式面向高考学生招生，为入选学子按照学科交叉、大类融合的原则安排宿舍，创建师生共有、共建、共享的文化场所和公共空间，实乃读书佳地。

如果你热衷于“不走寻常路”，清华能够安放你充满活力的青春。清华在全国率先推出的技术创新创业辅修专业，由经管学院发起成立的创新创业教育平台 x-lab，基础工业训练中心主办的 iCenter、i-Space、创 +，以及清华与企业联手开辟的“兴趣团队”都可以帮助学子实现创新创业梦想。在 2016 年第二届“互联网 +”大学生创新创业大赛中，清华共有 3 支团队从 12 万余个报名项目之中脱颖而出，进入全国总决赛，并获得一金二银的优异成绩，获奖数量在全国高校里名列前茅。

如果你渴望背上行囊出国闯荡，清华能够打开通往四海八荒的“传送门”。2016 年，清华有近 2400 名在读本科生、4600 余名在读研究生通过多种方式踏出国门。仅国际联合培养项目一项，清华 2016 年就新增了 11 个国际化项目。还有 2016 年秋季学期刚开学的苏世民书院、首批学生已经入学的位于西雅图的全球创新学院、蓬勃发展的清华 - 伯克利深圳学院，也让清华学子在读研时拥有更多选择。

如果你喜欢在实验室或书斋里埋头研究，清华能够带领你认识一大群学术达人。清华 SRT 计划（大学生研究训练计划）到 2016 年已推行 20 年，60% 以上的本科生在读期间参加过一项以上的项目。清华还于 2016 年正式推出荣誉学位制度，希望通过高挑战度课程的学习和科研创新训练来提高学生的学术志趣。

回首 2016，清华“私人订制”硕果累累；展望 2017，清华“私人订制”将为学子提供更多可能。

Tsinghua's "Personal Tailor" Programs Offer Infinite Possibilities

When viewing the scenery in Tsinghua, the views vary from place to place. The scenery, as the culture of Tsinghua University, is broad and profound. As Confucius teaches students in accordance of their aptitudes, Tsinghua provides each student with distinctive personal training modes, giving unique landscape on their journey of growth.

If you focus on learning, Tsinghua presents you with a vast ocean of knowledge. Each year, Tsinghua offers you more than 9000 available courses with valuable instructions from numerous top-notch teachers. 53 courses have been listed in the first "National Excellent Sharing Courses" announced by Ministry of Education in July 2016. The network resources are free and available to the public. By the autumn of 2016, Tsinghua had launched 196 online MOOC courses, the largest amount among that of worldwide colleges and universities in the recent two years. In addition, Tsinghua has opened 121 mixed teaching courses, achieving a combination of online courses and off-line lectures, guaranteeing students greater flexibility in their studies. In 2016, the Xinya College enrolled its first cohort of student from High School Graduates. The College arranged students' accommodation according to the principle of cross-discipline and subject fusion, producing a cultural venue and public space which is owned, built and shared by teachers and students, constituting a palace that is perfect for learning.

If you are keen on unusual ways, Tsinghua can steer your ambitious youth. Tsinghua firstly introduced the minor of technical innovation and entrepreneurship. School of Economics and Management has launched the x-lab, an innovation and entrepreneurship education platform; Fundamental Industry Training Center has also hosted the iCenter, i-Space, i+; and the "Interest Team" was jointly developed by Tsinghua University and enterprises; all projects above help students realize the dream of innovation and entrepreneurship. In the second Internet + College Students Innovation and Entrepreneurship Competition in 2016, 3 teams from Tsinghua stood out from over 120,000 projects and entered the national finals, they won one gold and two silver prizes, reaching the top place in national universities.

If you desire to go aboard for adventures, Tsinghua can open you the portal to the entire world. In 2016, nearly 2400 undergraduate students and over 4600 graduate students in Tsinghua University have stepped out of the country in a variety of ways. Only in the term of international cooperative training, Tsinghua added 11 international projects in 2016. Other projects like the Schwarzman Scholars opened in 2016 autumn, Global Innovation Exchange in Seattle, which has enrolled its first cohorts of students, and the well-developed Tsinghua-Berkeley Shenzhen Institute, have also provided more options for Tsinghua graduate students.

If you love working in the laboratory or doing study research, Tsinghua will introduce you to a large group of academic experts. By 2016, Tsinghua SRT program (Students Research Training program) has already been implemented for twenty years; over 60% undergraduate students have participated in more than one project during their study. Besides, Tsinghua launched the honorary degree system officially in 2016, allowing students to improve their academic interests by learning quite challenging courses and innovative research training.

Looking back at 2016, "personal tailor" in Tsinghua has made great achievements. While looking forward to 2017, "personal tailor" in Tsinghua will provide students with more possibilities and opportunities.

Translation and revision | Raj Lamar

Image | Song Chen

4 月 27 日

供稿 | 数学系

文字 | 刘兰

图片 | 宋晨

清华大学数学学科 90 周年庆：歌行砥砺，华章再续

四月的清华园桃红柳绿，春意正浓，清华大学数学学科迎来了建立 90 周年的庆祝活动。数学系和丘成桐数学科学中心共同举办庆典大会、系庆学术论坛、系庆晚会等系列活动，海内外历届系友共襄盛举，与在校师生共睹清华数学学科新貌，同叙师生情谊。

从 1927 年清华大学数学学科创建到 1952 年全国高等院校院系调整，清华数学一直是中国数学的一面旗帜，涌现出以陈省身、华罗庚为代表的蜚声中外的数学大师。经历了从院系调整到复建的特殊历史时期，1979 年清华大学成立应用数学系，1999 年更名为数学科学系，清华数学学科不断发展壮大。

过去十年间，清华数学学科在更高水平上进入了快速健康发展的新阶段。清华数学成为高端人才培养和前沿科学研究的主导学科之一，也是国家基础科学人才培养和学术研究的重要基地、清华大学建设世界一流大学的重要基础。

作为学校发展数学学科的重大战略举措，清华大学数学科学中心于 2009 年 12 月正式成立，聘请国际著名数学大师丘成桐先生担任中心主任。为推动中国数学学科的发展，教育部于 2014 年底正式批准依托清华成立“清华大学丘成桐数学科学中心”。在丘成桐先生的指导下，清华数学系对人才培养和课程设置进行改革，教育部创新人才培养计划——清华数学学堂班由丘成桐担任首席教授。

在加强本科生和研究生培养的同时，以数学系和数学科学中心为基地，学校建立了包括东润丘成桐中学科学奖、丘成桐大学生数学竞赛、新世界数学奖、晨兴数学奖、四位数学大师冠名讲座、华人数学联盟及世界华人数学家大会等“一条龙”人才发掘培养和科研交流平台。

栉风沐雨九十载，歌行砥砺；春华秋实满庭芳，华章再续。在新的时期和机遇下，清华数学有信心建设成为国际数学领域优秀人才培养和原创科学研究的第一流基地，也将会是千千万万清华数学人永远热爱的家园。

Tsinghua's Mathematical Sciences Discipline Celebrated Its 90th Anniversary

April ushered in vibrant colors, spring is in the air. Tsinghua's Mathematical Sciences Discipline saw countless activities being held to commemorate the Discipline's 90th Anniversary. The Department of Mathematical Sciences along with Yau Mathematical Sciences Center jointly celebrated academic forums, events and much more so that friends both at home and abroad were able to come together to remember the history, the current look and the future of the Discipline.

Tsinghua University's Mathematical Sciences Discipline is one of the leading disciplines of talent cultivation and cutting-edge scientific research. Whether it is the construction of Tsinghua as a world-class university or the development of Chinese Mathematical Sciences or the cultivation of leading talents, the Discipline has always made continuous contributions.

Tsinghua's Mathematical Sciences Discipline has a glorious and long history. In the early years, the Discipline made great success from 1927 to 1952. It also experienced special stages of adjustment and reconstruction from 1952 to 1979. In 1979, Tsinghua set up a Department of Applied Mathematics and then changed the name to the Department of Mathematical Sciences in 1999. This marked a new stage of vigorous development. It has been proven that with continuous efforts, this Department has developed into China's top Department for Mathematical Sciences.

In the past decade, the Discipline has developed at a rapid and smooth pace. It has launched itself into various stages. Among them, the Mathematical Science Center was formally established in December 2009 and internationally renowned mathematician Shing-Tung Yau became the center's director. At the end of 2014, the Ministry of Education formally approved the establishment of "Tsinghua University's Yau Mathematical Sciences Center" . The Department of Mathematical Sciences also engaged Shing-Tung Yau as Chief Professor of "Mathematics Class of Tsinghua Xuetang" .

It has been 90 years and the song will only continue. Regardless of the seasonal changes, new periods and opportunities will always be waiting for the Discipline. The 90th Anniversary not only give us a chance to reflect upon the past history, the struggles and developments, and it also provide us with much confidence and ambition for the Discipline's better future!

Contributor | Department of Mathematical Sciences

Translation and revision | Min Weiyuan

Image | Song Chen

4月28日

文字丨梁乐萌
图片丨赵存存、李娜

世界，清华与你同行

2016 年的“马约翰杯”篮球赛场上，几个肤色各异、衣着统一的身影格外引人注目。他们身着蓝色队服，衣服上印有相同的五个字——“苏世民书院”。

2016 年 8 月，来自 31 个国家的 110 位年轻人从全球申请者中脱颖而出，成为首届苏世民学者，进入苏世民书院学习。作为清华新百年发展的重要举措，苏世民学者项目旨在培养具有全球视野并理解中国的未来世界领导者。2016 年秋季学期，苏世民书院共接待来访交流 3000 余人，包括各国政要、大学校长、院长和知名学者等，成为清华展示自我、面向世界的一扇窗口。

在 2016 年 3 月的博鳌亚洲论坛上，清华宣布发起亚洲大学联盟。一年来，学校领导率团访问泰国、印度尼西亚、马来西亚、新加坡等地，一次次握手交谈，一笔笔描绘出亚洲高等教育崛起的愿景。2017 年 4 月 29 日，亚洲大学联盟成立大会暨首次峰会将在清华举行。正如邱勇校长所说，“高等教育不应该只有西方一种声音”，为实现持久和平、共同发展的“亚洲梦”，清华责无旁贷扛起了高等教育的引领之旗。

2016 年，具有里程碑意义的《清华大学全球战略》制订并启动实施。从课程融合、项目合作到校地共建，清华将“引进来”与“走出去”有机结合，全面提升国际化办学水平。全球创新学院首栋教研大楼在西雅图正式奠基，主办首届“中以大学校长论坛”和“中以创新论坛”，倡议发起“中英高等教育人文联盟”，与深圳市合作共建清华大学深圳国际校区……一系列国际化办学举措铺陈开来，有力提升了清华的国际影响力。

而教育的国际化并不是简单的你来我往，更是深度交流与融合。2016 年，清华从学校和院系层面共同努力，搭建平台，拓展资源，通过交换学习、假期实践、海外实习等项目，帮助年轻人将视线从菁菁校园投射到全人类共同的命运。17 位清华人利用假期前往东非，探察这片神秘土地上的中国元素。当贫民窟孩子口中喊出“你好，中国”时，他们感动得热泪盈眶。与此同时，越来越多的留学生走进中国农村，感知基层的呼吸……

在 2016 年苏世民书院开学典礼上，校长邱勇引用了惠特曼的诗句：“把所有的过去都置于身后，我们来到了一个更新、更强大的世界，一个多样化的世界。”与世界同行，越来越国际化的清华将为学子放眼全球、放飞梦想提供更加广阔的舞台。

Tsinghua and the World: Looking Back at 2016

At a basketball tournament during the Ma Yuehan Cup sporting event, one can't help but notice a few players on court. They are of different skin colors. On the back of their team jerseys were clearly printed the words "Schwarzman College" .

In August, 2016, students from 31 countries, totaling 110 were admitted into the Schwarzman Scholars Program. The Schwarzman Scholars program is an important milestone in Tsinghua's "New Century" toward globalization. Its aim is to cultivate future world leaders with a global view and an understanding of China. In fall of 2016, the Schwarzman College received more than 3,000 visitors, including former state leaders, university presidents, academic deans and renowned scholars. The college is the world's window into Tsinghua.

Earlier that same year in March, during the Bo'ao Forum for Asia in Hainan, China, Tsinghua University announced the initiative to establish the Asian Universities Alliance. Within a year, Tsinghua officials have visited Thailand, Indonesia, Malaysia and Singapore to form partnerships, paving the way for the rise of universities in Asia. The first summit of the Asian Universities Alliance will be held in Tsinghua University on April 29th this year. As the President of Tsinghua University Qiu Yong said "Higher education should not only bear the voice of the West" , To prolong harmony and achieve a collective rise toward an Asian dream, Tsinghua has shouldered on the task of leading the progress of higher education in Asia.

From the diversification of classes, cooperation in academic programs to co-establishing campuses, 2016 was a landmark year for Tsinghua in attracting foreign talents and going global, forwarding the university's path toward globalization. The year 2016 also saw the ground-breaking of the first teaching and research building for the Global Innovation Exchange in Seattle. Tsinghua also organized the first "China-Israel University Presidents Forum" and "China-Israel Innovation Forum" and built the Shenzhen Global Campus. These are all a step forward in Tsinghua's vision for globalization.

However, the globalization of education is not simply a matter of collaborations between universities. It's also about broad-based exchanges and integration. In 2016, through the work at the university administration and departmental level, the university established platforms and increased funding for student and scholar exchange programs, practical training during semester breaks, and study aboard programs. These have broadened the views of Tsinghua students, bringing their learning from the heart of Tsinghua campus to the world. During the same time, more and more international students are going into the villages of China, experiencing life at the grassroots level. Also, during the winter break this year, 17 Tsinghua teachers and students traveled to East Africa, visiting Chinese companies and operations in that little-known place. When the local African children greeted them with "Hello, China" , the students brimmed with joy and appreciation for the warm welcome.

During Schwarzman College's inaugural commencement ceremony in 2016, Tsinghua University President Qiu Yong quoted Walt Whitman: "All the past we leave behind; We debouch upon a newer, mightier world, varied world." Walking in step with the world, a more globalized Tsinghua will give scholars a grand global vision and a place that enables dreams to soar.

Translation and revision | Alexis See Tho

Image | Zhao Cuncun, Li Na

4月29日

文字丨张智伟

图片丨宋晨

清华发起成立亚洲大学联盟

2017 年 4 月 29 日，由清华发起成立的亚洲大学联盟（简称“AUA”）在清华园宣告诞生。除了联盟成立大会和校长论坛，AUA 高等教育展、青年创新工作坊等系列活动丰富了首届 AUA 峰会的形式与内涵，也为即将到来的清华 106 周年校庆增添了开放创新的色彩。

在一个多月前举行的博鳌亚洲论坛 2017 年年会上，清华大学校长邱勇宣布了亚洲大学联盟即将成立的消息。作为特邀嘉宾，邱勇在“未来的教育”分论坛上指出，亚洲正在经历快速发展时期，亚洲大学应该抓住机遇提升教育和科研水平，充分发挥人才培养、科学研究、社会服务、文化传承创新和国际交流合作的职能，为地区发展和全球治理贡献亚洲智慧。为此，清华大学联合亚洲十余所代表性高校共同成立亚洲大学联盟。联盟将促进亚洲高等教育领域的合作创新与文化交流，共同培养根植于亚洲多元化文化环境的青年领袖人才，整体提升亚洲区域高等教育质量和科技创新能力，推动亚洲高等教育的崛起。

邱勇校长表示：“高等教育不应该只有一种声音，西方的教育有成功的地方，但是我们认为东方的教育思想也有很多值得大家传播、传承和珍惜的内容。”2016 年春季，清华大学对外宣布将牵头发起成立亚洲大学联盟，得到了亚洲众多高校的积极响应。2016 年 9 月，联盟筹备会议在北京成功举行，会议审议通过了联盟章程草案，并就联盟的组织架构、运行模式和项目活动等达成了共识。

亚洲大学联盟创始成员包括清华大学、北京大学、香港科技大学、韩国国立首尔大学、日本东京大学、泰国朱拉隆功大学、缅甸仰光大学、马来西亚马来亚大学、新加坡国立大学、印度尼西亚大学、斯里兰卡科伦坡大学、印度理工学院孟买分校、阿联酋大学、沙特国王大学与哈萨克斯坦纳扎尔巴耶夫大学 15 所高校。

作为联盟发起者和创始成员之一，致力于走向“更国际、更创新、更人文”的清华大学正以更加开放的姿态吸引着世人的目光。2016年，清华首次制订并启动实施《清华大学全球战略》。

大学是传承文明、播种希望的殿堂，是培育和实现梦想的地方。面向未来，清华和她的伙伴们抱持着同样的初衷——虽然来自不同国家和地区的高校在历史、文化、民族和传统上存在多样性，但相信亚洲大学联盟可以通过更加创新的方式，团结发展、互相支持，在大学走向未来的变化阶段，通过亚洲大学之间的交流合作，提升亚洲大学在全球范围的话语权，共同培养面向未来的杰出人才，对亚洲乃至世界的发展产生积极影响。

AUA Officially Launched at Tsinghua

On April 29th, 2017, Fifteen Asian universities including Tsinghua University have launched the Asian Universities Alliance (AUA) in Beijing. In addition to the establishment of the Alliance and the Presidents' Forum, AUA Higher Education Exhibition, Youth Innovation Workshops and other activities enriched the first AUA Summit. These inaugural events hosted by Tsinghua have added even more reasons to celebrate Tsinghua's 106th Anniversary.

At the annual meeting of 2017 Boao Forum in March, Tsinghua University President Qiu Yong announced the news of the establishment of AUA. As a special guest of the "Future Education" forum, President Qiu Yong mentioned that Asia is experiencing rapid development and Asian universities should seize the opportunity to enhance levels in education and research. Asian Universities should also play a bigger role in training, scientific research, social services as well as the promotion of cultural heritage, international exchanges and cooperation. Motivated by this Tsinghua University along with fourteen other Asian universities jointly established the AUA which promotes cooperation and cultural exchanges and aims to contribute to regional development and global governance. Together, the universities cultivate leaders of tomorrow and ensure that they are deeply rooted in the diverse cultural environment of Asia. Together, they will promote the quality of higher education and technological innovation and ensure that higher education in Asia continues to develop in the future.

"Higher education should not have only one voice. Western education is also successful but I do believe that there are Eastern educational philosophy and heritage that deserves to be cherished also." said President Qiu. In September 2016, AUA's preparatory meeting was successfully held in Beijing. Organizational structure, operational model, project activities and many other factors were discussed and a consensus was reached.

The founding members of the Asian Universities Alliance includes Tsinghua University, Peking University, Hong Kong University of Science and Technology, South Korea's National University of Seoul, Japan's Tokyo University, Thailand's Chulalongkorn University, Myanmar's Yangon University, Malaysia's University of Malaya, National University of Singapore, University of Indonesia, Sri Lanka's University of Colombo, India's Institute of Technology Mumbai, UAE University, King Saudi University and Kazakhstan's Nazarbayev University.

As one of the founding members of the alliance, Tsinghua University is striving to become more innovative, more international and more humanity-oriented. Tsinghua attracts the world through an open manner and in 2016, Tsinghua issued and launched the first *Tsinghua University Global Strategy*.

University is the cradle of talents and a witness to the developments of civilization. They play a huge role in cultivating and realizing dreams. Facing the future, Tsinghua and her partners holds the same intentions - although colleges and universities from different countries vary in their history, culture and traditions, they also share much in common. AUA is seen as ground-breaking way for collaboration and development. Through exchanges and multi-level cooperation between universities in Asia, outstanding talents will not only contribute to the development of Asia but also have a positive impact on the world.

Translation and revision | Min Weiyuan

Image | Song Chen

4月30日

文字 | 刘书田

图片 | 唐蓓蓓

摄影 | 李睿、李兆麒

清华大学106周岁生日快乐！

走过106年风风雨雨，清华园又一次迎来一年中最美的时节。

在校庆日里，体育运动总是最好的“集结号”。正值“马约翰杯”田径运动会六十周年，“为祖国健康工作五十年”的口号早已深入清华学子的内心。灿烂的阳光下，学生们聚集在东大操场，共同享受运动的激情和快乐，回归体育的精神，收获意志的胜利，奔向清华更加美好的明天。

在校庆日里，丰富多彩的学生社团大放异彩。“清社年华”学生社团校庆嘉年华是每年不可缺少的学生活动。这场由近100家学生社团共同筹办的盛大“游园会”，分布在紫荆操场、大礼堂、新清华学堂等地，不仅为同学们带来一场有趣的社团文化盛宴，更唤起了校友们对于社团活动的青葱记忆。

无论是各条战线上的校友，还是在校的师生，创新的因子始终渗透在共同的血脉中。校庆当天，各类学术论坛相继举行，一大批实验室对外开放，以学术创新点染春天的暖风。今年的“挑战杯”学生课外学术科技作品展吸引了来自各院系、兴趣团队、企业等的300多件作品参展，对接创意大赛决赛、创业嘉年华，共同成为校庆日一道靓丽的风景线。

在小树林里，在大礼堂前，在新清华学堂广场上，一场场音乐会、演出和联欢活动精彩纷呈。国标队翩翩起舞，民乐队奏响乐章，校友合唱团、教师合唱团、学生艺术团相映生辉，欢快的音符在春风中回旋飘扬。

无论是走进开放的图书馆和实验室，徜徉于学生社团嘉年华的缤纷热情，还是流连在各种学术、文化或艺术展览中，回家的校友们无处不能感受到古老校园的全新风采，无处不能感受到“90后”学子们的青春律动。

随着不断向“更创新、更国际、更人文”的方向迈进，古老的清华园逐渐成为一座焕发国际魅力的家园，清华精神在校友心中薪火不灭。因为在今天，我们有个共同的名字——清华人！

Tsinghua University: Happy 106th Birthday!

After 106 years of ups and downs, Tsinghua ushered in the most beautiful season of the year again.

On this anniversary, sports are always the best event for collective celebration. Ma Yuehan Cup for track and fields is in its 60th anniversary. "To work healthily for 50 years for our motherland" is no longer just a slogan but a philosophy entrenched deep in our hearts. Under the bright sun, the students gathered at the Eastern Playground and they ran. They ran around the picturesque campus. They enjoy the joy of sports and regain that energetic and active spirit. They work together towards a better tomorrow, a better Tsinghua.

It is during such festive days that all sorts of wonderful student associations seized their chance to shine. The Tsinghua Student Associations Carnival is a must during such activities every year. Nearly a hundred student organizations jointly organized the grand Party which made its mark at Zijing, the playgrounds, the Auditorium, the New Auditorium and other places. Not only does it offer us an interesting cultural feast for the students, it also evokes memories of their university days for the numerous alumni.

Whether it is the alumni or teachers, or students, innovation and that Tsinghua spirit is that bond that always link everyone together. During the Anniversary, Schools and Departments held academic forums. Many laboratories were also open to boost academic innovation.

This is the new Spring. This year's "Challenge Cup" which features the science and technology exhibition from the students' extracurricular activities attracted more than 300 entries from various schools, departments, interest groups, enterprises as well as exhibitors. Such creative and entrepreneurial contests along with Tsinghua's Anniversary is a beautiful scenery for all to enjoy.

In the gentle breeze, Tsinghua held many performances. The Tsinghua Alumni Choir, the Teachers' Choir, The Students' Art Troupe, music concerts, ballroom dancing, folk music and much more added great happiness to the warm atmosphere!

Whether it is walking around the libraries and laboratories or witnessing the enthusiasm from the student carnival, or lingering around the calligraphy and photography exhibition, alumni can sense the energy of the young Tsinghua students and the familiar campus.

With constant changes and under the goals of creating a "more innovative, internationalized and humanity-oriented" Tsinghua, the ancient Campus is gradually becoming a charming international home for all. The only thing that stays the same is that Tsinghua spirit which is alive in the hearts of every alumni. Today, we have a common name - the people from Tsinghua!

Translation and revision | Min Weiyuan

Image | Tang Beibei

Photographer | Li Rui, Li Zhaoqi

5月8日

原作者 | 刘蔚如

改写 | 杨茂艺

图片 | 薛雅芳

清华科研关键词：改革·创新·引领

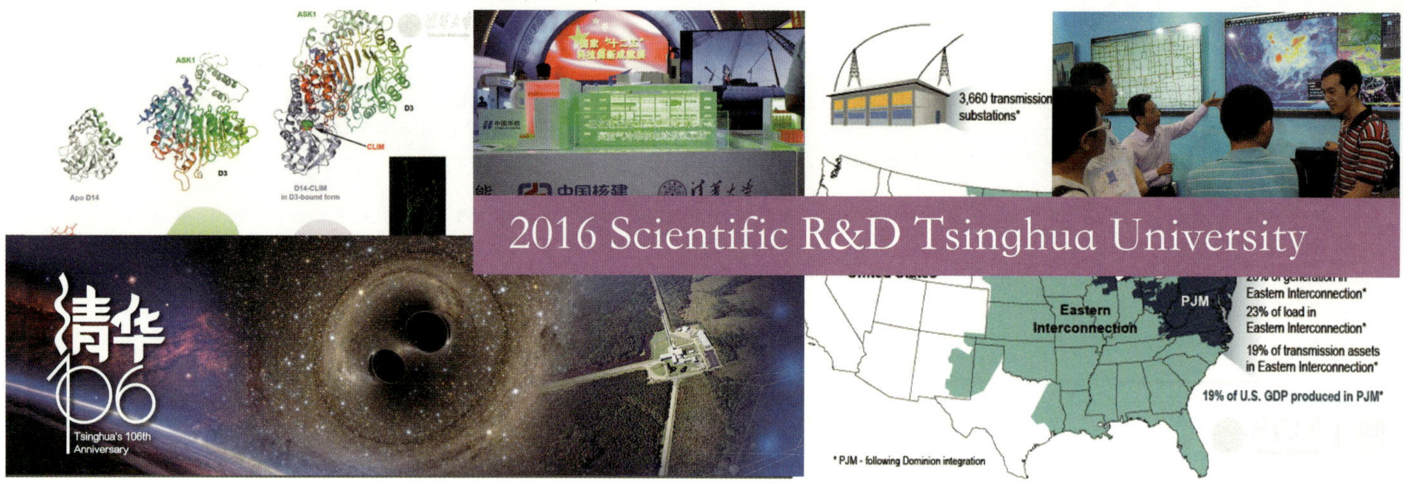

2016 年，在国家科技体制改革全面推进的背景下，清华召开了第 17 次科研工作讨论会，发布《清华大学关于深化科研体制机制改革的若干意见》，清华科研体制机制改革正式启动，聚焦学科交叉、军民融合、前沿部署和科技成果转化，创造有利于创新的学术生态。

这一年，在前沿基础研究领域，清华共申请国家自然科学基金 1646 项，立项 591 项，位居全国第一。11 名教师获得杰青基金资助，17 名教师获得优青基金资助；重点项目（含联合基金）、重大项目（含中德合作）共 88 项获得资助；在延续原有的 6 个创新群体的基础上，又新增创新群体 2 个。

过去一年里，清华师生取得了一系列科研成果，在国际顶级学术期刊发文多篇，SCI 论文数量保持增长。施一公研究组在《科学》连续发表研究长文，报道剪接反应中 5 个关键状态剪接体复合物的高分辨率结构；向烨研究组与合作者在《科学》在线发文阐述了两种针对埃博拉病毒人源中和性抗体的作用机制。李群仰课题组研究了界面摩擦对于二维材料的独特机理，荣登《自然》；周树云、陈曦等首次发文报道破坏洛伦兹不变性的第二类外尔半金属二碲化钼的拓扑费米弧实验证据，见于《自然物理》。

时空是不变的主题，计算机则是人类智力飞跃的见证。2016 年，清华作为激光干涉引力波天文台（LIGO）科学合作组织（LSC）在中国大陆的唯一成员，为引力波信号的探测做出了贡献；薛巍、付昊桓团队的“千万核可扩展大气动力学全隐式模拟”论文荣获国际高性能计算应用领域最高奖——“戈登·贝尔”奖。

面向国家战略需求，清华继续推进与大型企业的合作，为提高我国经济社会发展水平做出积极贡献。清华控股旗下北京辰安科技股份有限公司研发的厄瓜多尔国家安全指挥控制系统在厄瓜多尔抗震救灾中发挥了重要作用，得到了习近平总书记的充分肯定；由核研院主持设计的全球首座模块式高温气冷堆示范工程首台主设备压力容器在山东荣成石岛湾核电站顺利吊装就位，60 万千瓦级模块式高温气冷堆核电站方案发布，标志着我国高温气冷堆技术从“863”时期的“跟跑”位置，到示范工程阶段的“领跑”位置，再到即将跨入商用阶段。一旦建成，它将成为国际首个商用高温气冷堆核电站。

人文社会科学领域也成果辈出。这一年，清华获国家社科基金重大招标项目立项 11 项，立项总数在全国排名第一。格非的《望春风》以最高票当选“《当代》长篇小说年度最佳”。

2016 年，清华 19 项科技成果获国家科学技术奖励，杨知行教授领衔的团队获国家科技进步奖一等奖。薛其坤院士获得首届未来科学大奖，施一公院士获得何梁何利基金科学与技术成就奖，钱颖一教授获 2016 年中国经济学奖……

知识无涯而令人代代探索，清华尊重一切可贵的智慧，也愿秉持开放合作的心态，在各学科前沿领域继续探索前行。清华的科研工作将继续强调“尊重学术权力、强化问题导向、促进开放合作、建设创新文化”的基本原则，全力推进科研体制机制改革，实现科学研究从跟踪到引领的跨越。

Overview: Tsinghua Innovative Research 2016

2016 is a year which saw comprehensive deepening of reforms in science and technology systems. From the central government to the local governments, from scientific research institutions to individual workers, policies surrounding science and technology has seen many fresh looks.

This year, in the forefront of basic research, Tsinghua Scholars applied for a total of 1646 National Natural Science Funds and established a total of 591 projects which puts Tsinghua first in the country. There are 11 teachers who received funding from "The National Fund for Distinguished Young Scholars" and 17 more who received funding from "The National Science Fund for Excellent Young Scholars" . Some of the key projects are united fund, some major projects are often international cooperation such as Sino-German joint projects. In total, 88 projects have been funded and on the basis of 6 innovative projects, 2 more has been added.

In the past year, Tsinghua's teachers and students have made a series of scientific research achievements. Shi Yigong's research group in *Science* published 5 conclusions on spliceosome while Xiang Ye's research discussed human antibody when faced with Ebola. Li Qunyang studied the unique mechanism of interfacial friction for two-dimensional materials and saw his work being published in *Nature*. Zhou Shuyun and Chen Xi reported on the first experimental evidence of the break-up of the Lorentz invariance and saw their work being published in *Nature Physics*.

In 2016, as the only member from Mainland China in LIGO, Tsinghua has made important contributions to the detection of gravitational wave signals. Xue Wei and Fu Haohuan's "Ten million Nuclear Extensible Atmospheric Simulation" project took home the ACM Gordon Bell Prize.

Tsinghua continues to lead and align herself with national strategy. Tsinghua promotes the cooperation of large enterprises with national projects and continues to make positive contributions to China's economic and social development level. One example is Beijing Chen An Technology Co., Ltd. who played an important role in the command and control system in earthquake relief in Ecuador was praised by president Xi Jinping.

When it comes to the field of humanities and social sciences, various major projects has taken first spot in the nation. 12 new scientific research institutions saw the emergence of many outstanding talents. Professor Ge Fei's novel *Spring Breeze* received the highest vote in *Dangdai* bimonthly and took home the "Top Novel" in our times.

In 2016, Tsinghua saw a total of 19 scientific and technological achievements with Tsinghua's professors such as Xue Qikun, Shi Yigong, Qian Yingyi and others being awarded national awards.

Knowledge is limitless and so is exploration. Tsinghua respects all valuable wisdom and is more than willing to uphold a style that is open and cooperative. This way, exploration and achievements continues.

Translation and revision | Min Weiyuan

Image | Xue Yafang

5月9日

行健新百年，共筑中国梦

供稿 | 校团委
文字 | 杨鹏成
图片 | 李娜

2016年，清华大学学生工作取得了累累硕果。清华大学立足于“价值塑造，能力培养，知识传授”三位一体的育人理念，紧密围绕学校人才培养的根本任务，在引导学生成长、助力学生发展中不遗余力、砥砺前行。

这一年，清华的思想政治教育更贴近学生生活。“深根计划”“固本计划”“领雁计划”等计划开展了一系列富有特色的活动，通过理论知识和社会实践两方面对学生进行思想政治教育。在思想政治宣传方面，以“小五爷园”“清华研读间”为代表的新媒体平台建设不断完善，传播清华精神，书写清华故事。其中，人物报道编辑成册，出版《清华少年说》一书，反响热烈。

学校继续加大对学术科研的投入力度：清华大学团委主办的“闯世界”计划共支持287名本科生前往全球84所大学或研究机构开展学术研修，每名学生平均研修61天；依托科研院投入500万元经费支持的大学生学术研究推进计划，年度支持项目147项，发表论文41篇，申请专利17项；“巅峰学者实验室”计划则专门支持研究生赴诺奖实验室开展短期访学。

清华创业教育和指导工作成绩卓著，获评全国高校创新创业典型经验高校。学生的创意想法受到更多人的关注。“脑泡”创新创意平台搭建上线，注册用户3200余人，累计发布创意1050条。“Seek for Seed”研究生创意大赛，开展线上创意众筹活动，推动创新灵感落地生根。在2016“创青春”大赛中，清华大学代表队取得了五金一银、全国第二名的优异成绩。

体育场上学生屡创佳绩，创造历史。首次打进中国大学生篮球联赛CUBA总决赛的清华大学男子篮球队，一举夺得2016年CUBA总冠军。清华女篮也荣获CUBA全国季军，取得历史最好成绩。清华大学田径队获得第54届首都高校田径运动会冠军，实现了甲组团体总分“七连冠”。“中国女排清华行”活动在与师生共话女排精神的同时，发出了“自强时代，自信中国”的时代强音。

清华原创话剧《马兰花开》走进中国人民解放军海军东海舰队，为海军官兵完美呈现了正式公演的第50场演出。学生艺术团获得北京大学生音乐节合唱、交响、民乐比赛一等奖第一名，并先后访问台湾大学、新竹清华大学、伦敦政治经济学院、高威大学等地，成为展示清华学子的“文化名片”。

过去的2016年充实又美好，在新的一年里，清华学生工作将继续探索工作方法，创新工作形式，立足清华育人理念，面向同学成长需求，为每一名清华同学的成长撑起一片蓝天。

Tsinghua Students' Work 2016 Review: Working Together towards the Chinese Dream

In 2016, Tsinghua students made fruitful results. Based on the integrated concept of "shaping values, improving training and passing down knowledge" , Tsinghua pays close attention to training of both staff and students. Helping students to grow is a continuous and crucial effort for Tsinghua University.

This year, Tsinghua's ideological and political education is closer to the life of the students. "Xiao Wu Ye Yuan" and "Tsinghua Research Rooms" became the representative of the new media platform. Establishment of these reflects not just Tsinghua's ongoing work but also continuous improvement. This not only helps to spread the Tsinghua spirit but also inform readers about the Tsinghua story. Stories and characters are written into a book called *The Sayings from Tsinghua Youths* which has since received great responses.

Tsinghua continues to increase investment in academic research. Sponsored by the Tsinghua University Committee of Youth League, the "Into the World" program has supported a total of 287 undergraduates so that they could carry out their academic training and research at 84 various universities and institutions around the world. On average, their training lasts for 61 days. 5 million are used for funding to support students with their academic research and to promote the program. Annually, there have been a total of 147 projects, a publication of 41 papers and applications for 17 patents. The "Top Scholar Laboratory Plan" was also set in place to support graduates to carry short-term visits and training at Nobel Prize laboratory.

Students' creative ideas are also important and thus deserves attention. "Brain bubbles" , a creative online platform saw more than 3200 registered users with more than 1050 different creative proposals. "Seek for Seed" , a graduate creative contest, not only organized online activities but also promoted innovation, allowing this spirit to take root. In the "Young Innovation" contest, the Tsinghua team took home 5 Gold and 1 Silver, placing them second out of the country for excellence in performance.

The students also made great achievements out on the field and made history with many events. For the first time, a member of the Chinese University Basketball League (Tsinghua Men's Basketball Team) took home the championship during the final CUBA match. Also in the same year, Tsinghua Women's Basketball came third which is the team's best result to date. Tsinghua's Track and Field team won the 54th Capital University Championship. This meant that such great result has been kept for 7 years straight. "China's Women Volleyball Team- Tsinghua Visit" made headlines and saw huge response from the teachers and students. They came together to celebrate their undying spirit and to welcome an era of "commitment and confidence" .

Students go out of the campus to communicate with the world. *Ma Lan Blossom*, Tsinghua's original drama was performed on board the Chinese People's Liberation Army Navy: East China Sea Fleet. It was a perfect presentation for the navy officers and also marked the team's 50th performance. The Art Troupe won the first prize at Beijing University's Student Music Festival in chore, symphony and folk music. They performed at the University of Taiwan, Hsinchu Tsinghua University, London School of Economics and Political Science, Galway University and many more. This is Tsinghua's "Cultural Card" .

2016 was exciting and 2017 will be even more enriching. Tsinghua traditions and spirit continues, it expands, it forges ahead and grows alongside the students who not only defines and carry on such spirit but also hold up the sky for Tsinghua and their country!

Contributor | Tsinghua University Committee of Youth League

Translation and revision | Min Weiyuan

Image | Li Na

5月10日

文字 | 冯婉婷

图片 | 李筱甜

百年清华，人文日新

过去一年，清华园里的人文氛围日益浓郁。从“人文清华”讲坛到清华艺术博物馆的成立，从“中英高等教育人文联盟”的发起，到一系列重大项目和研究成果的推进，都标志着学校在传承百年清华的人文历史、开辟新清华人文格局的路上步履愈坚。

“人文清华”讲坛是清华大学在2016年“更人文”的进程中迈出的具有代表性的一步。论坛在传承历史文脉的基础上，着重呈现清华的新人文成果，遍邀当代人文大家，在标志性建筑新清华学堂定期开讲，阐述其经典学说、独特思考和重大发现，构建一个人文思想持续发声的公共空间。

寄托了几代清华人期待的艺术博物馆也在2016年正式开馆，开启了清华人文艺术新篇章。艺术博物馆凝聚了几代清华学人的夙愿，展示了清华大学的人文传统、人才成长和人杰培养。它以“彰显人文、荟萃艺术、涵养新风、化育菁华”为己任，坚持中西融汇、古今贯通、文理渗透，力图通过不懈努力打造一座世界一流的大学艺术博物馆。

2016年，清华还与国际、国内多所高校合作，倡议发起“中英高等教育人文联盟”，开启了中英人文教育合作交流新篇章。

继往开来，2017年对于清华人文建设而言具有更重要的意义。2017年，是清华人文建设良好发展势头继续延续的一年；2017年，也是清华大学人文学院正式成立五周年。虽然今天的清华人文学院是在2012年从原有的人文社会科学学院分离而来，但它的历史悠久，成果颇多。早在1925年建立国学研究院时，清华人文就有梁启超、陈寅恪、王国维、赵元任四位国学大家，有“独立之精神、自由之思想”的宝贵精神财富。进入新世纪以来，新成立的人文学院适应新时期对学术研究和人才培养的要求，把握时代和社会发展的新契机，积极开展国内外学术合作和交流活动，与北美、欧洲、亚洲等许多国家和港澳台地区有广泛的学术交流和项目合作。

进入新百年的清华大学，正在“更创新、更国际、更人文”的道路上不断迈进。百年清华，人文日新，清华大学正在传承优良人文传统，加强大学文化建设，促进人文社会科学与其他学科的交叉融合，争取为国家发展、人民幸福、人类文明进步做出更大贡献。

Tsinghua Enters New Phase for Humanities After a Century of Establishment

From Forum on Tsinghua Humanitas, to the establishment of Tsinghua Art Museum, China-UK Association for the Humanities in Higher Education and the establishment of the humanities program, the past year has seen Tsinghua's focus on the teaching and studying of the humanities, pushing forward a series of major academic programs and research. These achievements illustrate the passing on of Tsinghua's legacy in the area of humanities, laying the foundation for Tsinghua's path toward a pursuit in the new century.

The Forum on Tsinghua Humanitas, which began in 2016, marks a step forward in Tsinghua University's path toward a focus in the humanities. The forum is built on the vision to continue Tsinghua's cultural legacy, and to highlight the university's progress in arts and culture. Guest speakers are invited to the university's symbolic building - the New Tsinghua Auditorium, for periodic talks and to share unique insights and important discoveries. These will enable discussions in the realm of arts and humanities in the public space.

The year 2016 also saw the birth of the Tsinghua Art Museum. The museum was a culmination of the dreams of generations of Tsinghua people. It not only fulfilled the university's long cherished wish for a cultural platform, it also demonstrated Tsinghua's commitment to arts and culture, the maturity of Tsinghua's cultural talents and its vision for nurturing great talents. The next step forward is to preserve Tsinghua's unique convergence of East and West, Ancient and Modern, Arts and Sciences, and strive for excellence to make it one of the best university art museum's in the world.

In 2016, the atmosphere of increased focus on humanities was not only present on Tsinghua campus, but also internationally. There were various collaborations with local and foreign universities, which led to the launch of the China-UK Association for the Humanities in Higher Education.

Moving forward, this year will be even more important for Tsinghua's New Century. The year 2017 will be one where Tsinghua will continue its efforts in education in the humanities, and this year will also be the fifth anniversary of the Tsinghua's School of Humanities. Even though the current School of Humanities was only established in 2012, where it used to be a part of the School of Humanities and Social Sciences, Tsinghua's teaching of humanities has had a long history.

As early as 1925, when the Tsinghua Academy of Chinese Learning was first established, Liang Qichao, Chen Yinque, Wang Guowei and Zhao Yuanren, four masters on Chinese Learning, were the forefront of independent thought and ideals. Going into this new century, the new School of Humanities will be adapted to the current needs and to nurture the next generation.

Entering the New Century, Tsinghua's vision is to be more innovative, more internationalized and more humanity-oriented. In this New Century, the university will also make strides in combining the teaching and appreciation for arts and culture with other disciplines and to be a leader amongst the best universities in the world. These are goals so that Tsinghua may contribute to the country, its citizens and nations around the world.

Translation and revision | Alexis See Tho

Image | Li Xiaotian

5月11日

文字 | 左炬暄
图片 | 李娜

“北京榜样”程京院士：健康梦，中国芯

在“2016北京榜样”颁奖典礼上，中国工程院院士、清华大学医学院教授、博奥生物集团总裁程京作为2016年十大“北京榜样”的获奖者率先登场。

清瘦的脸上略显严肃，一副近视镜后面的眼神深邃而坚定。面对台下的掌声与欢呼声，程京说出了自己作为科学家和企业家的梦想：“我希望在‘健康中国’的建设中，处处能见到我们的‘中国芯’，用我们的‘中国芯’为全国人民的健康福祉提供有力的技术保障。”

他口中的“中国芯”其实是一种生物芯片——它就像一个微型检测器，可以通过检测人体样品（血液、尿液、唾液等），来判断胎儿是否健康，预测人体是否容易罹患某些疾病等。

1999年，程京放弃了他在美国生物芯片领域获得的成就与地位，毅然回国。从一无所有起步，程京带领博奥生物集团研制了生物芯片类产品及配套仪器数十项，在《自然·生物技术》等国际权威杂志发表SCI论文130余篇，出版中英文专著8部，获国内外发明专利200余项、欧盟CE证书25个，建立国家标准5项、行业标准7项。

程京并不满足于科研成果上的创新拓展，他一直在想：“老百姓怎么才能真正获得实惠？怎么才能用得上这些创新成果呢？”

他的回答是：“要把科研成果转化成低成本的商品，大批量地用于医院和百姓家庭。”科技成果转化的道路却并不简单。2003年“非典”爆发，程京率领团队战斗在抗击“非典”的第一线，在无数人选择离开的时候，他和他的团队选择留下。整整一周四处奔波取样、检测、做标本，程京和他的团队终于研制出专门用于SARS病毒检测的基因芯片。这是生物芯片在国内临床应用的启航。

后来，他们又研究出遗传性耳聋基因检测芯片，通过采集新生儿样本检测是否有致聋基因。这一技术目前已在国内20个省区市推广，完成了对200多万名新生儿的免费筛查。

程京说：“我们是‘填沟’的一代，中西方在技术方面的差距，需要一代又一代人用智力、精力去弥补。”也正是这样不计得失的潜心研究和创业实践，才一步步推动实现了中国人的“健康梦，中国芯”。

“2016 Beijing Role Model” Cheng Jing: Biological Chip Is for a Healthy Future

At the “2016 Beijing Role Model” Awards Ceremony, Cheng Jing was elected as 2016’s “Top Ten Beijing Role Models” . As a member of the Chinese Academy of Engineering, a professor at Tsinghua’s School of Medicine and the Director of National Engineering Research Center for Beijing Biochip Technology, he took the lead on the stage.

With a slightly serious look on his face, his eyes remained firm behind a pair of glasses as the applause and cheers continued during the ceremony. Cheng Jing spoke about his dream of being both a scientist and an entrepreneur. He said: “I hope to contribute to the field of healthcare for my country. I hope that ‘Chinese chips’ can be seen and used for the health of our people.”

The “Chinese chips” that he spoke about is actually a biological chip. Biochip is like a micro-detector. It can detect human samples such as blood, urine, saliva, etc. It can determine whether the fetus is healthy and predict whether the body is susceptible to certain disease etc.

In 1999, Cheng Jing gave up his status and achievements in the field of biochip in the United States and decided to return home. Starting from scratch, Cheng Jing led Capital Bio Corporation and developed bio-chip products as well as supported dozens of medical devices and instruments. He has published more than 130 SCI listed papers in internationally renowned publications such as *Nature Biotechnology*. Also, he has published a total of 8 monographs and achieved more than 200 patents at home and abroad. He also made 25 EU CE Certificates and set national standards 5 times and within the industry, 7 times.

Innovation in science and technology is a theoretical expansion and it is one which Cheng Jing is not satisfied with. He has been thinking: “How can people really find access to the services and can they really use our innovation achievement?”

His answer is: “We need to turn the results of scientific research into low-cost goods that are produced in large quantities for hospitals and people to use.” The transformation of scientific and technological knowledge into a more practical way is not an easy one. In 2003, SARS outbreak, Cheng Jing led his team to fight against SARS. They remained at the front line in the epicenter of this epidemic while many chose to leave. After a whole week of sampling, testing and experiments, his team finally developed a gene chip for SARS virus detection. This biochip was used at a large scale in the nation during such crucial times.

Later, they also developed a genetic deafness gene detection chip. By collecting neonatal samples, they are able to detect whether there are genes for deafness in an newborn child. This technology is currently being promoted and used in 20 provinces and municipalities. Currently, more than 200 million newborns have access to free screening.

Cheng Jing said: “We are a generation where gaps exist between Chinese and Western technology. Intelligence, diligence and passion is needed from generations of people in order to close this widening gap.” Such study and refinements in entrepreneurial practices is needed to achieve a “dream of health with Chinese biochips” .

Translation and revision | Min Weiyuan

Image | Li Na

5月12日

文字 | 杨鹏成

图片 | 任帅

施滉：真理所在，即趋附之

清华大学图书馆老馆大厅北壁上，嵌着一面白底金字的大理石纪念碑，碑上刻有这样的诗句："他是清华最有光荣的儿子，他是清华最早的共产党员，他为解放事业贡献了生命，施滉的革命精神永垂不朽！"

施滉进入清华的第二年，俄国十月革命胜利的消息传来。在新思潮的影响下，施滉开始关心中国的社会问题。1918年，他和同学组织了"暑假修业团"（后更名"修业团"），其宗旨是"振作我们的精神，尽我们所能尽的力量，来肩负文化运动底责任，以为社会改造之导火线"。从此，施滉踏上了强国的求索之路。

五四运动爆发后，现实的斗争使施滉认识到民族的危机、社会的黑暗。1920年，施滉和"修业团"成员们决心唯救国真理是从，"真理所在，即趋附之"，将"修业团"改名为"唯真学会"，施滉被推为会长。学会宗旨是"本互助和奋斗的精神，改良社会，以求人类底真幸福"。

经过不断探索，施滉逐步向着救国真理迈进。1924年，标志着国共第一次合作的国民党一大在广州举行时，施滉等三人受到孙中山先生和李大钊先生的热情接待和亲切教导，这更加坚定了他们为劳苦大众谋幸福的信念，并对马克思主义产生了兴趣。同年7月，施滉赴美留学，公开支持孙中山的"三大政策"，认为中国要坚持走共产党的道路。

真理在前方，即使危机重重，也要挺身向前。1927年，"四一二"政变前夕，当时美国的一些国民党右派在华侨中公开进行分裂革命的活动，施滉在这危急关头毅然加入了共产党，决心为实现共产主义奋斗终生。同年，还有六位同学加入了共产党，他们成为清华留美生中最早的一批共产党员。

1933年冬天，施滉因叛徒出卖而在北平被捕，随即被押解到南京。在狱中，他坚贞不屈，不改自己的追求与理想，痛斥反动派的罪恶行径，坚信革命必胜，共产主义一定会实现。1934年初，施滉被杀害于南京，年仅34岁。

积极探索，追求真理，言行一致，勇于实践，是施滉为人的特点。他以短暂而辉煌的一生，实践了"真理所在，即趋附之"的誓言。

Shi Huang: The Truth Endures

There is a poem engraved on a white marble monument situated to the North side of Tsinghua Library. It reads: "He is Tsinghua's most glorious son. He is the earliest member of Tsinghua's Communist Party. He gave his life to the liberation of his nation. Shi Huang's revolutionary spirit lives on!"

During the second year of his study at Tsinghua, the news of the victory of the October Revolution in Russia arrived and it was under such influences that Shi started to care about his nation's own social challenges. In 1918, he and his classmates organized the "Summer Vacation Study Group" (later renamed "The Mission"). The purpose is to "cheer on our spirit, do our best to fulfil our responsibilities and carry on social transformations" . From that moment on, Shi embarked on his journey to support and strengthen his most beloved nation.

Yet, after the outbreak of the "May Fourth Movement" in Beijing, the reality of the struggles made Shi realize what crisis is like and the darkness that lurks in the society that he lives in. In 1920, Shi Huang and members of "The Mission" became determined to keep truth intact. The name was changed to "The Truth Society" with Shi taking up the position of the President of the group. Their motto was "Assistance and struggle needed to improve society and to help all to find happiness in the end" .

After a preliminary examination, Shi gradually made his way to save his country through seeking the truth. In 1924, Shi and three other people were warmly received in Guangzhou by Sun Yat-sen and Li Dazhao. They became even more determined and were quickly interested with Marxism. In July in the same year, he went to study in the States and openly supported Sun Yat-sen's "Three Principles of the People" . Shi believes that China should stick to the path initiated by the Communist Party.

The truth is right in front of them even during times of troubles and chaos. On the eve of the "April 12th" coup, some KMT in the States opening began to seek a split. At this critical time, Shi decided to join the Communist Party. At the end of the year, 7 students joined the Communist Party. They became the first group of Tsinghua CPC students in the United States.

In winter 1933, he was arrested in Beiping (Beijing) after being betrayed by a traitor and ended up in Nanjing. In prison, he was unyielding and never changed his pursuit and ideals. He denounced the evils of the reactionaries and was convinced that the revolution will win in the end. Communism will be achieved. He was killed in Nanjing in early 1934 and was only 34 years old.

His active exploration and pursuit of the truth reflected his courageous character and fighting spirit. In his short and glorious life, he practiced the oath of "The truth" .

Translation and revision | Min Weiyuan

Image | Ren Shuai

5月15日

文字 | 冯婉婷

图片 | 赵存存、陈稳杰

邺架轩开业：清华是个读书的好地方

“清华不是读书的好地方。”著名古典文学专家、清华大学校友余冠英曾在20世纪30年代写下这句话，细数清华园里的花草鸟兽水系山石之美，用先抑后扬的笔法赞美清华园的人杰地灵。春夏之交的清华满园花开，生机盎然，不过正如余冠英所说，美景处处让人流连，并不意味着这里不是读书的好地方——随着校园浸润式阅读体验中心“邺架轩”的开业，清华正在成为更加美好的读书之地。

4月23日是世界读书日，也是清华首个浸润式阅读体验中心——“邺架轩”正式面向公众开放的日子。“邺架轩”取名自清华校歌中的“左图右史，邺架巍巍”“肴核仁义，闻道日肥”，意在通过阅读滋养身心，培育精神丰满的清华人。邺架轩位于清华大学图书馆北馆（李文正馆）G层，包含了500余平方米的图书展出与阅览空间和100余平方米的沙龙讲座空间。近百家出版社最新出版的近30000册精品图书在这里展出，设有清华专区、老北京风物专区、二十四史专区等专题书架。

清华大学党委副书记邓卫在邺架轩开业仪式上谈到，邺架轩区别于一般的书店，聚焦思想文化领域的书籍，其目的在于希望清华同学有意识地培养自己、引导自己向思想文化领域的前贤、名著致敬，使人文精神成为清华学生科技创新发展和进一步走向国际化的底蕴和灵魂。同时，邺架轩“服务阅读，引领阅读”的宗旨，也使得其在未来发展的过程中不仅仅是清华师生“选书、购书的好场所”，更将为大家带来“读书、品书的好回忆”。学校将邀请知名教授组成导师组，专门负责指导、组织学生的读书活动，开展读书沙龙和学术讲座，让邺架轩成为爱读书的清华人的好去处。

“水木清华，人文日新”。20世纪20年代国学四大导师王国维、梁启超、陈寅恪、赵元任等一批人文学术名家先后汇聚清华园，在中国近代学术史上留下了深远影响。迈向新百年的清华大学更加注重人文教育，“邺架轩”以“体现文化担当，传播先进思想与优秀文化”为理念，倡导“好读书、读好书”的生活方式，致力于打造“更人文”的清华大学校园文化氛围。正如邓卫在讲话中所说：“学校希望让两个习惯伴随清华同学的一生：一是喜欢锻炼，二是喜欢阅读。前者强身健体，后者丰满精神，都会让人受益终身。”

Ye Jia Xuan Reading Center Opening: Enjoy the Pleasure of Reading

"Tsinghua is not a good place to read books." once wrote a renowned classical literature expert, Professor Yu Guanying in 1930's, describing the beauty of Tsinghua Yuan (Tsinghua campus) that distracts the mind from poring over books. The grass and flowers, the birds and animals, and the waters and hills make the campus irresistible. In the rising and falling strokes of his words, he praised Tsinghua, a place with great minds and fine beauty. This April marks the season as described in Professor Yu's writings. The campus is filled with blossoming flowers, full with signs of life, but what amazes people is not only the beauty of the campus but also the opening of Ye Jia Xuan, an experiential reading center, creating a more conducive reading environment.

April 23rd was the World Book Day and it was also the official opening of Tsinghua's first experiential reading center, Ye Jia Xuan, that combines guided book reading, literary discussions and talks. The name "Ye Jia Xuan" comes from the lyrics of Tsinghua's school song that embodies the hope that with daily reading habits, Tsinghua students and faculty's lives would be enriched. Ye Jia Xuan is located on the ground of Tsinghua's North Library (Li Wenzheng Library). It occupies a 500 square meter area which is the exhibition and reading space and a 100 square meter space which is for discussions and talks. It carries nearly 30,000 books from about 100 publishers with special collections on Tsinghua, old Beijing and the Twenty-Four Histories, which chronicles ancient history from 3000 BC to the Ming Dynasty in 17th Century.

Deputy Party Secretary of Tsinghua University Deng Wei said during the opening ceremony of Ye Jia Xuan that it is not a typical book store but a place that congregates books rich in cultural thoughts and he expressed his hope that Tsinghua students will have great appreciation for important classics, making the spirit of the humanities the foundation for Tsinghua's innovation, advances in technology and internationalization. Ye Jia Xuan also aims to promote reading and in the coming days, it will not only be a good place for Tsinghua students and faculty to purchase books but also a place that create fond memories of reading and critiquing books together. Some future plans for the center include forming a tutor's group led by accomplished professors to give students reading guidance, organize reading events, discussions and talks. These activities will make Ye Jia Xuan a book haven for Tsinghua's students and faculty.

In the early 20th century, four masters on Chinese Learning Wang Guowei, Liang Qichao, Chen Yinque and Zhao Yuanren were all from Tsinghua University, and had profoundly influenced the history of academia in modern China. In Tsinghua University's step toward a new century and the university's focus on humanities education, Ye Jia Xuan reflects the university's new focus, and plays a role in spreading progressive ideas in culture and arts. The reading center is also to promote a reading lifestyle and a humanities-focused atmosphere on campus. As Deng Wei said: "I hope that when fellow Tsinghua students leave this university, they will have two habits that will stick with them for life: a love for exercise, and a love for reading. One is for the body and the other for the mind and spirit."

Translation and revision | Alexis See Tho

Image | Zhao Cuncun, Chen Wenjie

Photographer | Zhang Bo, Yang Yong, Hu Jiawei

5月16日

文字丨胡颖
图片丨唐蓓蓓
摄影丨张博、毛子卿

庆106岁诞辰，清华开放百个实验室

4月底的清华园阳光明媚，春和景明，清华大学迎来了106岁生日。分散在世界各地的清华人纷纷整装出发，赶赴这场春天的约会。在清华园的每一个角落，都可以看到“回家”的人们络绎不绝、纷至沓来。“我以前从来不知道陶瓷居然还能做成这样，简直是太有趣了！”一位随父母前来参观美术实验室的小朋友由衷地感叹道。不同学科、各具特色的开放实验室，让校友们和前来参观的社会各界人士充分体会到学术创新的力量。

为迎接106岁华诞，清华大学开放了低维量子物理国家重点实验室、智能空间系统实验室、生物膜与膜生物工程国家重点实验室等100个实验室，囊括理科、工科、社科、人文和艺术等不同的专业类别。同时，苏世民书院、艺术博物馆、图书馆和天文台等多个展馆、学院也面向广大清华校友开放。理工的严谨，科技的精锐，人文的浪漫，艺术的美妙……人们走进开放的实验室、学院、展览馆，徜徉在科技、人文与艺术交融的海洋之中。

值得一提的是，此次校庆开放的实验室，除了体现清华理工类优势学科的科研成果外，还充分展现了人文学科的风采。此次校庆开放的实验室中，外国语言文学系的同传实验室、法学院的模拟法庭实验室、新闻学院的实验教学中心和经管学院的行为与沟通实验室，都分外吸引眼球，集中展现了清华大学近年来人文社会学科所取得的发展成果。而美术学院开放的实验室，更是给校友带来了强烈的视觉冲击和艺术创造的全新体验。在一些展品前，许多校友久久驻足欣赏，大家纷纷表示，它们不仅体现了清华校园文化的丰富多元，更是对清华中西融汇、古今贯通、文理渗透的办学风格的极佳诠释。

“参观实验室、走进博物馆，学校好的资源对外开放，让我们能够身临其境地感受到学校的发展，感到很振奋。”1992级自动化系校友罗海滨激动地说。

100个实验室像100扇开放的窗口，人们在这里与科学、人文和艺术的使者相会，一瞥学术与智慧之光。而在过去、现在和未来的每一天，它们都在不断积累和凝聚新的知识、技艺、思维与成果，为正在阔步走向世界一流的清华注入全新的活力。

A Hundred of Tsinghua Laboratories Open to the Public on Homecoming Day

End of April, Tsinghua campus is filled with the warmth and colors of spring. Tsinghua welcomes her 106th Birthday. From all over the world, Tsinghua Alumni hurried to the campus to celebrate this special occasion. In every corner of Tsinghua Campus, you can see many who have "returned home" . "I didn't know that ceramics could be made into this. This is really interesting!" said a child who visited the campus with his parents. Every laboratory is different and brings with it new creative experiences for all visitors. Visitors stroll into the campus and remember their once student years and bear witness to the continuous growth, developments and contributions made by their university.

To celebrate Tsinghua's 106th Anniversary, various labs were made open to the public. Whether it is the State Key Laboratory of Quantum Physics, lab for biological engineering, multi-media function rooms for the School of Journalism and Communication, art hub for the Academy of Arts and Design or key locations for other professional categories, visitors are able to set foot into these places for the first time. At the same time, alumni are able to visit a number of pavilions, observatories, libraries and museums. Whether it is science and technology, engineering or arts and humanities, people are able to appreciate and take on board the beauty of all these subjects.

It is worth mentioning that at the opening ceremony of the laboratory, in addition to showcasing Tsinghua's advantages in the science and engineering disciplines, it also reflects the strength of arts and humanities subjects. Amongst the labs are the lab for simultaneous translation for the Department of Foreign Languages and Literatures, a mock court room for the Department of Law, multi-media function room for the School of Journalism and Communication and a communication lab for the School of Economics and Management. More than just being attention-grabbing, these labs reflects the development and achievements of arts, humanities and social science disciplines. The open lab of the Academy of Arts and Design has strong visual impact and offers a new experience for art creation for the alumni. In some of the exhibits, many alumni have commented on the diversity and richness of the campus culture. East meets West, tradition meets contemporary times, Tsinghua is a fusion of all these qualities.

"It's exciting to visit labs, walk into museums and have such resources at our disposal. We can really feel the development of our university, and of course, we are extremely excited for her." said Luo Haibin (1992 Alumni from the Department of Automation).

100 labs are like 100 open windows where people meet with the messengers of science, art and humanities to pursue wisdom. Whether it is the past or the present, or perhaps tomorrow, people will constantly be accumulating new knowledge, skills and achievements so that they can advance and add new vitality into Tsinghua.

Translation and revision | Min Weiyuan

Image | Tang Beibei

Photographer | Zhang Bo, Mao Ziqing

5月17日

原作者 | 李婧
改写 | 方之澜
图片 | 梁晨

开放交流时间：营造更有温度的校园文化

“钱老师，您认为女性在科研中会遇到哪些困难和挑战？”“钱老师，在面临两难选择时，更应该听取别人的意见，还是坚持自己的想法？”……学生们一连串“犀利”的问题，让中国工程院院士、清华大学环境学院教授钱易一向安静的办公室顿时热闹起来。2017年4月10日下午，11名学生来到钱易的“开放交流时间”，请师长分享人生阅历、传道授业解惑。原定一小时的交流时间最后延长至两个多小时，同学们仍意犹未尽。

相似的场景发生在大约半个月前，校长邱勇、校党委书记陈旭分别首次开设“开放交流时间”（Open Office Hour），与同学们面对面交流。大家围桌而坐，聊校园生活和建设，谈学习和科研感受，现场气氛热烈而活跃。同学们纷纷表示，老师们定期留出开放交流时间给全校同学，是让大家感觉“很棒”的一件事，这在同学们心目中留下了向自己信任、敬爱的师长请教的美好记忆。

“开放交流时间”是清华创新人才培养模式的改革新举措之一。为建立有温度的校园文化，强化师生互动，促进跨学科交流，学校制订了《清华大学开放交流时间制度》，教师公布可以开放交流的时间和地点，全校学生都可在此时间到约定的地点与其交流。2017年3月12日，学校发布《关于开展“开放交流时间”的通知》，附上全校48个院系和单位、1614位教师的开放时间安排表。

随着活动的展开，开放交流的内容和形式也在不断丰富：一对一答疑、微沙龙、座谈讨论纷纷“出炉”；办公室、教室、校内咖啡厅，都能看到师生交流的身影；课程答疑、专业指导、出国计划、时事热点、人生选择、个人感情……学生们不仅收获了学术建议，还能听师长们讲故事、聊生活，倾心相谈。

在这样的交流活动中，学生和老师都收获颇丰。清华大学历史系学生张铭雨说自己是“开放交流时间”的受益者——在一周内与3位不同专业的老师交流课题，对交叉学科的推进研究帮助很大。社会学系教师严飞认为，通过开放交流，无论老师还是学生，都更有机会接触到自己领域以外的学术思想和观点，共同交流碰撞，保持更旺盛的学术生命力和活力。材料学院教授李正操的话代表了很多教师的心声：“期待下一次‘开放交流时间’的到来，像等候朋友一样等待学生敲响办公室的房门。”

Open Office Hours Build Stronger Student-Faculty Relationships

"Professor Qian, what difficulties and challenges would a female researcher face? " "Professor Qian, when faced with a dilemma, should we listen to other people's opinions or stick to what we think is right?" Students' series of difficult questions to the Academician of the Academy of Engineering and Tsinghua's School of Environment professor, Qian Yi, turned her usually quiet office lively. On an April afternoon, 11 Tsinghua students visited Professor Qian Yi's office as part of the university's Open Office Hour initiative to hear her share life experiences, impart wisdom and answer questions that students may have. What was meant to be an hour-long meeting went on for over two-hours.

A similar scene was taking place in Room 109 at Tsinghua Xuetang about half a month earlier. In the room, 16 students were sitting in a circle, and in the middle of the circle was the Tsinghua University president, Qiu Yong. It was Qiu Yong's first open office hour with the students. The students came prepared, and started off talking about campus life and their studies and research. After two hours of discussion, many wished that the meeting could go on. The president himself agreed that the time was "very rewarding" .

Such scenes are the result of one of Tsinghua's new initiative — Open Office Hour. The program was launched to create a more caring campus environment, to strengthen student-faculty relationships and enable interaction among different disciplines. Through the program, faculty members announce the time and location for an open hour and any student from the university can show up at the designated time and location to meet the professor. A notice was sent out university-wide on March 12nd, detailing the open hours of all 1614 faculty members from 48 departments and schools in Tsinghua.

Aside from the university president Qiu Yong and academician Qian Yi, Tsinghua University's Party Secretary Chen Xu was also a part of this new initiative, receiving positive feedback from students. As the program matures, the discussion topics and structure evolved to playing one to one Q&A, engaging in salons, and forum discussions. Offices, classrooms and cafés on campus, became gathering spots for faculty and students having Q&A sessions on courses, discussing professional development and sharing about studying abroad plans, current events, life choices and personal relationships. Students not only receive academic advice, they also had the opportunity to learn about the faculty members' life experiences and literally talk about anything under the sun.

Faculty and students learned much through these interactions. A history major Zhang Mingyu considers himself a beneficiary of the Open Office Hour program. "My interactions with three professors from different majors this week have greatly helped my interdisciplinary research." Li Zhengcao, a professor from School of Materials Science and Engineering is pleased and welcomes the continuation of such a program. "I look forward to the next open office hour," Li said, "Waiting for the students is like waiting for a friend to knock on the door of my office."

Translation and revision | Alexis See Tho

Image | Liang Chen

5月18日

文字 | 刘书田

图片 | 李娜

艺术与科技的交融，让“非遗”传承回归生活

每个钟情于非物质文化遗产（“非遗”）的人，都不禁有这样一个问题：“非遗”正逐步遭受着市场和机器的挤压，如何才能将这些灿烂的文化瑰宝传承、活化，并融入现代生活？

走进清华大学传统工艺与材料研究实验室，倾听艺术与科技碰撞的声音——在这里，也许你会找到答案。

传统工艺与材料研究文化部重点实验室 2016 年 12 月由国家文化部批准成立。实验室以国家级非物质文化遗产名录中的传统美术和传统技艺为依据，以非遗传承人群为合作和服务对象，依托清华美院一流专家团队、各工艺实验室及清华其他院系科研力量，借助现代科技手段，为传统工艺的传承、利用、发展和创新提供科学依据，促进传统工艺振兴。

陶瓷、漆艺、金工、织绣印染、笔墨纸砚等传统工艺门类涉及的天然原材料和传统技艺都是实验室的研究对象。在承接文化部、教育部“中国非遗传承人群研修研习培训计划”的过程中，清华美院的专家们让传承人走上讲台、走进图书馆、走进教学实验工坊，拓宽思维，让传统工艺从“墙上”回归生活。在这里，艺术与科学相融合，使得“非遗”不再曲高和寡，而是能够融入现代生活。

近 3 年来，实验室取得了一系列科研成果，包括 13 项国家专利、64 篇学术论文，10 部著作等；并与工艺美术行业近百家企业建立产学研合作机制，完成企业委托横向课题 21 项。实验室还与以传统工艺研究见长的日本、韩国、英国、德国等国形成了稳态的学术交流机制，成为国内首个从材料入手、融合艺术与科学的传统工艺科研平台。

绛丝与蜀绣结合的时装、曹氏宣纸经现代设计转化而成的灯罩、河南钧瓷与青海银器传承人合作研制的茶具……每年的“非遗进清华”活动总能吸引众多关注。而这一件件交汇着传统与现代、融合着艺术与科学的作品，都成为实验室未来发展的宝贵财富。

实验室一直秉承着“非遗传承一定要回到日常生活”的信条，而使“非遗”工艺迸发出时代火花更是实验室的期盼。“从对材料和技艺的基础科学研究入手，破解古代工艺精品的制作奥秘，拓宽传统工艺在现代生活中的应用范围，将促进中国传统工艺行业迈上一个新台阶。”实验室副主任陈岸瑛说。

Key Laboratory of Traditional Craft Techniques and Materials Research: Blending Art and Technology

Lovers of intangible culture have all had one burning questions: How can we bring to life, pass on and immerse the brilliance of cultural heritage into our daily lives in an age where consumerism and machines reign?

Perhaps an answer could be uncovered in Tsinghua's Key Laboratory of Traditional Craft Techniques and Materials Research, where art and technology collide, merge and become one.

Established in December, 2016 by China's Ministry of Culture and working according to the national directory of intangible cultural heritage, the laboratory was tasked by the ministry to provide a scientific foundation for the passing on, adoption and development of traditional craft techniques. The laboratory is a collaboration among experts in Tsinghua's Academy of Arts and Design, craft research laboratories and scientific researchers from various other departments.

In the past, misunderstandings between culture and technology have significantly affected the production of creative cultural works. This misunderstanding and barrier have also prevented the application of technology in the domain of culture. In discussions about culture, intangible cultural heritage was considered as merely occupying the sphere of arts, with little connection to technology. With the establishment of this key laboratory, it has created a platform for the intersection between art and technology.

Research in the laboratory focuses on Chinese traditional craft and techniques and natural materials such as pottery, lacquer art, metalworking, embroidery and dyeing, writing brush, ink stick, ink slab and calligraphy paper. Through the marriage of art and technology, these Chinese cultural heritage will no longer be reserved only for the cultural elites but can be easily immersed into daily life.

The laboratory brought together numerous illustrious artists who were led the effort and poured out great efforts on this project. For the past three years, the laboratory acquired 13 national patents, published 64 academic papers and ten books and completed 21 horizontal studies. The laboratory also worked together with about 100 companies in the art industry to create a framework for easier collaborations. These efforts resulted in a growing recognition for China's intangible cultural heritage domestically and internationally, being showcased on the world's stage.

Costumes made out of silk weaving and Sichuan embroidery, lamp shades crafted using Xuan paper (a high-quality Chinese paper traditionally used for calligraphy and painting) , Henan's porcelain combined with Qinghai's silverware into tea sets made by cultural inheritors - these are attractions that takes central stage at Tsinghua's annual event celebrating China's cultural heritage and they attract great crowds of art lovers. These cultural works represent the convergence between the traditional and modern, art and technology and have become priceless experiences to draw on for the future development of the laboratory.

The laboratory has always held closely to the belief that China's intangible cultural heritage needs to return to everyday life amongst the common folk. And it is the hope of the laboratory and the expectation of culture lovers that these cultural heritages would one day ignite a spark in the modern-day art scene.

Translation and revision | Alexis See Tho

Image | Li Na

5月19日

文字 | 梁乐萌

图片 | 梁晨

马约翰故居：体育，从庭院出发

在清华二校门与邮局之间，道路东侧是一处不高的四合院，青瓦灰墙，悠闲的老人或好奇的游客经常三三两两从墙根下走过。这就是照澜院 16 号，现为清华大学纪念品服务部。然而，它还有另外一个身份——马约翰教授故居。

马约翰是我国近代著名体育教育家。1914 年，31 岁的马约翰来到清华任教，一直到他 83 岁高龄去世，马老将 50 余年的光阴投注于清华的体育事业，清华浓厚的体育传统自他而起。如今，全校性体育赛事“马约翰杯”依然以他命名。

1914 年秋天，马约翰应聘到清华任教，成为照澜院 16 号的主人。初到清华，马约翰教授英文、化学，却出于对体育事业的挚爱转而教授被时人轻视的体育课。他要求清华学子“不仅念书要好，体育也要好；功课要棒，身体也要棒”。清华曾规定体育为 4 年的必修课，不及格或缺课 8 次不能毕业或出洋。日后的文学教授吴宓在校读书时，就曾因跳远不及格被马老“扣留”，半年后补试及格方准予出国。

马老以身作则，坚持运动，鼓励大家不必抱怨房子太小，利用一切空间锻炼。照澜院 16 号庭院成为他早晚习武操练的园地。他早上 6 点起床，先在院子里做一套自编徒手操，再练太极拳和太极剑，晚上临睡前还到室外做深呼吸以提高睡眠质量。直到 80 岁高龄，他仍然体力充沛，白天工作八小时，夜晚学习两小时。

照澜院 16 号不仅是马老运动的场所，还是历史时刻的见证。痛感于 20 世纪二三十年代体育道德低下，马老把清华、北大、燕京、辅仁、师大 5 所大学的体育教师请到照澜院家中，商定成立“五大学体育组织”，共同培养优良的体育风气。新中国成立前夕，北平许多体育教师听信“共产党不要体育”的谣言心怀疑虑。马约翰反复劝说那些忧心忡忡的教师们，打消了他们的怀疑，坚定了大家的信念。

1952 年院系调整后，马约翰迁居胜因院 31 号，新居来访者与求教信仍是不断。而马老总抽出时间回信，详细传授自己的运动经验。每星期，马老都会到机关、学校、工厂作报告，反复讲解运动的意义，具体讲述锻炼身体的方法，往往讲到深夜才回到清华的家中。“我要献出全部精力，为发展祖国的体育事业而奋斗！”马老说。

如今，照澜院 16 号内出售着琳琅满目的纪念品，而房屋本身亦是对马老、对清华百年体育事业深沉的纪念。

Ma Yuehan's Residence: Continuing Tsinghua's Sporting Spirit

Towards the East side of the road that divides Tsinghua's Old Gate and the Post Office lies a courtyard. Not very high with green tiled roof and gray walls, retirees and tourists often walk past it during their visits to Tsinghua. This is NO.16 of Zhao Lan Yuan and currently Tsinghua's Souvenir Center. This was also Professor Ma Yuehan's former residence.

Ma Yuehan is a renowned modern sports educator. In 1914, 31-year-old Ma came to teach at Tsinghua and stayed there until his death at the age of 83. For 52 years, he has dedicated his time to sports education at Tsinghua. Tsinghua owes the strong sports tradition to Ma. Today, the university's sports event also known as "Ma Yuehan Cup" is named after him.

In the autumn of 1914, Ma was appointed to Tsinghua to teach and moved into No.16 of Zhao Lan Yuan. At the beginning, he taught English and chemistry but due to his interest and passion in sports education, he brought awareness to the often overlooked PE course. He made PE a compulsory course during the 4 year study and no one is allowed to fail or be absent from the classes. Anyone who fails will not be able to graduate or go overseas for their studies. Ma wanted all Tsinghua students to not only "be academic but be also sportive" . Students must "excel in class and in sports" . When Professor Wu Mi was an undergraduate student at Tsinghua, he failed his long jump. He then was "detained" by Mr Ma and was only allowed to further his studies overseas after passing the test 6 months later.

Ma Yuehan set a good example to his students and maintained exercise and sports. He encouraged others to not complain about the size of their room since that is no excuse for a lack in daily training. No. 16 of Zhao Lan Yuan became his training ground. He would wake up every day at 6a.m. and start off the day with his own set of exercise then Tai Chi. Before going to bed, he would take deep breaths and exercise again. Even at the age of 80, he remained energetic and would work for 8 hours by day then study for 2 hours at night.

No.16 of Zhao Lan Yuan is not only his training ground but also the witness to the history of our university. During the 1920s and 1930s, sportsmanship was overlooked so Ma set up a "Five Universities Sports Alliance" from his home. These five consisted of Tsinghua University, Peking University, Yenching University, Fu Jen Catholic University and Beijing Normal University. On the eve of the liberation, many sports teachers in Peking heard the rumor that the Communist Party does not want to include sports in the education system. Ma repeatedly persuaded these anxious teachers and dispelled their doubts.

After the national departments adjustment, Ma moved into a new residence and visits along with letters remained constant. He would reply to every letter and share with others his teaching experiences in the field of physical education. Every week, Ma would write reports and contribute to the establishment and philosophy of PE at Tsinghua. Talks would go well into the night. He used to say, "I want to devote all of my time and energy to the development of sports and PE and no doubt, to my beloved motherland."

Today, No.16 of Zhao Lan Yuan is a souvenir center yet the house itself will always be the home of Tsinghua's sporting spirit and a way for us to remember Mr. Ma Yuehan.

Translation and revision | Min Weiyuan

Image | Liang Chen

5月22日

文字 | 刘书田

图片 | 陈稳杰

特等奖学金获得者张祎蕊：大学生活是一场旅行

“大学的生活就像一场旅行，相比于展示终点的美好，我更希望从起点出发，与大家分享一路风景。”2016 年清华大学特等奖学金答辩会上，来自机械 33 班的张祎蕊将自己的科研之路娓娓道来。

初入清华，听闻着园子里的各类“传奇”事迹，张祎蕊开始思索自己的未来。大一是她寻梦尝试的开始，张祎蕊完成了电脉冲触感反馈数据手套控制机械手项目的“牛刀小试”，她发现了自己的兴趣所在，决定朝着科研的方向走下去。

做出决定后，张祎蕊联系了系里的温诗铸院士。促膝长谈中，她被温老师对科研的热忱所感动和鼓舞。世界上近三分之一的能源损耗于摩擦中，探寻其中的过程和能量转化是一项重要的工作，张祎蕊决定加入到摩擦发光的课题研究中。

大二是张祎蕊筑梦的攻坚时期，每日与她相伴时间最久的便是实验室。最煎熬的时候，张祎蕊经常在暗室实验到凌晨两三点。首次实现摩擦发光定量调控时，她更是通宵实验，第二天凌晨五点才走出实验室。她说，那是她见过的最美的清华。

凭借不懈的努力，张祎蕊的科研有了起色。但她并没有满足于此，而是积极申请了学校的“闯世界”计划，分别赴伯克利加州大学和斯坦福大学进行海外学术研究。本科期间她发表了四篇 SCI 及国际会议论文，做了一次国际会议口头报告，独立完成三篇共计 58 页、16000 词的英文学术报告。斯坦福的教授这样评价她：“祎蕊一个暑假的研究成果超过我们很多研究生一年的成果。”通过海外学术科研，张祎蕊丰富了课题研究经历，开拓了国际视野。

除了自己的进步之外，张祎蕊也希望能感染到更多的同学。她曾担任学习委员，加入系科协，“因自己能有所贡献而欣喜”。

作为 2016 年唯一一位获得本科特奖的女生，张祎蕊谦虚地说：“清华有很多优秀的女生，我只是其中幸运的一位。”

如今，张祎蕊正在申请赴海外读博，继续研究能源材料领域的相关课题。愿她始终怀着对科研的赤子之心，在学术的道路上继续探索，实现自己的科研之梦。

2016 Top Grade Scholarship Winner: Zhang Yirui and Her Journey

"University life is like a journey. Rather than to present the epic finish, I much prefer to share with others the whole journey." This came from the speech made by Zhang Yirui, the 2016 Tsinghua Top Grade Scholarship for Undergraduate Students recipient and a student from the Department of Mechanical Engineering.

Zhang has already heard about some Tsinghua stories and was eager to make her own. She began to think about her own campus life, and during the first year, she embarked on her dream. After completing a project and experiment on Data Glove Control of Robot Hand with Force Telepresence, Zhang found her interest and decided to make it her scientific research direction.

After making this decision, Zhang contacted Academician Wen Shizhu and was moved and strongly encouraged by his enthusiasm. Nearly a third of the world's energy is lost in friction thus, exploring energy conversion and the process of it is an important work.

The second year is a crucial year for Zhang to continue with her dream. During the toughest of times, Zhang would always be in the lab until early morning. Whether it is 2a.m. or 3a.m., she would be in the dark room, testing and trying to refine her work. The first time that she achieved quantitative control of friction light was an overnight experiment. She finished at 5a.m. the following day and for Zhang, "That was the most beautiful Tsinghua that I've ever seen."

With unremitting efforts, Zhang's research has improved. However, she did not stop from here. She applied for Tsinghua's "Top Open" program and headed to University of California at Berkeley and Stanford University to further her research. During that time, she successfully published four SCI listed and other International Conference papers as well as an international conference oral report and three English research papers totaling some 16000 words and 58 pages. One Stanford Professor made this comment about Zhang, "Her research result for this summer is equal to one year of research result from many graduate students." Through such overseas academic research experience, Zhang not only enriched her own understanding but also gained an international perspective.

In addition to her own progress, Zhang also hope to influence and encourage others. She has served on the learning committee in her class and joined the Science and Technology Association because she finds joy through contributions.

As the only female student of the 2016 Top Grade Scholarship for Undergraduate Students recipient, Zhang said humbly, "There are so many excellent girls in Tsinghua. I'm just one of the lucky ones."

Now, Zhang is applying to pursue her Ph.D overseas so that she could continue with her studies in energy materials. Still with her heart in scientific research, she is continuing to explore and realize her scientific dream.

Translation and revision | Min Weiyuan

Image | Chen Wenjie

5月23日

文字 | 刘书田

图片 | 薛雅芳

无偿献血：清华人十五载血脉相承

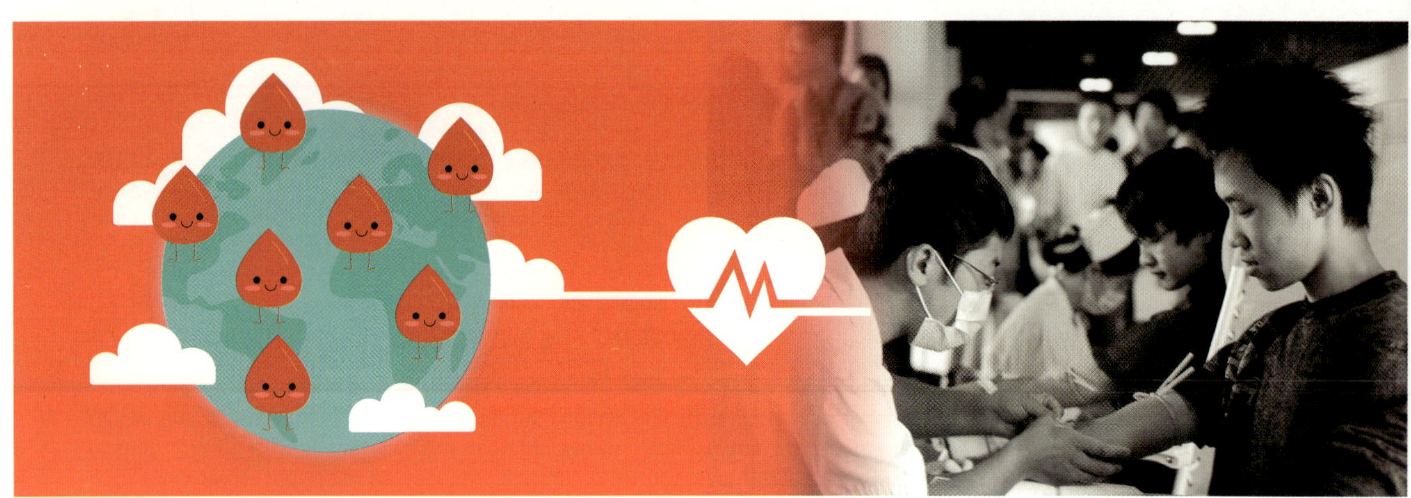

2017年4月9日，清华大学红十字会学生分会在紫荆学生综合服务楼开展“青春的献礼”大型无偿献血活动，本次大型无偿献血专场活动中，共有440名学生及教职工成功捐献全血492单位（每单位=200毫升），另有42人次成功捐献成分血42单位，68人捐献血样加入中华骨髓库成为志愿者。此次献血活动首次引入了成分血捐献项目，标志着清华的无偿献血工作又迈出了重要一步。

2002年，清华开始实行无偿献血，使献血从义务和责任向无偿和奉献转变。时任清华大学红十字会学生分会会长蒲光诚回忆道：“我们没想到，参与无偿献血的同学会如此之多。”前期对于献血人数不足、同学意愿不强烈的担心全都消散了，同学们排起长队，每个人脸上都洋溢着兴奋。

2008年，汶川地震，举国哀悼。而仅仅20小时过去，清华师生就挽起衣袖献血，只为能在灾区多挽救一条生命。那一年，清华师生贡献了北京血库应急支援汶川灾区近1/6的血量。

从2013年开始，为了让更多同学能够有机会参与其中，园子里每年都会组织4次主题献血活动：初入清华的“第一次”、年终的“岁末愿望清单”、校庆日前后的“青春的献礼”以及学业丰收时的“毕业·纪”。

为了使无偿献血活动更加温暖高效，清华大学红十字会还建立了无偿献血报名网站，可以实现献血时段预约、历次献血记录的查询等功能，每位同学在参与献血后都会获得对应自己的献血纪念卡和订制纪念品，献血活动越来越丰富，献血人数不断增加，但献血的初心从未改变。

15年来，两万多名清华人参与其中，共同谱写了一条血脉相承之路。紫荆学生公寓服务楼门前的献血队伍已成为每一代清华人共同的记忆，无私奉献的志愿精神与公益文化也深深影响着清华学子。而从清华人身体中流淌出来的汩汩鲜血，更将带着温度与热情传递下去，为更多人带来生命的活力。

Red Cross Blood Donation: 15 Years of Tsinghua's Support

On the 9th of April, 2017, Tsinghua University's Red Cross Society launched a large-scale voluntary blood donation event at the Zijing Service Center.

This large-scale special event saw a total of 440 students and faculty members successfully donating 492 units of blood (one unit =200 ml). 42 people successfully donated 42 units of blood component and 68 people also became volunteers to China's bone marrow bank. This event marks an important step for Tsinghua's dedication to blood donations.

In 2002, Tsinghua began to implement voluntary blood donations. Donations went from obligations and responsibilities to being voluntary, free and a form of dedication.

"We didn't expect to have so many students participating in unpaid blood donation." recalled Pu Guangcheng, former President of Tsinghua's Red Cross Society. In the early stage, worries about shortages of blood donors and the willingness of students being blood donors were quickly dispelled. Students lined up and their faces were all filled with excitement.

In 2008, the nation mourned for the lives lost at Wenchuan earthquake. After only 20 hours, Tsinghua teachers and students rolled up their sleeves and raced to save lives at the disaster zone. That year, Tsinghua contributed to 1/6 of the total blood bank Beijing gave to Wenchuan.

From 2013, in order to allow more students to have the opportunity to participate in blood donations, the campus organized 4 blood-related theme events. They are: "The First Time" for the freshmen, "Wish list" at the end of the year, "Our Young Contributions" before the Homecoming Day and "Graduation Joy" around graduation time.

In order to increase efficiency, Tsinghua's Red Cross Society established a registration site for blood donations. Appointments could be made, records can be checked, inquiries are answered and each student who participated in blood donation can receive customized memorabilia after every donation. Blood donation events are becoming more and more abundant and donor numbers are soaring.

During the past 15 years, more than twenty thousand Tsinghua people were blood donors. The blood donation team outside the Zijing Service Center has become a common memory of every generation of Tsinghua students. The spirit of volunteerism and public welfare culture are deeply entrenched in all. It is not just blood that Tsinghua has continuously donated but also care, warmth and enthusiasm.

Translation and revision | Min Weiyuan

Image | Xue Yafang

5 月 24 日

文字 | 张译丹
图片 | 梁露文

清华 x-lab：做创新时代的探路者、引路者、带路者

结束了一上午的课程，清华大学计算机系人工智能研究所自然语言处理实验室硕士研究生武彬走出教学楼，匆匆赶往食堂与自己的团队碰头，准备即将到来的清华 x-lab“校长杯”半决赛。除了是清华大学的学生，武彬还有另外两个身份——清华 x-lab 在培育团队“超满意”的项目发起人、北京超满意科技有限责任公司创始人兼 CEO。

走在树林荫翳的校园马路上，那个背着双肩包的男生骑车与你擦肩而过。他带领团队创办的八度阳光科技有限公司可能刚为你的新家安装了清洁高效的光伏屋顶，也可能你的手机里安装了他创办的“米公益”APP……在清华，创新创意创业的浪潮正吸引着众多学子一试“弄潮”，而清华 x-lab，则为广大师生校友打造了三位一体的三创生态平台。

作为创意创新创业教育的探路者，清华 x-lab 于 2013 年 4 月 25 日正式启动。它依托清华大学经济管理学院，由经济管理学院、机械工程学院、美术学院、医学院、新闻与传播学院等 14 个院系合作共建，并与清华科技园、清华企业家协会、清华控股、盛景网联和中关村发展集团建立了战略合作伙伴关系。经过不断探索和实践，通过聚合学校各个领域中对创新创业有涉猎、有想法的师资力量，形成一股稳定合力。2016 年，清华 x-lab 荣获全校教学成果一等奖。2017 年 3 月，作为清华首批本科生教学改革项目，x-lab 顺利通过结题鉴定。

作为创意创新创业教育的引路者，清华 x-lab 为万千拥有创业理想的个人、团队提供了系统全面的教育教学平台和通道。四年来，清华 x-lab 通过学分和非学分课程、国际联合教学项目、训练营、名师讲座、对话企业家、线上慕课等多种形式的教育教学模式，拓展了学生们在三创领域的视野和知识面，建立了对创意创新创业团队进行筛选和早期指导的体系，制订了多阶段训练与培育的方法。

作为创意创新创业教育的带路者，四年来，清华 x-lab 硕果累累。目前，平台累计共接收项目团队超过 1000 个，涌现出诸多发展比较突出的优秀团队，例如“八度阳光”团队、“米公益”团队、“淘氪”空气净化器团队、“孕橙”团队等。他们中有的获得了李克强总理的点赞，有的经历了发展中的波折逐渐走上了稳步向前的道路，优化了商业模式，获得了投资并逐步开拓市场。

走在创新的大道上，清华 x-lab 正在为更多三创人才引路，为更多三创教育平台带路。

Tsinghua x-lab: Leading the Way in the Innovative Era

After a morning of courses, Wu Bin, postgraduate student of Natural Language Processing Laboratory of Artificial Intelligence Institute under the Department of Computer Science and Technology of Tsinghua University, went out of the teaching building and rushed to the canteen to meet his team for the preparation of the forthcoming Tsinghua x-lab "President Cup" semifinals. In addition to the identity as a student of Tsinghua University, Wu Bin has two other identities, which are project sponsor of Tsinghua x-lab in the training team "Two Thumbs Up" , and founder and CEO of Beijing Two Thumbs Up Technology Co., Ltd.

Walking in the shade of woods on the road of the campus, a boy carrying a bag who rides and passes you by, may be the founder of Beijing Sunlectric Technological Co., Ltd., which has just installed clean and efficient photovoltaic roof for your new house, or may be the founder of APP "Ricedonate" installed in your phone. In Tsinghua University, the wave of innovation, creation and entrepreneurship is attracting a large number of students to give it a try, and Tsinghua x-lab, is creating a platform for all the students, teachers and alumni.

As a pathfinder of innovation, creation and entrepreneurship education, Tsinghua x-lab was officially launched on April 25th, 2013. Relying on School of Economics and Management in Tsinghua University, Tsinghua x-lab was jointly constructed under the cooperation of 14 schools, including School of Economics and Management, School of Mechanical Engineering, Academy of Arts & Design, School of Medicine, and School of Journalism and Communication, etc., and it also established a strategic partnership with TusPark, Tsinghua Entrepreneur & Executive Club, Tsinghua Holdings, Shengjing Technology and Zhongguancun Development Group. Through continuous exploration and practice, by gathering teachers with experience and ideas on innovative entrepreneurship from various fields of university, a stable joint force was formed. In 2016, Tsinghua x-lab won the first prize in university-level teaching achievement, and at the same time, it was one of the first undergraduate educational reform programs of Tsinghua which passed the concluding identification.

As the guide of innovation, creation and entrepreneurship education, Tsinghua x-lab provides comprehensive and systematic education and teaching platform and channel for thousands of individuals and teams with entrepreneurial ideals. For four years, Tsinghua x-lab, through the credit courses and non-credit courses, internationally cooperative teaching projects, training camps, lectures given by famous teachers, dialogues with entrepreneurs, online MOOC and other forms of education and teaching modes, has expanded students' horizon and knowledge in the field of innovation, creation and entrepreneurship, established screening and early guidance system for creative and innovative entrepreneurship teams, and developed a multi-stage training and cultivation method.

As the leader of innovation, creation and entrepreneurship education, in the past four years, Tsinghua x-lab has made numerous achievements. Until now, the platform has received more than 1000 project teams in total. A number of excellent teams with outstanding development also emerged, such as "Sunlectric" team, "Ricedonate" team, "Ms. Beauty" air purifier team, "Shecare" team and so on. Some of them won the praise of Prime Minister Li Keqiang, and some experienced the twists and turns in the development, but gradually embarked on the way forward, optimized business model, obtained investment, and opened up the market step by step.

With innovation, Tsinghua x-lab is guiding the way for more talents and leading the way for more education platforms of innovation, creation and entrepreneurship.

Translation and revision | Raj Lamar

Image | Liang Luwen

5月25日

文字 | 杨茂艺

图片 | 唐蓓蓓、霍巍

“万园之园”的数字化重生

圆明园始建于康熙年间，曾经是康熙给四皇子胤禛的赐园。胤禛继位为雍正皇帝后，圆明园成为一座皇家园林，此后作为五朝皇帝理政的场所。经过乾隆、嘉庆等皇帝的扩展，圆明园曾以其 340 多公顷的占地规模、100 多处景区、各式奇珍异宝藏品与丰富的文化内涵享誉世界。而这座被雨果誉为“东方梦幻艺术典范”的园林，在 1860 年遭英法联军焚毁，后终成废墟。重建与否，多方争议不休。

作为梁思成的学生，清华大学建筑学院教授郭黛姮始终坚持“建筑遗产保护与阐释其历史价值并重”的原则，想满足人们“亲眼见证”的情感期待——自 1999 年起，郭黛姮带领团队勘查、测绘已有的遗迹，研究考古发掘成果，同时深入挖掘史料，结合《圆明园内工则例》、帝王所写的诗词、《穿戴档》、《起居注》等古籍记载，从历史与文化的角度解读园中不同景区的构成。

“如果说建筑是石头的史书，那么圆明园就是用园林造就的一部活生生的社会文化史。”郭黛姮这样评价。

进一步地，团队结合 1933 年、1965 年、2002 年的圆明园地形图，样式房遗存图纸和书画作品等史料，研究了圆明园的景区设置、山形、水系、建筑艺术与花木配置特点。这些研究也极大深化了人们对清代皇家园林的认识。

然而，郭黛姮并不仅仅满足于文本成果：“一直以来，学界和业界对圆明园的研究仅限于发表某一学科领域的相关文章，缺乏全面的研究。我们要全面地解读圆明园的造园特点、景区建构模式、建筑造型、山石、花木特色。”于是，她带领着团队又走向了跨学科的数字复原工作，借助虚拟现实、三维建模等现代科技力图让圆明园“活”起来——从对样式房建造技术分析到残损构件的虚拟拼接，从不同类型建筑的形象、所处环境的特点，到植物景观的配置手法的变化，再加上各个景区在不同年代产生的变化，均需细心推敲，精益求精，一一呈现出来。有的景区最多出现了六个不同的时空单元，使人们从景观的变化中领会了每位帝王不同的审美理想和情趣，看到了圆明园活的历史。

目前，团队已经精准复原圆明园 60% 的景区，研发出集定位、导航、音频讲解于一体的“圆明园移动导览系统”、将遗址与历史复原场景进行同屏对比的“增强现实”iPad 导览。同时，团队仍在扩大数字修复的范围并尝试推出“感映现实”“创新现实”两大新项目。

15 年的岁月中积淀着 80 多位专业人员的辛勤与智慧，时光的星轨里，安放着 2000 余件历史档案、4000 余幅复原设计图纸与 2000 余座数字建筑模型。倘若百年历史是静止不动的躯体，那么这些有理想、有毅力的清华师生则是古老血管中热情涌动的血液，向我们展现出旧日烟云中别样的生机。

The Digital Rebirth of the Old Summer Palace

The Old Summer Palace was first built during the reign of Emperor Kangxi. Taking up more than 340 hectares with more than 100 sites and points of interests, the garden complex is filled with all kinds of treasures as well as numerous rich connotations. This "ideal model of dreamy Oriental art" regarded by Victor Hugo was plundered, burnt and looted in 1860 by the British and French troops. The site was abandoned after the Eight-Nation Alliance and debates over, whether it should be re-built has been ongoing.

As the student of Professor Liang Sicheng, Professor Guo Daiheng from Tsinghua's School of Architecture has always adhered to the principle of "architectural heritage protection and interpretation of its historical value" . She wanted people to "see the sight and feel the emotions" . Thus, since 1999, Guo and her team has been continuously exploring, surveying and mapping existing documents, ancient texts and historical data to note down and compose different historical interpretation of the Old Summer Palace.

"If architecture is the history of stone, then the Old Summer Palace is a living social and cultural documentation of history through the form of a garden." said Guo.

The team combined 1933, 1965 and 2002 topographic maps of the Palace. They referred to old drawings, paintings and calligraphy works to study the design, architecture, drainage systems, modelling and use of stones, flowers and plants within the garden complex. These studies have greatly deepened our understanding of the royal Qing gardens.

However, Guo has more goals to achieve. She said, "academic research has been limited to only publishing articles about the Old Summer Palace." So, she led the team to complete a digital restoration of the garden. With the help of modern technology, virtual reality and 3D modelling of the Old Summer Palace, the garden came "alive" . Everything from the rooms to the landscape to the colours, carved patterns, and designs on the woodworks, decorations, and wide arches to ponds... all are there for you to see. More than 10 programs are needed to restore a landscape. The team members are always meticulous when producing such works.

At present, the team has accurately restored 60% of the Old Summer Palace and developed a set of audio explanation system along with a "Yuanmingyuan mobile navigation system" . There is an IPAD "virtual reality" tour where various landscapes and points of interests come alive in this historical restoration. At the same time, the team is still expanding the scope of digital restoration and trying to launch two new "reality" projects.

15 years of works.

Undying efforts and wisdom from more than 80 professionals.

Altogether, more than 2000 historical archives, 4000 restored drawings and 2000 digital models.

Yes, this has been the work so far. If 100 years sits motionless throughout the long history of human civilization then these workers who constructed such magnificent sites is like bringing us another life and an undying passion.

Translation and revision I Min Weiyuan

Image I Tang Beibei, Huo Wei

5月26日

文字编写 | 张铮

图片 | 李筱甜

清华历史上的人和事：钱锺书是这样做读书笔记的

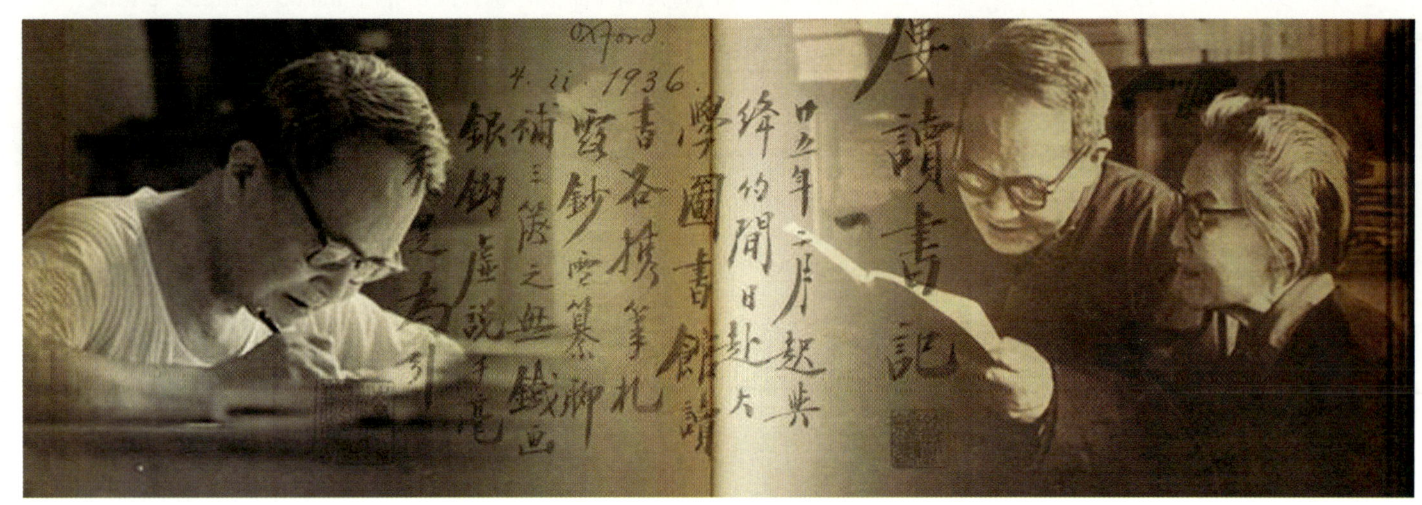

题记：

对爱书之人而言，对读过的书进行系统整理，高效做好读书笔记以加深记忆是十分重要的。本文节选自杨绛先生为《钱锺书手稿集》（商务印书馆出版）所作的序，文中详述了钱锺书先生是如何读书、做笔记的。从前辈学人的记述中，我们可以了解老一代清华人是如何做学问的，也能从中借鉴读书学习的方法。原文作于2001年5月4日。

许多人说，钱锺书记忆力特强，过目不忘。他本人却并不以为自己有那么“神”。他只是好读书，肯下功夫，不仅读，还做笔记；不仅读一遍两遍，还会读三遍四遍，笔记上不断地添补。所以他虽然读书很多，但不易遗忘。

他做笔记的习惯是在牛津大学图书馆（Bodleian——他译为饱蠹楼）读书时养成的。因为饱蠹楼的图书向例不外借。到那里去读书，只准携带笔记本和铅笔，书上不准留下任何痕迹，只能边读边记。

做笔记很费时间。锺书做一遍笔记的时间，约莫是读这本书的一倍。他说，一本书，第二遍再读，总会发现读第一遍时会有很多疏忽。最精彩的句子，要读几遍之后才发现。

锺书去世后，我找出大量笔记，经反复整理，分出三类。

第一类是外文笔记（外文包括英、法、德、意、西班牙、拉丁文）。除了极小部分是锺书用两个指头在打字机上打的，其余全是手抄。笔记上还记有书目和重要的版本以及原文的页数。他读书也不忽略学术刊物。凡是著名作家有关文学、哲学、政治的重要论文，他读后都做笔记，并记下刊物出版的年、月、日。锺书自从摆脱了读学位的羁束，就肆意读书。英国文学，在他已有些基础。他又循序攻读法国文学，从15世纪到19世纪而20世纪；也同样攻读德国文学、意大利文学的历代重要作品，一部一部细读，并勤勤谨谨地做笔记。这样，他又为自己打下了法、德、意大利的文学基础。以后，他就随遇而读。他的笔记，常前后互相引证参考，所以这些笔记本很难编排。

第二类是中文笔记。这部分笔记支离破碎，而且都散乱了，整理很费功夫。他这些笔记，都附带自己的议论，亦常常前后参考、互相引证。以后的笔记他都亲自记下书目，也偶有少许批语。中文笔记和外文笔记的数量，大致不相上下。

第三类是“日札”——锺书的读书心得。日札共23册、2000多页，分802则。每一则只有数目，没有篇目。日札基本上是用中文写的，杂有大量外文，有时连着几则都是外文。不论古今中外，从博雅精深的历代经典名著，到通俗的小说院本，以至村谣俚语，他都互相参考引证，融会贯通，而心有所得，但这点“心得”还待写成文章，才能成为他的著作。《管锥编》里，在在都是日札里的心得，经发挥充实而写成的文章。例如：《管锥编·楚辞洪兴祖补注》18则，共95页，而日札里读《楚辞》的笔记一则，只疏疏朗朗记了16页；《管锥编·周易正义》27则，共109页，而日札里读《周易》的笔记，只有一则，不足12页；《管锥编·毛诗正义》60则，共194页，而日札里读《毛诗》的笔记二则，不足17页。

这大量的中、外文笔记和读书心得，锺书都“没用了”。但是他一生孜孜矻矻积聚的知识，对于研究他学问和研究中外文化的人，总该是一份有用的遗产。

Stories of Tsinghua People: Qian Zhongshu's Note-taking Methods

Preface:

For those who love reading books, they know it's very important to systematically sort books and efficiently take notes. This article was written by Yang jiang, excerpted and adapted from the preface in Manuscript of Qian Zhongshu (published by Commercial Press), which explained how Mr. Qian Zhongshu read books and took notes. From her narration, we can see how the elder Tsinghua academicians conduct research, we can also learn from their methods of reading.
The original text was written on May 4th, 2001.

Plenty of people had earlier said that Qian Zhongshu had great memory and could remember things extremely quickly, but he never thought he was talented. He just loves reading, devotes plenty of time towards it and also takes notes; He doesn't only read a book once or twice, he reads it multiple times and enriches his notes. That's the primary reason he can remember the minute details from each and every book he reads.

He formed his habit of taking notes when he studied in the Oxford University library (Bodleian building). Since the library forbids the borrowing of books, he would have his notebook and pencil to take notes while reading.

Taking notes also consumed a lot of his time; in fact it took double the time of what he spent reading the books. He said, when reading a book for the second time, he usually found that he neglected some contents during the first-time of reading. He also thought that the most precious moments in a book is only found after reading it more times.

After Qian Zhongshu passed away, I found a large amount of his notes. Once I got to sorting them out, I arranged them into three different classifications.

The first classification is notes in foreign languages (the written foreign languages include English, French, German, Italian, Spain and Latin). Only a small sample of the notes was from the printer, most of them were manuscripts. There are bibliographies, important versions and page numbers on the notes. Qian Zhongshu never ignored academic journals; he would make notes when reading every important thesis related to literature, philosophy and politics by famous writers and record the specific date when the journal was published. Since Qian Zhongshu got rid of the restriction of conquering degree, he started reading recklessly. After laying a basic foundation in English literature, he gradually began to read French literature published from 1400s to the 20th century; He also read German and Italian literature and diligently made notes. Gradually he built wide knowledge in French, German and Italian literature. His notes were connected to each other because he would always cite and reference them to each other; that's why it's very hard to compile his notes later.

The second type classifications are Chinese notes, which are all scattered and extremely difficult to compile. His Chinese notes have his own comments where he also cites and references them to each other. However, his later notes have bibliographies with rare comments. The number of Chinese notes and notes in foreign languages is roughly the same.

The third type is "Rizha" — It's Qian Zhongshu's reading summary and diary. Rizha has 23 volumes, more than 2000 pages and 802 items. The items only had numbers without any chapter headings. Most of the Rizha were written in Chinese, a few were in foreign languages. We can see from Qian Zhongshu's Rizha that he read a lot of famous classics throughout the ages, common novels and slangs, he referenced to and cited one note with another, and all of his notes were closely connected. It is his thoroughly understanding of the books and notes that contributed toward his essays.

Though Qian Zhongshu has passed away, his massive notes and diaries guided later generations to make good notes and encouraged them to study efficiently. For the people who have researched on Qian Zhongshu's learning methods and Chinese and foreign culture, his notes are precious heritage.

Translation and revision I Anish Vincent Pandey

Image I Li Xiaotian

5月31日

供稿 | 新雅书院

文字 | 曹莉、张伟特、陈潇宁、王静姝、邓佳怡、杨茂艺

图片 | 赵存存、李娜

志合者，不以山海为远——清华大学新雅书院侧记

“锐意其新，茹涵其雅。初成书院，风物秋华。”2014 年 9 月，清华大学为开拓通识教育的新局面而设立新雅书院，来自建筑、生科、法学、电子、汽车和钱学森力学班等专业的 200 余名学生成为最初的见证者和参与者。2016 年 5 月，经校务会议讨论通过，新雅书院正式走上实体化运行的轨道。同年 8 月，来自全国 30 多个省市的 65 名大一新生入主新雅书院，成为四年学籍尽在书院的第一届本科生。从此，清华大学校园里多了一群“东西一视，文理同察”的新雅人。

“寻找心中的瓦尔登湖，传递大学宁静的力量”；“又博又专，愈博愈专，既新又雅，常新常雅”；“大学之大，不在其学广而无所不包，而在其学通而无所不达”；“新雅书院拒绝平庸，拥抱梦想，是志向远大者的学习共同体”——校长书记、院长总监和每一位师长的谆谆教诲、殷切期望是同学们的集体记忆和精神力量。

“新雅的通识课有两种：有一种关于知识，这类课既是艺术也是科学的；有一种关于成己，这类课既是科学也是艺术的。这种时候，你是一块顽石，人文的力量会透过石胎，去浸润最深底的美玉。”彭中尧同学这样评价新雅的课程和同学们。

从“大学之道”到“自我、他人与社会”，从“《史记》研读”到“英国文学的人文理解”，从“艺术的启示”到“物理学”，从每周一本经典著作的阅读到两万字的读书报告，从微积分线代到量子物理，新雅学子经历了一次又一次文理交融、学科交叉的“光荣蜕变”。老师们春风化雨，点石成金；同学们心领神会，结伴而行。

“通达成新，识智方雅。”同学们对新雅、对通识的理解是打开知识和能力大门的钥匙。连上三届“艺术的启示”课程的李睦教授提起新雅，便按捺不住心中的欣喜：“新雅学生的确与众不同，也许是因为知道自己需要‘通识’、需要‘拓展’，所以他们较少‘固执己见’，对于新的事物他们显现出了更多的好奇、更多的智慧以及更多无畏。”讲授“科学发展与人类文明”的刘兵教授说：“当你给学生足够的压力时，你会发现学生超出预期的能力。”

“新雅，新雅，就是一个让我们不断自我更新，进而逐步接近‘雅’的地方。”短短一个半学期，“新雅”二字已深深地烙在新雅 2016 级每个人心中。同学们用多种独特的方式诠释新雅，探求新雅，体验新雅，展示新雅——“天工人代、启梦未来”“经纶于道、致用于实——从新雅书院到大类招生”“邂逅书店、感悟阅读”“以诗词的名义，趁最美的年华”“不器 FM 电台”等活动围绕“书”“诗”“学”等书院特色主题频频展开，全部的创意和巧思都来自学生自己——既得益于新雅，又丰富了新雅。

夙兴夜寐、风雨兼程。同学们在新雅收获的不仅仅是挑战，还有成全。邓佳怡同学感慨道：“新雅一年，让我意识到此前曾错过了多少，而又差点将错过未来多少。小至每门通识课上每一点欣怡的领悟，之后回顾时每一处惊喜的能力飞跃，大至对本科教育的彻底改观，对人生与自我的重新审视，新雅都给予了我莫大的成全。”

“清华新雅，兼怀天下。”对此，孔祥瑞同学深有感触：“老师们希望我们真正明白选择新雅，就是选择挑战；希望我们拥有超越一般学生的视野与志气；希望我们不要被所谓的潮流裹挟，而要去思考二十年、三十年之后，假若我们成为那个决定我们周遭环境的大学掌舵者，我们应该怎么做、又为什么要这么做。”

70 个人，15 个专业（含政经哲 PPE、智能工程与创意设计 CDIE 两个交叉专业），8 个大类。同学们在选定专业之后，将以更坚定的步伐，走进“跨学科学习、跨文明思考、跨专业交流”的自然状态。“由新而雅，由专而精，由通而达”；“由学科交叉而思想激荡，由通专融合而全面发展，由勇敢探索而壮美人生”，2016 级新雅人以及即将考入新雅的同学们将迎来更多、更高的新起点和新里程。

无通识不新雅，无专业不新雅，无守成不新雅，无创新不新雅！

Xinya College: Aspirations and Commitments

In September 2014, Tsinghua University established Xinya College as a reform program to further advance liberal education. Nearly 200 students from architecture, life science, law, electronics, automotive and mechanical engineering and Qian Xuesen Experimental class joined the college and became the first to witness and participate in this new endeavor of undergraduate education. In August 2016, 65 freshmen from more than 30 provinces and cities were admitted directly into Xinya through national entrance examinations. These students will study for four years and be the first batch of undergraduate students at Xinya.

"Xinya College says 'no' to mediocrity and aims at building up a community of liberal learning for those who have larger aspirations and commitments." This motto forms the corner stone of Xinya's collective memory and intellectual strength.

"Xinya College has two kinds of liberal arts courses: one is about knowledge which contains both arts and sciences. The other is about yourself. You are a stone that can be penetrated by the light of humanities and science. You would weather through the tough road with the lighthouse ahead of you." said Peng Zhongyao, a freshman when asked about the teachings and the curriculum.

From "The Idea of the University" to "The Self, the Other and the Society" , from "The Book of History" to "Humanistic Approach to English Literature" , from "Inspired by Art" to "The Study of Physics" , students are constantly exposed to various topics and subjects, being classics or contemporary literature, linear algebra or quantum mechanics, every reading and writing assignment, every calculation and experiment, is a chance for the students to experience a "glorious metamorphosis" . Teachers are there to facilitate such wonders and progress.

"Access to liberal arts education, integrated learning and interdisciplinary studies is what Xinya stands for." Students' understanding of the college and its idea of holistic education is the key to open the door for new knowledge and greater achievements. Li Mu, a professor teaching "Inspired by Art" at Xinya cannot contain his joy: "Xinya students have the passion and willingness to learn more. They are open minded and most happy to accept new ideas and thoughts. They show more curiosity, intelligence and are fearless when faced with the unknown." "When you give the students pressure, you'll find that students' performances are greater than expected." says Liu Bing, who teaches "Science and Human Civilization" .

"Xinya is about self-cultivation." After one and a half of semester study at Xinya, Xin(which means new) and Ya (which means beautiful cultivation) have been deeply carved in the hearts of all 2016 students. Students interpret, explore, experience, and manifest Xinya in their own unique ways through activities and events bearing special liberal arts features. "Documenting Xinya" , "Encountering Bookstores" , "In the Name of Poetry" , "Human Intelligence and Future" , "Liberal FM" , are a few examples among many.

Day and night, students feel both pressure and satisfaction. Deng Jiayi who is going to study CDIE(Creative Designing and Intelligence Engeneering) wrote: "One year at Xinya makes me realize how much I had missed in the past and how I might have missed for the future. From each class performance to a transformative understanding of what undergraduate education and life should be like, Xinya teaches me everything that meet up with my imagination of a great university."

"While basing at Xinya, we actually have the whole world in sight." Kong Xiangrui, a student who is going to study PPE (Philosophy, Politics and Economics) understood Xinya this way, "Xinya expects us to truly understand its idea and mission. Once we have chosen Xinya, we have chosen both opportunities and challenges. We will become what we truly want to be and are getting ready to lead instead of following the suit. Perhaps in 20 to 30 years' time when we might have the chance to run a university, we would know what should be done and why."

70 students, of 15 concentrations covering 8 disciplinary categories, are soon to embark on a new journey of more surprises and pleasures that are "interdisciplinary and cross-cultural" , "innovative and challenging" . Xinya's special fusion allows a holistic education for those who aim high and can achieve more.

Contributor | Xinya College

Translation and revision | Min Weiyuan

Revision | Cao Li

Image | Zhao Cuncun, Li Na

6月1日

供稿 | 热能工程系
文字 | 蒋佩妍
图片 | 宋晨

“长城友谊奖”获得者罗忠敬：探寻燃烧之美，搭建科学桥梁

日前，清华大学燃烧能源中心主任、美国工程院院士、美国人文与科学院院士罗忠敬教授获得北京市2014—2016年度北京市外国专家“长城友谊奖”。

罗忠敬教授一生潜心学术、探寻燃烧之美。从美国普林斯顿到清华一路走来，他心中更多了一份促进中外燃烧界学术交流、推动清华带领中国走向国际燃烧学界前列的使命与责任。从此，在清华的课堂、办公室、国际会议现场……都能看到他孜孜不倦的身影。

罗忠敬教授与清华的缘分始于1983年，这一年，他首次来华访问，通过徐旭常教授接触到清华大学热能工程系，并得知中国燃烧学研究发展较慢的重要原因之一，是国内对国际上所取得的最新进展了解滞后。从此，罗忠敬与清华结下了不解之缘。2000年至2004年，罗忠敬担任国际燃烧学会主席，鼓励中国燃烧学者加入国际燃烧学会，并积极促成清华在2010年举办第33届国际燃烧学会议。2009年，热能系姚强教授与罗忠敬教授商讨能否在清华大学建立并指导一个燃烧学研究中心。罗忠敬被清华的诚挚态度所鼓舞，也为研究中心的宏图所打动，于是接受了这个挑战。

2010年8月，清华大学燃烧能源中心成立，罗忠敬任主任。中心旨在通过引进国际高水平人才、开展燃烧基础理论和应用基础研究，建设成为国际领先的燃烧学研究和教育机构。经过六年多的建设，覆盖化学和流体力学、具备交叉学科特征的燃烧学研究基地雏形初现，燃烧能源中心以热能工程系、汽车工程系和航天航空学院作为共建单位，目前在岗教师14人，其中包括3名“千人计划”入选者、7名“青年千人计划”入选者。

2012年，清华“先进燃烧能源科学与技术创新引智基地”成立，作为中国教育部和外国专家局联合组织的“高等学校学科创新引智计划”2013年度的建设项目立项，罗忠敬担任基地学术大师。

从2012年开始，燃烧能源中心每年开设清华—普林斯顿燃烧学暑期学校，由国际顶尖学者授课，每次吸引国内外近400人参加，他亲力亲为地参加暑期学校的活动策划、教师邀请和授课等工作，甚至特意把自己积累多年的讲义带回中国，厚厚的讲义装满了整个旅行箱。

2013年，清华热能系聘请若干流体力学的国际领先学者组成讲席教授组，为学生开设国际一流的流体力学课程，他担任讲席教授组组长。2016年，清华热能系、航院、汽车系三个院系和燃烧能源中心共同建立“能源动力工程烽火班”，每年遴选优秀学子与美国普林斯顿大学本科生交换培养。罗忠敬作为该班首席教授，为“烽火班”第一年招收的25名新生讲授第一堂专业课，为年轻的学子开启绚烂的燃烧之门。他目光灼灼，笑容慈祥，不仅在课上以深入浅出的语言带领同学们一览燃烧科学的灿烂风光，还在课后请大家吃比萨，关心他们入校之后的学习生活。他鼓励同学们与“火”为友，保持对燃烧科学的好奇心和热爱，享受研究的乐趣。

探寻燃烧之美，搭建科学桥梁，终身与“火”为友的罗忠敬依然壮心不已。他播撒下星星火种，为中国燃烧学熠熠生辉的明天而不懈努力。

Chung K. Law: Explore the Beauty of Combustion and Build a Scientific Bridge

Director of Tsinghua University's Center for Combustion Energy, Fellow of AAAS and Academician at the American Academy of Arts and Sciences, Professor Chung K. Law was awarded the Beijing Municipality 2014—2016 Great Wall Friendship Award, a special award for foreign experts in China.

Chung K. Law has devoted his life to learning and exploring the beauty of combustion. From Princeton to Tsinghua University, he has a mission and responsibility to promote academic exchanges between China and the world as well as to promote Tsinghua and ensure she will lead China into the forefront of the international combustion industry. Since then, whether it is in the Tsinghua classrooms, or offices or international conference sites, one can always see his tireless presence.

Professor Chung K. Law's fate with Tsinghua began in 1983 during his first visit to China. He came into contact with Professor Xu Xuchang from Tsinghua's Department of Thermal Engineering and realized that the main reason why China is experiencing slow developments in the field of combustion energy is due to the lag of China's domestic understanding with those in the international arena. Since then, Chung K. Law and Tsinghua forged an unbreakable bond. From 2000~2004, Chung K. Law served as Chairman of The Combustion Institute and encouraged Chinese scholars to join the institute and actively rallied Tsinghua on so that he could host the 33rd Conference on Combustion in Tsinghua in 2010.

In 2009, Professor Yao Qiang from the Department of Thermal Energy discussed with Chung K. Law about whether it is possible to establish and oversee a combustion research center at Tsinghua University. Chung K. Law was encouraged by the sincere attitude of Tsinghua University and was moved by the great plan of the research center. He gladly accepted the challenge.

In August 2010, the Center for Combustion Energy at Tsinghua was established and Chung K. Law was appointed director. The center aims to build the world's leading combustion research and education institution through the introduction of international talents as well as teachings in basic combustion theory and applied research. After six years of construction and covering chemistry and hydromechanics, the interdisciplinary characteristics of combustion research was established and two departments and one school became involved. They are the Department of Thermal Engineering, Department of Automotive Engineering and the School of Aerospace Engineering. There are currently 14 teachers, including 3 selected to be part of the "The Thousand Talent Plan" and 7 selected to be part of "The Thousand Youth Talent Plan" .

In 2012, Tsinghua's "Advanced Combustion Energy Science and Technology Innovation Smart Base" was established. China's Ministry of Education and Foreign Experts Bureau jointly organized the "Tertiary Education Engineering Plan" in 2013 and Chung K. Law served as the Academic Master.

From the beginning of 2012, an annual program was formed between Princeton and Tsinghua. As a combustion science summer school, courses are taught by leading international scholars both at home and abroad. Every time, the event attracts nearly 400 people. Chung K. Law would participate in every aspect of the work and he would personally attend the planning and activities of the summer school. He would invite teachers into the program and would carry years of his accumulated notes back to Chinese. These thick notes filled suitcases after suitcases.

In 2013, Tsinghua's Department of Thermal Energy invited leading international scholars of hydromechanics to form a group of professors who can assist in the teaching of a class for future students. Chung K. Law served as the Chairman of the group. In 2016, the two departments and one school jointly set up the "energy and engineering beacon class" . It is an annual selection of outstanding students with undergraduates from Princeton University being part of the cultural exchange. As the chief professor, Chung K. Law taught the first lesson for the 25 freshmen enrolled in the first "beacon class" . He certainly opened a door for these young students. His eyes always shine with care and not only does he try to use layman's language to ensure that his brilliant students excel in the study of combustion, he also likes to catch up with them and chat about their life in general over snacks and pizzas. He encourages his students and young friends to retain their "fire" , to keep on having curiosity, to have passion for combustion science and to enjoy their studies.

To explore the beauty of combustion energy and set up a scientific bridge has been the aspirations for Chung K. Law. "Fire" became his lifelong friend and he has kindled the burning bright future for China's learning and research in this field. His effort is ongoing and unremitting.

Contributor | Department of Thermal Engineering

Translation and revision | Min Weiyuan

Image | Song Chen

6月2日

文字 | 冯婉婷

图片 | 郭祥

清华北院，幽香如故

酷暑初消北园深，小雨偶来草地淋。
劲风古柏在歌晚，石堆山脚展现新。
点点翠竹千般绿，几条小路尽文人。
花台透露红珠落，彩蝶双飞护粉尘。

这首题为《北院幽深》的佚名诗作将清华北院的幽深精致与古朴氛围描写得淋漓尽致。

北院住宅区，位于清华图书馆以北，是清华创建前首批开工建造的高标准教员住宅。它由墨菲（H. K. Murphy）等美国建筑师设计，与清华学堂、同方部同期兴建，1909 年开工，1911 年竣工。其 8 栋住宅与 1 座会所呈“7”字形分布，为单层砖木结构的西式建筑，建筑面积 3484 平方米。每栋住宅有房间 5 个以上，客厅宽敞明亮，南向朝阳为整面玻璃窗，与向外延伸的廊窗相连，室内卫生设备齐全。后院附建家务侍服人员用房。

北院幽深，不仅在于它时代久远与柏竹清幽的环境，更在于它负载着清华百年历史。清华最初作为留美预备学校，中国教员与美国教员间存在严重的不平等，美观的北院住宅主要供美籍教员居住，被讥称为“小租界”“美国地”。中国教员则困居旧舍或苦于无房，为争取平等居住权，中国教员们组成“清华教职员俱乐部”和“清华华员大学会”，要求学校添建住宅。至 20 世纪 20 年代中期，学校陆续建成南院、西院住宅，教职员住宅紧缺的矛盾才得以缓解。

随着清华改办大学以及民族教育独立进程的推进，中国教员逐渐成为清华的主要力量，北院转为一批著名学者的居所，梁启超、叶企孙、萨本栋、陈岱孙、施嘉炀、蒋廷黻、王文显、陈福田、叶公超、浦江清、朱自清、黄子卿等 30 余位教授相继成为这里的主人，北院幽深的文人意境缘此而生。

梁启超曾在北院 2 号度过了由政坛返归学术人生的最后三载；叶企孙曾在北院 7 号居住 27 年，他让自家厨师将厨房办成小食堂，留学回国的年轻教师常来进餐，借此交流思想、议论校政；叶公超在清华外文系任教期间，住在北院 11 号，他在南窗外种植了毛竹，赋名寓所“竹影婆娑室”……

虽然如今的北院建筑多已不存，唯北院 16 号朱自清旧居孑立于校河河畔，遗址成为一片芳草地。但是透过起伏的草坪和幽深的长廊，依稀可以看到曾经的北院：天气好的时候，几乎每天都有清华美院的学生在此端坐写生。水彩，水粉，素描……北院的幽深景致成为许多学子笔下的精美作品，也见证了清华的人文历史。

Charm and History at the North Yard of Tsinghua University

When the heat of summer disappeared at the North Yard,
The light rain came to wet the meadow,
The gale chants with cypresses,
The rocks are heaped at the foot of the hill,
Green bamboos are showing vitality,
Scholars are crowding in alleys,
Dew is dripping from petals,
Where butterflies are embracing pollen.

This anonymous poem entitled “The Peaceful North Yard” fully expresses the peaceful delicacy and elegant atmosphere at the North Yard of Tsinghua University.

The residential area of North Yard, located in the north of Tsinghua Library, was one of the first high-standard faculty residences built before the founding of Tsinghua University. Designed by H.K.Murphy and other American architects, it started construction in 1909 and completed in 1911, over the same building period of Tsinghua College and Tongfang Department. The eight houses and one clubhouse were designed in a shape of “7” , all of which are single-layer masonry-timber structures built in western style with a construction area of 3484 square meters. Each house has more than 5 rooms: the living room is spacious and bright, and there's a south-facing French window connected to the porch windows which extend outwards, and the sanitary facilities inside are well equipped, while the helpers room is in the backyard.

The charm of North Yard lies not only in its long history and quiet environment, but also in the history of Tsinghua University it reflects. There were gross inequalities between Chinese staff and American staff when Tsinghua initially served as a preparatory school for overseas students in the United States. For the well-built north residential area was primarily offered to American staff, this place was ridiculed as “Tiny Concession” , “Land of the American” . Chinese staff were trapped in old houses or suffered from lack of housing. Striving for equal rights of residence, they formed "Tsinghua Staff Club" and "Tsinghua Chinese Association" to appeal for new residences. By the middle of 1920s, the problem of staff housing shortage was solved after the construction of South Yard and West Yard.

With the development of founding of Tsinghua University and the independence of national education reform, Chinese staff gradually became the main force of Tsinghua, and North Yard started to be residences for a number of famous scholars: Liang Qichao, Chi-Sun Yeh, Adam Pen-Tung Sah, Chen Daisun, Shi Jiayang, Chiang T'ing-fu, J.Quincey-Wong, Fook-Tan Chen, George Yeh, Pu Jiang-qing, Zhu Ziqing, and so on, a total of more than 30 professors. The scholar cultural at North Yard was therefore generated.

Liang Qichao spent his last three years of academic life at No.2 of North Yard; Chi-Sun Yeh had lived for 27 years in No.7 of North Yard, he outfitted kitchen as a small canteen for young returned teachers to exchange ideas and discuss college administration; George Yeh lived in No.11 of North Yard when he was on faculty of Department of Foreign Languages, he planted bamboo outside the south window, and named his house “Bamboo Apartment” .

Most buildings in North Yard had been destroyed, only the No.16, former residence of Zhu Ziqing, stands near the river, the site has now become a meadow. But the old North Yard can still be sensed through the undulating lawn and long porch: whenever the weather is good, students of Academy of Arts and Design will sketch at the door: watercolor, gouache, sketches... The peaceful scene of North Yard has become outstanding works of many students, which also witnessed the humanistic history of Tsinghua University.

Translation and revision | Raj Lamar

Image | Guo Xiang

6月5日

文字 | 左烜晅

图片 | 薛雅芳

赵小凡：拿下特等奖学金的博士妈妈

2016 年 12 月，在清华大学研究生特等奖学金答辩会上，来自公共管理学院的赵小凡格外引人注目。2016 年 9 月份生下一个宝宝的她，刚刚升级为“妈妈博士生”。

在来到清华之前，赵小凡在斯坦福用五年时间拿下了环境工程学士、管理科学与工程硕士。之后她来到伯克利加州大学的农业与资源经济系攻读博士，荣获仅授予全校 4% 新生的伯克利奖学金。一年后她顺利通过博士生资格考试，继续攻读伯克利的博士是顺理成章的事。

但就在这个时候，赵小凡决定放弃读博回国发展。

有人问赵小凡，为什么不在美国读环境或者能源政策方向的博士而选择回到中国呢？她说：“既然是做中国的政策研究，终究要回归到中国的土地上。否则做的研究永远无法‘接地气’。”

回到国内，赵小凡加入了齐晔老师所领导的气候政策研究中心，跟随他工作了两年。在此期间，她参与撰写了一年一度的《中国低碳发展报告》。她终于找到了适合自己的“土壤”——分析与评估中国的低碳发展政策才是她真正的研究兴趣所在。于是，2013 年 9 月，赵小凡“重起炉灶”，在清华公管学院跟随齐晔老师开始了第二次读博生涯。

她深入调研地方政府节能主管部门，走访钢铁、建材、石化、化工、电力等高耗能行业的几十家企业，收集了大量一手资料，并且对调研对象进行持续多年的跟踪研究。这个过程漫长而辛苦，即使在怀孕期间，挺着大肚子的赵小凡还坚持外出调研，只为获得第一手的研究资料。

尽管花费的时间很长，但是渐渐地，她稳扎稳打的前期工作逐渐显现出成效。从成果上来看，目前她已有 6 篇成果论文先后发表在 SCI/SSCI 收录期刊上，其中 3 篇论文是第一作者。这些论文都是节能政策领域少有的基于一手调研的实证研究。

特奖答辩的时候，赵小凡说博士期间要“写一篇优秀的博士论文，生一个健康的孩子”。如今，这位特奖妈妈正在学业、家庭的收获之路上继续前行。

Doctorate Mum Zhao Xiaofan Wins Top Grade Scholarship Award

December 2016, Zhao Xiaofan from Tsinghua University's School of Public Policy and Management received special attention as she received her Top Grade Scholarship Award. She just had a baby in September, 2016, and is now both a "mother and a doctor" .

Prior to Tsinghua, Zhao spent 5 years at Stanford University getting her BA degree in Environmental Engineering and a Master in Science Management and Engineering. She later went on to study a Ph.D in Agriculture and Resource Economics at University of California, Berkeley. She was awarded the Berkeley Scholarship for new students, which was only awarded to top 4% students. After one year, she passed the Ph.D exam, so naturally speaking, she should have continued her study at Berkeley.

But, Zhao decided to give up on her Ph.D and return back to China.

People asked her why not stay in the States to further her study instead of returning back to China? She replied: "Since my research is on policies in China then I must conduct it in China or else it won't be too aligned with the subject matter."

Back at home, Zhao joined the Climate Policy Initiative headed by Professor Qi Ye and worked alongside him for 2 years. During this time, she contributed to the *Annual Report on China's Low-Carbon Development*. She finally found the "soil" that suited her—the analysis and assessment of China's low-carbon development policy is where her real interests lie.

Therefore in September 2013, Zhao Xiaofan started her second Ph.D study at Tsinghua's School of Public Policy and Management under the guidance and teaching of Professor Qi Ye.

Her in-depth research took her to examine several local government departments in charge of energy conservation, steel, building materials, petrochemical, electric power and other industries. She investigated dozens of enterprises and collected a large number of first-hand materials and followed up on her research subjects. The process was long and arduous and even during pregnancy, Zhao would continue with her research and head to the front-line to gather first-hand research results and analyses.

It took a long time but gradually, her steady work began to show results. From it, she ended up publishing 6 papers in the SCI/SSCI listed journals, 3 of which she is the first author. These papers are a rare empirical study in the field of energy-saving policy making.

When applying for the Top Grade Scholarship Award, Zhao said that during her Ph.D, she wants to "write a superb doctoral thesis and have a healthy baby" . Today, this super mum is achieving both!

Translation and revision | Min Weiyuan

Image | Xue Yafang

6月6日

供稿 | 航天航空学院

文字 | 杨茂艺

图片 | 宋晨、何名暖

探寻航院校庆开放实验室：玄秘星空、精妙大脑与蓝色风洞

2017 年 4 月 29 日，沐浴着孟夏的第一缕阳光，我骑行在纤尘不染的荷清路上，不时望见三五成群好奇的游客。显然，校庆日开放活动使得校外人士也有机会一览清华风貌和丰富的学术科研成果，我心中小小的骄傲与幸福霎时涤荡开来。

作为一名修了李路明教授主讲的“飞天的奥秘”课程的文科生，我选择他主持的神经调控技术国家实验室作为此次实验室探秘之旅的首站。

在航天科技领域，实验室研制的航天员质量测量仪、生理信号测试盒等仪器设备已装备于从“神八”开始的飞船，为航天员在太空的健康保驾护航。更让人惊奇的是，实验室自主研制的用于治疗帕金森病的脑起搏器已经植入了超过 3500 名患者的体内。将一根精密的电极长期植入大脑，一直刺激大脑，你能想象吗？这可是让我们成为万物之灵的大脑啊！

我是怀着这种极端的好奇来探寻这个实验室的。一个个精密的部件、一件件自主研发的仪器好像在诉说着它们诞生的历史、艰辛和功效，而这些都记录着实验室过去 17 年来一步一个脚印的不懈努力与追求。看到视频中一个个因重新自主控制身体而露出重生般笑容的“帕友”们，我不禁由衷赞叹科技的神奇，这些摆放在玻璃柜里的脑起搏器是多么不可思议——只需将电脉冲释放到脑内核团，就能抑制异常神经信号，改善患者的运动功能，为成千上万的神经疾病患者带来福音。

从探索玄秘星空到聚焦人类精妙的大脑，李路明教授带领着团队将载人航天技术应用在医疗器械领域，开拓了中国神经调控研究新疆域，使我国成为全球第二个能够生产制造脑起搏器并将其大规模运用于临床的国家。介绍人员告诉我，清华研发的脑起搏器于 2009 年实现首例临床植入，2016 年获得欧盟 CE 认证，开始走向世界。同年，实验室与《科学》杂志设立全球首个神经调控学术奖（Science-PINS Prize of Neuromodulation）。

听完老师细致的讲解后，我伫立在实验室门口，望着这些埋头工作的研究人员和那些看似朴素却耗人心血的实验仪器，遥想远方的天穹，也思考着那些被疾病所折磨的患者。或许，他们就像一颗颗就要从轨道上坠落的星体，凭借着科技的助推器，重新焕发出生命的光彩。

告别了综合科技楼，我又来到了航院流体力学所的风洞实验室。临近中午的酷热暑气令人难受，可一进实验室就有一股强大的凉风扑面迎来，原来是一座 0.5 米的直流式风洞的吹风效果（风洞面向校内外教学科研机构开放）。结合风洞实验室内的尖端流体力学及动力学测试设备，如 Hot wire，PIV，测力天平，dSPACE 虚拟控制实验平台等，可进行与流体力学相关的实验，如湍流边界层实验、壁面流动摩擦阻力实验、流动阻力实验、流致振动及颤振实验、绕流流场结构实验、机翼气动力及流场实验等。

经过博士生师兄的介绍，我了解到眼前这个天蓝色的风洞只能算是风洞家族中的“小家伙”。航院较大尺寸的风洞坐落在河北清华发展研究院，实验段口径为 1.2 米的正方形，是回流式的低湍流度风洞，最大风速可达 90 米 / 秒，最低湍流度为 0.08%。实验室利用直播技术可以将远在廊坊的风洞现场传递到清华校园，在每学期的“飞行器基础实验”课上，学生们都有机会去现场观摩。

“光说不练假把式，我来给你们演示一下涡流实验。”师兄笑道。眼见他拿起一瓶甘油注入上方的液体添加器里，下方用细线吊了一个摆锤。接着，他又启动了风洞，通电。瞬间，甘油燃烧产生的烟雾被卷入气流，宛若千万缕对称的银丝，形成美丽的旋涡。师兄继续介绍说：“这是烟线，一种流动显示技术。”

几个小时的航院实验室之旅着实让人兴奋，也让我深刻体会到科研工作对精准、精密的追求。一路参观中，还有许多高中生、校外各界人士也在聆听实验室的介绍。真希望明年校庆能继续开放实验室的活动，让更多人得以一览清华科研的魅力！

Explore Open Laboratories of the School of Aerospace Engineering: Mystery Stars, Secret Brain, Blue Wind Tunnel

On April 29th, 2017, bathed in the first ray of the summer sun, I cycled along the Heqing Road, time to time looking past the curious visitors. Obviously, the anniversary's opening events provided outside people an opportunity to admire the scenery in Tsinghua, to meet our rich academic achievements, through which our inner pride and happiness get satisfied.

As a liberal arts student who takes the "The Mystery of Flying Apsaras" course given by Prof. Li Luming, I chose his National Engineering Laboratory of Neuromodulation as the first stop of my discovery trip.

In the field of space science and technology, devices developed by the laboratory such as astronaut mass measurement, physiological signal test box have been equipped in spacecraft starting with "No. 8 of Shenzhou" , escorting astronauts' health in space. Even more surprising, its self-made Beep Brain Stimulator, designed to treat Parkinson's disease has been implanted in more than 3500 patients. It's hard to imagine such a sophisticated electrode was implanted into the brain and constantly stimulates the brain, helping us dominate the world.

I came here with such extreme curiosity. Those sophisticated components and self-developed instruments were telling the history, hardships and achievements of their birth, which recorded tireless efforts and pursuit of the laboratory in the last 17 years. When I saw Parkinson's disease patients in the video smiling for regaining control of their bodies, I couldn't help but admire the magic of science and technology, how unbelievable these Beep Brain Stimulators are - only releasing the electric pulse into cerebrum nucleus, then allowing abnormal nerve signals to be inhibited to improve motor functions of patients, therefore benefiting thousands of patients in China's with neurological diseases.

From exploring mystery stars to focusing on human brains, Prof. Li Luming with his team has applied manned space technology in the field of medical devices, expanding the research of neuromodulation in China, making China the second country in the world to manufacture Beep Brain Stimulator and use it in clinical practice on a large scale. From the interpreter, the Beep Brain Stimulator developed by Tsinghua was firstly put in clinical use in 2009 and won CE certification of European Union in 2016, after which it spread across the world. Also in 2016, the laboratory and *Science* jointly set up the world's first Science-PINS Prize of Neuromodulation.

After hearing the careful interpretation from the teachers, I stood in the laboratory door, looking at the working researchers and those seemingly simple but painstaking experimental instruments, thinking of the stars as well as those patients tortured by diseases. Maybe they are like stars, which were about to fall from the orbit, shining again because of the booster of science and technology.

Leaving Comprehensive Technology Building, I moved to the wind tunnel laboratory in the Institute of Fluid Mechanics. Although the temperature at noon was insufferable, a strong cool wind greeted me at the moment I stepped into the wind tunnel laboratory. It was an open-looped wind tunnel with the working section of 0.5m×0.5m (it serves the wind tunnel tests for both scientific study and engineering testing). Combined with some advanced flow mechanics and dynamics testing facilities such as Hot wire, PIV (Particle Image Velocimetry), force balance, dSPACE virtual controlled platform, the wind tunnel lab can carry out a lot of flow mechanics experiments, e.g. turbulent boundary layer measurements, turbulent flow friction measurements, flowdrag measurement, flow-Induced vibration and flutter measurement, flow structures behind bodies and aerodynamic forces of wings.

After a brief introduction given by a Ph.D student instructor, I realized that this wind tunnel is just "little guy" in the wind tunnel family. The bigger one is placed in Tsinghua University's Development Research Academy Institute in Hebei, which working section is a square with a side length of 1.2m. That close-looped wind tunnel has the minimum turbulent density of 0.08% and the maximum velocity of 90m/s. The experiments could be viewed online at Tsinghua campus through a system named "wind tunnel testing live broadcasting based on internet plus" . In each summer term, students chosen the course "Fundamental Experiments of Aircrafts" have the opportunity to explore the wind tunnel by themselves.

A few hours of the laboratory trip was really exciting, whether the hardworking researchers or complicated instruments, they all represented the technical pursuit to precision and accuracy. Among the visitors, most were high school students, outside staff, who were carefully listening to the laboratory introduction. I really hope that the open laboratory events are kept during next year's anniversary, so that more people can enjoy Tsinghua's interesting researches!

Contributor | School of Aerospace Engineering

Translation and revision | Raj Lamar

Image | Song Chen, He Mingnuan

6月7日

文字 | 左烜晅

图片 | 赵存存、薛雅芳

跨越时空：平均年龄 93 岁的一次朗读

2017 年 4 月 15 日，在清华大学 106 周年校庆前夕，中国焊接领域的泰斗级专家潘际銮院士做客《朗读者》节目，携手 12 位清华大学和西南联大校友共同朗读《告全国民众书》。这 13 位先生的年龄加起来超过 1200 岁，平均年龄 93 岁。

1935 年，“一二・九”学生运动正如火如荼地开展着，由清华大学救国会起草的《告全国民众书》向全国人民喊出“华北之大，已经安放不得一张平静的书桌了”的爱国宣言。当时的青年学子，如今已经成为耄耋老人。

在《朗读者》节目中，潘际銮回忆了卢沟桥事变后背井离乡的际遇，他深情地说：“我的家就是清华，无论走到哪里，清华都是我的根。”

今年 90 岁高龄的潘际銮先生，与《告全国民众书》中所说的一样，一生都在“尽力之所及，为国家民族做一点实际工作”。现为中国科学院院士、清华大学教授的他，曾经创建了我国高校第一批焊接专业，长期从事焊接专业的教学和研究工作，是我国自行建设的第一座核电站（秦山核电站）的焊接顾问，也为保证我国第一条时速 350 公里的高速列车在 2008 年北京奥运会前顺利开通做出过重要贡献。

在场外录制视频参与朗读的钱易先生今年 81 岁，仍工作在教学第一线。作为环境工程学科奠基人陶葆楷的学生、国学大师钱穆的女儿，钱易先生一生成就斐然。回顾自己一路走来的学术人生，她朴素地说：“我的一生，谈不上任何的成绩，够不上大师的帽子。但有一点，我觉得非常有收获，就是当了一辈子教师，将近 60 年，很享受。”虽然承担了繁重的科研任务和社会工作，但钱易从未离开教学一线。“环境保护与可持续发展”每年为全校本科生开课，被评为国家级精品课程。

88 岁的彭珮云先生，1945 年考入西南联大社会学系。她曾先后担任过全国人大常委会副委员长，全国妇联主席、名誉主席等职务。59 岁到国家计划生育委员会履职，她说：“既要促进人口与资源、环境、经济、社会的协调发展，又要实现可持续发展。这就是要求我们抱着对国家民族负责、对子孙后代负责的高度政治责任感和使命感，深入实际进行调查研究，不断探索我国人口发展的客观规律。”

节目中，13 位先生共同朗读：“我们的胸怀是光明的：要以血肉头颅换取我们的自由！”场内外的和声与回响，记录了他们浓烈的青春，镌刻下他们深沉的热爱，更将他们报国、教书、育人的事业继续传递下去。

Marching Out of Time: Reading at an Average Age of 93

On April 15, 2017, at the occasion of the 106th anniversary of Tsinghua University, Mr. Pan Jiluan, a leading authority in China's welding field, attended the TV show *Readers* together with twelve alumni from Tsinghua University and Southwest Associated University to read *Report to The Nation*, a famous proclamation of National Salvation Association of Tsinghua University during the December 9th Movement.

In 1935, during the December 9th Movement, *Report to The Nation* drafted by the National Salvation Association of Tsinghua University appealed to the nation that, "even a quiet desk cannot be placed in the vast land of North China" . Those young students of the past have now become respected elders.

In the show, Pan recalled his drifting experience after the Lugou Bridge Incident with affection, "Tsinghua is my home, and no matter where I go, I am rooted to it."

This 90-year-old man, as what was written in *Report to The Nation*, has devoted all his life to "doing practical things for the nation and the country with all of one's strengths" . As an academician of China Academy of Sciences and a professor in Tsinghua University, he created China's first welding specialties in colleges and has been engaged in long-time work of teaching and research in the field. He was the welding consultant of China's first self-built nuclear power station (Qinshan Nuclear Power Station), and made great contributions towards ensuring the smooth opening of our first 350km/h high-speed train before the 2008 Olympic Games.

Prof. Qian Yi, who recorded the reading video outside the site, is still teaching at the age of 81. As a student of Tao Baokai, the founder of environmental engineering, and daughter of Qian Mu, master of Chinese culture, Qian Yi has made remarkable achievements throughout her entire life. Recalling her academic life, she sighed, "In retrospect, I dare not to speak of any achievements nor claim myself a master. But there's one point I feel very fruitful of, that is, I've been a teacher for nearly 60 years and I really enjoy it." Bearing heavy scientific research and social work, she never left the classroom. The curriculum "Environmental Protection and Sustainable Development" , which is launched for undergraduate students every year, has been rated as a national quality course.

Peng Peiyun, 88, was admitted to the Department of Sociology of Southwest Associated University in 1945 and later served as vice chairman of the Standing Committee of the National People's Congress, the Chairman and Honorary Chairman of the All-China Women's Federation. At the age of 59, she started to work in the State Family Planning Commission. She said, "It is necessary to realize sustainable development and promote coordinated development of population, resources, environment, economy and society. This requires us to hold a high sense of political responsibility and sense of mission in charge of the country, nation and the future generations. We should conduct deep investigations and studies in matters, and constantly explore the objective laws of China's population development."

Now, thirteen elders read together, "our hearts are bright: we must exchange for our freedom with flesh and blood!" The surrounding harmony and echoes recorded their passionate youth, engraved their deep affections, and passed on their ambitions for serving the country, imparting knowledge and educating the people.

Translation and revision | Raj Lamar

Image | Zhao Cuncun, Xue Yafang

6月8日

供稿 | 地学系
文字 | 杨鹏成
图片 | 郭祥

地学系张强教授：探究空气污染复杂来源

据全球疾病负担研究估计，$PM_{2.5}$ 的长期暴露导致中国 2013 年有 90 余万人过早死亡。面对空气污染带来的巨大健康威胁和经济损失，我们迫切需要知道空气污染的来源到底是什么、人类活动在其中扮演怎样的角色，清华大学地学系张强教授致力于回答上述问题。

“在中国，先进和落后的技术同时存在。快速的工业化和城市化使我国目前的大气污染排放源成为世界上最复杂、时空变化最迅速的污染源体系。如何准确估算中国人为源排放的时空分布一直是一个难题，这给政府精准施策、科学治理空气污染造成很大困难。”张强说。

针对这一问题，张强和他的团队以区域大气污染源高分辨率排放清单技术研发为主要目标，针对我国污染源技术水平跨度大、构成复杂且更替速度快的特点，在动态排放清单方法学、高分辨率排放清单数据、排放时空分布变化影响因素等方面开展了一系列研究。

大气污染物排放清单是指各种排放源在一定时间跨度和空间区域内向大气排放的大气污染物的量的集合，一套完整的大气污染物排放清单是识别污染来源和制定减排控制方案的重要基础。

经过多年的努力，张强和他的团队建立了动态的排放清单方法学体系，开发了全国尺度动态更新的大气污染物排放清单、建设了在线排放清单技术平台，在国内外得到广泛的应用。据不完全统计，目前国内 80% 以上的空气质量数值预报系统都采用了张强团队开发的排放清单数据，他们的清单数据也通过网站推送给中国环境监测总站以及全国各省市的空气质量预报预警系统。

张强的团队分析了经济增长、技术进步、污染控制等各类社会经济因素对中国人为源排放变化的驱动力。他们发现，近年来，我国空气质量总体改善，二氧化硫、氮氧化物和一次颗粒物排放量显著降低，但细颗粒物冬季重污染问题突出，空气质量仍面临严峻挑战。

“粗放的经济发展模式和不合理的产业结构导致人为源污染物排放持续增加，是中国出现严重空气污染问题的根本原因。解决空气污染问题不能单纯依靠末端治理，必须通过能源结构及产业结构调整实现长期持续减排。”张强说。

Professor Zhang Qiang: Exploring the Complex Sources of Air Pollution

A global burden of disease study shows that long-term exposure of $PM_{2.5}$ has led to more than 900,000 premature deaths in China in 2013. Faced with huge health threats and economic losses from air pollution, we urgently need to know what exactly the source of air pollution is and how human activities play a role in this phenomenon. Professor Zhang Qiang from Department of Earth System Science at Tsinghua University aims to tackle and answer this question.

"In China, advanced and backward technologies exist at the same time. With the fast industrialization and urbanization, air pollutants in China have been changing rapidly in terms of spatial and temporal dimensions, which pose a great challenge on the quantification work. The unified emission inventory technology in China has created great difficulties for government to make precise policies and scientific managements of air pollution." said Professor Zhang.

In order to solve this problem, Zhang and his team establish an emission inventory technology for regional air pollution. This model is developed using technology and process based methods, which resolves the quantitative relationship between emissions and technology turnover. They conduct a series of studies on the up-to-date dynamic methodology and high-resolution emission processing system.

Air pollutants emission inventory refers to quantify the emissions from all kinds of emission source within a certain time span and region scope. Complete emission inventories are essential to identify emission sources and necessary for policy making and air quality management.

After years of efforts, Professor Zhang Qiang and his team set up an up-to-date dynamic emission inventory system at a national scale. The developed online emission inventory platform has been widely used at home and abroad. According to incomplete statistics, at present, more than 80% of air quality numerical forecasting systems adopts their emission inventory, and their inventory is also used in many air quality forecasting and warning systems, including China National Environmental Monitoring Centre, local monitoring stations and environmental protection agencies.

Zhang and his team analyzed the driving force of various socioeconomic factors, such as economic growth, technological progress and pollution control. They found that, in recent years, China's overall air quality has improved with significate emission reductions of sulfur dioxide, nitrogen oxide, and primary particulate matter. However, air pollution during winter is still a big problem, which pose a great challenge on air quality improvement.

"Extensive mode of economic development and unreasonable industrial structure have led that anthropogenic emissions continue increasing, which is the fundamental cause of severe air pollution problems in China. To solve this problem, it is twin important to install advanced end-of-pipe control measures and conduct energy and industrial structure adjustments to achieve continuous and long-term emission reductions." said Professor Zhang.

Contributor | Department of Earth System Science

Translation and revision | Min Weiyuan

Image | Guo Xiang

6月9日

文字 | 张智伟

图片 | 宋晨

张奚若：学问要往大处着眼

1947 年，《清华周刊》请张奚若为 36 周年校庆题词，他挥笔写就：“学问要往大处着眼，不然就是精深也是雕虫小技。”

张奚若是哥伦比亚大学政治学硕士，1925 年回国后，曾任清华大学、西南联大政治系主任。虽然在他的一生中，专职做大学教授的时间并不太长，但他的教学获得了学生和同事的极高评价。

身为政治学系主任，每逢学期开始，他都亲自指导学生选课，并在每个学生选完课的表格上签上自己的名字。上课时，他头戴礼帽，架一副宽黑边眼镜，手持拐杖，给人的印象是严肃乐观、和蔼可亲、平易近人。

张奚若很注重引导学生关注社会问题，他在多次场合引导青年人：“思想的方向和技能的应用，都要朝着一个中心目标，那就是——人民的福利。”他还说：“举凡一切政治上、经济上的重要设施，必须以人民为出发点，而且以人民为归宿。我们今日若谈社会问题，必须以全体人民的利益，作为最重要、最基本、最后的目标。”

1932 年 6 月，张奚若在清华大学毕业典礼会上代表教授会向学生致辞，提出三点意见：奋斗、续学、耐劳。尤其是关于“耐劳”，张奚若说：“这一点是特别对本校同学说的。我们常听到校外人对清华的批评，都说清华的同学，成绩的确比别的学校好些，但是缺点在不能吃苦，不肯吃苦。所以，我希望诸位出校之后，抱定为社会服务的宗旨，把个人的享受看轻些。”

除去言辞上的引导外，张奚若本人的学术研究、社会活动也成为鼓励青年人“往大处着眼”、关心社会问题的典范。《张奚若文集》中所收集的发表于 1927 年至 1946 年的文章，很大一部分属于时评和政论，集中表达了他关心国运、鞭挞腐朽的强烈心情和不畏强权、不顾一身安危的非凡勇气。由于性格刚直、经常对社会问题发声，张奚若被好友徐志摩称为“有名的炮手”。

在清华任职期间，张奚若吸引、鼓舞了一大批青年学生。2001 年 6 月，时任总理朱镕基在辞去清华大学经济管理学院院长的告别会上，回忆当年在清华求学时的情形：“我们也很喜欢去张奚若先生家里，坐在地上，听张先生纵论天下，大骂国民党。我后来做班长、学生会主席，读了很多很多书，我的共产主义信仰就是在那时候建立的。”

陈岱孙评价张奚若是“合志士与学者于一身的人物”。如今，这位鼓励学生“做学问要往大处着眼”的志士、学者早已远去，但他留给了后人无尽的怀念与追思。

Zhang Xiruo: Knowledge Is About Being Far-sighted

1947's *Tsinghua Weekly* edition, which corresponded with the 36th Anniversary of Tsinghua University, asked Zhang Xiruo for an inscription. "Knowledge is about being far-sighted otherwise it is just insignificant."

Zhang Xiruo has a Master in Political Science from Columbia University. After returning home in 1925, he served as the Head of the Department of Political Science at Tsinghua and National South-west Associated University. Although he did not serve as a full-time university professor for very long, his teaching approaches and philosophy has earned him high praises from both students and colleagues.

As the Head of the Department of Political Science, he would personally guide the students in their course selections at the start of every new semester. He would also sign his name on every student's document indicating the completion of course selections. In class, his hat stays on his head, his glasses are in black frame and his hand always rests on a walking stick. The impression that he gives is both stern yet approachable, optimistic and amiable.

Zhang Xiruo is very focused on guiding his students to focus on social problems. He repeatedly said: "How we think and the application of our skills must move towards a common goal. What is that? The welfare of the people." He also said, "All political and economic aspirations must be about meeting the needs of the people. The social issues that we discuss today must be the interests of the people and most importantly, it must remain our final goal."

In June 1932, Zhang Xiruo gave a speech on the behalf of all professors at the Tsinghua Graduation Ceremony. He put forward three points: "To endure hardship, to continue learning and to work hard." This especially applies to the students. "We often hear people criticize Tsinghua and say that although the students have better marks than others, they are not as hard working and unwilling to endure hardships." "I hope that after graduation, you will keep in mind the importance of social responsibility and be more selfless through lowering the importance of having personal comfort and enjoyment."

In addition to his parting words, Zhang Xiruo's own academic research and involvement in social activities allowed him to tell his students to "be more far-sighted" , so they can take on more social responsibilities and gain awareness. In *Zhang Xiruo's Collection of Works*, many are his commentaries and political theories which focused on his concerns for his nation, the challenges that lies ahead and his courageous voice for addressing various social issues. Zhang is often dubbed by his friend Xu Zhimo as that "famous solider" .

During his time at Tsinghua, Zhang Xiruo attracted and encouraged a large number of young bright students. In June 2001, when Premier Zhu Rongji resigned from his post at Tsinghua's School of Economics and Management, he recalled his time at Tsinghua. "We all love to visit Mr Zhang because we enjoy sitting on the floor of his humble dwelling and listen to his views on Kuomintang and much more."

Chen Daisun said that "Zhang is both a warrior and a scholar" . Now, this important figure has left us but his memories and words live on.

Translation and revision | Min Weiyuan

Image | Song Chen

6月12日

文字 | 刘兰

图片 | 任帅

特等奖学金获得者张晓声：专注科研，多元发展

“科学的诗意和美好，鼓励我一直前行！”“做光学领域最前沿的研究，造国家所需最精密的仪器，要成为一名纯粹而优秀的‘工科男’。”清华大学精仪系2013级本科生张晓声站在特奖答辩的讲台上，用自己严谨的治学态度和对科学的热爱征服了在场评委，成为2016年清华大学特等奖学金获得者。

张晓声的身上，满载各种荣誉——学业方面，三年平均学分绩年级第一，曾连续两年获清华大学国家奖学金等；科研方面，以第一作者身份在SCI期刊发表两篇论文，其中一篇在光学领域重要期刊《光学快报》发表，拥有“光栅单色仪虚拟仪器自动控制软件V1.0”的软件著作权等；社会工作方面，曾获社会工作优秀奖学金、献血先进个人等。

张晓声评价自己：科研为他获得特奖打下基础，多元使他脱颖而出。

与科研结缘，始于张晓声大一下学期参加的大学生研究训练计划项目（SRT）——飞秒激光高精度测距。2016年9月，他取得较大科研成果——以第一作者的身份撰写的论文，仅仅23天即被光学领域重要期刊录用。三年间无论多忙，张晓声从未间断实验室的研究工作，每个寒暑假都至少安排三周时间留在学校做实验。尤其在9月份发表论文之前，他利用期末考试复习的间隙，加班加点做实验、测数据，一整个暑假都没有回家，最终在美国暑期研修期间完成论文撰写。

初试牛刀时，张晓声亦觉茫然，甚至在遇到实验精度等问题时深感挫败。然而，他明确知道自己喜爱思考、乐于钻研的性格适合做科研，并对科研有着浓厚的兴趣，于是在老师和实验室前辈的帮助下，张晓声在科研道路上披荆斩棘、精益求精。如今即将本科毕业的他，选择去美国继续攻读光学博士学位，希望学习更多专业知识，探索新的方向。

“今年特奖候选人中有很多科研突出的同学，我的优势可能在于有社会工作等方面的广泛经历，让自己的发展更加多元。”张晓声说。与张晓声一起获得今年本科生特奖的热能系学生刘一锋是“八度阳光”科技有限公司的创始人，公司在太阳能光伏发电领域获得了八项专利授权。在张晓声看来，刘一峰的获奖也体现了近年来特奖评选对学生创新创业和多元发展的关注。

清华大学特等奖学金设立于1989年，是学校授予在校学生的最高荣誉，一批批特奖获得者成为在校生们学习的榜样。作为一个优秀的群体，他们大都对自己的人生目标有比较清晰的认识，并有好的学习生活习惯帮助他们达成目标。

Top Grade Scholarship Winner Zhang Xiaosheng: Focus on Scientific Research and Develop with Diversity

"The poetry and beauty of science encourage me to move forward!" "Conducting the most cutting-edge research in the optical field and making the country's most precise instruments, requires a pure and excellent engineer." Zhang Xiaosheng, 2013 undergraduate from the Department of Precision Instrument in Tsinghua University, standing on the podium of Top Grade Scholarship, with his rigorous scholarship and love of science, conquers the present judges and becomes the Top Grade Scholarship winner among the undergraduates of Tsinghua University in 2016.

Zhang Xiaosheng is loaded with various honors. In respect of academic performance, his GPA in three years ranked first and he also won the national scholarship of Tsinghua University for two consecutive years; in respect of scientific research, he has published two papers in SCI listed journals as the first author, one of which is published in *Optics Letters*, an important journal in the optical field, owning the software copyright of "grating monochromator virtual instrument automatic control software V1.0" ; in respect of social work, he has won the social work excellence scholarship, and blood donation advanced individual, to name a few.

When talking about himself, Zhang Xiaosheng said, scientific research lays a foundation for his special scholarship winning, but diversity makes him stand out from the rest.

The ties formed with scientific research starts from Zhang Xiaosheng's participation in the project of Student Research Training (i.e. SRT) named "femtosecond laser high-precision ranging" in the second semester of the freshman year. Up to September 2016, he made a bigger scientific research achievement—the paper written by him as the first author is included by an important journal in the optical field after merely 23 days. Within three years, no matter how busy he was, Zhang Xiaosheng never suspended the research work in the laboratory, and arranged at least three weeks in each winter and summer vacation to do experiments in the university. Especially before the publication of the paper in September, he took advantage of his spare time during the final exam review to conduct experiments and measure data by studying overtime. He did not go back home in the entire summer vacation, and ultimately completed his paper during the summer training period in the United States.

During his first attempt, Zhang Xiaosheng also felt at a loss, even in the event of experimental accuracy, he felt frustrated. However, he clearly knows that his character of the love for thinking and studying makes him more suitable to do scientific research, and he has also has vast interest in conducting scientific research. Therefore, with the help of teachers and laboratory predecessors, Zhang Xiaosheng has overcome difficulties and pursued excellence on the way of doing scientific research. Now in the face of graduation, he chooses to go to the United States to continue his study in the optical field for a doctor degree, hoping to gain more professional knowledge and explore new directions.

"This year, there are many Top Grade Scholarship candidates who have given outstanding performances in scientific research, while I may have extensive experience in some other aspects, making myself more diversified and granting me more relative advantages." Zhang Xiaosheng said about himself. As much as Zhang Xiaosheng understands, in recent years, the Top Grade Scholarship of Tsinghua University pays more and more attention to diversification. Just like in the case of Liu Yifeng, who is the Top Grade Scholarship winner from the Department of Thermal Engineering, he once suspended his schooling and started his own business, and his start-up company "Beijing Sunlectric Technological Co., Ltd." has obtained authorization of eight patents by far.

Top Grade Scholarship of Tsinghua University was established in 1989 and it is the highest honor awarded by the university to the students. Top Grade Scholarship winners have also become models among Tsinghua students. As an outstanding group, most of them have a clear understanding of their goals in life, and their outstanding learning capabilities and living habits also help them achieve their ultimate goals.

Translation and revision | Raj Lamar

Image | Ren Shuai

6 月 13 日

供稿 | 绿色大学办公室

文字 | 蒋佩妍

图片 | 宋晨

绿色清华“三联画”：绿色教育，绿色科技，绿色校园

夏至未至，园里园外的林木早已亭亭如盖，似大片黛绿泼墨于宣纸之上。在以“节能有我，绿色共享”为主题的第 27 个全国节能宣传周（2017 年 6 月 11 日至 6 月 17 日）以及第 5 个全国低碳日（2017 年 6 月 13 日）前夕，5 月 26 日，中央政治局就推动形成绿色发展方式和生活方式进行了第 41 次集体学习。习近平总书记在主持学习时强调，推动形成绿色发展方式和生活方式是贯彻新发展理念的必然要求，必须把生态文明建设摆在全局工作的突出地位。

清华早在 1998 年便提出“绿色大学”建设构想。经过近 20 年的绿色发展，描绘出一幅由“绿色教育”“绿色科技”和“绿色校园”组成的绿色清华“三联画”。

“绿色”在教育，打造全方位、多层次、国际化的绿色教育体系。据不完全统计，全校有 26 个院系每学年开设 240 余门绿色课程，其中 140 余门为非环境专业，还与耶鲁等名校强强联手，开设环境专业双学位项目。读万卷书，行万里路。除了教室里名师大家的谆谆教诲，校园处处都能够看见绿色行动的足迹：环境友好科技竞赛、学生绿色社会实践和绿色社团活动……这些以绿色教育为旨的实践，吸引了上万人次参与，涌现出了灿若繁星的品牌成果，将绿色教育打造为清华的一张精美“名片”。

“绿色”在科技，发挥优势学科资源，推进绿色科研。近 10 年来，清华累计承接了 2000 余项绿色科研项目，超过 50 个院系单位参与其中，一大批重要的绿色科研成果令人瞩目。科研过程清华同样重视，开展了清洁生产审核，不断推进科研过程绿色化。在学科交叉、交流合作方面，还成立了生态文明研究中心等跨学科研究机构，与校外单位共建清洁煤炭研究院、清华伯克利能源与气候变化联合研究中心等，为国家和区域绿色发展服务。

“绿色”在校园，建设资源节约型、环境友好型绿色校园。太阳能、地热能等清洁和可再生能源为清华所用，废弃自行车被回收再生，雨水收集池和中水处理站也建成使用。进步无止境，清华还在继续完善能源管理体系，努力将能源管理水平提升至国内高校领先水平。

“景昃鸣禽集，水木湛清华。”如今的清华园，三季有花、四季常绿。1280 种树木，20 余万株乔灌木，128 万平方米的绿化，54.8% 的绿化覆盖率，使其成为北京无可替代的一片“绿肺”，为这颗繁忙的心脏源源不断地输入新鲜氧气。

在新的历史背景下，绿色大学建设将深入贯彻五大发展理念，以生态文明建设为契机，不断深化和拓展绿色大学建设内涵和外延，将新发展理念融入人才培养的各个环节。

Green Tsinghua: Education, Technology and Campus

Summer has yet to arrive and the trees at Tsinghua has already covered the campus and provided an early escape from the incoming heat. Under the theme of "Energy Saving and Sharing the Greenery" and as part of the 27th National Energy Saving Week (June 11 to 17, 2017) and the 5th National Low-Carbon Day (June 13, 2017), the Political Bureau of the Central Committee undertook a group study with regards to green development on the eve of the 26th of May, 2017. President Xi Jinping stressed that green development and lifestyle is a crucial concept and such focus must be fully implemented.

As early as 1998, Tsinghua has put forward the idea of constructing a "Green University" . After nearly 20 years of development in this area, education, technology and campus have been shaped to suit this green development.

Green Education: Multi-dimensional

According to statistics that have yet to be completed, there are more than 240 "green" courses from 26 different Departments. Many courses include double degree programs taught in joint collaborations with world-class universities such as Yale University. "He who knows much travels far." So apart from coursework, there are also many social practices, green activities and other related education events. These "green" activities saw tens of thousands of participants and supporters.

Green Technology: Promoting resources and green research

Over the past ten years, Tsinghua has undertaken more than 2000 green research projects and collaborated with more than 50 institutions. Tsinghua has also made a large number of important green research achievements and continues with such related promotions. In terms of interdisciplinary exchanges and cooperation, research centers were also formed along with joint research to tackle issues involving green energy and climate change etc. Such examples can be seen in the formation of research units for cleaner coal usage, joint new energy research with Berkeley and much more.

A Green Campus: Building an efficient and environmentally friendly campus

Tsinghua uses clean and renewable energy, such as solar and geothermal energy. Abandoned bicycles are recycled, rainwater are collected and water treatment stations are also put into use. Tsinghua continues to improve her energy management system and strive to set a positive example for other tertiary institutions to follow.

Today's Tsinghua campus is filled with greenery. With more than 1280 kinds of trees, more than 200,000 shrubs and 1.28 million square meters of greenery which covers 54.8% of Tsinghua, it's really a part of the "green lungs" for Beijing.

A green university offers an opportunity to deepen and expand the importance of green development for not just China but also the world.

Contributor | Green Office of Tsinghua University

Translation and revision | Min Weiyuan

Image | Song Chen

6月14日

文字 | 胡颖

图片 | 薛雅芳、杨思维

老师当“绿叶”，同学变“红花”——一堂别开生面的思政课翻转课

“今天我们一起学习的这堂思政课，可以说是别开生面，老师当‘绿叶’，同学变‘红花’，角色转换很到位，翻转课堂很成功，是一场思想交锋的精神大餐。”在亲临清华大学一线教学课堂、聆听了一堂马克思主义学院副教授冯务中主持的思政讨论课后，教育部党组书记、部长陈宝生这样感慨道。

2017年4月20日，教育部党组、清华大学党委理论学习中心组全体成员深入清华大学一线课堂，与70多名本科生一起上了一堂以“‘质疑改革开放’思潮之解析”为主题的讨论课。该门思政课以混合式教学模式开展，由学生自主观看“学堂在线”上的慕课视频、教师课堂讲授、师生小班讨论和学生课下作业四部分组成。

教师引导环节中，冯务中首先简要介绍了混合式教学的四项要素、课程的作业构成和考核方式、“翻转课堂”概念的由来以及他的“导客为主”教学理念，使大家能从宏观上了解清华思政课的混合式教学改革。随后的教学环节中，冯务中从方法论的角度说明了如何解析一种社会思潮，并使用“学堂在线”开发的免费智慧教学工具——“雨课堂”对同学们进行了相关测试和调查，其结果可以即时呈现于大屏幕上，使大家一目了然。课上还开通了弹幕让大家实时评论，课堂气氛因此变得更加活跃。在学生展示阶段，同学们展开了激烈的辩论，各抒己见，侃侃而谈，集中展现了清华学子的社会问题思考深度和临场发挥能力。“老师当‘绿叶’，同学变‘红花’”的教学理念，在这个“翻转课堂”中得到了充分实践。

陈宝生在点评中充分肯定了清华大学思政课采取“基于慕课的混合式教学模式”的创新和效果，评价这堂课“配方”新颖，问题意识强，体现了时代特色和社会关注的焦点；“工艺”精湛，将教师、学生和课堂主题紧密联系到一起；“包装”时尚有特色，运用现代技术手段，体现了清华大学思政课建设取得的成绩。

目前，清华大学“马克思主义基本原理”“中国近现代史纲要”“毛泽东思想和中国特色社会主义理论体系概论”“思想道德修养与法律基础”四门本科生思想政治理论课已全部实现了线上线下相结合的混合式教学，线上部分的选课人数累计突破17万人次。从“冷门”到“抢手”，从国内到国际，清华思政课打破常规，勇于创新，敢于突破，结合时代的发展不断更新自我，这背后，是清华以混合式教学模式推动思政课改革的一系列创新之举。

习近平总书记在全国高校思想政治工作会议上的重要讲话中指出，做好高校思想政治工作，要因事而化、因时而进、因势而新，要运用新媒体新技术使工作活起来，推动思想政治工作传统优势同信息技术高度融合，增强时代感和吸引力。清华这堂别开生面的思政课，正是这样的呼应之举。这不仅是一堂利用现代技术增强思政课时代感和吸引力的思政课，也是一次展现清华学子风采、体现清华师生教学相长的精彩活动。

Special Ideological and Political Course: The Teacher Will be the Green Leaves and the Students Will Become Red Flowers

"Today, you can say that this ideological and political lesson is special since the teacher will be the green leaves and the students will become red flowers. Roles were reversed and this change is successful. This is both an academic and spiritual feast." Chen Baosheng, Minister of Education made this comment after personally participating in the lesson taught by Associate Professor Feng Wuzhong from the School of Marxism.

On the 20th of April 2017, Chen Baosheng along with Chen Xu (Tsinghua's Party Secretary), Chen Cungen (Vice Secretary of State Organs Work Committee of the CPC), Qiu Yong (The President of Tsinghua University), and others participated in the ideological and political course alongside about 70 Tsinghua students. Taught by Feng Wuzhong and under the theme of "Analyzing the Questioning trends about Reform and Opening-up" , this integrated teaching mode require students to go online to attend class, watch lectures, participate in small classroom discussions and complete assignments after class.

Associate Professor Feng Wuzhong briefly introduced the integrated teaching mode along with the various tasks, assignments and exams. He also explained the "role reversal" concept and the importance of "guiding" students to undertake their own learning. Such explanations helps many to understand the reforms and direction of the current ideological and political course. During his teaching, Feng explained how to analyze social trends through the methodological view and combined multi-media means to give an overview of the related subjects for his students. The utilization of the "bullet screen" acts as a visual stimuli during learning and also a visual platform for exchange and feedbacks. This only helps to make the lesson more lively. Students are encouraged to participate in active dialogues when presenting their work which requires them to have deep analysis of the various social issues. "Teachers will be the green leaves and students become the red flower" is Feng's teaching philosophy and has come into full swing during such new lessons and subsequent changes.

During his speech, Chen Baosheng fully affirmed the effectiveness of Tsinghua's ideological and political course. This "hybrid class" with such innovative approaches allow various "formulas" to take effect and tackle problems and encourage students to make analysis and come up with solutions that reflects the challenges faced in our era. "Such craftsmanship" is made possible through the links amongst teachers, students and the discussed themes. "Packaged" well and integrated with multimedia technology, this fully reflects the achievements made by Tsinghua.

At present, four of Tsinghua's undergraduate ideological and political theory course: "Basic Principles in Marxism" , "Outline of Modern Chinese History" , "Introduction to Mao Zedong's Thoughts and Theory" and "Moral Education and Legal Foundation" has fully realized a combined hybrid course consisting of both online studies and elective subjects. So far, 170,000 students have signed up for the courses. From China to the World and from being initially somewhat "unpopular" to now being the "hottest" course around, such teaching breaks traditional rules and reflects a push for innovative education reforms.

Following what President Xi Jinping said about the importance of ideological and political work in tertiary institutions, striving in such matters is crucial for all participants. New topics, new media and fusing traditional teachings with modern technology is required to ensure it is up-to-date and thus interesting. Tsinghua's efforts is a reflection of the hopes expressed by President Xi. This is not only about making the coursework interesting but also about ensuring that both teachers and students at Tsinghua can enjoy the course and grow along with it.

Translation and revision | Min Weiyuan

Image | Xue Yafang, Yang Siwei

6月15日

化学系石高全教授领衔石墨烯研究项目获国家自然科学奖二等奖

供稿 | 化学系

文字 | 梁乐萌

图片 | 宋晨

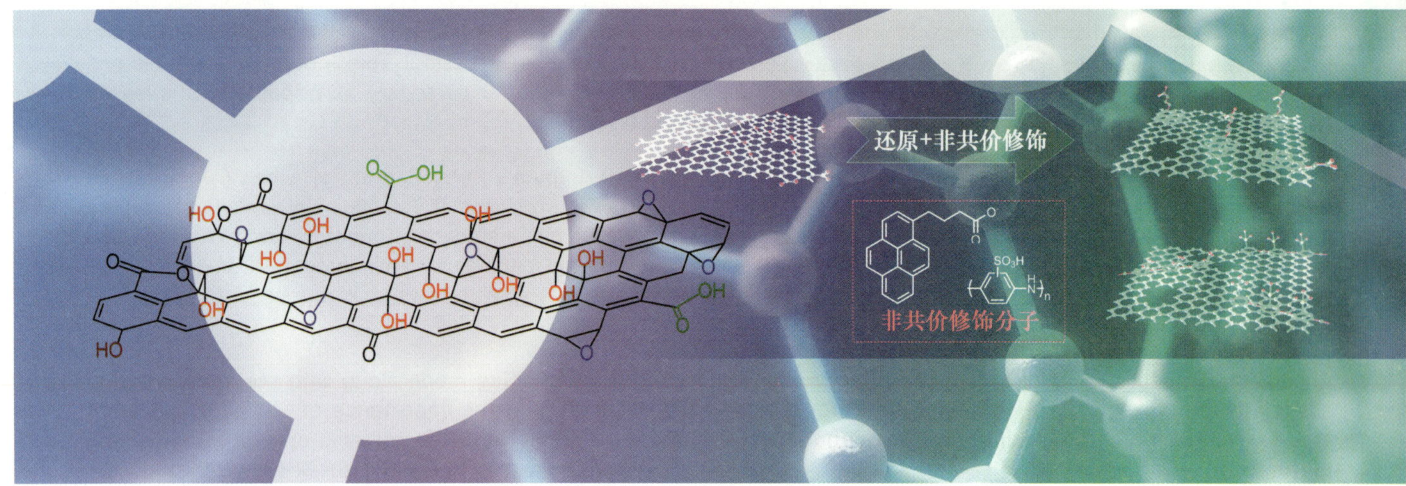

自 2004 年于英国曼彻斯特大学实验室首次被成功制备以来，仅由一层原子构成的石墨烯因其特殊性质，成为物理、化学等多个学科关注的热点。在 2016 年度国家科技奖励大会上，清华大学化学系石高全教授等完成的“化学修饰石墨烯可控组装与复合的基础研究”获得了自然科学奖二等奖。

石墨烯从结构上可以看成是二维共轭高分子。特别是化学修饰石墨烯作为新型共轭高分子构筑基元，已成为高分子学科新的生长点以及知识与技术创新的源头之一。

石高全教授的这一项目主要研究了化学修饰石墨烯的大分子行为，提出了石墨烯化学修饰与组装、复合的新方法，为揭示化学修饰石墨烯结构与性能的关系、构建新型石墨烯功能材料提供了知识积累、理论基础与技术支撑。该项目还着眼于探索新型石墨烯材料在能源领域中的应用，不仅是材料化学学科的重大理论突破，对于推进石墨烯工业化进程也有着关键意义。

该项目成果在国际上获得高度认可，20 篇主要论文被引用次数均位居该领域世界前 1%，并曾应邀在《先进材料》《能源与环境科学》等国际著名期刊发表综述。该项目阶段性研究成果还曾获中国 2013 年度高等学校科学研究优秀成果奖（自然科学）一等奖。除石高全教授以外，清华大学化学系徐宇曦、李春、白华、吴穹也是该项目主要完成人。

国家自然科学奖授予在数学、物理学、化学等基础研究和信息、材料、工程技术等领域的应用基础研究中，阐明自然现象、特征和规律，做出重大科学发现的中国公民。获得这一奖项的人员或项目都在科学上取得重要进展，达到国际先进水平，并为学术界所公认和引用，在推动本学科发展同时，对经济建设、社会发展有较大影响。

Professor Shi Gaoquan from the Department of Chemistry Was Granted State Natural Science Award for Graphene Research

Since being successfully prepared by the University of Manchester in 2004, graphene, which is composed of only one layer of atoms, has been a focus in chemistry, physics and other subjects due to its unique property.

Graphene can be regarded as a 2D conjugated macromolecule with huge molar mass according to its structure. Particularly, chemically modified graphenes (CMGs) are new members of conjugated polymers, having become a newly developing branch of polymer science and an abundant source of knowledge and technology innovations.

Professor Shi's project primarily studied the macromolecular and supramolecular behaviors of CMGs. Especially, the self-assembly and hybridization of CMG sheets, the fabrication and applications of CMG-based functional films, gels and composites were investigated. The project provides knowledge accumulation, theoretical basis and technical support to reveal the relationship between CMG structure and property, to construct new functional materials of graphene. The project also focused on the application of new graphene materials in the fields of energy, which is not only a theoretical breakthrough in material chemistry but also plays a key role in promoting the industrialization of graphene.

The results of the project were recognized internationally. Citations of twenty major papers were ranked in the top 1 percent worldwide in the field. The project was also invited to publish reviews on high profile journals including *Advanced Materials*, *Energy & Environmental Science*, etc. The periodical achievements of this project obtained the 1st grade award of natural science of Chinese Education Ministry (CEM) in 2013. Beside Professor Shi, Xu Yuxi, Li Chun, Bai Hua, Wu Qiong from the Department of Chemistry also played a vital role in the project.

China's State Natural Science Award is granted to Chinese citizens who have clarified natural phenomena, characteristics and laws, made major scientific discoveries in basic research of mathematics, physics, and chemistry and in applied basic research of information, materials, engineering. Citizens or projects, which win this award, have all made significant progress in science and met international cutting frontiers. They were universally recognized and cited by academic circle, promoting development of the discipline as well as economics and society.

Contributor | Department of Chemistry

Translation and revision | Raj Lamar

Image | Song Chen

6月16日

供稿 | 招生办公室

文字 | 校长办公室

图片 | 李娜

邱勇校长：有你的清华会更好——致2017年高考考生的邀请信

亲爱的年轻朋友们：

水木清华，人杰地灵。在这个美好的日子里，我代表清华大学向你发出诚挚的邀请，欢迎你加入清华人的行列，在美丽的清华园开启新的人生旅程。

清华大学是一所有梦想的大学，也是帮助青年学子圆梦的地方。在106年的发展历程中，清华培养了一大批学术大师、兴业英才、治国人才。一代代清华人在这里浸润于创意迸发的研究实践，砥砺于中西融会的思想碰撞，陶冶于人文日新的文化氛围，自信地走上人生更广阔的舞台。站在新百年新起点的清华大学，正在朝着更创新、更国际、更人文的目标迈进，致力于培养具有全球胜任力的拔尖创新人才，帮助每一个青年学子成就梦想中的自己。

更创新的清华，助你提升人生的高度。

创新决定未来，创新的意识、创新的能力极大地拓展人生的空间。清华今年将49个招生专业整合为16个大类，通识教育与专业教育相结合的培养模式，将使你发现自己真正的兴趣所在，更准确地找到适合自己的专业发展方向。师生自由探讨的“开放交流时间”（Open Office Hour），让你有充足的机会与各个领域的前沿学者、学术大师面对面，在交流中迸发出思想的火花。多种多样的创新教育平台与课外兴趣团队，让你在身边最优秀的同学中找到志同道合的小伙伴，开启思维与实践的探险。

更国际的清华，助你拓展视野的广度。

一个人要完善自己，不仅要有深厚的知识，更要有宽广的见识。不仅要读万卷书，更要行万里路，广交五湖四海的朋友，学会在多元文化环境中与不同经历背景的人交流合作。清华正在实施全球战略，丰富多彩的国际交流合作项目可以让你的足迹遍布世界各地，充分体验不同文化的魅力。你既可以去欧美发达国家的世界一流大学访问交流，也可以参加清华全球南方文化浸润系列项目，深入到非洲西海岸与南洋诸岛等发展中国家。你还有机会参加国际组织人才训练营，为未来投身联合国、世界银行、世界贸易组织做好充分的准备。

更人文的清华，助你永葆心灵的温度。

人文的价值，不仅在于丰富个体的生命体验，更在于能为我们生活的世界带来温暖。清华有着深厚的人文传统和实力日益提升的人文社会学科，我们希望，你不仅能获得经世济民的本领，更能成为一个有情怀、有担当的人。定期举办的“人文清华”讲坛，让你有机会聆听学术大师的演讲，和他们一起沉思时间、守望传统、追问正义、探讨幸福。新建成的艺术博物馆，可以让你在其中净化心灵、陶冶情操，欣赏科学与艺术的深度融合，感受人类追求真善美的信念与力量。深度阅读计划和宁静的书香校园，让你养成爱读书、读好书的良好习惯，在与智者的对话中思考人生。

亲爱的同学，我无比激动地期待着你的到来。在这里，我们将共同见证一个更加美好的清华。如果你要问我：“清华有多好？”我会告诉你：“有你的清华会更好！”

邱勇

清华大学校长

二〇一七年六月

The President of Tsinghua University Qiu Yong's Letter to 2017 Prospective Students—a Tsinghua with You Is a Much Better Tsinghua

Recently, Tsinghua University's President Qiu Yong issued a sincere invitation to the 2017 prospective students. He welcomed and asked them to join Tsinghua so that they can start an exciting and beautiful chapter in their lives.

In the letter, Qiu said that Tsinghua is a university filled with dreams. It is also a place to help young students find and fulfil theirs. During 106 years of development, Tsinghua has produced a large number of academicians, scholars, experts and professionals. Generations and generations of Tsinghua people have immersed themselves in innovative research, collided with both Eastern and Western ideas and knowledge, navigated through the new and the different and confidently marched ahead on a bigger platform and stage in their lives. When it comes to the new century, you are faced with an era that is more innovative and international where more and more talents are nurtured to have social awareness and global competencies. Tsinghua is here to support every student so that they can achieve their goals and dreams.

In his letter, "more innovative" , "more internationalized" and "more humanity-oriented" are the three directions that not only reflect the charms of Tsinghua but also the support that one can have. "A more innovative Tsinghua can help to broaden your horizons. A more internationalized Tsinghua can help you venture far and a more humanity-oriented Tsinghua can turn you into an even better person."

Qiu Yong wrote: "My dear students, I look forward to your arrival. Here, we can witness a beautiful Tsinghua. If you ask me, 'How good is Tsinghua?' I'll tell you, 'A Tsinghua with you is a much better Tsinghua!'"

Translation and revision | Min Weiyuan

Image | Li Na

6月19日

文字 | 杨晨晞

图片 | 李娜

15年，清华大学博士生学术论坛在路上

4月的清华园，春意盎然，水木明澈。走在学堂路主干道上，会发现路边多了一条亮丽的风景线——博士生学术论坛15周年展板。

始于2002年，清华大学博士生学术论坛已经走过了15年的时光。15年前，100位机械系博士生的相聚拉开了博士生学术论坛的序幕。15年久久为功，论坛不断发展壮大，成为清华园里学术交流的一大特色平台。

清华大学博士生学术论坛是主要面向博士生、教师广泛参与的学术交流活动，由清华大学研究生院和研究生工作部主办、校研究生会承办，15年来逐步形成包括院系论坛、校级论坛（两岸论坛）、专题论坛、全国论坛、国际论坛等在内的博士生学术论坛体系。500期学术论坛，18000余场学术报告，50000余名师生参与，清华大学博士生学术论坛在过去的15年间取得了令人瞩目的成绩。在这里，聊学术，拓思维，不论什么专业，总能找到一款适合你自己的"学术大餐"。在轻松愉悦而又火花四射的交流氛围中，学术志趣逐渐形成、学术思想不断浸润，学术志向得到激发。

学术永远是每位博士生最重要的主题。如今，师生间发散性、无障碍的学术争鸣和相互启发已经成为清华大学博士生学术论坛的核心特征，为每一个志在以学术为时代创新做贡献的博士生提供了思想交锋、创新融合的平台。

与清华大学博士生学术论坛15周年纪念大会同期举行的，还有以"交叉融合，创新时代"为主题的2017清华大学博士生学术论坛暨第七届两岸清华研究生学术论坛。师长们分享学术经验，两岸学生也在交流中拓展了自己的心胸与视野。

更好的清华，离不开更好的博士生教育。15岁风华正茂，让我们共同期待博士生学术论坛以15年、500期为契机，更加沉稳而奋进，成为清华以国际一流水准办好博士生教育的一张重要名片。

15 Years, Tsinghua University's Doctoral Student Academic Forum Still Well on the Road

April, Tsinghua Campus is filled with the colors and sights of spring. As one walks on the main road in the Tsinghua Campus, there is a huge board—Celebrating the 15th Anniversary of Tsinghua's Doctoral Student Academic Forum.

Started in 2002, Tsinghua University Doctoral Student Academic Forum has gone through 15 years of changes and developments. 15 years ago, 100 Doctoral students from the Department of Mechanical Engineering came together to start the first Academic Forum. For the next 15 years, the forum continues to grow and develop into a major platform for all academic exchanges.

Tsinghua University Doctoral Student Academic Forum is mainly for doctoral students and teachers to be involved in related activities. Organized by Tsinghua's Graduate School and Graduate Student Council, various forums from thematic ones to national ones to international ones have been held with success. 500 academic forums and 18,000 academic reports with more than 50,000 participants, the forum has made remarkable achievements during the past 15 years. Here, one can extend discussion and deepen analysis. No matter what the subject and profession may be, there is always a way for you to have your own "academic feast" . It is under such relaxing atmosphere that communication and academic thinking is promoted and students are inspired.

Academics is always the most important topic for every doctoral student. Nowadays, open academic exchanges and mutual inspirations between the teachers and doctoral students have become the core characteristic of this academic forum. It provides students with a platform for ideological discussions and innovative exchanges.

Translation and revision | Min Weiyuan

Image | Li Na

6 月 20 日

供稿 | 外文系

文字 | 杨晨晞

图片 | 宋晨

摄影 | 何名暖

同声传译实验室：培养更国际、更顶尖的外语人才

106 周年校庆之际，清华大学同声传译实验室迎来了一群崭新的青春面孔——清华附中的学生代表们。他们在老师和志愿者的引导下，来到这个校庆开放实验室，进行同声传译的尝试与体验。

清华大学同声传译实验室始建于 2010 年，是为了适应外文系培养高水平面向国际的顶尖外语人才而建。同声传译实验室位于第三教学楼三段 3505，是一个具有交替传译和同声传译教学、学生自主学习、多媒体课件演示及制作、模拟国际会议等功能的综合性实验室。

同声传译实验室由主会场和同传间两部分组成。会场部分可容纳 24 人，供教师进行课堂教学使用，模拟会议中则作为观众座席。同传间共四间，每间设两个译员席位，可供多组学生同时练习，也可以满足国际会议中多语种同声传译的需要。

无论是会场还是同传间，每个座位均配备计算机和语音终端。教师可以通过计算机对整个实验室的使用情况进行全方位的掌控，同时进行不同教学模块的切换管理以及发布翻译任务，监督每个学生的翻译状况，还可以选择单独交流以达成最好的教学效果。语音终端则可以通过不同按键进行音视频输入输出的控制，进行多种模式的翻译自主学习、开展交互式翻译练习、模拟会议场景等。

同声传译是一项高难度、高标准、高要求的技术，是译员在不打断讲话者讲话的情况下，不间断地将内容口译给听众的一种翻译方式。因其即时、准确、效率高等要求，需要精通外语和母语、知识面广阔同时应变能力强的高水平专业人才。随着清华全球战略和国际化办学的不断推进，对高级别学术会议的口译人才和外语人才的需求也愈加旺盛。

清华大学一直致力于为渴求提升外语能力和翻译水平的同学提供良好的平台。清华外文系不仅为英语专业和英语双学位的同学开设会议口译课程，还为全校同学开设了包括口译在内的相关翻译课程。课程设置和同传实验室的建设使用均以国际一流翻译专业为标准，并得到了包括国际翻译家联盟（FIT）前秘书长、国际译联会刊 Babel 主编弗朗斯·拉伊特（Frans De Laet）教授在内的多位专家的现场指导。今后也将继续为有效提高学生外语水平和翻译能力、为国家和时代培养更多高水平翻译人才做出更多贡献。

2017 年 4 月 29 日上午，在清华举行的亚洲大学联盟成立大会上，我们就看到了同声传译员的风采，他们为来自亚洲十余所大学的代表架起了沟通的桥梁。相信通过同声传译实验室的精心培育，清华园中会走出更多在国际舞台上发光发亮的同声传译人才。

Simultaneous Interpretation Laboratory—the Cultivation and Training of Talents Who Are More Sharp and International

April 29, 2017, Tsinghua's Simultaneous Interpretation Laboratory ushered in a new group of young faces—student representatives from Tsinghua High School. At the 106th Tsinghua Anniversary Celebration, Tsinghua High School organized a group of student representatives to visit the Tsinghua's Simultaneous Interpretation Laboratory and experience the world of interpretation.

Tsinghua's Simultaneous Interpretation Laboratory was founded in 2010. It was designed to meet the needs of the Department of Foreign Languages and Literatures and to train high-level foreign language talents. At 3505 in the third Teaching Building, the laboratory is a comprehensive one with language teaching such as consecutive and simultaneous interpretation. The lab allows students to learn on their own and with multi-media facilities, various functions could be offered to improve student learning.

Simultaneous Interpretation Laboratory consists of two parts. The meeting hall can accommodate 24 people for classroom teaching. There are four simultaneous interpretation booths at the back of the room and each can accommodate two interpreters. Audiences can sit and participate as well. Such rooms helps to meet the needs of interpretation practices and theory works.

Whether it is in the meeting hall or in booths, it is equipped with computers and interpretation machines for everyone to use. Through the computers, teachers can make full use of the laboratory control system and at the same time, switch modules, assign interpreting tasks, monitor student learning and progress and give instructions through individual channels. The interpreters can control the audio input and output and complete different types of exercises. Apart from supervised individual practice, students can also self-study, collaborate with others and organize mock conferences by using the training module.

Simultaneous interpretation is a difficult and demanding skill often requiring the translator to display a high-standard in his or her techniques. It is a way of interpreting the content to the audience without interrupting the speaker's speech. Because of its immediacy, accuracy, efficiency and other characteristics, high level of proficiency in foreign languages is needed along with broad knowledge and adaptability. At the same time, globalization and the strengthening of internationalization means that Tsinghua is becoming more focused in cultivating globally competent talents and language professionals.

As Tsinghua University endeavors to improve the level of foreign languages and interpreting skills for her students, the Simultaneous Interpretation Laboratory is providing a good platform for students to explore their interests and unleash their potentials. Conference interpreting and translation courses offered by the Department of Foreign Languages and Literatures are available for English majors as well as students from other departments. The curriculum and the construction of the laboratory is a reflection of the highest interpretation standards. In addition, along with other experts and professionals, the former Secretary-General of the International Federation of Translators (FIT) and editor in chief of *Babel*, Professor Frans De Laet visited the lab to provide guidance. In the future, the lab will continue to make more contributions to the improvement of students' foreign language proficiency and interpretation ability. It will train more top-level interpreters for our motherland and generation.

At the inaugural meeting of the Asian University Alliance in the morning of the 29th of April, we saw the talents of simultaneous interpretation who became the bridge that linked valuable exchanges amongst the Asian universities. With the Simultaneous Interpretation Laboratory, we believe that Tsinghua will cultivate more talents and fine interpreters for the near future.

Contributor | Department of Foreign Languages and Literatures

Translation and revision | Min Weiyuan

Image | Song Chen

Photographer | He Mingnuan

6 月 21 日

文字 | 刘书田

图片 | 唐蓓蓓

夏至：昼晷已云极，宵漏自此长

夏至乃夏之初，公元前 7 世纪，先人采用土圭测日影，就确定了夏至。《礼记》中记载了自然界有关夏至节气的明显现象——鹿角开始脱落，蝉儿开始鸣叫，半夏、木槿两种植物逐渐繁盛开花，万物进入了蓬勃生长的时机，争先恐后地释放积蓄已久的活力。

夏至时的清华园别有一番景致。学堂路上的树木郁郁葱葱，充满着青春的气息；荷塘上漂浮的圆圆荷叶，透映出青翠的生命力；水木清华旁的柳枝随风飘拂，摇曳生姿——清华园在艳阳照耀下，流光溢彩。

晴朗夏至的清晨，倚靠在情人坡前长廊里，和身边的人说着悄悄话；散步于球场前的雕塑园内，一览各式各样的花开。暴雨突袭的午后，适合窝在寝室里睡个好觉，伴随着雨滴敲打阳台的声响，欣赏这一曲夏至交响。

夏至自古便是诗人们的咏吟对象。唐朝权德舆曾云："璿枢无停运，四序相错行。寄言赫曦景，今日一阴生。"而"水木清华"借以得名的"景昃鸣禽集，水木湛清华"这句诗，似乎也描绘着夏至前后的景况。

夏至的到来，标记着天气真正进入暑热阶段。在我国，这一天全年白昼最长，其后日照时间一天天缩短，民间也有"吃过夏至面，一天短一线"的说法。倘若在园子里遇上夏至日，不妨去听涛园打一份辣得够味的担担面，或是去丁香园来碗香喷喷的烩面，给予这最灿烂的节气一个小小的仪式感。

夏至亦是毕业的季节，下个决心早早起来追逐朝阳的升起，伴着晨曦微光留下与园子的合影，顶着烈日来一杯清爽的绿豆沙冰，夕阳西下再去操场踢一场球。随着夜幕降临，大雨突袭，潇洒地挥一挥衣袖，带着对园子的留恋离开……那时清华园的夏至日，将成为定格在大学记忆里最后且最美的画面。

Celebrating the Summer Solstice at Tsinghua

Summer solstice is the beginning of the summer. In 7th Century BC, the ancient Chinese used tugui (土圭) or a gnomon plate to measure the length of the sun's shadow to determine summer and winter solstice. *The Book of Rites* recorded three events in nature as summer solstice approaches, where deer's antlers begin to fall off, cicadas begin to sing, Pinellia, a plant native to East Asia, and hibiscus gradually flourish and bloom. Everything springs to life and goes into full-swing.

Summer solstice on Tsinghua campus is like no other places. The Xuetang Road where bikes whiz by and students stroll along is lined with lush trees, bringing an atmosphere of youth and vibrance. Lotus leaves float delicately on the surface of the famed imperial Lotus Pond, the swaying willow branches next to Shuimu Tsinghua bids visitors a welcome. Radiance from the sunlight fills all corners of the campus.

An early morning on summer solstice is the best time to lie on the green slopes of Qingren Po next to the North Library, chat away with a companion, or wander around the courts and park, naming all the flowers. If a storm steals an afternoon out away, it then becomes an opportune time to stay in bed and enjoy a good nap that's accompanied by raindrops—the song of a summer solstice.

The arrival of summer solstice marks a change in weather and the arrival of high temperatures. It is the longest of day in a year in China, and daytime following summer solstice shrinks to shorter hours. A Chinese folk saying goes "eat strings of summer noodles, every day is a strand (of time) shorter" . If you're out on the paths on campus on a summer solstice, why not go to Tingtao canteen for a bowl of spicy Dandan noodles or to Dingxiang canteen for a bowl of fragrant braised noodles, to give this most brilliant season a little sense ritual.

Summer solstice is also graduation season. Determine to rise early to chase after the sunrise and at the first rays of the morning sun, take a photo around campus. When the sun is scorching hot, grab a cup of refreshing iced mung bean. At the setting of the evening sun, catch a game of soccer at the field. In the evening, when it rains unexpectedly, be carefree and untroubled. Bring with you cherished memories on this campus as you leave. In that moment, summer solstice at Tsinghua will be a frozen frame in time and it shall be the last and most beautiful picture in your memory of campus.

Translation and revision | Alexis See Tho

Image | Tang Beibei

6月22日

文字丨拜喆喆

图片丨梁晨

摄影丨何名暖

曾哲妮：清华，我的“刷新”之旅

湖南省优秀学生干部、雅礼中学团委副书记……进入清华时，曾哲妮身上带着耀眼的光环。2017年夏天，她卸下光环，踏入了梦想已久的清华园。曾哲妮用“刷新”二字给园子里的一年经历作了注解。

阅读是种自我刷新

进入新雅书院时，曾哲妮对于通识教育怀着懵懂的认知和期许。然而，当她在开学伊始就拿到一整套简・奥斯汀的作品，同时开始准备《史记》研读时，内心不无惶恐。“好在新雅给予了我真诚善意的老师与宁静沉潜的氛围。”渐渐地，厚重的书本转化为思想的积淀，和同窗的交流也让知识更加立体。她和舍友在寝室聊遥远的鲧禹传说、聊历史与绝对真实…… “新雅改变了我。”哲妮说。在她看来，自己无甚天分，但努力与进步都被老师们看在眼里——她的《史记》研读作业被收作范本，“自他社”报告登上了新雅公众号……

饮水思源的公益梦

园子里的生活不止诗和远方，哲妮的目光离不开“公益”二字。创建属于新雅书院的公益社团“雅志协会”是她这一年最为骄傲的事。一切从零开始，她和伙伴们组织周末支教、开展线上分享会、完成10家福利机构调研……新雅的公益项目在清华能够后来居上，过程的艰辛自不必说，这样的过程对曾哲妮来说却是幸福的：“能在新雅的成长日记中留下自己的一笔，就是最大的意义。”从雅礼中学毕业，卸下母校带来的光环，曾哲妮和雅礼的故事却在续写。她担任了情系母校的雅礼支队长，联系三十余所兄弟学校为母校的学弟学妹服务，收获了“近几年来最好最扎实的一届雅礼蓝”的评价。

从“子所雅言，诗书执礼”到“水木湛清华”，从情系母校到投身新雅公益，她始终怀抱着饮水思源的责任感，“是清华让我扎根、成长。”

从激扬文字到人工智能

按照新雅书院的课程设置，哲妮即将面临专业分流的选择。她坚定地选择了自动化专业，想要成为“能‘修洗衣机’也能‘激扬文字’的非典型工科女”。通识课程的学习让她在技术之外更加关注人文关怀和科技伦理：“我希望能在推动人工智能发展的同时，保护人类免遭可能的‘生存危机’。”哲妮的理想中有一种改变世界的决心：“这种决心并不是随口乱说。有了决心，还需要历练出改变世界的力量，新雅给我提供了种种历练的机会。”她期待着在园子里拥有更多的“刷新”之旅。

Zeng Zheni: Hitting the "Refresh" Button in the Tsinghua Experience

Outstanding Student Cadre from Hunan Province, Vice Secretary of the Communist Youth League at Yali High School... when she was admitted into Tsinghua, Zeng Zheni already had such titles around her. Last summer, she said goodbye to these past titles and started her study at Tsinghua. This had always been her dream. Zeng used the word "refresh" to define her year at Tsinghua.

Reading is a way to "refresh" oneself

When entering Xinya College, Zeng had great expectations for the general education that awaits her. However, once she started to read about Jane Austen' work and was asked to also read up on the *Records of the Grand Historian*, she felt a sudden sense of fear. "Thankfully in Xinya we had great teachers and the quiet environment." she later recalled. Gradually the thick books and ideas developed into rich accumulation of thoughts. Besides, sharing personal insights with classmates enabled her to have more comprehensive understanding about knowledge. Along with her roommates, she would chat about the stories that they had just read, the authenticity of the historical records... . "Xinya changed me." said Zeng. In her view, she had little talent however the effort and progress displayed by Zeng allowed her reports to be selected as templates or published on Xinya's Social Media Account... .

The source of her charity dream

Campus life is also about social responsibility and in Zeng's view, charity is important. Creating a charity-based account called "Yazhi Association" became one of her proudest accomplishments this year. Starting from scratch, she and her team organized weekend trips to teach migrant children voluntarily and they would share their experiences online. Furthermore, they accomplished investigations about 10 welfare agencies... . The process was not easy but for Zeng, it was more sweet than bitter. "The greatest accomplishment is being able to leave behind a footprint of my growth." Since graduating from Yali High School to her time in Tsinghua, her active role in social events continues and she always embraces this sense of social responsibility. "Tsinghua allowed me to take root and grow."

Artificial Intelligence

In accordance with Xinya's curriculum, Zeng is faced to picking her major and professional direction. She firmly chooses the major of automation and she wants to become "a typical female engineering student who knows how to 'fix a washing machine' and how to 'write a poem'." General education lets her pay more attention to human concern and ethic of science and technology. "I want to protect humans from possible survival crises and at the same time, push forward the development of artificial development." Zeng's goal is not something that comes in passing. Once she makes up her mind, she has every intention to completing it. She wants to have the power to change the world and Xinya gave her this opportunity for exercise. She hopes to find more chances to hit the "refresh" button during her time at Tsinghua.

Translation and revision | Min Weiyuan

Image | Liang Chen

Photographer | He Mingnuan

6月23日

文字 | 张智伟

图片 | 郭祥

世界和平论坛：为世界安全这个古老命题寻找新的钥匙

2017 年 6 月 24 日至 25 日，以“应对国际安全挑战：合力、担当、变革”为主题的第六届世界和平论坛将在清华大学举行。在 2017 年上半年国际安全形势面临诸多不确定性和严峻挑战的背景下，此次世界和平论坛备受关注。

“在国际社会缺乏有效领导进行全球治理时，各国应该团结协商，展开无领导式安全治理的合作；地区性大国应该更多地承担起维护本地区秩序的责任；此外，冷战后国际秩序背后主导的价值观——自由主义观念正不断受到冲击，由此可能引起国际规范的改革。国际社会只有携起手来，本着‘合力、担当、变革’的精神，加强对话与合作，才能塑造一个更加和平与安全的世界。”世界和平论坛秘书长、清华大学国际关系研究院院长阎学通如此解释本届论坛的主题。

世界和平论坛由清华大学主办、中国人民外交学会协办，是中国举办的第一个高级别非官方国际安全论坛，至今已经走过了五个年头。论坛聚焦世界和平与安全，成为目前世界上非官方、国际安全论坛中最具影响力的论坛，吸引了来自多国的原政要和智库领导人参会。

过去五届中，论坛主题从首届的“各方共赢：和平、安全、合作”，到第二届的“世界变革中的国际安全：和平、发展、创新”，再到 2016 年的“共同安全秩序：合作、包容、开放”，每年都有新的变化。逐年更新的主题贯穿着论坛追逐始终的目标：“高层目标上，希望通过这样的平台，能够提出国际战略领域新的概念、新的研究思想，并取得一致；中层目标上，希望会议能够呈现出百家争鸣的局面，把各自新的概念陈列出来，即使这些新的概念并非一定是共识；最后，也是最低层的目标，是增强国际安全意识，提高民众对于维护世界和平的关注。”

各国现任或原政要、智库领导、专家的发言，为当前全球热点问题提供了思考火花和解决方案。例如首届世界和平论坛就提出了“自己安全也要让别人安全，自己发展也要让别人发展”的思想，论坛还首次提出中国的外交政策应该是大国的外交政策，这些后来都逐渐成为被国际社会普遍接受的思想。

在 2017 年的世界和平论坛上，与会者将围绕全球性、地区性和专题性三类安全问题进行有针对性的讨论，国际秩序面临的挑战、反建制主义思潮、大国关系、反导问题、核不扩散、恐怖主义等议题将得到与会者的关注。

正如人民网此前的一篇评论所言，“（论坛）将为世界和平与安全这个古老命题的解答找到新的钥匙”。

World Peace Forum: Finding a New Key for the Age-old Propositions of Global Security

From June 24th to 25th, 2017, the 6th World Peace Forum with the theme of "The Challenges of International Security: Cooperation, Responsibilities and Change" will be held at Tsinghua University. Under such context of uncertainty and the serious challenges faced by the international community when it comes to issues relating to security especially in the first half of the year, this year's World Peace Forum has received much more attention than usual.

"In the absence of effective leadership and global governance when it comes to tackling global security issues, countries should unite, consult one another and cooperate. Regional powers should also assume the responsibility to maintain order. In addition, the concept of liberalism is constantly undergoing disruptions and turbulence which may result in various reforms. The international community should join hands and embody the spirit of 'cooperation, responsibilities and change' to strengthen dialogue and cooperation in order to bring more peace and stability to the world." This explanation was given by Prof. Yan Xuetong, the Secretary-General of the World Peace Forum and the Dean of Tsinghua's Institute of International Relations.

The World Peace Forum, organized by Tsinghua University and co-organized by the Chinese People's Institute of Foreign Affairs, is the first high-level non-official international security forum held in China. It has been around for nearly five years. The Forum focuses on world peace and security and has become the most influential forum in the world's security forums. It attracts participations from international leaders, experts and think tanks. In the past five sessions, the theme of the forum started with the First Session's "Win-Win Situation: Peace, Security and Cooperation" to the Second Session's "International Security in the world of change: Peace, Development and Innovation" , to 2016's "Common Security Order: Cooperation, Tolerance and Openness." Every year, something new is discussed at the forum. The theme aligns with the goal of the Forum: "The goal is that through such platform, new concepts and research ideas in the field of international strategy could be put forward and agreed upon. The new concept is not necessarily a consensus. Moreover, it is about enhancing international security awareness and raising public awareness of the maintenance of world peace."

Key speeches and statements made by political leaders, think tanks and experts provide solutions and plans to tackle such discussed topics. For example, the First Forum put forward the idea that "If one is to be safe then others must be safe as well. If one develops then others must also develop." The forum also put forward for the first time that China's foreign policy should be the policy of a big nation and gradually become accepted by the international community.

In the forthcoming 2017 forum, participants will focus on global, regional and thematic security issues. The challenges facing the international order, anti-colonialism, and relationships amongst various international powers, anti-missile issues, nuclear non-proliferation, terrorism and many more will become the focus for the participants.

As the *People's Daily Online* said in a previous comment: this forum is about "finding a new key for the age-old propositions of global security."

Translation and revision I Min Weiyuan

Image I Guo Xiang

6月26日

原作者 | 吕婷

改写 | 胡颖

图片 | 宋晨

清华国学研究院院长陈来：优秀传统文化的传承者

陈来在清华有两个身份，既是人文学院哲学系教授，又是国学研究院院长，他笑言："我给学校打两份工，也是一种'双肩挑'。"

清华在1925年成立清华学校研究院国学门，以王国维、梁启超、赵元任、陈寅恪"四大导师"为首的国学大师荟萃一堂。由于种种原因，国学院于1929年停办。令人欣慰的是，老国学院的精神和学术传统在八十年后再一次焕发光彩，2009年清华复建国学研究院，陈来出任首任院长。

"中国主体，世界眼光"，是清华复建国学院时设立的宗旨，也是陈来对未来国学研究的期许，更是对老清华国学院衣钵的继承。陈来说："'中国主体'是要突出我们中国人对中国文化历史的理解，国学院本身就是一个彰显主体性的概念。我们要在与世界文化、与世界性的中国文化研究的密切沟通中确立起自己的地位。"

作为在中国传统文化相关领域长期耕耘的学者，陈来对于优秀传统文化的价值有着更加强烈的认同感，也有着身体力行的捍卫与弘扬。"中华民族的发展离不开中华文化的不断浸润和滋养，中华文化对中华民族的成长、发展和复兴有着重要意义。没有任何东西能取代它的影响，来给人民提供价值观、归属感、人生目标和精神追求。"

党的十八大以来，陈来一直注重学习、宣传和阐发习总书记关于传统文化的论述。2015年10月，陈来承担了中宣部马克思主义理论研究和建设工程重大课题"中华优秀文化的创造性继承及创新性发展研究"，多次在《人民日报》《光明日报》发表文章，阐述弘扬中华优秀文化的基本内涵及其现代价值。在著作《中华文明的核心价值——国学流变与传统价值观》中，陈来对中华文化产生发展的历史、中华文化的当代价值以及社会主义核心价值观的根源进行了全面的阐释。作为一名有着45年党龄的老党员，他还从专业的立场，积极为党中央建言献策，尤其关注社会主义核心价值观的建设。陈来强调，社会主义核心价值观的培育与弘扬不能脱离优秀传统文化空洞地来谈，一定要结合中华传统美德的涵养与实践。

关注人的精神生活、民族的发展复兴，是65岁的陈来笔耕不辍的重要动力。在国学研究之路上，陈来满怀着对国学的眷眷深情，同时也保持着攻坚克难的拳拳之心。这位当代儒者，立足传统却不守旧，吸取西学而不盲从，立志为中华文化的当代价值立言修德。

Dean of the Tsinghua Academy of Chinese Learning Chen Lai: Inheriting the Excellence of Our Traditional Culture

Chen Lai has two roles at Tsinghua. He is both a Philosophy Professor at the School of Humanities and the Dean of the Tsinghua Academy of Chinese Learning. "I have two jobs at Tsinghua so I carry two responsibilities on my shoulders." he said.

In 1925, Tsinghua established the Academy of Chinese Learning. "The Four Masters" who became in charge of the Academy were Wang Guowei, Liang Qichao, Zhao Yuanren and Chen Yinque. Due to various reasons, the academy was suspended in 1929. However, it was gratifying to note that the spirit and academic tradition of the Academy has been brought back after 80 years. In 2009, Chen Lai became the Dean of the Academy.

"The Chinese Focus, A World Vision" became the motto of the Academy. It is also Chen Lai's expectation for the Academy and furthermore, a Tsinghua heritage. Chen said: "The Chinese Focus is about highlighting Chinese understanding of Chinese culture and history. We want to set up our own cultural research center with both a Chinese and world focus."

As a scholar in the field of traditional Chinese culture, Chen has a stronger sense of identity and understands the value of traditional culture. "The development of the Chinese nation depends on the constant nourishment, growth and development of the Chinese Culture. Nothing can replace it. The goal is to give people value, a sense of belonging and spiritual pursuit." he said.

Since the 18th CPC National Congress, Chen Lai has focused on President Xi's discussions and hopes for traditional culture in China. In October 2015, Chen undertook the major project "The Research on Creative Inheritance and Innovative Development of Chinese Culture." His work has been frequently published on *People's Daily* and *Guangming Daily*. In his book *The Core Values of Chinese Civilization - Rheology and Traditional Values*, Chen Lai sets out to explain the development of Chinese culture, the contemporary value as well as the cause of existing socialist values. As a member of CPC for 45 years, he stated that socialist values cannot be separated from traditional culture. It must be integrated with the practice of traditional Chinese virtues.

The spiritual life of the people and the rejuvenation of China are the two most important driving force for the 65-year-old. Filled with great love for his country, Chen sets out with the initial goals in mind. As a scholar, he upholds tradition yet never allowing it to become too conservative. He absorbs Western views and teachings but refrain from being blinded by it. He is determined to maintain the contemporary value of Chinese culture.

Translation and revision | Min Weiyuan

Image | Song Chen

6月27日

原作者 | 程曦、吕婷
改写 | 刘书田
图片 | 李筱甜

追记清华大学水利系教授谷兆祺：化作滴水汇江河

生命中的每一天应该怎样度过？秉持怎样的信念才能心安无悔？什么才是最宝贵的财富和快乐？清华大学水利系教授谷兆祺用他普通而不平凡的人生做出了自己的回答。

水利是谷兆祺向祖国许下的终身之约。他一生奔走在万里江河之间，"真刀真枪"做水利。从1958年参加密云水库建设工程开始，一直到古稀之年，谷兆祺都坚持亲赴施工现场检查指导。爬大坝、钻隧洞、进电厂、攀闸门、睡帐篷、查阅资料、核算结构、取样实验、现场检测……攀上爬下是他的工作常态。他把全部心血都投入到工程现场中，甚至连身体健康和生命安全都置之度外。谷兆祺不仅走遍了祖国的江河湖海，还在改革开放后多次走出国门，带回国外先进的水电工程经验，为亚洲多个国家的水利项目做出了重要贡献。

退休后的谷兆祺心中始终牢记老校长蒋南翔"争取至少为祖国健康地工作五十年"的教导，他组织一些有经验的离退休教师共同撰写了《水利水电工程经验及案例分析》一书和相关的100多篇文章，系统总结了清华水利系50多年在科研、设计、生产方面的知识积累。直到病重前夕，谷兆祺一直在为国家的水利事业贡献全部的光和热。

教育公益事业也是谷兆祺一生的牵挂。20世纪90年代初，他经常利用出差间隙，到附近的农村小学看望学生。从1998年到2008年，谷兆祺坚持每学期向易县希望小学捐款，从未间断。在易县清华希望小学、阜平县同心希望小学，谷兆祺这个名字已经成为一条纽带，将关爱和善意源源不断地传递下去。在谷兆祺的带动下，他的家人和学生们也参与到扶贫助学活动中。有的学生义务为希望小学讲课、为教师作培训；有的学生已在美国生活工作多年，仍然坚持每年资助希望小学的贫困生。

2016年7月，病榻上的谷兆祺委托夫人陈方来到清华校友总会，捐赠多年积蓄80万元，设立"清华校友—谷兆祺励学基金"，资助经济困难、学习勤奋的学生完成学业，成材报国。谷教授身后，按照他的遗愿，家人又把他最后一个月的退休工资和近20万元丧葬费悉数捐入励学基金。

走到人生边上，谷兆祺选择了一切都"不留"。他像一滴晶莹剔透的水珠，汇入江河，渗入泥土，润物无声，用一生的学识、坚守和奉献，诠释了一名普通知识分子的责任与追求。

Remembering Gu Zhaoqi: a Selfless Professor in the Department of Hydraulic Engineering

How should life's many days be spent? What beliefs and convictions would lead to peace of mind instead of regrets? Gu Zhaoqi, Tsinghua University professor in the department of Hydraulic Engineering lived his simple yet extraordinary life to answer those questions.

Hydraulic Engineering was Gu Zhaoqi's lifelong covenant with his country. His whole life was spent running between the rivers and the streams, involving himself in the fieldwork of hydraulic engineering. Since 1958, when he participated in the construction of the Miyun Resorvoir to his seventies, he would insist on inspecting the construction sites where climbing up a dam, drilling tunnels, visiting power plants, sleeping in tents, gathering samples and conducting on - site experiments were part of his work routine.

He delved into work on the construction site, sometimes even to the detriment of his health and safety. Not only did Professor Gu covered the width and length of China's rivers and lakes, he also traveled abroad after the China's economic reform in the 1980s to bring back advanced hydraulic engineering technology, making great contributions to many countries in Asia.

After his retirement, Professor Gu Zhaoqi kept the words of former president of Tsinghua University, Jiang Nanxiang, close to heart: "To work healthily for 50 years for our motherland." He organized some experienced retired professors to co-write a book called *Hydraulic Engineering Experiences and Case Analysis* and wrote more than a hundred related articles and systematically organized fifty some years' worth of the university's scientific research, design and production in hydraulic engineering. Up until his last days, he was a major contributor in the field of hydraulic engineering in China.

Public education was Gu Zhaoqi's other passion. In the early 1990s, he would take advantage of his spare time during his work-related trips to visit elementary school students in nearby rural areas. From 1998 to 2008, he faithfully donated to Hope Elementary School in Yi County in Hebei Province, a province neighboring the city of Beijing. To those in Hope Elementary School and Fuping County's Tongxin Hope Elementary School, Professor Gu's name has become a link that see the passing on of care and goodwill to these students. Under the influence of Gu Zhaoqi, his family and students were also involved in poverty alleviation projects. Some of his students volunteered to teach the young students and train teachers at these elementary schools, while others who have been living the U.S. for many years, continue to provide financial aid to the students at these schools.

Laying on his sickbed in July of 2016, Gu Zhaoqi entrusted his wife, Chen Fang, through the Tsinghua Alumni Association, to donate 800,000 yuan of his life savings to establish a scholarship fund to help students with economic difficulties to complete their studies. At the end of his days, his family again donated his final month's retirement salary and almost 200,000 yuan allocated for his funeral expenses to the scholarship fund, fulfilling his final wishes.

Until the end of his life, Gu Zhaoqi had chosen to leave nothing behind. He is like a glistening and pure drop of water, flowing into the rivers, moistening the earth and quietly giving life to all. He has used a lifetime of knowledge, perseverance and dedication to live out the responsibilities and pursuits of an intellectual.

Translation and revision | Alexis See Tho

Image | Li Xiaotian

6月28日

文字 | 梁乐萌

图片 | 霍巍

毕业纪念品：可触摸的清华记忆

毕业衫有四种款式，图案绘制在布料上，仿佛记忆烙印在心口；二校门和“THU”字样环成小小一枚戒指，戴在手上，锁住四年时光；印章轻轻按下，庄严地证明对你的爱意，倾诉的话全在纸上，奈何纸短情长……

是情物，也是信物，这些就是以“三生有幸，且歌且行”为主题的清华三字班毕业纪念品。

随着天气渐暖白昼渐长，又一个满载着毕业离情的夏天悄然到来。从前抱怨油腻的食堂，突然想再多“吃”几次；平日熟视无睹的荷塘清波，突然想再多看几眼。“当时只道是寻常”，上课的铃声，北馆的书香，礼堂前排的长龙，一切突然变得那么珍贵。可回忆抓不住，时光太匆匆。

于是，把回忆凝结在物件中，将带有浓浓清华气息的纪念品，作为日后追忆的凭据。从“清华味道”“窗里窗外”“毕业巡礼”“毕业时刻”四款毕业衫，到以“THU”和二校门为主题元素的毕业戒指、印章，再到印有清华风物的纪念杯，毕业纪念品的价值远远超出了实用的范畴，成为毕业生手中可触可感的一份清华记忆。

就像纪念杯的广告词所说：“这一杯，我们敬最好的时光。”

毕业纪念品是清华的传统。每一年的纪念品都是独一无二的，除了慰藉思情，也是一代清华人身处的时代的缩影。从2011年到2017年，纪念品的图案由繁到简，纪念衫也展现了不同时代审美的变化。而2013年的“八天七夜”主题纪念衫，更是讲述了九字班同学用八天七夜的时间排练出国庆60周年“毛泽东思想”标语方阵的共同故事。

“既然留不住最美的清华时光，不如留住最真的清华记忆。”2017年毕业纪念品的广告词中这样写道。“时光的脚步从不停留，从今天开始，幸福地向前走。”毕业不是终点，而是全新的起点。愿三字班带着纪念品中承载的清华记忆，带着刚入园子的赤诚初心，不停奔跑，向着更高更远的方向。

也许某一天，在世界一隅，换上在箱底沉睡许久的毕业纪念衫，转过街角却看到相同的身影。“嘿，你也是三字班的？”

Graduation Souvenirs: Your Tangible Tsinghua Memory

There are four styles to this year's graduation shirt. Their designs on pieces of fabric are like patterns inscribed on the heart. A ring with Old Gate and the words "THU" engraved, putting it on a finger is a reminder of four years of memories in Tsinghua. A seal that gently presses onto paper, it's a sign of love expressed with words. It's as if pieces of paper are too small to imprint the deep affections felt.

These are the momentos designed for this year's graduating class, the class of 2013. They are like gifts from a lover and a souvenir for safekeeping.

With the weather getting warmer and days going longer, the season of graduation has arrived and summer vacation is not far off. Back then, greasy food in the canteens used to be a constant complain. But now it's as if I want to eat at the canteens for my last few meals on campus. Usually, I would turn a blind eye to the lotus pond and the green slopes. But now I see myself stealing a few more glimpses of them. At that time, everything seemed mundane. But now the sound of the class bell, the smell of books in the North Library and the long lines in front of the Auditorium, these have all suddenly become so precious. But the memory of them are so faint, time has passed by too hastily.

So these memories can be compressed and stored in these momentos. Use them, which carries with it wonderful memories from Tsinghua, as a reminder of your time here. The four designs of the graduation shirt, a ring with "THU" and the Old Gate engraved, a seal stamp and a Tsinghua mug, these are graduation souvenirs that has a value beyond its practical uses. They are the students' tangible reminders of their memories at this university.

It's like what the graduation mug says: "In this life, we will remember our best time."

Creating graduation souvenirs is a tradition of Tsinghua. Every year's souvenirs are unique. They not only serve as a comfort to longing hearts, but also an epitome of a generation of Tsinghua students. From 2011 to 2017, the designs of momentos range from complicated to simple, which show the aesthetic changes in different generations. In 2013, the "eight days and seven nights" themed commemorative shirt was about the story of classmates who had eight days and seven nights to rehearse a slogan formation named "Mao Zedong Thought" for the 60th Anniversary of the founding of the PRC.

"Since the most beautiful time in Tsinghua cannot be retained, why not keep a tangible and true memory of Tsinghua." 2017 graduation souvenirs advertisement wrote. "The footsteps of time never stay, so from today forwards, move forward happily." Graduation is not the end, but a new starting point. May the class of 2013 carry with them the Tsinghua memory, and their hearts for the university when they first entered as freshmen. And may they strive forward toward a higher and farther goal.

Perhaps one day, in some corner of the world, when you put on the graduation shirt that has been stuffed in the bottom of your suitcase for years and turn around a corner on the street, you will meet someone with the same shirt and call out: "Hey, are you also from the class of 2013?"

Translation and revision | Alexis See Tho

Image | Huo Wei

6月29日

文字 | Larry Han

图片 | 梁露文

苏世民书院这一年，重新定义了我对中国的了解

题记：

作为清华新百年推进教育国际合作交流的标志性项目和清华全球战略的重要举措之一，清华大学苏世民学者项目即将欢送她的首批毕业生。在此，我们诚邀首批苏世民学者 Larry Han 用中英文双语写下他在清华、在苏世民书院一年来的体验与感受，分享他对中国、对清华不断深入的认识和情感。

2017年7月1日早晨，我将与各个院系的清华研究生一起庆祝毕业。当天下午，我将与同班同学从苏世民书院毕业，开始我的新生活，希望实现苏世民学者项目的愿景，为创造一个更加繁荣和平的世界做出贡献。作为在美国北卡罗来纳州出生长大的华人，毫无疑问，我可以说，今年在清华的经历重新定义了我对中国的了解。

清华的人才荟萃和国际化程度给我留下了深刻的印象。不管是听世界一流教授施一公的尖端研究报告会，还是跟国家最优秀的青年深入探讨，清华的顶尖人才储备赢得了我最高的尊重，清华的国际化努力也印证了中国在推进经济全球化上的责任和担当。苏世民学者项目就是清华国际化的典范。我个人惊喜地经历了清华的国际化进程，包括帮助新投入使用的清华大学艺术博物馆翻译展品标签，为新华网的两会介绍视频提供英语画外音，以及作为欧盟高级代表 Federica Mogherini 的 Top Talk 的官方记者。

在中国生活、学习和旅行，使我更新了对中国创新创业的旧假设。像很多美国同胞一样，我承认自己低估了中国技术创新的质量和速度。例如众所周知的微信，它不是简单的聊天工具，而是一个具有完整生态系统的应用，其中有众多创新都超过其美国竞争对手。“三国鼎立”的百度、阿里巴巴、腾讯，以及华为、小米、步步高都改写了各自领域的许多旧“信条”。在人工智能领域，本土化的科大讯飞是一家提供语音识别软件的公司，因其无可挑剔的翻译功能赢得了无数奖项。在交通运输方面，中国商用飞机开始与美国波音和欧洲空客竞争；中国的高速铁路已经超越了日本的新干线；摩拜和滴滴都在重建共享出行的概念。尽管在不久之前，还有不少美国人认为中国的创新创业受到诸多限制，但我有太多证据证明，我应该更新自己对中国创新创业的过时假设。

最令我鼓舞的是有机会与来自世界各国的学者讨论交流，尤其是过去一年对包括美国总统大选等在内的一系列国际问题的研讨，还有参加书院赴西安和郑州的考察项目的经历。坦白说，中国共产党对我来说曾经一直有点神秘。通过与中国学者的非正式聊天和正式的研讨，我现在不仅对共青团的工作有所了解，对中国共产党也有了更进一步的认识。

随着我在苏世民书院的一年学习经历即将结束，我不禁怀念同学们之间相处时那种温暖和深厚的情谊。一起参加“一二·九”合唱比赛和激烈的“马约翰杯”体育比赛等全校性的重要活动，我们的感情无疑得到了加强。我们非常感激清华如此热情地欢迎我们。即便今年秋天开始，我将到剑桥大学攻读战略运营管理专业的硕士学位，而后到哈佛大学生物统计系攻读博士学位，但我保证，我不会让我的这一段宝贵的中国记忆蒙尘。通过我在医院管理和传染病方面的研究，未来我会努力与中国决策者和机构合作，发展更健康的城市和更好的公共卫生。

清华大学，苏世民书院，你们将永远在我心中拥有一个特别的位置！

A Reflection on My Year at Schwarzman College, Tsinghua University

On the morning of July 1, 2017, I will celebrate graduation with fellow Tsinghua graduate students. Later that afternoon, I will walk across the podium with fellow Schwarzman Scholars as we set out on our own adventures, seeking to fulfill the vision of the Schwarzman Scholars program to create a more prosperous and peaceful world. As a Chinese-American born and bred in North Carolina, my time as a Schwarzman Scholar at Tsinghua University has redefined my understanding of China.

I have been deeply impressed by the immense talent and internationalization of Tsinghua. From cutting-edge research by world-class professors like Shi Yigong to in-depth discussions with the brightest young minds of China, I've been astounded by the quality of Tsinghua's immense brain power. I have also been pleasantly surprised to see the internationalization efforts of Tsinghua, which parallel China's championing of globalization at the national level. The Schwarzman Scholars program has been a major hub of the internationalization process as Tsinghua continues to ascend the global university rankings. My own experiences with this internationalization movement include translating exhibit labels at the newly-opened Tsinghua University Art Museum, providing the English voice-over for Xinhuanet's Two Sessions introduction video, and being the official note-taker for a Top Talk event by High Representative of the European Union, Federica Mogherini.

Living, studying, and traveling in China have led me to revise many of my old assumptions about China's technological innovation. Like many Americans, I admit to having underestimated the quality and speed of China's technological innovation. The innovation goes beyond the well-documented case of WeChat, an all-in-one app that has surpassed its American competitors. The three kingdoms of Baidu, Alibaba, and Tencent, along with Huawei, Xiaomi, and BBK Electronics are re-conceptualizing many old tenets in their respective fields. In the realm of artificial intelligence, the homegrown Iflytek is a company that produces voice recognition software, winning numerous awards for its uncanny translation ability. In transportation, COMAC is looking to compete with Boeing and Airbus, the high-speed rail system has already surpassed Japan's Shinkansen, and Mobike and Didi are reimagining ridesharing. It wasn't so long ago that the consensus view in the United States was that China stifled innovation with its limits on freedom of speech. Technological advances have come in spite of restrictions, and the evidence base is strong enough for me to update my outdated assumptions.

Finally, it has been heartening to discuss with global scholars, particularly with so many international issues occurring this past year, including the presidential election in America. To be frank, the Chinese Communist Party had always been a bit of a mystery to me. Through informal chats and seminars by the Chinese scholars at Schwarzman College, I have learned about topics of importance to the Communist Youth League. Coupled with deep dives in Xi'an and Zhengzhou, these experiences have taught me a great deal about how the CPC functions.

As my year at Schwarzman College comes to an end, I reflect on the warmth and depth of comradeship we have formed. Our bonds of affection have no doubt been strengthened by participation in university-wide events such as the December 9th chorus competition and the intense Ma Bei sports events. We are so thankful that the university has welcomed us with open arms. As I head off to the University of Cambridge in the fall for an MPhil in Strategy, Marketing and Operations, followed by a Ph.D. in Biostatistics at Harvard, I promise not to relegate my China experience to the past. Through my research in hospital management and infectious diseases, I will actively engage with policymakers and institutions in China to develop healthier cities and better public health. Tsinghua University and Schwarzman College, you will forever hold a special place in my heart.

Author | Larry Han

Image | Liang Luwen

6 月 30 日

文字 | 拜喆喆

图片 | 宋晨

毕业季：没有人是佩妥剑再入“江湖”

大学岁月倏然，毕业生们常用一句“剑未佩妥，出门已是江湖”道尽离别的不舍和步入社会的忐忑。其实，没有人是佩妥剑再入江湖，我们只是从未意识到转身入江湖时，已经在园子里习得了最妥帖的“招式”和“心法”，那才是“行走江湖”的行囊。

大二暑假，我和好友留在园子里备考英语，听了一整个夏天的蝉鸣。那段努力却悠然的日子里，我们为《清新时报》写过一篇《书剑清华》。文章讲的是清华院系的分分合合，像是江湖帮派的更迭变换，“清芬挺秀，华夏增辉，这片江湖总为万人景仰，各个院系都有独门秘籍。一眼看去，都是书生意气；细思之下，又全是江湖豪情……”那时，园子就是爱好武侠的我们眼里的江湖，带给我们七分希冀与三分忐忑。

四年后却发现，这片所谓的“江湖”，其实是小菜鸟真正踏入江湖前拜师学艺的那座山。我们在这里修炼面对未来的“招式心法”：专业课是未来“上阵”的块块基石，是不能含糊的第一课；校园马拉松的汗水，带来“无体育，不清华”的活力能量；“一二・九”合唱是最后一次宏大的“集体叙事”，我们放声歌唱，努力和身边的人保持着一致的音调与节拍；海外研修与交换学期一次次告诉我们这世界很大，未来充分无限可能；大礼堂的电影和新清华学堂的各种演出，告诉我们诗和远方触手可得……从每片叶子到每个春夏秋冬，这里像一座巨大的鸟巢，给你时间成长，等你羽翼渐丰，许你海阔天空，然后叩谢师恩，“下山游历”。

站在清华路回望，你发现你终于理解了它的自强不息——清晨指向八点的时针与望不到尽头的车流，藏着一颗颗信仰未来的灵魂；你发现你终于体会到它的厚德载物——你在红楼，我在西游，有人攀登书海，有人踏遍世界，做出最合适的人生排序题；你接受了江湖有黑白两道，但你也发现，更多的人，只凭一份热爱也能在其中悠游自在。你发现你终于可以看到整个世界，内心忠于自由，也依然执着于兼济天下。没有人是佩妥剑再入江湖，当你最后一次唱着校歌哭出来，园子只跟你说，勇敢向前走吧！

Graduation: Entering into "Jianghu" from Tsinghua

University comes to an end and those who are graduating often say that "as soon as I step out, I find myself in this place called 'Jianghu'." The uncertainty that awaits us all and that hint of sadness at having to say goodbye to Tsinghua is felt by everyone. Actually, no one is ever fully prepared when they find themselves in an unfamiliar "Jianghu" . Yet, we have already learnt much during our times at Tsinghua. We are already prepared to face it.

My summer vacation during my second year at Tsinghua was spent studying English with my friend. We listened to the chit chats of the cicadas all summer and for us, that period of hard work became a lasting pleasurable memory. We wrote an article called "Books and Swords at Tsinghua" for a university publication which detailed the many stories of Tsinghua which to us somewhat a "Jianghu" . Like "Jianghu" , the many changes of schools and departments at Tsinghua are like the many Kung Fu divisions all with their unique features and secrets. Take one look and you see the faces of scholars and academics but deep down inside every one of them, they are all like martial artists, legendary fighters and heroes..." Yep, Tsinghua is like the Jianghu filled with a community of fighters and heroes...a place gave us 70% of aspirations and 30% of uncertainty.

Four years later, what I found is that this "Jianghu" is in fact the hidden oasis for us rookies to learn from the real masters before we enter into the real society, the real "Jianghu" . We learn, we experiment, we refine and we practice all the "secrets" . This is where we lay down the foundations for a future where many challenges and battles will require us to display high standards and great professionalism. This is not something that we should overlook. The marathon reflects the great sport tradition at Tsinghua ("No sports then no Tsinghua"); The December 9th choir is the last grand gathering where we sing with all our hearts in sync with the beat around us; international exchanges even for one semester reminds us that the world is huge and limitless; the performances shown at the Auditorium reminds us that art is always within our reach... every leaf and every season, Tsinghua is like a huge nest where we grow then take flight and seek out our own skies... we thank our masters and it is time to "venture out and explore."

When it's time to say goodbye to Tsinghua and as we look back, we realize what "Self-Discipline" is. It is the rush of traffic and colours of the bikes at 8 am throughout the campus; it is the students and their dreams; You slowly realize what "Social Commitment" is as well - no matter where you are, where you go, what you see or what your life becomes, you accept the rules of "Jianghu" and you also realize that the more people there are, the more passion and energy you have. You see the world as it is and know that deep down, you still have much freedom inside of you. When you sing the school song for one last time, Tsinghua will only tell you to march ahead with courage.

Translation and revision I Min Weiyuan

Image I Song Chen

7月3日

文字 | 清橙

图片 | 宋晨

热烈庆祝中国共产党清华大学第十四次党员代表大会胜利召开！

盛夏的清华园，阳光灿烂，枝叶葳蕤。在清华大学全面深化综合改革，推进“双一流”建设，实施“十三五”规划，致力于构建学校新百年发展新格局的关键时期，中国共产党清华大学第十四次党员代表大会于 2017 年 7 月 6 日至 7 日隆重举行。

自 2012 年第十三次党代会以来，清华大学党委深入学习贯彻党的十八大和十八届三中四中五中六中全会精神，以习近平总书记系列重要讲话精神和 105 周年校庆贺信精神为指引，团结带领全校师生员工锐意进取、扎实工作，学校党的建设和世界一流大学建设迈出了新的坚实步伐，新百年发展实现良好开局。

让我们共同庆祝中国共产党清华大学第十四次党员代表大会胜利召开，期待新一届清华大学党委团结带领全校师生员工，更加紧密地团结在以习近平同志为核心的党中央周围，高举旗帜，改革创新，攻坚克难，开拓进取，向着迈入世界一流大学前列的目标奋力前行，为国家富强、民族复兴和人类文明进步做出新的更大贡献！

扫一扫，查看清华大学第十四次党员代表大会新闻专题：

Celebrating the Success of the 14th Party Congress of Tsinghua University of the CPC

The Tsinghua campus is filled with sunshine and greenery during summer. Tsinghua is currently undergoing a process of comprehensive reforms which includes the "Double First-rate" strategy as well as "The Thirteenth Five-Year Plan." Committed to playing a major role in the construction of a new century, such development of the new model comes at a critical period. The 14th party congress of Tsinghua University of the CPC will be held from July 6th to July 7th, 2017, with great success to discuss such issues.

Since the 13th party congress of Tsinghua University of the CPC in 2012, Tsinghua's CPC Committee has thoroughly studied and implemented the spirit of the 18th CPC National Congress and the Third, Fourth, Fifth and Sixth Plenary Session of the 18th Central Committee of the CPC. President Xi Jinping spoke about the new strategy needed for governance with special focuses on strengthening ideological and political work, promoting science and technology and education, deepening a strategy for cultivating talents and ensuring future development is innovation-oriented so that the important progress of achieving a world-class university could be greatly accelerated.

In accordance with President Xi's hopes for Tsinghua which was stated in his Tsinghua's 105th Anniversary letter, Tsinghua is setting the correct direction and she adheres to her goals in cultivating the right talents who will serve the nation. Reforms and innovations will be earnestly implemented. Teachers and students are united to produce solid results and push for vigorous developments.

Let us celebrate the success of the 14th Congress and hope that the new Committee will unite and lead such reforms. The innovative spirit displayed by the teachers and students as well as scientific construction and ideological and political work continues to build a world-class university with outstanding achievements to greet future success of the 19th CPC National Congress.

Translation and revision | Min Weiyuan

Image | Song Chen

7月10日

文字｜张译丹

图片｜赵存存、梁露文

清华艺术博物馆“奇妙日”：从莫奈到苏拉热

日前，“从莫奈到苏拉热：西方现代绘画之路（1800—1980）”展览正在清华大学艺术博物馆举行。展品包括莫奈罕见的圆形《睡莲》等51件风格各异的西方艺术代表性作品，均来自法国圣埃蒂安大都会现当代艺术博物馆的馆藏。除了莫奈、库尔贝、马蒂斯、毕加索、杜布菲、苏拉热这些人们耳熟能详的艺术名家，展览还展出了很多不为人熟知却产生了重要影响的西方艺术家的作品。古典主义、印象主义、立体主义、超现实主义以及抒情和几何抽象主义等，一系列风格流派的激变在清华汇聚，共同展现出1800年至1980年间西方艺术走过的“现代之路”。

据展览中方策展人、清华大学艺术博物馆副馆长杨冬江介绍，展览按时间和风格分为六大主题单元，分别是：“对风景的新感知”“西方艺术中的人物与肖像”“从立体主义革命到纯粹主义”“超现实主义、梦境与无意识”“回归物质”“在具象与抽象之间”。这也是继“对话达·芬奇”和“从酒神赞歌到阿卡迪亚：马库斯·吕贝尔茨作品展”之后，清华大学艺术博物馆主办的又一次重量级的艺术巡礼特展。

光影潋滟，睡莲、水面和树的倒影，细腻中有着微妙的对比，环形的样式让视觉范围更为集中，画面空间仿佛被无限打开。1907年至1908年间，莫奈面对他在法国吉维尼住所的水面，创作了仅有4幅的圆形《睡莲》。拒绝透视、抛弃水平面，追随着稍纵即逝的光色变幻……这些被莫奈称为“水的风景”的装饰性处理，强调与自然的灵性沟通，彻底改变了欧洲传统绘画的习惯准则，预示着20世纪中叶艺术家们所进行的探索实践。

至第一次世界大战前夕，艺术家们又开始通过木板、线条、形状和颜色之间的联系，将想法和感受转至画布上，逐渐摒弃绘画的具体主题，艺术成为人们寻找“纯粹”的通道。在皮埃尔·苏拉热的《1979年6月19日画作》这幅经典的“黑画”中，黑色几乎覆盖整个画面成为主宰，乱刀的划痕打乱了水平条纹的肌理。他强调黑色所反射的光线，“将黑色从黑暗汇中解放出来”，成为对“纯粹”的大胆探索。

从莫奈到苏拉热，众多西方现代艺术中的代表性作品像一系列闪回的镜头，在清华大学艺术博物馆成为一个系列，带领我们回望那个时代多变的历史轨迹和深刻丰富的文化意蕴，展现出艺术对人类生活永恒的激情表述。

此次展览持续到2017年8月31日。

A Wonderful Day at Tsinghua Art Museum: from Monet to Soulages

Recently, the "From Monet to Soulages: The Road of Western Modern Painting" exhibition has been taking place at Tsinghua Art Museum. It also includes Monet's rare artwork—the circular *Water Lilies*. The exhibition's 51 representative artworks of various styles came from France's St Etienne Metropolitan Museum of Modern and Contemporary Art. Besides the well-known artists like Monet, Courbet, Matisse, Picasso, Dubuffet, Soulages, works of artists who were less famous but exerted significant influence on western art were also included. A variety of genres such as classicism, impressionism, cubism, surrealism, lyricism, geometric abstraction and so on, converged at Tsinghua, jointly depicting the "modern road" of western art from 1800 to 1980.

According to Yang Dongjiang, Chinese curator of the exhibition and deputy director of Tsinghua Art Museum, the exhibition consists of six themes divided by time and style: *A New Perception of Landscape*, *Figures and Portraits in Western Art*, *From Cubism Revolution to Purism*, *Surrealism*, *Dreams and Unconsciousness*, *Back to Materials*, *Between the Concrete and the Abstract*. This is yet another heavyweight art exhibition held by Tsinghua Art Museum after the exhibition of "Dialogue with Leonardo da Vinci" and "From Dithyrambe to Arcadia Exhibition of Markus Lupertzy" .

Light glitters on ripples, water lily and trees have been reflected on water, there are subtle contrasts in the delicate portrayal, the circular format increasingly concentrates the visual range, and the image space seems to be expended to infinite extent. From 1907 to 1908, inspired by the water on his residence in Giverny, France, Monet created only 4 pieces of circular *Water Lilies*. Discarding perspective and horizontal plane, following the fleeting light shift... These decorative approaches, which were called "landscape of water" by Monet, emphasize spiritual communication with nature, completely changing the traditional standards of European painting, indicating thinking and practice of artists in the middle of the twentieth century.

Right before the First World War, artists began to express their thoughts and feelings on the canvas by making connections between woods, lines, shapes and colors, the specific theme of painting was also gradually abandoned while art became the tunnel to "pureness" . In the classic art of Pierre Soulages, *Paintings at June 19, 1979*, the entire image was almost completely covered black and the scratches of knife broke the texture of the horizontal stripes. He stressed that the lights reflected by black, the work of "freed black from darkness" , was therefore a bold exploration into "pureness" .

From Monet to Soulages, various representative works of western modern art formed a series at Tsinghua Art Museum, flashing back the changeable historical tracks and profound cultural implication of that period, highlighting the eternal passion of art for human life.

The exhibition lasted until August 31, 2017.

Translation and revision | Raj Lamar

Image | Zhao Cuncun, Liang Luwen

7月17日

春去夏犹清，美味伴暑假

文字 | 杨茂艺

图片 | 赵存存、薛雅芳、杨思维

摄影 | 杨茂艺

绘制 | 李叶蔚、任帅

一直以来，“食堂菜”就是我们心中的“第九大菜系”。头戴白帽的厨师、汇集南北特色的菜肴、密密麻麻的食堂桌椅、人手一袋的清华酸奶……食堂，总是伴随着五味杂陈的期待融入清华学子的记忆。转眼暑假已至，操场绿地上仍热气蒸腾，尚未归家的小伙伴们，既无缘江南水乡之幽凉又不可得高原晚风之劲爽，如何是好？不妨就在园子里尽享消夏美食，与食堂来一次美妙的邂逅。

紫荆二楼凉菜

《闲情偶寄·饮馔部》有言：“制菜之法，摘之务鲜，洗之务净。”自2005年清华饮食服务中心在长白山设立了首个绿色食品采购基地以来，学生的碗碟里总能有源源不断的新鲜蔬菜。这盘木耳色泽黑褐而口感柔软，薄而有弹性，配以西兰花与土豆丝后，只消用香醋与鸡精轻轻一拌，便令食者顿觉清爽。而那一盘火腿肉，则用利刃切成薄片，瘦肉鲜明似火，辣椒油也恰到好处，一筷一片，毫无肥腻汁液屏障胸脯之感。两份凉菜搭配相宜，可谓佐酒进粥之佳品。

清芬鸡丝凉面

南米北面，常也。这学期，以面食闻名的清芬园在川渝窗口推出了别出心裁的新品——鸡丝凉面。将熟鸡肉用花椒料酒去腥后手撕成丝，再将过了凉水的面条铺在盘中，加上擦丝的黄瓜与酥脆的花生末和鲜嫩的豆芽菜，用芝麻酱油和红油勾芡，最后撒上葱段，便成就了这一盘黄灿灿的鸡丝凉面。此面可谓将肉类蛋白、主食淀粉、青葱绿意都占全了，油盐酱醋等调和料皆归于面，能为那些酷爱面食的同学驱走烦忧。

紫荆三楼绿豆紫薯芋圆

消夏食物怎能不提清热解暑的绿豆呢？性凉味甘的绿豆遇上晶莹剔透的紫薯芋圆，加入冰糖水后又添几分甜滑。从泡制绿豆到捣碎紫薯，一碗碗盛载的都是手艺精湛的师傅为同学们精心打造的幸福。

观畴一楼蒸凤爪

木制蒸屉里放上一碗烂熟的豉汁凤爪，凤爪在白色灯光的照耀下格外诱人。经过大油炸熟的凤爪要在冷水里浸泡两个小时左右以达到“皱皮”的美感，再淋上用八角、五香粉、麻油和老抽等调料配成的卤水，加入颗颗饱满的花生粒，蒸上几分钟的时间，便能成就一道酥软美味。这道粤菜以恰到好处的温度，在夏日黄昏消散酷热，令人食欲大增。

以食堂优劣来评断大学质量未免有失公允，可清华食堂总是在不经意间给我们带来惊喜，筷箸刀叉起落之时，有别样风景……观畴听涛厨浪起，紫荆桃李菜色溢，清芬丁香肴爽口，玉树芝兰汤鲜品。年年盛夏，岁岁精心，食在清华，不负白衣。

This Summer, Tsinghua Launched New Dishes

All along, canteen food takes the place as "the Ninth Cuisine" in our hearts. (Traditionally, China's regional cuisines are divided into eight cuisines — Anhui cuisine, Cantonese cuisine, Fujian cuisine, Hunan cuisine, Jiangsu cuisine, Shandong cuisine, Sichuan cuisine and Zhejiang cuisine). The white chef's hat, the culmination of north and south cuisines, the tightly packed canteen tables and chairs and a bag of Tsinghua yogurt in hand. The canteen, with its multitude of flavors had always been a fond memory of Tsinghua students. Without realizing it, summer has come, the rising temperatures on the green fields on campus has become commonplace. For those who have not gone home, those who have not gone to the cooling village towns, what can they do? Why not enjoy fine summer dishes in the canteens and experience a culinary adventure.

Zijing 2nd Floor — Cold Dishes

In a classical Chinese text, *Xian Qing Ou Ji*, it states that freshness of ingredients is a must. In 2005, the Tsinghua Catering Service Center set up its first food procurement center in Changbai Mountain in the northeastern region of China. There is always a steady stream of fresh vegetables in students' dishes. This piece of black fungus has a soft texture, it's thin yet flexible. Gently mixed with broccoli, potato julienne, a swirl of black vinegar and chicken essence, the dish is refreshing. On another plate is thinly sliced ham, its meat lean and fresh with a fiery red color. Tossed with some chili oil, even after many slices, it doesn't taste greasy. These two affordable cold dishes are pairs perfectly with a bowl of porridge or a glass of wine.

Qingfen - Cold Noodles with Shredded Chicken

Rice in the south, wheat in the north. This semester, the Qingfen canteen that is known for its wheat-based dishes launched a Sichuan-Chongqing stall that introduced innovative new dishes. An example is the cold noodles with hand-shredded chicken. The chicken is marinated in cooking wine then hand-torn into thin shreds. The cold noodles are then placed in the middle of the plate, topped with chicken shreds, thinly sliced cucumber, crunchy crushed peanuts and bean sprouts, a sprinkle of scallions and a swirl of sesame oil and soy sauce. It's a complete dish with meat for protein, noodles for carbohydrate and green vegetables, perfect for the noodle lovers out there.

Zijing 3rd Floor — Mung bean and purple taro dessert

Talking about summer food, how can we miss mung beans, the traditional ingredient that relieves the heat of summer? Sweet and refreshing mung beans are paired with round balls of purple taro with some crystal sugar water. From the soaking of mung beans to the mashing of the purple potato, a bowl of this dessert is a craftsmanship of the master chefs created for the joy of students who will taste it.

Guanchou 1st Floor — Steamed chicken feet

In a wooden steamer, is a bowl of cooked chicken feet. Under the bright lights of the canteen, it looks particularly tempting. After deep frying the chicken feet, they are soaked in cold water for two hours or so to achieve the "wrinkled skin" — a desired texture. Then star anise, five-spice powder, sesame oil and dark soy sauce becomes a brine that will infuse the chicken feet with flavor. On top of the chicken feet, peanuts are added and they are steamed for a few minutes, creating a dish that has a contrasting texture of crunchy peanuts and silky smooth chicken feet. This Cantonese dish is perfect for a summer evening, increasing appetites.

Using the quality of canteens to determine the excellence of a university is not a fair and equitable judgement. But the Tsinghua canteens always pleasantly surprise us. At the rise and fall of chopsticks, forks and knives, this sight, whether in the kitchens of Guanchou or Tingtao canteen, or the multitude of colorful dishes at Zijing and Taoli canteen, or the refreshing dishes at Qingfen and Dingxiang canteen, or the freshness of what Yushu and Zhilan offers, every year and every summer, eating at Tsinghua becomes better.

Translation and revision I Alexis See Tho

Image I Zhao Cuncun, Xue Yafang, Yang Siwei

Photographer I Yang Maoyi

Drawing I Li Yewei, Ren Shuai

7月24日

文字 | 张译丹

图片 | 宋晨

赵元任故居：想国想家，教我如何不想他

从二校门继续向南，天上飘着微云，斑驳的荫翳跳跃在照澜院诸多院落灰白的砖瓦上。1 号院里坐着一位摇着蒲扇的老人，她远远地看着在二校门前开心地拍照留念的人们。有三三两两的游客会朝着这一带幽静雅致的院落走来，他们是否也循着大师的足迹而来？老人笑了，哼起了歌，歌儿是这么唱的："天上飘着些微云，地上吹着些微风。微风吹动了我的头发，教我如何不想他？"

照澜院 1 号是清华"国学四大导师"之一——赵元任先生的故居。赵元任先生是中国现代语言学先驱，被誉为"中国现代语言学之父"，同时也是中国现代音乐学先驱，"中国科学社"的创始人之一。1920 年，他留学回国在清华教授物理、数学和心理学课程，后赴哈佛任讲师；1925 年，重返清华园任教，并与夫人杨步伟安家在清华园照澜院 1 号。在这里，先生埋头伏案、潜心树人，讲授方言学、普通语言学、音韵练习等课程，并指导学生从事研究。谈笑有鸿儒，国学巨匠陈寅恪先生就常常来赵家"蹭饭"，清华学生们都难忘赵元任夫妇在清华园营造的多彩的学术生活氛围。而赵元任先生，始终难忘故国和故园。

1920 年，新文化运动先驱刘半农先生在去国怀乡之际，挥笔写下《教我如何不想她》这首感情深沉的诗，1926 年赵元任先生将此诗谱曲使之广为传唱。1938 年后赵元任先生一直侨居美国，但每逢清华校友聚会，赵元任先生必定参加，并且总要唱起清华校歌，唱起他自己谱曲的那首歌："燕子你说些什么话？教我如何不想她？"

1973 年和 1981 年，赵元任先生两次携家眷回国，几乎全部的日程都用来"想他"——故国、故院、故校和故知。1981 年，赵元任先生在探访故居时曾深情地说："去国不久的人，不懂得思恋故土的深情！"临别之际，他频频地说："我还要来的，我还要来的……"清华园照澜院 1 号故居，凝聚着他对故国故园最深的眷恋。

2014 年 9 月，赵元任先生的女儿赵小中将父亲长年弹唱使用的钢琴捐赠给清华大学。赵女士表示，这架钢琴对赵元任先生来说意义非凡，而清华自始至终是赵元任先生家国情结的起点，这样的缘分独一无二、无可替代。清华大学将这架钢琴视为清华宝贵文化财富和深厚文化积淀的见证。

"啊！西天还有些儿残霞，教我如何不想她？"余晖就要散尽，院内也掌灯了，不知过一会儿陈寅恪先生是否会来叩响赵家的宅门？

先生之风，山高水长，教我如何不想他？

Former Residence of Zhao Yuanren : His Nation, His Home, His Deep Affection

Forwarding south through the Old Gate, the sunlight filters through light clouds, casting mottled shade on the gray walls of Zhaolan Yard. An old woman shaking a fan in No.1 yard gazed across at visitors in front of the gate, most of them were taking pictures, in twos and threes. They would come towards this quiet and elegant courtyard, did they follow the footsteps of masters? She smiled, humming the tune: "Light cloud drift above in the sky, over the land wafts a light breeze. The light breeze stirs my hair, how could I not miss her?"

No. 1 of Zhaolan Yard was the former residence of Mr. Zhao Yuanren , one of "four masters of Chinese Learning" in Tsinghua University. Known as the "father of modern Chinese linguistics" , Mr. Zhao Yuanren was a pioneer of modern Chinese linguistics. He was also one of the pioneers of Chinese modern musicology and one of the founders of the Science Association of China. In 1920 he returned to China to teach physics, mathematics and psychology at Tsinghua University. Later he left for the United States for further studies. He returned to Tsinghua in 1925 with his wife, Yang Buwei, and settled at No. 1 of Zhaolan Yard, southwest of Tsinghua campus. In this vary place, he dedicated to imparting knowledge of dialect, general linguistics, phonological exercises, and guided students to engage in research. Talking with friends, chatting with scholars, Mr. Chen Yinque, the giant master of sinology, would often "drop over" Zhao's home. The music was flowing from his fingers, the notes were dancing at his tongue, even after they left, the fantastic academic atmosphere created by Mr. Zhao and his wife was still kept in the memory of Tsinghua students. However, what's long kept in his mind was always his motherland and Alma Mater.

In 1920, the pioneer of New Culture Movement, Mr. Liu Bannong, wrote the poem "How Could I Not Miss Her" with deep longing of disintegrated country. in 1926, Mr. Zhao Yuanren composed a tune for the poem and made it widely popular. Mr. Zhao had lived in the United States since 1938, but whenever there was a Tsinghua alumni reunion, he would always attend, singing the school song of Tsinghua and his own art: "Swallow, what are you saying? How could I not miss her?"

In 1973 and 1981, Mr. Zhao had twice returned to China with his family, the schedules were filled with "missing" — motherland, college and old friends. During the visit to his former residence in 1981, Zhao said with deep feeling, "Those who left not for long do not understand the deep affection about homeland!" Before they parted, he repeatedly expressed. "I will come back, I will come back..." The No.1 of Zhaolan Yard in Tsinghua campus embodied his deepest attachment to the homeland.

In September 2014, Zhao Xiaozhong, daughter of Mr. Zhao Yuanren , donated her father's beloved piano to Tsinghua University. She said the piano was of great significance to Mr. Zhao Yuanren , while all along; Tsinghua was the starting point for his home affection. Such a fate was unique and irreplaceable. Regarding this piano as a valuable cultural treasure and profound cultural inheritance, Tsinghua University will constantly promote its culture-oriented effects.

"Sparse sunset clouds linger in the western sky, how could I not miss her?" The last ray of sunlight was verging into darkness; lights in the courtyard were lightened, would Mr. Chen Yinque knock at the door in a while?

The charm and elegance of Mr. Zhao lasts long and forever, how can I rid my mind of him?

Translation and revision | Raj Lamar

Image | Song Chen

7月31日

文字 | 方之澜

图片 | 梁晨

于婉莹：给你不一样的手绘清华

画面里似乎是正午时分，七八辆自行车随意停放在路灯下，周围是茂盛繁密的松树。初看这幅画，最先惊诧于画面里大片墨色的铺展。但若细细看来，更发现其中不易之处——看似洒脱豪放的墨色下，松树的每根针叶，都异常清晰。

这是于婉莹的“手绘清华”系列作品之一。她的朋友甚至不相信这是用水性笔所作，为此，于婉莹专门将作画过程用 GIF 图记录了下来。于婉莹创作了很多这样的画作。最初，她画的都是校园里的标志性景观：二校门、水木清华、荷塘、清华学堂……后来，她将眼光投向那些校园里的寻常场景。从亲密依偎的自行车到日晷上繁复精细的花纹，从图书馆前的圆形路灯到荷叶簇拥着的汉白玉拱桥，这是清华人眼中的清华，唤起每个与这个园子有密切交集的人的记忆。

于婉莹已经在清华待了七年，而她的水性笔绘画创作，灵感源于在法国巴黎游学的经历。当时她创作了一幅关于塞纳河景色的长卷作品，随性随意，展示出一种特别的艺术意境。回到清华后，她行走在校园里，看见一些场景，“觉得清华园的美，也可以用水性笔的艺术创作方式呈现出来”。

她每画一幅画，基本都是用水性笔直接从一个局部开始展开刻画。由于绘画条件的特殊性，她的大部分作品需要根据照片资料进行创作，每张作品从构思到完成需要三天至四天的时间，每天工作大概五小时以上。于婉莹伏案用水性笔细细描绘，画面由一个空荡荡的框架，从局部到整体，不断填充细节，完成之时便是一幅让人惊叹的画作。

于婉莹的绘画，还表现了一些我们能够感受到但却看不到的东西。她用黑白颜色去概括万千色彩变化，描绘了清华的朴素和沧桑；她用线条去描绘的形状，画出的，不仅是清华的景色，还有清华的自信和荣耀。“看到其中几张就能感觉到，这是一个大气的学校。”

在导师李睦眼里，于婉莹是他带的几个研究生里非常不同的一个：“尤其是，她的绘画非常不同——艺术品最核心的价值就是不同，如果是重复的东西，就无从谈起好坏，不同的作品至少具备了成为好作品、优秀作品的可能。”

于婉莹的艺术创作历程，也是清华精神在她笔下的一个缩影。而她表示，清华系列的创作还会一直进行下去。

Yu Wanying: Here's an Amazing Hand-painted Tsinghua Campus

The picture presents a scene of noon: several bicycles parked under the streetlights, surrounded by lush pines. At first glance at the painting, you may wonder about the dark color spread over the image. But a deeper look will show its rare quality—every single pine needle is extremely clear under the bold and unconstrained style.

The painting is one of the series of "Hand-painted Tsinghua" works made by Yu Wanying, a postgraduate student from the Academy of Arts and Design. To convince her friends that the work was actually done with an ink pen, Yu even recorded the painting process with the help of GIF images. Similar works have been created numerous times. At first, Yu painted all the landmarks of the Tsinghua campus: The Old Gate, Shuimu Tsinghua, Lotus Pond, Tsinghua Xuetang... and later, her emphasis was gradually placed on the ordinary scenes: from rows of bicycles to intricate patterns on the sundial, from the round streetlights in front of the library to the white marble arch bridge embraced by lotus leaves. That is the Tsinghua University in the eyes of Tsinghua students, arousing the intimate memories of the campus.

Yu Wanying has been in Tsinghua University for seven years, and her ink-pen painting was inspired by her experience of studying in Paris. During that period, she created a long scroll of the Seine River scenery, which presented a unique artistic conception. Upon returning to Tsinghua, she walked around the campus and saw the scenes, "I thought that the beauty of Tsinghua Campus could also be displayed in an artistic creation by the use of ink pen."

For each of her paintings she starts with a part directly depicted by an ink pen. Given the particularity of drawing conditions, most of her paintings were created on the basis of photographs, with every piece of work typically taking three to four days to complete, and she mostly worked for more than five hours a day. The image was in fact completed step by step, an empty frame was depicted first, and then, from smaller parts to the entire picture, with more added details, eventually a fine piece of art would be created.

Yu's paintings also express subtle aspects that can only be felt. She adopts black and white to summarize the changing colors, depicting the simplicity and vicissitudes of Tsinghua University. She uses lines to portray the ever-changing shapes, drawing not only Tsinghua University's scenery, but also the confidence and glory of Tsinghua. "You can sense a grand university through a few of her paintings, ultimately magnificent."

But according to Li Mu, Yu Wanying's supervisor, Yu is a very special one among her graduate students: "In particular, her paintings are very different, and differences are definitely the core value of art. One work cannot be rated as good or not if it's a duplicate, difference at least preserves the probability for a piece of art to be an excellent one."

The creative process of Yu's art also illustrates the evolution of Tsinghua spirit. And she also confirmed that her series on Tsinghua is bound to continue....

Translation and revision I Raj Lamar

Image I Liang Chen

8月7日

文字 | 杨茂艺

图片 | 薛雅芳

立秋：朱明送夏，少昊迎秋

立秋，晋代文人潘尼有云："朱明送夏，少昊迎秋。"即火神祝融送走酷暑，秋神少昊迎来清秋的时节。转眼间，清华学子的漫漫暑假尚在继续，而秋却已翩翩来到，为 2017 的余年装点风华。

八月里，学堂路两侧的青葱草木仍迎着骄阳生长，你我手中的那杯酸梅汁也还入口冰凉。只是不知从何时起，肃清之西风忽至，吹落了几缕柳絮，蒸发了些许暑气，铺陈出秋的步履痕迹。在这三伏天的尾声里，何不缓步清华园中，共赏秋的容颜……

或许，秋最早是从二校门的青砖白柱间溜进的，随着太阳直射点的南移而腾跃，和日晷一起痴心地等候渐短的白昼。待到流霞漫天时，则又卧于大礼堂的铜面穹顶上聆听晚蝉的心声。若是不够，她次日还要去那荷塘流连，在湖畔的秋韵里徜徉，打量那一颗颗凝滞的晶莹的白露。以及，用她那拂起红荷绿袖的轻风吹散荒岛咖啡的浓香，给倏忽降温的黎明一点暖意。

沿着大雁飞翔的痕迹，欣然地，她又看到满壁的爬山虎：灰褐色的老枝上卷须繁多，蜿蜒的藤茎向老教授的书窗探去，像极了求知的顽童。一场清雨过后，原本绿意盎然的叶开始泛红，叶脉上的纤毛温柔地向着白云招手。成簇的叶宛如秋天的朗读者，摩挲之间，用沙沙絮语流淌出一段段动人的"秋事集锦"。

仍是好奇于清华景色，她又看到路上三五成群的骑行的学子——他们穿着薄薄的或是纯色或是方格的衬衣，背着轻便的帆布包或手拿几本书刊，微笑着聊天，用天南海北的语音交谈，回应着"秋燥衣巾轻"的诗篇。

小径青苔、飞鸟银杏、球场呼号、琴房笛音，经行处皆有秋的魅影。渐渐地，秋风四起，空气里飘来了银耳莲子羹的甜香或山药排骨汤的清润。终于，清华初秋的夜沉醉在一片闪耀之中，她安静地坐下来，陪忠诚的恋人们细数繁星。

好一场秋梦，一切事物都在秋天优雅的呼吸声里随和了起来。不知不觉地，我们将短袖短裤收进衣柜，不再渴望那一杯绿豆冰沙，擦干曾经的毕业泪水……用满满的元气和轻盈的心情走入下一季，走入了 2017 的清秋。

Autumn Begins: Goodbye to Summer, Hello to Autumn

Autumn begins. Pan Ni, scholar and poet of the Jin Dynasty once said that the time around Lunar July is when one "say goodbye to summer and eventually welcome the arrival of autumn" . The Fire God bid the heat farewell and the God of Autumn make preparations to usher in the new season. Tsinghua students are still enjoying their summer break but in a blink of an eye, autumn has arrived to cover the rest of 2017.

In August, the green grass on both sides of the main campus roads still grows under the sun. Our cups of sour plum juice is still cold and refreshing. The wind from the west started to blow, the onslaught of heat began to be on its last breath and traces of autumn emerged. During these days, a stroll around the campus shows all the beauty possessed by this new season.

Perhaps, autumn drifted into the campus through the Old Gate. Perhaps she hitched a ride alongside the last of the sun rays. When clouds cover the sky, she rests alongside the bronze domes of the Auditorium, listening to the cicadas and all of their songs. If this was not enough, she would head over to the lotus pond, watch the white dews in the morning and listen to all of her songs throughout the day. The light wind caresses the green sleeves of the trees, it carries the aromas from the campus café and brings much needed coolness to months of heat.

Guided by the wild geese, autumn saw the lizards climbing along the campus walls, the overhead grey branches, like curious schoolboys, hanging outside the windows of the teachers' offices. After rain, the green leaves turn red and waves gently at the white clouds. She watches on the Tsinghua students as they, wear their new shirts, take school bags and books, make their way around the campus in a cheerful fashion. They speak with enthusiasm in their respective accents, like an autumn choir.

The birds, the football fields, the colors and songs...all sights of autumn. The arrival of autumn during Tsinghua's nighttime is a quiet one. She sits alongside those who, like her, enjoys watching the stars and the campus at night time.

We wake up from this autumn dream, we put away our summer clothes and no longer yearns for that cool drink and summer treat. Instead, we march towards the next academic semester...this new autumn of 2017

Translation and revision | Min Weiyuan

Image | Xue Yafang

8月14日

文字 | 蒋佩妍
图片 | 李娜

无体育，不清华：清华体育小史

清华建校之初，曾以“三好学校”著称：校舍好、英文好、体育好。清华学生体育好，“强迫运动”功不可没。1931 年出版的《国立清华大学二十周年纪念刊》所刊《清华二十年来之体育》一文阐述了“强迫运动”其法：

“……于每日下午四时后，将全校各处寝室、自修室，以及图书馆、食品部等处之大门一律关锁，使全体学生到户外运动场，投其所好，从事运动。……此法行至民七体育馆已落成，体育课改为正课后为止，是为清华强迫运动时期。”

除此以外，清华还制定了检查锻炼效果的具体标准，例如 1919 年《清华一览》“体育课程”篇章阐述的“体育实效试验法”，规定试验注重“康健”“灵敏”“泅水术”“自卫术”和“运动比赛时具有同曹互助之精神并能公正自持不求徼幸”，体育不及格者则不能毕业。

国民形象代表着国家形象，国家强大自国民强健伊始。新中国成立之后，清华从 1953 年起率先实行劳卫制。为保证学生有充足的锻炼时间，清华更改作息时间，集中上午上课，并规定每日下午的体育锻炼时间不得安排其他活动。

老校长蒋南翔身体力行推动清华体育发展，于 1957 年提出“为祖国健康地工作五十年”，而这也成为清华人持之以恒的动力与追求。直到 20 世纪八九十年代，每到下午四点半，校园广播便会响起：“同学们，走出宿舍，走出教室，去参加体育锻炼，保持强健的体魄，争取为祖国健康地工作五十年！”操场上、道路旁，随处可见奋力挥汗的身影，整个校园洋溢着生命的活力。

清华对于体育的重视，绝不仅是为了让学生掌握一些运动技能，而是为了培养学生完善的人格，实现“体魄与人格并重”。新世纪到来之后，即使本科学制由五年缩短为四年，清华的体育课时却不减反增。2003 年和 2006 年，清华的“游泳教学”和“大学体育”课程分别被评为北京市和国家级精品课程。

在丰富课外体育活动方面，清华也成果颇丰。从 1999 年起，“马约翰杯”田径运动会扩展为贯穿全学年、涵盖多种项目、具备广泛参与性的综合性体育系列活动，堪称举校瞩目的体育盛典，截至 2017 年已历 60 届。在百余个学生社团之中，体育类社团占三分之一，会员人数列各类社团之首。马拉松是近年来群体性体育活动的又一抹亮色，每年吸引数千人参赛。

无体育，不清华。蔚然成风的体育锻炼，是一支由清华人创作的慷慨激昂的进行曲，永恒奏响于清华的过去与未来之中。

No Sports, No Tsinghua: Tsinghua's Sporting History

When Tsinghua was being established, Tsinghua was known for excelling in three areas: school facilities, English and a sporting culture. Tsinghua students are good at sports because of the "compulsory movement" . In the Journal of *20th Anniversary of the Founding of Tsinghua University* and under the article of *20 years of sporting culture and history at Tsinghua University*, this "compulsory movement" was described in more detail:

"... after 4 p.m. daily, the dorms, study halls, library and all other buildings are locked so that students are forced to exercise and engage in sporting tournaments in the various playgrounds scattered across the campus...this applies for everyone. PE lessons became a formal and compulsory lesson for every student which cements Tsinghua's sporting culture."

In addition to this, Tsinghua made criteria to PE which was documented in 1919's paper on PE curriculum. In the chapter, the teaching and learning of PE was made to be effective. It paid close attention to health, self-defense, teamwork and sportsmanship. Students who fail in sports are not allowed to graduate at all.

The image of the people represents the image of the nation. A country is strong if her citizens are strong. Since the founding of the People's Republic of China and ever since 1953, Tsinghua has been the first to mold a system that "supports the labor and sporting needs of the nation." In order to ensure sufficient exercise time, Tsinghua altered the daily schedule so that students spend the day studying and the afternoon exercising.

The Dean of Tsinghua University Jiang Nanxiang promoted sports in Tsinghua and in 1957, he proposed "To work healthily for 50 years for our motherland." This has become the driving force and pursuit of the Tsinghua people. Until 1990's, at 4:30p.m. every day, the students would walk out of the classroom and take part in all sort of physical exercises. This is more than just sports but to uphold the tradition and culture of Tsinghua. Playgrounds, campus grounds...you can see people exercising...the campus is filled with vitality!

Tsinghua University attaches great importance to sports, not only to enable students to master some athletic skills, but to cultivate their character and personality. After the arrival of the New Century, even though the undergraduate system was shortened from five years to four years, Tsinghua's physical education class has not been cut. In 2003 and 2006, Tsinghua's "Swimming" and "PE" courses were rated as top quality courses throughout Beijing and the Nation.

Tsinghua has also made a lot of achievements in the field of extra-curricular activities. Since 1999, "Ma Yuehan Cup" extended to include track and field. Various games has spanned throughout the whole year. Gradually, Tsinghua saw more participation of comprehensive sporting activities from every student and faculty. By the end of 2017, annual events have welcomed her 60th Anniversary. Among more than 100 student societies, sport clubs accounts for over a third. Membership in these clubs are always the highest out of the whole university. The Campus Marathon is another popular event that has attracted high participation rate from people in recent years.

No sports, no Tsinghua. This is the culture, tradition and passion of the Tsinghua people. It stays for the past, the present and future.

Translation and revision | Min Weiyuan

Image | Li Na

8月21日

文字 | 梁乐萌

图片 | 赵存存

致七字班新生：欢迎你，在更好的清华园

你拖着行李箱，昂首挺胸或是稍有些紧张羞涩地踏进清华园。我们微笑着看着你，你是整个园子的焦点。

欢迎你，七字班的新同学！清华园等你很久了。

收拾停当，来园子里逛逛吧。初秋的荷塘清波荡漾，芙蓉争妍，朱自清曾在荷畔漫步，写下如秋水般清新婉转的篇章；照澜院似家常院落般平凡，赵元任、陈寅恪、钱伟长等大师却曾居住于此，在艰苦的年代治学不辍；阳光洒在蓝色的西大操场，马约翰曾带领学生跑步跳远，留下“无体育，不清华”的运动传统……漫漫106年岁月，清华积淀了厚重的底蕴与优良的传统，等待你的到来。

今天迎接你的，是一个比昨日更好的清华园。作为第一批通过大类招生来到清华的同学，你的面前是更广博的知识天地，通识教育与专业教育的结合，将帮助你更准确地找到适合自己的专业发展方向；“开放交流时间”的设立，让你有更充足的机会与大师面对面碰撞思想；苏世民学院不断成长，全球南方文化浸润项目继续开展，更多的交换学习、假期实践、海外实习机会则给你放眼全球的可能，与全人类同呼吸共命运……时代在发展，清华也在变化，以更创新、更国际、更人文的姿态迎接你的到来。

一纸紫色的录取通知书，是一份共度四年的许诺。在这四年里，你可以聆听国内外大师的讲座，饱览图书馆的书籍；可以潜心学术科研，为人类智慧添砖加瓦；可以投身创新创业，结识伙伴，增长才干；也可以加入丰富多彩的社团，让青春的每一秒过得更加精彩……“青春如初春，如朝日，如百卉之萌动，如利刃之新发于硎，人生最宝贵之时期也。”愿你不忘初心，珍惜时光，一步一步向着未来的“学术大师、兴业英才、治国人才”迈进。

邱勇校长在给2017年高考生的信中写道：“有你的清华会更好”。清华欢迎你，不仅期待你成为她的一部分，更相信你可以成为她的下一个骄傲。挥别高中，清华是一个新的平台、新的起点。希望你在汲取清华给予你的滋养的同时，不为前人所囿，为她增添新的故事、新的亮色！

欢迎，七字班！加油，七字班！

To the Class of 2017: Welcome to a Better Tsinghua

Dragging along a suitcase, with head held high or perhaps a little nervous and shy, you set foot on Tsinghua campus. Today, you are the focus of the whole campus and we are pleased that you have made it.

Welcome, Class of 2017! Tsinghua has been awaiting your arrival.

Get away from unpacking in your rooms and come out for a stroll. In August, water in the lotus pond ripples with beautiful lotus flowers. Well-known author, poet and former professor of Chinese language at Tsinghua, Zhu Ziqing, once strolled by the pond writing his famous essays. In the humble and ordinary-looking Zhaolan Yard was where academics such as Zhao Yuanren , Chen Yinque and Qian Weichang once lived and persisted in research during challenging times in the country. The blue tracks of the West Playground brightened by sun rays are where Ma Yuehan, a former Tsinghua physical education reformer, trained his students in sprinting and long jump, leaving behind the motto "No Sports, No Tsinghua" and a strong sporting tradition on campus. In 106 years, Tsinghua has formed a strong heritage and fine traditions, waiting for your arrival.

Awaiting you is a Tsinghua that is better than yesterday's. As the first batch of students after the admission reform this year where majors were grouped into wide categories, what is in front of you is a world where there is greater access to knowledge. With the combination of liberal arts and professional education, you will be able to better determine your future direction in your majors. Initiatives such as "Open Office Hours" - to allow greater opportunities for students and professors to conduct face-to-face academic discussions; the continued improvement of the Schwarzman Scholar program, further development of the Tsinghua Global South Culture Immersion Series, more study abroad exchange programs, field trips during semester breaks and internship opportunities abroad, giving you the possibility to see the world and share a common destiny with all humanity. Along with the development of our times, Tsinghua has also been changing. We have become more innovative, more internationalized and more humanity-oriented, to meet your arrival.

The purple admission letter is a four-year promise. In the next four years, you will listen to lectures by domestic and foreign experts, enjoy library books to your heart's content; devote yourselves to academic research, contribute to the wisdom of mankind, join in innovation and entrepreneurship, make friends, grow your abilities; join the numerous student clubs and associations, and making every second of your youth marvellous.

"Youth is as the early spring, as the sun and the sprout of a hundred flowers, as the sharp blade just off a grind stone. It's life's most valuable years." May you not forget your first love when you walked into campus. Cherish your time here and step by step, strive forward to become masters in academia, outstanding professionals and the pillars of the country.

Qiu Yong, the President of Tsinghua, in his letter to the 2017 batch of students taking the university entrance exam wrote: "With you, Tsinghua will be better." Tsinghua welcomes you. Not only do we look forward to you becoming a part of Tsinghua, we also believe that you can become her next pride. Bid farewell to high school. Tsinghua is a new platform, a new starting point. As you learn from the nourishment in Tsinghua, may you not be limited by your predecessors, but add to Tsinghua new stories, and new glories! Welcome Class of 2017! Go Class of 2017!

Translation and revision | Alexis See Tho

Image | Zhao Cuncun

8月28日

文字 | 拜喆喆

图片 | 任左莉

蔚然百年的清华学风

毕业季期间，许多清华学子的朋友圈主题变成了“查重”二字。清华大学对于本科生论文文字的复制比要求整体在 5% 以下，一些院系甚至有着 0% 的规定。这样的严格要求是清华历来的传统，校园内洋溢着的严谨学风是一道有着百年历史脉络的风景。

在 1911 年建校伊始颁布的《清华学堂章程》，就对学生成绩评定、升级、毕业做出了明确规定，例如高等科学生两科以上不及格会被降班，降班两次即出堂。根据 1924 年《清华周刊》的统计，建校历年来只有约四成学生能够按期毕业。改办大学后，清华延续了认真教学、严格要求的风气。尤其是理工学院保持了较高的淘汰率，1930 年理学院甚至只有三成学生顺利毕业。

较高的淘汰率与严格的考试密不可分。然而严格的考试仅仅是教师们的教学手段，让学生们在付出心血的过程中学到知识、提高本领才是目的。20 世纪 30 年代，土木系二年级的把关教师会在 5 分钟必须答完的小测试中不断大声地催促学生“快！快！”，借此训练未来工程师在紧张气氛下冷静思考和精确计算。蔡方荫教授常对学生说：“不能因为我放松这一门课的把关，而丢了清华的脸！”

师者的严格要求背后是对学生的殷切期望和关心爱护。就读于西南联大的汪家鼎院士这样回忆：“老师们一方面坚持标准，另一方面又为了不耽误多数学生毕业，不辞辛苦地在暑假中开课，便于不及格的学生重读和其他学生选读。”爱好京剧的机械系学生唐世一的考卷上，曾被以铁面无私著称的刘仙洲批过一句“以后要多多读书，少唱戏”，关爱督责之情溢于言表。

新中国成立后，清华学子肩负起对国家和民族的责任，教师认真教学，学生刻苦读书，努力为事业打下坚实基础。从保存和发扬老清华对功课严格要求的好传统，到 20 世纪 80 年代对“严谨、勤奋、求实、创新”的清华学风的正式表述，从“优良学风班”的建设到激励教师以身作则的师风师德建设……正是由于清华始终坚持严谨教学、严格要求，同学们珍惜光阴、用功学习、严格磨炼，才保证了清华毕业生具有较高的素质，日后在社会上肩负大任。

著名学者季羡林曾在当年的日记中对清华频繁的考试牢骚满腹，而到了晚年，他却满怀感激地自问：“我同广大的清华校友一样，现在所以有这一点点知识，难道不就是在清华园中打下的基础吗？”

One Hundred Years of Study at Tsinghua University

As graduation approaches, many Tsinghua students had the words "plagiarism check" displayed on their social media accounts to remind themselves and others about the strictness that comes with graduation at Tsinghua University. Tsinghua's overall requirement for plagiarism in final papers for undergraduate students should be less than 5%. Some departments and schools have a 0% policy. This strict requirement and rigorous style has been a part of the century-long Tsinghua tradition.

As early as 1911, the establishment of the Tsinghua School started to have clear provisions with regards to student performance assessment, graduation requirements, exemptions and much more. One rule was if the student failed in more than 2 subjects and are downgraded to a lower class rank then they will be asked to leave Tsinghua. According to the statistics from 1924's *Tsinghua Weekly*, only about 40% of students were able to graduate on time. Teaching and studying at Tsinghua remained firm, rigorous and demanding. This is especially true for those studying the science disciplines where elimination rates are high. In 1930, only 30% of the students from the School of Sciences were able to graduate on time.

The higher elimination rate is inseparable from the strictness surrounding exams. However, it is not the only method used by the teachers to ensure that students are able to learn and apply the needed knowledge. In the 1930s, Civil Engineering teachers would start shouting the words "Quickly! Quickly!" when there are only 5 minutes to go in the quizzes. This is to train the students to remain calm under stress and to still maintain accurate calculations which is often needed during actual work. Professor Cai Fangyin often said to the students: "I'm not going to be lenient since I don't want to lose Tsinghua's face!"

Despite being strict, the teachers are caring. Wang Jiading said, "The teachers are strict but on the other hand, in order to not cause delay to the students' graduation, they would always give up their holidays and hold more courses. That way, those students who have failed a course and require more support can find time to catch up during the break." Tang Shiyi, a Civil Engineering student who loves Peking Opera once had the comments "Please study more and sing less opera" written on the paper. Deep down, the teachers are cruel only to be kind.

After the founding of New China, Tsinghua students shouldered the responsibilities of supporting their motherland. The teachers took teaching seriously and the students studied hard to ensure that they have a solid foundation which will fully prepare them for work in the future. "To be rigorous and diligent, to seek the truth and always be innovative" became the style of Tsinghua University. This has continued and encouraged all teachers to set the example in teaching and talent developments.... it is precisely because Tsinghua always adhered to a rigorous style of teaching and strict requirements that the students cherished their time at Tsinghua and immerse themselves fully in their studies.

Mr Ji Xianlin, had frequently complained about Tsinghua's frequent tests in his diary. But In his later years, he looked back and felt grateful since "Like my other Tsinghua classmates, all that I know now came from the foundations that I made during my time at Tsinghua. Is it not?"

Translation and revision | Min Weiyuan

Image | Ren Zuoli

9月4日

文字 | 杨晨晞

图片 | 郭祥

“清华创客”王世栋：让每个人的3D创想变成现实

“没有清华，就没有我的今天。”今年夏天硕士毕业的清华大学汽车工程系校友、紫晶立方科技有限公司创始人王世栋回忆自己的创业之路时，难以忘怀清华给予他的培育和帮助。

王世栋看上去有着典型的清华工科男的内敛气质，但是却在竞争激烈的全球3D打印市场上，凭借自己的研发力量开辟了一条全新的道路。“一开始我和其他几位创始人租了一个小屋子，没课的时候我们就跑去组装机器。好不容易组装出了第一台差不多勉强能用的3D打印机，我们就用这台原始机器来打印我们需要的更好的零部件，再用打印出来的零件组装更好的机器。我们只能不断更新设计方案，不断挑战前一个成果，才能实现更大的突破。”在王世栋看来，正是清华良好的求学氛围，促使自己养成了勇于创新、善于思考、挑战自我、脚踏实地的品质。

除了精益求精的产品质量，王世栋对产品售后服务的强烈责任感和一丝不苟的精神，也源自“清华印记”。“只要卖出去的机器出了一点点问题，我就浑身起鸡皮疙瘩，满脑子只想着赶紧去帮人把问题解决了。”王世栋说，“因为自己是清华的学生，所以越来越觉得必须要用更高的标准来要求自己。”这份“与校俱来”的责任与担当，促成了王世栋团队在产品上的执着与成功。

创业遇到困难时，清华亦是他获得力量的源泉。“在创业初期，很多时候投资人无条件支持我，仅仅是因为他们知道我是清华的学生，相信我有足够的研发能力。还有些清华校友在不算特别了解我的情况下，毅然出资支持我创业。创业的过程充满艰辛，但也一直让我感动，可以说是清华成就了我的今天。”在谈到对未来有什么期许时，王世栋首先想到的就是“反哺”：“如果将来发展良好，我一定会竭尽全力支持和帮助我的学弟学妹们，就像当初那些校友们无条件支持我创业一样。”知足感恩，饮水思源，清华精神在王世栋的创业过程中起到了无可替代的作用。

2014年10月，扎克伯格来到中国，当他在清华见到王世栋时，不禁用中文连夸“很厉害”。在世界各国纷纷为争取3D打印领域核心竞争力布局时，王世栋带领团队杀出了一条“血路”。清华培养了他行胜于言、以身作则的品格，那些平日在校园里点点滴滴的积累，都成为日后王世栋在3D打印领域“异军突起”的有力支撑。

王世栋的目标是将低成本高质量的3D打印机送入寻常百姓家，“创立可与国际巨头抗衡的民族3D打印企业，让每个人的3D创想变成现实”。

Tsinghua Maker Wang Shidong: Materializing Everyone's 3D Creative Imagination

"Without Tsinghua, I wouldn't be where I am today." recalls Wang Shidong of his path in entrepreneurship, a master alumnus of Tsinghua University's Department of Automotive Engineering. It is difficult to forget the training and help he received from Tsinghua.

Wang Shidong has the typical look of a Tsinghua engineering student and an introverted temperament. But in the globally highly competitive 3D printing market, he has opened up a new path for himself thanks to his research prowess. "At first, I rented a small room with several other co-founders," Wang reminisces, "and when there's no class, we would assemble our machines there. We finally assembled our first 3D printer which we could barely use. We used this first 3D printer to print out better parts that we need, and from the better parts printed out even better ones to assemble a better printer. We continued to update the design and continue to challenge previous results to achieve greater breakthrough." Tsinghua's learning environment has developed courage within him - courage to be innovative, to think, to challenge himself and the virtue of humility.

In addition to producing excellent products, Wang Shidong also has a strong sense of responsibility to provide excellent after-sales service. This came from the "Tsinghua" label on him. "Even when the machines have small problems, my whole body would tremble and my brain would only think of how to help the customers solve the problem." Wang Shidong said, "because I am Tsinghua student, I'm becoming more convinced that we need to ask for a higher standard from ourselves." It is because of this sense of responsibility that contributed to the success of the product by Wang Shidong and his team.

When he met with difficulties, Tsinghua gives him limitless strength and support. "In the early days of entrepreneurship, investors often support me unconditionally, simply because they know that I'm a Tsinghua student, and they believe that I have sufficient research and development capabilities. And there were also Tsinghua alumni who didn't know me, yet offered funding to support my business," Wang recalls, "The entrepreneurial journey is full of hardships, but it has moved me. I can say that it's Tsinghua that has made me who I am today." Speaking about his future, Wang Shidong said the first thing he would do when he is financially able is to support future Tsinghua students, just as he received unconditional support from Tsinghua alumni when he first started his business. Contented and thankful, the Tsinghua spirit has played a huge role that is irreplaceable.

In October 2014, Mark Zuckerberg, CEO of Facebook, came to China and he met a student named Wang Shidong in Tsinghua. Using Chinese, Zuckerberg uttered the words "very powerful" to describe Wang Shidong. In a world where the 3D printing market is extremely competitive and has superseded China, Wang Shidong led his team and blazed a new trail. The values he learned in Tsinghua has taught him that actions speak louder than words, to lead by example, and to embrace love for the country. The mundane and seemingly ordinary days on campus little by little had accumulated in him and became Wang Shidong's pillar of support when he began his 3D printing venture.

Wang Shidong's goal is to produce low-cost but high-quality 3D printers for the homes of ordinary folks. He wants his company to be a national company that can compete with the international giants in the 3D printing market, materializing every person's 3D creative imagination.

Translation and revision | Alexis See Tho

Image | Guo Xiang

9月11日

文字丨杨鹏成

图片丨梁晨、杨思维

“清华大学新百年教学成就奖”颁奖

在 9 月 8 日召开的清华大学 2017 年庆祝教师节大会上，环境学院钱易院士、机械系教授曾攀、公共管理学院教授程文浩、人文学院教授彭林、社会科学学院教授阎学通、体育部教授赵青、计算机系副教授邓俊辉、电机系副教授于歆杰等 8 位教师荣获首届“清华大学新百年教学成就奖”。

他们中有的先后 7 次被全校研究生推选为“良师益友”；有的写得一手漂亮书法，把教学变为一门精致的艺术；有的潜心体育教学 30 年，全面负责“大清体校”门类繁多、量大面广的“大学体育”……他们是不忘初心、不知疲倦的“良师”，又是享受教学相长、感觉后生可“慰”、深受学生景仰的“益友”。

作为清华教育教学改革的新举措，今年新设立的“新百年教学成就奖”指向了倾情投入教学、教学效果享誉度高的一线教师。获奖者由各大院系部门和师生校友提名“海选”而出，无关职务、职称，覆盖各个年龄层面。奖项汇聚了清华园中让人感念难忘的恩师言行和他们“口碑爆表”的课堂实况，也充分体现出清华对一线教学的倾注和对师风师德的重视。

“新百年教学成就奖”与“青年教师教学优秀奖”和奖励近百名教师的“年度教学优秀奖”，共同组成了清华奖励一线教师的“三驾马车”，折射出学校蓬勃发展的盛况。“所谓大学者，非谓有大楼之谓也，有大师之谓也”，如今的清华园大师云集、人才济济，一门不起眼的基础课，也许就会成为学生一生中最难忘的记忆。

一流的教师带来一流的课堂教学，一流的本科教育构成一流大学的底色。清华大学副校长、教务长杨斌表示，长期以来，广大清华教师对于教书育人工作有着强烈的使命感和内生动力。作为综合改革的重要内容，清华正在深度推进教育教学改革，希望通过转变育人理念，让教师担负起学生价值塑造的主要责任，通过言传身教感染学生，用人格魅力和学识魅力陶冶学生的情操；并从体制机制上鼓励教师更多地投入教学，营造和保持重视教学、重视人才培养的良好环境氛围，把价值塑造、能力培养、知识传授“三位一体”的教育模式落到实处，不断培养出更多优秀人才。

Tsinghua University New Century Teaching Achievement Award

On September 8th, 2017, Tsinghua University celebrated the 33th Teacher's Day. During the celebration, Professor Qian Yi from the School of Environment, Professor Zeng Pan from the Department of Mechanical Engineering, Professor Cheng Wenhao from the School of Public Policy and Management, Professor Peng Lin from the School of Humanities, Professor Yan Xuetong from the School of Social Sciences, Professor Zhao Qing from the Division of Sports Science and Physical Education, Associate Professor Deng Junhui from the Department of Computer Science and Technology and the Associate Professor Yu Xinjie from the Department of Electrical Engineering were the recipients of the First "Tsinghua University New Century Teaching Achievement Award" .

Some of them have been elected 7 times as the "top mentor" by graduates. Some write excellent calligraphy, some turn teaching into a fine art, some has been devoted to physical education for well-over 30 years and held great responsibility to ensure that sports remain large-scale and available for all... These educators never forgot their initial goals and worked tirelessly in the field of teaching and learning. They injected much energy and passion into teaching and are seen as "a good friend" by many of their students.

As a new initiative in Tsinghua's Education and Teaching reforms, the "New Century Teaching Achievement Award" brings attention to front-line teachers who have demonstrated what education is and upheld their teaching philosophies. Winners of the Award were selected by both the teaching staff and students from all schools and departments. One's titles, positions, age and other factors were not taken into account. Everyone placed their votes and re-lived the memories of their favorite teachers. Tsinghua place huge importance on the quality and make-up of the teaching staff. This award reflects just that.

The "New Century Teaching Achievement Award" and the "Young Teacher Teaching Excellence Award" as well as the "Annual Teaching Excellence Award" forms the main drive in recognizing the efforts and quality of Tsinghua teachers. Such recognitions reflects the vigorous development made by the university. Now, Tsinghua is filled with masters, talents, academicians and experts in their respective fields. Those fundamental and seemingly easy courses might perhaps become the most memorable experiences in a student's life.

First-class teachers bring first-class teaching and first-class undergraduate education provides the backbone for a first-class university. Tsinghua University's Vice President Yang Bin said that for a long time, the majority of Tsinghua teachers made great achievements in teaching due to their continuous dedication towards education. As an important part of the comprehensive reform, Tsinghua is deepening reforms in education and teaching. The hope is to transform the concept of education. Teachers take on the main responsibility of shaping values for students and through one's words and deeds, students are encouraged and inspired. It is with charisma and academic charm that student sentiments are cultivated and maintained. Institutional mechanisms are set in place to encourage teachers to invest more in teaching so creativity flows and attention are placed in providing a good environment for personnel training and development. Shaping correct values, Cultivating comprehensive skills and ensuring the correct transfer of knowledge will be implemented and fully maintained so that more talents can be cultivated and Tsinghua can play an even greater role in the nation's education reform.

Translation and revision | Min Weiyuan

Image | Liang Chen, Yang Siwei

9月12日

文字 | 杨晨晞
图片 | 唐蓓蓓

行为与沟通实验室：打造自我实验、自我提高的平台

无论在大学校园里还是工作单位中，“无领导小组讨论”都是选拔人才的重要面试形式。因为这一面试形式被认为能够有效考察面试者的沟通与表达能力、自信程度、进取心、情绪稳定性、反应灵活性等多项全方位能力。同学们在面试前不妨来到经管学院，在行为与沟通实验室测试一下，看看自己究竟能够在无领导小组讨论中发挥出怎样的水平吧！

清华大学行为与沟通实验室位于经济管理学院 128 室。实验室“潜藏”在伟伦楼和舜德楼之间的小花园一角，却有着一方自己的小天地。进入实验室，映入眼帘的是一个会议圆桌，看起来简洁大气，实际上却“暗藏玄机”。圆桌会议的环境背后，是一整套对参与实验的人进行准确记录的设备。实验室配备有音视频信息发布设备、实验用计算机、固定摄像机、桌面摄像机、超强指向性话筒和三基色柔光灯。这些设备能够准确发布实验内容，并全方位记录下实验者的表情与动作，达到记录实验者沟通行为的目的。

除了实验室主体外，与实验室隔着一层透明玻璃的是配套的观察室，同时还有一间设备间，专门用来放置对实验室设备进行控制的一整套高水平的音像摄制及制作系统。在软件方面，实验室还拥有组织行为与人力资源测评系统。优良的硬软件设施，使得实验室拥有了教学科研等多重功能。

行为与沟通实验室为经管学院的教师教学提供了良好的平台，也为人力资源管理、行为学、整合营销、管理沟通等课程建设提供了教学、观摩、讨论和评价的环境。组织行为与人力资源测评系统渗透到了经管学院各类教育项目（包括 MBA 培养项目、管理培训项目等）的相关课程中。同时行为与沟通实验室也为经管学院学生提供相关技能培训。经管学院本科生培养方案中有一门名为“中文沟通”的课程，就会到行为与沟通实验室进行“无领导小组讨论”的学习与实践。在给定的题目下，同学们发表各自的观点，进行沟通与交流。与此同时，多台无死角的摄像机将每一个人的表情动作记录下来，用做素材进行教学，在另一侧观察室里的老师也会结合实际案例进行分析和讲解。通过这样的亲身体验和案例教学，同学们的表达与沟通能力得到了显著的提升。

实验室还为经管学院教师进行纵向、横向的课题研究提供了便利，为其他院系的相关研究提供了支持。其可供用于研究的方向，有包括团队小组研究、多人决策与工作效率研究、人力关系研究、现代媒体效果评估研究在内的十余个方向。

在这个实验室中，实验者本人同时也是被实验者，来参与实验的人便在自我实验与被实验的循环中不断提升自我。行为与沟通实验室为提升学生各项能力提供了学习与锻炼的机会，为培养出更多优秀的、符合社会和时代发展需求的人才提供了共享平台。

Behavior and Communication Laboratory—a Platform for Self-experiment and Self-improvement

Either it be in the university or in the work place, "leaderless group discussion" is an important form of interview for talent selection. This is because this form of interview is considered to effectively test the interviewee's ability to communicate and express, self-confidence, aggression, emotional stability, response flexibility and other comprehensive abilities. On the laboratory-opening day of Tsinghua University anniversary, you might as well come to the School of Economics and Management and test how well you can play in the leaderless group discussion at the Behavior and Communication Laboratory.

The Behavior and Communication Laboratory in Tsinghua University is located at Room 128 of the School of Economics and Management. The laboratory hides in the corner of a small garden between Weilun Building and Shunde Building, but has its own space. Entering into the laboratory, you can see a round table for meetings, which looks simple but classy, and keeps secrets under cover. Behind the scene of round meeting table, there is a complete set of equipment for accurate records of participants in the experiment. The laboratory is equipped with audio and video information publishing device, computers for experimental use, fixed cameras, desktop cameras, super-directional microphone and three-color soft lights. These devices can accurately publish the experimental contents, and record the observer's expressions and actions in all directions, achieving the aim of recording the observer's communication behaviors.

In addition to the main part of laboratory, connected with the laboratory through a layer of transparent glass, there is a supporting observation room, as well as an equipment room with a complete set of high-level audio and video filming and production system, which controls the equipment in the laboratory. As for the software, the laboratory also has software packages with regard to organizational behavior and human resources evaluation system and related statistics. Excellent hardware and software facilities make up the laboratory's own teaching, scientific research and other multiple functions.

The Behavior and Communication Laboratory provides a solid platform for teachers' teaching in the School of Economics and Management, and provides teaching, observation, discussion and evaluation environment for curricula construction such as human resources management, behavioristic practices, integrated marketing, and management communication, etc. At the same time, it also provides relevant skills training for the students in the School of Economics and Management. In the training program of undergraduate students in the School, there is a course titled "Chinese communication" , which will be applied in the learning and practice of the "leaderless group discussion" at this behavior and communication laboratory. With a given topic, the students express their views and communicate with each other, and at the same time, several no-dead-end cameras will record each person's facial expressions and actions, which will be used as materials for teaching. Teachers in the observation room will also analyze and explain aspects concerning the actual cases. With this, the actual case and personal experiences will help the students significantly improve their expressing and communicating abilities.

The laboratory also facilitates the vertical and horizontal research of teachers in the School of Economics and Management, and provides support for relevant research in other schools. It can serve more than ten research directions including team group research, multi-person decision-making and work efficiency research, human relations research, and modern media effects evaluation research.

In this laboratory, the observer is also the human subject at the same time, and the person who participates in the experiment constantly conducts self-improvement in the cycle of conducting experiment and being experimented. The Behavior and Communication Laboratory provides opportunities for learning and exercises to enhance students' abilities, which makes the qualities of students in the School of Economics and Management, even all Tsinghua students, become fully developed, and makes more excellent talents in line with the development needs of the society and times to be cultivated.

Translation and revision | Raj Lamar

Image | Tang Beibei

Photographer | He Mingnuan

9月13日

文字 | 胡颖

图片 | 宋晨

彭凯平：幸福是一种有意义的快乐

“幸福不是虚幻的概念，也不是简单的满足，幸福不是有钱就可以，也不是靠别人就能给予，幸福更不是独善其身。幸福其实是一种有意义的快乐。”

在最新一期的“人文清华”讲坛中，清华大学社会科学学院院长、心理学系主任彭凯平与上千名观众分享了他从积极心理学角度“求解幸福”的思考和感悟。彭凯平曾任伯克利加州大学终身教授、社会心理学专业主任，他是文化心理学的奠基人之一，也是清华心理学系复建的领军人物，近年在国内大力推动积极心理学。

在一个半小时的演讲中，彭凯平用幽默生动的语言为大家剖析了关于幸福的常见误区以及当代中国社会所面临的心理危机。当天，场外还有数十万观众收看了“人文清华”讲坛的在线直播，感受这场思想传播的盛宴。

在彭凯平看来，幸福不是虚幻的概念，也不是简单的满足，更不仅仅是心灵鸡汤，它有脑科学的定位，有神经递质的作用，有经济的、社会的各种效用，也有看得见、摸得着的生理变化。幸福和收入、高学历、年轻美貌没有必然的关系，对幸福最起作用的其实是美好的人际关系，是至爱亲朋的支持，是社会交往的技巧。

在 2017 年 3 月联合国发布的世界幸福报告中，中国仅排名第 79 位。对此，彭凯平分析认为，中国人民在生活自由度方面毫不逊色，幸福排名不尽如人意的主要原因是一些社会心理指标，例如社会公益水平偏低、社会信任度不高以及主观幸福感不足等。正是在中国积极构建社会正能量、增强老百姓幸福感的大背景下，彭凯平一直在思考清华心理学系应该如何在促进中国社会发展和人民幸福方面做出自己的贡献。

彭凯平表示，心态建设、心态发展、心态调整是中国在改革开放、经济进步之后必须补的一门课程，清华心理学系愿意在科技心理学、积极心理学领域做出全新的探索。因此，彭凯平牵头成立了世界上第一个幸福科技实验室，希望能够利用清华的跨学科优势，培育出世界领先的积极心理学学科。

演讲在美国著名黑人爵士乐歌手阿姆斯特朗的名曲《如此美好的世界》中结束，这是彭凯平心爱的曲子，也传递出他对幸福、美好的积极求索。

Peng Kaiping: Happiness Is a Form of Meaningful Joy

"The concept of happiness is not a fantasy. It is not easy to fulfil. Happiness is not about having money or depending on others. Happiness does not belong to just one person. Happiness is a form of meaningful joy."

Night of the 5th of June, 2017, Professor Peng Kaiping (the Dean of Tsinghua's School of Social Sciences) attended The Forum on Tsinghua Humanitas, and shared with the audience his positive views on "happiness" and all related sentiments. Peng was a professor of social psychology at the University of California, Berkeley and as one of the founders of cultural psychology, he was one of the driving forces behind the re-establishment of the Department of Psychology at Tsinghua. In recent years, Peng has been vigorously promoting psychology in China.

In his 90 min speech, Peng used vivid and humorous language to pinpoint the common mistakes that people make about the concept of happiness as well as the psychological crisis facing contemporary Chinese society. In addition, hundreds and thousands of audiences watched this live forum online.

According to Peng, the concept of happiness is not a fantasy. It is not easy to fulfil. It is more than just chicken soup for the soul. It is also science. It has a neurotransmitter effect and many economic and social changes. Happiness has no link with income, education levels, age and beauty. What works best for happiness is positive interpersonal relationship, support from love ones and positive skills in social interactions.

In 2017's UN World Happiness Report, China ranked 79th. Peng believes that a shortage of social public welfare donations, the lack of basic social trust and low levels in the perception of well-being for individuals are all major causes of dwindling happiness in China. The entire Chinese society needs to actively build a positive social energy and enhance the backdrop for ordinary happiness. Peng has been thinking about how Tsinghua could be the leader in making social progress and developing social happiness for the country.

Peng stressed that mentality, development and adjusting the state of mind is a compulsory course for China after fast economic progress accelerated by the country's reform and opening up policies. Tsinghua's Psychology Department is willing to be the advocate for positive psychology and scientific movement. Therefore, Peng took the lead to establish the world's first "H+ (Happiness, Health & Harmony) Lab" . He hopes that it could take full advantages of Tsinghua's interdisciplinary technology to improve the teaching and learning of the psychology department.

The speech ended with Louis Armstrong's *What a wonderful world*. This is Peng's favorite song. It conveys his active and positive pursuit for happiness.

Translation and revision | Min Weiyuan

Image | Song Chen

9月14日

文字丨左炟晅

图片丨任帅

周济团队：用钻研挑战材料王国的不可能

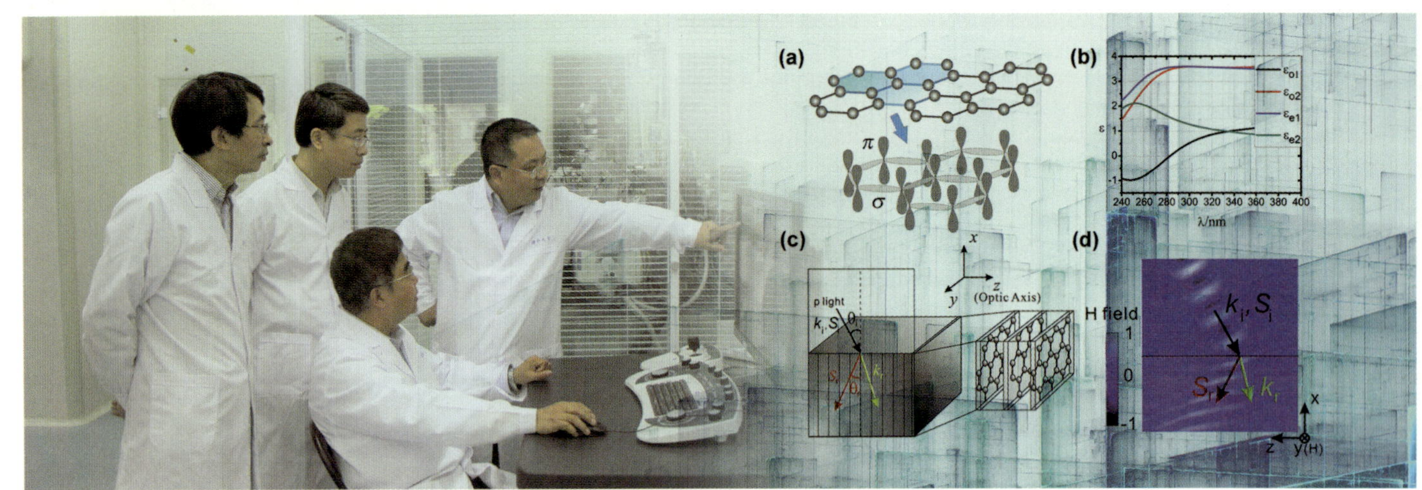

在2016年度国家科学技术奖励大会上，周济和他的团队凭借“非金属基超常电磁介质的原理与构筑”项目获得国家自然科学奖二等奖。

超常电磁介质的探索，最初始于20世纪60年代苏联科学家韦谢拉戈提出的一个思想实验。韦谢拉戈发现，假如有同时具备负介电常数和负磁导率的物质，即负折射率，电磁波的传播行为将会发生根本性改变。然而，由于自然界中并不存在该材料，该想法在当时并未得到人们的过多关注，直到20世纪90年代末，一位英国科学家提出利用金属人工结构阵列实现这一想法，并于世纪之交被实验验证，超常电磁介质才自此诞生。然而，受制于金属基体的固有特性，高损耗、各向异性、难以调控以及光频材料难以制备成为困扰此类材料发展的壁垒。

为了解决此问题，周济团队在研究之初选择利用超材料与自然材料的融合，发展非金属基超常电磁介质。

2008年，在西班牙的一个小镇上，周济见到了仰慕已久的韦谢拉戈教授，他向其介绍了自己团队正在进行的研究。“韦谢拉戈教授最初的思路也是在传统介质中实现超常电磁响应，但最终得出的结论是不可能。”周济回忆道。

令韦谢拉戈难以想象的是，他曾经认为“不可能”的这个想法多年后在一群中国科研者手中成为现实。

回想起科研攻坚的那段日子，周济感触最深的有两点：一是学科交叉，把相关学科的精髓原理巧妙应用到本学科中来；二是要敢于打破常规，尝试别人认为不可能实现的目标。

十余年间的艰难困苦和心血汗水，周济视之淡然。“每位从事科学研究的人，都已经习惯了不断遇到问题、不断解决问题、进而不断探索的过程。在科研中不断积累经验和加深认知可以帮我们形成大致的方向感，一步一步不断有所进步和发现。”周济表示。

最终在“超材料与自然材料融合”的思想指导下，借助非金属材料中丰富的电磁极化机制，周济团队初步创建了非金属基超常介质的原理框架和构筑策略，为超常介质这类新世纪出现的新型材料的系统探索和器件应用提供了新的范式。

谈及多年来从事材料研究的体会，周济认为：“做科研，首先要有科学精神，要有独立思想。不要盲从文献，不要迷信权威，也不要有功利目的。”

“中国正在从科学大国向科学强国转变的转折点上，过去我们做科研总是跟在别人的后面，今后这种跟风式的研究已经没有多大意义了。只有在很多领域都做出原创性成果，才能成为真正意义上的科技强国。”周济说。

Zhou Ji: Challenging the Impossible in the Material Kingdom

In the National Science and Technology Award Conference of 2016, the State Natural Science Award (2nd class in Materials Science) was awarded to Prof. Ji Zhou and his group, for the significant achievements in research project entitle "The principle and construction of non-metallic metamaterials" .

The initial exploration of the abnormal electromagnetic medium dates back to 1960s. A Russian physicist, Dr. Victor Veselago, proposed an assumption that if the permittivity and permeability of the materials became negative simultaneously, namely, negative refractive index, many general physical phenomena would fundamentally be changed. However, such an abnormal property can hardly occur to natural existed materials and Veselego's assumption was still a scientific fiction in the following 40 years. Nowadays' metal based metamaterials, despite of the exhibition of a negative index, are always troubled by the high loss, anisotropy, nontunable, and the incredible challenge to keep the property at optical frequency.

To crack this nut, Prof Zhou's group started their research by fusing metamaterials with natural materials to develop non-metal based abnormal electromagnetic metamaterials.

In 2008, at a small town in Spain, Prof. Zhou met the distinguished pioneer Prof. Veselago, to whom he introduced the team's ongoing research. As Zhou recalled, "Prof. Veselago's initial thought was to achieve such an abnormal electromagnetic response in conventional media, however, the answer was quit negative."

Beyond the imagination of Veselago, the idea once considered to be a "fiction" has become a reality after a few years of hard work by the group of Chinese researchers.

At the crucial stage of the research, Zhou was deeply impressed by these two points: one is inter-discipline, that is, properly applying essential principles of relevant disciplines to a specific one we are focusing; the other is to break the limit from conventional mental set, and try something impossible.

Paying more than ten years' hard work and efforts, Zhou treated it peacefully. "All scientists have been used to the endless processes of encountering problems, solving problems, and continuing to explore. By accumulating experience and improving our recognition, we start to have our own direction and make progress gradually towards it."

Finally, based on the idea of "combining metamaterials and natural materials" , and study on the various electromagnetic polarization mechanism in abundant nonmetallic materials, Zhou's team initially framed the principle and built the strategy of non-metallic abnormal electromagnetic media, providing a new paradigm for the explorations and applications of metamaterials and metamaterials based systems which emerged in this new century.

Regarding to the experience in these years' research, Zhou believed that "A scientific research requires a scientific spirit and independent thinking. We can not just following the literature, or always obey claims from authority or even for a utilitarian purposes."

"China will be transformed into a scientific and technological power in the world. In the past, mostly we had to follow the trends of the science from the developed countries and can hardly make a breakthrough by such a way. Eventually we start to make original innovations and achievements in all different fields and we may proudly say our country is a scientific and technological power." said Zhou.

Translation and revision | Raj Lamar

Image | Ren Shuai

9月15日

文字 | 张智伟

图片 | 任帅

温馨雅室别样红——梁思成林徽因故居

如今的清华大学新林院 8 号，居住了几户人家和商户，正房前新修了偏房，如果不是院内小店门前那块“梁林故居”的招牌，很难引起行人额外的注意。

而在 70 多年前，这里的沙发上坐过金岳霖、陈岱孙、周培源夫妇、张奚若夫妇，热烈的讨论此起彼伏，话题广泛，涉及哲学、美学、艺术、社会、城市规划等领域，吸引了不同年龄、不同院系的教员和学生。在这里，梁思成、林徽因为深夜造访的两位解放军代表在地图上标出了北平重要的古建筑，划出了禁止炮击的地区，也正是这一晚，“他们和共产党的感情一下子就亲密起来了”。新中国成立后，这里的绘图桌又见证了他们带领清华建筑系教师设计新中国国徽和人民英雄纪念碑方案的身影……

新林院，是清华早期的教授住宅，建于 1934 年，起初被称为“新南院”，抗日战争胜利后，由朱自清提议，改为“新林院”。1946 年，清华大学复员北平，决定增设建筑工程学系，梁思成受邀任教授兼主任，新林院 8 号成为梁思成、林徽因夫妇在清华园的居所，直至 1954 年，他们迁居胜因院 12 号。他们在新林院的邻居，包括周培源、陈岱孙、俞平伯、潘光旦等最有学识威望的大师们。

当时的新林院 8 号，小院周围砌了低矮的砖垛略作围护，四周花木扶疏，阳光自林荫透过。正房十分高大，前檐砌出拱形雨篷，冬天要烧四个大火炉取暖；正房与后院之间是教授们余暇聚会的场所，相邻几个小院围合成的空场地供孩子们嬉戏，也时常放映露天电影。

迁居新林院 8 号的梁家保留了“午后茶聚”习惯。每天下午 4 点半开始，金岳霖、陈岱孙、张奚若夫妇和建筑系师生相继到来，各类话题无不在他们讨论之列。女儿梁再冰至今仍清楚地记着：“我每周回到新林院 8 号时都发现，这里是一个各种活动——学术的和生活的中心。”

1948 年末的一个晚上，政治学系教授张奚若带着两个解放军代表登门请教梁林夫妇，诧异又惊喜的他们为解放军代表绘制了保护北平文物建筑的目录。此后，建筑系教师为南下解放军编写了全国文物建筑保护单位目录，最大限度保护了文物建筑。新中国成立后，他们又热情地投入到了国徽和人民英雄纪念碑的设计工作中。那时，梁再冰记忆中的新林院 8 号客厅，“到处是红、金两色的国徽图案，沙发上、椅子上摆满了国徽”，“感受到家中浓重的‘国徽氛围’”。

20 世纪 50 年代初，梁思成又带领建筑学系师生投入到“为新中国创造新建筑”的各项实践中，完成了中南海怀仁堂改建设计、第一个五年计划的城市规划等多项建设。

见证与凝聚了一段传奇的新林院 8 号，也因与新中国建设的特殊情缘，多了一份独特的历史意义，给后人留下无尽的追思与遐想。

No. 8 of Xinlin Yard: Witness of New China's Architectural History

A few households and merchants occupy the present No. 8 of Xinlin Yard in Tsinghua University. The new-built wing-rooms stand in front of the principal room, where, if there wasn't a sign reading "Former Residence of Liang Sicheng and Lin Huiyin" , it would be hard for people to see the place.

However, about 70 years ago, here on the couch, Jin Yuelin, Chen Daisun, Zhou Peiyuan and wife, Zhang Xiruo and wife once had heated discussions upon a wide range of topics: philosophy, aesthetics, art, society, city planning and so on, attracting Tsinghua faculty members and students of various age and departments; right here, Liang Sicheng and Lin Huiyin met two representatives of People's Liberation Army, marking the important ancient buildings on the map, highlighting the areas free of shelling; also in this very evening, "They got close to the Communist Party" , and stayed in Beijing after the founding of New China, contributing to the protection and construction of ancient Chinese buildings; here on the table, the New China's national emblem and the reconstruction program of Zhongnanhai's Huairen Hall were designed... .

Xinlin Yard, early residence of Tsinghua professors, was built in 1934 and initially named "Xinnan Yard" , later after the victory of Anti-Japanese War, proposed by Zhu Ziqing, the name was changed to "Xinlin Yard" . In 1946, Tsinghua University moved back to Beijing and established the Department of Architectural Engineering. Liang Sicheng was invited to be a professor and the director, since then the No. 8 of Xinlin Yard became the residence for him and his wife Lin Huiyin until they moved to the No. 12 of Shengyin Yard in 1954. Their neighbors in Xinlin Yard include Zhou Peiyuan, Chen Daisun, Yu Pingbo, Pan Guangdan and other respected masters of knowledge.

A low brick wall and luxuriant plants, cracks of light filtered through the branches and leaves, surrounded the yard at that time. The principal room is tall with arched awning, four stoves are needed in winter to keep the house warm; between the principle room and the backyard, there's a leisure place for professors, and the open space, which was enclosed by adjacent several small courtyards, was for children to play and was much frequented for projecting outdoor movies.

As the host of Xinlin No.8, Liang's family kept the routine of "afternoon tea time" , when Jin Yuelin, Chen Daisun, Zhang Xiruo and wife, and teachers and students of the Department of Architecture would all be the guests. All kinds of topics would be discussed. Their daughter, Liang Zaibing, still vividly recalls that, "When I returned to the No.8 of Xinlin Yard each week, I found out there was an active center for a variety of academic and life activities."

In 1948, before the liberation of Beijing, Zhang Xiruo, professor of the Department of Political Science, guided the two representatives of PLA to Liang's house. Sudden and surprised, Liang Sicheng and Lin Huiyin drew the catalogue of Beijing's ancient buildings. Soon after, the Department of Architecture had compiled the collection of national cultural relics for the PLA heading for the South China, to maximize the protection of cultural relic buildings. After the founding of New China, Both of them were fully devoted to the design work of the National Emblem and the Monument to the People's Heroes. According to Liang Zaibing, in the living room of the house, "Everything was covered red and golden patterns of the national emblem, even the sofa and chairs were covered by that" , and "I was feeling a strong patriotic atmosphere with the national emblem" .

Thereafter, Liang Sicheng has led the Department of Architecture to get involved in the practice of "create new architecture for the New China" , completing a variety of constructions including the design of Zhongnanhai's Huairen Hall and the city planning of the first Five-Year Plan.

Having witnessed a legend, the No. 8 of Xinlin Yard, also due to its special links with New China's construction, leaves a unique historical significance for later generations to memorize.

Translation and revision | Raj Lamar

Image | Ren Shuai

9月18日

文字 | 胡颖

图片 | 宋晨

钱易：最大的幸福是后生可“慰”

中国工程院院士、清华大学环境学院教授钱易在几代清华学子心中留下了共同的记忆。从青丝到白发，如今已经 81 岁高龄的她，仍然躬耕于三尺讲台，当之无愧地成为清华首批“新百年教学成就奖”获得者。

钱易出身书香门第，国学大师钱穆是她的父亲、著名科学家钱伟长是她的堂兄，她是中国工程院第一批院士，也是清华大学第一个女院士。正是因为家风的传承，钱易爱上教师这个职业：“我想最大的影响，是我们都把做教师作为一个非常享受的职业。”

1959 年留校任教以来，钱易培养的学生数不胜数，很多已成长为环境工程领域的中流砥柱。在清华的一方讲台上，她一站便是近 60 年，为教育和环保事业奉献了一生。她从 1998 年起开设的“环境保护与可持续发展”被评为国家级精品课程，因为选课学生太多而从一年一次改为一年两次。如今，年过八旬的她仍然活跃在教学一线，除了参与讲授国家级精品课程“环境保护与可持续发展”和“生态文明建设十五讲”两门公选课，还坚持每年单独开设新生研讨课“环境与发展”，每学期八次，每次两小时，持之以恒地为环保教育发声。她曾获国家级教学名师奖、央视“最美教师”称号，三次获清华大学“良师益友”奖。每学年所授课程的学生数近 1000 人次。

已届耄耋之年的钱易教授不仅未离开教学一线，还把讲台搬到了更大的地方。她是倡导建设“绿色大学”第一人，活跃在各种学术会议和咨询会议、干部培训班上，呼吁政府及公众关注循环经济、生态文明建设、可持续发展。

对于自己一路走来近 60 年的教学生涯，钱易感叹道：“我的一生，谈不上任何的成绩，够不上大师的帽子。但有一点，我觉得非常有收获，就是当了一辈子教师。”不管有多忙，钱易的日程表上永远把学生排在第一位。“中国老说‘后生可畏’，但我更愿意说的是后生可‘慰’，‘欣慰’的‘慰’。看到学生们取得了骄人的成绩，一个一个超越了我，就是我最大的幸福。”

Qian Yi: Surpassed by Excellent Students Is Great Happiness

Qian Yi, an academician of the Chinese Academy of Engineering and a Professor at Tsinghua's School of Environment has left a common memory in the hearts of several generations of Tsinghua students. The changes in her hair marks her age yet at eighty-one years old, she is still up at the podium giving her lesson. No doubt, she fully deserves the Tsinghua New Century Teaching Achievement Award.

Born into a family of scholars, Qian Yi's father is Qian Mu who is a master in Chinese Learning. The famous scientist Qian Weichang is her cousin and she is one of the first batch of academician of the Chinese Academy of Engineering. She is also Tsinghua's first female academician. It is because of such traditions that inspired Qian to fall in love with the teaching profession. "I wish to have the biggest impact on the lives of others. I thoroughly enjoy this occupation."

Since 1959, Qian has trained and nurtured many students who later became talents in their field of work and the main backbone in the field of environmental engineering. Using the platform at Tsinghua University, she stayed and taught for 60 years. She has devoted her entire life to education and environmental protection. She started to teach her course "Environmental Protection and Sustainable Development" from 1998 which was selected as a National Quality Course. Since too many students selected the course, it was changed from being taught only once a year to twice a year. Despite being over 80 years old, she is still actively teaching at the forefront. In addition to the two courses ("Environmental Protection and Sustainable Development" and "The construction of Ecological Civilization"), she continues to teach freshmen every year in her fundamental course "Environment and Development" . Every semester, this course is taught a total of 8 times and every lesson lasts for 2 hours. For Qian, this is her way of ensuring that environmental education thrives. She has won the title of "National Teaching Award" , CCTV's "Most Beautiful Teacher" and much more. Nearly 1000 students are enrolled each academic year in the coursework and it is her efforts that made her the three-time recipients of Tsinghua's "Best Mentor" Award.

Professor Qian Yi is supposed to go into retirement due to her age yet she remains in the teaching podium and only seeks to expand her teaching. She is the first person to initiate the construction of a "Green University" and has remained active in various academic conferences, consultation meetings and cadre training courses all with the aim to call on the government and the public to pay closer attention to economic development, ecological civilization and sustainable development.

When it comes her near 6 decades of teaching career, Qian said: "All my life, I cannot say that I've made any achievements nor can I say I can be called a Master. There is one thing that is for certain and that is, it is such a rewarding feeling that I can dedicate my life to being an educator." Regardless of how busy she is, Qian always put her students first. "When I see that my students have made such remarkable achievements and results, this becomes my greatest form of happiness."

Translation and revision | Min Weiyuan

Image | Song Chen

9月19日

文字 | 杨茂艺

图片 | 李娜

曾攀：把“有限元”讲得“出神入化”

机械系教授曾攀曾获得7届清华大学研究生“良师益友”荣誉称号，在今年的教师节庆祝大会上，他又获颁首届“清华大学新百年教学成就奖”。

曾攀主讲研究生学位课“有限元分析”和“弹塑性力学”。课堂上，他以其渊博的学识、清晰缜密的思路和深入浅出的讲述，将数理推导烦琐枯燥的课程讲得环环相扣、引人入胜，使学生系统掌握相关理论的同时，对理论和问题的本质有更深层次的认识。

授课24年来，曾攀最为人称道的是可以将艰深复杂的有限元分析及应用课程讲得“出神入化”。他还有一个特别之处是上课不依赖PPT，而是将有限元分析课上漂亮的推理一笔一画地写在黑板上，被同学们称赞为“完美”板书，让人印象深刻。

除了在教学科研上指导同学们，曾攀还十分乐于和同学们分享个人的工作心得。比如出版教材的经历，包括从一开始的素材积累到后来系统整理，再到最终的审查定稿，他都毫无保留地告诉学生们，让学生了解一本教材是如何从最初的想法到最终诞生的。在他看来，这也是学术培养的一部分。

对于正式出版物，他显得格外“较真”，每一个插图都仔细修改，每一条附录都认真核对，字斟句酌，一丝不苟。曾攀告诉学生，既然是拿出去给别人看的东西，就一定不能放过任何疑点，这样才是对读者负责，也是对我们自己负责。

Zeng Pan: Bringing Mechanical Engineering Classes to Life

Upon receiving Tsinghua University's 7th Annual "Best Mentor" Award, Professor Zeng Pan of the Department of Mechanical Engineering was recently named the recipient of the New Century Teaching Achievement Award.

Zeng mainly teaches two master's degree courses, "Finite Element Analysis" and "Elasto-Plastic Mechanics" . In the classroom, Zeng's broad knowledge, clear and thoughtful ideas in his lecture, made what could have been dry topics come to life, drawing in his students' attention. His teaching also helps students to systematically understand theories and at the same time have a deeper understanding of the problem sets.

In his 24-year teaching career, Zeng is well-known for clearly explaining the complexities in the Finite Element Analysis and its application to a level that is almost perfection. Another difference in Zeng's teaching is that he does not rely on PowerPoint slides in his class. Rather, he writes out the logical reasoning on the blackboard, or what his students call "perfection" . Zeng's teaching leaves students with a deep impression.

Other than teaching and mentoring students in classes, he is often delighted to share with the students his personal experiences in his work. An example is his experience writing teaching materials, from gathering resources in the preliminary stages to systematically organizing the materials and to the final review. He generously shares with students how a textbook is written from the initial idea to the final product. In his view, this is also part of academic training.

For other publications, he also diligently checks each illustration, each item in the appendix, and meticulously looks over every word and sentence, leaving nothing to chance. Zeng told his students, "If it's something that will be read by other people, we cannot be unsure of any of its content. This is what we should do to be responsible to the reader and also our own faithfulness to our duty."

Translation and revision | Alexis Soo Tho

Image | Li Na

9 月 20 日

文字 | 冯婉婷

图片 | 李娜

程文浩：教学是生命，是信仰

清华大学公共管理学院的一间教室里，程文浩教授正在讲述抗日战争时期民族实业家卢作孚先生保全西迁民族工业、破解军粮匮乏之困局的故事。他细致诉说着卢作孚如何以“三段接力法”完成宜昌大转移的壮举，声音有些哽咽。教室里非常安静，大家沉浸在这段震撼人心的抗战史诗中，有些同学甚至感动得流下眼泪。

这是程文浩主讲的“公共管理”课程的最后一讲。在以卢作孚的经典案例讲授并行、串行管理等知识时，应同学们的要求，程文浩讲述了这个动人的故事。下课铃声响起后，不少同学依旧沉浸在故事中不愿离去，一些同学守候在教学楼前，等待着与他合影留念。

用丰富有趣的大小案例，让学生迅速领会相对抽象的概念，是程文浩讲课时的一大特色。他讲课极富感染力，尤其注重将历史事件融入公共管理教学，深受同学们喜爱。程文浩在课上信手拈来的各种实例，离不开他平时的用心积累。每当在日常生活中看到有用的事例，他会马上掏出手机拍摄；平时读到与课程内容相关的文章，他也会立即复印下来，带到班上发给同学们阅读。

朴实、准确、精练、有力、幽默的语言风格，是程文浩讲课时打动学生的“另一招”。“语言是重要的教学工具。为了让同学们能够在轻松愉快的气氛中掌握知识，我平时积累了许多与课程相关的幽默素材，时不时抖个小‘包袱’，寓教于乐，效果明显。”程文浩认为，教师要形成独特的个人教学风格，离不开教学语言这个重要元素，而教学语言风格的形成同样需要长期的磨砺和积累。

程文浩躬耕讲坛 15 年，先后获得清华大学青年教师教学优秀奖、学术新人奖、良师益友奖等奖项，曾在北京市高校青年教师教学基本功比赛中为清华拿回第一个文科组一等奖冠军。今年教师节庆祝大会上，程文浩又获颁清华大学首届“新百年教学成就奖”。但是在他看来，教学并不能用奖项来衡量，“对我而言，教学是生命，是信仰”。

Cheng Wenhao: Teaching Is Life, Teaching Is Faith

In a classroom at Tsinghua's School of Public Policy and Management, Professor Cheng Wenhao was telling the story of Lu Zuofu who as a Chinese entrepreneur, stood by and layed a huge role in saving his country during the Anti-Japanese War Period. He carefully explained how Lu devoted his whole life to saving the country through industry and education. He got all chocked on just talking about it. The classroom was very quiet, the students sat there and were all transported back to those tough years upon hearing Cheng's words. Several students were even moved to tears.

This is the last lecture of Professor Cheng's Public Administration Course. Talking about Public Policy and Management through the famous example of Mr. Lu Zuofu, Professor Cheng shared with his class the touching story and even after the lesson ended, many students were still so immersed in the story. Some waited in front of the teaching building... . waiting to take a photo with Professor Cheng.

Using interesting cases and a wealth of knowledge and information allow students to quickly grasp the concept of something that is relatively abstract. This is the main characteristics of Cheng's lessons. His lectures are very popular and influential due to his deep interest in integrating historical events into his public management courses. Whenever he spot useful examples that could be used in his lessons, he would immediately take out his phone to take a photo or grab his notebook to write it down. Any articles related to the course content that he would come across will always be photocopied and recorded. He shares all of his findings in class.

Another characteristic of his lessons are that they are always delivered in a humorous, simple, accurate and concise format. "Language is an important teaching tool. In order to let the students master the knowledge in an easy and happy way, I've collected many humorous materials that could be taken out from time to time to make the lesson more fun and relaxing. The effect is obvious." Professor Cheng believes that teachers should form a unique teaching style and this is inseparable from language. Such style requires refinement and time.

Professor Cheng has taught for 15 years and have been awarded on many occasion teaching awards and various Tsinghua and Beijing prizes. He took first place in a Young Teachers Teaching Award organized by the Beijing Municipality. This year, he took home the "Tsinghua University New Century Teaching Achievement Award" . But for Cheng, teaching is not about awards. He said: "For me, teaching is life, teaching is faith."

Translation and revision I Min Weiyuan

Image I Li Na

9月21日

文字 | 杨晨晞

图片 | 宋晨

彭林：清华学生太优秀，老师多努力都不过分

"我是一名虔诚的国学推广者。"这是清华大学历史系教授彭林给自己的定位。彭林主要从事中国古代文献与学术思想史的教学和研究，核心是对儒家经典"三礼"（《周礼》《仪礼》《礼记》）的研究。

1999年进入清华大学后，彭林深感教书育人责任之重大，"孟子说人的一生有三种快乐，父母俱存，兄弟和睦，得天下英才而教育之。站在清华的讲台上，面对个个优秀的学子，你就会觉得，老师无论多努力都不过分。"对待课程建设，他坦言要有"十年磨一剑"的意识，语不惊人死不休。

彭林讲授的"文物精品与文化中国"和"中国古代礼仪文明"都是耗尽心血、反复锤炼而成的国家级精品课。他近几年新开的"民族文化与民族命运"课，也经十几年沉潜反复、精心打造，成为清华"学堂班"的"荣誉课程"，它们都深受学生喜爱。三年前，彭林去德国海德堡讲学，一名德国青年专程驱车两三百公里见他，说自己特别喜欢看彭林在edX上的网络课程"文物精品与文化中国"。

"讲中国文化，自己先要追根刨底，只有把自己感动了、震撼了，才会让学生感动和震撼。"彭林说。有一次，一位理工科的同学在课堂上向彭林提问："老师，你们这种学科有什么用？"彭林挺直了腰板，朗声说道："我很惭愧，既不会造机器，也不会盖房子，但是，我们这个学科是塑造民族精神和民族灵魂的！"课堂上几百位同学听后掌声雷动。

清华学子是懂彭林的，他们这样评价："在清华如果没有听过彭林老师的课，那简直是悲哀。彭林老师的课如果用一个词来形容，就是'震撼'。"还有学生说："彭老师的课是振聋发聩的寻根之学，是文化和心灵的碰撞。"

在彭林的课堂上，老师的讲授与同学的学习达到了一种相得益彰、浑然一体的境界。彭林欣慰地说："我特喜欢教师这个职业，喜欢在黑板前边讲边组织语言的那种惬意。当在讲解的某个瞬间突然擦出火花来时，那种陶醉真没法形容！"

Peng Lin: Tsinghua Students Are So Good, and It Is Perfectly Fine That Teachers Work Hard

"I am a pious advocate of sinology." This is how the history professor Peng Lin sees himself. Peng Lin is mainly engaged in the teaching and academic research of ancient Chinese literature. The core of his work lies in the Confucian classics known as the "Three Li" . They are *Zhou Li*, *Yi Li* and *The Book of Rites*. Apart from being a scholar, he is also a teacher. "I love teaching and I find absolute joy in teaching and organizing languages in front of the blackboard. When I am giving an explanation and suddenly the sparks fly, that sort of euphoria is difficult to use any words to explain."

This year, Mr. Peng Lin won the "Tsinghua University New Century Teaching Achievement Award" . This award highlights and encourages the embodiment of having both solid knowledge and a loving heart which is the spirit of being a teacher. As one of the eight teachers to first win such an award, Peng has made great contributions in promoting the establishment of the Liberal Arts discipline.

Having taught in Tsinghua for 18 years, Peng Lin has added much atmosphere to the university. In 1999, Tsinghua University became a part of the "Project 985" . Keeping in mind the need to become an international first-class university, Tsinghua has gradually begun to rebuild her Liberal Arts discipline. It is in that year that Peng Lin was invited to teach in Tsinghua. Harboring the dream of making Tsinghua a top and "first-class institution" , Peng threw himself completely into the teaching profession.

It is after years of hard-work and refinement that Peng has realized his goals of making his two courses ("Cultural Relics and Chinese Culture" and "Ancient Chinese Etiquette") a part of the National Quality Course. In recent years, his course "The culture and destiny of the nation" became a top course at Tsinghua and is greatly loved by his students. This cannot be achieved without hard and meticulous work.

In Peng's class, teaching and learning are not separate entities but one. A student once said: "In Tsinghua, if you haven't attended Peng's course then it is simply a pity. If we are to find one word to describe his course, it would be awe-inspiring!" Another student made a comment that "Professor Peng's course allows one to go in search of our roots. It allows our mind to collide, to think and confront aspects of our culture." For Peng, his lecture has a strong sense of rhythm. It is like one smooth wave after another.

"When you are teaching and faced with so many good students, you will work hard naturally." When it comes to the construction of his own coursework and curriculum, his persistence and endurance earned him great respects within Tsinghua. Peng does not see himself as being just an educator, one who only passes down knowledge. He has high expectations. When science and engineering students asked about the point of having such a course in Tsinghua, Peng would say "It is with sadness that I am unable to make machines and build houses. However, this course is about shaping the spirit and the soul of our nation."

Translation and revision I Min Weiyuan

Image I Song Chen

9月22日

文字 | 拜喆喆

图片 | 薛雅芳

华罗庚：天才出于积累，聪明在于勤奋

曾在清华任教的数学家华罗庚仅有初中学历，但他一生发表了数学研究论文 200 余篇，出版专著和科普性著作数十种，为我国数学科学的发展和普及工作做出了重要贡献。人们说他是数学天才，然而华罗庚自己认为：“天才出于积累，聪明在于勤奋。”

初中毕业后，家境贫寒的华罗庚开始了半工半读的自学生涯，用五年完成了高中和大学初年级的全部数学课程。1931 年，他发表的文章得到清华大学教授熊庆来的赏识，被调到清华数学系任助理员。在清华人才济济的环境中，华罗庚立下一个宏愿：以过人的努力，追求自己的成就。“人家受的教育比我多，我必须用加倍的时间以补救我的缺失，所以人家每天八小时工作，我要工作 12 小时以上才觉得心安。”

后来，当被问及成功的秘诀时，华罗庚从不提及自己的天分，他认为“天才出于积累，聪明在于勤奋”。基于勤奋与努力，华罗庚在清华只用了五年时间，就从助理员成长为助教，进而到英国剑桥大学研究深造，并在进修的两年里完成了十余篇论文，深得著名数学家哈代的赞誉。

华罗庚不仅在治学上勤奋严谨，对于国家，他更是满怀一腔赤诚。新中国成立后，华罗庚放弃国外的优厚待遇毅然回到清华任教，并在途经香港时写下了《致中国全体留美学生的公开信》，大声疾呼：“为了抉择真理，我们应当回去；为了国家民族，我们应当回去……”

华罗庚为培养新中国数学家和骨干队伍做出了杰出贡献。中科院数学所初建时，他兼任所长，对年轻的研究人员严格要求。每天黎明，华罗庚会去研究人员的宿舍敲门，一起讨论问题或是讲课；有时睡到半夜，他会把学生叫起来，把白天题目中的问题再讲一遍。严师出高徒，在他的悉心培养下，以万哲先、陆启铿、王元、陈景润等为代表的一批年轻人迅速成长起来，共同开创了中国数学研究的新格局。

1965 年后，华罗庚开始思考如何让数学直接为经济建设服务。他用最通俗的语言，将改进工艺与管理的“优选法”和“统筹法”讲解给普通工人听，用近 20 年的时间跑遍了中国几乎所有省市，不顾劳累与病痛投入到数学普及的工作中去。

1985 年，华罗庚到日本讲学，倒在东京大学的讲坛上，他一直工作到了生命的最后一刻。正如挽诗中所说：“将军死在战场，学者死在书房，可敬的你，耗尽心血一腔，光荣地死在科学的讲坛上。”

Hua Luogeng: Genius Comes from Accumulation, Intelligence Comes from Diligence

Despite only having a junior middle school education, the Professor and Mathematician Hua Luogeng had published more than 200 papers, monographs and dozens of popular works in the field of mathematical research. He has made important contributions to the development of mathematical science in China. People often say that he is a mathematical genius but Hua believes that "Genius comes from accumulation, and intelligence comes from diligence" .

After graduating from junior high school, Hua, who came from a poor family began a life of part-time work and study. He spent 5 years completing all high school and university coursework in mathematics. In 1931, his publication caught the attention and gained much praise from Tsinghua Professor Xiong Qinglai. He was subsequently, transferred to the Department of Mathematics to work as an assistant. Surrounded by talents, Hua made a promise to himself: "I will make extraordinary efforts to achieve my own goals!" "They have received greater education than me so I must double my efforts in order to make up for the losses. So if people only work for 8 hours every day, I need to work 12 hours every day!"

Later, when asked about the secret of his success, Hua Luogeng never mentioned his talents since he believes that "Genius comes from accumulation, and intelligence comes from diligence" . With 5 years of hardwork, Hua went from an assistant to going abroad to study at the University of Cambridge. During his 2 years at Cambridge, he has completed a dozen papers and won the praise of renowned mathematician, G.H. Hardy.

Not only was Hua hardworking in his research and development, he also held great love for his country. After the founding of New China, Hua gave up his work overseas to teach at Tsinghua. In Hong Kong, he wrote "An open letter to all the Chinese students who studied abroad in America" from which he advocated the need to return home, "We must return for our ideals. We should return home for our country and people."

Hua Luogeng has made outstanding contributions to the training of new Chinese mathematicians. When the Institute of Mathematics was founded by the Chinese Academy of Sciences, he served as Director of the Academy and was very strict with young researchers. Every day at dawn, Hua Luogeng would go to the researchers' dormitory and knock on their doors to start his discussion on the questions and findings raised during the lectures. Sometimes he would call upon students in the middle of the night and ask about what they have learnt during daytime. It is under such strictness that many of his students grew and created a new talent pool of Chinese mathematicians. Some of them are Wan Zhexian, Lu Qikeng, Wang Yuan, Chen Jingrun and much more.

After 1965, Hua Luogeng began to think about how to make mathematics into a tool to directly serve the economic construction of the country. He used the most basic of language to improve technology and management. He explained his plans in "optimization" to the ordinary workers and spent nearly 20 years to popularize mathematics.

In 1985, Hua Luogeng went to give lectures in Japan and he fainted on the teaching podium due to exhaustion. He worked until the last minute of his life. As what is said in a poem for him: "A general dies on the battlefield and a scholar dies in his study room. You have dedicated your entire life to academics and research and you have given your life to science."

Translation and revision | Min Weiyuan

Image | Xue Yafang

9 月 25 日

文字 | 刘书田

图片 | 李娜

阎学通："为人"是一辈子的学问

阎学通出生在一个知识分子家庭，书香浓厚，耳濡目染，从小就认为做学问是一件非常崇高的事情，并将踏实做学问当作自己一生的追求。现任清华大学国际关系研究院院长、博士生导师的阎学通，既是一位广受社会关注的学者，又是一位深受学生敬重的老师。

阎学通在国际关系理论研究领域自成一家，被公认为中国国际关系学界倡导科学方法论和预测国际形势的著名学者。将预测国际形势作为最大乐趣的阎学通，以其研究成果观点尖锐、逻辑清晰著称于中外学界。而在学生眼里，阎学通是一个简单纯粹的人，每天早出晚归，学术几乎是他唯一的乐趣。

阎学通的课堂总是"人满为患"。在他教授的"国际关系分析"通识课上，教室常常在上课前半小时就被早早占满，来晚的人不得不站在过道里听课。"看起来温文尔雅的阎老师，一上课声音清脆、妙语连珠，课堂氛围十分活跃。"阎学通的学生"粉丝"这样评价道。

阎学通的学生常常在网络学堂上提出各种各样的问题，有的还写邮件与他交流。"每学期，多的时候在网络学堂一门课就能收到 100 封学生邮件。"阎学通深知这是学生对自己的信任，因此他尽可能地回复同学们的问题，并在下一堂课将有代表性和典型性的问题拿到课堂上详细讲解。

阎学通在传授知识的同时，也十分注重启发学生独立思考。为了做到这一点，他经常与学生进行思想交流。阎学通认为，头脑风暴、思想撞击，不但有助于学生提高认识能力，也有助于老师提高自身能力。

阎学通曾被评为清华大学先进工作者、"十佳教师"和"良师益友"等。在学生评教中，他的学生曾这样写道："阎老师很幽默，讲的东西内容丰富、涵盖深广，而且他总能用一种非常通俗的方式让我们理解、接受那些看起来困难的知识。他是治学严谨的学者，更是值得信赖的默契朋友。"

在阎学通看来，对学生的指导并不仅限于学术和学习，比学术更重要的是为人。"一个对社会负责的人不仅要有自立的知识，还要有自立的能力，为人正直就是这种能力中最重要的部分。"阎学通说："老师对学生最殷切的希望不仅是学有所成，更是有完整的人格。'为人'是一辈子的学问，也是人生最重要的课程。"

Yan Xuetong: Learning Integrity Is a Lifelong Pursuit

Yan Xuetong was born into an intellectual family. Growing up with books and in a cultural environment, he thought that being in academia is a very noble pursuit and decided early on to devote his life to research. As the Director of the Institute of International Relations, Yan is a widely known scholar and a well-respected professor among students.

As a notable scholar in the field of international relations theory, Yan is widely-recognized in China as a promoter of scientific methodology and predictor of the international relations situations. He enjoys studying and predicting international relations situations and his research is lauded in China and internationally for his sharp and logical analysis. Yan, according to his students, is a simple and modest scholar that works day and night and academic work almost seems to be his only source of pleasure.

Yan's classes are always full. For his "Analysis of International Relations" class, the classroom is usually filled half an hour before the class starts. Those who are late can only stand in the aisle. "He looks like a soft and gentle professor, but when he starts teaching in class, his voice is loud and crisp, interspersed with humor. The atmosphere is really fun." one of his students said.

His students often pose questions on his class' online forum. Some even send him emails. "Every semester, I can receive up to 100 emails from students." Yan said. He knows that these show that the students trust him. So he tries to reply to every students' question and sometimes share commonly asked questions in class for in-depth discussion.

Yan understands that teaching is not only about passing knowledge to another generation. He tries to inspire students to have their own views. To achieve this, he often hold discussions with discussions. He thinks that brainstorming and clashing of ideas are useful for students to increase their level of awareness and also helpful for his own improvement.

In the past, he had been named as Tsinghua's most progressive employee, a "Top Ten Teacher" , "Best Mentor" and other awards. His students say "Professor Yan is very humorous, and his lectures cover a wide range of topics. He is able to use simple language to explain complex concepts so that we are able to digest what seems very complicated. He is a serious scholar but also a trustworthy friend."

In Yan's eyes, his guidance to students is not limited to academic studies and research, but what's more important is the students' character and behavior. "A responsible citizen is not only one who is knowledgeable, but also one who has abilities. Integrity is the most important in these abilities." Yan said.

Yan added that, "A teacher's most earnest hope for students is not only that they learn something but that they have a good character. Integrity takes a lifetime of learning, but it's also the most important lesson in a person's life."

Translation and revision | Alexis See Tho

Image | Li Na

9 月 26 日

文字 | 梁乐萌

图片 | 李娜

赵青：清华体育传统是从教的力量源泉

“做教师是我学生时代的梦想，非常幸运从事了喜爱的职业——一名体育教师。我将继续坚守一线教学工作，争取为祖国健康工作五十年。”谈及从教感受，赵青这样说。

自 1987 年来到清华大学体育部，赵青潜心体育教学工作已有三十年。

清华大学常被同学们戏称为“五道口体校”，体育的重要性可见一斑。作为主管教学工作的体育部副主任，赵青一手负责量大面广的“大学体育”课程。同时，她三十年如一日地坚守在教学一线，先后开设“沙滩排球”“软式排球”“气排球”等课程，深受同学们的喜爱，是许多学生排球技术的启蒙教师。

“言传身教”是赵青在教学上对自己的要求。她坚持“育人至上，体魄与人格并重”的体育教育观，教学中不仅教授专项技术，更注重培养学生的集体意识和拼搏精神，从而达到“育人、育心、育体”三位一体的教学效果。她坚持在每节沙滩排球课前浇灌场地。夏日炎炎，沙地表面往往已达到四五十度的高温，脚经常被烫出水泡，但是为了营造良好的场地环境，她一做就是十六年。有心若此，沙滩排球课在历年教学评估均为优秀，并被评为清华精品课。

排球教学之外，赵青还带领体育部的部分教师承担了航天航空学院飞行员班的航空体育课程。赵青与“飞班”的缘分起于一次“意料之外”。“飞班”的同学经常在东大操场训练，赵青很认真地观察了一个学期的时间，发现了一些不太科学的训练内容，热心的她忍不住从办公室冲到操场上给出建议。这次“意外”后，身为体育部主管教学的副主任和一名一线教师，赵青的教学激情和责任感油然而生。她主动向航院申请承担航空体育课程，想为学校联合培养做出一名体育教师的贡献。这一带就是三年，“飞班”同学都把她当作航院的老师看待。

此外，赵青自 1990 年担任校女排教练至今，关心每一位队员的成长。50 多岁的她身体力行，摸爬滚打，与队员一起练技术、一起练素质，为同学们树立了榜样，女排队员们都亲切地称她为“赵妈”。“赵老师不仅是教练，还会给我们讲为人处世的道理。”女排队员、新闻学院学生何韵琪说。赵青不仅教授技术技能，更注重队伍建设，清华女排成绩在全国名列前茅，曾获得全国大学生沙滩排球冠、亚军（专业组），泛波罗的海大学生运动会沙滩排球季军等优异成绩，并连续 7 年获“清华大学优秀队”称号。

赵青曾连续 7 次获清华大学教学成果一、二等奖，还曾获得“清华之友”优秀青年教师一等奖、“马约翰”优秀体育教师奖、宝钢优秀教师奖等荣誉。2017 年，赵青荣获首届“清华大学新百年教学成就奖”。

耕耘三十年，赵青说：“清华大学优良的体育传统是我从教的力量源泉，教学工作是我的最爱，我爱学生们，教学工作和学生们是我不断前行的动力。”

Zhao Qing: Tsinghua's Sports Tradition Is the Source of Motivation as a Teacher

"Becoming a teacher was my dream as a student. I'm so lucky to be doing a job I like — being a physical education teacher. I will continue to be at the frontline of teaching and to work toward the famous saying 'To work healthily for 50 years for our motherland' . " said Zhao Qing. Since joining the Division of Sports Science and Physical Education at Tsinghua University in 1987, it has been a labor of love for Zhao Qing the past three decades.

Students often call Tsinghua the "Wudaokou Sports School" because the importance of sports is evident in the university. As the division of sports' deputy dean in charge of teaching, Zhao Qing is responsible for a wide range of sports courses in the university. In her three decades of service, she has also set up courses such as beach volleyball, soft volleyball and air volleyball, which are favorites of many students.

"Words and deeds" are requirements that Zhao Qing place on herself in her duty as a teacher. She insists that education must come first, but physical exercise and character development are equally important. In teaching, she does not merely focus on techniques, but places equal emphasis on cultivating students' teamwork and fighting spirit, in order to educate "the person, the heart and the body." In her beach volleyball class, she insists that the court is watered before the start of the class. During the summer days, the court surface easily exceeds 40 degrees Celsius, causing blisters on her feet. The beach volleyball class consistently receives high ratings from students and is dubbed a Tsinghua gem.

Zhao Qing not only taught classes within her major - volleyball, but also led some teachers in the division of sports to take on the task of training pilots from the School of Aerospace Engineering. Her teaching at the School of Aerospace Engineering came from an unexpected event. The student pilots used to train at the East Track and Field. Zhao Qing had carefully observed their training for a semester and discovered some unproven training techniques. As an enthusiastic teacher, she once rushed to the field from her office to give the students some suggestions. After this incident, her passion and sense of responsibility as a teacher led her to take the initiative to apply for the training of the student pilots. She wanted to make a contribution to the university and the aerospace program as a good physical education teacher. It's been three years and the teachers and students there sees her as one of their own.

In addition, Zhao Qing has been the university's women's volleyball coach since 1990. She takes time to care for the growth of each member, and even though she is in her fifties, she leads by example during trainings, often involving herself in vigorous physical exercises done by the students. She is affectionately called Mother Zhao by the women's volleyball team members. "Teacher Zhao is not only a coach, she also teaches us about life," said He Yunqi, a student of the journalism school and a member of the women's volleyball team. Zhao Qing teaches not only volleyball techniques, she also pays attention to team building. Tsinghua's women's volleyball team is among the best in the country and has won first prize at the national varsity beach volleyball competition and other exceptional achievements. For seven consecutive years, the women's volleyball team has won the Tsinghua University Outstanding Team award.

In her three decades of teaching career, Zhao Qing has won numerous teaching awards such as first and second prizes for the Tsinghua University Teaching Achievement Award, the Friends of Tsinghua award, and the Ma Yuehan Excellent Sports Teacher Award. In 2017, she was honored with the university's inaugural New Century Teaching Achievement Award.

After laboring for three decades of teaching, Zhao Qing shares, "Tsinghua University's excellent sports tradition is the source of my motivation as a teacher. Teaching is my love and I love the students. They motivate me to go forward."

Translation and revision | Alexis See Tho

Image | Li Na

9 月 27 日

文字 | 刘兰

图片 | 宋晨

邓俊辉：精致的趣味，师者的情怀

“二十年前选择从教，是因为深知自己最擅长什么；但要真正把书教好，更需坚守自己对这份事业的挚爱。‘知者自知，仁者自爱’，正是我的使命与目标。”——清华大学计算机系副教授邓俊辉这样总结自己的教学理念。

2017 年教师节庆祝大会上，邓俊辉获颁首届“清华大学新百年教学成就奖”。在邓俊辉看来，旨在奖励教学一线优秀教师的“新百年教学成就奖”可谓是一股“清流”。而他本人亦如清华理工科院系中的一股“清流”，为师讲究精致和趣味，让知识和情怀细细流淌进学生的心中。

邓俊辉教书有“奇招”，他用精致诠释趣味。他会用“左右互易”——一个出于你的视角做出的手势，讲解复杂的算法原理与过程。他常常把文学、哲学知识引入课堂，比如从《红楼梦》的章法入手，讲解二叉树的迭代遍历算法。他的教材和讲稿，虽然内容繁多，但索引精准详细且趣味横生，讲稿中多是插图，教材中代码也是“活”的。他开设的慕课在学堂在线数百门慕课中名列前茅，他还专门编写了一个简洁、实用的课堂讲授辅助工具，并借助它高质量地制作了两门慕课。

邓俊辉为师有风范，他用精致诠释敬畏。他称自己 20 年从未点过名，但绝不承诺放弃这一权力。他把学生编程作业的每一道题都交给查重系统，在他的课堂上，学生们深刻体会到对知识、规则和公平的那份敬畏与尊重。他舍得花时间去了解每位学生的情况，有位计算几何课上的学生曾评价“他是我所知的大学期间唯一会逐个查看每个人的大实验代码的老师”。

邓俊辉兴趣爱好广泛，他用精致诠释情怀。他酷爱书法，书写的小品并不容易求得，但却愿意送给成绩突出、进步显著的学生。他还是中国象棋的个中好手，曾斩获全校教工冠军，有时也会刮净胡子“混迹”于学生的“马杯”赛事当中。

有人说邓俊辉是个“有腔调”的老师，但他更认同自己的“精致”。这精致是一种执念，更是师者的情怀。

Deng Junhui: Bringing Delicacy into Teaching

"Twenty years ago, I chose to teach because I know what I'm good at. However, in order to really teach well, one needs to stick to our principles. 'You need to know and love yourself first', this has been my mission and lifetime goal." This is Associate Professor Deng Junhui's teaching philosophy, and he's from Tsinghua's Department of Computer Science and Technology.

On June 30th, 2017, the First "Tsinghua University New Century Teaching Achievement Award" was released and Deng became one of the eight recipients. There were no lengthy and confusing application nor was there any self-promotion and pretentious marketing. In Deng's view, this Award is like a breath of fresh air. Teaching and learning with elements of fun helps to make knowledge more interesting and the students more engaged.

Deng Junhui has a couple of teaching tricks up his sleeves. He would use gestures to explain complex algorithm theories and would bring philosophical knowledge into the classroom such as using a chapter from *A Dream in Red Mansions* to explain the binary tree traversal algorithm approach. Although his teaching materials and lectures are heavy in content, the index is always interesting and accurate. Illustrations and graphics fills the pages making this difficult course more simple and "alive" . His online class received great praises from the students due to the simple approach, teaching aids and quality of the lesson layout.

Deng Junhui has his own teaching style. Students often don't have high expectations for his exams. "After an intensive battle for 2 hours, getting 40-50 is already good enough." Students are often "injured" in his class yet this does not mean that people lose their respect for him. Apart from the strictness, Deng also has a tremendous sense of responsibility and respect for his students. He takes the time to understand the situation of each and every one of his students. A student once said that "during my entire time at Tsinghua, Professor Deng is the only one who checks all the students' experimental codes."

In addition to being a teacher, Deng also places emphasis on personal interests. He loves calligraphy and began to practise the art of calligraphy with his friends, colleagues and students through the use of Wechat. He is also a great Chinese chess player and had won many school championships. Sometimes, he would also participate in the students' "Ma Yuehan Cup" Race.

Some people say that Deng Junhui is an "interesting and unique" teacher. He sees himself as being "delicate" . This is his concept and sentiments.

Translation and revision | Min Weiyuan

Image | Song Chen

9月28日

文字 | 蒋佩妍

图片 | 宋晨

于歆杰：执匠人之心，铺设育人“电路”

选修过“电路原理”的学生，想必都不会忘记于歆杰授课时因聚精会神而微微皱起的八字眉，以及那宛若电流一般富有感染力的声调。经过“海选”，这位清华大学电机系副教授获得了2017年清华首届“新百年教学成就奖”。

“电路原理”是清华第一门大规模开放的在线课程（Massive Open Online Course,MOOC,简称“慕课”）。身为主讲教师，于歆杰可谓鞠躬尽瘁。为了“拴住”学生的心，他进行了网络视频用户行为分析。当发现随着视频长度的增加，观众的专注程度会在6分钟至10分钟内跌入谷底，他便将传统的90分钟课程浓缩为一个个简短的小故事，并精心设计起承转合，安排巧妙的伏笔与“陷阱”。通过与在线学习者的交流，他不断调整教学思路，根据学生的兴趣增补知识点，反复雕琢课程。

“于老师做事情既专注又负责，可谓废寝忘食。”于歆杰的学生、2015级硕士生班瑞说，“做‘慕课’期间，有次都下半夜了，于老师还在网上发布视频，教大家如何在电脑上画电路图。这种敬业的精神特别令人感动。”

针对线下的传统大班授课，于歆杰也敢于做第一个“吃螃蟹的人”。为了克服学生人数众多导致老师难以深入了解每位学生学习情况的问题，于歆杰使用智慧教学工具“雨课堂”，将手机转变为学习工具，释放了学生学习的主动性和积极性。

如今，于歆杰的学生遍布世界各地，不仅有“90后”，还有“50后”“60后”。“我是非常热爱教学的，喜欢和同学们在一起。当你完全抓住了学生的思维，无论是线上还是线下，那一刻他们抬起头，视线正对着你，这种四目相视交流的快乐是难以言表的。当你经过充分准备，激情四射地完成讲授后，你在讲台上接受他们发自内心的称赞和鼓掌，在线上看到他们由衷的肯定，这种快乐不是金钱能够衡量的，也正是我在教学中获得的最大乐趣！”于歆杰说。

西山苍苍，东海茫茫，先生之风，山高水长。于歆杰以一颗赤诚的匠人之心铺设了广阔的育人“电路”，孜孜不倦地将新鲜知识和前行动力输送到每一位学生的心中。

Yu Xinjie: Sharing His Greatest Joy in Teaching

Students who have taken “Principles of Electric Circuits” would certainly remember Yu Xinjie’s wrinkled eyebrows when he concentrates and the infectious tone in his voice that’s electrifying. After many rounds of selection from a sea of candidates, this Tsinghua University associate professor was named one of the recipients of the inaugural “Tsinghua New Century Teaching Achievement Award” .

“Principles of Electric Circuits” was Tsinghua’s first mass open online course (MOOC). The course, which is offered on edX, has Yu Xinjie as the main instructor. As a teacher, he can be described as one who spares no effort in helping students understand his class. In an effort to retain his student’s interest in the class, he conducted an analysis of the behavior of online video users and discovered that with the increase of video length, audiences’ level of concentration would decline and eventually taper off within six to ten minutes. Armed with that knowledge, he decided to divide the traditional 90-minute video course into carefully designed bite-size short stories and that’s easier for students to follow along. He also constantly refined the course. Through interaction with the online learners, he adjusted his teaching method and included additional content to suit the interests of the students.

He is a devoted and responsible teacher, his students say. “There was once during the period of the online course, Teacher Yu was still posting videos online even though it was past midnight to teach students how to draw an electric circuit diagram on the computer.” said Ban Rui, a master’s student. “That kind of dedication is very touching.”

For offline classes, Yu Xinjie was one who dared to “be the first to eat crabs” (a saying popularized by Lu Xun, a renowned Chinese writer in early 20th Century, that describes someone courageous who dare to attempt something new). In order to gain a better understand of his students learning progress in a large class, Yu Xinjie introduced a teaching tool called “Rain Classroom” where he turned each students’ mobile phones into a learning tool, enabling them to take more initiative and be more enthusiastic about the class.

Today, Yu Xinjie’s students are found all over the world. There are not only the ones born in the 1990s, but also those born in the 1950s and 1960s. “I am very fond of teaching and I like being with students.” Yu Xinjie shared. “When you attract the students’ attention, whether it’s an online or offline class, the feeling at that moment when they raise their heads to look you in the eye because they understood, is hard to describe. When I receive affirmation from the students, that kind of joy is not something that can be measured with money. These are my greatest pleasures in teaching.” Yu Xinjie said.

The Western Hills, the vast East Sea, the gentlemen’s manner is as high as the mountains, far-reaching as the waters. Yu Xinjie, with a sincere heart of a craftsman is paving a way for Tsinghua student and the society that carries new knowledge and passion to the hearts of every student.

Translation and revision I Alexis See Tho

Image I Song Chen

9月29日

文字 | 甘泽霖

图片 | 赵存存

一封家书

父母亲大人膝下:

展信如晤。

转眼间，我已经在清华度过了一个多月的时光，我的大学生活也在忙忙碌碌的骨干培训和军训中开始了。我很好。不知道这一个多月的时间里，你们在一千多公里外的福建过得又如何。

中秋节又快到了，我很想回到福建见你们，可是从北京返乡路途遥远，舟车辗转劳顿，而且假短心长，所以我决定今年就不回去了。

仔细想来，这已经是我们不在一起度过的第四个中秋节了。高中三年，我离开南平去厦门读书，从此过上了只见故乡冬夏、不见春秋的生活，而短短的中秋假期，也不足以让我回到南平过上一个安稳的团圆夜。于是一年一年的中秋节，都是那一轮明月陪着我，也陪着你们。一年又一年，当我默默地站在窗边，听着轮渡呜咽的汽笛，看着那玉白色的月亮时，我总想着张若虚那句“愿逐月华流照君”，可惜这是一个唯物的世界，我只能祈祷着每一个中秋月夜，都能有着千里共婵娟的浪漫。

今年我来到了一个全新的环境，没有了鼓浪波涛，只有北方干燥的空气，可我仍然有着和那时相似的心境。有人说中秋是每一个中国人心中永恒的诗句，此言得之。我想今年中秋之时的我，也许就该站在紫荆公寓的阳台上，看着明月，把栏杆拍遍，再回味着那句“愿逐月华流照君”了吧。

你们常教育我不要做一个汲汲于私利的人，我自己也总想为他人做一些事情。来到清华，我发现这所学校里有许许多多和我一样的同学——离开了原生家庭，来到遥远的清华追寻自己的梦想，也学习着如何担当清华人的责任。和他们一起生活，让我进一步感受到了何为爱国奉献的清华品格，也让我更加明白家国之间的关系在青年身上应该如何实现和谐与平衡。

选择清华，就是选择了一种责任。这种责任或许很小，只是要我好好学习，努力做到又红又专，成为对国家有用的人；这种责任或许也会很大，不但要完善自己，还要努力成为一个可以引领时代风气、推进社会变革的人，要成为一个唯物史观下的英雄。

我又不由自主地想到以后的中秋节。

因为我发现，无论是上述的哪种责任，它们都代表着一个简单的事实：我们相聚的时间将越来越少，也许我们很难再有一个可以团圆的中秋了，也许我们以后都只能够一同看那圆月而思念着彼此了。

可能思念将让我们在同一轮明月下一起忧伤，可能家乡的呼唤会让我在月夜中辗转反侧。可我相信这一切都是值得的。青年马克思曾在《青年在选择职业时的考虑》一文中写道：“在选择职业时，我们应该遵循的主要指针是人类的幸福和我们自身的完美。”其实不只是对于选择什么样的职业，对于选择什么样的人生，这句话也同样适用。我们或许都隐约知道，其实从我离家远赴清华的那一刻起，我就已经选择了一种不同的人生，这也许是一段注定要把我从你们身旁拉走的人生，可我也相信这种人生将会让我有机会成为更完美的自己，也让我能为祖国、为人民、为全人类的幸福做出更大的贡献。而我相信你们对我前路的企盼也是如此。

中秋和国庆都即将来临，在此预祝你们中秋节、国庆节快乐。我的确又不能在你们身边陪伴你们，但请你们看看天边的那轮月亮，那月光之中，一定流淌着我对你们的思念，以及我坚定的决心和一个光明的未来。

敬颂

崇祺

你们的儿子：甘泽霖

2017年9月29日

A Letter to Home

My dearest parents,

In a blink of an eye, I have spent over a month in Tsinghua University. My busy university life started with training and military drills. I am doing well. Are you well when I am thousands of miles away from home?

The Mid-Autumn Festival is fast approaching and I, after enduring three weeks of tough military training, would very much love to see you both in Fujian. However, the journey from Beijing is a long one which is why I have decided not to go back home this time.

Actually, this is the fourth Mid-Autumn Festival without the both of you. During my senior high school years, I left Nanping to study in Xiamen. That marked the start of my days when I only was able to spend Winter and Summer days in my hometown. Back then, the short Mid-Autumn Festival days were not sufficient for the trip back home nor enough for a real family reunion. Thus, during every Mid-Autumn Festival, the moon stays by my side and quietly watches us on. Year after year, I stayed by my window and listened to the sounds of the incoming ferries. I would look up at the bright white moon and I could hear Zhang Ruoxu (a poet) whispering the words "I hope that the moonlight could guide me towards you" into my ears. Unfortunately, all I could do is to hold onto that romantic thought of sharing the beautiful moon with you through miles apart.

I have arrived at a new environment this year. Surrounded by the dry northern air, I found myself in a similar mood like all those years ago. Some say that the Mid-Autumn Festival is the eternal verse for every Chinese people. I think this year, I'll spend the festival standing by my window in Zijing Building, staring at the moon and hearing Zhang Ruoxu's words again.

You often teach me to be selfless. I always want to do something for others. After coming to Tsinghua, I found that many of my classmates left their homes and travelled far to enter into this prestigious university so that they could pursue their dreams and also learn about responsibilities. When I'm with them, I could feel a strong sense of patriotism and dedication not only to Tsinghua but to the nation. This is really the Tsinghua character. I've also come to realize the relationship that young people have with their motherland and how one could achieve this through harmony and balance.

I choose Tsinghua. I choose responsibilities. It might be small to the point that it is only about me studying well and becoming a talent in my field so that I could help my country. Yet, it could be a huge one. Just like what Professor Liang Qichao said to us Tsinghua people, not only am I going to be more patriotic and professional in my field, I also need to make contributions and changes to this society and era that I live in. I could be a hero. I could leave behind my footprint and be remembered by history.

Now, I can't help but think of all the future Mid-Autumn Festivals that we will have to go through.

I know that regardless of what kind of responsibilities I was talking about, there lies only one simple truth: we will spend more and more time apart. Perhaps, we will never have a chance to spend Mid-Autumn Festival together again. Perhaps we can only use the moon as our way of remembering and loving one another on this special day. I believe that it is worth it! Karl Marx wrote in his paper when he was young that "In the choice of our occupation, we should follow the main indicators of human happiness and our own perfection." In fact, it is not only about making decisions for our occupation but also what kind of life we wish to live. Perhaps we know that our lives have changed forever on the day we bid farewell to our hometown. I will not be by your side. Yet, I believe that this kind of life will allow me to perfect myself and find that better me. Perhaps I'm able to make contributions to my country, my people and the world. I believe that this is your hopes for me as well.

As National Holiday and Mid-Autumn Festival approaches, I wish you endless happiness. I cannot be by your side but do look up at the moon and know that the moonlight is filled with my thoughts and love for you. It is also a reflection of my own determination to do well in the future.

Affectionately yours,
Gan Zelin

Translation and revision | Min Weiyuan

Image | Zhao Cuncun

10月9日

文字丨左烜晅

图片丨宋晨

全球胜任力课程——走在“一带一路”上的课堂

今年暑假，来自清华大学的38名师生以新开设的“全球胜任力海外实践课程”为依托，分赴“一带一路”沿线国家开展“丝路新探”海外社会实践项目，在伊朗、哈萨克斯坦、乌兹别克斯坦和柬埔寨4个国家开启学习与探索之旅。

“丝路新探”是清华大学面向“一带一路”沿线国家设立的海外社会实践项目，属于新开设的“全球胜任力海外实践课程”，参与学生可获得3学分、96学时的课程认定。

今年暑假，该项目从全校报名的300余名同学中，选出35名本科生、硕士生和博士生，涵盖文理工科等10余个学科，在新闻与传播学院胡钰教授、公共管理学院楚树龙教授、医学院程峰教授的分别带领下，赴伊朗、哈萨克斯坦和乌兹别克斯坦、柬埔寨开展调研。

随着经济影响力的与日俱增，中国元素在中亚地区随处可见。

在伊朗的伊玛目广场上，一位给自己取名叫“马云”的当地人，用汉语招呼人们到店里欣赏传统的波斯地毯。他说：“我在中国南昌学习过汉语，想成为和马云一样的大企业家！”

2017年5月，来自“一带一路”沿线20国的青年将移动支付、高铁、电子商务、共享单车评为中国改变当代世界的四样“法宝”。“中国对世界的影响力，再也不是千百年前的丝绸与茶叶，而是涵盖硬件基础设施、网络信息服务、便捷互惠生活的新生活方式。”看到伊朗沿街店铺挂出的支付宝二维码、汉语广告牌，经管学院学生惠泽华感慨道。

除了“新四大发明”，此行的支队长、新闻与传播学院硕士生万宁宁对街头巷尾的中国企业标志印象深刻：“华为、海尔、中兴、中石油等标志随处可见；阿斯塔纳世博会的中国馆外排起了长长的队伍；超市里有从中国大量进口的糕点糖果等，这些都是我来之前没有想到的！”

“我希望同学们掌握真正的全球视野而不仅是欧美视野，掌握真诚的跨文化尊重而不是对弱者俯视、对强者仰视的跨文化摇摆。也正因如此，我希望同学们用自己的脚来丈量世界的土地、用自己的眼来观察世界的真实。”伊朗支队带队教师、新闻与传播学院党委书记胡钰总结本次课程时说。

伟大的文明各有不同却又殊途同归，而文化的相互交流与理解是提升其他一切交往的文化根基。让学生们走出校园、走出国门，引导他们培养全球视野、坚定中国立场、树立清华观点，这正是“丝路新探”海外社会实践项目的主旨。

Global Competence Course on the Belt and Road

During Summer vacation this year, 38 teachers and students from Tsinghua University, with "global competency overseas practice curriculum" as the backing, undertook learning in Iran, Kazakhstan, Uzbekistan and Cambodia.

"New Silk Road" is Tsinghua's way of being involved in social practice projects initiated in the Belt and Road countries. Students can undertake the 96hr course "Global Competence on Belt and Road" and subsequently receive 3 credit points.

This year, 35 out of more than 300 undergraduates, master's and doctoral students from more than 10 schools such as arts and engineering were selected to take part in the project. They were led by Professor Hu Yu from the School of Journalism & Communications, Professor Chu Shulong from the School of Public Policy and Management and Professor Cheng Feng from the School of Medicine for their research in Iran, Kazakhstan, Uzebekistan and Cambodia.

In Iran's Imam square, a local man who named himself "Jack Ma" , beckoned people to his store to admire his collection of traditional Persian rugs. "I've studied Chinese in Nanchang and I want to be a big entrepreneur like Jack Ma!" he said.

Due to growing economic influences, Chinese elements are everywhere in Central Asia. In May, youth from twenty countries along the Belt and the Road ranked mobile payments, high-speed railways, e-business and bike sharing apps as the four key tools for China to change the modern world. "China's influence on the world is no longer the silk and tea of a thousand years ago, but a new way of life covering hardware infrastructure, Internet services and the conveniences that such services can bring to our lives." said Hui Zehua, after seeing Alipay QR codes and Chinese billboards in the shops along the street.

Wan Ningning further added, "Huawei, Haier, ZTE, PetroChina and many more can be seen everywhere. Moreover, the Chinese Pavilion at the Astana Expo is always accompanied by long queues and of course, lots of cakes and sweets imported from China. I never thought that it would be like this!"

"I hope that students will master true global vision not only from European and American perspectives, but also one that is sincere and cross-cultural. Because of this, I hope that students will use their own feet to measure the world's size and scope and use their own eyes to see the reality." Professor Hu Yu said these words after the completion of the Iranian chapter.

Great civilizations have different methods and cultural exchanges, and understanding are the foundation to enhance all other ways of communication. Students need to develop a more global perspective, one that has Chinese elements. This is one of the objectives of the "Global Competency Overseas Practice Curriculum" .

Translation and revision | Min Weiyuan

Image | Song Chen

10月10日

文字 | 胡颖

图片 | 赵存存

清华国际本科新生拓展营：感受中华文化，传递清华精神

这个夏天，来自韩国、马来西亚、美国、日本、加拿大、缅甸、新加坡等35个国家的300余名国际学生成为清华2017级新生。在中国学生军训时，国际学生也要参加为期三周的“国际本科新生拓展营”，内容包括中国语言与文化课程、体能训练、入学教育系列讲座以及新生集体活动。

今年的国际本科新生拓展营是清华的第一次尝试，也是国内高校的首次尝试。拓展营旨在加强中外新生的交流融合，帮助国际学生适应环境，顺利开始本科学习生活。这一安排，也体现了清华对中外学生趋同管理的要求。

从传统的太极拳到排球、轮滑、棒球、健美操等，在清华的运动场上，国际新生们按照体育老师的指导，挥洒汗水，迸发激情。

除了体育课程，清华还为国际新生们带来了他们的第一堂中国语言和文化课。他们不仅学习语法的使用和句子的结构，还要细心品味中国话平上去入的变化和中国字横竖撇捺的笔法。汉字、成语，交通出行中的文化内涵，北京历史文化，饮食与中国文化，中西方语言表达异同……多样的文化课程从不同角度展现了中华文化的博大精深。

以往，国际学生同学的报到时间比中国学生晚，往往没有足够时间适应生活习惯、语言文字上的差别。对于国际新生而言，拓展营的文化课堂是了解中国传统与摩登文化的最佳途径，也是在清华园中扎根中国文化的良好契机。

听完一节课，韩国学生王采衍感慨良多：“中国传统文化的内涵极其丰富，几千年锤炼下来的才是这个民族的精华。”

来到古都北京，这些国际学生期待着有更多机会了解北京本地的文化。无论京腔京韵还是胡同庙会，都召唤着他们内心深处的憧憬，也需要他们用更多的时间去领略体会。“清华在各方面的细致安排给我留下了深刻的印象。我非常期待在这所充满活力的大学中开始自己的学习生活。”来自美国的秦荣表示。

与往年相比，今年清华大学来自欧美和“一带一路”沿线国家的生源大幅增加，国别覆盖率显著提高，生源结构呈现更加多样化发展的趋势。一张张异国面孔，跨越半个地球的距离，梦想的红线将他们连在一起。2017，一个更加“国际范儿”的清华正在出发。

International Undergraduate Enhancement Camp : Feel the Chinese Culture and the Spirit of Tsinghua

This summer, more than 300 international students from 35 countries, including South Korea, Malaysia, United States of America, Japan, Canada, Myanmar and Singapore became Tsinghua's new 2017 undergraduate students. During the Chinese students' military training, the new international students need to attend a three-week orientation programme, or "International Undergraduate Enhancement Camp" , the content includes Chinese language and culture courses, physical training, lecture series and other new collective activities.

This enhancement camp is the first attempt made by Tsinghua for universities in China. The camp aims to strengthen the exchange and integration between Chinese and foreign students. It will help international students to adapt to their new learning environment so that they can begin their undergraduate studies with ease. This arrangement also reflects Tsinghua's goal in the convergence of Chinese and foreign students.

From traditional Taichi to volleyball and roller skating, baseball, aerobics and so on, international students are required to follow the guidelines and sweat it out. In addition to physical education, Tsinghua has brought these international students their first Chinese language and culture lessons. Not only do they study the usage of grammar and the structure of sentences, they also need to carefully try out the dialects and sounds of the language as well as the twists and turns and mannerism in writing the Chinese characters. Chinese characters, idioms, cultural connotations, Beijing's history and culture, cuisine and Chinese culture... Various cultural courses reflect the great depth of Chinese culture from multiple perspectives. In the past, international students stated that often, they did not have enough time to adapt to the differences between Chinese and foreign languages.

For the international freshmen, expanding the understanding of culture from such camp activities is the best way to learn about Chinese tradition and modern culture. Furthermore, it is also a good opportunity to take root in Chinese culture during one's time in Tsinghua.

After listening to a class, Korean student Wang Caiyan sighed deeply: "The connotation of Chinese traditional culture is extremely rich and the essence of this nation has been tempered by thousands of years of history.

Since these students are in Beijing, they will need to know more about Beijing's local culture: Beijing hutong, temple fair etc. These students will need more time to absorb 5000 years of history and culture. "I was deeply impressed by the meticulous arrangements made by Tsinghua. I'm looking forward to my life in this dynamic university." said US student Roan Henry Guinan.

Compared with previous years, students from Europe, USA and most notably- those from the Belt & Road initiative participating countries came to study at Tsinghua. Faces and interesting minds that flew halfway across the globe have many dreams connecting them together. In 2017, a more Internationalized Tsinghua University is right before our eyes.

Translation and revision | Min Weiyuan

Image | Zhao Cuncun

10月11日

文字 | 刘书田

图片 | 薛雅芳、杨思维

全球创新学院教研大楼在西雅图落成启用

想象有这么一个地方——来自世界各地的学生可以通力合作、共同创新，那里既充满大学学术的无限活力，也满载业界拼搏的实践真知。这是2015年清华大学、华盛顿大学和微软公司合作创建全球创新学院时的愿景。而今，这一愿景正在变成现实。

2017年，当地时间9月14日上午，全球创新学院教研大楼落成启用及开学典礼仪式在美国西雅图举行，这是清华大学推进实施全球战略的又一里程碑。

2015年9月23日，中国国家主席习近平访美期间曾专程到西雅图看望学院工作人员并赠送水杉，寓意中国高等教育"走出去"的自信、对两校友谊长青的祝福和对全球创新学院茁壮成长的期待。随着教研大楼的落成使用，水杉也拥有了自己的新家——移栽至教研大楼的门前。水杉是中国特有的树种，被誉为植物王国的"活化石"。两年来，在工作人员的细心呵护下，水杉长势喜人。

教研大楼使用面积约一万平方米，地面三层、地下二层，配备最先进的教学和科研设施，专门为全球创新学院项目配置了设计工作室、创业孵化中心、电子原型实验室、演示空间以及西雅图地区其中一个最大和最全面的制造工坊。楼内还特别建设了清华厅，厅内充满着浓郁的清华气息，让人仿佛置身于清华校园。

全球创新学院是中国高校在美国设立的第一个综合性教育科研平台，不仅搭建起中美、东西之间的交流桥梁，更重要的是推进技术创新领域的教育革新，为人类科技进步和发展提供人才支撑。

两年来，全球创新学院在各方关注下稳步发展，洛桑联邦理工学院、香港科技大学、印度科学理工学院、韩国科学技术院、台湾大学、以色列理工学院、蒙特雷科技大学及不列颠哥伦比亚大学等8个学术机构成为学院的学术合作伙伴，来自中国和美国的15个商业机构给予大力支持，它们将与清华大学、华盛顿大学和微软公司等三家创始成员一起，携手共创学院的美好未来。

The GIX（Global Innovation Exchange）Building in Seattle Opens

Imagine a place where students from all over the world can collaborate and innovate together. Imagine that this place is filled with endless vitality, endeavours, knowledge and of course struggles. This is the shared vision created in 2015 by Tsinghua University, Washington University and Microsoft. The GIX or Global Innovation Exchange Institute used to be a vision. It is now a reality.

Morning of September 14th (local time), 2017: the Opening Ceremony of the GIX Building was held in Seattle. This marked another milestone and important step in the implementation of Tsinghua university's global strategy.

On the 23rd of September 2015, Chinese President Xi Jinping's paid a visit to Seattle during his trip to the United States. He visited the staff of the institute and offered his well wishes and confidence in the positive steps that China could take to ensure that her higher education institutions can go abroad and connect with the international community. He offered his sincere wishes for the Institute and saw his gift (the metasequoia) being moved to its new home. It is a unique tree species in China and is regarded as the "living fossil" of the plant kingdom. It is now standing in front of the door of the GIX Building.

The GIX building has an usable floor area of about 10000 square meters. There are a total of 5 floors with 2 being underground. It is equipped with the most advanced teaching and research facilities. Whether it is design studios, business incubation centers, electronic prototype laboratories and other innovative spaces, it is certainly one of the largest and most comprehensive manufacturing workshop in Seattle. There is also a Tsinghua Hall which is filled with the spirit and flavours of Tsinghua. It automatically makes you feel like you are back in Tsinghua.

GIX is China's first comprehensive scientific research platform in the United States of America. It not only is the bridge between China and America but most importantly, it is crucial in promoting technological and educational innovation. It helps to provide and nurture talents to support scientific and technological progress and human development.

For the past two years, GIX has developed steadily and collaborated with école Polytechnique Fédérale de Lausanne (EPFL), Hong Kong University of Science and Technology (HKUST), the Indian Institute of Technology (IITs), Korea Advanced Institute of Science and Technology (KAIST), Taiwan University (NTU), Technion-Israel Institute of Technology, Instituto Tecnológico de Monterrey, and the University of British Columbia. Supported by 15 commerical institutions from China and America and many other associations, every one is working towards the creation of a brighter future not only for GIX or for each other but for the world.

Translation and revision I Min Weiyuan

Image I Xue Yafang, Yang Siwei

10月12日

文字 | 冯婉婷

图片 | 李筱甜

清华大学艺术博物馆开馆一周年，迎来设计者马里奥・博塔

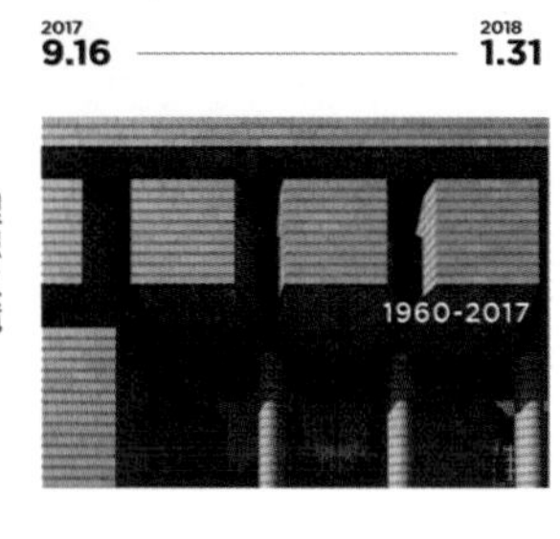

2016年9月，达・芬奇的60幅手稿真迹漂洋过海，成就了清华大学艺术博物馆开馆的华美启幕。

2017年9月，时值艺术博物馆开馆一周年，国际建筑大师、艺术博物馆的设计者马里奥・博塔在这座由他自己设计的博物馆里，举办了他在中国大陆的第一次个人建筑艺术回顾展。

“作为一个建筑师，其实很难在自己设计的场馆里展现自己的作品，令我高兴的是，这座建筑不仅外部由我设计，而且内部展览也是我个人的作品。”马里奥・博塔在致辞中表达了这次展览对他个人的特别意义。本次展览的主题是“理想之境：马里奥・博塔的建筑与设计1960—2017”，集中展示马里奥・博塔1960年至2017年间的部分建筑和设计作品，是博塔建筑设计思想的一次集中呈现。

“理想之境”四个字来源于博塔的设计风格和理念。作为国际级建筑大师，博塔的建筑理念充满人文性和理想性。他融合了严谨的理性主义传统和深厚的历史文化底蕴，用富有时代特色的当代建筑语言回应久远的历史记忆。

在2001年底清华大学艺术博物馆的国际方案征集活动中，博塔的建筑事务所从国内外众多知名设计单位中脱颖而出，不仅仅是因为其自身出众的创造力，更因为他们的设计方案考虑到了清华大学的传统文化和教学模式，注重建筑与周边环境的关系，营造出符合高校环境和符合可持续发展理念的校园空间。

除了艺术博物馆，清华大学人文图书馆也是博塔为清华大学设计的地标性建筑，这两大建筑都融合了博塔个人的设计想法和清华的人文底蕴，理解并表达了清华大学的深厚文脉。

清华大学一直与博塔有着深厚的友谊，这一次展览不仅对于博塔本人有特别意义，对清华也有着别样的意义。

“每一位来到清华大学艺术博物馆的人都会首先被这座建筑的宏伟气势所震撼，缓缓上升的步行阶梯把展厅有机地整合在一起，观众拾级而上，仿佛走向艺术的圣殿。”艺术博物馆馆长冯远表示，清华大学艺术博物馆充分体现了博塔建筑作品精准、和谐与平衡的特点，本身就是博塔的一件艺术精品。艺术博物馆在一周年之际迎来了她的设计者，是一件值得被纪念的事情。

Tsinghua University Art Museum Welcomes Her Designer Mario Botta for 1st Anniversary Celebration

September, 2016, 60 original manuscripts of Leonardo da Vinci traveled across the ocean to be unveiled at the grand opening of the Tsinghua University Art Museum(TAM). This September, the art museum is graced by an exhibition of the artwork of Swiss architect and designer of the Tsinghua University Art Museum, Mario Botta. The exhibition is Botta's first in China and the first that showcases solely his designs.

"As an architect, it's hard to believe that my exhibition will be in a building I designed," Botta said. "What makes this really special is that externally, this building is a mark of my design, and internally, it houses my personal artwork." Botta added during his speech at the opening ceremony of the exhibition. The title "The Realm of Idealism: Mario Botta Architecture and Design 1960-2017" focuses on his designs between 1960 and 2017 and features his core architectural ideas.

"The Realm of Idealism" encapsulates Botta's style and philosophy in design. As an internationally renowned architect, Botta's architectural philosophy is filled with humanism and idealism. He combines the rationalistic tradition and deep historical and cultural heritage with contemporary architectural designs to give respond to history.

In 2001, at the open solicitation of the Tsinghua University Art Museum, Botta's architectural firm stood out from other well-known design firms in China and internationally. His design not only showed outstanding creativity, but it also incorporated Tsinghua's traditional culture and teaching philosophy — to highlight the relationship between architecture and the environment and to create a campus that meet standards for sustainable development.

In addition to the art museum, the Tsinghua University Humanities Library is also a landmark of Botta' s design for Tsinghua University. Both buildings combine Botta's design ideas and Tsinghua's humanistic heritage, expressing the humanistic context of Tsinghua.

Tsinghua has always had a deep friendship with Botta. This exhibition is not only especially significant to Botta, but also to the university.

"Every person who walks into the Tsinghua Art Museum will be amazed by its magnificence and grandeur." said Feng Yuan, head curator of the art museum. "Walking up the gradually ascending ladder to the exhibition halls, the visitor is integrated into the space, as if walking into a sacred temple of the arts." Feng adds.

The Tsinghua University Art Museum fully embodies the precise, harmonious and balanced nature of Botta's architectural design. The building itself is a fine piece of artwork by Botta. To have the museum's designer here for its first anniversary is an absolute privilege and a moment worthy of commemoration.

Translation and revision | Alexis See Tho

Image | Li Xiaotian

10月13日

文字 | 左烜晅

图片 | 任帅

回忆园中好风景——梅贻琦故居

梅贻琦1889年生于天津，1909年投考第一批庚款留美生被录取，在美读电机工程。1915年，梅贻琦到清华任教，1931年出任校长。陈岱孙曾评价梅贻琦："他一生的业绩和清华结合在一起。"

在清华期间，梅贻琦先后住过工字厅及照澜院（原旧南院）5号，成为校长后又住过甲所。每一处，都见证了老校长的清华往事。

工字厅始建于1707年，以它为主体建筑的清代皇室园林即是清华园，距今已有300多年历史。如今，砖红色大门和牌匾上的"清华园"三个大字依旧是校园中的一处风景，浓郁的文化气息与清华悠久的历史交织在一起。

建校初期，工字厅各院房屋除行政办公场所以外，多是教师住宅。刚到清华的梅贻琦教授数学、物理，住在工字厅西偏院。每当深夜，透过灯光，人们总能看到他埋头备课的身影。

1922年秋，梅贻琦搬进旧南院5号。旧南院始建于1921年，由10所西式丹顶洋房和10所中式四合院组成，是清华大学早期的教授住宅群，当时称为南院，1946年后改称照澜院。当时"旧南院的西北角和东南角各有一个通向院外大路的门，……从旧南院的西北门可以走向二校门"。吃午饭时，邻居赵元任的夫人杨步伟有时就会把路过的梅贻琦邀进屋里共餐。

1926年春，梅贻琦成为教授会推举的首位教务长。他着手改组和调整大学部，把"两科（普通和专门）制"改为学系制，设17个学系；制定新《组织大纲》，为民主治校奠定了制度基础，使清华具备了一所正规的、有特点的大学的雏形。

1931年，梅贻琦出任校长后住进甲所。甲所位于工字厅以南，始建于1917年。其间树林成荫，花木拥簇，周边环境极为清雅，又离办公场所很近，是当时专供校长居住的处所。

梅贻琦一生清廉，自住进甲所就放弃校长在生活中的特权（如公家供给的一切日用物品和两吨煤）。清华档案馆现存有梅贻琦用废旧纸张起草的公文，彰显了他一贯的节俭作风。庚款基金雄厚但他不苟分文，他说："清华有点儿钱，要撙节着用在图书、仪器、请教授上。""清华向来有一种俭朴好学的风气，我希望今后仍然保持着。"

基于梅贻琦"所谓大学者，非谓有大楼之谓也，有大师之谓也"的办学理念，校园内汇聚着各家各派的学术思想。20世纪30年代近百位教授就聘于清华，尽是学界知名学者。梅贻琦一生情系清华，曾用"生斯长斯，吾爱吾庐"来描述对清华的情感。

Former Residence of Mei Yiqi: in the Garden of Memory

Mei Yiqi was born in Tianjin in 1889. In 1909, he was admitted as one of the first overseas students to study in the United States, majoring in electrical engineering. In 1915, he started teaching in Tsinghua University and became President of Tsinghua University in 1931. In regard to Mei Yiqi, Chen Daisun once commented, "His lifetime performance was in harmony with Tsinghua."

During the period, Mei Yiqi lived in the Gongzi Hall and No. 5 of Zhaolan Yard (formerly called the Old South Yard). After becoming President of Tsinghua University, he had once resided in Building A. Each place is testimony of the former president's Tsinghua story.

The Gongzi Hall, built in 1707, has a history of over 300 years, it is the royal garden based on which is the Tsinghua Garden. Today, the brick-red gate and the characters on plaque, "Tsinghua Garden" is still a campus landscape, demonstrating a combination of culture and history.

In the early period of Tsinghua University, except for administrative office, the Gongzi Hall primarily served as housing for lecturers. Mei Yiqi was initially teaching mathematics and physics in Tsinghua and he lived in the west yard of Gongzi Hall. Often at night, through the lights, his dedicated figure could always be seen.

In the fall of 1922, Mei Yiqi moved into the old South Yard No.5. The Old South Yard house was built in 1921. Composed of 10 western crowned houses and 10 Chinese courtyards, it was an early residence for professors in Tsinghua and was called "South Yard" then and renamed as "Zhaolan Yard" after 1946. At that time, "each of the northwest corners and the southeast corners had a gate leading to the out-courtyard avenue... From the northwest gate of the yard, you can walk to the Old Gate". Sometimes at noon time, neighbor Yang Buwei, Zhao Yuanren's wife, would invite Mei Yiqi who was passing by for lunch.

In those days, Mei Yiqi was elected as the first dean who was working on reshuffling the undergraduate teaching. He changed the "two-subject system (general and specialized)" to an "academic system" which contained 17 departments; meanwhile, he formulated a new "general structure", laid the systematic foundation for democratic governance and enabled Tsinghua to truly transform into an embryo of a standard, featured university.

In 1931, Mei Yiqi moved into to Building A, after serving as the President of Tsinghua. Building A, built since 1917, is situated in the south of Gongzi Hall and it is an independent western villa similar to Building B and C. The villa was surrounded by plants and close to the office, making it an ideal choice for residence.

Mei Yiqi was a righteous man who abandoned principal's privileges in daily life (such as public supply of all daily items and two tons of coal), and the existing documents in university archive, drafted on waste paper, highlights his consistent frugality. With regard to the great amount of boxer indemnity fund, he said: "Tsinghua University has to budget the money for books, appliances and professors." "Tsinghua has always remained an atmosphere of thrift and curiousness, and I hope this will continue into the future."

Based on Mei Yiqi's philosophy "the reason why a university is a university lies in the professors, not the buildings", the campus brings together various different kinds of academic thinking. In 1930s, Tsinghua employed nearly 100 professors, all of who are academic scholars. Mei Yiqi's entire life was attached to Tsinghua. He had used the words "here I was born, here is where I grew up, here is where I love to be" to describe his deep affection to Tsinghua.

Translation and revision | Raj Lamar

Image | Ren Shuai

10 月 16 日

文字 | 张译丹

图片 | 任帅

张强课题组：化学领域版“小蝌蚪找妈妈”

伴随着电子产品对大众日常生活的渗透，人们对于储能电池的需求日益增长，也对储能电池提出更高的储能和安全性要求。在各类体系中，金属锂是研究下一代电池负极材料的热点对象，但是，目前金属锂负极在充放电过程中易形成针状或树枝状的锂枝晶，这会给电池体系带来不可逆的容量损失，甚至可能会穿过隔膜而导致电池正负极内部短路，埋下电池过热自燃等安全隐患。科研工作者们为解决这些重点问题从多角度进行了诸多尝试，但收获有限。近日，《德国应用化学》（*Angewandte Chemie International Edition*）选取的一张中国传统国画封面，寓示着清华大学化工系张强课题组在金属锂负极形核和无枝晶生长领域取得了新进展。

封面图传达的正是张强课题组此次关于金属锂负极形核和无枝晶的核心思想：“亲锂位点定向形核”。国画传统水墨风绘制出大家耳熟能详的“小蝌蚪找妈妈”故事，而在化学版本的故事中，小蝌蚪通过“锂”就能轻松找到青蛙妈妈，正如同在充电过程中，锂离子以掺氮石墨烯为骨架，实现稳定的、无枝晶的金属锂沉积：锂离子优先定位在导电亲锂的掺氮位点并沉积形成均匀、密集分布的金属锂形核点。在后续充电过程中，锂离子将基于这些均匀、密集的形核点进行沉积，从而避免了普通铜箔上形核点过度分散造成的金属锂枝晶生长行为。这一新型金属锂负极结构不仅实现了无枝晶的高安全性金属锂沉积特性，还表现出了优异的电化学性能。

为抑制金属锂负极的枝晶生长，张强研究团队加强与相关领域团队的合作，通过与美国德雷塞尔大学的尤里・高果奇研究团队、华中科技大学江建军研究团队的合作探究，提出纳米金刚石共沉积策略来调控锂离子的形核和沉积行为。

近年来，张强课题组在金属锂负极研究领域，通过原位手段研究固态电解质面膜，采用纳米骨架、人工固态电解质界面膜、表面固态电解质保护金属锂、调控金属锂的沉积行为、抑制锂枝晶生长，实现金属锂的高效安全利用。其相关研究成果发表在《微尺度》（*Small*）、《美国化学学会・纳米》（*ACS Nano*）、《化学评述》（*Chemical Reviews*）等众多知名期刊上，并申请了一系列发明专利。张强课题组的研究被认为是在金属锂负极形核和无枝晶生长领域取得的重要突破性进展。

Zhang Qiang's Team: Chemical Version of "Baby Tadpoles Looking for Their Mothers"

With the wide applications of electronic products, the demand for rechargeable batteries is increasing in the aspect of high energy density and strict safety requirements. Lithium metal is strongly considered as the next-generation anode materials among various electrode materials. However, lithium dendrites are always obtained on lithium anode during the charge/discharge process, which induces high irreversible capacity loss of battery systems and may even cause short circuit, leaving security risks such as spontaneous combustion caused by overheating. Many efforts have been devoted to address this challenge, however, the controllable Li plating is a black box. Recently, a traditional Chinese styled cover of *Angewandte Chemie International Edition* indicated that Zhang Qiang, professor of Department of Chemical Engineering, Tsinghua University, and his team have made breakthroughs in lithium metal cathode nucleation and non-dendrite growth.

The cover image conveys the core idea of Zhang' s research on lithium metal cathode nucleation and non-dendrite growth: "Lithiophilic sites guide nucleation" . Traditional Chinese paintings depict the famous tale of "Little Tadpoles Looking for Their Mothers" , and in the chemical version of this story, the little tadpoles can easily find their mothers through "lithiophilic sites" . In the charging process, the nucleation of lithium ions is guided by the nitrogen heteroatoms. Lithium ions will be deposited based on these homogeneous and dense nucleation sites during the following charging process, thus avoiding the dendrite growth of lithium metal caused by excessive decentralization of nucleation sites on ordinary copper foil current collector. Such lithium metal cathode structure not only guarantees the high security of non-dendrite lithium metal deposition, but also exhibits superb electrochemical performance.

To restrain dendrite growth of lithium metal cathode, Zhang's team deepened their cooperation with other groups. By joint efforts of Yury Gogotsi's team from Drexel University and Jiang Jianjun's team from Huazhong University of Science and Technology, they proposed nano-diamond deposition strategy to regulate nucleation and deposition of lithium ions.

In recent years, Zhang's team has made numerous efforts towards the safe lithium metal cathode through stable solid electrolyte interface by situ methods, protecting lithium metal with 3D scaffolds, artificial solid electrolyte interfaces and exterior solid electrolyte. The lithium metal plating is regulated and the dendrite growth is retarded, which renders the cell with high efficiency and safe utilization. Relevant research results have been published on *Small, ACS Nano, Chemical Reviews* and other high impact journals and a series of invention patents have been applied for their achievements. The study done by Zhang Qiang's team is considered to be a major breakthrough in the fields of lithium metal cathode nucleation and non-dendrite growth.

Translation and revision | Raj Lamar

Image | Ren Shuai

10月17日

文字 | 杨晨晞

图片 | 刘雨田

全运赛场上的清华“学生兵”

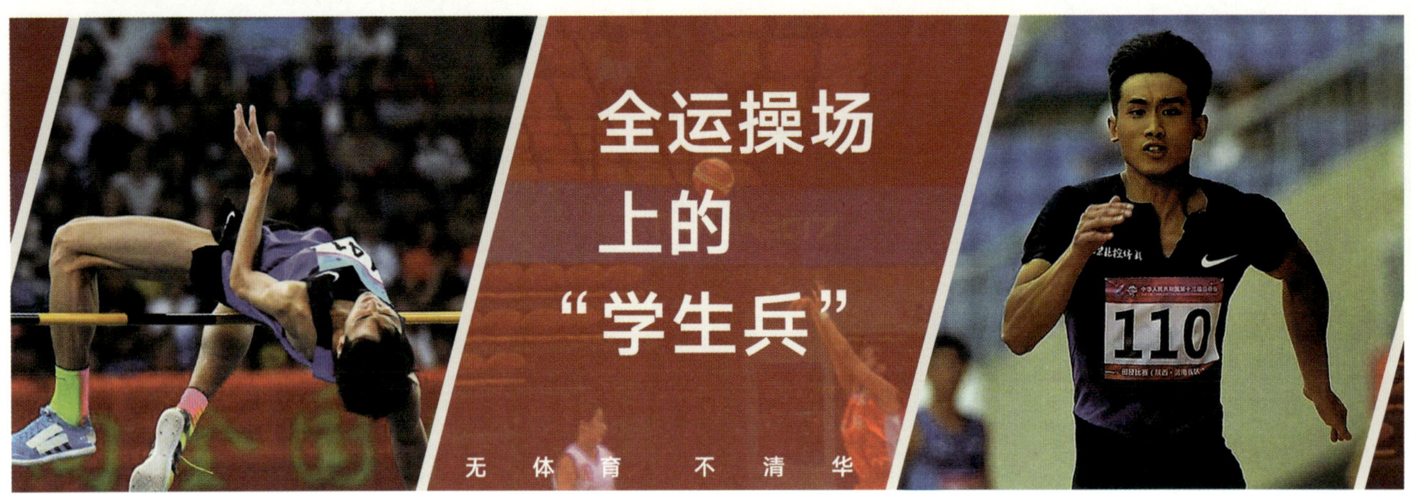

日前，清华学子王宇在天津卫冕全运会男子跳高冠军；李志鹏摘得男子跑跳二项全能金牌，由清华学生组成的男子 4×100 米接力队获得预赛第二……如火如荼的全运会赛场上，来自清华的“学生兵”正在形成一股力量。

2017 年全运会，仅在田径赛场上，来自清华大学的选手就有 23 人。自 2001 年清华学子首次参加全运会以来，此前四届，清华的运动健儿已经获得了 5 枚全运会金牌。

在不少人眼中，运动员一般要功成名就了才会去大学“镀金”，成为“运动员学生”。但王宇们却不一样，他们和普通学生一样，要通过考试进入大学，要在大学读书、住校，是真正的学生运动员。

1996 年起，清华大学的相关培养计划开始由“运动员学生”向“学生运动员”过渡，将不同体育项目进行不同类别划分，按照不同标准进行选拔，立足自己培养体育人才。在清华，“学生运动员”只有下午 3 点到 6 点半训练，训练之余就和正常学生一样，上课、做作业、考试，而训练和比赛耽误的课业都需自己补上。但在王宇看来，学习和训练完全不矛盾。“训练累的时候，用学习来调整和分散注意力。反过来也一样。正好互补，时间一点也不浪费。”

20 世纪 90 年代，清华大学提出过“业余赶专业”的口号，即用业余身份赶上专业运动员的成绩。但若要实现这个目标，必须进行专业训练。因而，清华在专业运动员必不可少的营养、伤病恢复、医疗保证等保障体系等方面，努力减少短板，给运动员创造最好的条件。

多年来，以清华为代表的高校对体育人才的培养已成为我国现有竞技体育体制和运动员培养模式的有益补充，也涌现出“眼镜飞人”胡凯、王宇等一批优秀运动员。虽然与专业队还有一定距离，但是，在未来道路选择中，学生运动员或可拥有更加丰富的机会。

少年强则国强，体育强则国强。希望在未来的全运赛场、世界赛场、奥运赛场上，能有更多学生运动员的身影，能有更多的清华学子创造佳绩！

Tsinghua's Students in the National Sports Game

Recently, Tsinghua Student Wang Yu won the Men's High Jump at the National Sports Game; Li Zhipeng won Gold as well and in the 4×100m relay, Tsinghua came second place... "Student Soldiers" became a formidable force at the National Games.

Tsinghua students attended the first National Sports Game in 2001. At the National Sports Game this year, 23 people from Tsinghua University participated in the track and field events.

In the eyes of many, athletes who have gained fame eventually attend university and become a so-called "athlete student" . However, students like Wang Yu are different. They need to pass exams in order to attend Tsinghua. They also need to study and stay within the campus, like real "student athletes."

1996 saw the start of Tsinghua's transition from "athlete students" to "student athletes" . Emphasis changed and along with it, the accompanying curriculum and teaching approach. Different sports are divided into different categories and selected in accordance to different criteria. In Tsinghua, student athletes only have training from 3 to 6 in the afternoon. Apart from this, they have the same schedule as any other normal student. They attend class, have exams and need to complete all course work. If training and competition cause a delay in their studies then it is up to themselves to catch up. For Wang, he does not see learning and training as conflicting. "When you are tired from training, use study to adjust and distract yourself. The same applies vice versa. It is pretty complementary and no time is wasted at all!"

In the 1990s, Tsinghua made a proposition and the slogan of "From Amateur to Professional." This refers to allowing students to reach a level as close to those of professionals as possible. For those who really wish to achieve this goal, they must undertake professional training. Tsinghua provides all round support for these athletes from nutrition to injury recovery to medicare and many other efforts which ensures that athletes are given the best of conditions for training.

Tsinghua's presence and emphasis on cultivating sporting talents has become the current system and training mode for athletes and students. We have now seen many remarkable athletes such as Hu Kai, Wang Yu and more. Even though they still need to catch up to those at a professional level, these student athletes have much more opportunities in the future to decide what they really wish to do.

Stronger youths means a stronger nation and strength in sports equates to strength in the motherland. We hope to have more student athletes in the future. We hope to see them in world competitions and even the Olympic Games. We also hope that Tsinghua students will make more achievements!

Translation and revision | Min Weiyuan

Image | Liu Yutian

10 月 18 日

文字 | 柳橙

图片 | 杨思维

清华师生喜迎中国共产党第十九次全国代表大会胜利召开！

在这金风送爽、硕果累累的季节，中国共产党第十九次全国代表大会于 2017 年 10 月 18 日在北京胜利召开。清华师生满怀喜悦和激动的心情，收听收看十九大开幕式盛况。

五年砥砺奋进，五年跨越发展。近五年来，学校党委带领全校师生员工，深入学习贯彻党的十八大、十八届三中四中五中六中全会精神，以习近平总书记系列重要讲话和 105 周年校庆贺信精神为指引，锐意进取、扎实工作，努力在创建世界一流大学方面走在前列，做中国高等教育的一面旗帜。

不忘初心，感悟改革发展；继续前进，凝聚奋进力量。站在新百年发展的历史新起点上，清华全校师生员工将认真学习、深刻领会、全面贯彻党的十九大精神，更加紧密地团结在以习近平同志为核心的党中央周围，高举旗帜，改革创新，攻坚克难，开拓进取，全面推进综合改革和“双一流”建设，为国家富强、民族复兴和人类文明进步做出新的更大贡献！

扫一扫，查看“喜迎十九大 砥砺奋进看清华”专题：

Tsinghua Teachers and Students Warmly Welcomed the 19th CPC National Congress

In this fruitful season, the 19th CPC National Congress was held on the 18th of October 2017. Teachers and students of Tsinghua University eagerly greeted and watched the opening ceremony of the 19th CPC National Congress.

It was five years of hard work and development!

For the past five years, Tsinghua University's Party Committee held onto the spirit gathered from four sessions of the 18th National Congress to deepen their study of the CPC. Using General Secretary Xi Jinping's speech and his letter for Tsinghua's 105th Anniversary as the guideline, we forged ahead with our solid efforts in making new strides in all development which offers a positive new chapter for the next 100 years.

Never forget our initial goals and always be aligned with our current revolutionary developments!

Let's march ahead and muster up all of our vitality and endeavors!

Standing at a new starting point in this most crucial phase of our development, the teachers and students of Tsinghua will fully implement the spirit of the 19th CPC National Congress. We hold our banners up high and with our eyes on reforms, innovation and always with our pioneering spirit, Tsinghua will make advancements and comprehensive reforms so that we can continue to make greater contributions to our national prosperity, our national development, our national rejuvenations and at a grander scale- the betterment of human civilization.

Translation and revision | Min Weiyuan

Image | Yang Siwei

10月19日

文字丨杨鹏成

图片丨李娜

砥砺奋进看清华·教育教学篇：努力培育肩负使命、追求卓越的人

不忘初心，感悟改革发展；继续前进，凝聚奋进力量。党的十八大以来，清华大学始终坚持以人才培养为根本，面向国家长远发展和重大战略需要，面向世界变革的未来趋势，努力培育肩负使命、追求卓越的人。

五年来，清华确立了“三位一体”模式，深入探索现代教育治理方式；从成效出发重构培养方案，给学生更多发展可能；加强通识教育，鼓励更多名师在清华开课；创新教学方法，从“以教为主”转变为“以学为主”；大力开展“三创”教育，构建高层次创新创业教育体系；完善研究生分类培养机制，造就领军创新人才；开放式办学，提升学生国际胜任力……砥砺奋进写华章，继往开来启新程。作为中国首批“双一流”建设高校，清华大学将继续行进在新百年波澜壮阔的新征程上，不断深化教育教学改革，为建设新时期中国特色的世界一流大学不懈努力奋斗！

扫一扫，查看详细报道：

努力培育肩负使命、追求卓越的人（一）（二）（三）

The Teachings of Tsinghua: Cultivating Talents and Always Be in the Pursuit for Excellence

In the recent 5 years, Tsinghua teachers and students have stood in unity and adhered to the philosophy of cultivating talents, which remains at the heart of Tsinghua. Tsinghua is set to support the country's long-term developments and meet all strategic needs. The mission of cultivating talents and always be in the pursuit for excellence is more crucial than ever when it comes to adapting to future trends and changes in the world.

Tsinghua has established and maintained a “Trinity Model” to further explore the management of modern education, the construction of effective training programs and giving students more possibilities in developments. It is needed to strengthen our understanding of education and to encourage more teachers to share their knowledge with the students of Tsinghua. New teaching philosophy and transition from “teaching as the focus” to “students as the focus” is just one aspect of this change. Education has been vigorously promoted to build an education system that consists of high-level innovation, internationalism and entrepreneurship. This open teaching style is all about improving the international competitiveness of students…to continue with our journey in gaining new results. As a top university in China, Tsinghua welcomes a new century of opportunities and growth. Tsinghua will continuously deepen teaching reforms and work towards becoming a first-class international university with Chinese characteristics.

Translation and revision | Min Weiyuan

Image | Li Na

10 月 20 日

文字 | 杨鹏成

图片 | 宋晨

砥砺奋进看清华·学术科研篇：推进科研体制机制改革，催生一流创新成果

科技兴则民族兴，科技强则国家强。党的十八大以来，清华大学认真学习贯彻党和国家的要求，深入实施科研体制机制改革，若干学科进入国际一流，科技创新能力和学术水平持续提升。

五年来，清华大学获得国家科技三大奖一等奖 6 项，文科成果获奖数和重大项目立项数目实现重要突破，高温气冷堆、下一代互联网、公共安全、大跨度钢 - 混组合结构等一批重大科研成果服务国家、造福社会。学校全面推动学科交叉，深度参与服务国家战略需求；进一步加强重大前沿项目部署，在国际学术前沿不断取得重大的标志性成果；不断强化校地合作平台建设，健全科技成果转化机制，推进对口支援工作，服务社会能力显著增强。

砥砺奋进，继往开来，清华大学将继续按照中央要求，深度参与国家战略，充分发挥人才优势和学术优势，坚持“顶天、立地、树人”的科研宗旨，把满足国家战略需要和引领国际学术前沿“两个战场”统一起来，不断深入推进科研体制机制改革，推动产生一流创新成果，为建设新时期中国特色的世界一流大学继续奋斗！

扫一扫，查看详细报道：
砥砺奋进看清华·学术科研篇：推进科研体制机制改革 催生一流创新成果

Tsinghua's Research Achievements: Scientific Research System Reform to Promote First Class Results in Innovation

Science and technology is tied to our people, our nation and above all, science and technology is strength. Since the 18th National Congress of the Communist Party of China, Tsinghua University studied and followed the needs of the nation and Party. In-depth reforms in scientific research are carried out to ensure that disciplines are internationalized and high in quality. Tsinghua works to ensure that the ability of scientific and technological innovations at an academic level will continue to see an ascent.

For the past five years, Tsinghua University took home six times the first prize in three National Science and Technology Awards. Major breakthroughs have been made in art achievements as well as crucial projects.The high-temperature gas-cooled reactor, the next generation of the Internet, issues concerning public safety, mixed composite structure and much more all reflect how Tsinghua's scientific research and achievements have brought much benefits to society and subsequently, allowed the university to serve the motherland. Tsinghua comprehensively promotes the merge of disciplines and participates in the implementations of national strategy. We will further strengthen the deployment of major frontier projects and continue to make iconic achievements in the international arena.

We will continue to strengthen the scientific cooperation between Tsinghua and the society. We will work to improve the transformation mechanism needed to apply out scientific and technological achievements.

Tsinghua will continue with our efforts and in accordance with the guidelines of the motherland and the Party, we will participate in the national strategy and give full play to talent and academic advantage. We will adhere to the scientific goal of "standing upright between heaven and earth with an indomitable spirit and nurture talents" to fulfill the needs of our nation. We will promote and produce first-class achievements in innovation and ensure that we persevere in this new period of making Tsinghua a top international university!

Translation and revision | Min Weiyuan

Image | Song Chen

10 月 23 日

文字 | 高原

图片 | 宋晨

砥砺奋进看清华·学生思政篇：点亮理想之灯，照亮前行之路

莲发藕生，必定有根。大学时期的青年正处在价值观形成和确立的关键时期，是一个人成长、成才的关键起点。清华大学始终高度重视青年学生的思想政治工作，在过去的五年里，清华的思政课堂发生了翻天覆地的变化，从传统课堂全面进入网络化、移动化、数据化、个性化时代。而清华推进、加强学生思政工作，变化的远不仅在课堂。坚持党建为先，开展思政教育；坚持全力推进“全员育人、全过程育人、全方位育人”。清华思政因事而化、因时而进、因势而新，将思想政治工作深入到校园生活的各个方面，打造起思想政治工作的坚强堡垒。

“为学生点亮理想的灯、照亮前行的路，激励学生自觉把个人的理想追求融入国家和民族的事业中。”这是习近平总书记对青年学生的殷殷期盼，也是清华新百年扎根中国大地、聚力改革创新、创建世界一流大学的动力源泉。

蓝图已展，号角吹响，让我们更加紧密地团结在以习近平同志为核心的党中央周围，高举旗帜，改革创新，为国家富强、民族复兴和人类文明进步做出当代清华人的更大贡献！

详细报道请点击：
砥砺奋进看清华·学生思政篇：点亮理想之灯 照亮前行之路

The Ideological and Political Work Towards Tsinghua Students: Lighting up a Path of Illumination

Our youthful years at university are crucial for the formation and establishment of values. It is a key starting point for the growth and success of an individual. Tsinghua has always attached great importance to ideological and political work of our young students. For the past five years, from traditional classroom layouts to one that is fully covered by digital and mobile networks, Tsinghua has made earth-shaking changes in the classroom, which has promoted and strengthened the ideological work towards students by adhering to the party's own guidelines.

Tsinghua continues to promote the ideological work towards students through the whole staff and ensure that this is all-rounded in our teaching and curriculum. We are committed to promoting an all-round education. As a result, Tsinghua University has become a strong fortress for ideological and political work by ensuring their presence in every aspect of campus life.

"Lighting up the light for students, illuminating the way forward and inspiring them to consciously pursue the ideals that one needs and thus, make contributions to the nation..." This is the expectation of President Xi Jinping and it is also the drive for Tsinghua to continue with her hard efforts in becoming a leading university on the international stage.

The blueprint has been set so let us unite more closely around the party and President to uphold the banner and final goals of our reforms. Let us remember the importance of innovation and the need to work towards national prosperity, rejuvenation and progress of human civilization. Let us continue to make progress and contributions for our society and nation.

Translation and revision | Min Weiyuan

Image | Song Chen

10月24日

砥砺奋进看清华·人事制度改革篇：激发人才引擎动力，助推世界一流大学建设

2013年，党的十八届三中全会做出全面深化改革的重大决定。清华、北大主动请缨，希望在国家深化教育领域综合改革中先行先试。全面深化综合改革的第一步，清华大学坚定地选择用人事制度改革来“破局”。

这是一场使命驱动的改革——高校是科技第一生产力和人才第一资源的重要结合点。深入推进人事制度改革，以此为突破口深化学校综合改革，不仅是清华新百年的发展需要，更是深度参与创新驱动发展战略实施、创建世界一流大学，为国家发展、人民幸福、人类文明进步作出贡献的需要。

从抵近教师人事制度“深水区”，到吹动一流大学建设人才队伍建设的“一池春水”，清华的人事制度改革着眼长远，通过一系列改革举措进一步解放和发展学校的先进生产力、解放和增强师生员工的创造活力，为“双一流”建设提供重要的助推力量。

扫一扫，查看详细报道：
砥砺奋进看清华·人事制度改革篇：激发人才引擎动力，助推世界一流大学建设

Tsinghua's System Reform of Human Resources Management: Stimulating the Engine for Talents and Boosting the Construction of a World-class University

In 2013, the Third Plenary Session of the 18th CPCCC made a major decision to comprehensively deepen reforms. Tsinghua University and Peking University have offered to take the initiative to deepen the comprehensive reform of education in the country. In the first step of such reforms, Tsinghua firmly adhered to and used a new system for human resources management and talent stimulation to break the ice.

This is a mission-driven reform: universities are important junctures with the most immediate scientific forces and human resources. Further promotion and using this as a breakthrough to deepen the comprehensive reform is not the only new developmental needs that Tsinghua requires for the next century. This is for an innovation driven strategy in the overall implementation that helps to form the fundamental ingredients to ensure that Tsinghua becomes a world-class university. Tsinghua works for our nation's development, one that meets the needs of the people and contributes to the progress of human civilization.

From venturing into the deep waters of talent stimulation and its connections to staff training to ensuring the continuous flow of the talent pool at Tsinghua, this reform is a long-term one. Through a series of measures, the liberation and development of the university in advanced productivity, opening up and creativity amongst both teachers and students will play significant roles in giving Tsinghua vitality and ensuring that Tsinghua retains her elite status.

Translation and revision | Min Weiyuan

Image | Song Chen, Yang Siwei

10月25日

文字 | 曲田

图片 | 郭祥、杨思维

砥砺奋进看清华·全球战略篇：风从清华来，吹向全世界

当下贯穿未来，教育连接世界。

党的十八大以来，从顶层设计到深耕细作，清华大学坚定不移地走世界一流、中国特色、清华风格的发展道路，制定并实施全球战略，稳步推进学校国际化建设，不断提升学校一流大学建设水平和全球影响力。

从大国到周边，从“一带一路”沿线国家到多边舞台……五年来，清华大学将学校发展置于国家现代化和经济全球化的大背景中，以更加开放的姿态积极参与全球人才与教育科研资源的竞争。这五年，国内国际，园内园外，清华人的身影忙碌而从容。这五年，国际社会更多地听到了清华声音、看到了清华智慧，面对全球治理格局深刻变化和中国高等教育深化改革的重大机遇，清华持续发力中。

扫一扫，查看详细报道：

砥砺奋进看清华·全球战略篇：风从清华来，吹向全世界

An International Look at Tsinghua: the Tsinghua Wind Blows to the World

Now and certainly into the future, education connects the world. Ever since the 18th National Party Congress of the CPC, from top level design to the tiniest details, Tsinghua, who aims to be a world class university with Chinese characteristics, has formulated and implemented its first global strategy. Tsinghua is promoting and marching ahead in the internationalization of the university to ensure that global influence and top quality in education is constantly maintained.

From big countries to neighboring countries and from the Belt and Road countries to a more multilateral stage... In the past five years, Tsinghua University has placed the development of education institutions in the context of national modernization and economic globalization. Tsinghua has adopted a much more open and extensive manner in education resources, talent cultivation and participation rate in global events and competitions.

For these five years, Tsinghua people made their presence known both at home and abroad. For these five years, the Tsinghua voice has been heard more often by the international community. They have witnessed the wisdom of Tsinghua and felt profound changes made under the framework of global governance and seizing the chance of deepening reforms in the Chinese higher education system. Tsinghua is marching ahead and displaying such continuous power.

Translation and revision | Min Weiyuan

Image | Guo Xiang, Yang Siwei

10 月 26 日

文字 | 冯婉婷

图片 | 赵存存

清华美院向帆:“艺术与科技的春天”就是当下

“为什么不呢？”当被问起为什么要参加比赛时，向帆这样反问道。

作为清华美院视觉传达设计系的副教授，向帆与软件工程师朱舜山合作的作品《数据追问——全国美展优化作品视觉化解读》入选了美国《科学》杂志官网举办的 2016 年度数据故事视频比赛最终名单。

在这个作品中，向帆和她的团队通过对获奖油画作品的视觉化分析，显现了色调、少数题材、作品名称、画幅、获奖经历等因素与获奖的相关度，提出了不同于传统视角的艺术观察新方法。当点击作品时，2276 张获奖油画作品随着音乐的节奏，如一些彩色的小斑点般在眼前铺陈而来，既能凌空鸟瞰一片斑斓的油画天地，又能瞬时俯冲而下观察每个作品的细节，为观众呈现了一种前所未有的观看油画的方式。

这个作品可谓计算机科学技术与艺术交叉研究的精彩案例。然而，向帆本人并非来自计算机专业，也不画油画。“我确实不需要获得油画奖项，我关注的是大型图像数据库，不仅仅是全国美展的，也不限于油画。”对向帆而言，图像是核心的考察样本形式之一，研究者的研究能力取决于对图像资料的分析能力。而基于当今数据视觉化方法，人类已经可以一次性观察上千、上万张图像，并通过交互的视觉化界面探索其中隐含的关系，这大大提升了研究的准确性。她的其他作品，譬如《地方节奏》和《春晚重构》，也是将图像与大数据相结合后进行视觉化呈现，这是她设计的核心思维。

与向帆同时出现在《科学》官网这份最终名单上的，还有美国宇航局视觉化实验室、美国洛斯阿拉莫斯国家实验室等科研机构的工作人员。其实对向帆来说，科学与人文的交融并不是件陌生的事——她自己就在《科学文艺》杂志的编辑部图书室长大，也曾有幸与叶永烈、童恩正等老一辈科幻文学作家们面对面。今天的清华大学和清华美院，一直积极鼓励艺术与科学交融的探索，类似向帆这样的研究项目出现，可以说是一种必然。在向帆看来，当年那些老先生们所向往的“艺术与科技的春天”，就是当下。

Xiang Fan: Now Is the Spring Time of Both Art and Technology

"Why not?" was Xiang Fan's reply when she was asked about her reason in entering the competition.

Last year, US based magazine *Science* announced the final list of 2016 Data Stories competition on their homepage. Tsinghua's associate professor Xiang Fan's work "Award Puzzle | How to win art awards in China" was on the list.

In this work, Xiang Fan and her cooperator Zhu Shunshan put forward new methods that are different from the more traditional methods in gaining perspectives for art observations. They try to release the relavence between winning national art awards and many factors of the oil paintings, such as the tone, the subject and award-winning experiences. When clicked, 2276 award-winning paintings along with the rhythm of the music are revealed in front of our eyes in the form of small colorful specks. Whether it is from a bird's eye view or a closer observation of each detail, audiences are presented with a different and unprecedented look at oil paintings.

This work is a wonderful example of the merge between art research and computer science and technology. However, Xiang is neither an expert in computer science nor an oil painter. "I don' t really need to win the oil painting awards. What I'm more focused on are large image database." For Xiang Fan, the image is one of the core test samples and the research result depends on the researchers' ability to make analytical conclusions from such image data. Based on current data visualization methods, humans can view tens of thousands of images at any one given time and most importantly, through the interaction of visual interfaces, they can explore this relationship which can greatly improve the accuracy of the research. Her other works, such as "Local rhythms" and "The reconstruction of the Spring Festival Gala" are also the visual presentation of a combination of images and big data. This is the core thinking behind her design.

Other winners appearing on the list of *Science* website are from the NASA's Scientific Visualization Studio, Los Alamos National Laboratory and more scientific institutions.

In fact, interdisciplinary is the essence of contemporary art. Science is no stranger to Xiang's work and involvement in art. Xiang said that she grew up in the reading room of a magazine called *Scientific Literature* and had the honor of meeting early science fiction writers such as Ye Yonglie and Tong Enzheng. In her opinion, "the spring time of Art and Technology" as the writers called is always here — Tsinghua and its Academy of Arts & Design always encourage the exploration of blending of arts and science. This may be one of the reasons why Xiang, as an associate professor in visual communication has been named by *Science*.

Translation and revision | Min Weiyuan

Image | Zhao Cuncun

10月27日

文字 | 刘书田
图片 | 宋晨

杨学诚：我这支蜡烛，不求点得长，只求点得亮

“我这支蜡烛，不要求点得长，只求点得亮。”1944年，年仅29岁的杨学诚用生命诠释了“蜡炬成灰泪始干”的奉献精神。

出生于湖北省黄陂县一个贫苦农民家庭的杨学诚天资聪慧，勤奋好学。在1934年以优异成绩考入清华大学物理系后，他每天“挟着课本、规规矩矩地按时到图书馆用功”，沉默寡言，很少参加课外活动。

直到1935年，一句“华北之大，已经安放不得一张平静的书桌了”的口号响彻清华园，清华广大的师生们纷纷投入到挽救民族危亡的爱国民主运动中，杨学诚觉醒了，他毅然走出书斋，渴望做一只燃烧的蜡烛，自觉勇敢地投身于伟大的爱国学生运动中，将个人的命运与中华民族的解放事业紧紧联在一起，希望能够照亮黯淡弱贫的祖国。

加入中国共产党，意味着杨学诚为实现“为人民服务”理想又迈出了重要一步。1936年秋天，他开始担任清华地下党支部书记。1938年，受党组织委派，杨学诚前往鄂中应城汤池建立革命武装，开辟鄂中抗日民主根据地。杨学诚这位学生出身、没有任何军事经验的年轻干部，怀着对革命事业的无限忠诚和一腔革命热情，用他过人的智慧和出色的组织才能，将一支只有13人、8条步枪的应城抗日游击队，逐渐发展成有数千之众的强大武装力量。

杨学诚在严酷的斗争中迅速成长为一名“深思熟虑、冷静沉着”“独当一面工作”的优秀干部，不舍昼夜地投入到工作中。敌后长期的艰苦斗争使他积劳成疾。1943年初，杨学诚从鄂南敌后返回江北时，已经身染重病。

同志们劝他休息时，他依然要坚持带病工作。听到他病倒的消息后，母亲和弟妹赶来看他。为了不增加组织的负担，杨学诚要家人们赶快回家。母亲临走时，组织上想给点路费，也被他拒绝了。在同志们眼中，杨学诚就是这样一个全心全意为大局考虑、却鲜为自己着想的人。

1944年3月7日，杨学诚在部队转移途中病逝于大悟山。这位优秀的清华学子、杰出的革命战士以对祖国和人民的无私奉献，真正做到了“鞠躬尽瘁，死而后已”，实践了他“这支蜡烛”光彩夺目的人生理想。

Yang Xuecheng: Like a Candle, I Only Desire It Burns Brightly

"Like a burning candle, I do not seek a long life; I only desire that it burns brightly." This is what Yang Xuecheng said in 1943, only one year before his death at 29. The words epitomized his desire for his life, one that carries a spirit of dedication, and like a candle, he longs for his life to be ashes and tears in dedication for a cause.

Born in a poor peasant family, Huangpi County, Hubei Province, Yang Xuecheng was naturally talented and intelligent, and was a studious young man. In 1934, due to his excellent exam results, he was admitted into the Department of Physics at Tsinghua University. His life in Tsinghua consisted of carrying a textbook under his arm and a daily routine of studying in the library. He was rarely a part of extracurricular activities.

Then 1935 arrived. A slogan "The expanse of North Chinese no longer has room for a quiet desk" resounded throughout Tsinghua campus, and when countless Tsinghua students and teachers joined in a patriotic movement amidst China's national crisis (Japanese invasion), Yang Xuecheng was awakened from his studies. He decided to abandon his books, for he was eager to become a burning candle that gives light. With courage, he joined a student patriotic movement, surrendering his individual fate to the greater cause of liberating China, and hoping to bring light to his weak and destitute motherland.

Joining the Chinese Communist Party for Yang Xuecheng meant that he has taken an important step toward realizing the ideal of "Service for the People" . In the fall of 1936, he began to serve as the secretary of the underground communist party branch at Tsinghua. In 1938, according to party organization, Yang Xuecheng traveled to Tangchi in Yingcheng, Hubei Province, to establish revolutionary armed forces and set up anti-Japanese bases in the area. As a student and young cadre, Yang Xuecheng had no military experience. But as he held on to his loyalty and passion for the revolutionary cause, he tapped onto his wisdom and extraordinary organizational skills, growing a small company of 13 people with eight rifles to a powerful anti-Japanese armed force numbering in the thousands.

In the harsh environment, Yang Xuecheng grew into a thoughtful and composed cadre who devoted himself to work day and night. The long and arduous struggle against the enemy however brought upon illness. At the beginning of 1943, when Yang Xuecheng traveled to the north of Yangtze from the southern enemy lines, he was already gravely ill.

When comrades advised him to rest, he insisted on working. Upon receiving news of his illness, his mother, brother and sister came to see him. To lessen the burden on the organization, Yang Xuecheng told his family to quickly return home. When his mother was about to leave, the organization wanted to help her with travel expenses but Yang Xuecheng refused the gift. In the eyes of his comrades, Yang Xuecheng was someone who thought it was more important to consider the organization's needs than his own personal needs.

On March 7th, 1944, while traveling with troops on route to a new base, he perished on Dawu Mountain. This outstanding Tsinghua student and revolutionary fighter who selflessly fought for his motherland, spared no effort until his dying day. He had lived out his fervent ambition for his life, to burn brightly.

Translation and revision | Alexis See Tho

Image | Song Chen

10 月 30 日

文字 | 杨晨晞

图片 | 李娜

“会飞的盒子”实践支队：带着山区的孩子飞到更远的地方

2017 年 12 月，由清华大学“会飞的盒子”实践支队同学设计的四川省广元市苍溪县万安小学校舍即将在位于山顶上的万安小学落成。

万安小学始建于 1982 年，其教学楼已有 25 年的历史，学校从学前班到六年级，每个年级仅有一间教室。2008 年汶川地震后，学校东侧校舍变为危房，学校只得将教学楼一层的教室改建为宿舍提供给学生。位于大山顶上的万安小学，是白驿镇唯一一所学校，教学和生活条件都十分艰苦。由于宿舍的限制，每个床位必须睡两到三个孩子才可满足孩子们的住宿需求，并且无法提供热水、洗澡等设施和条件。尽管条件艰苦，但是每个孩子都在尽力维护校园的环境，每天早起打扫校园，上课认真学习。环境再艰苦，也不能挡住他们对知识的渴望。

“会飞的盒子”是在中国青少年发展基金会支持下设立的公益项目，旨在为贫困地区上学路途遥远的中小学生提供轻便安全的新型宿舍。万安小学校舍是“会飞的盒子”公益项目实施以来的第七所“盒子”，由清华大学建筑学院、土木工程系和建设管理系的 20 多名同学设计完成，由四川省广元市苍溪县教育与科学局和苍溪县团委提供一部分资金支持，扩大规模以满足万安小学 170 名学生的住宿需求。校舍同时配备多功能活动室、浴室和卫生间，全方位保障学生的生活需求和质量。

作为发起方和主要参与方，清华大学“会飞的盒子”实践支队分设计团队、支教团队、调研团队三支力量。设计团队主要负责校舍的设计工作，支教团队负责为孩子们带去课内外学习资源，调研支队则对当地的教育扶贫政策进行调研。实践支队总队负责掌控进度，结合专业知识，在流程优化、风险预测、方案设计、政策调研与反馈等方面起到了关键作用。实践过程中，同学们不仅着眼于保障当地学生的生活质量，也通过切身的居住体验来优化校舍设计，围绕“盒子”建造开展了学生素质拓展、走访式在地调研、物资购置等工作，不仅要让孩子们住在更加舒适的“盒子”里，更要让教育资源进一步平衡，尽最大的努力帮助他们摆脱贫困限制。

“The Flying Box” Team: Take Children in the Mountainous Area Fly Farther

In December 2017, a new schoolhouse built by “the flying box” team from Tsinghua University will be completed in Wan'an Primary School, Cangxi County, Sichuan Guangyuan.

Founded in 1982, Wan'an Primary School has a teaching building that has served for 25 years; from pre-school to sixth grade, each grade has only one classroom. After Wenchuan earthquake in 2008, the eastern schoolhouse became a dilapidated building, therefore the school had to change the first floor of the teaching building into a student dormitory. Located on top of a mountain, Wan'an Primary School is the only school in Baiyi Town, which faces tough living and teaching conditions. Due to the limited conditions, two to three children have had to share one bed to meet the demand of student accommodation, and there is no facility to provide hot water for showers. Even in such harsh conditions, all of the children are trying their best to maintain a positive campus environment, they clean up the campus every day and study hard; their desire for knowledge is not diminished by the outside environment.

“The flying box” is a public welfare project supported by the China Youth Development Foundation (CYDF), committed to providing light and safe dormitories for students living far away from school in poverty-stricken areas. The “flying Box” in Wan'an Primary School is the seventh “box” of the project. Over 20 students from Tsinghua's School of Architecture, Department of Civil Engineering and Department of Construction Management designed it; Bureau of Education and Science and Youth League Committee in Cangxi County provided a segment of financial support. The construction is committed to expanding the housing area to meet the accommodation needs of 170 students in Wan'an Primary School. At the same time, the house is equipped with a multi-functional room, a bathhouse and toilet, and meets the overall living demands of students while significantly improving their quality of life.

As a sponsor and major participant, “The flying box” team of Tsinghua University consists of a design team, volunteering teachers and a research team. The design team is in charge of design work of the schoolhouse; volunteering teachers bring all kinds of learning resources for the local students; research team conducts surveys on local education-oriented poverty alleviation policy; the headquarters controls the progress with professional knowledge, and play a key role in procedure optimization, risk prediction, plan design, policy research and feedback. During the practice, team members not only focus on providing local students' good life quality, but also optimize the design through personal living experiences. Besides the building construction, they carried out works in student quality development, local interview survey, material purchase work, ensuring children to live in a more comfortable “box” , to further balance educational resources, breaking the limits that poverty has placed.

Translation and revision | Raj Lamar

Image | Li Na

11月1日

文字 | 冯婉婷

图片 | 宋晨

王步高：清华园的诗风词韵，离不开他的心血灌溉

在清华，王步高老师开设的“大学语文”“诗词格律与创作”等几门文化素质课曾被同学们认为是最难选到的热门课程，不少同学经历了几个学期的抢课才能选上。但凡听过王老师讲课的人，无一不被他渊博的学识和强大的人格魅力所吸引。

王步高早年在南京大学德语专业学习，后到吉林大学、南京师范大学攻读古典文学专业，并成为词学大师唐圭璋的入室弟子。他的诗词写作课在东南大学享有盛誉，在高校人文素质教育界亦素有口碑。2009 年春，从东南大学退休的王步高受清华邀请，到清华开设“诗词格律与创作”“大学语文”等四门文化素质课。2016 年底，王步高因生病回南京休养至今。

王步高在清华任教的时候，一学期上 9 学分的文化素质核心课，工作量比很多没退休的老师都大。他每天早上 5 点起床，每逢周三晚的“诗词格律与创作”课，他从一早开始就一遍遍地批改检查学生作业。忙到吃不上饭的他只在中午去楼下的食堂买两个玉米，中午吃一个，晚上吃一个。他每堂课的 PPT 都有两三百页，每每有新的灵感和思考，他都不忘往 PPT 里加入新的内容，在他任教的八年里一直如此。清华的一线教师一般每年 96 个学时就满工作量了，但王步高每年都讲 288 个学时。

王步高对课程的敬业负责让同学们由衷佩服和敬仰，但却并没有因此让学生和他产生距离感。每逢佳节，王步高都会邀请学生到家中，一二十人一起包饺子、玩诗词游戏，其乐融融。他常用“震撼”与“自愧不如”这样感情色彩浓烈的词汇，形容自己在清华授课的体验。他要求上他课的学生在期末时必须指出他的课程与他所编写教材中有待改进的地方，目的是为了和同学们互相学习、共同进步。“在这些后生面前，我绝不敢以真理的化身自居，必须谦逊、低调，活到老，学到老。”王步高如是说。

生病之后王步高回到南京休养，挂念老师的同学们往往会凑好时间一起去探望他。养病期间的王老师记忆力仍然极好，他记得每一批来看望他的清华师生，并笑着关心同学们的近况，和每个来看望他的同学握手、合影。虽然离开了教学一线，但他却始终惦念着清华的同学们。王步高说自己特别喜欢清华的学生，从来没后悔过来清华。

编者后记：

2017 年 11 月 1 日下午，突然传来王步高老师当天中午在南京逝世的噩耗，我们不胜悲痛。去世之前，王步高老师念念不忘清华的同学们，十分怀念清华的课堂，还准备将“诗词格律与创作”拍成慕课留给清华同学们。没想到，这一去竟成永别。谨以此文悼念为清华文化素质教育付出辛勤汗水和心血的王步高老师，他的师风诗韵、他对莘莘学子的满腔热爱将永远留在清华师生心中，王老师一路走好！

Wang Bugao: The Poems of Tsinghua, a Part of His Soul

In Tsinghua, Wang Bugao's courses "Chinese" "Poetry and Writing" and other literary lessons were all widely received by students. However, they are also known to be the hardest lessons to enroll in due to its popularity. Many students had to go through several semesters to finally gain successful admission. All who have attended Wang's lessons have all been captivated by his profound knowledge and personality charm.

In his early years, Wang studied German at Nanjing University and then went onto his studies in the classics at Jilin University and Nanjing Normal University. He became a disciple of Master Tang Guizhang. His poetry writing class enjoyed a high reputation in Southeast University and also in the humanities circles amongst all tertiary institutions. In the spring of 2009, Mr. Wang, who retired from Southeast University, accepted an invitation from Tsinghua to open four courses such as "Poetry and Writing" and "Chinese" . At the end of 2016, Wang went to Nanjing to recover from an illness.

When Mr. Wang taught at Tsinghua, his nine credits of course work saw enormous workload. In fact, it was a lot more than those teachers who have not retired. He gets up at five every morning, and on Wednesday evenings, he would check work and all related notes. He would mark students' work from the early morning; he would forget to have lunch. He would often buy two corns and save one for lunch and one for the evening. Every one of his PowerPoint is 200 to 300 pages long. Every page has fresh ideas and he would keep on adding in new contents into his lessons. He has been doing this for 8 consecutive years. Most Tsinghua teachers need to fill in 96 hours of teaching time every year but for Mr. Wang, his total racked up to be 288 hours.

Mr. Wang is dedicated to the curriculum and to his students. He is greatly respected and admired by all. All felt close to him. During every festival and special occasions, Mr. Wang would invite students to his home and in groups of 10 to 20; they would make dumplings, play poetry-related games and listen to music. He often uses words like "surprising" and "rather ashamed" to describe his experience at Tsinghua. He always made a request for his students to point out areas for him to improve on. "When I'm faced with these students, I must remain humble and continue to learn until the end." said Wang.

Wang returned to Nanjing to recover from his illness and many of his students went to see him. Despite being sick, he remembered everything and could name all of his visitors. He would chat and joke around with the students, ask about their studies and take photos with them. Even though Mr. Wang is no longer teaching at the frontline, he still misses the students and Tsinghua. He said that he is particularly fond of Tsinghua students and never had any regrets about his time in Tsinghua.

Editor's Note:

Afternoon of November 1, 2017:

We received the sudden news of the passing of Professor Wang Bugao. He passed away in Nanjing around noon. Professor Wang always placed Tsinghua students in his heart and truly misses his class at Tsinghua. He was ready to turn his lessons in "Poetry and its creation" into a MOOC course for all Tsinghua students to see. We did not anticipate such a farewell. We dedicate this to Professor Wang, to his continuous efforts and to his dedication in teaching. His knowledge and love for his students will remain in the hearts of us Tsinghua people. May you rest in peace Professor Wang!

Translation and revision | Min Weiyuan

Image | Song Chen

11月2日

文字 | 冯婉婷
图片 | 薛雅芳

数学系扈志明：当一名教师一直都是我的心愿

1993 年 8 月，从中科院数学所博士毕业的扈志明脚踩三轮车，带着全部家当来清华报到，实现了他做一名教师的心愿。一转眼，他已经在园子里任教 24 年，送走了一批又一批优秀学子。

“做教师的想法始于高中阶段。”高中时期扈志明的成绩曾从入学时的倒数上升到了毕业时的名列前茅，在他看来，这离不开任课老师们的帮助，尤其是他的班主任，也是他的数学老师。从那时开始，扈志明就产生了将来当一名教师的想法。进入大学后，他接触了更多认真负责的老师，他们的为学、为人更加坚定了他的这一想法。

来到清华后，扈志明始终不忘以自己的老师们为榜样，希望自己能对学生有所帮助。对他而言，作为教师，“用心”是做好工作的基础和保障，用心向老教师请教，用心向同辈学习，用心掌握教学要求，用心组织教学内容，用心完成教学过程，更要用心关爱自己的学生。

身为数学科学系的副教授，扈志明多年来一直工作在教学第一线，开设了“微积分 B”“微积分 B”（MOOC）等课程，每年学生评教他的课程都稳居前 5%。他上课极有个性，讲课语速快、从不打磕绊，不需看讲稿、例题信手拈来，拓展的内容不需多想就能脱口而出。但是，同学们从来都不会因为老师语速快而跟不上节奏，因为扈志明思路清晰，能帮同学们很好地理顺知识。除此之外，每次课前他都会绕着教室转圈，热心地为同学们答疑，确保及时解决同学们遇到的难题。

在清华 105 周年校庆之际，扈志明获得了“清华大学新百年基础教学教师奖”，喜悦的同时他又深觉责任和使命重大。他认为，作为教师能够获得同学们的认可是最重要的。“能在清华教书是幸福的”，扈志明说清华有最好的学生，也有比较宽松的教学环境，老师在完成课程基本要求的基础上，有很大的发挥空间。他对自己教过的每一届学生都十分喜爱和感激，“同学们的包容和认可是我积极工作的主要动力，他们的好学也激励着我不断学习、不断进步”。

除了高质量的课堂教学，扈志明也十分关注学生在课外的情况。他告诉学生们，只要有问题，随时都可以和他联系。他也经常参加学生们的课外活动，希望通过不同场合、不同主题的交流，让同学们更好地了解大学的学习、大学的文化。“老师对学生的影响是多方面的。”扈志明希望自己不仅是站在讲台上的导师，也是同学们在课堂外的朋友。

Department of Mathematics, Hu Zhiming: Being a Teacher Has Always Been My Wish

August 1993, Hu Zhiming, a graduate from the Chinese Academy of Sciences was on his tricycle and brought along with him everything that he owned. It was then that he started his teaching career with Tsinghua. He has fulfilled his dream. In a blink of an eye and 24 years later, he has sent away groups after groups of some of the most talented young minds in the country.

"The idea of becoming a teacher started in high school." Hu was top in his class. In his view, such achievements could not be separated from the dedication and help from his own teachers. His head teacher, who was also his math teacher, was the source of inspiration for Hu. After he went to university, he came in contact with many more hardworking teachers and that eventually cemented his dream of becoming one of them.

When Hu came to Tsinghua, he never forgot his teachers and the example that they set for him. He hopes that through his own actions, he is able to help his own students. For Hu, being a teacher is about setting your "heart" in the right place. You need to do a good job and not only consult your colleagues but also learn from your peers, know what is required and ensure that the teaching content, process and goals are met. In the end, one needs to ensure that students are cared for and catered to.

As an Associate Professor of Mathematical Sciences, Hu has been at the frontline of teaching for years. His "Calculus B" course has seen his students rank his class in the top 5%. He speaks fast yet never stumbles. He does not need to read any lecture notes and has a lot to say. Although the pace is fast, no one is left behind. All the students are able to keep up with his pace and find much needed information and clarity from his lessons. Moreover, he would circle around the classroom and enthusiastically answer all of the students' questions to ensure that all problems are timely resolved.

On the occasion of Tsinghua's 105th Anniversary, Hu won the "Tsinghua Centennial Fundamental Teaching Award" . He is fully aware of his sense of responsibility and mission. He believes that being recognized by the students is the single most important thing in the world. "I'm happy that I'm able to teach at Tsinghua!" Hu said that Tsinghua has the best students and a very relaxed teaching environment. Apart from teaching, teachers also have a lot of room and space to grow. He cares and is grateful for all of his students and believes that "it is their tolerance and recognition that drives and inspires me to be hardworking and a teacher who is continuously learning and making changes."

In addition to paying attention to the students in class, Hu is also concerned about their extracurricular activities. His students could always reach him and he would also take part in some of these activities. He hopes that his students can better understand the culture and meaning of university through different occasions and topics. "The influence that teachers have on students is multi-layered." Hu doesn't only want to be that teacher up on the podium but also a friend outside the classroom.

Translation and revision | Min Weiyuan

Image | Xue Yafang

11月3日

文字丨刘书田

图片丨李娜

“双一流”背景下的一流本科教育：清华倾全力培养肩负使命、追求卓越的人

本科教育是大学人才培养的根本，一流本科教育是一流大学的底色。

清华大学始终将本科教育置于学校的基础性、全局性地位，始终把培养适应社会发展的一流人才视为重中之重。

第 24 次教育工作讨论会后，清华大学以全面深化综合改革为契机，重点推进本科教育教学改革，提出并实施价值塑造、能力培养和知识传授“三位一体”的教育理念，在建立高水平师资队伍、教学资源、培养过程、学生发展、质量保障等各方面开展了一系列改革创新和探索实践。

清华恢复教学委员会并成立了本科生课程咨询委员会，吸引学生参与顶层设计；从成效出发，在充分调研的基础上进行了重在“增加学生自主性、提高挑战度”培养方案重构。围绕培养目标，清华建立了以通识教育为基础、通专融合的本科教育体系；不断创新线上线下的教学手段和方法，聚名师、建名课、出名教材；加强生师互动，构建有温度的教育；扎实开展科研训练，建立高层次创新创业教育体系，努力培养拔尖创新人才；坚持全过程国际化培养，提升学生国际胜任力；坚持全过程全方位育人，重视个性化发展。

面向未来，清华将继续走中国特色、世界一流的发展道路，坚持“中西融汇、古今贯通、文理渗透”的办学风格和“又红又专、全面发展”的培养特色，坚持立德树人、改革创新，为迈向世界一流大学前列而努力奋斗。

扫一扫，查看详细报道：

清华：倾全力培养肩负使命、追求卓越的人

Tsinghua: Top Undergraduate Education Aligned with "Double World-class" Development

Undergraduate education is the basis of talent training at a tertiary level. A top-class undergraduate education is the foundation for any top university. Tsinghua University has placed great emphasis on the development and sustained improvement of her undergraduate education. Tsinghua has made it a top priority to train the best talents to adapt to social developments and national progress.

After the 24th Tsinghua Education Conference, Tsinghua placed forward a comprehensive reform plan with the aim to promote and deepen reforms in undergraduate education. Whether it is talent training or implementing education philosophies or establishing high-quality teaching staff, resources and pedagogy that focuses on students' development, Tsinghua has made it her mission to maintain quality assurance and building a culture that is innovative and holistic.

Tsinghua established an undergraduate course advisory committee to attract students to participate in the curriculum design process. The new cultivation programme aims to "increase student's autonomy and raise the challenge" .

Based on the cultivation objectives, the university has established a new undergraduate education system, which is based on general education, and combines literature education with specialty education. Online and offline teaching innovations are widely made. The best resources, the best teachers and the best environment are all applied for cultivating talents. Interactions between students and teachers are strengthened. Research training programme is carried out and a high-level system of innovation and entrepreneurship is built to train innovative talents. Tsinghua keeps the undergraduate education truly internationalized, and continues to enhance the students' international capabilities. Tsinghua continues to cultivate talents through the whole staff and ensures that this is all-rounded in the teaching and curriculum. Tsinghua also takes care of all the students' personalized development.

For the future, Tsinghua will continue to head down the path of becoming a leading university with Chinese characteristics. We will adhere to the "integration of East and West, the past and future" and adopt teaching characteristics that is "Chinese, specialized, and comprehensive" . Our reforms and innovations will ensure that we are always working towards being a top university in the world.

Translation and revision | Min Weiyuan

Image | Li Na

11 月 6 日

原作者 | 曲田

改写 | 杨鹏成

图片 | 李娜

聂建国院士：传递土木工程的广博与厚重

清华大学土水学院土木工程系结构实验大厅与普通实验室有些不同，它更像是真实的、繁忙热闹的建筑工地。在这个“工地”里，每天都能看到一位头戴安全帽、身穿工作服的老师行走其中，耐心询问实验进展、细致指导学生科研，夜以继日，倾心付出。

他是清华大学土水学院教授聂建国院士。多年来，他把所有精力都奉献给了祖国的土木工程事业，取得了一系列重大创新型成果，培养了一大批组合结构优秀人才。不管是科研，还是教学，他都全心全意地付出。

“我的体会是讲课效果‘没有最好，只有更好，永无止境’。在我看来，毅力也是对能力的一种补充，为了讲好课，追求卓越，我还会不断努力。”这是聂建国的工作态度，也是他的人格写照。

近年来，聂建国主要担任两项本科教学工作：一是为土木系本科新生上第一堂专业概论课，二是为本科毕业班学生上第一堂专业前沿课。任务不多，但意义重大，一头一尾，正好是本科生整个学习生涯中最关键的两个时间点。

“第一堂专业概论课无疑是对本科新生最重要的一次专业启蒙，我希望这堂课能为他们种下第一颗梦想的种子，甚至能成为他们终生难忘的回忆。”然而，刚开始讲课时并没有预想中的顺利，面对一群对专业毫无概念的高中毕业生，一些原本非常精彩的案例却无法引起他们的共鸣。为了更好地与这些初入科研殿堂的学生“共情”，聂建国开始尝试站在他们的角度重新思考问题，回想自己还是懵懂少年时如何被土木工程所吸引，又如何凭借兴趣长期沉浸于土木工程的研究与实践。

“这些思考给了我不少灵感。我决定从学生们最熟悉的生活讲起，从带给他们温暖幸福的小家到求学的校园，再到来清华一路上看到的交通基础设施，努力让学生们体会，每天看似理所当然的生活都离不开土木工程的恩泽，就如同水和空气，我们有时并不在意，但却非常重要。”就这样，从生活中的一点一滴讲起，聂建国将土木工程的广博与厚重、无与伦比的魅力润物细无声地传递给了年轻学子。“我希望这两堂课能成为清华土木人永久的回忆。”聂建国说。

Academician Nie Jianguo: The Improvement of Teaching Is a Never-ending Journey

The experiment lab in the Civil Engineering Department is somewhat different from other labs. It looks more like a busy construction site. On site, a professor in safety helmet and work uniform, can be frequently found walking about, inquiring about students' progress in their experiments and giving guidance in research; it's a devotion that goes on day and night.

A member of the Chinese Academy of Engineering, Cheung Kong Distinguished Professor, and Director of the Key Laboratory of Structural Engineering and Vibration of Ministry of Education, Professor Nie Jianguo's passion is in teaching. Over the years, he has devoted all his energy to the advancement of civil engineering in China. He has made a series of major innovative achievements and trained a great number of outstanding talents. Whether it is scientific research or teaching, he works at them wholeheartedly.

"My experience is that there is no best method to give a lecture, only a better method, the improvement of teaching is a never-ending journey. Perseverance has helped where my abilities were lacking. In order to teach better and achieve more excellent results, I will continue to work hard." Professor Nie reflects on his work over the years. His words reflect his work attitude and his personal character.

Professor Nie mainly teaches two undergraduate courses. The first is introducing the civil engineering major to freshmen, and the second is for graduating students on cutting-edge topics in civil engineering. The task may not seem big, but they are of great significance. They are at the two most critical points of an undergraduate student's learning career at Tsinghua.

"The first introductory class on civil engineering undoubtedly provides the most important insight into the major, and I hope that the class will sow the seeds of students' first dream and perhaps even be a lesson that they'll remember for life." However, the lectures didn't go smooth-sailing at the very beginning. Teaching a group of high school graduates who has no idea about civil engineering, wonderful case studies fail to excite them. In order to better empathize with these students who will delve into scientific research in the future, Professor Nie began putting himself in their shoes and recalled how he was attracted by civil engineering when he was a teenager and how he immersed himself in the research and practice of civil engineering.

"These thoughts gave me a lot of inspiration. I decided to talk about the most familiar things in life to the students. For example, how civil engineering gave them a warm and happy little home, their beautiful campus, and the transportation infrastructure that brought them all the way to Tsinghua. My aim was for students to realize that civil engineering is so intertwined with our daily lives and it's as important as water and air to mankind. Although we do not think much of it, civil engineering is inseparable to our modern lives." In this way, bit by bit, Professor Nie's lectures have attracted young students. "I hope these two courses will become lifelong memories of civil engineering students in Tsinghua University." Professor Nie said.

Translation and revision | Alexis See Tho

Image | Li Na

11月7日

文字 | 杨晨晞

图片 | 赵存存、郭祥

假如清华只有 100 个本科生

穿梭于上下课拥堵的车道间，面对食堂窗口前长长的队伍不由踟蹰……每一个清华学生，总是不断在周围追求卓越的人群中找到认同感、归属感，又难免有自己心中的小小迷茫。假如，清华只有 100 个本科生，每个清华“小本”又应该怎样在这 100 人中发现自己呢？

假如清华只有 100 个本科生，他们会是这样的组成：100 人中会有 68 位男生，32 位女生。而按照学科分类，理科生 13 人，文科生 22 人，工科生 65 人；根据招生类型，则有 1 位来自飞行员班、1 位文体特长生、1 位来自港澳台地区、7 位艺术特长生、4 位国防或定向生、10 位保送生、21 位自主招生生源和 55 位统招生。从地区来看，西部有 21 人、中部 30 人、东部 47 人、港澳台地区 1 人、外国 1 人。

多样而丰富的构成，使得清华学生的属性更加多元，各具特色又不乏共性的学生一起在园子里成长，产生的奇妙的化学反应给清华增添了独特的色彩。

假如清华只有 100 个本科生，他们会做些什么呢？

100 人中 61 人每周做作业和预习的时间超过 10 小时；在每周课程拓展学习时间方面，20 人超过 10 小时，其中 9 人超过 15 小时。本科生中，12 人每周投入课外学术科研活动超过 10 小时，其中 8 人超过 15 小时。每 4 个本科生中，有 1 个同学修读双学位。每学年，有 4 人读过 20 本以上教科书，有 8 人读过 20 本以上专业专著，有 4 人读过 20 本以上文学作品。每学年都有 11 位本科生参加海外交流。

学习是清华学生课余时间的第一首选。是课上课下的双重努力，使得他们能够不断刷新、提升自己的专业素养。学术和科研占据了清华本科生大量的时间，而这些精力的投入也使得他们能在知识的海洋中尽情畅游，收获属于自己的成果。

假如清华只有 100 个本科生，他们在学习之余还会做些什么呢？

100 人中投入最多的体育锻炼项目，12 人打篮球、6 人踢足球、29 人跑步、12 人游泳。29 个同学每天使用网络超过 6 小时。58 位同学谈过恋爱。凌晨 12 点，27 人已经安然入睡，凌晨 2 点，5 人还在为梦想奋斗。需要放松的时候，32 人选择运动，32 人选择读书，15 人选择吃东西，10 人选择购物，36 人选择看电影和演出，6 人选择唱歌……每个人的选择不止一种。32 人做一份社工，24 人做两份社工，15 人做三份以上社工。关于未来，有 33 人打算出国学习，56 人想留在国内深造，8 人想工作，1 人想创业，还有两人继续寻觅。

学习之外，清华学生还有着充实和精彩的课余生活。清华足够大，给你广阔的舞台，每个人都把自己的时间献给了自己最热爱的事情，满怀期许，朝着想成为的那个自己努力奋进。

你，是否在这 100 人中找到了自己的影子呢？

创意及数据来源：

“小五爷园”微信公众号

If Tsinghua Had Only 100 Undergraduates

Caught between the congested lanes before and after class, faced with the long hungry queues in the cafeterias.... every Tsinghua student is looking for a sense of identity and belonging. Inevitably, there are also times when one feels lost. If Tsinghua had only 100 undergraduates, then how can each of them find themselves amidst the many?

If Tsinghua had only 100 undergraduates, they would be like this: There would be 68 boys and 32 girls. There would be 13 science students, 22 humanities students and 65 engineering students. 1 would be from the aviation class. 1 would be a literature, musical or sports talent, 1 would be from the Hong Kong, Macao and Taiwan regions, 7 would be art talents, 4 would be students especially trained for national defense, 10 would be students recommended for immediate admission, 21 would have gone through self-admission and 55 students would have been admitted through the traditional way. Geographically, 21 students would be from Western China, 30 would be from Central China, 47 would be from the East, 1 would be from the Hong Kong, Macao and Taiwan regions and 1 would be from overseas.

Tsinghua students are certainly all about diversity. Despite their rich backgrounds, they seek common grounds while putting aside differences. Their energy and relationship is like that wonderful chemical reaction or something mystical that links everything together under one name: Tsinghua. The color that they all wear is certainly unique.

If Tsinghua had only 100 undergraduates, what would they do?

61 students would be doing their homework and preview for more than 10 hours per week; 20 people would have spent more than 10 hours to expand their study every week, and 9 people would have surpassed 15 hours. 12 undergraduate students would have spent more than 10 hours per week in extracurricular academic research, 8 of them would have exceeded the 15-hour mark. 1 out of every 4 undergraduates would be studying for a double degree. In each academic year, 4 would have read more than 20 textbooks, 8 would have read more than 20 more professional and academic literature while 4 people would have read more than 20 literary works. Every year, 11 undergraduates would have participated in the overseas exchange program.

During the students' spare time, studying would be their first choice. It is the in class and out class determination and hard work that allows them to continuously refresh and improve their professional quality. Academic and scientific research occupies a large amount of time in Tsinghua. Such energy enables them to swim freely in the sea of knowledge so that they could harvest their own achievements.

If Tsinghua had only 100 undergraduates, what would they do in their spare time?

Most people would be playing sports. 12 would pick basketball, 6 would pick football, 29 would be running and 12 would be swimming. 29 students would surf the net for more than 6 hours per day. 58 students would be going on dates. At midnight, 27 would be asleep. At 2a.m. 5 people would be still fighting for their dreams. When it is time to relax, 32 people would choose to exercise, 32 would pick reading, 15 would eat, 10 would go shopping, 36 would go and watch movies and 6 would sing...Everyone has more than one choice. 32 students would do one type of social work, 24 would go for two and 15 would attend more than 3 social work activities. When talking about the future, 33 would study abroad, 56 would stay in China, 8 would start work, 1 would want to be an entrepreneur and 2 would be still planning their future.

Apart from studying, Tsinghua students have a rich life out of the classroom. Tsinghua is a big stage and everyone is his or her own actor. Whatever you want and love to do, you can go for it.

Now, have you found yourself?

Originality:

WeChat Official Account "xiaowuyeyuanthu"

Translation and revision | Min Weiyuan

Image | Zhao Cuncun, Guo Xiang

11月8日

文字 | 胡颖

图片 | 宋晨

本科教学大家谈

本科教育是大学人才培养的根本，一流本科教育是一流大学的底色。围绕一流本科教学的使命与特点，结合自身从教经历，清华大学航天航空学院党委书记、国家级教学名师获得者、“万人计划”教学名师李俊峰，航天航空学院教授、青年教师教学基本功比赛资深指导教师薛克宗，教育研究院常务副院长史静寰，建筑学院副教授、北京高校青年教师教学基本功比赛一等奖获得者郑晓笛畅谈了自己的感受、体会与思考。

李俊峰表示，自己心目中的一流本科教学应该是学校、院系、教师以培养肩负使命、追求卓越的人为共同目标，三方共促，环环相扣，形成合力。在课堂上，教师们认真对待课程教学，学生主动谋求全面发展，学校全方位关爱学生、积极引导学生成长成才。课堂外，学校始终把教书育人作为发展的第一要务，采取丰富有效的管理措施，不断持续推进改进机制；学校、院系积极回应学生发展的灵活性、多样性需求，以及学生的个性化成长路径。

薛克宗认为，清华的青年教师对教学工作抱有极大的积极性，同时也存在一些问题，包括较少对学生的深入研究、较少对“知识森林”的俯视、较少双向互动，以及较少对批判性思维和创新精神与能力的培养等。清华通过参加和举办青年教师教学基本功比赛，开展广泛深入、反复多次的集体研讨和教学大交流，强调对“教学创新点”的提炼，凸显在教学中引入的新见解、新成果、新材料和新设计，开辟了提升青年教师教学水平的一条新路。

史静寰指出，清华在长期的教育实践过程中，始终坚持以人才培养为根本任务，致力于培养肩负使命、追求卓越的人，使学生具备健全人格、宽厚基础、创新思维、全球视野和社会责任感，实现全面发展和个性发展相结合。2014 年出台的《清华大学关于深化教育教学改革的若干意见》明确提出实施价值塑造、能力培养、知识传授“三位一体”的培养模式。史静寰的党龄和教龄均已有 40 余年，她深感党员与教师这两个角色的初心与使命有着很高的契合度，决心“不忘初心，牢记使命”，不懈践行清华人才培养理念。

郑晓笛说，在哈佛攻读学位时，著名生态学家理查德・福尔曼教授带领学生们在酸果蔓地里打滚，那种与大地融为一体的感觉震撼了她的心灵。因此在设计课的教学中，她特别强调学生对场地的深入调研。参加青年教师基本功比赛，则使她有机会更加全面系统地反思教学本质，推敲讲授内容、逻辑与形式。清华的学生是中国未来重要的设计者与建设者，通过宽口径、国际化、通识教育与专业教育相结合的本科学习，要能既扎根于我国的现状与特点，又敢于挑战世界前沿的研究领域；既脚踏实地，又具有家国情怀与国际视野。为了实现这样的培养目标，年轻的郑晓笛正在教书育人的道路上不断前进。

扫一扫，查看相关专题：

Experts Share Essentials of Undergraduate Teaching at Tsinghua

Undergraduate education is the foundation of talent cultivation; excellent undergraduate education produces top universities. Around the topic of undergraduate teaching and what makes a well-rounded education, four experts in the field of education share from their experiences and their thoughts on teaching as a mission. Li Junfeng is the party secretary of the School of Aerospace Engineering at Tsinghua, a recognized state-level teacher and a recipient of a teaching award from China's education ministry; Xue Kezong is a professor in the School of Aerospace Engineering at Tsinghua and an advisor of young teachers' education skills competitions; Shi Jinghuan is the Executive Vice-Dean of the Institute of Education at Tsinghua; Zheng Xiaodi is an associate professor in the School of Architecture at Tsinghua and first prize winner of the Beijing Universities Young Teachers' Education Skills Competition.

Li Junfeng shares that to him, the university, departments and teachers should work together toward a common goal in a first-class university, cultivating students who shoulder the historical responsibility and pursue excellence. In the classroom, teachers ought to take their courses seriously, while students should proactively pursue overall development in their education. Outside the classroom, the university must consider teaching and educating its people a top priority and adopt effective measures to improve management of the university. The university and respective departments should actively respond to constant changes in students' development, their diverse needs and their individual needs.

Xue Kezong thinks that the young teachers in Tsinghua are very enthusiastic about teaching. However, there still exist some problems - they need to explore the students' in-depth needs, take an overlook view on the "knowledge forest" , enhance two-way interaction between students and instructors, cultivate the students' critical thinking and innovative abilities etc. Through participating and holding the young teachers' teaching skills competitions, Tsinghua has carried out extensive seminars and interactions about teaching skills between colleagues and teachers from different disciplines, highlighting "innovative points" in teaching, encouraging young teachers to involve new opinions, research advancements, new resources and new designs which obviously enhance their teaching skills.

Shi Jinghuan pointed out that in Tsinghua's long-term plan for education, it has always focused on holistic nurturing of students as its main task. In its mission in education, the university is committed to produce students who possess a good character, a strong intellectual foundation, an innovative mindset, a global perspective and a social responsibility. The goal is to educate well-rounded individuals not just in academics but also as a person. An education reform paper by Tsinghua in 2014 suggested the implementation of a "trinity" cultivation mode that focuses on the shaping of values, the cultivating of skills and the imparting of knowledge. Professor Shi who has been both a Communist Party member and a teacher for more than 40 years thinks that the goals of the party and a teacher are very compatible, in that both calls for emphasis on the mission, which in this case is in cultivating talents and well-rounded individuals in Tsinghua.

Zheng Xiaodi shares that when she was studying at Harvard University, the famous ecologist Richard Forman had his students roll on a cranberry field. The experience of being one-with-nature amazed her. Ever since then, in the design course, she places special emphasis on students' in-depth research of a site. Participating in the young teachers' teaching skills competition gave her an opportunity to reflect on the nature of teaching more thoroughly and systematically, by evaluating her teaching content, logic and form. She believes that Tsinghua's students are important future designers and builders of China. Through broad-based and international education and professional training, they should be able to understand China's status quo and Chinese characteristics, meanwhile has the ability to challenge forefront research fields in the world; These students will possess a pride for the country yet have an international perspective and that is the goal for Zheng Xiaodi's continual work in education.

Translation and revision | Alexis See Tho

Image | Song Chen

11月9日

策划 | 《新清华》编辑部

文字 | 杨晨晞

图片 | 唐蓓蓓、梁晨

绘制 | 杨思维、王汐月、薛雅芳

清华本科生的一天

清华像座城。园子外的人经常好奇，清华的学生每天都是怎样度过的？园子里的人可能也会好奇，不同的人在做些什么事情？不妨跟随我们的镜头，看看清华本科生日常生活的一种“打开方式”吧！

清晨 6：30，迎着朝阳来到草坪旁，或走进各教学楼设立的晨读间，取出一本《大学》与志同道合的小伙伴一同诵读，在书声琅琅中开启元气满满的一天。在听涛园吃完丰盛有营养的早餐后，提前半小时到达图书馆门口等候开馆。尽管才早上 7：30，排队的人早已一百有余，在清华最可怕的事情恐怕是抢不到图书馆的座位了吧。8：00，来到“信号与系统”的课堂上，全新的互动课堂模式下，每当有不懂之处，便用手机发送弹幕至投影仪，所有疑难第一时间得到解决。11：00，来到六教和同学们一起讨论小组作业，专门的讨论教室能将“可变形”的桌椅拼接成圆桌样式，讨论氛围瞬间提升。

中午 12：00，在学堂路上骑着自行车，两侧各类讲座、社团、创新创业活动的展板不断擦肩而过。不经意间瞥见一个吸引人的标题——“全球南方文化浸润项目——去印度，去埃及”，数不胜数的国际交流机会让人心驰神往。13：00，来到紫荆食堂，本科生课程咨询委员会的同学们喜欢在这里进行“头脑风暴”，提炼选题、设计问卷、开展教学调研，推动清华教育教学改革的步伐。14：00，来到游泳馆，在清华体育课的丰富“菜单”中选择了跳水课，站上跳台、克服恐惧，收获的不仅是体育素养，更是体育精神。15：30，到达艺术博物馆参与志愿讲解，与不同背景的观众分享每一件艺术品背后的故事。16：00，利用“开放交流时间”与老师讨论一下实验进展。学校 1000 多位教师公开“开放交流时间”，为同学们提供了与大师、名师面对面交流的机会。

17：00，到实验室投入 SRT（“大学生科研训练计划”）或是兴趣团队的项目研发，培养创新思维，激发创意火花。17：30，来到紫荆操场，伴着夕阳加入阳光长跑的行列，“为祖国健康工作五十年”从不是一句空洞的口号。18：00，来到蒙民伟楼，参与排练以“两弹一星”元勋邓稼先为原型的清华原创话剧《马兰花开》。20：00，回到宿舍，登录全球最大的中文慕课平台——清华大学“学堂在线”进行线上学习，足不出户，全球知识尽在掌握。21：00，走出宿舍，来到紫荆操场享受一场紫荆风情夜——点亮牛奶灯，挥动荧光棒，品尝清茶小点，欣赏吉他伴唱……在游戏中博弈脑力，在欢笑中收获友谊。

当又一个黎明到来，又是全新美好的一天。在这座全球最美校园里，莘莘学子每天的生活忙碌而充实，每一个时间空间都能激发各种志趣，所有人都享受奔涌向前的每分每秒，努力拓展无限精彩的可能。

扫一扫，查看微信长图：

One Day as a Tsinghua Undergraduate Student

Tsinghua is like a city. Many people are curious about what life is like for the Tsinghua students. Many Tsinghua people are also curious about what their peers are up to. So let us take a look and see what 24hr in Tsinghua feels like.

6:30a.m.: I chased the sunrise to do some reading. Along with my classmates, we started to read a classical book together. After a wonderful and rich breakfast at Tingtao Cafeteria, we went to the library 30 minutes before opening time. Despite being only 7:30a.m., over a hundred students have lined up already. Perhaps the most frightening thing at Tsinghua is not being able to find a seat at the library.

8a.m.: I arrived at my "Signal and System" course and under the new interactive classroom model, any problem could be solved with a simple touch of your mobile phone.

11a.m.: I went to Building 6 to have a discussion with my classmates. The foldable tables and chairs can be formed into an oval and certainly any other shape. It was a lively conversation.

Noon: I rode my bike along the campus road and went by numerous banners and posters advertising lectures, associations, panels, exhibitions and other innovative programs. At a glance, I spotted a rather attractive banner that reads— "Tsinghua Global South Culture Immersion Series — Let's go to India and Egypt" . Such countless opportunities for international exchange are simply fascinating.

13:00: I went to Zijing Cafeteria to refine research topic and questionnaire design with members of the Undergraduate Courses Advisory Committee to promote Tsinghua's education reform.

14:00: I went diving at Tsinghua's swimming pool. Tsinghua's PE courses offer students a variety of choices. I learnt to overcome my fears and always sustain Tsinghua sporting spirit.

15:30: I went to the Tsinghua University Art Museum as a volunteer to explain the story behind each artwork to the audience.

16:00: I went to discuss my lab research progress with my teacher during their open office hours. Tsinghua's 1000 plus teachers have provided much convenience for students to seek guidance and advice during such open hours.

17:00: I went to the lab to continue my R&D in the SRT project. This helps me to develop my manipulative ability and innovative capability.

17:30: I went for a run with the sunset at Zijing Playground. "Work healthily for our motherland for at least 50 years" is not an empty slogan.

18:00: I went to Mengminwei Building to rehearse and participate in the original drama named "MaLan Flower Blossoms" , which tells the story of Deng Jiaxian—a leading organizer and key contributor to the Chinese nuclear weapon programs.

20:00: I returned to my dorm and went online to study excellent courses on the platform xuetangx.com. This is the world's largest Chinese MOOC platform for online learning. I have knowledge in the palm of my hands without even leaving my room.

21:00: I walked out of my dorm to enjoy the colors, sights, food and sounds on the Zijing Playground. "Zijing Leisure Night" which held in every Friday evening provide music, games and even open-air movies, friendships are formed amidst the laughter.

After waking up from the previous slumber, a new and wonderful day awaits. In this stunning campus, the daily lives of students are always filled with vitality. Every space inspires interest and everyone is rushing towards something that they enjoy. Every minute...every second...all who call Tsinghua home find the endless opportunities both inspiring and interesting.

Translation and revision | Min Weiyuan

Image | Tang Beibei, Liang Chen

Design | Yang Siwei, Wang Xiyue, Xue Yafang

11 月 10 日

文字 | 张译丹

图片 | 薛雅芳

张仃：先生之风，山高水长

“如果我们把 20 世纪中国文化界比喻为苍穹星空的话，张仃先生无疑是一颗十分辉耀和独特的星辰……”在“张仃百年诞辰纪念展”开幕式上，清华大学艺术博物馆馆长冯远的致辞是这样开始的。明亮而宽敞的展厅中，你可以看到白发苍苍的老人拄着拐杖，在张仃晚期的焦墨山水画前伫立良久，也可以看到背着书包的女孩拿着蜡笔临摹《哪吒闹海》。

2017 年，是原中央工艺美术学院（现清华大学美术学院）院长，杰出的革命文艺家、艺术教育家张仃先生（1917—2010）100 周年诞辰。文艺精神，薪火相传，由中国文联和清华大学联合主办的“张仃百年诞辰纪念展”共分 7 个单元，展出张仃先生 70 余年艺术人生中的历史照片以及漫画、年画、工艺美术、电影动画、焦墨山水画、书法等作品近 300 件，全面呈现了张仃与中国革命和中国文艺事业休戚与共的一生，回望张仃献身中华民族伟大复兴的高远境界，展示他一生对文艺为人民服务创作宗旨的坚守。

张仃是中国具有重要影响力的杰出革命文艺家。20 世纪 30 年代，他创作的漫画是民族解放运动的“潮流”，激励和呼唤中华民族的奋起和解放。在延安，他是解放区“新年画运动”的发起人，他的艺术创作活动为革命事业的发展和艰苦生活岁月增添了文化活力。新中国成立后，张仃参与了新中国国徽和政协会徽的设计工作，成为新中国国家形象艺术设计“顾问”，更在国际舞台上通过艺术传递新中国的魅力。张仃还是中国壁画艺术复兴的举旗人，改革开放之初，他领衔主持的国家重大项目北京首都机场壁画群创作，以多元的艺术创新和民族艺术风格震动海内外，迎来中国文艺的春天。到了晚年，他又在焦墨艺术领域独辟蹊径、别开一派，再创中国焦墨山水画的艺术高峰，让人敬仰。

张仃也是新中国美术教育的开拓者、艺术设计教育的奠基人，他坚守民族文化自信，探索有中国特色艺术教育、艺术思想、艺术风格体系。由他创建和开拓的具有中国特色的艺术设计教育体系和办学思想，不仅影响了一个历史时代和几代学子，对现当代国内外艺术设计教育也具有重要的影响力。张仃是艺术教育界融合古今中外艺术和教育思想精华，勇于实践、探索、创新的一面旗帜。

Revolutionary Artist and Art Educator Zhang Ding: His Spirits Last Forever

The curator of Tsinghua University Art Museum, Mr. Feng Yuan started his speech at the opening ceremony of Zhang Ding's Centennial Birth Exhibition by saying, "If we compare the 20th century Chinese cultural circles to the sky, Mr. Zhang Ding is undoubtedly a sparkling star..." In the grand exhibition hall, you can find old men with rods obsessed by Zhang's coke ink landscape works of his later period; you can also see girls with backpacks imitating Zhang's work of "Prince Nezha's Triumph Against the Dragon King" with crayons.

This year marks the 100th anniversary of the birth of Zhang Ding (1917—2010), curator of Central Academy of Art and Design (Now the Academy of Arts Design, Tsinghua University), outstanding revolutionary artist and art educator. To commemorate and inherit Mr. Zhang's spirits, Tsinghua University and China Federation of Literary and Art Circles hosted the Zhang Ding's Centennial Birth Exhibition. The exhibition is divided into seven parts showing pictures of Mr. Zhang's 70-year art life and nearly 300 pieces art works like cartoons, New Year paintings, arts and crafts, movie animation, coke ink landscape and calligraphy. This exhibition is a comprehensive presentation of Zhang's contribution to Chinese revolution and Chinese arts, highlighting his devotion to the great rejuvenation of the Chinese nation, showing his persistence in creating art works for the general public.

Zhang Ding is an outstanding revolutionary artist. In 1930s, Zhang took part in the national liberation movement with his brush as a weapon, inspired and called for the rise and liberation of the Chinese nation. In Yan'an, he was the initiator of New Year Painting Movement in the liberated area. His artistic creation poured cultural vitality into the development of revolution and hard life. After the founding of New China, Zhang got involved in the design work of the national emblem and the emblem of CPPCC. He became the consultant of art design of new China image and spread the glamour of New China in the global platform. Zhang was also a person who held the banner of art restoration for China's mural painting. After China' s Reform and Opening up, he is the project leader of mural painting artwork in Beijing Capital Airport, which shocked the world with diverse artistic innovation and national art style. In his later years, Zhang developed a new style for coke ink landscape, climbing to yet another pedestal.

At the same time, Mr. Zhang Ding was the pioneer of art education in New China and the founder of art design education. He stuck to the confidence of national culture and explored art education, art thoughts and art style system with distinctive Chinese features. Especially, the art design education system founded by him and his educational ideology not only affect an era and several generations, but also exert vital influence on contemporary art and design education at home and abroad. They combine the tradition and the modern times, China and the western world, art and science, while focusing on practice, exploration and innovation.

Translation and revision | Raj Lamar

Image | Xue Yafang

11月13日

文字 | 梁乐萌

图片 | 梁露文

“八度阳光”创业团队：以光汇电，助力扶贫

“炙热明亮的阳光转化成如蛇般流动的电流，想一想就觉得好美。”2008年，家乡受汶川大地震波及，整个地区停电，正上初一的刘一锋望着夏日灿烂的阳光这样想。

清华大学热能系2013级本科生刘一锋从14岁起就关注太阳能发电问题，他在高中时设计的太阳能房子曾获“中美清洁能源技术竞赛”一等奖第一名。通过“拔尖计划”进入清华大学后，刘一锋在匹配的导师和科研训练项目支持下继续进行太阳能材料研究。

大二时，刘一锋休学成立了“八度阳光”科技有限公司。在与地方负责人的交谈中，刘一锋多次听到他们诉说脱贫的难题。“电作为一种硬通货，可以持续地给老百姓带来收益。”刘一锋意识到，“八度阳光”也可以为产业扶贫贡献一份力量。

2017年4月，“八度阳光”参加了教育部依托中国“互联网+”大学生创新创业大赛举办的“青年红色筑梦之旅”实践活动，带着创业项目来到革命圣地延安实地考察。延安位于黄土高原中南地区，光照资源良好，“阳光扶贫”之路自此起步。

经过多方沟通，“八度阳光”决定将太阳能发电站直接建在扶贫户的屋顶，建站资金主要由企业、政府、银行三方承担。电站建成后，老百姓只需对电池板进行简单护理，将发出的电卖给国家，每年可获得约5000元的电费收益和清洁能源补贴，并可持续获益25年。

“八度阳光”团队已在河北、陕西、安徽等地建立电站，并计划两年内助千户百姓脱贫。同时，他们也在不断进行技术更新。团队研发出的柔性晶硅太阳能材料已达到国际领先、国内最高的22.09%转化效率，拥有核心专利51项，获各类奖项100余项。

2017年8月15日，参加“红色筑梦之旅”的八度阳光等青年创业团队收到了习近平总书记的回信。总书记在信中勉励他们并寄语广大青年：“扎根中国大地了解国情民情，在创新创业中增长智慧才干，在艰苦奋斗中锤炼意志品质，在亿万人民为实现中国梦而进行的伟大奋斗中实现人生价值，用青春书写无愧于时代、无愧于历史的华彩篇章。”

收到总书记的回信，“八度阳光”团队倍受鼓舞。“我们‘90后’终将承担起时代的重任，将梦想变为现实。”刘一锋说。

Eight Sunshine Startup Team: Lighting the Way for Poverty Alleviation

"It's just beautiful to think that bright sunlight could be transformed into electric currents." Liu Yifeng has been thinking about this ever since his hometown was affected by the Wenchuan Earthquake. Electric cut meant that the whole area suffered a blackout.

Liu has been focusing on solar energy and power generation since he was 14 years-old. He won awards in his high school competition with a solar house design as well as coming first in the Sino-American Clean Energy Technology Competition. After being admitted into Tsinghua's Talent Program, he carried out his studies in solar energy and materials with support from his mentor and the research curriculum.

In his second year at Tsinghua, he decided to cease his studies. During this time, he started his company "Beijing Sunlectric Technological Co. LTD" (Eight Sunshine). During his chats with many people, Liu repeatedly heard about the difficulty of poverty alleviation. "Electricity, as a form of hard currency, can continue to bring benefits to the people." Liu realized that his company can offer support and help to alleviate poverty.

In April 2017, The Eight Sunshine Team participated in a practice activity to Yan'an with the theme of "Trip to Realize the Red Dream." It was organized by the Ministry of Education and accompanied with the "Internet+ University Students' Innovative and Entrepreneurship Competition" . Yan'an, located in the heart of the plateau with bountiful sunlight, is where the team's "road to poverty alleviation" began.

After a lot of dialogue, the Eight Sunshine team decided to build a solar power station directly on the roof of those in need. Construction and all related costs were borne by three parties: the company, the government and the banks. After completion, locals are required to simply maintain the power plant then sell the generated electricity back to the government. Annually, they are able to receive 5000 yuan for the electricity along with clean energy subsidies. Such sustainable profit could be continued for 25 years.

the Eight Sunshine team has established power stations in Hebei, Shaanxi and Anhui provinces, and plans to lift thousands of people out of poverty within two years. They are also constantly updating their technology. The team's self-developed flexible crystalline silicon solar material has achieved the highest conversion efficiency in China (22.09%). They have now gained 51 core patents and received more than 100 awards.

On August 15th, 2017, President Xi wrote a reply letter to university students' teams which participated in the "Trip to Realize the Red Dream" , he encouraged them to "firmly plant your feet in our country, to understand the national conditions and know what the people need. Maintain and push your innovative and entrepreneurial spirit and weather through any challenges and struggle that you may face. May you realize your goals and achieve your Chinese dream" .

Liu and his team were deeply inspired by President Xi's reply. "This world will eventually belong to the post-90s generation. It is time to turn this dream into a reality!" said Liu.

Translation and revision | Min Weiyuan

Image | Liang Luwen

11 月 14 日

文字 | 杨鹏成

图片 | 李娜

“赤子初心”致敬党的光辉历史

翻雪山、过草地，一幅幅浮雕将人们引入那段豪迈昂扬的征程；国庆阅兵、山河辽阔，一张张画作描摹出一个伟大复兴的中国……近日，由教育部指导并委托清华大学主办、清华大学马克思主义学院承办的首届全国高校思想政治理论课“赤子初心”大学生艺术作品巡展在清华大学正式启动，青年学子们用绘画、书法、雕塑、工业设计等艺术形式，抒发着他们的“赤子初心”。

此次巡展是 2017 年高校思政课教学质量年工作的重要组成部分，也是高校学生思想政治理论课学习成果展示系列四大主题活动之一，旨在增强学生学习思政课的主动性、积极性，提升学生对思政课的参与度，提高大学生对思政课的获得感。活动共收到全国高校近 600 件参赛作品，经评审遴选出 400 件作品参加展览，其中包括清华大学 2017 年春季学期“中国近现代史纲要”课程上 200 余位同学的课程作业。他们经过 16 周的课程学习后，以绘画、书法、雕塑、染织、陶瓷、海报、工业设计、诗歌和摄影等多样的艺术形式，编织成一幅幅栩栩如生的历史画卷。活动后续还将赴浙江、陕西等地高校巡回展览。

在贯彻落实全国高校思想政治工作会议精神、提高高校思想政治理论课教学质量的时代主题背景下，教育部社科司指导清华大学等高校将“全国思想政治理论课学生艺术作品巡展”作为探索“因材施教”新模式、展现思政课独特魅力、创建全国高校思想政治理论课文化平台的重要创新举措，通过这一新型的大学生思政课文化艺术创作活动，推动大学生日常思想政治教育与思政课建设深度融合。

自 2011 年以来，清华大学马克思主义学院已连续举行六期思政课学生艺术作品展，每年的作品展围绕一个主题进行创作，六届思政课大学生艺术作品展的主题分别是 2011 年“百年印象”、2012 年“人间正道”、2013 年“寻梦中国”、2014 年“峥嵘岁月”、2015 年“山河浩气”和 2016 年“雄关漫道”。每一年新入学的学生都会参与到这类艺术创作中，用实际行动向党的百年光辉历史致敬。

Art Exhibition Pays Respects to Party History

One after another relief sculpture take its observers over snow-capped mountains and grass plains, depicting Long March, the heroic journey undertaken by Communist Party members decades ago; paintings after paintings portray China's national rejuvenation through a military parade on National Day, and the country's vast rivers and mountains. These are some artworks recently displayed in a national college art tour that started-up in Tsinghua.

The exhibition showcases the works of students from ideological and political theory courses throughout the country for the first time. The art tour was commissioned by the Ministry of Education of China and organized by Tsinghua University's School of Marxism. Varied art forms - painting, calligraphy, sculpture and industrial design, were produced by students under the theme "The Pure and Original Hearts" (Chizi Chuxin), a popular phrase used to remind the Party to stay true to its founding mission.

The art exhibition tour is an important part of increasing the teaching excellence of ideological and political courses in 2017. It is also one of the four major activities under an initiative to increase students' participation and enthusiasm in learning Marxist ideology and politics courses, and enhance their learning experience in such courses. The activity received almost 600 entries from colleges and universities across China and 400 works were selected by judges to be a part of the art tour.

Some works included are class projects of 200 Tsinghua students from the "Introduction to Modern Chinese History" class in Spring 2017 semester. After 16 weeks of class, the students weaved Chinese history into vivid pictures in diverse art forms — painting, calligraphy, sculpture, weaving, ceramics, posters, industrial design, poetry and photography. The traveling exhibition will make stopovers at Zhejiang, Shaanxi and colleges and universities in other provinces.

Under the theme of carrying out the spirit of the National Conference on Ideological and Political Work in Colleges and Universities, and to improve teaching quality of ideological and political courses in tertiary education institutions, the Social Science Division of the Ministry of Education guided Tsinghua and other universities to use activities such as the art exhibition tour to tweak teaching methods according to students' needs.

This new model aims to show the unique charm of ideological and political courses. Such activities are also useful for the creation of a cultural platform of national ideological and political theory courses. Through these new activities for undergraduate ideological and political education classes, culture and arts can be integrated and used to promote daily ideological and political education of college students.

Since 2011, the School of Marxism at Tsinghua University has held six consecutive art exhibitions showcasing thematic art works of students of ideological and political courses. Every year, new students participate in such art creation, paying tribute to the party's glorious history with manifest representations.

Translation and revision | Alexis See Tho

Image | Li Na

11 月 15 日

文字 | 左烜晅

图片 | 李娜

筑梦成网，织就光明未来

电力是现代文明的标志之一。而在位于四川西部的阿坝州壤塘县宗科乡，全乡供电主要依靠一个小水电站，由于电力质量不稳定，宗科乡中心校的许多电教设备无法正常使用。学校晚间没有电力供应，给学生的学习和生活带来诸多不便。

2017 年夏天，经过十余天的紧张施工，由清华大学电机系、工业工程系、计算机系学生组成的“梦之网”实践支队终于为宗科中心校送去了一份光明。

4 年，7 所小学，230 余块光伏电池板，70 余名队员，累计建设共 65 千瓦的光伏微电网，超过 600 名藏乡师生受益——“运用专业知识为国家带来一些改变”，这正是“梦之网”实践支队的初心。

2014 年 3 月，植根于清华人的社会责任和专业梦想，电机系的同学们发起成立了“梦之网”实践支队，期望通过搭建新能源微电网，为国家无电、缺电的偏远地区提供必要供电。

第一次到达海拔 3800 米的玉龙西小学时，队员们的高原反应非常强烈，加上严酷的天气考验，“梦之网”工程变得非常困难。在雨雪中，队员们一个一个地整理冰冷的设备，扛着五六十斤的太阳能电池板爬上屋顶。就在队员们最疲惫的时候，一群藏族老乡送来了热腾腾的酥油茶，让他们感受到了浓浓温情。奋战 10 天后，“梦之网”计划的第一批同学终于完成了通电工程。

此后三年里，“梦之网”支队继续奉献爱心，将光明带到了四川省甘孜藏族自治州雅江县木绒乡新卫村小学、阿坝藏族羌族自治州阿坝县柯河乡中心校、新疆喀什地区塔什库尔干县马尔洋乡中心校等七所小学，建设共 65 千瓦的光伏微电网，直接惠及 600 余名师生。

“梦之网”支队还通过清华校友资源积极联合社会爱心企业和人士，累计争取到社会公益赞助 100 余万元，总计 80 余名清华师生参与其中。

“我们希望能改变一代人的生活方式与观念，而不仅仅是一套设备、一点微光。”这是“梦之网”队员们的心声。

梦，终会醒来；但梦想，只要开始，便永远不会停止。

Dream Grid, Building a Bright Future

Electricity is the symbol of modern civilization, but in Zongke Town, in Western Sichuan, the whole town relies on a small hydropower station for power supply, while the power quality is not stable. Many audio-visual devices in the town's central school are out of service, and the school is short of power supply at night, which exerts a lot inconvenience on the study and lives of the students.

After days of efforts, a group of Tsinghua students from the "Dream Grid" team built up the brightness for the Central School of Zongke Town.

4 years, 7 primary schools, more than 230 pieces of photovoltaic panels, more than 70 team members have built up 65kw of photovoltaic micro grids, benefiting over 600 Tibetan teachers and students.

"Using our knowledge to make a difference for the country." This is the original intention of "Dream Grid" .

In March 2014, shouldering social responsibility and professional dreams of Tsinghua's electrical engineering discipline, 9 students in the Department of Electrical Engineering formed a team, "Dream Grid" , expecting to provide necessary power supply in remote areas by building a new-energy micro grid.

At Yulongxi Primary School which is 3,800 meters above sea level, the team suffered an intense altitude reaction when they first arrived. What's worse, affected by the harsh weather, the "Dream Grid" project endured a tough start. In the freezing rain and snow, the team carefully sorted out all the devices, moving fifty or sixty jin of solar panels to the roofs. When they were exhausted, Tibetan villagers came with hot butter tea, which warmed their body and heart. Eventually, after 10 days of hard work, the first members of "Dream Grid" completed the power-supply project.

In the next 3 years, "Dream Grid" continued to beam the light to seven primary schools and built up 65kw of photovoltaic micro grids in areas such as Xinwei Village, Kehe Town, Maeryang Town... benefiting more than 600 teachers and students.

"Dream Grid" unites social volunteers with Tsinghua alumni resources, accumulating welfare funding of more than 1 million yuan from enterprises and persons. A total of more than 80 Tsinghua teachers and students have joined the project.

As one team member said, "We want to change the way people live and think, not just a set of devices or a glimmer of light."

Natural dream will eventually wake up, but people's dream, as long as it begins, will never stop.

Translation and revision | Raj Lamar

Image | Li Na

11月16日

文字 | 刘书田

图片 | 任帅

清华大学张学工团队入选首批“人类细胞图谱计划”项目

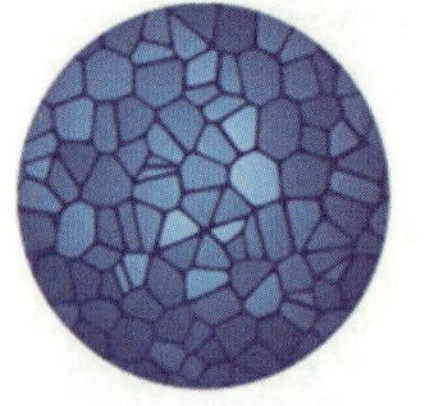

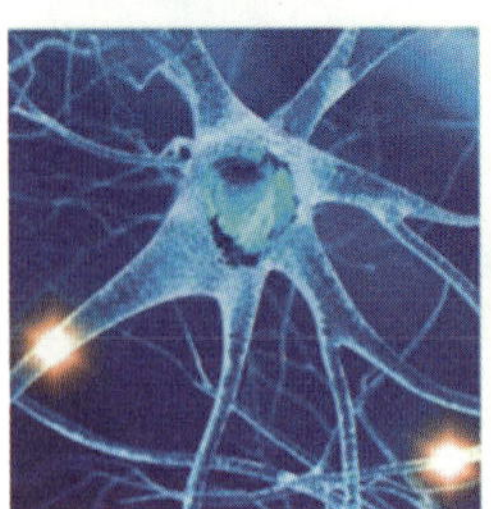

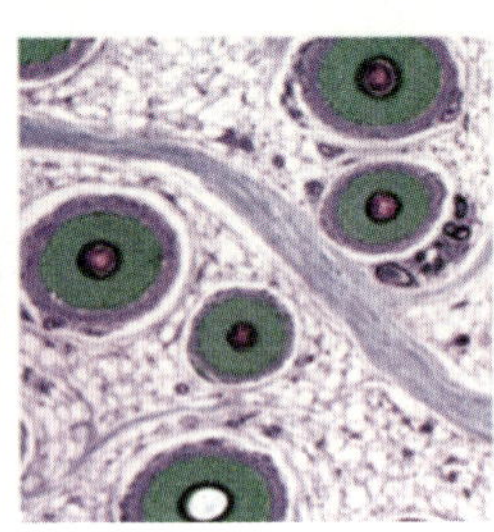

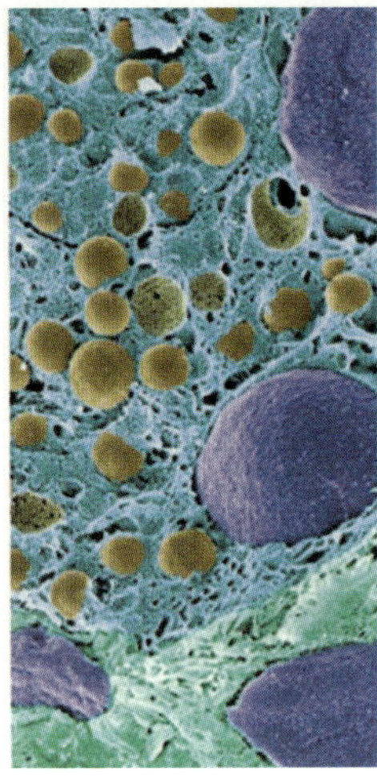

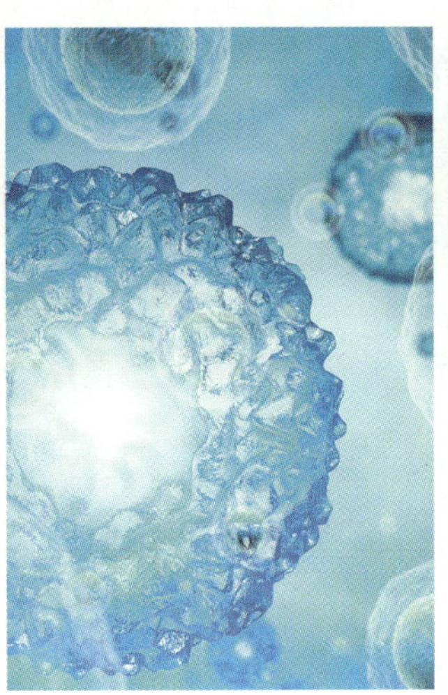

美国太平洋时间2017年10月16日，与“人类基因组计划”相媲美的“人类细胞图谱计划”首批拟资助的38个项目正式公布。清华大学教授张学工负责的项目作为其中唯一一个由中国科学家承担的项目，从全球范围内征集的近500个项目中脱颖而出。

“人类细胞图谱计划”是一项大型国际合作项目，致力于建立一个健康人体包含的所有细胞参考图谱，包括各种细胞类型的基因组、转录组、表观基因组特性以及它们的数目、位置、相互关联等。该计划是由Facebook创始人马克·扎克伯格和妻子普莉希拉·陈成立的CZI（Chan Zuckerberg Initiative）基金会发起并资助的，通过全世界范围内优秀的生物学家、技术专家、病理学家、医学专家、计算机科学家、统计学家等共同讨论提出的一个具有划时代意义的大科学项目。

目前的项目是一年期的预研究，肩负着探索整个计划如何开展的重任。这批项目的主要任务是建立完成整个图谱所需各种技术和工具的基准参照。“现在是一个宏大的计划的开始，是整个计划中非常激动人心的时刻。”张学工说。

从十几年前起，张学工及其团队便开始把研究重点放在转录组分析的生物信息学方法和对各种转录组的分析上，在用RNA测序进行转录组分析方面发展了一系列生物信息学方法，并在国际同行中得到了很多有效应用。

对人类各种类型的细胞进行单细胞测序研究是“人类细胞图谱计划”中的核心内容，生物信息学分析在其中肩负着至关重要的作用。由于单细胞测序技术发展迅速，这一方面极大地促进了整个领域的发展，另一方面也导致目前一些分析方法缺乏系统深入的推敲。张学工在此次申请中提出，在“人类细胞图谱计划”中对差异分析、聚类等核心问题的生物信息学方法进行系统的研究，这是整个计划中非常重要的基础工作。

CZI基金会组织多位遗传学家、基因组学家、分子生物学家、医学家、细胞生物学家、生物化学家、系统生物学家和生理学家对近500份申请进行了评审，筛选了全球38个项目进行首批资助。作为中国目前唯一入选的团队负责人，张学工表示，希望能够不辜负大家的期望，在这个重大的国际合作研究计划中做出应有的贡献，也希望通过这个预研究项目，将来能够引导更多中国团队加入“人类细胞图谱计划”的研究。

Zhang Xuegong Team of Tsinghua University Is Selected in the "Human Cell Atlas" Program

On October 16th, 2017, PST, the 38 projects to be funded by CZI (Chan Zuckerberg Initiative) as the first batch of projects in the Human Cell Atlas (HCA) program were announced. The importance of the HCA program is believed to be comparable to that of the human genome project (HGP). The project of Dr. Zhang Xuegong, professor of Tsinghua University, is the only project led by a Chinese scientist, selected from nearly 500 applications worldwide.

The Human Cell Atlas Project is a large international collaborative project initiated by CZI, founded by Mark Zuckerberg, the founder of Facebook and his wife Priscilla Chan. It is dedicated to create a set of reference maps of all cells of a healthy human being. The maps will include genomic, transcriptomic and epigenomic characteristics of various cell types, as well as their quantity, location and interrelationships, etc.

The current projects are one-year pilot-studies with the task of exploring how the entire project shall be carried out. The main task of these projects is to establish benchmarks for multiple technologies and tools needed for building the atlas. "It is the beginning of a grand plan and a very exciting time." said Zhang Xuegong.

From more than a decade ago, Dr. Zhang and his team began to focus their research on bioinformatics methods for transcriptome analyses and their applications on various types of transcriptomes. A series of bioinformatics methods have been developed for transcriptome analyses using RNA sequencing, which have been widely applied by many scientists in the world.

Single-cell sequencing of various types of human cells is at the core of the HCA program, where bioinformatics analysis plays a crucial role. Single-cell sequencing technology has developed very rapidly in recent years. The rapid development has greatly promoted the progress of entire field. But on the other hand, methods rushed for analyzing the generated data are lacking systematic and in-depth development. Dr. Zhang proposed in his project to systematically study the involved bioinformatics methods especially those for differential analysis and clustering. This is of crucial importance for the whole program.

The current batch of projects were selected among nearly 500 applications after being reviewed by a number of geneticists, genomics, molecular biologists, medical scientists, cell biologists, biochemists, systems biologists and physiologists, Dr. Zhang said that as the only team in China that has been selected, he hopes to live up to the expectations from the community, and hopes that this pilot project will make valuable contributions to this major international cooperative program and will be able to guide more Chinese teams to join the effort in the future.

Image | Ren Shuai

11 月 17 日

文字 | 梁乐萌

图片 | 郭祥

清华大学第一级学生：为人垂一范，为学报国恩

1925 年 9 月，清华学校如往年一样举行秋季始业式——入学典礼。与以往不同，这次参加始业式的学生中除了留美预备部的学生外，还有新设大学部和研究院招收的第一批学生。

在此之前，清华一直是为接受庚款的学生专设的留美预备学校。改办大学的计划最早由清华学校第二任校长周诒春于 1916 年提出，他主张摆脱对“西人所提供的学术刺激”的依赖，实现学术独立，申请呈送外交部不到一月即获批准。1925 年，清华学校设立大学部，并成立国学研究院，向完全大学过渡。当年 9 月，清华招收大学普通科一年级学生 132 人，实际报到 93 人，即为清华大学历史上的第一级学生。

相对于留美预备部的旧制生，大学部所招学生被称为新制生。按照当时的习惯，新制生按入学年代的先后，依次被称为第一级、第二级……直到西南联大时期入学的学生，才改为按毕业年代称“×××× 级”。

作为清华完全以培养本国人才为目的接收的第一批学生，“清华第一级”人才济济、名家辈出。文有中国最早从事外国文学研究的李健吾、最早把毛泽东著作译成英文的翻译家许孟雄；理有中科院学部委员周同庆、袁翰青、夏坚白、张大煜；“两弹一星功勋奖章”获得者王淦昌也是清华大学第一级学生。

1925 年，中国仍处在北洋政府统治和帝国主义侵略的双重黑暗之中。身处特殊历史时期，清华大学第一级学生多有着强烈的爱国热忱和使命感、责任感。韦杰三在“三·一八”惨案中牺牲，临终犹言：“我心甚安，但中国快要强起来呀！”如今，在清华校河畔“三·一八”烈士墓址旁，仍矗立着刻有他名字的大理石断碑。王淦昌受命参加研制原子弹时铿锵有力地说：“我愿以身许国！”施士元谢绝恩师居里夫人的挽留，执意回国任教，后来的中科院学部委员中有十几名是他的学生，其爱徒吴健雄更被誉为“美籍华裔的居里夫人”。

清华第一级学生身负民族危难的十字架，怀抱“科学救国、教育兴国”之理想；他们视学习为追求科学真理，顽强而不畏一切地走到底，攀登学术高峰奋斗不止。“长将一寸身，衔木到终古。”王淦昌近 80 岁转向氟化氪激光聚变研究，年届 90 岁又关注防雷科技，热情支持激光引雷的基础研究。

第一级学生有着很强的服务精神和团结能力，对学校更是爱之甚笃而望之弥切，积极参与清华初期的改革。他们自言：“语其内，则清华生命之创新，吾级应负重责；语其外，则中国独立教育之得失，亦将取征于吾人。”

为学报国，为人垂范。作为清华学生的杰出代表和后人的光辉榜样，清华第一级学生的优秀品质届届相传、发扬光大，成为清华宝贵的精神财富。

First Class of Tsinghua: for Oneself, for Others and for the Nation

In September 1925, the Tsinghua School held its autumn opening event — Freshman Orientation Day. In contrast to the past, students who took part in this event not only included those bound for studies in the United States of America but also the first group of students for Tsinghua's new departments and graduate school.

Back then, Tsinghua was a preparatory school. Mr Zhou Yichun, the second Dean of Tsinghua School, proposed changes back in 1916. He advocated for academic independence and stimulus and found his proposal approved by the Ministry of Foreign Affairs in less than a month. In 1925, Tsinghua established its College Department and started its research institute on Chinese Learning before transitioning into a university. In September of that year, Tsinghua admitted 132 students. 93 students showed up and they became the first batch of students for Tsinghua University.

Compared students in the old Tsinghua program, these new enrolments were called the new students. Back then, students were allocated into their classes based on the year of their admission. So they were named First Class, Second Class etc. It was not until National Southwest Associated University that students were allocated into classes based on their graduation year.

Many alumni of the First Class were very well-known. Filled with experts and talents in their respective fields, you have Li Jianwu, the first to study foreign literature in China. Xu Mengxiong was the first to translate the works of Chairman Mao into English. You also have other big names and academicians such as Zhou Tongqing, Yuan Hanqing, Xia Jianbai and Zhang Dayu. Wang Ganchang, the recipient of the "Two Bombs and One Satellite Meritorious Award" was also from the First Class of Tsinghua.

In 1925, China was faced with imperialist aggression. During such historical period, the First Class of Tsinghua had a strong sense of patriotism and sense of responsibility. Wei Jiesan, who perished during the March 18th Massacre, uttered these words before he passed away: "I feel very peaceful but China, rise up and be strong!" A marble tablet, with inscriptions of his name, still stands today in the Tsinghua Campus. When Wang Ganchang was appointed to participate in the research and development of China's atomic bomb, he said "I will give myself to my nation!" Shi Shiyuan declined Madame Curie's offer and decided to return to China to take up teaching. His student Wu Chien-Shiung was dubbed "the Chinese Madame Curie" .

The First Class of Tsinghua found themselves at the crossroads. They embraced the notion of "save the nation with science and revive our motherland with education." They saw learning as the pursuit of scientific truth. They saw learning as ever-lasting with no expiration date. When Wang Ganchang was about 80 years old, he turned his attention to laser fusion research and at the age of 90, he embarked on his research of lightening protection technology.

These students were very dedicated and united. They participated actively in the reforms of the school. They said: "We should shoulder the responsibility of both Tsinghua's innovation and China's independent education."

Learn to contribute to the country and become a model, this is what Tsinghua spirit requires. The First Class of Tsinghua provided a shining example for all to follow. Their outstanding qualities have been passed on. This precious Tsinghua spirit must and will always be uphold by all.

Translation and revision | Min Weiyuan

Image | Guo Xiang

11月20日

供稿 | 地学系

图片 | 任左莉

清华领衔团队斩获世界高性能计算最高奖“戈登·贝尔”奖，创新战略 + 学科交叉打造一流超算平台

2017 年 11 月 17 日，在美国丹佛举行的全球超级计算大会（SC2017）上，由清华大学地球系统科学系付昊桓副教授等共同领导的团队所完成的“非线性地震模拟”荣获“戈登·贝尔”奖（ACM Gordon Bell Prize），实现了中国在此奖项上自 2016 年首次获奖后的蝉联夺冠。

设立于 1987 年的“戈登·贝尔”奖是世界高性能计算应用的最高奖。它由美国计算机协会（Association for Computing Machinery, ACM）于每年 11 月在召开的超算领域顶级会议上颁发，奖励时代前沿的并行计算研究成果，特别是高性能计算创新应用的杰出成就。

付昊桓领衔的另一项工作“全球气候模式的高性能模拟”，也成功入围今年“戈登·贝尔”奖的最终决选。这两项工作，与 2016 年 11 月 25 日中国首获“戈登·贝尔”奖的获奖论文“千万核可扩展大气动力学全隐式模拟”一样，都是以“神威·太湖之光”作为重要依托平台，“神威·太湖之光”也由此成为世界高性能计算最高奖的孵化平台。

“四连冠”，彰显硬件绝对实力

位于国家超级计算无锡中心的“神威·太湖之光”由清华大学负责运营。它的峰值计算能力为每秒 12.5 亿亿次，持续计算能力为每秒 9.3 亿亿次。

在 2017 年 11 月 13 日发布的最新一期全球超级计算机 500 强的榜单中，“神威·太湖之光”连续第四次夺冠；中国的超算上榜总数又一次超过美国，夺得第一。这既表明了“神威·太湖之光”的绝对实力，也再一次彰显了中国在超算硬件领域的世界领先地位。

多学科交叉，打造神威国产软件生态

2015 年夏天，当清华大学的团队进驻到还未完全建成的国家超级计算无锡中心时，冲击世界顶尖的“戈登·贝尔”奖似乎还是个遥远的梦想。

“神威·太湖之光”全国产的机器设计，以全新的片上融合异构的众核芯片，带来了性能与能耗效率的大幅提升。但是，与众不同的硬件架构，也意味着所有主流的科学计算和工程计算软件都无法在这台新的超级计算机上直接运行，软件生态相对匮乏。

相对落后的软件生态，对于致力于神威平台的应用软件团队，既是挑战，更是机遇。2015 年的 7 月，无锡最热的时节，来自清华大学、北京师范大学以及国家海洋局第一海洋研究所的三十多位老师和同学，面对模式上百万行的计算程序，悄然展开了国产应用软件研发的第一次征程。

三个月的集中研发，使团队中计算机专业的同学们逐渐成为大气、海洋模拟的专家，而地学专业的同学们也逐渐成为国产神威平台的专业“码农”，最终造就了三个月完成百万行代码移植、十万多行代码重构及重新设计的奇迹。事后看来，这一批计算机与地学交叉型人才的培养和形成，成了日后清华团队在神威平台上应用成果开花结果的关键。

经过了一年多的集中开发，在国内几十所大学及研究机构的通力合作下，到 2017 年，良好的神威国产软件生态终于形成，拥有超过十几种可扩展至全机的科学及工程应用软件。

清华团队中的一部分老师同学继续与北京师范大学和山东大学组成联合研究团队，致力于大气模式在神威平台上的重构设计与大规模优化计算；而另一些老师同学则与山东大学、南方科技大学和中国科学技术大学等单位形成了一支新的交叉队伍，短短几个月的时间，就完成了基于“神威・太湖之光”的地震模拟全过程软件平台。

方法创新，多应用世界领先

荣获今年“戈登・贝尔”奖的《基于“神威・太湖之光”的 18.9-PFlops 非线性地震模拟：实现对 18Hz 和 8m 情景的描述》，由清华大学地球系统科学系、计算机系与山东大学、南方科技大学、中国科学技术大学、国家并行计算机工程技术研究中心和国家超级计算无锡中心等单位共同完成。团队中共有 5 人来自清华大学。

地震模拟工具可以实现对地震发生过程的重现与模拟，是科学家理解地质构造与地震发生与传播原理的重要工具，对于降低与预防地震灾害所带来的巨大损失具有重要作用。地震模拟工具还可以与其他技术相结合，用于对地震高发区的基础设施进行合理规划与设计，以提升城市规划的安全性，防患于未然。

基于“神威・太湖之光”强大的计算能力，研究团队成功地设计实现了高可扩展性的非线性大地震模拟工具。此工具实现了高达 18.9-PFlops 的非线性地震模拟，是国际上首次实现如此大规模、高分辨率、高频率的非线性可塑性地震模拟；还首次实现了对唐山大地震（M7.8, 1976）发生过程的高分辨率精确模拟，可以更好地理解唐山大地震所造成的影响，对未来的地震预防预测研究具有重要的借鉴意义。

此外，以付昊桓为第一作者的另一入围研究“全球气候模式的高性能模拟”，则采用了从进程到线程的一整套优化方案，对具有海量代码任务的经典大气模式 CAM 进行了重构设计，将其成功地移植到国产平台上，并利用数百万核规模对 25 公里分辨率实现了每天计算 3.4 年的模拟。对模式的动力框架部分，更是实现了千万核规模下 750 米的分辨率，以及 3.3-PFlops 的计算性能。基于该成果，团队实现了对卡特里娜飓风整个生命周期的准确模拟。该工作的成功完成，对未来面向 E 级（百亿亿次）计算系统的应用开发具有重要借鉴意义，并在程序设计、优化方法等方面提供了宝贵经验。

创新驱动发展，助力新时代中国特色社会主义伟大建设

在 2016 年 11 月 25 日与“戈登・贝尔”奖获奖项目“千万核可扩展大气动力学全隐式模拟”团队中清华大学成员的座谈中，邱勇校长指出，“神威・太湖之光”及其应用研究，是清华大学服务国家创新驱动发展战略的重要体现，是学校交叉学科发展的优秀成果。

未来，清华大学的科研团队将继续依托“神威・太湖之光”，在地球系统模拟、生物医药、机器学习、航空航天、工业制造、新材料和新能源等多学科领域深入开展高性能计算应用研究，在建设世界一流大学、实施十九大报告提出的创新驱动发展战略、加快建设创新型国家等方面发挥更加积极的作用。

A Tsinghua-led Team Won "Gordon Bell Prize" (the World's Most Prestigious Award in High Performance Computing)

On November 17th, 2017, a Chinese team won the 2017 ACM Gordon Bell Prize at the Supercomputing Conference (SC2017) held in Denver, USA. The winning research was entitled "18.9-PFlops Nonlinear Earthquake Simulation on Sunway TaihuLight: Enabling Depiction of 18-Hz and 8-Meter Scenarios" , led by Associate Professor Fu Haohuan in the Department of Earth System Science, Tsinghua University, with collaborators from six institutes. After winning this award for the first time in 2016, Chinese scientists achieved a consecutive winning of this outstanding award.

Founded in 1987, the Gordon Bell Prize is known as the most significant award in high-performance computing (HPC). It was presented annually by the Association for Computing Machinery (ACM) at the top conference in the field of supercomputing in November to reward cutting-edge parallel computing research, especially the outstanding achievements of innovative applications based on high-performance computing facilities.

Besides the work that won the Gordon Bell Prize, another work led by Fu Haohuan, "Redesigning CAM-SE for Petascale Performance" , was also selected as one of the three finalists of the Gordon Bell Prize. the Sunway TaihuLight supercomputer has become the incubator of the Gordon Bell Prize.

"Four consecutive championships", highlighting the absolute strength of the hardware

Located at the National Supercomputer Center in Wuxi, Jiangsu, China, Sunway TaihuLight is a Chinese homegrown supercomputer operated by Tsinghua University with over 10.5 M heterogeneous cores. This machine has a peak performance of 125 PFlops and a sustained performance of 93 PFlops.

In the latest release of the Top 500 List (November 13, 2017) that ranks the world's most powerful supercomputing facilities, Sunway TaihuLight ranked No.1 for the fourth consecutive time. China surpassed the United States once again in the total number of supercomputers of the TOP 500 List, highlighting China's leading position in the world for supercomputer hardware.

Multidisciplinary efforts, to create Sunway software ecosystem

When the research team from Tsinghua first arrived at the National Supercomputing Center in Wuxi in the summer of 2015, the Gordon Bell Prize seemed to be an unreachable dream.

The complete homemade processor design of Sunway TaihuLight has brought significant improvement in both computing performance and power efficiency. However, its unique hardware architecture also means that all major scientific and engineering computing software cannot be used on this supercomputer directly. The software ecosystem for the homemade hardware was very limited.

The limited software ecosystem brings challenges but also opportunities for the application software development team for Sunway architecture. In July, 2015, the hottest season of Wuxi, over 30 professors and students from Tsinghua university, Beijing Normal University, and the First Institute of Oceanography of National Bureau of Oceanography, started to work with the migrations of millions lines of code in the climate models to this homegrown system. A challenging journey toward developing an ecosystem for the Sunway architecture has begun since then.

After 3 months of intensive research and development, the students majored in computer science became experts of atmospheric and ocean simulation, while the students majored in geosciences also gradually became professional programmers of Sunway TaihuLight. Finally they created the miracle of migrating millions lines of code and refactoring hundreds of thousands lines of code. In hindsight, the training of a group of young multi-disciplinary talents during the three months was the key to the successful application by the multi-institute team on Sunway TaihuLight.

After more than one year of application development, with the joint efforts of many universities and research institutions in China, a reasonable application software ecology is formed, with over ten science and engineering application software packages that can scale to the full machine with over 10 million cores.

A part of Tsinghua team continued to form a joint team with Beijing Normal University and Shandong University, and continued to work on the refactoring and redesign of the atmospheric model for Sunway TaihuLight. Meanwhile, another part of the Tsinghua team formed a joint team with Shandong University, Southern University of Science and Technology, and University of Science and Technology of China, and accomplished the earthquake simulation software framework on Sunway TaihuLight within three months.

Innovative methods with multiple world-leading applications

The research project named "18.9-PFlops Nonlinear Earthquake Simulation on Sunway TaihuLight: Enabling Depiction of 18-Hz and 8-Meter Scenarios" was awarded the 2017 ACM Gordon Bell Prize. This was a joint project by the Department of Earth System Science and the Department of Computer Science and Technology, Tsinghua University, and researchers from Shandong University, the Southern University of Science and Technology, the University of Science and Technology of China, the National Research Center of Parallel Computer Engineering and Technology, China, and the National Supercomputing Center, Wuxi, China.

Earthquake simulation tools can reproduce and simulate the process of earthquakes. It is an important method for scientists to understand the principles of geology, earthquake occurrence and propagation, and plays a significant role in reducing and preventing the huge losses caused by earthquake disasters. Seismic simulation tools can also be combined with other technologies to rationally design the infrastructure for high-seismic areas, in order to enhance the safety of urban planning.

Based on the powerful computing power of "Sunway TaihuLight" , the research team succeeded in designing and implementing a highly scalable non-linear large-scale earthquake simulation tool. This tool achieves a performance of up to 18.9-PFlops for nonlinear earthquake simulation, and for the first time in the world, achieves such large-scale, high-resolution and high-frequency non-linear plasticity earthquake simulations. It is also the first time to achieve a highly accurate simulation of the Tangshan earthquake (M7.8, 1976), which can help to better understand the impact caused by the Tangshan earthquake and provide insights and reference for future earthquake research.

In addition, the other finalist work, also led by Dr. Fu Haohuan, "Redesigning CAM-SE for Peta-Scale Performance" , applied a full set of optimization methods to refactor and redesign the classical atmospheric model CAM-SE for Sunway TaihuLight. The redesigned version can use up to millions of cores, and achieves a simulation speed of 3.4 SYPD (simulated years per day). The redesigned dynamic core can support a high resolution of 750m, and achieves a computing performance of 3.3-PFlops. Using the redesigned CAM software, the team achieved an accurate simulation of the entire lifecycle of Hurricane Katrina. The successful completion of this work is of great reference significance for future application development of Exa-scale computing systems, and provides valuable experience in programming, optimization methods and so on.

Innovation-driven development helps the great construction of Socialism with Chinese characteristics

On November 25th 2016, during a panel discussion with members who won the 2016 Gordon Bell Prize based on the work titled "a fully implicit solver for atmospheric dynamics" , Qiu Yong, the president of Tsinghua University, pointed out that Sunway TaihuLight and its application research are important demonstration of Tsinghua University's service to national innovation-driven development and an outstanding achievement in the development of interdisciplinary research.

In the future, the research team at Tsinghua University will continue to develop high-performance computing applications in multidisciplinary fields such as earth system simulation, bio-medicine, machine learning, aerospace, industrial manufacturing, new materials and new energy research etc., on Sunway TaihuLight. The supercomputer will play a more active role in helping build world-class universities, implementing the innovation-driven development strategy and accelerating the building of an innovative China.

Contributor | Department of Earth System Science

Image | Ren Zuoli

11月21日

文字 | 冯婉婷

图片 | 刘雨田

清华美院实验室：艺术“美”梦实现的地方

众所周知，清华拥有一批高水平的理工科实验室，但是很多人不知道，在清华美院这样一个艺术类学院，也有着众多有趣的实验室。它们特色鲜明、设施完备，不仅是重要的实验实践教学基地，更是清华美院向校内其他院系同学甚至校外人士开放的窗口之一。

清华大学艺术与设计实验教学中心，作为北京市及国家级实验教学示范中心、校级实验教学中心、清华大学一级实验室，依托于清华美院建设和管理，已建设成为国内艺术与设计领域涵盖专业面最广，理念与模式先进，综合性、交叉性、创新性最强的实验教学平台。中心目前有 29 个不同的实验室，涵盖了艺术设计、工业设计、工艺美术、绘画、摄影及信息设计等专业领域，实验设备一流，本科生人均实验室面积等综合资源条件处于国内高校同领域领先位置。

与众多理工科实验室相比，美院实验室也是同学们教学和实践的重要场所，他们在这里用专业的仪器设备进行日常实验、实践。例如玻璃工艺实验室拥有箱式窑炉、热熔窑、预热窑等国际先进设备，整个实验室按照玻璃艺术的制作工艺流程分成了窑制、吹制、装饰、灯工、冷加工和模具成型六个主要教学实践区域，同学们在这里创造出许多玻璃日用品、工艺礼品和精美首饰。与此同时，美院实验室还为同学们的艺术创作提供了更广阔的空间，例如摄影实验室包括大摄影棚、小摄影棚、传统暗房、数字工作间、设备库等场所，还配备了化妆间、模特淋浴间等，不仅为学生专业课程及日常练习提供空间设备，也为广告摄影、大画幅摄影、人像摄影、时尚摄影等多方面的实践与艺术创作提供了专业平台。

每年的校庆开放日，清华美院都会定期开放一定数量的实验室供校内外人士参观。每年前来参观美院实验室的团队、个人络绎不绝，参观的过程中有美院同学担当讲解的志愿者，有秩序地组织一批批参观者前往一个个实验室，向他们介绍各个实验室的基本情况，带领他们观看实验室里老师同学的日常创作过程和杰出作品。美院实验室的特色风采以及丰厚内涵广受校内外各界好评。

除此之外，实验教学中心还承担着清华美院 9 个系（艺术史论系除外）所开设的各类专业必修课、选修课，以及面向全校开设的艺术素质课程的实验教学任务。艺术与设计实验教学中心在发展过程中逐步形成完善的实验教学体系与创新的实验教学模式，建立了与高层次、复合型、可持续发展的艺术设计人才培养相适应的综合创新型实验实践教学平台，不仅是高质量艺术人才的培育基地，也是清华美院对外的一张别具特色的“名片”。

相关链接：清华美院实验教学中心的一流技术装备

清华美院实验教学中心拥有先进的技术设备，服务于教学、科研及创新开发。其中包括用于拍摄汽车等大型实物的国际顶级 15 米长德国巴赫调频灯光系统，是全世界第四套、全中国唯一一套；用于动画、影视制作的国际顶级的 Vicon 光学式运动捕捉系统；用于陶瓷烧制的国际顶级水平的进口高温电窑炉；14 台世界领先的德国纳博热玻璃窑炉，可完成不同体量玻璃铸造、热熔、热塌陷等工艺；用于石版画制作的国际一流的进口平板 / 石板印刷机；照明与色彩实验室自主设计的模拟日光和自然光的照明系统一套，技术指标达到国际同类产品的水平；纤维艺术实验室自主设计的世界最大的手工楼式编织机。

The Laboratories of Tsinghua Academy of Arts and Design: Where Art Dreams Come True

As everyone knows, Tsinghua owns a variety of high-level scientific and engineering laboratories; but what people may not know is that, as an art school, Tsinghua Academy of Arts and Design also has many interesting laboratories. With distinctive features and complete facilities, they are not only important practical teaching bases, but also open windows to students from other schools and visitors.

As a national and Beijing municipal experimental teaching demonstration center and first-class laboratory of Tsinghua University, the Experimental Teaching Center of Arts and Designs, under the construction and management of Academy of Arts and Designs, has become an experimental teaching platform covering the largest specialty scope with the strongest comprehensiveness, interaction and innovation in the field of arts and design in China. The center currently has 29 different laboratories, covering art design, industrial design, arts and crafts, painting, photography, information design and other fields, showing a leading position among all domestic universities in terms of resources like advanced devices and lab spaces for undergraduates.

Compared to scientific and engineering laboratories, laboratories in Academy of Arts and Design are also essential places for students to learn and practice. They carry out daily practice and experiments with professional instruments in the laboratories. For example, equipped with box-type kiln, melting kiln, preheater kiln and other advanced devices, the glass art laboratory is divided into six major practicing areas in accordance with the processing procedure of glass art: heating, blowing, decoration, lighting, cold processing and modeling, where students created various glass necessities, craft gifts and exquisite jewelries. The uniqueness of such laboratories is that they provide broader spaces for students to perform artistic creation. For example, photography laboratory is equipped with a large studio, a small studio, a traditional darkroom, a digital workshop, a device library and a dressing room, a showering room, etc., not only to provide a platform for student's specialized courses and daily work, but also to offer a professional space for practices and artistic creation in advertising photography, large format photography, portrait photography, fashion photography and other aspects

Every year, on the opening day of Tsinghua's anniversary, Tsinghua Academy of Arts and Design regularly opens a number of laboratories for public visitors. A continuous stream of groups and individuals come to the laboratories. Students from Academy of Arts and Design serve as volunteer instructors to guide visitors, introduce basic information of the laboratories, and show them the daily creation process and outstanding art works of the teachers and students in the laboratories. The distinctive feathers and rich connotation of those laboratories are highly recognized by the general public.

In addition, the experimental teaching center also hosts the experimental teaching tasks of compulsory courses, elective courses and art courses offered for the whole university, covering all nine departments of Academy of Arts and Design (except for Department of Art History). With development, the center has gradually formed comprehensive experimental teaching system and innovative experimental teaching mode, to become not only a training base of high quality art talent but also an attractive brand of Tsinghua Academy of Arts and Design.

Translation and revision | Raj Lamar

Image | Liu Yutian

11月22日

文字 | 拜喆喆

图片 | 李筱甜

小雪：盼望

“小雪，十月中，雨下而为寒气所薄，故凝而为雪。小者，未盛之辞。”在小雪节气之后，常常会有初雪。而这个节气最让人期待的，也莫过于“开始下雪”这四个字。雪是一种很矛盾的意象。它寒冷，却最容易让人联想到温暖。前人在这个时节，拥一方小暖炉，看着几欲下雪的天气，为友人温一杯酒，煮一壶茶，如今，我们也从这个季节开始盼望园子里的第一场雪。

一直觉得中外对雪的氛围的刻画是不同的。《情书》中的雪是漫长而无法遨游的白色森林，见证的爱情带有凉意和日本美学色彩；在《冰雪奇缘》的镜头里，雪是一切奇妙的起点;《纳尼亚传奇》的积雪里藏着勇气、力量与征服，背后是对自然的探索和敬畏。而在中国，寒江垂钓的茫茫冰雪，是与天地的对话；边塞诗中千树万树绽放的“梨花”，在冰雪里传递着暖意豪情；民间谚语里的雪，则总是带着对生命和丰收的希冀。

汉朝哲学家董仲舒在《春秋繁露·阴阳出入上下》中说：“小雪而物咸成，大寒而物毕藏。”这个时节为传统中国的农耕社会赋予了一种惜时耕耘的勉励。北方习惯在这个时节开始腌制过冬的泡菜，南方开始为冬小麦保暖。而园子里的学子们，也要开始耕耘期末的“好收成”了。

农谚里常提到的“小雪雪满天，来年必丰年”，让人在细密而迅速融化的小雪时节里看到了希望和期待。若能于下雪时偶遇这个时节成熟的雪柿子，白色世界里平添一抹艳红，就再可爱不过了。

我们期待春日归来，却也准备好了迎接冬日凛冽。因为可以融雪煮新茶，温酒候故友；因为可以拥有满室暖意和滚烫热闹的火锅；因为学堂路上又停驻了甜蜜蜜的糖葫芦，食堂里又添了热腾腾的红薯。

园子里的银杏落了，便又是期待初雪的时候了。

Yearning for Light Snow

"Light Snow- October -It rains- It becomes cold- It becomes snow." In the Chinese Solar Term, Light Snow is often something that most people yearn for. Of course, it marks the start of "snow" and reminds us just how contrasting the image of snow can be. Snow is cold yet it is also a reminiscent of warmth. People gather around the heater and chat either over hot tea or traditional wine. And now, we all look forward to the first snow in Tsinghua too.

Snow always brings about a different feel and certainly its perception differs both at home and abroad.

In *Love Letter*, snow is a thick and untraveled white forest. It bears witness to the cold, the love and a certain sense of Japanese aesthetics. In *Frozen*, snow is the catalyst of something magical. In *The Chronicles of Narnia*, snow stands for courage, strength and conquest. What lies behind it is exploration. In classical Chinese poems, snow is like a white blanket covering all rivers and streams, a messenger between heaven and earth, as well as thousands of lively pear flowers... In Chinese proverbs, snow always bring the hope of life and a new round of harvest.

Light Snow is a season that offers much encouragement for the traditional Chinese farming society. Northern China is used to pickling pickles at this time of year, while peasants in the South are starting to keep the wheat warm for the coming winter. Tsinghua students are also beginning to look ahead for the good "harvest" in the final exams.

Light Snow is often seen as a good sign of harvest, as the old saying goes, "if there're snows in the sky, next year has got to be bountiful" . In the thin and rapidly melting snow lies much hope and expectation for the coming year. What is interesting is that the late-maturing persimmons are just ripe so it adds much adorable red delights to a world of whiteness.

We look forward to the return of spring but we are ready to welcome the winter as well. Because snow can be melted to make tea, it is a great chance to catch up with old friends. With the hotpot in the middle of the dining room, how marvelous would it be to dine amongst friends, happiness and warmth? Meanwhile, the Tsinghua Campus is filled with the sight of candied haws and the aroma of sweet potatoes.

The ginkgo leaves have fallen, and now is the time to welcome the first snow in this winter...

Translation and revision | Min Weiyuan

Image | Li Xiaotian

11 月 23 日

文字 | 梁乐萌

图片 | 宋晨

当数字技术遇上甲骨文——清华美术学院陈楠设计汉仪陈体甲骨文

两条弧线构成的“方舟”上，载着象、狗、羊、龟等各种动物，写实与象征意味并存，艺术的美感中蕴含着童稚的趣味。细细看去，画面中的每一个形象都是一个原始的文字，这就是陈楠设计的“数字化甲骨文”。

如今，“汉仪陈体甲骨文”字体让每个人都可以使用这种古朴生动的文字，创作属于自己的内容。

清华美院视觉传达设计系副主任陈楠自 1999 年起致力于“数字化甲骨文”设计，意在将技术与艺术、传统与创意相结合，揭示甲骨文所蕴含的几何之美和网格秘密。他创作的“数字化甲骨文”艺术作品先后在首届艺术与科学国际作品展、北京国际设计周暨首届北京国际设计三年展等活动中展出，并出现在中国邮政官方发行的《甲骨文 · 吉祥成语》系列贺年明信片上。

在进一步推广“数字化甲骨文”过程中，陈楠与汉仪字库合作，设计了“汉仪陈体甲骨文”字体。这是国内外第一套甲骨文设计字库，也是第一套不以书写作为主要功能的字库，它将设计开发重点放在文化衍生与推广上，在商业开发的同时担负起文化传承责任。正如陈楠在公众号“陈楠工作室”中所写：“甲骨文字就像是一台商朝的照相机，我们的先民将目光触及的万事万物化为龟甲上形象的文字符号，这些质朴的图案文字成为我们与祖先跨时空交流的桥梁，向我们展现了一幅千年前的远古图卷。”

2017 年 9 月 28 日，由清华大学中国古文字艺术研究中心和汉仪字库联合主办的“再造 · 甲骨——现代设计语境中的远古文字”汉仪陈体甲骨文字体设计展在 751 时尚回廊举行，这也标志着“汉仪陈体甲骨文”字体在汉仪字库中正式发布。在甲骨字体之外，展览还展出了甲骨文十二生肖徽章、甲骨文手机壳、甲骨文真丝小方巾等跨界创意产品，形成系统的文化视觉体系。

陈楠认为，甲骨文既是中国优秀的传统文化符号，又是符合当今设计潮流的创意字符。2017 年 11 月，陈楠工作室新推出《生肖甲骨文》和《甲骨有表情》两套手机表情包，通过年轻化、时尚化的趣味性“玩转甲骨文”。

习近平总书记在哲学社会科学工作座谈会上的重要讲话明确指出：“要重视发展具有重要文化价值和传承意义的‘绝学’、冷门学科……还有一些学科事关文化传承的问题，如甲骨文等古文字研究等，要重视这些学科，确保有人做、有传承。”陈楠的数字化甲骨文字库设计与文化衍生创意正是这种文化传承的生动“缩影”。2017 年 11 月 9 日，《人民日报》在文化版刊登采访文章《甲骨文成了创意源代码》，专题报道陈楠团队关于甲骨文的创意设计。

Chen Nan's "Digital Oracle Bone Inscriptions" Design: When Digital Technology Meets Oracle Bone Inscriptions

The "ark" above the two arcs is loaded with animals such as elephants, dogs, sheep and tortoises. It is both realistic and symbolic. This art is beautiful with a hint of one's childhood. In detail, each image contains a primitive text- this is Chen Nan's "Digital Oracle Bone Inscriptions" design.

Today, the "Hanyi Chen Style Oracle Bone Inscriptions" font makes it possible for everyone to create their own content using this ancient and vivid text. His "Digital Oracle Bone Inscriptions" art has been successively exhibited at international arts and science shows, Beijing International Design Week and much more. His designs also appeared on China Postal New Year Card under the title of "Auspicious Oracles" .

Chen Nan from Tsinghua Academy of Arts and Design has been committed to "digital oracle Bone Inscriptions" design since 1999. It was his aim to combine technology with art and tradition with creativity to reveal the beauty of the oracle and the fineness of its geometry and grid.

In the process of further promoting the "digital oracle bone inscriptions" , Chen Nan cooperated with Hanyi Font Library and designed the "Hanyi Chen Style Oracle" . This is the first set of work on oracle characters font. Apart from promoting Chinese culture, it also bears the responsibility of cultural bone inscriptions inheritance. Just like what Chen Nan wrote in the "Chen Nan Studio" social media account: "Oracle bone inscriptions script is like a camera. Our ancestors first noted down such texts on the shells of tortoises and these patterns are now a bridge or an ancient map, allowing us to find and connect with them."

On September 28th, 2017, Tsinghua University's Ancient Chinese Characters Art Research Center and Hanyi Font Library jointly organized the event "Re-inventing Oracle — Modern Design in the Context of Ancient Words" . The "Hanyi Chen Style Oracle" were on display at the 751 corridor which also marked the official launch of this set of work. In addition to the oracle, the exhibition also featured creative products such as the Chinese oracle zodiac emblem, oracle mobile covers, oracle silk scarves and many other cultural goodies.

Chen Nan believes that the oracle is both a traditional cultural symbol of China and a creative character that conforms to the current design trend. In November, Chen Nan Studio launched two sets of mobile phone emojis called "Oracle of the Chinese zodiac" and "Oracles have facial expressions" which greatly appealed to the younger generation.

During his speech on philosophy and social science works, President Xi Jinping said, "we should pay more attention to the unpopular disciplines and subjects...to all those with important cultural value and heritage significance. There are also some issues related to cultural inheritance, such as oracles and other ancient languages...we need to ensure that it is kept alive and that it would be passed on for our future generation." Chen Nan's digital oracle database and design are the epitome of this cultural inheritance. On November 9th, 2017, *People's Daily* conducted an interview with Chen Nan, and a report named "Oracles as a Creative Source Code" was published in their cultural edition.

Translation and revision I Min Weiyuan

Image I Song Chen

11 月 24 日

文字 | 拜喆喆

图片 | 李娜

清华最早的图书馆：梦开始的地方

每当回忆起负笈清华的光阴，清华人总不由地深情提及图书馆。现在的清华图书馆是一个新老建筑完美衔接的楼群，其老馆之东翼即是清华最早的图书馆。

在清华学校建校初期，清华学堂大楼北面平房中曾有一个仅三间房的图书室。1913 年，周诒春校长提出把清华改办成独立大学，后兴建包括图书馆在内的四大建筑。当时的清华人把新建的图书馆称为“大图书馆”，它建于 1916 年至 1919 年间，建筑面积 2114.4 平方米。拾级而上迈入大铜门，眼前是宽敞明亮的大厅，进入后面的书库，深邃宁静，缥缃盈架。如今，这里依旧是清华学生自习的好去处和毕业留影不可错过的一站。

除了建筑风格，大图书馆的管理也十分先进。首任图书馆主任戴超（字志骞）曾在纽约州立图书馆专科学校进修，他和一批接受过相关专业教育的工作人员为图书馆的早期发展做出了重要贡献。

图书馆于 1930 年至 1931 年间进行了扩建，形成了后来老馆之中部大厅和西翼。由杨廷宝（1921 届校友，与梁思成一起被誉为“南杨北梁”）设计，建筑面积 5588.56 平方米。扩建部分与原有者浑然一体，很难看出是先后建造的，被公认为扩建工程中的杰作。

20 世纪 30 年代的清华园，是“天堂应是图书馆模样”的最好注解。学生除了阅读专业书籍，更多的时候是在博览群书。杨绛先生（1933 级研究生）在《我爱清华图书馆》中讲道：“我在许多学校上过学，最爱的是清华大学；清华大学里，最爱清华图书馆。”文学大师钱锺书 (1933 届) 曾立下“横扫图书馆”的志愿，图书借阅卡上几乎必有他的名字。厚积薄发使得他的巨著《管锥编》出版，震动学术界，而其参考书目竟多达万种。与钱老同届的著名作家曹禺也几乎读遍了馆中有关戏剧的图书，年仅 23 岁的研究生曹禺在“西文阅览室大厅的东北边，靠近借书台的长桌”上写出了第一部中国式的话剧剧本《雷雨》。

清华图书馆哺育了一代又一代的清华学子。它经历着不断的完善和扩建，变迁中永远不变的是开馆前门口那长长的、悄然无声的队伍，不变的是清华学子一以贯之的勤奋与好学。

Tsinghua's Earliest Library: The Place Where Dreams Begin

Every time you recall the early Tsinghua years, the library makes a strong presence in the memories of all Tsinghua people. The current Tsinghua library is a perfect bridge between the old and new building. The east wing of its old building is the first library in Tsinghua.

In the early days, there was a three-room library in the north side of the Tsinghua Xuetang building. In 1913, President Zhou Yichun made proposals to transform Tsinghua into an independent university. Included in the new construction were four main buildings with one being the library. Tsinghua people at that time called this the "Big Library" . Built between 1916 and 1919 and with a building area of 2114.4 square meters, a spacious bright hall greets all after students have ascended the stairs and past the gate. The further you go the quieter it is. Today, it is still a good place for self-study. It is also featured in everyone's graduation photos since memories must be preserved.

In addition to her architectural style, management was also very advanced. The first Director Dai Chao had advanced studies in New York State Library. Along with a group of professional staff members, they have all made important contribution to the early development of the library.

The library expanded between 1930 and 1931, which made it become the central hall and west wing of the "Old Library" today. Yang Tingbao (1921 Tsinghua alumnus and took his place alongside another architecture master Liang Sicheng) was the designer. With a building area of 5588.56 square meters, the expansion was more an integration since it is not easy to spot the change. Although expanded, it has kept true to its original design.

Tsinghua in the 1930s was the best annotation of "what heaven should look like is a library" . Apart from the more serious studies, it is also a place for all book lovers. Yang Jiang (1933 graduate student) wrote: "I have studied in many universities. My favorite is Tsinghua. My favorite building in Tsinghua is the library." Literature master Qian Zhongshu (Class of 1933) once made a goal of devouring all the books at Tsinghua. His name has always appeared on the borrowing card. His *Limited Views* (Guanzhui Pian) that has once caused a storm in the literature world could not have been written without his insatiable appetite for what is being kept at Tsinghua's library. Cao Yu, a famous writer wrote the first words of his script *Thunderstorm,* sitting at a desk in the library. That was one of the first scripts for Chinese Modern drama.

Tsinghua library has nurtured generations of students. It has undergone continuous improvement and expansion. There will always be a long and silent line in front of her every day. It remains unchanged: the library and the diligent spirit of the Tsinghua students.

Translation and revision | Min Weiyuan

Image | Li Na

11月27日

文字 | 冯婉婷

图片 | 梁晨

“挑战杯”特等奖“天格计划”：基础科学也可以很“酷”

2017年4月，由来自清华大学工程物理系、物理系、航天航空学院等院系同学组成的“天格计划”学生团队，凭借“空间分布式引力波暴电磁对应体探测网”项目夺得了清华大学第三十五届“挑战杯”学生课外学术科技作品竞赛特等奖。“天格计划”不仅仅只是一个“挑战杯”竞赛作品，更是一个目前仍在进行的、挑战基础科学前沿领域的学生项目。

来自清华大学工程物理系的团队负责人温家星介绍说，“天格计划”的目标是探测引力波暴在伽马射线波段的电磁对应体，即短伽马射线暴。计划将在2018年发射第一颗功能验证型卫星，在未来的五年内还将逐步发射，最终形成由10~24颗微纳卫星组成的探测网络。

传统的伽马射线探测卫星由于受地球遮挡，无法实现对伽马射线暴法的全天覆盖探测，而“天格计划”团队所提出的利用立方星平台搭载先进闪烁体探测器、多颗微纳卫星组网探测的方案，能够实现对短伽马射线暴真正的全天覆盖探测，并可通过时间延迟和流强调制的方式实现有效定位，可保证不错过任何一次与引力波暴发成协可探测的短伽马射线暴，有着重要的科学意义。

“除此之外，项目还有一个非常重要的意义，即对同学的培养。”温家星说，该项目是一个完全的学生项目，他是团队中年龄最大的人，但在去年10月团队成立之初，他还只是一名大四本科生。“天格计划”团队目前由30多名清华本科生和部分外校学生组成，他们来自各个年级、不同院系，因为兴趣聚集在一起。团队内高年级同学主要负责具体的技术攻关，低年级同学负责科学理论的探索；不同院系同学按照专业特点分成科学、载荷、卫星三个小组，在项目运行过程中分工协作。温家星说，希望通过这个项目让本科同学意识到基础科学研究并不遥远，鼓励大家勇敢尝试。

一年来，团队在一步步取得成果的同时，也遇到了不少具体的困难，比如怎么解决探测器在太空中的稳定性问题、如何实现对低能γ射线的高效探测等。“幸运的是，我们得到了许多老师的竭力帮助。”温家星说。

正如指导老师冯骅所说，像“天格计划”这样融合科学与工程技术的项目，既可以让学生接受基本的科研训练，从而适应从课堂学习到科研第一线的转变；也将为学生今后参加国家级科学工程奠定良好的基础，让同学们亲身体会到基础科学也可以很“酷”。

The “Challenge Cup” Top Grade Award — “Grid Project” : Basic Science Can Be Really Cool

In April 2017, the “Grid Project” started by students from Tsinghua University's Department of Engineering Physics, Department of Physics and School of Aerospace Engineering took home the Top Grade Award of Tsinghua's 35th “Challenge Cup Award”. It is more than just a competition work, but a project for students to overcome challenges through applying teamwork, analytical thinking and their understanding of basic scientific knowledge.

Wen Jiaxing, who is from Department of Engineering Physics, is the team leader of the “Grid Project” . He said that the goal is to detect the electromagnetic counterparts of gravitational waves at gamma ray, namely short gamma ray bursts. The plan is to launch the first functional verification satellite in 2018. Satellites will be launched gradually over the next five years, eventually forming a probe network of 10 to 24 micro-nano satellites.

Due to being blocked by earth, traditional gamma probe could not achieve a round-the-clock coverage of gamma ray detection. The “Grid Project” team proposed using cubic star platform with advanced scintillation detector to achieve a micro-nano satellite network system, which allows such holistic coverage and detection. Such findings have important scientific significance.

“In addition, the project's main aim is to cultivate students.” said Wen. The “Grid Project” is a complete student project. At present, Wen is the oldest in the team yet at the start of the team's founding last October, he was still a senior student. Comprised of more than 30 undergraduate students from Tsinghua and other universities, they are united due to sharing a common interest. The senior students are mainly responsible for specific technical research while the junior students are responsible for the exploration of scientific theories. Coming from different departments and with varying specialities, students are divided into three groups: science, payloads and satellites. Wen Jiaxing hopes that the project will allow undergraduates to realize how important basic scientific research is and encourage them to give it a try.

Over the past year, team achievements were obtained one step at a time. The team also met with many difficulties from finding ways in solving the problem of the stability of detectors in outer space to realizing efficient detection of low-energy gamma ray. “Fortunately we have many teachers who are offering us help.” said Wen.

Just like what instructor Feng Hua said, the “Grid Project” is an integration of science and engineering projects. It allows students to not only refine their basic scientific research skills but also ease the transition from theory work in the classroom to practice at the frontline. It helps to lay a good foundation for students to participate in future national scientific projects. They will find that even basic science can be really “cool” .

Translation and revision I Min Weiyuan

Image I Liang Chen

11月28日

文字 | 梁乐萌

图片 | 李娜

清华学生手语社：用手画出彩虹，让爱成为行动

大礼堂的灯光亮了起来，舞台上的演员安静无声，双手行云流水般做着复杂流畅的动作。这是 2017 年清华精密仪器系学生节“纳米纪元”中一个特殊的节目，演员们用手语带来一首“唱给整个园子的情歌”——清华版《成都》，而他们都来自清华学生手语社。

清华学生手语社成立于 2006 年 3 月，是由清华学生自主创立，以促进聋健交融为己任，并在校团委指导下进行自主管理的学生公益社团组织。“用手画出彩虹，让爱成为行动”一直是社团的核心理念，他们致力于运用手语、宣传手语、普及手语，为听障人和健听人搭建沟通的桥梁，以达到“聋健融合”的理想目标。

手语教学是清华学生手语社最重要的日常活动。手语社每两周交替举办一次手语小班和一次手语歌小班，前者教授生活中常用的手语，旨在培养用手语进行交流的能力；后者则由具有一定手语水平的核心社员根据《中国手语》自己编排手语歌进行教学，希望通过手语歌这种形式让普通人感受到手语的美。此外，手语社还定期举办手语文化讲座，并曾组织聋健定向越野、手语文化节、聋人文化电影赏析等活动，参与院系学生节表演也是他们普及手语文化的重要途径。

教学和演出只是手语社活动的一部分，他们还与公益组织合作，以实际行动关心、帮助听障人士，尤其是少年儿童。手语社定期前往位于北京的莎莉文聋哑儿童康复中心和专为聋生设立的北京启喑实验学校，为孩子们送去书籍、进行交流，让听障儿童得到实实在在的帮助，也让社团同学们对无声世界的生活有了切身体会。

从 2006 年成立到现在，清华学生手语社已经走过了 11 个年头。“在这里，我们实践助聋心愿，分享着同一个梦想——促进健听人与聋人朋友平等交流。”现任会长黄景洋说。他希望未来能够有更多同学加入聋健交流圈，一起学习手语、推广手语。

Sign Language Association: Use Hands to Paint Rainbows, Transfer Love into Action

The Auditorium lightened up, and the actors on the stage were silently performing complex gestures with their hands. This was a special program as part of the 2017 "Nano Age" Student's Day of Department of Precision Instrument, Tsinghua University. Actors used sign language to play "a love song for Tsinghua Campus" — "Chengdu" Tsinghua edition. They all came from Tsinghua Sign Language Association.

Founded in March 2006 by students, Tsinghua Sign Language Association is a public welfare organization aiming to promote interaction between the deaf and the general public, it is self-managed under the guidance of the Youth League Committee. "Using hands to paint rainbows, transferring love into action" has always been the core concept of the association. They are committed to bridging the communication between the deaf and the hearing people through using and publicizing sign language, so as to achieve the integration of the two groups.

Sign language teaching is the most important daily activity of the sign language association. The association alternately hosts a language class and a song class every two weeks. The former class teaches daily-used signs to cultivate basic communication ability; core members in another class design and teach songs composited according to *Chinese Sign Language*, hoping ordinary people can feel the beauty of sign language through the songs . In addition, the association regularly holds cultural lectures on sign language, and organizes the deaf-hearing orienteering, sign language festival, the deaf movie appreciation and other activities. Participating in the performances during the Students' Day is also an essential part of promoting sign language.

Besides teaching and performance, the association works with public welfare organizations to offer help for hearing-impaired people, especially young children. They regularly visit Sullivan Rehabilitation Center and Beijing Qi Yin Experimental School, communicate with children there and donate books. These activities provide hearing-impaired children with practical help, and also allow association members to experience lives in a silent world.

Since established in 2006, Tsinghua Sign Language Association has been through 11 years. "This is where we devote to help and share our mutual dream—to promote equal communication between the deaf and the general public." association leader Baoky Kingyang Huang said. Looking forward, he expects even more students to join them, learning and advocating sign language.

Translation and revision | Raj Lamar

Image | Li Na

11月29日

文字 | 杨茂艺

图片 | 李娜

初探电子系微纳光电子学实验室：光子的世界，精致的诺言

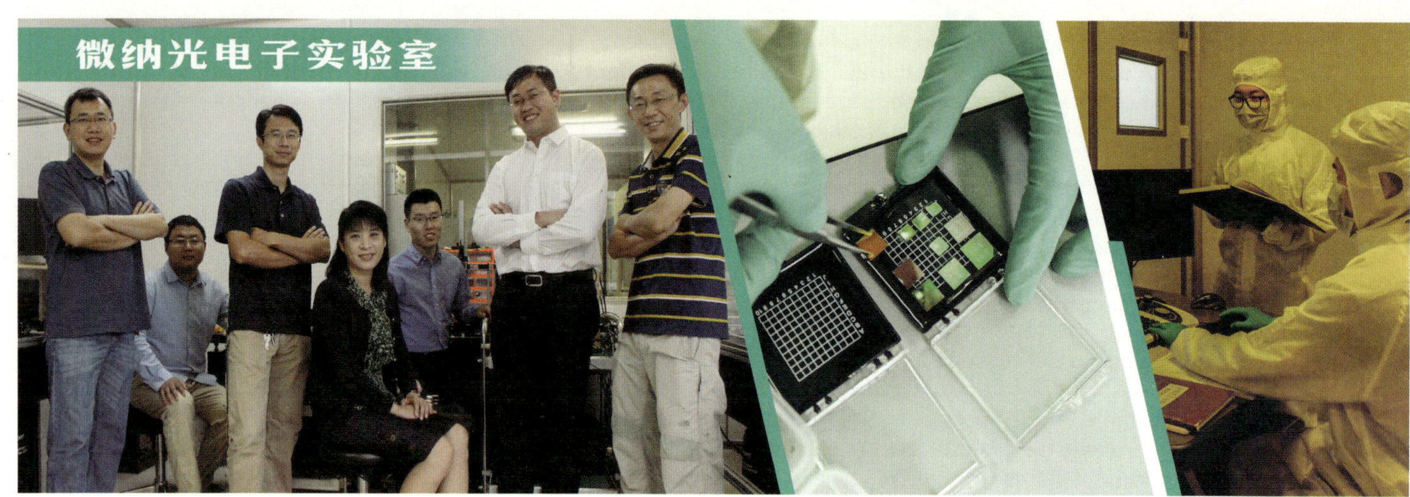

深秋十月的校园已是冷风阵阵，单薄的毛衣早已不能御寒。我哆嗦着走进罗姆楼，心里满是对电子系的期待，却也有几分胆怯——“微纳光电子学实验室”？如何断句？难不成是“微纳光／电子学／实验室”？

诸君莫笑，微纳光电子学是一门研究微纳结构中光子与物质相互作用的交叉学科，研究成果可应用于信息、能源、环境、生物医学等诸多领域，包括我们熟知的量子通信、太阳光伏等。此实验室成立于 2004 年，至今已走过 13 个年头，科研方向大致分为：光子／光声晶体、光通信波段的光量子器件、硅基集成器件、表面等离子激元及其应用这四大类。研究团队包括长江学者特聘教授黄翊东、张巍副教授、冯雪副教授、刘仿副教授、崔开宇副教授，以及 20 余名博士、硕士研究生。

穿戴上洁净服，进入实验室，我立刻被明亮的白色基调和纤发不落的整洁所吸引——450 平方米的洁净间被设计为流动的迷宫，各个房间可通可隔，大面积地块上致密地安放着手动光纤耦合台、等离子体增强化学气相沉积器等仪器，转角门廊处则有特殊气体压力瓶、气泵和压缩机等设备——整个空间设计巧妙、精心布局，让人顿觉美好。

环顾四周，皆是线缆密布的操作台和白框黑屏的显示器，一切精致的部件都在安静的实验室内呼吸。当我靠近显微镜时，却没有看到老师们所说的“重要的样品芯片”——冯雪副教授告诉我：“实验室里研究的器件和结构都是很细微的，肉眼自然是看不见的。”诚然，做微纳结构的研究是需要耐心和细心的。一片边长几毫米的芯片的诞生，从模型设计、电子束曝光，到离子刻蚀加工、去胶、磨片，再到测试总共需要至少 3 周时间。冯雪笑着说：“学生们步入研究生阶段后，首先就要经历‘粉碎阶段’，他们会知道做实验不同于做题……完成一次芯片的制备和测试，既需要对于仪器和设备的熟悉，又需要自身对于大量数据的数理直觉。”

实验室最新科研成果当属“集成无阈值切伦科夫辐射芯片”——如何降低产生切伦科夫辐射的巨大电子能量阈值是几十年来的科学难题。2014 年，刘仿副教授研究发现，利用双曲超材料可以实现无阈值的切伦科夫辐射。历经两年多反复地实验锤炼后，刘仿于 2017 年在《自然·光子》杂志上正式发表了这一研究成果，并颠覆了人们对于传统自由电子光源的认识，使得在芯片上研究飞行电子与微纳结构的相互作用成为可能。

不知不觉中，短暂的两小时很快过去了，实验室里的整洁环境、认真工作的学生和风趣博学的老师们都给我留下了深刻的印象。这里好似一片思维与实践的沃土——师生们在这里模拟、假设、试验，每一步都看似单调枯燥，但却最终孕育了精致的作品，践行着他们对微观光子世界“解密”的诺言。

The World of Photons: What Is the Micro-nano Optoelectronics Lab Like?

It is well into the fall season on campus where a thin sweater is no longer warm enough. Shivering, I walked into the Rohm Building that houses Tsinghua's Department of Electronic Engineering. My heart is filled with excitement but was also somewhat nervous. I am visiting the "Micro-nano Optoelectronics Lab." It's a mouthful to even say it. What is micro-nano optoelectronics?

Micro-nano optoelectronics is an interdisciplinary research of the interaction of photonic and matter in micro and nano structures. Research results can be applied to many fields such as information technology, energy, environmental science, biomedicine, including hot topics such as quantum communication and solar photovoltaic. The laboratory was established in 2004 and for the past 13 years, its research directions can be broadly divided into: photon and photoacoustic crystal, optical communication wavelength optical devices, silicon-based integrated devices, surface plasmon and the application of these four class. The research team includes Professor Huang Yidong (Changjiang Scholar), Associate Professor Zhang Wei, Associate Professor Feng Xue, Associate Professor Liu Fang, Associate Professor Cui Kaiyu, and more than 20 master and doctoral students.

Putting on clean clothes and walking into the laboratory, I was immediately drawn in by the bright white lights—400 square meters of clean rooms are designed to flow like a maze. Each room can be separated and large areas are filled with manual fiber-optic couplers, plasma-enhanced chemical vapor deposition and other instruments. In a corner, there are special gas pressured bottles, air pumps and compressors—the entire space is cleverly designed and carefully laid out, giving immediate good vibes.

Looking around, there are cable-covered consoles and white blank displays, all the delicate components are breathing in a quiet laboratory. When I approached a microscope, I did not see what the professors called "important chip samples." So Associate Professor Feng Xue had to enlighten me. "The components and structures studied in the laboratory are very microscopic, things not visible to our naked eyes," he said. It is true what they say, that research on micro-nano structure requires patience and care. For the birth of a chip length of a few millimeters, from model designing, electron beam exposure, to ion etching process, to glueing, grinding and then to the test requires a total of at least 3 weeks.

"After students enter the post-graduate phase, the first step is to go through the 'breaking point' where they realize that conducting experiments is wildly different from solving a problem set. To complete the preparation and testing of a chip not only requires a certain familiarity with instruments, but also their own mathematical intuition in dealing with large amounts of data." said Feng with a smile.

The latest scientific research in the laboratory is on integrated threshold-less Cherenkov radiation chip. Finding a method to reduce the huge electron energy threshold that produces Cerenkov radiation has been a scientific puzzle for decades. In 2014, Associate Professor Liu Fang found that the use of hyperbolic metamaterials allows for a threshold-free Cerenkov radiation. After more than two years of intensive experiments, Liu published the research results in *Nature Photonics* in 2017 and subverted the recognition of the traditional free electron light source, making it possible to study the flight on the chip and the interaction of electrons with the micro-nano structure.

Without realizing it, my two-hour visit had come to an end. I was impressed with the neat environment in the laboratory, the serious and hardworking students coupled with entertaining and knowledgeable professors. Here is a fertile land of theory and practice, professors and students are simulating, testing hypotheses, and conducting experiments. Although every step seems monotonous and boring, but it promises to culminate into an exquisite workmanship that 'decrypts' the microscopic world of photons.

Translation and revision | Alexis See Tho

Image | Li Na

11月30日

原作者 | 曲田
改写 | 杨鹏成
图片 | 李娜
摄影 | 何名暖

航天航空学院教授郑钢铁：钢铁是怎样炼成的

郑钢铁 1960 年出生，1988 年加入中国共产党，现任清华大学航天航空学院教授、飞行器设计研究所首任所长。主要研究领域为飞行器系统与结构设计、结构动力学与控制。他解决了“风云二号”卫星、中巴资源卫星、月球着陆器、运载火箭等航天器关键技术问题，为卫星的发射成功和着陆器准确着月做出了贡献。

2016 年夏天，航天航空学院教授郑钢铁带博士生胡展外出做试验，在回学校的路上，一场车祸从天而降，郑钢铁身受重伤，不得已截肢失去了右腿。

“我们是靠头脑生活的，只要脑袋没坏，日子就都能过下去！”事发后，当胡展去看望郑钢铁时，郑钢铁开口安慰他。听到这句话，胡展忍不住流下了眼泪。“老师乐观的精神状态真的深深触动了我。”

康复期的两个多月时间里，郑钢铁一点儿没有闲着，每次学生来探望他，汇报近期学业与科研情况是必做的“功课”。刚被医生允许使用电脑，他便一刻不耽误地批改起了学生的论文。更令人惊喜的是，在平日与大夫交流的过程中，病床上的郑钢铁又酝酿出了一个新的大学生研究训练计划课题——手术机器人。

郑钢铁说：“当经历了人生变故后，会越发珍惜自己曾拥有的东西。”这其中，他付出多年心力的清华大学大学生研究训练计划便是其一。

清华大学的大学生研究训练计划（Students Research Training，SRT 计划）旨在提高学生学业挑战度，培养学生的研究能力和自主探索精神，激发他们的学术志趣。在郑钢铁看来，SRT 计划考验的是学生全方位的能力。“这需要学生智商与情商相互配合，共同发力。”郑钢铁解释说，“学生的智商和情商不只是两个抽象的概念，在科学研究过程中，智商和情商是两种包含具体指向的能力。智商包括知识的综合运用能力、自主学习能力、科研能力和动手能力；而情商则指的是团队合作能力、工作态度和作风、意志和勇气等。这些要素对每一个参与大学生研究训练计划的同学都至关重要。”

作为奋战在 SRT 计划中的一位“老兵”，郑钢铁坚持指导本科生做科研已有十余年，实现了将航天科学技术寓于 SRT 计划项目，将航天教学和学生科研训练相结合。在这一过程中，郑钢铁始终坚持“三位一体”的育人理念，倾心付出，收获满满。

如今，SRT 计划已经成为本科生参与学术科技活动、培养创新精神和实践能力的重要平台。郑钢铁说，自己愿意继续做 SRT 计划苗圃中一位兢兢业业的“农夫”，看着一棵棵小苗生根发芽、茁壮成长，这便是他最大的快乐。

Prof. Zheng Gangtie from the School of Aerospace Engineering: How Is Steel Tempered?

Zheng Gangtie, born in 1960, joined the Communist Party of China in 1988. He is now the professor of Tsinghua University and the first director of Aircraft Design Institute. His primary research fields are system and structural design, structural dynamics and control of aircrafts. He has solved the key techniques of "FY-2C" Satellite, CBERS, lunar lander and rocket launcher, contributing to the successful launch of satellites and accurate landing of the lander.

In the summer of 2016, Zheng Gangtie took Ph.D. candidate Hu Zhan out for an experiment. On the way back to Tsinghua, a traffic accident befell on him. Zheng was seriously injured and had to amputate his right leg.

"We are living in our brains, as long as the mind is okay, we can still go on with life!" Zheng consoled Hu Zhan who came for a visit. Hearing so, Hu couldn't help but cry, "His optimism deeply touched me."

During the two months of convalescence, Zheng never stayed idle, whenever a student came to visit him, a report of recent studies and scientific research would be a necessary "task" . Having just been allowed to use computer by the doctor, Zheng corrected the students' papers without any delay. What's even more surprising was, inspired by communicating with the doctor in a daily basis, Zheng, who was on the sickbed, has brewed a new program for Students Research Training, called surgical robot.

Zheng said, "When you have experienced misfortunes in life, you value what you once had even more." One of them is the Student Research Training of Tsinghua University, for which he has devoted numerous years.

The Student Research Training (SRT) aims to improve students' academic challenges, cultivate students' ability in research and spirit of independent exploration, and stimulate their academic interests. Zheng believes that the SRT project concerns the full range of the students' abilities. "This requires students' IQ and EQ to come together and make joint efforts." Zheng explained, "IQ and EQ are not just two abstract concepts. In the process of scientific research, they are two specific abilities. IQ includes the comprehensive use of knowledge, independent learning, ability in scientific research and practice, while EQ refers to teamwork, work attitude and ethics, will and courage. These factors are critical to each and every student involved in SRT."

As a "veteran" in SRT, Zheng has directed undergraduates for scientific research for over ten years. He embedded aerospace technology in the SRT project, combining aerospace teaching with students' research and training. Zheng completely dedicated his life for the cause and eventually all of the dedication paid off.

Today, SRT has become an important platform for undergraduates to participate in academic and technological activities, and to cultivate innovative spirit and practical ability. Zheng said that he'd like to continue playing a "farmer" in the nursery of SRT, seedlings saplings and watching them to grow; that's what would make him the most content.

Translation and revision | Raj Lamar

Image | Li Na

Photographer | He Mingnuan

12 月 1 日

文字 | 拜喆喆

图片 | 梁晨

西区体育馆：清华精神的“见证者”

两年前的冬天，当学子们从逸夫馆旁的林荫道经过时，发现清华西北边增添了一抹湛蓝，呼应着蓝色天空，显得分外有活力——那是翻新了跑道的西大操场。而它西侧的西区体育馆，是清华的第一个体育馆。蓝色新跑道与砖红色老体育馆的对话，有一种奇妙的历史感。

西区体育馆是清华早期四大建筑之一，分为前馆和后馆两部分。前馆建于 1916 年至 1919 年，由墨菲设计，泰来洋行施工，外表采用西方古典形式，馆前有陶立克式花岗岩柱廊；十多年后建成的后馆和前馆巧妙相接，建筑风格浑然一体。

清华素有重视体育的传统，西区体育馆在清华体育运动史上更有着独特地位。体育馆建成伊始，学校即开始正规的体育教学，直到 20 世纪 80 年代，它一直是清华师生室内体育活动的重要场所，迎来了一批又一批清华体育健儿。清华师生在各种运动会上取得的骄人成绩，西区体育馆功不可没，它曾不断汇聚着我国体育界的精粹——我国体育先驱马约翰、曹霖生、李剑秋等都曾在此长期执教；在远东运动会斩获篮球冠军的孙立人、邓健飞，在全运会上获得项目冠军的罗庆隆等都是清华学子。1958 年，清华成为最早通过全国“劳卫制”锻炼标准的高校之一。

沉默的西区体育馆背后还蕴藏了层叠的历史脉络，见证了园子里许多重大历史事件的发生。

1919 年，北京爆发了反帝爱国的“五四”运动。次日，全校学生在体育馆前召开全校大会，高呼“收复失地”“废除 21 条”等口号，决定 6 日起罢课。5 月 9 日又在馆内举行“国耻纪念会”，宣誓“愿牺牲生命以保护中华民国人民、土地、主权”。1935 年 12 月，“一二·九”运动爆发，清华学生发出了“华北之大，已经安放不得一张平静的书桌了！”的呐喊，积极参与了游行请愿。次年，团结一致的清华人同包围清华园的国民党反动军警在西区体育馆进行了机智而勇敢的斗争。抗战期间，体育馆被日军毁坏，直至新中国成立后才恢复原貌。

百年春秋，西区体育馆迎送了一代代清华人。她陈旧简朴的砖红色墙壁是清华体育运动的摇篮，更是清华园历史沧桑的时代见证——见证着清华历久弥新的体育精神，更见证着清华人执着坚韧的爱国热情。

The West District Gymnasium: a "Witness" to the Tsinghua Spirit

Two years ago, when students went pass YiFu Hall or Tsinghua's Library, they noticed a sea of blue towards the Northwestern area of the Tsinghua campus. This blue echoes the color of the sky and adds much vitality to the scenery. That newly renovated runway and that red gymnasium at the west end of Tsinghua is in fact the first gymnasium of Tsinghua University.

The West End Gymnasium is one of the four earliest buildings in Tsinghua. It was divided into two parts: the front and the back. The area at the front was built in 1916—1919 and was designed by Murphy. It was constructed in the western classical form with ceramic colonnade right at the front of the building. The area at the back was built more than 10 years later. However, there are no clear distinctions between the two. It was a perfect match in style and design.

Tsinghua University attaches great importance to sports. The West District Gymnasium has a unique position in its sports history. Tsinghua started with regular physical education right at the same time when the building was being first constructed. Right up to the 1980s, it remained the place for indoor sports activities. Many proud achievements were made by the teachers and students. The gymnasium was the gathering place for countless athletes and sport stars: Ma Yuehan, Cao Linsheng, Li Jianqiu and more taught at the gymnasium and athletes such as Sun Liren, Deng Jianfei and Luo Qinglong were all once Tsinghua students. In 1958, Tsinghua became one of the first universities to achieve the national "Physical Fitness standards" .

In addition to being Tsinghua's sporting cradle, the quiet gymnasium is also a very historical place. It has witnessed many historical events.

In 1919, the anti-imperialist "May Fourth" movement broke out in Beijing. The following day, the whole university held a general assembly in front of the gymnasium. Slogans were chanted, views were exchanged and it was the place when they decided to go on strike on the 6th of May. On the 9th of May, a National Humiliation Memorial was held vowing to "make sacrifices so that we could protect the people, the motherland and the sovereignty of China." In December 1935, the December 9th Movement erupted and saw much petitioning and participation from Tsinghua students. The following year, Tsinghua people fought bravely against the KMT police at the site of the West District Gymnasium. During the Anti-Japanese War, the gymnasium was destroyed by the Japanese army and was only restored after 1949.

The gymnasium said hello and goodbye to generations of Tsinghua students. Her simple red brick wall was, is and always will be the cradle for Tsinghua's sporting spirit. She has witnessed much history, Tsinghua spirit and acts of patriotism. She is an integral part of Tsinghua University.

Translation and revision | Min Weiyuan

Image | Liang Chen

12 月 4 日

文字 | 张静

图片 | 宋晨

李稻葵做客“人文清华”讲坛：在新时代用新思维看待中国经济

2017 年 11 月 2 日晚，清华大学经济管理学院弗里曼讲席教授、清华大学经济管理学院中国与世界经济研究中心（CCWE）主任李稻葵做客“人文清华”讲坛。这位认为“最热闹、最集中、最能引起全球关注的社会经济变化就发生在中国”的经济学家，在“人文清华”讲坛上分享了他对于中国经济的新看法。

党的十九大报告指出，“中国特色社会主义进入新时代，我国社会主要矛盾已经转化为人民日益增长的美好生活需要和不平衡不充分的发展之间的矛盾。”步入新时代之际，中国经济呈现出了新的特点及新的挑战。

李稻葵认为，中国经济的首要特点为超大规模的实体经济，巨大的产品量使中国经济更有底气，但储蓄过剩也带来了管理挑战。要素相对成本大逆转是中国经济的另一特征，如今的劳动力不再廉价，呈现出了价格上涨的趋势，资本和资金相对充足，获得技术已经不难，资本也不再短缺。此外，国民需求日渐高端化与多元化，正如十九大报告中所言，国民更加追求美好生活。

党的十九大报告为中国经济的发展描绘出了非常值得期待的蓝图，李稻葵用经济学的数据为现场观众做出了形象的“翻译”：“2020 年中国人均收入应该能够达到 1 万美元，非常接近世界银行所定义的高收入国家的门槛。中国人可以骄傲地说，我们没有拖全球经济发展平均水平的后腿了。”

从另外一个维度来看，2020 年绝对不只是收入水平提高，更重要的是全面消灭贫困，从过去非常贫瘠的、生活条件很恶劣的农村，要转向现代化的、比较富裕的新农村。

李稻葵也用经济学的语言描绘了另外两个时间节点——到 2035 年，中国将跨入高收入国家的行列，进入中大型国家 30 强，人均 GDP 达到美国的 50%，人均收入水平相当于西班牙。到 2050 年，中国将进入中大型国家 20 强，人均 GDP 将占到美国的 70%，人均收入水平相当于法国。

李稻葵强调，我们不仅要讲中国的经济故事，还要有中国的理论：“我们的初衷是办好中国的教育，同时发扬光大中国的现代科学，包括社会科学和人文学科。推动中国的社会科学包括经济学理论的创新，这是我们的初心，也是我们清华社会科学学者的使命！”

“人文清华”讲坛是清华大学发起的大型思想传播活动，其目标是推动建设更创新、更国际、更人文的清华新百年。讲坛定期邀请优秀人文学者，在标志性建筑新清华学堂发表公众演讲，阐述其经典学说、独特思考和重大发现。

Li Daokui Attended the Humanitas Tsinghua Forum: New Thinking for China's Economy in the New Era

In the evening of November 2nd, 2017, Li Daokui, Freeman Chair Professor and Director of Centre for China in the World Economy of Tsinghua's School of Economics and Management, gave a speech at the Humanitas Tsinghua Forum. This economic expert, who believes that "the most active, the most concentrated, and the most global-concerned social and economic changes happen in China" , shared his views on China's economy.

Report of the 19th National Congress of CPC states that, "As socialism with Chinese characteristics has entered a new era, the principal contradiction facing Chinese society has evolved. What we now face is the contradiction between unbalanced, inadequate development and the people's ever-growing needs for a better life." Entering a new era, China's economy presents new features and new challenges.

Li Daokui believes that, the primary feature of China's economy is the solid strength coming with super-large scale real economy and huge amounts of products, but surplus savings in turn brings management challenges. The reverse of relative factor cost is another feature of China's economy. Nowadays, the labor force is no longer cheap, labor price is on a rise; capital and fund are relatively abundant, technology is more available, and there are no more shortages of capital. In addition, the national demand appears to be increasingly high-end and diversified, indicating that, just as the Report states, people are pursuing a better life.

The Report depicts a promising blueprint for the development of China's economy. Prof. Li Daokui has vividly interpreted that with economic data: "In 2020, China's per capita income will reach 10,000 dollars, very close to the threshold of high income countries defined by the world bank. The Chinese are proud to say that we have not dragged the global economy on average.

In another regard, what can be achieved by 2020 are not only the raise of income, but also more importantly, the eradication of poverty. Rural areas that poor and limited in living conditions, will be transformed to modern well-off countryside.

Li Daokui also described other two time points in economic way: By 2035, China will be a member of high-income countries and rank in the top 30 among large counties; the per capita GDP will reach 50 percent of that of the United States, equivalent to that of Spain. By 2050, China will rank in the top 30 among large countries; the per capita GDP will reach 70 percent of that of the United States, equivalent to that of France.

Looking forward to this blueprint, Li Daokui also put forward the new challenges facing China's economy. He stressed that we should not only talk about China's economic story, but also China's theories, "Our intention is to run Chinese education well, our intention is to introduce and carry forward modern Chinese science, including social sciences and humanities. Our mission is to give impetus to China's social science, including the innovation of economic theories. This is our original intention, and this is Tsinghua University's mission!"

Humanitas Tsinghua Forum is an innovative communication event held by Tsinghua University, aiming to empower the construction of a more innovative, internationalized, and humanity-oriented Tsinghua. The forum regularly invites excellent humanists to give public speeches at the renowned New Tsinghua Auditorium, sharing their classical theories, unique thinking and major discoveries.

Translation and revision | Raj Lamar

Image | Song Chen

12 月 5 日

文字 | 张译丹

图片 | 梁露文

十年星星之火，初成燎原之势

2007 年，第一期“星火计划”开班；十年后的 2017 年，第一批“星火”学员刚刚博士毕业不久，已经在自己的学术领域初露锋芒——“星火计划”的全称是“科技创新，星火燎原”清华大学学生创新人才培养计划，“星火”二字来源于“星星之火，可以燎原”，由学生处、教务处、校团委共同发起推动，每年主要面向大二本科生招募，采用“四阶段、五环节”的培养模式，旨在通过整合校内外各种相关资源，凝聚起一个跨专业、跨年级的学生兴趣共同体，培养出新一代有代表性的拔尖学术创新人才。

2017 年 5 月 27 日晚，“科技创新，星火燎原”清华大学学生创新人才培养计划十周年年会举行，“星火班”学员与往期校友学员齐聚一堂。年会以“iSPARK・峥嵘十年”为主题，用“百舸争流”“欣欣向荣”“十年树木”“似水流年”四个版块展现十年来“星火班”学员的学术科技创新成果，共同回顾“星火”十年的故事。

2007 年 10 月，针对本科生科研创新能力不足的问题，学校基于因材施教的理念，整合全校资源，启动了“星火计划”。作为资历最老的首批学员，香港中文大学助理教授、2005 级汽车系校友郭平在年会上分享了自己作为第一批“吃螃蟹的人”的记忆，以及此后人生道路中与“星火”难解难分的情缘。

十年一路走来，“星火计划”的影响日益提升——“星火班”的海外研修资源面向全校学生开放，逐步发展演变成为“闯世界”计划；成立“星火俱乐部”；以“星火班”自主立项研究为蓝本正式设立了清华大学大学生学术研究推进计划……十年一路走来，“星火”成长成熟了许多，但不变的，是其始终强调兴趣为主、创造环境、因材施教、个性发展的培养思路。

年会上，学员们纷纷通过展示自己的创新成果，为“星火计划”送上十周年生日礼物：“星火”八期学员、2011 级电子工程系校友姚颂讲述了他作为联合创始人创办深鉴科技有限公司后，在深度学习硬件加速领域中取得成果的经历。两位“星火”十一期的学员，2015 级材料学院本科生张翱和 2015 级人文学院本科生王浩宇分别展示了他们的申请项目——“量子点的合成策略探究及其光电应用探究”和“清代满文《西医人身骨脉图说钦定骼体全录》译编”。

十年星星之火，已初成燎原之势。二十年、三十年后，清华“星火”必将更加耀眼！

Ten Years of "iSpark" , It is Just the Beginning

The first "iSpark" class was established in 2007. In 2017, this first group of students who have just graduated from their doctoral degree have begun to show their true talents in their respective fields. This talent class is derived from "Scientific and Technological Innovation" —the full name being Tsinghua University Students' Innovative Talent Training Program. This talent class is also known as "iSpark" since a spark is all that is needed to start something big. Jointly sponsored by the student affairs office and various other units, recruitment is mainly targeted at the sophomores. The training mode of "Four stages - Five cycles" aims to integrate all kinds of related teaching resources to cultivate a new generation of top innovative academic talents.

On the evening of May 27, 2017, "Tsinghua University Student Innovation Talent Training Program's 10th Anniversary Annual Conference" welcomed the gathering of the proud alumni. With "iSPARK Eventful Decade" as the conference theme, the achievements made by the students during the past decade were showcased in four segments.

In October 2007, when faced with the bottleneck of scientific research and innovation in the undergraduate students, Tsinghua decided to use the available resources to start a plan in cultivating talents. As the first batch of the most senior students, Guo Ping, the assistant professor at the Chinese University of Hong Kong and 2005 Alumni from Tsinghua's Department of Automotive Engineering, shared with all the earliest and fondest memories of the special talent class.

During the past ten years, the class has gained great results. Opportunities to boost international experience has been made available for students at Tsinghua including all research and development resources. The "Top Open" program and an "iSpark" club were also established.

At the annual meeting, students presented their academic achievements as gifts to celebrate the 10th Anniversary of the program. 2011 alumni Yao Song shared his achievements in deep learning hardware acceleration as co-founder of an electronic engineering company. 2015 alumni Zhang Ao from School of Materials Science and Engineering and 2015 alumni Wang Haoyu from School of Humanities respectively displayed their research work.

Ten years of the "iSpark" program is more than just a spark since it will surely continue for the next 20-30 years and more.

Translation and revision | Min Weiyuan

Image | Liang Luwen

12月6日

文字 | 杨茂艺
图片 | 任左莉
摄影 | 何名暖

探访核研院核化学化工实验室：从岁月的溶液里萃取记忆

能源问题，是人类共同面临的世纪难题。相比于化石燃料、太阳能、风能、水能等传统能源，核能因其高度浓缩性和废物少量性而日益受到人们关注。然而，使用核能所产生的废物虽然量少，却有着很高的放射性，为了从中提取出宝贵的铀、钚资源，减少废物量，我们不得不对核电站生成的乏燃料进行后处理。

清华大学核研院位于北京西北郊，整个园区依山而建，松柏常青，静谧隐蔽。核化学化工实验室建于 20 世纪 60 年代，最早研发我国核武器用钚提取技术。目前主要研究方向是先进的核燃料循环技术，包括高放废液的分离处理、高温堆核燃料后处理等。

短短一上午，实验室老师带我参观了放化实验室的热室、放化工艺实验室、液闪测量室、水法工艺实验室、化学实验室、有机合成室等实验场所，并向我展示了通风柜、离心萃取机、手脚沾污检测仪、混合澄清槽、脉冲萃取柱、萃取剂合成装置以及老式机械手、手摇计算器等实验设备和仪器。不得不承认的是，随着时间的侵蚀，房间内照明亮度普遍不够，许多设备表面落了一层尘埃。但老师们却用实验室的历史提醒我，核燃料后处理技术的发展是一段众多人为之付出努力的漫长历史。

20 世纪 50 年代，苏联曾帮助中国援建核燃料后处理厂，提供的是技术相对落后的沉淀法，但在工程关键时期，苏联撤走所有专家，国家核工业相关部门束手无策。与此同时，清华工程物理系师生选择了当时最先进的磷酸三丁酯溶剂萃取法为主攻方向，开展深入研究。1964 年，中央拨专款在清华“200 号”工地建造热化学实验室以进行萃取法的可行性验证，并于 1966 年完成了全流程热验证实验。基于这些成果，我国决定放弃沉淀法，采用自主研发的萃取法建设核燃料后处理厂，并在 20 世纪 70 年代达到国际先进水平。20 世纪 70 年代末，实验室开始关注高放废物处理问题，开发了用三烷基氧膦从高放废液中萃取分离锕系元素的中国 TRPO 流程，并持续开展了几十年的深入研究，正在积极推广其工业应用……

风举千阳，叶落成蹊。沉淀了无数科研攻关记忆的“200 号”是如此宁静，那暖黄色的光和一座座孤独的楼所交织而成的美又是如此无言，只留下绿叶灰墙诉说历史。当我离开核研院的那一瞬间，一丝感动涌上心头——泛黄的记忆之中埋藏着艰难与勇敢的故事，是前辈们孜孜以求的真实写照。我们不应当忘了，这个远离清华园的地方。

The Laboratory of Nuclear Chemistry and Nuclear Chemical Engineering: Extracting Tsinghua's Distant Past in Nuclear Chemistry Research

The problem of energy is a problem that mankind has had to face for centuries. Compared to traditional sources of energy such as fossil fuels, solar energy, wind energy and water energy, nuclear energy has drawn increasing attention because of its high concentration of energy and minimal amount of waste. However, the waste generated from the production of nuclear energy is highly radioactive, but in order to extract valuable energy from uranium and plutonium, we have to reprocess nuclear fuel (fuel elements no longer usable and removed from reactor) generated at nuclear power stations.

The Institute of Nuclear and New Energy Technology of Tsinghua is located in the northwestern suburbs of Beijing. The entire park sits on a hillside with evergreen pines, quietly hidden. The Laboratory of Nuclear Chemistry and Nuclear Chemical Engineering was built in the 1960s. Its earliest use was to provide weapons-grade plutonium for China. At present, its main research directions are to improve the solvent extraction method, improve high-temperature reactor related technology, nuclear fuel cycle and nuclear pore membrane technology.

In a short morning, Director Wang of the Lab took me along to visit the radiochemical laboratory, radiochemical technology laboratory, liquid measurement flash chamber, dry chemical laboratory, chemical laboratory, and the organic synthesis room. He also showed me experiment equipments and instruments such as fume hood, centrifugal extractor, old mechanical scale, hand and foot detector, hand calculator, simulated liquid water tank, mixed clarification tank, pulse extraction column, and extractant synthesis device. I have to admit that, due to decay over time, the room's lighting conditions are generally poor, and many equipments are covered under a layer of dust. However, Director Wang reminds me of the history of the laboratory: the development of nuclear fuel reprocessing technology has a long past.

In the 1950s, the Soviet Union promised China to build a reprocessing plant, which provided a backward precipitation method with low yield and poor separation effect. It is difficult for units within the state nuclear industry department to implement this method. At the same time, faculty and students from Tsinghua's Department of Engineering Physics chose the most advanced tributyl phosphate solvent extraction method as their main research direction. In 1964, China's central government approved the construction of a thermochemical laboratory at Tsinghua No. 200 site to prove the feasibility of the extraction method.

In 1966, upon the completion of the thermal experimental research, the central government decided to adopt the extraction method to build factories, which greatly enhanced China's post-industrial technology. In 1970, nation-states began signing a nuclear non-proliferation treaty. In the late 1970s, the trialkyl phosphine oxide extraction method was invented. Through years of research, a process with high separation efficiency called TRPO was completed for using high-level liquid waste.

Strong wind lifts the autumn leaves onto a path. The No. 200 site is tranquil showered with the beauty of a warm golden sunlight. The lonely building had left behind green leaves and a gray wall, and the structure reminds me of Tsinghua's distant past. When I left the the Institute of Nuclear and New Energy Technology, a wave of emotions surged within my heart - under the yellowed memories are buried stories of hardship and bravery, an authentic portrayal of our predecessors' lives. We should not forget this place though it is far from Tsinghua campus.

Translation and revision | Alexis See Tho

Image | Ren Zuoli

Photographer | He Mingnuan

12月7日

文字 | 刘书田

图片 | 赵存存、刘雨田

二十四节气之大雪

大雪，农历二十四节气的第二十一个节气，标志着仲冬时节的正式开始。古人云："大雪，十一月节。大者，盛也，至此而雪盛矣。""大雪为节者，形于小雪为大雪，时雪转甚，故以大雪名节。"这是大雪节气的由来。

隆冬时节，风总是紧紧地裹着人们奔跑，让你无处躲藏。呼啸的冷风吹过，感受到冬天肃穆的气息。枝头的枯叶已稀疏零落，剩下一群鸟儿站立在枝头。然而幸运的是，在某个清晨走出寝室，"忽如一夜春风来，千树万树梨花开"就会真实地呈现在你的面前。

人们说，一下雪，北京就变成了北平。每个人都期待着清华园的第一场雪。清秀动人的水木清华，当一景一物均染上了银白，校园的每一个角落都可以称作银装素裹的世界了。朦胧中的大礼堂散发着高雅的气息，清华学堂的古老建筑在雪天的映衬下更显得有几分书斋味道，荷塘月色披上了一层轻薄的白色棉被，二校门宛若和雪景融为一体。

雪后的清华园，静谧安宁，古朴典雅，不禁让人想起那些旧时光。"绿蚁新醅酒，红泥小火炉。晚来天欲雪，能饮一杯无？"下雪的夜晚，与两三好友相约，围炉沏茶，谈经论道，诗书重读，畅谈理想。年轮循环至仲冬，雪落处，喧嚣折尽，一切劳心劳形都显得不合时宜。忙碌了一学年的莘莘学子进入了期末考试备战阶段，而古人的那颗平常心则深深感染着他们，在这个园子里读书做事，安静笃定，岂不幸哉！美哉！

大雪是"进补"的好时节，素有"冬天进补，开春打虎"的说法。瑞雪兆丰年，大雪节气正是韬光养晦的好时节。飘雪，是大自然的馈赠。踏雪寻梅，寒梅正艳，仿佛已经闻到春天的气息。不禁感慨一句：冬天到了，春天还会远吗？

Heavy Snow, the 21st Solar Term of the Year

The Heavy Snow is the 21st term of the 24 traditional Chinese solar terms. It refers to winter and a period when the weather gets even colder than that in Light Snow.

In winter, the wind is always there...chasing and following us wherever we go. It sure reminds us of how cold it is. The last few leaves that lie motionless on the ground and that last flock of birds are perhaps the last sight that we have of autumn. However, we all know that after a few months, spring will greet us all.

People say that when it snows, Beijing becomes Peking. Everyone looks forward to the first snow in Tsinghua when every corner and inch of the campus is covered by a white blanket. An elegant atmosphere descends upon the lotus pond, the old Gate and all of the Tsinghua buildings. Despite being under this blanket of snow, there still lies a burning desire for knowledge, research and academic pursuits.

Tsinghua is tranquil after the snow. Simple and elegant, it reminds all of those distant memories. On a snowy night, two or three friends gather around the stove, drinking tea, reading and chatting about life. The snow outside reminds all that it's time for the final exam and as they look at the sight of their dear campus, nothing can quite beat this white serenity.

Heavy Snow is also a good time for "replenishing." There is a saying that "winter is replenishing time so that one can remain energetic throughout spring." Snow is also a gift from nature since it also marks the start of spring and all of its colors. If winter comes, can spring be far behind?

Translation and revision | Min Weiyuan

Image | Zhao Cuncun, Liu Yutian

12月8日

文字 | 刘兰

图片 | 宋晨

忆“一二·九”运动骨干、清华大学校友陆璀

“一二·九”运动发生于1935年12月9日。那一天，一批青年学生走上街头，用满腔的爱国热血向社会各界发出振聋发聩的呼喊，大大唤起了中国人民的觉醒。在这场动员全民族抗战的爱国主义运动中，青年学生发挥了重大作用。

1935年12月21日，邹韬奋主编的《大众生活》第一卷第六期的封面、封底上刊登了两张闻名中外的“一二·九”运动群众集会照片。照片上，一位女学生手执大号话筒，慷慨激昂地向学生和市民群众发表演说、宣传抗日。这两张照片的主人公是当时清华大学社会学系大四的学生陆璀，那一年，她刚刚21岁。

在“一二·九”运动爆发前，陆璀已经是清华园里的一名活跃分子。她经常担任“清华女生时事讨论会”的主持人，编辑策划女生宿舍救亡壁报。此外，她还秘密学习了《八一宣言》，积极宣传和实践中国共产党的抗日主张。1935年，陆璀担任清华大学学生救国委员会委员。

在1935年12月9日和12月16日抗日救亡的示威游行中，陆璀走在队伍的最前列，并于12月9日临危受命，代表北平学联向大家发表演讲。12月16日，在行进被阻于宣武门外时，她勇敢地从城门底下爬进城内开门。不过，在即将打开城门的紧要关头，她遭到军警的痛打，并被带到了警察所。就在警察所，陆璀接受了美国著名记者埃德加·斯诺的采访，才有了之后引人瞩目的《中国的贞德被捕了》这一独家新闻。

1936年，陆璀赴上海参加全国学生救国联合会筹建工作，同年及1938年，陆璀受组织委派出国，以全国学联代表的身份先后参加了在日内瓦和纽约举行的两次世界青年大会，并在两次会议期间和陶行知等同志一起辗转奔波于美、英、法、加等国，不遗余力地向华侨和国际友人宣传中国的抗日救亡运动。

2015年2月，陆璀在京逝世，享年100岁。她一生节俭，将个人积蓄捐给母校清华大学设立助学金，帮助家庭贫困的学生完成学业。生前她曾多次回到母校，谆谆教诲现在的年轻学生：“一是要有爱国之心；二是要有报国之志；三是要有建国之才；四是要有卫国之能。”爱国、报国、建国、卫国，这正是陆璀一生的真实写照，也是她对清华学子的深情厚望。

忆往昔岁月峥嵘，感今朝盛世繁华，望来日任重道远。重新聆听投身革命的父辈们走过的烽火硝烟，除了感动与感恩，青年学子更应当勇于担当，将清华人始终如一的家国情怀与责任传承下去。

Lu Cui: Backbone of the December 9th Movement

On December 9th, 1935, a group of patriotic and young students took to the streets, exclaiming to all levels of society to fight against Japanese invasion. The rally aroused the awakening of the Chinese people and began the mobilization of the entire nation. Throughout the counter Japanese movement, young students played an important role.

That same month, on December 21st, 1935, the cover and back cover of *Public Life* (a weekly magazine that publicized counter-Japanese war efforts) featured two photos of the now famous December 9th movement known both in China and overseas. One of the photos depicted a female student speaking to students and citizens through a loud speaker. The protagonist of these two photos is Lu Cui, a senior student of the Department of Sociology at Tsinghua University, who was just 21 years old that year.

Lu Cui was an active member of movements on Tsinghua campus even before the December 9th Movement broke out. She often served as the host of the Tsinghua Female Current Affairs Symposium and was the editor who planned national salvation posters for female dormitories on campus. In addition, she also secretly studied the "August 1 Declaration" and actively publicized and implemented Communist Party of China's anti-Japanese propositions. In 1935, she served on Tsinghua University's Students National Salvation Committee.

Demonstration parades took place on December 9th and December 16th, 1935. Lu Cui marched in front of the ranks and bravely climbed into the city from the bottom of the city gate to unlock the gates when the march was stopped at the city gate on December 16th, 1935. However, at the critical juncture of opening the city gate, she was beaten by the military police and taken to the police station. At the police station, Lu Cui accepted an interview with Edgar Snow, a famous American reporter, and afterwards, news spread that "China's Joan of Arc was arrested" .

In 1936, Lu Cui went to Shanghai to participate in the preparation for the National Students Salvation Alliance. In the same year and in 1938, Lu Cui was appointed by the organization to go abroad to participate in the World Assembly of Youth held in Geneva and New York and in her capacity as a representative of the National Students Salvation Alliance. During these two meetings, along with Tao Xingzhi and other comrades, they have spared no effort in spreading news to overseas Chinese and international friends in the United States, Britain, France and Canada about the counter-Japanese national salvation movement.

In February 2015, Lu Cui died in Beijing at the age of 100. She had lived a frugal life, and donated personal savings to her alma mater, Tsinghua University to set up grants to help students with financial problems to complete their studies. She had continually returned to Tsinghua where she advised young students: "First, we must have a patriotic heart; second, we must have the ambition to serve the country; third, we must have the abilities to build the nation; and fourth, we must have the capabilities to protect our country." Those words are a true portrayal of Lu Cui's life, and also her affectionate expectations of Tsinghua students.

While listening to the stories of predecessors who took part in the revolution, in addition to being touched and grateful, young students should have the courage to carry the burden and inherit the patriotic responsibilities as a Tsinghua person.

Translation and revision | Alexis See Tho

Image | Song Chen

12月11日

文字 | 杨晨晞

图片 | 李娜

2017年清华大学特等奖学金获得者胡耀文:“大满贯”是怎样炼成的

“后来我意识到，如果不学物理的话，我会后悔一辈子。”2017年清华大学本科生特等奖学金答辩会上，一位意气风发的少年话音未落，台下便响起雷鸣般的掌声。

这位激情澎湃的少年叫胡耀文，来自清华大学物理系物理42班。

胡耀文本科前三年的平均学分绩为94，在物理专业排名第一。2017年1月26日，胡耀文把大学里最想集齐的四颗“龙珠”悉数收入囊中——在“分析力学”“量子力学（1）”“电动力学”“统计力学（1）”这四门物理系最核心的必修课里达成全部满分的“大满贯”。平时，胡耀文被同学们称为“耀神”。

对于胡耀文来说，学业、科研、社会工作和实践“串联”起了他的大学生活，也使得他在迷茫中逐渐找到方向。

起初，通过高考进入清华的胡耀文来到竞赛高手如云的物理系时，自信心也曾受到过冲击。但不服输的他一边调整心态，一边一步一个脚印地往前走着。相较于选择多门课程但却浅尝辄止，他选择把少数几门课学好学精。功夫不负有心人，到了大三，胡耀文的学年平均学分绩97.7分，成为全年级第一，外加“四大力学”全满分，充分证明了他对待专业知识的态度和能力。

在修好课内课程的同时，胡耀文也早早地开始了科研。“我不打算把自己的科研局限在某一个领域中，也不想把自己囿于纯粹的理论或实验研究中。”胡耀文说，他希望尽可能多地去尝试。于是，从最开始尝试凝聚态理论方向，到接触量子信息方向，再到大三赴哈佛大学暑期研究尝试量子光子学，他不断挑战着自己，在这三个完全不同的领域中，胡耀文均完成了第一作者的论文。目前，胡耀文共发表SCI期刊论文九篇，其中包括以第一作者在《物理评论A》(Physical Review A)、《科学报告》(Scientific Reports)和《物理学报：凝聚态物质》(Journal of Physics: Condensed Matter)发表的3篇论文。

大学生活丰富多彩，胡耀文选择用社会工作和实践作为“调味剂”。他曾作为团委实践组的组员参与社会工作，同时担任学习委员，在期末举办复习会，讲解重难点，撰写总结文档，服务同学并与大家共同进步。

谈到在清华度过的本科时光，胡耀文说自己最大的收获不是学业和科研上的硕果，而是在清华的摇篮中找到了自己真正想做什么。尽管迷茫动摇过，但随着自己的成长，他最终明白，自己是真的喜欢物理。“一方面，物理研究拓宽人类的知识边界，是一份宏大的事业，我想要为这份宏大的事业出一份力；另一方面，学者应该有学者的责任和担当，我希望自己的研究也能够造福人们的生活。在我看来，研究的格局和品味，才会在未来真正定义自己是一个怎样的科学家。”胡耀文说。

Hu Yaowen, The Recipient of 2017 Tsinghua Top Grade Scholarship: The Grand Slam

"Then I realized that if I do not learn physics, I'll regret for that forever." Applause continued and filled the air at the end of his speech. This happened on the 7th of November, 2017, the day of the defense meeting of 2017 Tsinghua Top Grade Scholarship candidates. So who is he?

This passionate youngster is Hu Yaowen from Class No.42 of Department of Physics, Tsinghua University.

Hu's grade point average for the first three years is 94. He is the Top1 student in Physics major. On the 26th of January 2017, Hu took home the "Grand Slam" by obtaining full marks in the "Analysis of Mechanics" "Quantum Mechanics (1)" "Electrodynamics" and "Statistical Mechanics (1)" courses. These are considered to be the four most important courses in the Department of Physics. Coming first and scoring full marks in these courses made him that "wizz kid."

For Hu, his studies, research and social work practices are all central to his university life. They also gave him much direction and clarity.

At first, Hu's confidence was shaken after being admitted into Department of Physics at Tsinghua University. He adjusted his mentality and took it one step at a time. Rather than signing up for a great deal of courses, he chose to focus on only a few of them and try to understand them as deep as possible. Hu was rewarded for his efforts since his grade point average for junior year was 97.7. Coming first in his grade and earning full marks in all four important courses are obvious the reflections of his professional knowledge and hard work.

Apart from his coursework, Hu also started with research. "I don't want to limit myself to a single field nor do I want to be stuck with only theoretical or experimental research." Hu wish to give everything a try. So, from work in condensed matter theory to quantum information to research in quantum photonics at Harvard University, he constantly pushed himself to tackle these three domains. As a result, he has completed first-author papers at all these three fields and published 9 journal papers, including 3 first-author papers in *Physical Review A, Scientific Reports* and *Journal of Physics: Condensed Matter*.

University life is rich and colorful. Hu was heavily involved with social work and as a member of the student committee, he undertook multiple social projects and completed reviews with the aim of helping his fellow peers.

For Hu, the biggest gift from Tsinghua are not academic results or scientific researches. It is that he found what he wants to do. Despite being lost for a while, being more mature makes him realize that he really loves physics. Hu said, "Researches in physics that broadening the boundaries of human knowledge is a huge process. I wish to be a part of this process. On the other hand, scholars also have their own responsibility to the society. I hope my research can also take care of the assistance on people's life at the same time. I think that, in the future, it is this kind of taste on research that define what kind of a scientist I really am."

Translation and revision | Min Weiyuan

Image | Li Na

12 月 12 日

文字 | 杨鹏成

图片 | 刘雨田、宋晨

清华大学学生粉刷匠工作室协会：改造校园，粉刷梦想

最近，北京市行知实验小学的孩子们在上学时发现，教室外面有不认识的哥哥姐姐在墙上进行创作——他们像魔法师一样把平淡无奇的墙面变成赏心悦目的艺术品，为孩子们的校园生活增添了许多乐趣，他们是由清华大学的学生组成的“粉刷匠”团体。

用自己的创意让校园变得多姿多彩，是清华大学学生粉刷匠工作室协会成立的初衷。协会于 2013 年 9 月成立，是由清华大学学生发起并运营的公益组织，致力于对儿童生活空间进行优化再造，通过墙面改造、室内设计、景观设计、儿童教育等方式，与师生共同营造多彩的生活环境，使儿童享受校园生活、快乐成长，为中国人居事业贡献自己的一点力量。

“我们坚持自己的公益理念，以改造生活环境的方式使儿童受益。”“粉刷匠”第五任会长洪冬玲在访谈中强调。“粉刷匠”是中国大陆第一个致力于儿童空间改造、校园环境美化的高校公益社团。自成立起到现在，“粉刷匠”与 16 个公益组织展开合作，足迹遍布青海、内蒙古、贵州等 14 个省份，已经改造 26 所学校，受益儿童约 7000 多人，累计改造墙面约 12500 平方米。“孩子们不仅能够在墙刷完之后享受更好的生活学习环境，在刷墙时也会参与进来，和志愿者产生友谊。”洪冬玲说。

除了打工子弟学校、贫困山区学校之外，“粉刷匠”还走进了社区、服刑子女学校、自闭症儿童疗养院等。四年来，“粉刷匠”获得了“清华大学十佳协会”“北京市优秀社团”“德年公益文化优秀社团”等 14 项公益奖项。协会的活动也受到了社会的关注，被搜狐网、网易新闻、CCTV13、凤凰网、凤凰卫视等多家媒体报道。

“花一个下午站在墙前静静地画画，身心会得到很大放松。”谈到她作为志愿者参加粉刷匠活动的感受时，洪冬玲说。自协会成立以来，“粉刷匠”共招募大学生志愿者约 760 人，同学们克服种种困难，把创意和努力带到了海拔 4000 米之上的青海果洛藏族自治州和经历过洪水的湖北恩施土家族苗族自治州，也在吉林省榆树市恩育乡幸福小学体验到了三天没有洗澡、每顿必豆腐和黄瓜的生活。在这项形式独特的公益活动中，志愿者奔赴祖国大地践行梦想、收获友谊。

2017 年，“粉刷匠”除了寻找学校进行粉刷活动外，还把粉刷对象放在了清华校内的建筑上。11 月底，经过为期两个月的筹备，粉刷匠协会的同学们在寒风凛冽的冬日徒手作画，为清华学堂地下研读间的 14 个采光井披上了彩绘新衣。“粉刷匠”们希望通过自己的努力，把校园变得更美，为同学们提供更好的学习生活环境。

KidStudio: Transform the Campus and Paint the Dream

Recently, the students of Xingzhi Primary School in Beijing's Haidian District discovered that many older brothers and sisters were outside working on their school walls. Like magicians, they transformed plain looking walls into beautiful artworks. They have added much color and fun to school life. These brothers and sisters are members of the KidStudio from Tsinghua.

Using creative ideas to make the school more colorful is the main work of the KidStudio. Founded in September 2013, it was launched and operated by Tsinghua students as a public welfare organization. The aim is to optimize the children's living space through renovation, interior design and landscape design. It is with great hope that together with the teachers, students are able to thrive in a colorful environment so that not only do they enjoy campus life but also find joy during their growth.

"We adhere to our own public welfare concept in finding ways to benefit children through reforming the living environment." Hong Dongling, the 5th president of the KidStudio stressed in the interview. The KidStudio is the first public welfare association dedicated to the improvement of children's learning environment. Since the establishment, the KidStudio has collaborated with 16 organizations and made its mark in Qinghai, Inner Mongolia, Guizhou and about 14 other provinces. They have made changes to 26 schools and over 7000 children have benefited from various projects supported and initiated by the association. Since now, about 12500 square meters of walls have been re-painted. Children can not only enjoy a better learning environment but also paint the walls themselves. They can use this opportunity to make friends with the volunteers.

In addition to schools for migrant children and schools in remote areas, the KidStudio also visit communities, nursing homes and special schools for children with autism. During the past 4 years, the KidStudio has won over 14 public service awards such as "The Top Ten Best Associations in Tsinghua" "Top Association in Beijing" and much more. It has also attracted the attention of our society and they have been reported by Sohu, CCTV13, Phoenix News, Phoenix TV, news 163 etc.

"Spend an afternoon standing in front of a wall and you realize how soothing it is." This is how Hong felt as a volunteer of the KidStudio. Since the establishment, 760 volunteers were recruited and students have overcome difficulties from visiting schools in Qinghai and Hubei. Whether it was going to schools located 4000m above sea level or working for three days without a bath and eating bean curd and cucumbers for every meal, the volunteers are forming friendship and realizing their dreams by going deep into the heart of the motherland.

This year, in addition to looking for new schools to paint, objects within Tsinghua's own campus have been the targets as well for the KidStudio. After 2 months of preparation, in late November, students from the KidStudio added bright colors to 14 light wells of Tsinghua Xuetang's underground study room. The KidStudio wants to make the campus more beautiful and through their work, they wish to create a much better learning and living environment for the students.

Translation and revision | Min Weiyuan

Image | Liu Yutian, Song Chen

12月13日

文字 | 原橙

图片 | 罗梦霞、杨思维

“为祖国健康工作五十年”提出60周年：清华体育精神60年的接力

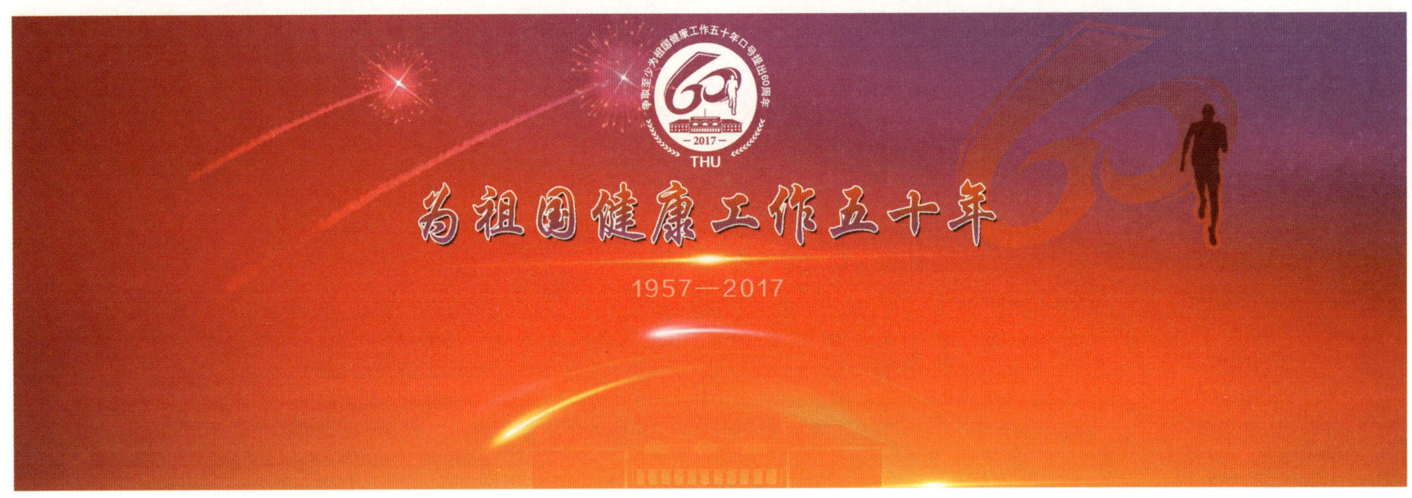

“为祖国健康工作五十年”，60年来，这是一代又一代清华人共同的口号和信念，激励着他们在漫长的人生中强健体魄，挑战自我，报效祖国，奔跑向前。

2017年12月10日上午9点，“为祖国健康工作五十年”提出60周年纪念大会在清华大学大礼堂隆重举行。教育部副部长田学军，国家体育总局副局长高志丹，北京市委副秘书长郑登文，教育部体卫艺司司长王登峰，中国大学生体育协会副主席华爱军，清华大学校长邱勇、校党委书记陈旭、党委常务副书记副校长姜胜耀、党委副书记过勇、学校老领导张孝文等出席大会。清华校友、奥运冠军邓亚萍、肖钦，体育健将蓬铁权、胡方纲，专程回母校参加纪念“一二·九”系列活动。现平均年龄74岁、曾以一曲《我爱你中国》在“出彩中国人”舞台感动千万中国人的上海清华校友合唱团，上百名毕业50年以上的老校友……他们以体育的名义重返曾留下自己青春汗水与拼搏记忆的清华园，与数百名师生代表一道，共话清华体育的“前世今生”，畅谈体育的迁移价值，传递不断发扬光大的清华体育精神。

会上，校长邱勇宣读了国务院副总理刘延东的批示。刘延东在批示中指出：“清华大学坚持‘育人至上，体魄与人格并重’的全面办学理念，为党和国家培养造就了大批德才兼备、全面发展的高素质人才。60年来，蒋南翔校长发出的‘为祖国健康工作五十年’的口号，激励了一代又一代清华人，产生了广泛的社会影响。希望你们深入学习贯彻习近平新时代中国特色社会主义思想，继续坚持重视体育工作的优良传统，不断总结经验，深化教育教学改革，为我国高等教育内涵质量的提升和人才培养发展继续谱写新时代的新篇章！”

陈旭在讲话中强调，要学习和继承口号中体现的强烈爱国主义精神、深嵌的全面发展的育人理念，以及指出的鲜明价值导向和努力目标。陈旭表示，体育是立德树人的重要载体，为祖国健康地工作50年，就是要在人生热情最高涨、精力最充沛、经验最丰富的各个阶段为党和人民的事业贡献自己的一切。

教育部副部长田学军在总结讲话时充分肯定了清华体育育人取得的成绩，强调要深入研究、深入挖掘“为祖国健康工作五十年”口号的内涵和精神，继承和发扬口号中蕴含的强烈的爱国情怀、全面发展的健康理念和自强不息的拼搏精神，努力开创体育工作的新局面，培养德智体美全面发展的社会主义建设者和接班人。

固体力学家、今年90岁高龄的黄克智院士以“健康是成功之本”为题，分享了自己受益于清华体育精神的经历和感悟。黄克智20岁大学毕业，至今仍坚持在教学科研第一线，已健康工作70年。他从40岁开始跑步，70岁学习游泳，72岁至今每天坚持打40分钟网球。“勤奋加健康，使我一生没有虚度。”耄耋之年的黄克智声音清亮、逻辑清晰缜密，他用自己70年健康工作的精彩人生，为清华师生树立了最好的典范。

清华自1911年建校至今始终重视体育，并将体育作为重要的学校传统和办学特色。60年前，1957年11月29日，在全校体育工作干部会上，蒋南翔校长提出“为祖国健康工作五十年”的口号，这句脍炙人口的口号从此成为清华人的奋斗目标。几十年来，这个口号不仅对清华，对全国高校以至对全社会都产生了积极而广泛的影响。

"To Work Healthily for 50 years for Our Motherland" : 60 Years of Tsinghua's Sportsmanship

"To work healthily for 50 years for our motherland" , this has been the slogan for 60 years. It has remained a common goal and spirit of the Tsinghua people. It has inspired and challenged them to continue making contributions to the motherland and most importantly: to make further advancements.

On December 10th, 2017, the 60th Anniversary of the slogan "to work healthily for 50 years for our motherland" was held at Tsinghua's main auditorium. During the day, Tsinghua's President Qiu Yong read out the approval letter from Liu Yandong, the Vice Premier of the State Council. Liu pointed out that Tsinghua has adhered to "maintaining the highest level of education, physical education is as important as positive character" . Tsinghua has, trained large number of top-quality talents for both the party and the motherland. For the past 60 years, the slogan "To work healthily for 50 years for our motherland" , first stressed by President Jiang Nanxiang has inspired generations after generations of Tsinghua students as well as generated a wide range of social influences. "We hope that you will continue to study hard and apply new ideas as stated by President Xi Jinping into your work. We hope that you will continue to adhere to the traditions of sports and deepen reforms in education. A new chapter will commence in the teaching and development of China's higher education sector and you will no doubt be an important part of this!"

Tsinghua alumni, Olympic Champion Deng Yaping, Xiao Qin and masters of sports Peng Tiequan, Hu Fanggang made a special trip back to their Alma mater. With an average age of 74 years-old, Tsinghua's Shanghai Alumni Choir, moved the hearts of many viewers. Alongside leaders from the Ministry of Education, National Sports Bureau, Beijing Municipal Party Committee, Chinese University Students' Sports Association as well as the current and former Heads of Tsinghua and hundreds of staff and students, they recalled and carried forward the sportsmanship of Tsinghua University.

"Health is the foundation of success" — this has been the experience of 90 years-old Huang Kezhi. After graduating from university at the age of 20 years old, he has always remained at the forefront of teaching and research for 70 years. He started running at the age of 40 and learnt how to swim at the age of 70. At the age of 72, he kept his daily habit of playing tennis for at least 40 minutes per day. "Hard work and health have kept me from wasting my life." said Huang. He has set the best example for Tsinghua teachers and students to follow.

Tsinghua University has always attached great importance to sports since its founding in 1911. It has made sports an important school tradition and a part of the curriculum. This has remained a top characteristic of Tsinghua. 60 years ago, on the 29th of November 1957, President Jiang Nanxiang put forward a slogan "To work healthily for 50 years for our motherland" at the Tsinghua Sports Cadre Conference. This popular slogan has since become the goal of every Tsinghua person. For decades, the slogan has had a positive and broad impact on Tsinghua as well as the whole society.

Translation and revision I Min Weiyuan

Image I Luo Mengxia, Yang Siwei

12月15日

文字 | 胡颖

图片 | 任帅

王文显：清华园里的“话剧教父”

在民国时期的清华园里，演话剧是一股颇有声势的文化风潮。学校将话剧作为学校美育以及健全学生人格的手段，学生也普遍认为演话剧能“增进阅历”，培养“刻苦勤劳之精神”，提高“分工合作”的能力。而对清华话剧活动影响最大的，是今人可能已经不太熟知的王文显先生。

王文显的故乡在江苏昆山，他的父亲儿时曾被李鸿章手下的“洋枪队”统帅戈登收留，后成为一名香港警察。王文显自幼随家庭辗转中英各地，英国文化在他身上打下了深刻烙印，做过他助教的李健吾称之为“一位循规蹈矩的上流人”。

王文显在清华任教22年之久，长期执掌被称为“戏剧家摇篮”的西洋文学系。1927年，王文显到美国耶鲁大学师从戏剧大师贝克教授学编剧。在此期间，他创作了英文剧《北京政变》和《委曲求全》，前者写袁世凯窃国之事，后者揭露高等学府内钩心斗角的阴暗面，一时享誉戏剧界。《委曲求全》被朱光潜称为“一种可惊赞的成就”，“他的观察老练而真切，他的嘲笑冷俏而酷毒”，在制造紧张的布局方面“几乎是无瑕可指”，在中国现代喜剧史上留下了极重要的地位。

王文显对中国话剧教育的影响同样深远持久。他主持制定的清华大学西洋文学系学程大纲及学科说明，列入了“戏剧概论”“莎士比亚”两门课程，“现代西洋文学”课程中也专设戏剧部分，这些课程都由他亲自主讲。1933年，他又加开了“近代戏剧”，专门讲授易卜生以后之戏剧。据听过课的季羡林回忆，王文显讲课比较枯燥，一句闲话也没有，下课铃一摇便合上讲义走人。但他却培养了中国现代话剧的一批中坚力量。做过王文显助教的张骏祥说，王文显的讲稿“扎扎实实，对于初接触西方戏剧的人来说，是个入门基础”。

教学之外，王文显还为清华积攒了大批戏剧专业书籍，包括曹禺在内的大量后辈都深受其益。他说：“我就是看他（王文显）买的戏剧书，钻研戏剧的。”可以说，王文显购置的这些书为清华话剧乃至中国早期话剧提供了丰富深厚的知识储备，成为无数后起之秀的精神花园。

John Wong-Quincey: Father of Stage Play in Tsinghua

Acting in dramas and plays in Tsinghua University during the Republic of China period (1912-1949) was quite a trendy cultural activity. Departments and colleges regarded drama as a means of aesthetic education and improvement of students' personalities. Students generally thought that drama can improve their learning experience, cultivate a hard-working spirit and enhance the ability of work together in teams. The person who has had the greatest impact on Tsinghua's drama activities was John Wong-Quincey, who was later revered as Tsinghua University's "Father of Stage Play" .

John Wong-Quincey's ancestral hometown is in Kunshan, Jiangsu Province. When his father was a child, he was, for a period of time, cared for by British officer Charles Gordon who was part of the Ever Victorious Army (Yang Qiang Dui), an army of Chinese soldiers trained and led by American and European officer corps. Later, Wong's father became a police officer in Hong Kong. Because of family circumstances, Wong lived away from his hometown since childhood, traveling between China and Britain. Naturally, the British culture left a deep impression on him. His teaching assistant Li Jianwu described him as "a conservative noble man" .

John Wong-Quincey taught in Tsinghua University for 22 years and has long been the Dean of Department of Western Literature, which was known as the "cradle of theatre" . In 1927, Wong went to Yale University in the United States to study screenwriting under Professor George Pierce Baker in the drama school. During this time, he wrote the English drama *Coup d'etat in Peking*, a play about Yuan Shikai and the political unrest and strife to abolish the Republican form of government, and *Compromise*, a story revealing the dark side of institutions of higher learning. Both of them became well-known works largely because they were the few serious attempts to accurately represent China to the Western world. *Compromise* was called "a marvelous achievement" by Zhu Guangqian. "His observations are sophisticated and real. His ridicule is rather cold and poisonous" , and "almost impeccable" in creating a tense plot. It has left a very big impact on China's modern history of comedy.

The impact of John Wong-Quincey on China's drama education is equally profound and lasting. He presided over the formulation of an outline of programs and disciplines of the Department of Western Literature at Tsinghua. He included courses such as "Introduction to Drama" and "Shakespeare" , and through his efforts, a course on modern western literature had special sections on theater added. He taught these classes himself.

In 1933, he added "Modern Drama" to teach plays written after Ibsen's time. According to Ji Xianlin, he recalled that Wong's lectures were boring and matter of fact, without jokes. When the bell rings, he would immediately wrap up and leave the classroom. Despite that, he has cultivated a number of backbone figures for China's modern drama. Zhang Junxiang, who was a teaching assistant of John Wong-Quincey, said that Wong's lectures "are a solid foundation and a good starting point for those who are introduced to Western drama for the first time."

Aside teaching, John Wong-Quincey also collected a large number of books on stage play for Tsinghua. These are well-received by the later generations of students, including Cao Yu. "I studied about stage plays by reading many books he (Wong) bought." Cao Yu said. We can say that the books purchased by John Wong-Quincey have provided a rich and profound knowledge base for the teaching of drama in Tsinghua and even for China in the early periods. His contributions have sowed seeds in many rising talents at Tsinghua.

Translation and revision | Alexis See Tho

Image | Ren Shuai

12 月 18 日

文字 | 田姬熔

图片 | 赵存存

“闯世界”本科生海外学术研修支持计划：学术人才的“清华设计，全球培养”

2017 年 8 月 21 日，清华大学物理系 2014 级本科生张锦苏从加州大学前往爱达荷州，在红鱼湖期待着百年一遇、横跨美国东西海岸的日全食。“那天学校里基本上一个人都没有，大家都到视野开阔的地方等着这次十分难得的天文现象。”她在几个月后回顾暑假在海外研修的经历，仍对这一天印象深刻。

2017 年，清华大学 408 名本科生在“闯世界”计划的支持下，奔赴海外 13 个国家、102 所科研机构参与交流和研修，张锦苏就是其中一员。

“闯世界”本科生海外学术研修支持计划，是清华大学团委自 2012 年发起，依托学校教务处国际大学生科研训练机化项目，面向全校大二、大三本科生开设的学生支持计划。学生根据自身兴趣，自主联系海外顶尖学术研究机构与知名学者，确定研修课题与计划，通过申请、选拔，在学校的经费支持下，参与海外学术研究与交流。

2017 年，在“闯世界”计划的支持下，同学们在海外进行了充实的研修并产出了优秀的学术成果。83 名同学前往世界排名前 5 名的学校进行研修，占总人数的 22%。截至目前，同学们共撰写论文 229 篇，其中已发表论文 22 篇，在审论文 59 篇，参与国际会议 41 人次，发明专利 7 项。

斯坦福大学 UGVR 项目（Undergraduate Visiting Research Program）每年在中国招收 18 人，今年清华有 13 名同学入选，获得 2017 年特等奖学金的电子系 2014 级本科生余天呈就是其中一位。在斯坦福一个月的研修中，除了知识性的学习，余天呈更享受的是通过与教授们的积极交流，感受到斯坦福浓郁的学术氛围：“大师们思考问题的方式给予我很多启发，也激励着我为成为他们那样的人而努力。”

今年的“闯世界”计划还支持了多名同学前往国际组织实习。新闻与传播学院的李子晗在暑假期间赴联合国教科文组织实习。从和平愿景到多元包容，从人文关怀到国际精神，在联合国为期 43 天的工作，让她对自己的未来有了清晰的认知：“‘走出去’对新闻专业的同学来说有很重要的意义，它能帮助我们更好地认清未来的努力方向。”水利系的周力和马睿则前往巴基斯坦卡洛特水电建设项目，参与了项目中混凝土拆模时间的论证研究，见证了“一带一路”上清华人的贡献。

社科学院的留学生青木哲也是清华大学未来动漫·游戏技术兴趣团队的前任理事长，今年暑假，他带领团队 23 名成员在“闯世界”计划的支持下前往日本 HAL 专门学校进行了为期 8 天的短期留学活动。在 HAL 的 8 天中，他们与日方学生一同学习开发工具、制作项目，在深度学习任天堂 3DS 开发系统后，制作出了独立掌机游戏作品。

“闯世界”计划实施五年来，已经成功支持了 1387 人次走向世界各地进行学术交流活动。“‘闯世界’计划为同学们提供了提升学术研究和自我认知的平台，同时也有效地激发了大家对学术研究的热情和自主性。”清华大学团委书记郦浩表示。

走向世界，开阔视野，用学术的语言与不同文明对话，与世界顶级学者一起进行学术交流与探索——“闯世界”计划希望能够支持清华学生在“走出去”后更好地“走回来”，站在学术前沿，推动学术发展。

"Top Open" Program: Cultivating Academic Talents in Global Culture

On August 21st, 2017, Zhang Jinsu left the University of California for Idaho. She sat and waited at Redfish Lake hoping to catch sight of the solar eclipse as it made its way across the east and west coast of American. "There were basically no one at the university that day, everyone was outside waiting to catch sight of this rare astronomical phenomenon." A few months later, Zhang still remembers this experience.

In 2017, 408 undergraduate students from Tsinghua participated in the "Top Open" Program and went to 102 scientific research institutions across 13 countries. Zhang is one of those students.

"Top Open" Program is a support plan for overseas academic training. Established by Tsinghua's Youth Committee in 2012, the program is open for sophomores and juniors. Students can contact academic research institutions and scholars from around the world in accordance to their own interests and apply for a chance for overseas research and exchange.

In this year's program, students fulfilled their training and made outstanding academic achievements: 83 students went on to study at the world's top 5 universities. As of now, 229 articles have been written including 22 that have been published, 59 under review, 41 people participated in international conferences and 7 inventions became patents.

Every year, Stanford's UGVR (Undergraduate Visiting Research Program) admits 18 people from China. 13 Tsinghua students were admitted this year and the recipient of 2017 Tsinghua Top Grade Scholarship, Yu Tiancheng is one of them. He spent a month at Stanford. In addition to study, he also had the chance to interact with the professors and got a taste of Stanford's academic atmosphere.

This year's program supported many students with a chance to undertake their internship at major international organizations. Li Zihan from the School of Journalism and Communication undertook a summer internship at UNESCO. From understanding the vision of peace to the embodying an international spirit, 43 days working for the United Nations has allowed her to truly understand what she wants to do in the future. "It is important for humanities students to venture out and see the world. You'll know about which road to take and what you wish to do. You'll also know what you are good at and what to contribute." Zhou Li and Ma Rui from the Department of Hydraulic Engineering anticipated in a hydropower construction project in Pakistan and were heavily involved with the research. They also witnessed the contributions made by Tsinghua people in the Belt and Road initiative.

Aoki Tetsuya from the School of Social Sciences was the former director of Tsinghua's Future Anime Games Technology Team. With support from the "Top Open" program, he led a team of 23 people to HAL College of Technology and Design in Japan for an 8-day exchange. During the 8 days, the students worked alongside the Japanese local students and had in-depth study of the Nintendo 3DS development systems. They also produced their own anime games work within 72 hours.

5 years since the launch of this program, 1387 students were supported and encouraged to take on board academic exchanges around the world. Whether it is academic research, study or a sense of self-awareness, "Top Open" program offered everyone a platform and inspired all to hold onto this enthusiasm and autonomy, which is important for academic research. Bing Hao, the secretary of Tsinghua's Communist Youth League said that "Top Open" program truly encourages undergraduate students to venture out.

To go into this world, to widen our views and gain a global perspective is crucial. One must have the ability to engage in academic dialogues with all civilizations and stay in conversations with top scholars from worldwide institutions. "Top Open" Program hopes that it can encourage Tsinghua students to gain self-improvement and remain at the academic frontier after their oversea exchange and experience.

Translation and revision | Min Weiyuan

Image | Zhao Cuncun

12 月 19 日

文字 | 杨晨晞

图片 | 宋晨

清华大学学生清源协会：运用专业知识，促进可持续发展

山西平遥县城往西，省道旁随处可见黄得发亮的向日葵，这里是梁家堡——很少有人知道，在这些茂盛的向日葵下面，是砷污染严重的地下水。2017 年 7 月，为了让村民喝上干净的水，20 多名大学生每天都在这条省道上往返，他们是清华大学学生清源协会的成员。

学生清源协会是一个由中外本科生、研究生共同组成的环境类公益社团，2012 年注册成立，目前协会交流群中共有 133 人，其中留学生约占四分之三。协会目前有饮用水安全、气候变化与可持续农业、可持续废物管理三个项目部门，旨在运用专业知识，促进中国的可持续发展。

饮用水安全部致力于将科研融入实践，为中国农村提供安全的饮用水，并改善人们对水安全的认知，提高对水安全的重视。2014 年至今，清源协会一直利用寒暑假到梁家堡实地考察并搭建慢滤池。今年夏天，部门成员再次奔赴当地，通过一周的实践完成了部分慢滤池的重建和升级，同时采取了更多水样，为后续实验提供数据。目前，清源协会的慢滤池项目已经逐渐成为一个涵盖实践、志愿、文化交流、学术、创业等多领域的全面发展的成熟项目。通过校外实践和返校后科学研究的结合，清源协会正为让更多人饮用安全放心的水而努力。

气候变化与可持续农业部主要关注全球气候变化问题、农业生产中的气候变化适应与减缓策略。2017 年 10 月 5 日至 7 日，由清源协会与北京师范大学模拟联合国协会联合主办的第二届模拟气候变化会议成功举办。来自 14 个国家 29 所学校的 71 名代表、12 名观察员以及 20 余名志愿者相聚清华环境学院，共商《巴黎协定》后全球气候行动走向，领略国际谈判的要义与魅力。大会上，清源协会成员围绕全球盘点机制与资金技术机制完善问题展开讨论，发表独到的见解，为气候变化问题而努力。

可持续废物管理部致力于改善农村的固体废物回收处理问题。部门目前正在运行三个项目：河南省平顶山湾李村农村垃圾及水资源管理项目、江西省新余市垃圾兑换超市项目与江西省新余市禽畜粪便资源化项目，三个项目都取得了不错的进展。清源协会通过不同地区的农村垃圾治理实践，积极探索规律、总结经验，为将来在更广阔的土地上进行垃圾治理而努力。

不断探索并将所学知识用于解决中国农村环境问题，继续在可持续发展领域发出清华声音、贡献清华力量，清源协会一直在路上。

Rural International Student Exchange of Tsinghua University: Using Professional Knowledge to Promote Sustainable Development in China

West of Shanxi's Pingyao county, you are greeted by rows after rows of bright sunflowers that stands alongside the highway. This is Liangjiabao and few know that under this lush sunflower field lies groundwater that have been heavily polluted by arsenic. In July 2017, more than 20 university students commute to the province every day just so "villagers could drink clean water" . They are members of RISE (Rural International Student Exchange) of Tsinghua University.

RISE is a student volunteer organization based on School of Environment, Tsinghua University. It is comprised of Chinese and foreign undergraduate and graduate students. Established in 2012, there are 133 people in the association with three-quarters being international students. The association currently has three project focuses—water safety, climate change & sustainable agriculture, and sustainable waste management. The aim is to use professional knowledge to promote sustainable development in China.

The Water Safety Department is committed to putting scientific research and theories into practice. The aim is to provide safe drinking water for rural China and at the same time, improve and increase awareness for water safety.

Since 2014, RISE has taken advantages of the winter and summer vacations to conduct fieldwork at Liangjiabao. During this summer break, members of RISE spent one week at the frontline and completed phases in the reconstruction and maintenance of low-cost water filters. They also took multiple water samples for data and subsequent experiments. At present, this water filter project has developed into a mature project at RISE which helps to comprehensively develop practicums, volunteering, cultural exchanges, academic research and entrepreneurship. By combining research and theory with practice, RISE is working towards providing more people with safe drinkable water.

The Climate Change & Sustainable Agriculture Department focuses on global climate changes as well as implementing beneficial strategies in agricultural production. On October 5th, 2017, the Second Model Climate Change Conference of Parties successfully welcomed 71 delegates from 29 schools across 14 countries. 12 observers and over 20 volunteers were also present. At Tsinghua's School of Environment, they started their discussion on climate change and necessary actions after the Paris Agreement. At the conference, RISE focused their attention on global stocktake, technology as well as financial mechanisms.

The Sustainable Waste Management Department works on solid waste management in rural areas. The department is currently running three projects on rural waste and water management in Henan and Jiangxi Province.

The three departments are growing and expanding. RISE continues to explore other applications, which could help to solve environmental problems in rural China, and Tsinghua's voice continues to be heard in the field of sustainable development.

Translation and revision | Min Weiyuan

Image | Song Chen

12 月 20 日

文字 | 杨晨晞

图片 | 梁晨

探访模拟法庭实验室：法学实践的第二课堂

走进法学院明理楼的大楼，你一定会被醒目的“模拟法庭”四个大字所吸引。不妨跟随我们走进模拟法庭，一睹法学学子在理论学习之外的实战风采。

模拟法庭位于清华大学明理楼 216 室，始建于 2001 年的模拟法庭已经走过了 16 个春秋。模拟法庭实验室最初按照西式的法庭风格特色而建，前方中间是法官席，与之相对的是陪审团，两侧设有辩论双方的席位。现在的模拟法庭则不仅可以根据需要随时进行中西式法庭的切换，还可以进行刑事庭、民事庭、行政庭和仲裁庭之间的转换，是标准的“多功能”模拟法庭。

法学本身就是实践性极强的学科，对于法学院的学生而言，模拟法庭自然是不可或缺的实践场地。为此，模拟法庭配备了先进的设施，为学生们提供更好的实践体验。法庭前方、后方和两侧共配备了四个摄像头，可以将法庭中各方的表现清晰地记录下来，作为教案进行研讨和观摩。齐全的多媒体设备与仿真度极高的法庭设置，让学生能够更加身临其境地学习和锻炼。

清华大学法学院本科生和硕士研究生的培养方案中，均列有在模拟法庭进行实践的必修课程。模拟法庭教学注重理论知识与法律实践紧密结合，培养学生综合能力素质，加强职业技能训练，有效地克服了传统法学教育模式的弊端，有利于实现法学教育的培养目标。通过模拟法庭的锻炼，学生不仅能够提升语言表达能力、逻辑思维能力、应变创新能力等基础能力，更能够培养法律事实识别与建构能力、法律文书制作能力、证据调查与运用能力、法庭陈述与辩论能力、司法速记能力、法律解释与推理能力和查阅法律文献能力等专业能力。模拟法庭一直在为培养面向未来的法学专业创新型人才做出贡献。

从 2003 年起，清华大学模拟法庭开始承办“理律杯”全国高校模拟法庭竞赛。从开办之初的十几所高校参与到如今数十支参赛队伍角逐，越来越多的法学学子从全国各地来到清华，感受这座模拟法庭的独特魅力。

除了日常教学和比赛外，模拟法庭实验室还是举办法学论坛的重要场所，每年都会有十余次国际性的大型学术研讨会在此举行，法学院师生们也经常到此聆听法学专业的相关讲座，享受一场场高水平的学术盛宴。

Moot Court Laboratory: the Second Classroom of Law Practice

Entering into the Mingli building of the School of Law, you will be attracted by the eye-catching characters "Moot Court" . On Tsinghua's laboratory-opening day, you might as well follow us to the moot court, and have a look at the great performance of law students in the actual combat besides theoretical study.

The moot court is located at Room 216 of Mingli Building, Tsinghua University. It was founded in 2001 and originally constructed in a western court style, with the judge's bench set in the front, jury on the opposite side and debaters' seats on two sides. Although the construction style was initially western, the current moot court can not only switch between Chinese and western style at any time according to the needs, but also switch to a criminal court, civil court, administrative court and arbitral court, so as to complete all the required tasks.

Law itself is a very practical discipline, and for law students, the moot court is an indispensable practice site. To this end, the moot court is also equipped with the most advanced facilities for students to have a better practical experience. Four cameras are equipped in the four directions of the court, which can clearly record the performance of participants in the moot court, as teaching cases for discussion and observation. A full range of multimedia equipment and a high simulation degree of court setting also allow students to become more immersive in study and exercise.

In the curriculum system for undergraduate and graduate students of School of Law, moot court practice is listed as a compulsory course. Through the training of the moot court, students can not only improve their expression ability, logical thinking ability, adaptability, innovation ability and other basic abilities, but also cultivate the abilities to identify and construct the legal facts, to write legal documents, to investigate and apply the evidence, to give court statement and debate, to take judicial record down in shorthand, to interpret the law, to consult legal literature, and other professional abilities. The moot court is making and will always make its contribution to cultivating brand new legal talents for the future.

From 2003, the moot court of Tsinghua University began to host the "Lee and Li Cup" National University Moot Court Competition, and this competition has become the most influential moot court competition in Chinese mainland. From participation by a dozen colleges and universities at the beginning to participation by dozens throughout the country now, more and more law students from all over the country come to Tsinghua to feel the charm of the moot court.

In addition to the daily use of teaching, the moot court laboratory is also an important site for scientific research and forums. Every year, more than ten times of large-scale international academic seminars are held here. At the same time, the laboratory also undertakes many domestic law-related lectures, so as to improve the service efficiency of the laboratory.

Translation and revision | Raj Lamar

Image | Liang Chen

12月21日

文字丨张译丹

图片丨梁露文、郭祥

鲍捷：老一辈科学家的影子，新一代赤子的心

午后冬阳正暖，清华北门的超市里，散步来买菜的大妈正在和摊主争论着哪种苹果更甜。年轻的博士生导师鲍捷轻轻笑着从他们身后经过——也许在不久的将来，只要拿手机轻轻一扫，就能知道想买的苹果是酸还是甜，喝的牛奶安不安全，食用的油是不是地沟油……他这么想着，慢慢走回实验室。

从读书时起，鲍捷就已经开始关注量子点在光谱仪领域的应用——光谱是物质的一种天然“指纹”，是其与生俱来的“身份证”。作为分辨光波的神奇“眼睛”，光谱仪能“一眼洞穿”物质内部的化学成分和相对含量。然而，传统光谱仪受光栅分光的物理原理限制，在实际中难以做到小于一本字典的大小，且造价昂贵，高达数万美元。因此，传统光谱仪一直是实验室的“专宠”，难以进入寻常百姓家。“量子点是能在非常宽的颜色范围内连续地获得不同颜色的材料，基于这一独特性，它是用来辨别物质颜色或光谱的绝佳材选。”鲍捷说。

鲍捷本科就读于清华大学化学系，博士阶段深造于美国布朗大学，4 年内学过材料、光谱等 4 个专业，博士后则在麻省理工学院从事量子点研究。跨学科的专业背景和长时间的观察思考，让鲍捷有了“后发优势”，他打破常规思维，以超然的研究视角“蹚”出了一条新路。量子点光谱仪受到了国内外业界学界的广泛关注。

“他身上有老一辈科学家的影子，怀着一颗朴素的爱国心。”课题组科研助理张大伟这样评价鲍捷。在美国时，鲍捷就在量子点光谱仪的研发上获得突破。凭借这一技术，他想要留在美国任教绝非难事。但是在接到清华的邀请后，鲍捷还是坚定地回到了祖国，回到了母校。归国之初，实验室里的设备跟不上，他就一一购置，逐渐搭建起完备的实验研究平台。在这里，他一次次地试验，成功研制出了量子点光谱仪，开了量子点和光谱仪巧妙结合的先河。现在，他又瞄准前沿领域，朝智能制造、智能传感、智能分析等领域迈进，准备攀登新的高峰。

聊起这位年轻的像大哥哥一样的导师，学生们有说不完的话。“鲍老师常常告诉我们，在算法精度上，别人能做到的，你们也要做到。”但他又很体谅学生，“我们实验室从不打卡，鲍老师不会强迫我们。如果学生状态不好，出去散心调整，他也不会介意。”博士研究生李思敏说。

鲍捷团队的实验室就像家一样，墙上贴着师生们的不少合影。照片上，鲍捷总是站在最外侧，你会以为他是个还在读书的学生，灿烂的笑容里有的是对未来的笃定。

Young Scholar Bao Jie Inheriting the Older Generation Scientists' Spirit

In a winter afternoon, some women in the supermarket of the north gate of Tsinghua Campus were arguing with dealers on which type of apple was sweeter. The young doctoral supervisor Bao Jie passed by and smiled, thinking someday, you will be able to scan the apple with your phone; that way you will know whether the apple is sweet, if the milk is healthy and whether the cooking oil is authentic or not. Dwelling on such thoughts, he strolled back to the laboratory.

Since his student days, Bao Jie has paid great attention to the application of quantum dots in spectrometer. Spectrum is a natural "fingerprint" of matter, an inherent "identity card" . Described as magic "eyes" , which can distinguish between light waves, a spectrograph can "see" (tell) chemical components and relative amount inside substances. However, limited by grating beam-splitting physics, traditional spectrographs cannot be made smaller than a dictionary. What's more, they are expensive—reaching prices as high as tens of thousands of dollars. Due to this, they have always been "exclusive" for labs and professionals—much beyond people's daily reach. "With quantum dots, one can obtain materials of different colors in a wide spectral range continuously, such a unique property makes quantum dots the most ideal material for making sensors to identify precise colors or spectra," said Bao Jie.

Bao Jie graduated from the Department of Chemistry, Tsinghua University and received his Ph.D from Brown University. Within four years, he studied in four areas including materials and spectroscopy. He then continued with his postdoctoral research on quantum dots at MIT. Interdisciplinary expertise and long-time research granted Bao Jie a "late-starting advantage" — he broke the conventions and explored a new method. Quantum dot spectrometer has been attracting wide attention from academia both home and abroad.

"He owns the spirits of the older generation of scientists." said Zhang Dawei, the research assistant of Bao's team. During his study in the United States, Bao Jie made the breakthrough in the development of quantum dots spectrometer. With such an achievement, Bao could easily land in a faculty position in the US. But upon receiving the invitation from Tsinghua University, he didn't hesitate for one minute before returning to China to pursue further studies at Tsinghua. At the initial phase of his career in China, the laboratory lacked advanced devices. Bao Jie established all the required devices and gradually set up a complete platform for experimental research. After countless experiments, Bao achieved the development of a quantum dot spectrometer, realizing the ingenious combination of quantum dots and spectrometers. Currently, he is focusing on the cutting-age fields, heading for smart manufacturing, smart sensing, intelligent analysis and so on, ready to climb to newer heights.

In the eyes of his students, this young mentor is more like a big brother. "Prof. Bao often tells us that when it comes to algorithm accuracy, if others can achieve it, you should also be able to." But he is also very considerate of his students. "We never have to swipe our cards in our laboratory and Prof. Bao never forces us to stick to a schedule. If we are not in a good mood, he doesn't mind if we relax ourselves." said Dr. Li Simin.

The laboratory is like a home, with a lot of pictures on the wall. In those pictures, Bao was always standing by his young students, with his bright smile filled with certainty for the future.

Translation and revision | Raj Lamar

Image | Liang Luwen, Guo Xiang

12 月 22 日

文字 | 杨茂艺

图片 | 李娜

饺子们，温暖整个冬天吧！

不知从何时起，清华园里的学生们换上了绒手套、厚护耳、雪地靴等全套越冬装备，三教的玻璃窗上浮现了温柔的雾水，图书馆的咖啡厅弥漫着卡布奇诺的醇香……冬至，踮着脚尖轻轻来到，是什么装点了这个节气的颜色和神韵，带我们领悟这昼短夜长的时分？是午后天空的那片蓝，抑或是梦中的那朵雪花，还是餐盘中的那几只胖饺子？

“冬至饺子夏至面”的习俗源自东汉，相传是为了纪念医圣张仲景冬至日舍药救人的善举。悠久的历史长河中，饺子曾被赋予多种称谓，如“汤中牢丸”“时罗角儿”“粉角”“扁食”等。饺子需精心制作——以冷水和面粉为剂，揉成面团、切成长条，用擀面杖推出饺子皮，包裹或荤或素的馅心，再捏成月牙形或角形。

近年来，随着伙食原材料价格和用工成本的不断上涨，清华大学饮食中心为了保障食堂饺子的正常供应，经过细致考察和论证，在 2010 年建成了机械化饺子生产线，引入和面机、馅料机等，不仅能标准化水和面的比例，还能把蔬菜和肉类原料切成颗粒状同时保留纤维感，提升馅心的品质。据采购科人员介绍，生产线每小时可生产 15000 个饺子。饺子一旦制好，先由工作人员分拣装盘，经过零下 35℃的速冻线，然后装箱、封箱，转入零下 18℃的冷库储存，之后便被陆续送往各大食堂，进入沸水之中翻滚煮熟。

猪肉大葱、猪肉芹菜、猪肉圆白菜、猪肉茴香、猪肉韭菜、牛肉胡萝卜……多种口味的饺子往往令驻足窗口的我们“选择困难”，看着一只只妥帖匀实、憨态可掬的饺子们被漏勺从热气腾腾的汤锅中捞起，再见它们一股脑儿地滑进铁方盘里，好不欢喜。若是再蘸上一点儿醇厚的陈醋或油香的辣子，放进嘴里，齿牙厮磨之中溢出浓郁汁水，肉的嚼劲儿配合着菜的清幽，被一片氤氲的水雾拥抱，霎时想起家乡的灶台、面粉、母亲、笑颜，一切的寒冷和凉意便驱散开去。饺子，承载了对游子的慰藉和相思，是这个百木凋零的日子里温暖的果腹之愉。

饺子作为传统食品别具风味。目前，学校饺子生产加工车间正在研发新品种的饺子，希望能为这个漫长的冬季再添一丝暖意。

Dumplings, Warm up This Winter!

I'm not sure when it began but students started to wear their warm gloves, ear muffs and snow boots in the Tsinghua Campus. Water mist appeared on the windows of teaching buildings and the smell of cappuccino filled the air of the library's coffee bar. The winter solstice arrived gently on her tippy toes. Is this the blue afternoon sky, or the snowflakes or the big dumplings that sits on our plates? The colors and charm of this solar term allow us to realize the hours that exist between shorter day and longer night.

The custom of "eating dumplings during the winter solstice and eating noodles during the summer solstice" originated from the Eastern Han Dynasty. It is said that it commemorates the benevolence of Doctor Zhang Zhongjing who is regarded as a saint. During its long history, jiaozi or dumplings are also known by many other names. The dumpling needs to be carefully crafted as well. The dough is kneaded with cold water and flour, then it is divided and turned into dumpling skins. The filling, whether it is meat and/or vegetables are placed within the dumpling skin then folded into a crescent shape.

Rising ingredient costs and increased labor costs prompted the establishment of a dumpling production line at Tsinghua. This is needed to ensure a normal supply of dumplings. Many machines were set up such as dough kneading machine, filling machine, etc., with a standardized method in cutting and shaping. According to the procurement officers of the dumpling production line, the production line can produce 15,000 dumplings per hour. Once the dumplings are done, staff sort them out and pack them in an environment that is minus 35 degrees Celsius. Dumplings are then sealed at minus 18 degrees Celsius.

Pork with onion, pork with celery, pork with cabbage, pork with leek, beef and carrot...Such wide range of dumplings are making it difficult for us to choose. The aunties behind the counters give us bowls after bowls of steamy dumplings, and when we finally take a bite of the dumplings, dip it into vinegar and then wait for juice and taste to seduce our senses — that familiar taste, the feeling of home, that reminder of my mother, those flour, those dumplings and that smile...yep... are all able to drive away any sense of coldness. Dumplings are more than just a bite but reminders of home, warmth and love.

Dumplings have special flavor as Chinese traditional food. At present, Tsinghua's dumpling production line is developing new varieties of dumplings in the hope that they will add a bit of warmth to this long winter.

Translation and revision | Min Weiyuan

Image | Li Na

12 月 25 日

文字 | 杨晨晞

图片 | 宋晨

2017 年清华大学特等奖学金获得者余天呈：做有人文精神的科学家

2017 年清华大学本科生特等奖学金答辩会上，余天呈的介绍人沈渊老师说，余天呈给他的第一印象是“电子系的典型学霸”。

余天呈来自清华大学电子工程系，的确是老师和同学们眼中的“学霸”。前三年学分绩位列电子系前三，连续三年获得国家奖学金，发表一篇期刊论文，入选 UGVR 斯坦福大学暑期科研项目，“星火”计划第十期学员……不过，余天呈更愿意用科研、艺体、人文这三个关键词来描述他的大学时光。“学霸”的标签背后，他立志成为一名兼具人文情怀和艺术修养的科学家。

科研为本，开拓国际视野。自大二起，余天呈就加入电子系沈渊老师的课题组，开始从事数据驱动的室内定位项目研究。得益于清华的全球战略，余天呈得到了两次赴美参与学术交流的机会。在美国威斯康星大学麦迪逊分校交换期间，他修习了包括 4 门研究生课程在内的 6 门课程，获得该校交换生最高荣誉。樊外堂（Waitang Fan）教授评价说：“他作为本科生，表现超过了课堂上所有的研究生。”在斯坦福大学暑期研修时，指导教师 Tsachy Weissman 教授评价说：“他在这一困难问题（高维谱估计）上的进展远远超出我们的想象，突破了我对该项目中最好学生的预期。”

艺体兼休，陶冶砥砺心智。余天呈是清华大学学生艺术团合唱队一队男高声部的成员，曾作为声部长先后参与了多次演出。在钻研学术的同时，艺术也给了他许多慰藉和启迪。他每每沉醉于多部合声的美妙统一，并且感到这与自己解决高维统计问题时使用的匹配技巧殊途同归。在清华浓厚的体育氛围的感召下，余天呈还养成了长期坚持锻炼的习惯，成为“马杯”舞台上的健美健将。

人文情怀，服务回馈清华。余天呈受益于清华人文精神的感染，也希望把这种精神更好地传播出去。在担任学生致知协会会长期间，他作为创办人之一发起了“爱读夜”系列活动，至今已有数千人次参与其中，成为校园里最受欢迎的读书活动。余天呈感激清华对他的塑造培养，更渴望把自己的成长经验也分享给他人。为此，他先后担任学习发展中心答疑坊队长和学习发展中心同辈咨询师，累计志愿工时 254 小时，被评为紫荆五星级志愿者，陪伴同学们攻克难关，一路成长。

“真正的事业不需要坚持，真正的理想谈不上忍耐。”余天呈在特奖答辩现场如是说。他希望自己一直做一个坚定而从容的人，成为人文与科学创新精神的践行者。

Winner of Tsinghua Top Grade Scholarship Yu Tiancheng: to Be a Scientist with Humanistic Care

On November 7th, 2017, in the defense meeting for Tsinghua's undergraduate Top Grade Scholarship, Associate Professor Yuan Shen brought up his first impression of Yu Tiancheng: "He's like a typical top student."

Yu Tiancheng, student of the Department of Electronic Engineering at Tsinghua, is indeed a top student in the eyes of his classmates and teachers. In his first three years, he ranked top three in his major and consecutively won national scholarships and a series of other scholarships. He published a journal paper and was selected for the Undergraduate Visiting Research (UGVR) Program at Stanford University, a summer research program. However, behind the "top student" label, Yu is determined to become a scientist with humanistic values and artistic accomplishments. He is more willing to use three key words to describe his time in college—scientific research, arts and humanities.

Since his second year at Tsinghua, Yu Tiancheng joined Yuan Shen's team to do research in data-driven indoor localization. Owing to Tsinghua's internationalization efforts, Yu was given two opportunities to participate in academic exchanges in the U.S.. During his study at the University of Wisconsin-Madison, he took 6 courses, including 4 graduate level courses, reaching the maximum number of classes available to exchange students. Professor Waitang Fan commented, "Despite being an undergraduate student, his performance outperforms even graduate students in my class." During his summer research program at Stanford University, his instructor, Professor Tsachy Weissman commented, "He ended up obtaining results more decisive and conclusive than that we thought was reasonable to expect for this highly non-trivial problem setting (high-dimensional spectrum estimation). He exceeded my expectation of even the very best students through this UGVR program."

Yu is a member of the tenor section of the choir in Tsinghua's Student Arts Troupe. He was once the vocals section leader and have participated in many performances. Arts has given him much relief from studies and at the same time provided much inspiration. While immersed in the wonderful harmony of multiple voices, he felt that the matching technique to achieve harmony is quite the same as the method he uses in solving high-dimensional statistical problems. He was also inspired to develop long-term adherence to exercise habits while immersed in Tsinghua's sporting tradition. He was admitted into the varsity bodybuilding team and won fourth place in the 80kg class in the annual Ma Yuehan sporting event.

Benefiting from the atmosphere of humanities at Tsinghua, Yu is hoping to spread this spirit. During his tenure as the president of Tsinghua's Student Association of Seeking Knowledge, he launched the "I-Do-It" reading club. Thousands of students have participated in it and it has become the most popular reading activity on campus.

Grateful for the cultivation he has received at Tsinghua, Yu hoped to share his experiences to others. He served as a peer counsellor and leader of a question and answer workshop at the Learning Development Center, accumulating a total of 254 hours of volunteer hours. He was also rated as a five-star volunteer for helping other students overcome difficulties in their studies.

Yu Tiancheng once said, "It's not about having perseverance or patience, a real cause is worth doing beyond all reasons." He always wish himself to be a scientist with innovation and love for the humanities.

Translation and revision | Alexis See Tho

Image | Song Chen

12 月 26 日

文字 | 左烜晅

图片 | 宋晨

本科生课程咨询委员会：学生是教改的主角

为更充分地发挥学生的主体作用，建立学生对本科教学质量的反馈机制，2014 年 12 月，清华大学本科生课程咨询委员会（简称“课委会”）在教务处指导下成立，成为校内第一个以学生身份参与学校教学管理和改革的委员会。

课委会的每位委员，都经历了从教学中的接受者向重要的决策建议者转变的过程。课委会在成立的三年时间内，推动了中期退课改革、课程大纲修订、部分院系培养方案修订、学分绩改革、小学期改革、Waiting List 选课法等提案的提出和落实。

首届课委会的 20 名学生委员来自理、工、人文、艺术等不同学科，年级覆盖大一至大四，接近一半人有出国交流经历，他们都是通过校内公开报名加入课委会的。用首届课委会主席卢森的话说，大家都很“厉害”，有学术大牛、竞赛大神，也有文艺特长生，有的有创意，有的有激情，个个特色鲜明。

课委会从成立伊始就保持高效运转——来自各院系的 20 名同学，不但超额完成课堂教学调研，还精心设计标志并申请微信公众号，定期发布同学们对于教学改革的意见建议。卢森当时是美术学院的本科生，经常利用就餐时间带领委员们去紫荆食堂地下餐厅——大家一起头脑风暴，用短短一个月提炼了十多个选题，设计“基础课改革调查”等问卷，一星期就回收了 786 份。

至今，由课委会组织并与教务处、各院系教学负责人共同研讨的正式会议近 20 次，提出的 35 个提案均得到广泛关注和反馈，并都在学校的教育教学改革中得到采纳和体现。

课委会曾经不止一次与学校领导面对面探讨教学大纲和课程特点，积极开展学业评价体系改革调研并协助推进学分绩改革。在广泛听取同学意见后，他们提出每学期学生可选择一门课不记录成绩、只记录通过与否，造福了广大“觊觎”其他院系专业课程却因担心成绩不佳而不敢“下手”的同学，对鼓励学生自主发展、做出更具挑战性的选择起到了有益作用。

“人才培养是大学的根本。教育教学改革要靠教师和学生两个主体，学生是教改的主角，改革要依靠你们。”邱勇与学生代表座谈时的这句话，一直激励着课委会委员们充分发挥主观能动性，投入这项富有开创性的光荣工作中去。

学于斯，长于斯，课委会委员们愿更好地为清华教改助力。

Advisory Committee of Undergraduate Courses: Students Are the Protagonists of Education Reform

The Advisory Committee of Undergraduate Courses (ACUC) of Tsinghua University was established in December 2014 in order to maximize students' main role and to ensure that a positive feedback mechanism could continue to ensure the quality of undergraduate education. It became the first committee to participate in education management and reform of the university.

From being the recipients of learning to policy makers and managers, the committee within three years of its establishment has actively participated in the promotion of reforms about syllabus revision, waiting list for electives and much more.

All of the students in the committee are recruited publicly. The first 20 student members of ACUC were from science, engineering, literature and art disciplines, from freshmen to seniors. Nearly half of them had experiences of going abroad. Lu Sen, the first chairman of ACUC said that everyone is a "legend" . Some are top in academics, some are winners of competitions, some are art talents, and all of them have their own specialty and creativity.

ACUC went straight to work right after its establishment. The 20 students not only completed the research about class teaching but also designed their Wechat account logo and regularly publish the opinions of their fellow peers. Lu Sen was then an undergraduate student from the Academy of Arts and Design. He and the other members always went into a long brainstorming session at Zijing Cafeteria. Within a month, they designed an investigation questionnaire on the reform of basic courses, and received 786 replies in a week.

So far, ACUC has held over 20 formal meetings with Dean's Office and teachers from the schools and departments. 35 proposals have been put forward and have gained much attention. At present, all of the proposals have been adopted in Tsinghua's education reform.

Furthermore, the students also discussed with Tsinghua's President Qiu Yong about the curriculum. They have promoted the reform about academic evaluation. Also they suggested that every semester, students could select a course that won't have its grades being included in the final result. That way, it encourages students to challenge and manage their own study.

Qiu Yong once said to the students, "Cultivation is fundamental to any university. The education reform depends on the teachers and the students. You are the main force behind such reform." His words inspired the students from ACUC to devote themselves to their creative work.

Translation and revision | Min Weiyuan

Image | Song Chen

12 月 27 日

文字 | 张译丹

图片 | 唐蓓蓓、李娜

戏曲进清华：给我一天，还你千年

一到秋冬，我们就会羡慕起古人的浪漫来：京城下了一场大雪，大观园中的姐妹们便割腥啖膻，把酒吟诗；梁兄与英台在红罗山书院三年朝夕相处中，想必也曾互邀“晚来天欲雪，能饮一杯无”；而霸王声声的“虞兮虞兮奈若何”，则为这本就肃杀的节气平添了一抹新愁……

这些场景如今一幕幕被还原到戏曲舞台上，从 2017 年 10 月起，名剧名角纷纷走进新清华学堂，献上了今冬穿越千年的视听盛宴。

戏曲作为中华民族传统优秀文化中的艺术瑰宝，具有很高的艺术欣赏价值和教育价值。戏曲艺术走进校园，有助于传承和发展中华传统文化，同时也将丰富校园文化建设，是美育的重要资源和载体。早在 2008 年，教育部就开始提倡“京剧进校园”。今年，中宣部、教育部、财政部、文化部又联合发布了《关于戏曲进校园的实施意见》，足以说明国家对戏曲艺术教育的重视。

为了使中华优秀传统文化艺术在校园生根、发芽，成为影响学生价值塑造的载体，由教育部艺术教育委员会指导、北京市教委主办，清华大学承办，北京市电视台、海淀文化委员会支持的“戏曲进校园——2017 校园戏曲节”在清华上演了持续三个月的“大戏”。

本次戏曲节中，八大剧种鸣锣开唱，江苏省演艺集团昆剧院的《桃花扇》、国家京剧院梅派经典《凤还巢》、上海京剧院折子戏专场《霸王别姬》、南京越剧团尹袁版《红楼梦》等众多优秀剧目相继登台，用中国声音演绎西方真情的京剧《圣母院》则为观众带来另一番全新体验。

中国评剧院原创评剧《母亲》在新清华学堂上演后，收获了校内外观众的一致好评。作为新编戏剧的优秀代表，《母亲》既贴近生活、语言浅显易懂，又底蕴深厚，戏剧唱腔独特。这部剧结合了和声唱法与话剧表演形式，让观众眼前一亮。剧中人物的家国情怀，也让清华观众们产生深深的共鸣。一位来自微电子所的观众表示，《母亲》带给她的是一场关乎回忆的洗礼——她出生在山东革命根据地，从小耳濡目染革命先辈的光辉事迹，剧中的很多场景都与祖辈向她讲述的故事相似，让她不由自主地产生亲切、庄重之感，也更加深刻地体会到自己肩负的时代使命。

大幕渐合，盛宴的回味依旧美妙。给我一天，还你千年余音袅袅……

Traditional Chinese Opera in Tsinghua: a Day in Exchange for a Thousand Years

At the arrival of fall and winter seasons, we begin to envy the romance of the ancients. when the capital was enveloped in thick snow, sisters in *A Dream in Red Mansions* held parties in the Grand View Garden; when Lovers Liang Shanbo and Zhu Yingtai spent three years at the Hongluoshan Academy, they should enjoy poems together; and when the Hegemon King said farewell to his concubine, it added some sadness to the harsh winter.

These are now scenes restored on the stage. Since October, famous names in the world of traditional Chinese opera have performed at the New Tsinghua Auditorium, opening up for many a winter feast of sights and sounds through a thousand years of Chinese opera.

As a treasure of Chinese traditional culture, Chinese opera is highly appreciated and has much educational value. As traditional Chinese opera makes its way into campuses, it will not only help to pass on and develop Chinese traditional culture but also enrich the campus culture. It is an important resource and bearer of arts and creative education.

In 2008, the Ministry of Education began to promote Peking opera on campuses. This year, the Publicity Department of the CPC, Ministry of Education, Ministry of Finance and Ministry of Culture jointly released an initiative to promote Chinese opera on university campuses. This demonstrates that the central government attaches great importance to the education of Chinese opera.

In order to spur the traditional Chinese culture and arts take root and flourish on campuses, the Chinese Opera Festival was held in Tsinghua since this autumn. The program was under the guidance of the Art Education Committee of the Ministry of Education, sponsored by the Beijing Municipal Education Commission and supported by Beijing TV Station and Haidian Culture Commission.

There are numerous outstanding repertoires in the Chinese Opera Festival, including Jiangsu Kun Opera Theater's *The Peach Blossom Fan*, the National Peking Opera Theater's *Phoenix Returns to the Nest*, Shanghai Peking Opera Theater's special performance of *Farewell My Concubine*, and Nanjing Yue Opera Troupe's *A Dream in Red Mansions*. Besides, there is a Peking opera version of *Notre Dame*.

Among them, China Pingju Theater's original work *Mother* won widely praises from the audience. As a good representative of modern Chinese opera, *Mother* is not only relevant to the present times with language that is easy to understand, but also keep the unique sprit of traditional Chinese opera. It combines vocal singing and drama performance, bringing fresh feelings to the audience.

"*Mother* is a reminder of the revolutionary times in Shandong and the achievements of our predecessors there." remarked an audience from the Institute of Microelectronics at Tsinghua. She added that many of the scenes were similar to the stories her predecessors told her, and gave her a sense of gratitude and respect.

Although the festival is over, the memory will last for a long time.

Translation and revision | Alexis See Tho

Image | Tang Beibei, Li Na

12 月 28 日

供稿 | 交叉信息研究院

文字 | 梁乐萌

图片 | 梁晨

交叉信息院金奇奂研究组刷新单量子比特储存相干时间世界纪录

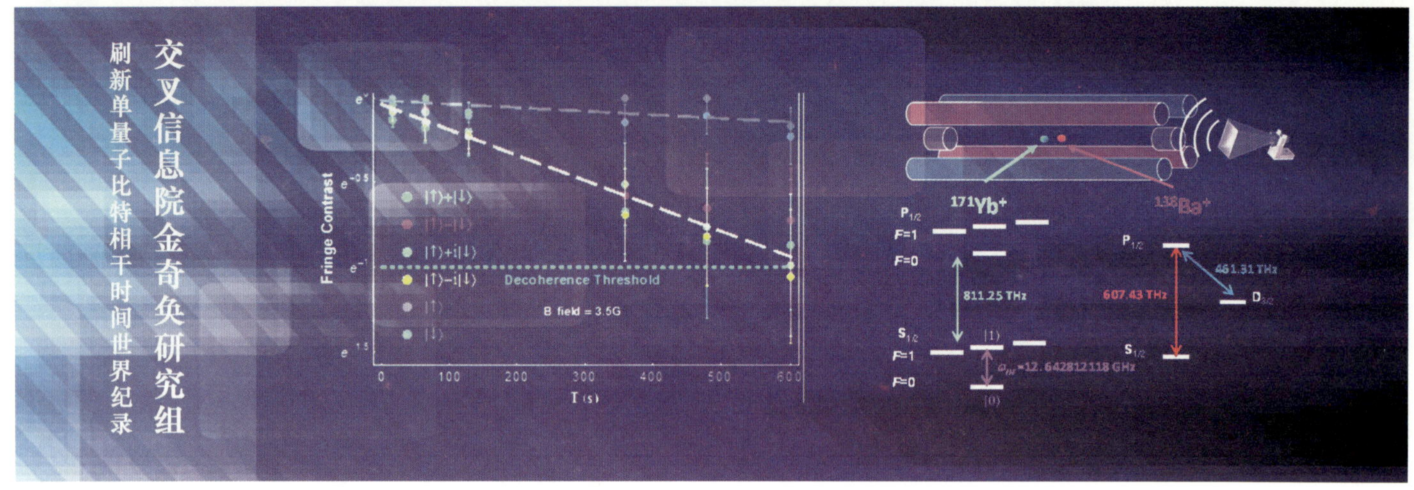

2017 年年中，交叉信息院量子信息中心金奇奂副教授研究组实现拥有超过 10 分钟相干时间的单量子比特储存，刷新了单量子比特相干时间的世界纪录，将此前纪录提高 10 倍。此工作的研究论文《相干时间超过 10 分钟的单量子比特储存》于 2017 年 9 月 25 日发表在光子学研究最高学术期刊《自然・光子学》上。

单量子比特是量子信息技术中的基本单元，只有拥有对其完整的操作能力，才能实现量子信息的储存、操作和读取。相干时间是量子信息技术中的一个术语，指量子信息储存的最大时间。金奇奂研究组此次实现了超过 10 分钟相干时间的单量子比特储存，虽然在离子系综系统和固体系综系统中曾观察到相近甚至更长的相干时间，但在单量子系统中，这是第一次。

单离子系统相干时间不长的主要原因是加热。在没有激光冷却的环境下，环境噪声可以加热离子，从而降低量子态探测的效率。此项研究在实验中利用协同冷却技术解决加热的问题，同时施加上千个动态解耦操作，以抵抗环境的磁场噪声和信号发生器的相位噪声，从而延长相干时间，单量子比特操作保真度达到 99.99%。

单量子比特相干时间研究的推进明确展示了量子信息储存技术的可行性，这也成为量子计算机的重要组成部分，尤其是基于离子阱技术的量子计算机，而离子阱技术是目前已知最接近实现大型量子计算机的技术之一。离子阱量子计算机架构由量子储存区域和量子操作区域组成，并通过移动离子来实现两个区域的连接。金奇奂研究组的成果将成为量子储存区域最为关键的技术。

同时，该成果也成为量子网络关键技术之一。量子网络是传输量子信息的通信网络，而离子光子纠缠是实现量子网络的重要途径。由于离子光子纠缠过程具有不确定性，为了保证足够小的误差，需要很长相干时间的离子以进行操作，此工作则为这一点提供了保证。

本研究的第一作者为量子信息中心博士生汪野，共同通讯作者为出站博士后廉茶铉和金奇奂副教授。

Kihwan Kim's Group from the Institute of Interdisciplinary Information Sciences Breaks the World-record in the Coherence Time of a Single Quantum Bit Storage

Prof. Kihwan Kim's trapped ion group at Center of Quantum Information of Institute for Interdisciplinary Information Sciences (IIIS) realized a single-qubit memory with over 10 minutes coherence time, which is the longest coherence time for a single qubit, the basic unit of quantum information processing. The work was published in *Nature Photonics* on Sep. 25th, 2017, which is entitled as "Single-qubit quantum memory exceeding ten-minute coherence time."

The actual quantum information processing is fundamentally based on the technology of coherent manipulation and detection of the basic unit, the qubit. Without the full accessibility to individual qubits, it is fundamentally inconceivable to store, operate and retrieve a quantum information. It has been a long quest to develop technologies to coherently process and detect a quantum information in a single qubit level. This time Kim's group report the coherence of over 10-minutes in a single-qubit system, which is an order of magnitude longer than the previous world record. Actually, similar coherence times in the ensemble of trapped ions were reported more than 20 years ago and even longer coherence times in the ensemble of solid state system were reported recently. Kim's group have brought the long coherence time seen in the ensemble to the single qubit level, a single ion.

The coherence time of a single ion is mainly limited by the reduction of state-discrimination efficiency from the heating of the qubit ion without any laser cooling. In the experimental demonstration, the problem is resolved by the sympathetic cooling. Then thousands of dynamical decoupling pulses were applied to extend the coherence time in the influence of magnetic field fluctuation with the gate fidelity of 99.99%.

The experimental result is the clear realization of the quantum memory zone, which would be the essential ingredient for the quantum computation and quantum computation based on the trapped ion technology, which is one of the leading candidates for a practical large-scale quantum computer. One scalable architecture for the ion-trap quantum computer would consist of memory zone and operation zone connected by ion shuttling. Kim's group's technique would provide the key technique for the realization of the memory zone in this scalable quantum computers. It is also an important technique for a quantum network based on ion-photon mapping, which performs in probabilistic way and requires long coherence time for the fault-tolerant performance.

Wang Ye, Ph.D. candidate in IIIS, is the first author and the corresponding authors are a former post-doc Dahyun Yum and Tenured Associate Professor Kihwan Kim.

Contributor | Institute of Interdisciplinary Information Sciences

Translation and revision | Raj Lamar

Image | Liang Chen

12月29日

文字 | 刘书田

图片 | 赵存存、宋晨、任天姝

2017，我们与清华一起走过

转眼之间，2018 的脚步近了。回顾 2017，我们曾一起见证过许多属于清华的精彩瞬间。

2017 年，“清华映像”共推出 185 期。它们像 185 扇彩色的窗口，每扇窗里都有一则属于清华的好故事。

在此，我们列出了当月访问量最高的 10 期选题，它们共同贡献了超过 40 万次的访问量（中文版）。这并不是因为它们有多特殊，恰恰相反，它们大多讲述的就是我们身边的人和事，是清华园里的日常，也是“清华映像”的日常。

这一年，我们继续追寻园子里的故居风物，在“清华名人名言”中感悟清华人的风骨与基因。

我们从造福失能者的脑机接口系统触摸到人工智能的温度，更为中国高温气冷堆技术从跟踪到领跑的跨越而自豪。

我们邀请苏世民书院首批毕业的“世界水手”写下他们在清华一年的满满收获，用手绘和动画呈现出清华本科生奔涌向前的每分每秒。

我们在 4 月见证了清华 106 周岁的荣耀（发起成立亚洲大学联盟、清华简《算表》入选吉尼斯世界纪录），在金秋为 8 位获得“新百年教学成就奖”的良师益友献上心中的赞叹与感恩。

团结的力量，创新的力量，开放的力量，人文的力量，交流的力量，榜样的力量，意志的力量，坚守的力量……在我们每个人之间传递、激荡、放大，让我们不孤独、不迷茫，更加有力前行。

不念过往，不畏将来。当我们在下一个工作日如期见面时，窗外已是新年的碧空与阳光。2018，我们来了！

2017“清华映像”月度访问量“十大”：

1 月 13 日《清华名人名言之梁思成：有所专而又多能，精于一而又博学》

3 月 30 日《高温气冷堆技术，中国领跑》

4 月 30 日《清华大学 106 周岁生日快乐！》

5 月 25 日《“万园之园”的数字化重生》

6 月 29 日《苏世民书院这一年，重新定义了我对中国的了解》

7 月 31 日《于婉莹：给你不一样的手绘清华》

9 月 28 日《于歆杰：执匠人之心，铺设育人“电路”》

10 月 31 日《医学院高小榕团队研发脑机接口系统：以意念与世界对话》

11 月 9 日《清华本科生的一天》

12 月 11 日《2017 年清华大学特等奖学金获得者胡耀文：“大满贯”是怎样炼成的》

The 10 Most-read Tsinghua Spotlights Stories of 2017

In a blink of an eye, we will approach the dawn of a new year. Looking back at the past twelve months, we have witnessed many remarkable moments belonging to Tsinghua University.

In 2017, Tsinghua Spotlights launched a total of 185 issues. They resemble 185 colorful windows, each window shows a good story in Tsinghua.

Here, we have listed the ten most-read stories in the month they were published, they were read more than 400,000 times (Chinese version). This is not because of how unique the stories were. On the contrary, most stories were about the people and things around us. They are the routine happenings on campus, and they are also the routine of Tsinghua Spotlights, a team that publishes a Tsinghua story every weekday on the Tsinghua website.

We pursued stories that tell of Tsinghua's tradition and culture this year. Through biographical stories of Tsinghua students and faculty members in the past and present, readers experienced the sentiment of Tsinghua people's character and spirit.

From a brain-computer interface system that benefits the disabled, we learned of progress in the field of artificial intelligence. We also witnessed a breakthrough in China's high-temperature cooled reactor technology, which was a significant milestone internationally and a source of pride for Tsinghua.

We also invited a graduate from the first cohort of Schwarzman Scholars to write his reflections on his year in Tsinghua, and featured a Tsinghua student's intricate hand-drawn depictions of Tsinghua campus. Yu Wanying's drawings brought to life the scenes so familiar to many Tsinghua alumni.

In April, we also witnessed the glory of Tsinghua University's 106th anniversary: the establishment of the Asian University Alliance and the admission of "Tsinghua Bamboo Slips" into the Guinness World Records. In September, we celebrated the dedication of eight faculty members who were awarded the Tsinghua New Century Teaching Achievement Award for their outstanding contributions.

The power of unity, innovation, openness, humanity, communication and exchange, good example, strong will and perseverance, are passed on to every one of us. May these stories inspire and strengthen us, and may we not feel lonely in our journeys or experience confusion. Rather, let us become a force that moves forward.

Don't be afraid of the future and don't miss the past. When we meet the next time, the view beyond the window will be a clear blue sky and sunshine. Here we come, 2018!

Top ten most-read Tsinghua Spotlights stories (Chinese version)

January 13 "Famous Quotations in Tsinghua History: Multi-Talented Yet a Specialist, Versatile Yet Master of One"
March 30 "China Takes the Lead in High-temperature Gas-cooled Reactor Technology"
April 30 "Tsinghua University: Happy 106th Birthday!"
May 25 "The Digital Rebirth of the Old Summer Palace"
June 29 "A Reflection on My Year at Schwarzman College"
July 31 "Yu Wanying: Here's an Amazing Hand-painted Tsinghua Campus"
September 28 "Yu Xinjie: Sharing His Greatest Joy in Teaching"
October 31 "Speaking to the World Through Brain Signals: Tsinghua Biomedical Engineering Team Pioneers Brain-computer Interface Research in China"
November 9 "One day as a Tsinghua Undergraduate Student"
December 11 "Hu Yaowen, The Recipient of 2017 Tsinghua Top Grade Scholarship: The Grand Slam"

Translation and revision | Alexis See Tho

Image | Zhao Cuncun, Song Chen, Ren Tianmei

后 记

在编校本书的过程中，重新翻阅 2017 年“清华映像”栏目每一期的图文，仿佛串联起它们从策划、收集素材、安排采写 / 设计、审稿 / 审图和发布的全过程。正是在每个环节中的点滴用心和日积月累，汇聚成了我们手里分量不轻的这本合集。在此，我们要郑重感谢每一位曾在这个过程中给予指导帮助、付出创意心血、提出中肯意见的师生校友和读者。

感谢清华大学领导对“清华映像”栏目一如既往的大力支持。

感谢清华大学信息化办公室为“清华映像”栏目奠定的坚实基础。

感谢清华大学美术学院张歌明老师团队、新闻与传播学院张莉老师团队为“清华映像”视觉设计和文字采写所做出的不懈努力和创新。这两个团队中既有在读的清华学子，也有已经毕业走上工作岗位的清华校友。“清华映像”呈现的一则则“清华好故事”，他们既是参与者、见证者，同时也是创作者、传播者。他们对清华、对“清华映像”栏目都有着非同一般的深厚感情，他们付出的，是难能可贵的创造性劳动。

感谢清华大学党委宣传部（新闻中心）领导班子和全体同仁给予“清华映像”的关心、爱护、帮助和支持。没有清华“大宣传”格局的整体架构和丰满血肉，就没有“清华映像”源流丰富的微循环。

感谢清华大学出版社石磊主任和责编梁斐对本书出版给予的热情支持和细致工作。

2018 年清华大学主页改版后，推出了更富视觉冲击力的轮播主页大图，“清华映像”栏目作为主页大图最重要的来源之一得以延续并发展。新版的主页大图（清华映像）进一步突出了叙事性摄影和高品质深度报道的分量，以更从容的步伐，努力为讲好清华故事、塑造清华新百年形象继续贡献力量。

凭借百余年厚重的积淀和改革创新的新发展，清华大学正满怀自信和力量，以更加宽广的国际视野、更加高远的历史站位、更加有力的实际行动推进中国特色世界一流大学建设。有幸身处这一史无前例的历史进程中，我们愿继续通过“清华映像”这扇窗口，守望并映照出清华大学前行路上的璀璨光华。

编者

2019 年 8 月于清华园